Government Public Relations

A Reader

PUBLIC ADMINISTRATION AND PUBLIC POLICY

A Comprehensive Publication Program

EDITOR-IN-CHIEF

EVAN M. BERMAN

Huey McElveen Distinguished Professor
Louisiana State University
Public Administration Institute
Baton Rouge, Louisiana

Founding Editor

JACK RABIN

Professor of Public Administration and Public Policy
The Pennsylvania State University—Harrisburg
School of Public Affairs
Middletown, Pennsylvania

Available Electronically

Principles and Practices of Public Administration, edited by
Jack Rabin, Robert F. Munzenrider, and Sherrie M. Bartell

PublicADMINISTRATION*netBASE*

Government Public Relations

A Reader

Edited by

Mordecai Lee
University of Wisconsin–Milwaukee
Milwaukee, Wisconsin, U.S.A.

CRC Press
Taylor & Francis Group
Boca Raton London New York

CRC Press is an imprint of the
Taylor & Francis Group, an **informa** business

Auerbach Publications
Taylor & Francis Group
6000 Broken Sound Parkway NW, Suite 300
Boca Raton, FL 33487-2742

© 2008 by Taylor & Francis Group, LLC
Auerbach is an imprint of Taylor & Francis Group, an Informa business

No claim to original U.S. Government works
Printed in the United States of America on acid-free paper
10 9 8 7 6 5 4 3 2 1

International Standard Book Number-13: 978-1-4200-6277-9 (Hardcover)

Library of Congress Cataloging-in-Publication Data

Government public relations : a reader / editor Mordecai Lee.
    p. cm. -- (Public administration and public policy ; 135)
  Includes bibliographical references and index.
  ISBN 978-1-4200-6277-9 (alk. paper)
  1. Government publicity--United States. 2. Communication in politics--United States. I. Lee, Mordecai, 1948-

JK849.G68 2007
352.7'480973--dc22   2007020045

Visit the Taylor & Francis Web site at
http://www.taylorandfrancis.com

and the Auerbach Web site at
http://www.auerbach-publications.com

Dedication

For my sister, Riva Lee Nolley, who in 1974 insisted that I take advantage of an opportunity to do government public relations instead of just writing about it.

Contents

SECTION I OVERVIEW OF GOVERNMENT PUBLIC RELATIONS

SECTION II PURPOSES OF GOVERNMENT PUBLIC RELATIONS: MEDIA RELATIONS

SECTION III PURPOSES OF GOVERNMENT PUBLIC RELATIONS: PUBLIC REPORTING

SECTION IV PURPOSES OF GOVERNMENT PUBLIC RELATIONS: RESPONSIVENESS TO THE PUBLIC

SECTION V PURPOSES OF GOVERNMENT PUBLIC RELATIONS: OUTREACH

SECTION VI CRISIS MANAGEMENT AS GOVERNMENT PUBLIC RELATIONS

SECTION VII THE EXTERNAL ENVIRONMENT OF GOVERNMENT PUBLIC RELATIONS

SECTION VIII THE EXTENDED PUBLIC SECTOR: PUBLIC RELATIONS BY NONPROFIT AGENCIES

SECTION IX FUTURE TRENDS IN GOVERNMENT PUBLIC RELATIONS

SECTION X   APPENDIX

Foreword

Just Another Day at the Office

It's Monday morning. You rush to get to the conference room on time for the weekly senior managers' meeting. You were recently promoted to the agency's management team and don't want to be late. While the atmosphere is usually a bit jocular, the mood seems totally different today. The agency head, as usual, starts the meeting exactly on time. She's unusually severe in her tone. You've never seen her like this. "We had a *really* bad week last week. *Something's* wrong. Cancel your appointments for the rest of the day. We're staying in this room until we figure out what it is and how to fix it." There's a quick hubbub while everyone grabs their cell or handheld and tells their assistants to cancel everything on their calendars for the day. When the agency head resumes the meeting she says, "Maybe the best way to start is to identify as precisely as possible exactly *what* is wrong." She slowly looks around the table. Each department head takes the hint. Going around the table, each summarizes the issues they tried to deal with last week, unsuccessfully.

The head of one of the service delivery divisions says, "Last week was the second week of our new program to help low-income people, but instead of being inundated with hundreds of applications as we had expected, we got a measly 43 sign-ups in the first week and — incredibly — only 29 last week. This is awful."

The manager of another major department talks about his difficulties enforcing a new regulatory policy. "I absolutely need 22 full-time inspectors to enforce the new law, but because of budget cuts, the hiring freeze and retirements, all I've got is seven people out in the field on any given day."

A third line manager had just kicked off a new abuse reporting hotline. Everyone in the agency was assuming that the line would be ringing constantly or that people would be posting anonymous tips on the Web site. "Something is wrong. On the hotline, we got only eight calls and on the Web site only six more tips," she said.

The press officer talks about bad press the agency got all weekend. "A reporter called late Friday afternoon and insisted on a comment by her deadline of 5:00 p.m. It was to be an exposé of how we supposedly screwed up in taking care of one of our clients. My secretary took the call and knew the information was sensitive, so she wanted to be careful that what we released was OK. I was off on Friday and couldn't be reached, even by cell or beeper. So, she scrambled around the top floor, but few senior executives were in their offices and the ones she found had no media experience. No one knew what to do. The only consensus was to touch base with you." Turning to the chief, he says, "And you were on a four-hour flight to the Coast. By the time you'd have landed, the reporter's deadline would have come and gone. So, my office only released a bland statement saying we were looking into it." The agency got a black eye in the local newspaper the next morning and, because it was a slow news weekend, the TV stations picked up the story and led with it for three days straight, including Monday morning drive time.

Next it was the turn of the legislative liaison officer. "We took a hammering at the appropriations hearing last week. Not a single member of the committee said anything positive about us. Just the opposite. The legislators were treating us like dead meat. They said they could underfund us and none of their voters would care. Our unpopularity with politicians was palpable in the committee room during the bill's mark-up."

It's like that all around the table. When everyone had spoken, the chief repeats her question: "What's wrong?" No one seems to have any answers or insights beyond what they've already said. As the newbie, you aren't sure if you should say anything. You've never talked at the senior management meeting before. But, with everyone else talked out, the boss looks at you. "OK, kid, any bright ideas from all that schoolin' of yours?"

You hesitate, not sure what to do. Finally, you decide you have to answer her question. You take a deep breath and then quickly blurt out, "We only have *one* problem: public relations." The room erupts.

Public Relations in Public Administration

In American culture, the term 'public relations' and its widely recognized initials, PR, have come to have a negative, even sinister, meaning. It generally means appearance over substance, use of misleading information over truth, manipulation over openness. "That's just PR," is a common put-down, virtually an assertion of lack of credibility. Furthermore, in the American political system, public relations has had several other negative connotations added to its meaning. Politicians are quick to criticize agency expenditures on external communications as a waste of money, a misspending of the hard-earned dollars that taxpayers have to pay the government. "You shouldn't need to do any PR," the self-righteous politicians will glibly lecture the agency head. "Just do your job." Other elected officials will claim that any public relations that a government organization engages in is a purely self-serving act of puffery, trying to 'look good' regardless of the merits. Back in 1970, President Nixon had issued a memo to the federal executive branch condemning agency public relations as "wasteful and self-serving." It was an apt summary of how most elected officials feel about PR in public administration, then and now. It doesn't seem to matter whether those politicians are in the legislative or executive branch; at the federal, state, or local levels. No one, it seems, is *for* government public relations.

It is the contention of this book that the negative image of public relations in American culture in general, and in American politics in particular, has invariably prompted several generations of public administrators to shy away from considering public relations as a management tool sitting in their toolbox available for use. In the same way that practitioners and professors think of the benefits of using budgeting, HR, strategic planning, and performance measurement to improve the work of a government agency, so too can public relations. It can be used to advance the substantive mission of an agency in ways that save money, staff, time, and effort.

Going back to the scenario of the senior staff meeting described previously, public relations can increase the utilization of governmental goods and services, promote voluntary compliance with new laws and rules, have citizens act as the eyes and ears of the agency, improve media relations, and strengthen the standing of the agency with the public-at-large. These are all management goals, unrelated to accusations of wasteful spending or self-serving activities. Exactly the opposite. The theme of this book is that public relations *is* public administration.

Some of the uses of public relations in government are pragmatic, intended to advance the mission of the agency, but in unorthodox ways that reduce costs. For example, public service campaigns are ways to influence public behavior ('buckle up') in a way that is less expensive than policing. Similarly, advertising the availability of new programs and services is a way to reach potential clients and customers through a wholesale approach, rather than the more expensive one-by-one retail effort. Another useful goal that can be accomplished through public relations co-opts the public to serve as the eyes and ears of an agency (such as 911 systems) rather than substantial increases in staffing that would otherwise be necessary.

Besides these pragmatic uses of public relations, external communications can also be used to advance the goals of democracy, the central characteristic that distinguishes public administration from business administration. These would be situations of 'information for information's sake' rather than to accomplish a more tangible management goal. Examples of this aspect of government public relations include reporting to the public on agency activities as a way of contributing to an informed public, disseminating information as a prelude to citizen participation in agency decision making, and listening to public opinion.

These preceding examples are of the different *purposes* of government public relations, which is how this volume is structured. There are eight distinct purposes that public relations can help accomplish in public administration:

1. Media Relations
2. Public Reporting
3. Responsiveness to the Public
4. (Outreach) Increasing the Utilization of Services and Products
5. (Outreach) Public Education and Public Service Campaigns
6. (Outreach) Seeking Voluntary Public Compliance with Laws and Regulations
7. (Outreach) Using the Public as the Eyes and Ears of an Agency
8. Increasing Public Support

The book is structured to highlight how these specific management purposes can be accomplished by using public relations. It is intended to be practical, useful to practitioners and students alike.

Uses of This Volume

Even though the news media and advances in public communications technologies are dominant trends in the 21st century, the profession of public administration has — oddly — given those subjects little attention. The last reader in government public relations was published in 1981. However, today's public administrators and students training to be future public administrators need to understand the crucial role that the news media plays in public life, how to deal with the media and, more generally, how external communications efforts can be used to advance the work of public agencies. Public relations is a tool of governance just like the many others in the manager's toolkit.

The book covers the theory, practice, and context of government public relations. Therefore, it is not a 'how-to' book, in the sense of providing instruction on, for example, writing press releases or planning an advertising campaign. Rather, it is for one level up from such a technically oriented training. It is intended to provide current practitioners and students in university-level courses with an understanding of the uses of public relations as tools to advance the goals of government (in contradistinction to politics).

The approach used here is comparable to the pedagogic premise used for other aspects of university-level professional training. For example, public administrators who are not HR specialists need to have a basic understanding of the role of public personnel administration as a management device. That is why most MPA programs offer a basic course in human resources management. This book is based on a similar premise. Even though an administrative agency would likely employ public information and media relations specialists, the middle- and top-level agency managers need to have a basic understanding of the importance, value, and uses of public relations and external communications.

As an introductory reader, the book presents an overview of the applications and benefits of public relations in public administration. As such, it could be useful to practitioners who are seeking to break the impasse of the status quo by using a management instrument that is often overlooked. Similarly, this book can be used as an introductory textbook in graduate and undergraduate courses in public administration. In some cases, it can be a primary textbook for courses on government public relations or on the broader subject of communications in public administration, comprising both internal and external communications. In a slightly different context, this book could be useful as a secondary text for political science courses on political communication and on tools of governance as well as for overview courses on public relations offered in schools and departments of journalism, communications, and public relations.

The structure of the book has been designed with these audiences in mind. Following an introduction to the general subject of government public relations (Section I), the focus shifts to some of the discrete purposes of public relations, so that their benefit to government managers can be made more tangible. They are on, respectively, media relations, public reporting, responsiveness, and outreach (Sections II–V). Public relations is also an integral part of crisis management (Section VI). Then, to counterbalance the depictions of these beneficial uses of public relations, there are some readings about the external context of government public relations. As with other aspects of public administration, the *publicness* of government management is the qualitative characteristic that differentiates it from business administration. In this case, the public environment of government public relations is an important parameter to keep in mind. This includes, for example, legislative hostility to agency public relations and the application of freedom of information laws (Section VII). Finally, with the public sector increasingly using nonprofit agencies to deliver government-funded services, it is also relevant and important to review the practice of public relations by nonprofit agencies, as part of the extended public sector (Section VIII). The last section of the book seeks to summarize the overall themes related to government public relations, along with an assessment of trends likely to affect its future practice, such as globalization and E-reporting (Section IX). An Appendix at the end of the book provides a comprehensive annotated bibliography of the historical literature on the relationship between public administration and the news media.

To assist students and instructors, I have written an introduction to each section. Each introduction provides an overview of the topic of the section and a short preview of the chapters to follow. Then, at the end of every section, I have prepared a list of discussion questions that can be used to help identify key points in the readings and a short list of additional published material that goes into more depth regarding the subject of that section. To accomplish a similar purpose, the Appendix presents an annotated bibliography of historical sources relating to public administration and the news media. These are classic writings that have informed all subsequent knowledge of the subject. As always, a deep historical understanding is important for those seeking to explore the topic beyond the material presented in the book.

The pieces selected for the reader were culled from the best *contemporary* writing about government public relations. I have limited the selections mostly to sources that have been published since the turn of the century. Of the 25 chapters, 20 were published since 2000, and the other five are from the 1990s. There is a rich historical literature about the practice of government public relations pre-1990, but these — while interesting — would not be particularly useful to the modern-day public administrator or university-level student. Those earlier writings can be found as cited sources in the endnotes to the chapters, in the short list of suggested additional readings found at the end of every section of the book, and in the Appendix.

I have also tried to tailor the readings to international as well as American audiences. Government public relations is a universal aspect of public administration. It is important to improving the quality of government regardless of locale. A majority of the chapters are written by American authors focusing on the U.S. public sector. However, many of the discussions in those chapters are easily applicable to other countries, especially to developed and Western-oriented nations. Therefore, non-U.S. readers should find many of those chapters to be relevant and useful to their context. I have also included some readings that discuss aspects of government public relations as they occur in other developed countries. Chapter 13 and Chapter 16 were written by U.K.-based authors and often use examples that are European. Chapter 14 discusses a citizen complaint process in Taipei, and Chapter 15 analyzes the operations of the Hong Kong ombudsman. So, conversely, while these chapters use international examples, I have chosen them because they are equally applicable to the U.S. context. Therefore, American readers should have little trouble visualizing those discussions in the environment of the U.S. public sector. Finally, Chapter 24, one of the two chapters in the concluding section of the book, seeks to draw international generalizations about public administration during these times of globalization, especially of media treatment of government. Given the pervasiveness of globalization both to developed and developing nations, the topic seemed to be an apt way to help summarize the book's focus on government public relations, whether in the United States or in other countries.

The book contains only two largely historical pieces, both about government public relations in the United States. Pinkleton's history of the Committee on Public Information during World War I (Chapter 4) is applicable to the contemporary reader because it provides a highly specific description of what an *all-out* government public relations effort would look like. My history of municipal public reporting in the United States (Chapter 11) helps give the modern-day reader a tangible sense of what a robust reporting effort would look like, based on the detailed examples from its earlier applications. Those examples continue to be relevant in the present.

As editor, I tried to maintain as light a touch as possible. Most changes were to assure a consistent style throughout the volume, which would be advantageous to the reader. Some of these modest changes included assuring standard citation formats and, for consistency purposes of having a uniform style throughout the volume, shifting spelling in a few chapters from British to U.S. style. In another effort to assure that the book would be as up-to-date as possible, I reviewed all the URLs that had been cited in the originally published materials and modified them as necessary so that they continued to be accessible as of 2007. Finally, given that the book seeks to integrate different aspects of public relations into a whole, I have inserted an editor's note flagging for the reader instances when one writer cites a source that was also selected to be a separate chapter in this book. I hope this will help readers gradually see how the various parts of the book are related elements of a bigger picture, components that synthesize well into a common theme.

Acknowledgments

Almost all of the readings selected for this volume were from blind-review journal articles, from encyclopedia entries, and from book chapters that had previously been published by Taylor & Francis or its corporate predecessors. This publishing house has an astounding copyrighted library of writings on public administration. As editor, I considered myself fortunate to be able to rummage though this virtual library and select the best for inclusion in this book. I found high quality and incisive pieces relating to all different facets of government public relations in the Taylor & Francis collection. My thanks to the in-house professionals who helped facilitate the preparation of this book, especially Rich O'Hanley. Rich and series editor and LSU professor Evan Berman were both enthusiastic supporters of the concept of this book from the start and they deserve the credit for shepherding it through to fruition.

Of all the copyrighted material contained in the book, only two come from sources other than Taylor & Francis. The two exceptions are both pieces that I had previously published and which I felt were instrumental to the theme of the book, fitting in well as bookends to the volume as the first and last chapters. The first chapter is an introduction to government public relations and the last is an assessment of ongoing trends in public reporting that are likely to impact the future direction of this aspect of government public relations (Chapter 25). Chapter 1 is a major rewrite of an article I had published in the free online journal, *Public Administration & Management: An Interactive Journal* [www.pamij.com], and the last chapter comes from a report funded by a grant from the IBM Center for the Business of Government in Washington, D.C. My thanks, respectively, to Aaron Wachhaus and Mark Abramson for facilitating re-use of those materials. Finally, three pieces in the book had been published by the federal government and therefore were not copyrighted. My thanks to the American taxpayers for funding such outstanding research.

Given my career-long interest in government public relations, about a third of the readings in the book are those that I had authored. I tried to be objective about these selections, rejecting most of my historical research as unhelpful for those seeking concrete and useful information about the practical application of public relations in government. In general, I hope that my own work selected for this volume, along with those of others, provides a comprehensive perspective on the many uses and benefits that public relations can offer the government manager, a theme I have been interested in since my graduate studies. This reader was a welcome opportunity to pull together many items of mine and from other sources that, hopefully, when published together here for the first time, provide a synthesis of the book's overall premise, namely that public relations can help public administrators accomplish the substantive missions of their programs.

Nothing I write could be accomplished without the eagle eye of Andrea Zweifel, the department's program associate. She has a talent that can seemingly spot a proofing error from a mile away. I was lucky to benefit again from her assistance.

I hope you will find this book interesting, practical, and helpful. I welcome feedback and reactions from readers: mordecai@uwm.edu.

Permissions

Chapter 1: Southern Public Administration Education Foundation, Inc. to reprint Lee, M., Public information in government organizations: A review and curriculum outline of external relations in public administration, *Public Administration and Management: An Interactive Journal*, 5, 183, 2000.

Chapter 25 and portions of the introduction to Section III: Rowman & Littlefield to reprint Lee, M., E-reporting: Using managing-for-results data to strengthen democratic accountability, in *Managing for Results 2005*, Kamensky, J.M. and Morales, A., Eds., Rowman & Littlefield, Lanham, MD, 2005, chap. 4; and IBM Center for the Business of Government to reprint Lee, M., *E-Reporting: Strengthening Democratic Accountability* (monograph), IBM Center for the Business of Government, Washington, DC, 2004.

About the Editor

Mordecai Lee is professor of governmental affairs at the University of Wisconsin–Milwaukee. He teaches graduate seminars in the Master of Public Administration and the Master of Science in Nonprofit Management and Leadership programs, including policy analysis, nonprofit management, and nonprofit advocacy. He also oversees the noncredit Certificate in Public Administration and Professional Certificate in Nonprofit Management offered by the university's School of Continuing Education.

Professor Lee has specialized in researching and writing about government public relations. His publications in that area include *The First Presidential Communications Agency: FDR's Office of Government Reports* (Albany: State University of New York Press, 2005) and about 20 articles in refereed academic journals, including *Public Relations Review* and *Journal of Public Affairs*. In addition, he is author of two other books relating to public sector history.

Before joining the academy, Lee was a practitioner of public relations in the public and nonprofit sectors. He served as an assistant to a congressman in Washington, D.C., was elected to three terms in the Wisconsin Legislature's State Assembly and two in the State Senate, and served as executive director of the Milwaukee Jewish Council for Community Relations.

Professor Lee graduated Phi Beta Kappa in political science from the University of Wisconsin–Madison. He received his Master of Public Administration and Ph.D. in Public Administration from Syracuse University. He wrote his dissertation while a Guest Scholar at the Brookings Institution in Washington, D.C.

Contributors

Tony Bovaird is on the staff of the Institute of Local Government Studies, University of Birmingham, Birmingham, United Kingdom. E-mail: T.Bovaird@bham.ac.uk

Don-yun Chen is associate professor of public policy and management, Shih Hsin University, Taiwan. E-mail: donc@nccu.edu.tw

Joy A. Clay is associate professor of public and nonprofit administration, University of Memphis, Memphis, Tennessee. E-mail: joyclay@memphis.edu

Edward J. Downes is associate professor of public relations, Boston University, Boston, Massachusetts. E-mail: edownes@bu.edu

James L. Garnett is professor of public policy and administration, Rutgers University–Camden, Camden, New Jersey. E-mail: garnett@crab.rutgers.edu

James E. Grunig is professor emeritus of communication, University of Maryland, College Park, Maryland. E-mail: jg68@umail.umd.edu

Amy Helling is associate professor of public administration and urban studies, Georgia State University, Atlanta, Georgia. E-mail: ahelling@gsu.edu

Behrooz Kalantari is professor of public administration, Savannah State University, Savannah, Georgia. E-mail: Kalantab@tigerpaw.savstate.edu

Kevin R. Kosar is an analyst in American national government, Congressional Research Service, Library of Congress, Washington, D.C. E-mail: kkosar@sprynet.com

Carlos Wing-Hung Lo is professor of management, Hong Kong Polytechnic University, Hong Kong, China. E-mail: mscarlos@polyu.edu.hk

Daniel W. Martin is professor of public administration, University of Baltimore, Baltimore, Maryland. E-mail: dmartin@ubalt.edu

Steve Martin is professor of public policy and management and director of the Centre for Local and Regional Government Research, Cardiff University, Cardiff, United Kingdom. E-mail: martinsj@cardiff.ac.uk

Bruce Pinkleton is professor of communication, Washington State University, Pullman, Washington. E-mail: pink@wsu.edu

Suzanne J. Piotrowski is assistant professor of public affairs and administration, Rutgers University–Newark, Newark, New Jersey. E-mail: spiotrow@andromeda.rutgers.edu

Robert Radvanovsky is a partner in the consulting firm Infracritical, Geneva, Illinois. E-mail: admin@infracritical.com

Joseph P. Viteritti is the Blanche D. Blank Professor of Public Policy, Hunter College, City University of New York, New York. E-mail: joseph.viteritti@hunter.cuny.edu

OVERVIEW OF GOVERNMENT PUBLIC RELATIONS

Introduction to Section I

The foreword began with a description of a crisis staff meeting at a government agency when everything seemed to be falling apart. The fictional narrative ended with the junior member of the agency's management team blurting out that the agency had only one problem, public relations. The purpose of this section is to identify what that answer meant. Government public relations is an oft-neglected tool in the toolkit of the public administrator. External communications programs can help an agency accomplish its goals such as marketing its services, notifying the public of new laws and programs, trying to modify public behavior to prevent problems, and benefiting from the citizenry serving as the agency's eyes and ears. These are some of the tangible purposes that government public relations can help accomplish. Besides that, as inherent to the public sector in a democracy, public relations helps fulfill the democratic obligations of the government manager, such as media relations and reporting to the citizenry. In total, the successful practice of government public relations can mobilize public support for an agency, helping secure it a more stable and safer future, thereby enabling it to better serve the public and the public interest (not necessarily the same).

Chapter 1 provides an overview of the theme of the book, namely the importance of public relations in government and how it can contribute to accomplishing the core missions of public sector agencies. The chapter focuses on the *purposes* of government public relations and how each purpose separately contributes to improved public administration.

James E. Grunig is the foremost academic theoretician of public relations in our times. He has developed a new model of public relations based on two-way symmetrical communications. In Chapter 2 he presents his basic theory and then he applies it more specifically to the public sector. Grunig's model is no mere theory. It is a practical approach to the practice of government public relations and presents an ideal goal that practitioners can, and should, strive for.

As a counterbalance to Grunig's theoretical approach, Chapter 3 is a tangible explanation of government public relations. Issued by the U.S. Office of Personnel Management, the federal government's HR agency, this is the job description used for public affairs positions throughout the national government. Given the size and scope of federal operations, this position description is a ground-level view of what public information officers do and the tasks they have. It also helps delineate those information-related activities that are, generally, not considered part of public relations, such as editing and publishing functions.

The last chapter in the section describes the work of the federal government's Committee on Public Information (CPI) during World War I. While historical narratives tend not to be very helpful for modern-day practitioners and students, this chapter is an exception. CPI's accomplishments continue to be relevant to our times. Established by President Woodrow Wilson with the entrance of the United States into World War I, CPI's scope of activities is a concrete demonstration of what a comprehensive and large-scale government public relations program would look like. CPI's mandate was to mobilize the civilian population in support of the war effort. The agency organized itself so that it would reach all U.S. citizens, relying on a systematic use of different media, different public relations methods, and outreach based on audience segmentation. While CPI was controversial with Congress (see Chapter 19 for a description of Congressional limitations on federal PR), it was effective in promoting the cooperation of the citizenry in the war effort. Nothing approaching the scope of CPI's public relations activities has ever been repeated in the public sector in the United States; certainly not the operations of the Office of War Information (OWI) during World War II. Students and practitioners of government public relations in the 21st century can continue to learn lessons from the work of CPI. It was government PR to the max. The lessons of CPI are in appreciating and learning from the systemic employment of public relations techniques by government. This historical case study shows us how public relations can help any government agency accomplish its goals and mission.

In all, after reading these four chapters, a better understanding of government public relations should emerge. Then, following this introductory overview, the next four sections of the book delve into more detail of some of the key purposes of these external communications programs in the public sector: media relations, public reporting, responsiveness to the public, and outreach/marketing.

Chapter 1

Public Relations in Public Administration

Mordecai Lee

Contents

Abstract: Public relations in public administration encompasses the use of information outside the boundaries of a government agency to accomplish administrative purposes. It is integral to the conduct of public administration, whether as a specialized activity or as an approach held by the agency's leadership. However, the contemporary curriculum in public administration education pays little attention to public relations. With the rapid expansion of the digital age and the information explosion, the importance of managing informational relationships in the 21st century is certain to increase. Public administration practitioners and educators need to broaden their scope of attention to embrace public relations.

Public relations can accomplish many different management goals and can be planned to reach specific audiences. Once a government manager has analyzed an external relations challenge and identified the purpose and audience involved, then the techniques for such an effort can be selected from standard menus available to the practitioner.

Status in Public Administration Education

Public relations is integral to the conduct of public administration. [1] The first textbook in public administration asked in 1926, "How can a working connection be maintained between the official and the public?" [2] Herring answered in 1935 that "the skillful and effective use of publicity is one of the essential devices of successful administration." [3] Within a year, he had already sharpened and broadened that statement from a generalized administrative focus on 'publicity' to the importance of "an office for the management of public relations." [4] Four years later, Woolpert stated that for municipal administration, "public relations problems are inseparable from the program of a city and…every member of the organization is, or should be, a public relations officer." [5] Some contemporary observers have concurred about the continuing value of this activity in public administration by noting — not necessarily approvingly — that public managers can effectively use citizen participation and other public outreach programs as "an instrument for the achievement of administrative objectives." [6]

Yet, until recently, public relations had no major part within contemporary public administration pedagogy. This author documented the disappearance of public relations from the graduate curriculum by comparing Public Administration textbooks from the 1920s to the 1950s with those of the 1980s and 1990s. [7] At the mid-point of the same time period of that textbook review, an international survey of curricula documented that public relations was rarely part of public administration training in institutions of higher education. An agency of the United Nations had sponsored a study of public administration education that included a summary of the curricula of 17 schools in 11 countries. Only four schools listed public relations, external relations or communication as a subject for study. [8] In 1997, Cleary updated his 1989 review of the curriculum of MPA programs. [9] In his original survey, he had "found little evidence of coverage of communication skills in these materials." Then, in 1997, he "continue[d] to find little evidence of coverage of these concepts." [10]

But then practitioners and scholars began calling for increasing the attention to external communication in public administration pedagogy. Kell described communication as "public administration's forgotten art." [11] Swoboda examined the literature on relations between public administrators and the media and concluded that it was "sparse," containing little applicable guidance to budgeting practitioners. [12]

Academic writers have made similar observations about the importance of public relations (and, in general, communications) to the public administrator as well as the paucity of such training in university curricula. In 1991, Waugh and Manns suggested that one of the modifications needed in the curriculum of public administration would be to teach "public administrators [how] to promote their services better and good communication skills are necessary to accomplish that public relations task." [13] In 1998, a joint committee of the National Association of Schools of Public Affairs and Administration (NASPAA) and the American Political Science Association's Section on Public Administration recommended that "those involved in shaping public administration curricula should work to ensure that managers more fully understand how to get their message out to the media." [14]

From the broader perspective of communications in general, Garnett observed that "a sizable gap exists between what government practitioners and students need to know about communicating and what training and reading are available to them." [15] Waldo called communication "a significant but neglected topic" in public administration. [16] Five years later, Garnett co-edited a comprehensive handbook that focused on the importance of communication in public administration and the need to have a greater research-based understanding of it. [17] He specifically called for an "increase [in] the salience of communication within public administration education." [18] Another writer declared that due to research-based scholarship, "public relations has become a respected domain within both the disciplines of communication and management." [19,20]

Another reason why public administration programs have begun to include public relations in their offerings is that nonprofit administration is looming larger within MPA programs which, in turn, has triggered the important link between effective nonprofit management and public relations. NASPAA's 2006 nonprofit education guidelines recommend including external relations as a "component topic" in the curriculum:

> The relationship between the organization and its constituents, how that is managed, and various interpretations of accountability should be included in the program. Within this context are principles of communication, public relations, general and social marketing, managing constituent groups, negotiation and conflict management, and strategic planning. This element also encompasses the role of mobilization of human resources and media relations for the purpose of public relations and advocacy and the principles and techniques of crisis management. [21]

Wish and Mirabella list public relations — within the larger rubric of 'fundraising, marketing and public relations' — as one of the seven major categories of a curricular model of nonprofit management education. [22] A survey of faculty, practitioners and students regarding the skills needed by nonprofit administrators listed public relations as one of eight 'most important' core subjects. [23]

Nomenclature

With a consensus gradually emerging that the general subject of external communications indeed is an important aspect of public and nonprofit management, then the next obvious question is *what* about public relations should students and practitioners of public administration know? As a first step, attention needs to be paid to titles, usage and meanings of words. The subject area of internal and external communication has been variously referred to as "communication in public administration," [24] "public agency communication," [25] "public sector communication," [26] and "administrative communication." [27] In their commonly understood meaning, "boundary spanning" would describe this endeavor well, but that title has already been appropriated by a separate and unrelated academic subject. [28]

This inquiry focuses on the narrower topic of out-of-house communication activities in public administration. The first modern social scientist to study this field in depth named it government publicity [29] or public relations in public administration. [30] Since then, it has been variously called promotion, [31] administrative public relations, [32] public affairs, [33] external communication, [34] and public relations management in government. [35] Other recent terms, but unlike the previous titles are not oriented to the public sector, include external affairs [36] and relationship management. [37] The activities and offices in public agencies that deal with the press have been called government information media [38] or government information systems. [39] A very common coinage is public information. [40–42] 'Public information officer' is often the personnel classification for someone working in that area. [43,44]

Literally, 'external relations' is a descriptive and accurate term for this activity. Some of its early uses, half a century ago, included its role in federal agencies during World War II, [45] in municipal administration, [46] and in federal regulatory agencies. [47] For example, a 2005 handbook on nonprofit management included discussion of the importance for leaders to spend time on external relations. [48] NASPAA's guidelines recommend that "external relations" be included in the curriculum of graduate level programs in nonprofit administration. [49] On the federal level, the National Aeronautics and Space Administration (NASA) has an Office of External Relations [50] and an office in the headquarters of the National Weather Service is "responsible for effective external relations, programs, and policies" related to its commercial weather support. [51]

However, despite its precision, the term *external relations* has never gained wide usage. Ditto for *external communications*. On the other hand, public relations is the generally recognized moniker for this field of activity, despite the negative meaning PR sometimes has in popular culture. [52] Still, the plain meaning of the words *public relations* captures perfectly the activity that a public or nonprofit administrator would be engaging in under this rubric: managing different kinds of communication relationships with different kinds of publics. Therefore, public relations it is. (However, for the sake of variety, this volume uses public relations, external relations and public information as synonyms.)

Organizing Principles for Government Public Relations

Public relations can be presented as an important component of the toolbox available to government managers to implement their goals. Some textbooks have presented this approach. For example, Dimock and Dimock — an influential textbook with multiple editions — observed that "public relations lies at the heart of administration." [53] In the fourth, and last, edition of that textbook the authors declared that "public relations is now an integral part of the philosophy of administration, and consequently not separate from the rest of administration." [54] A more recent textbook explains that "agencies also engage in public relations not only to generate greater political support for their activities but also to help clients, regulatees, and others to understand what they do." [55]

A key decision point is to select the optimal organizing principle for an external relations curriculum. In their presentation of a broader curriculum in communication, Waugh and Manns' focus on skills and competencies. [56] For example, in the sections of their curriculum that would be relevant to external relations, they emphasize learning the skills of written communication and of oral communication. Similarly, Garnett's approach focuses significant attention on the direct and indirect ways to communicate with external audiences. [57] The difficulty with this common skills-centered focus is that students are presented with a seemingly sterile checklist of technical ways to conduct external communication, but this is largely disconnected from the administrative situations that call for such skills or the purposes those skills help accomplish. A shift in focus from the 'how' to the 'why,' 'what for' and 'to whom' helps integrate the uses of external relations into the broader goals of a public manager.

It is my contention that skills and techniques flow from goals. When a practitioner is able to identify the variety of situations in which the external relations focus can help accomplish administrative goals, then the act of picking-and-choosing specific tools to use in any particular situation is a logical outgrowth of the goal itself. Skills and techniques emerge logically from a situational analysis of the specific problem facing the manager and the benefits of the external relations perspective. Therefore, I argue that the organizing principle of the public relations curriculum needs to be on the ends rather than the means.

With the approach that focuses on reviewing management issues through the perspective of external relations, a curriculum would first focus on the actual purposes of public relations and, after that, on the audiences of external relations and the techniques to communicate with them. In other words, after the public administrator has identified an administrative goal ('what'), the next decision is the purpose ('what for'), followed by a selection of specific audiences ('who'). The final decision is the choice of the optimal techniques ('how') that contribute to reaching the goal and the purpose.

Purposes of Government Public Relations

A central organizing principle of communication is to identify, as specifically as possible, the *purpose* of any communication effort. This approach can be of special utility to public administrators because of the different reasons that the manager may seek to use the tools of external relations. Different methods logically emerge when trying to accomplish distinct purposes. From analysis of purpose flows the particularistic and logical decision about methods of communication in a given situation. Hence, the specific decision of how to do external relations emerges naturally from the reason that it is being relied upon. I suggest that government public relations has eight distinct and identifiable purposes: (1) media relations, (2) public reporting, and (3) responsiveness to the public, followed by four separate and distinct purposes involving outreach activities, namely (4) increasing the utilization of services and products, (5) public education and public service campaigns, (6) seeking voluntary public compliance with laws and regulations, (7) using the public as the eyes and ears of an agency, and, finally, (8) increasing public support.

Certainly, sometimes an intended *purpose* of a public relations activity can have an impact on another separate purpose. For example, a *consequence* of reporting or a public service campaign might have the side effect of increasing public support for an agency. But, simultaneously, it can also trigger legislative hostility (see chap. 19). My recommendation is to focus on the primary and planned purpose for a public relations initiative. While thinking through side effects can be helpful for an overall analysis, the driving force in decision making should be what is attempted to be accomplished, i.e., what the main purpose is.

Media Relations

The most common purpose of the external relations activity of a public administrator is to deal with reporters, who usually have a negative predisposition when covering government agencies. According to Gates and Hill, "the popular media is often filled with complaints that the bureaucracy is out of control." [58] Most public managers experience receiving a phone call from a reporter seeking information or a quote — and generally dread it. [59] Yet, according to Viteritti, "no high-level public manager can survive the crossfire of public discourse without learning how to deal with the press." [60]

The obligation to cooperate with the press is a combination of the publicness of public administration [61,62] and the constitutional expectation that the media would serve "as an instrument of democracy." [63] However, contemporary journalism is less and less a serious conveyer of news about government. [64] Instead, the orientation of reporters seems more a "hunt for government scandals…'Waste-fraud-and-abuse' has become a single word in the media." [65] According to the spokesperson for the State Department, "journalists get much more excited when they find an example of error than they do when they find an example of success." [66]

To paraphrase the bestseller, administrators are from Jupiter and reporters are from Mercury. [67] For the Romans, Jupiter was patron deity of the state, in charge of laws and social order. The annual festival at the Jupiter temple was in thanks for the preservation of the state. On the other hand, Mercury was the bearer of messages who was eloquent of expression, but cunning and unpredictable. The two are bound to get into conflict and are destined to struggle with each other for eternity. For example, the public administrator is assimilative in orientation, seeking to emphasize continuity and precedent. When explaining, the administrator is likely to use phrases such as "just like," "related to" or "an outgrowth of." On the other hand, the reporter's focus is distributive, seeking to communicate startling and new information as quickly and as broadly as possible. The journalist is seeking to use such phrases as "controversial," "disagreement" and "different" — vocabulary that is generally anathema to the government manager. [68] In administration, specific details are crucial, while the media focuses instead on the larger issues or themes. [69] These bedrock differences contribute to an inherently dissatisfied attitude by administrators when conducting media relations. If the media is not interested in government, then administrators need to learn new strategies to fulfill their obligations in a democracy. [70]

Public Reporting

As part of the public sector, government agencies have a general obligation to report to the public on their activities. This form of direct reporting to the citizenry is different from the oversight function of elected officials to whom agencies are formally accountable. The origins of public reporting date back to the establishment of public administration early in the 20th century. [71] Current examples of this activity include agency annual reports, websites updated with information about the activities of the agency and informational material sent to public libraries for the citizens to take based on their individual interests. The Government Finance Officers Association sponsors a Popular Annual Reporting Award to encourage public agencies to produce financial reports that are understandable to the lay public and thus promote democratic accountability. [72]

Responsiveness to the Public

Public relations, and communication in general, entails two-way communication. [73] Agencies can use public relations to be responsive to their stakeholders. Organizationally, governments need to be 'good listeners,' to hear the underlying messages that the public is sending. Public opinion is a powerful force in democracy and public administrators need to know what it is saying to them. As entities in the public sector, government is also expected to promote citizen participation in its activities, as one more way to advance the interests of democracy.

Public administration is enhanced when government agencies hear the message sent by the public and choose policies and programs based on that information. For example, the U.S. Mint had failed with its introduction of the Susan B. Anthony dollar coin. However, a stakeholder, the vending machine industry, very much wanted a dollar coin to be widely used. So, the Mint conducted in-depth research about public preferences before introducing a new version of the dollar coin. [74] At every U.S. Postal Service branch is a brochure entitled, "Let's hear from you… We want to know if we met your needs today." Similarly, advances in electronic communication greatly enhance the ability to learn from the messages that the agency is receiving. [75]

Outreach: Increasing the Utilization of Services and Products

Like all other producers of goods and services, government agencies need to market their programs. [76,77] With increasingly innovative channels for delivering government services, administrators can no longer count on the "we're the only game in town" attitude. For example, building public awareness of available public services helps maximize the usage of the service and accomplish its public purpose.

Another element of marketing is to provide quality service to customers, whether they can take their business elsewhere or not. Public managers need to review all aspects of the experience that their customers have when they come in contact with the agency. Small details, such as the wording and location of signs, the availability of information and seating arrangements are all critical elements for a positive interaction. [78] This service orientation is a manifestation of the two-way aspect of public relations.

Outreach: Public Education and Public Service Campaigns

By using paid and free media coverage, an agency can accomplish its mission and reduce its expenditures by encouraging behavior that has broad social approval and reflects widely held values. [79,80] The most widely recognized example is the campaign by the U.S. Forest Service to reduce fires in national forests through the Smokey the Bear campaign. By encouraging a change in public behavior regarding use of fires while camping, the Forest Service was able to reduce the demand on its fire suppression infrastructure.

Outreach: Seeking Voluntary Public Compliance with Laws and Regulations

Agencies can reduce their regulatory costs by engaging in public relations to encourage voluntary compliance with the new laws, regulations and programs they have been assigned to administer.

This is a cost-effective approach to the implementation phase of the policy process. A common example is the effort by the U.S. Postal Service to inform the public about an increase in postal rates as a way to reduce the number of letters that have to be pulled from the mail stream and returned for "postage due." Another example is the effort by prosecutors to notify the public about a new aggressive policy of increasing criminal charges for crimes committed with guns. One of the prosecutors was quoted as explaining, "If those people don't know about it, how's it supposed to serve as a deterrent to them?" [81]

Outreach: Using the Public as the Eyes and Ears of an Agency

Government agencies can encourage citizens to serve as their eyes and ears, thus reducing the need for staffing. For example, when a person chooses to call 911 in an emergency, he or she has been co-opted effectively by the police and fire departments to serve as a member of its 'informal' organization. Incentives for participation can vary from self-interest, to self-satisfaction, to rewards. The key to the success of this function is that citizens are familiar with their potential role as an extension of the agency, an awareness accomplished through public relations. For example, a Wisconsin sheriff said that he could not afford to put deputies on patrol for drunk drivers all the time. Instead, he created a program called Mobile Eyes that pays drivers who use their cell phones to notify deputies of probable drunk drivers they observe. Callers receive $100 for calls that result in an arrest for drunken driving. [82] New digital communication technologies permit citizens to report the location of a pothole and then to expect that the agency will respond promptly to their report. [83]

Increasing Public Support

At mid-century, Graham declared that "the art of achieving and maintaining support for sound public policies is as much a part of public administration in a democracy as is the execution of policies." [84] Government units can use a wide variety of communication techniques to try to increase the support they have with the public. [85] In 2000, the Pew Research Center for the People & the Press conducted a survey to gauge the favorability ratings of individual federal agencies and found significant variations. [86,87]

For example, in an attempt to gain favorable ratings, the armed services will cooperate extensively with the production of movies that will enhance their image and decline to cooperate with movies that would put them in a bad light. [88] Some agencies, especially in law enforcement, organize citizen academies to inform local leaders about their activities. Other agencies create 'Friends of' groups, to have a network of supporters available when needed.

However, attempts to woo public support can backfire as well. This reflects the external environment of government public relations. Politicians have a fingertip feel for the public mood. They can sense when an agency is particularly popular or unpopular with the public. Therefore, agency efforts seeking public support can trigger attacks from elected officials who are its adversaries and do not want it to gain this support. Opponents of the Forest Service's policy to limit logging attacked its public communications plan. [89] A U.S. senator, when opposing military public relations, explained that "There is something basically unwise and undemocratic about a system which taxes the public to finance a propaganda campaign aimed at persuading the same taxpayers that they must spend more tax dollars to subvert their independent judgment." [90]

In summary, it is valuable for public administrators to be able to distinguish between the different purposes of external relations because the attainment of a specific goal would necessarily call for a specific, even ad hoc, mix of techniques and audience orientations that are most appropriate for that particular purpose.

Audiences

The other central organizing principle of communication — besides the purpose of the public relations activity — is to identify, as specifically as possible, the intended audience of the communication effort. This approach can be of particular utility to public administrators because of the multiple external stakeholders in an agency's world. Each distinct audience has different needs and interests. Therefore, through audience analysis a public manager can more precisely focus on the identifiable audiences that have a particular stake in the issue at hand. From audience analysis flows the specific decisions about methods of communication in a given situation. For example, one demographic group may have a predominant focus on oral communication, while another may be a newspaper-reading one. In such a case, the specific decision of how to do external relations emerges naturally from the audience analysis. For the practice of public relations in government, the universe outside the agency can be segmented into six discrete audience categories.

1. Customer Relations: Individuals and groups who are 'consuming' the agency's goods or services. This perspective, of viewing citizens who interact with an agency as identical to customers, clients and consumers in the private sector, has some limitations. However, for purposes of communication, this category is helpful, as it differentiates this audience from other elements of the public with which the government agency might be interacting.

2. Community Relations: The term 'community' is so overused in American parlance that it has virtually been emptied of any meaning. However, the phrase 'community relations' has tended to have a more specific and understood usage. It focuses on interacting with minority and under-represented populations and, separately, it relates to citizens who live in close proximity to a specific government facility. In this meaning, as a subset of public relations, community relations focuses on audiences that would have a highly identifiable interest in a particular agency activity, not because they are consumers of the organization's goods and services, but because of their racial/ethic status or because of where they are physically located.

3. Interest Group Relations: Organized special interest groups that are particularly attentive to the work of an agency. In some cases, these groups would not be consumers of the agency's product, but, nonetheless, they have intense interest in the work of the agency, whether for economic, ideological or other reasons. For example, the snack food industry may not be inspected by an Agriculture Department, but has significant interest in the department's nutritional recommendations. A prisoner rights advocacy group would not be a consumer of correctional services, but for reasons of mission would be attentive to the operations of the correctional institution.

4. Citizen Relations: This covers interaction with the undifferentiated public-at-large. As taxpayers, they are the funders of the agency. As voters, they are the 'shareholders' of government. And as members of the polity and the source of sovereignty in democracy, they are the owners of government.

There are two other audiences that are external to a government agency. While they can be relevant to a public relations orientation, they generally are not the responsibility of public relations offices. However, for the senior administrator, regardless of who does what, it is important to be aware of all external audiences that would be relevant for any particular public relations initiative. These two other audiences are:

5. Liaison with Elected Officials: Legislative bodies usually exert more power over administrative agencies than the chief elected executive. [91,92] Therefore, appropriate management of the flow of information between an agency and its legislative body is vital. This activity is variously called "congressional relations," "legislative liaison," "board relations," etc. Similarly, the agency needs to perceive that a different audience with which it interacts is the chief elected executive of any particular level of government, such as "White House relations," "executive office relations," etc. Finally, sometimes there are other elected officials who have substantive oversight powers, such as a comptroller, with whom an agency liaises.

6. Intergovernmental Relations: This includes relations with other agencies at the same level of government or other levels of government. It is generally done through direct communication, although agencies sometimes do this indirectly, by using media coverage to communicate with other agencies or other levels of government. [93]

Techniques

After identifying and analyzing the purpose and the audience for an external relations effort, it then becomes timely for the public administrator to focus on the different techniques of external communication that would be most suited for the given situation. Garnett provides a comprehensive listing and explanation of the primary techniques of external relations.

- Direct Communication
  - Face-to-Face Contact
  - Telephone Calls
  - Written Publications
  - Television Programs
  - Films and Videos
  - Computers and Computer Disks
  - Actions and Decisions
- Indirect Communication
  - News Media
  - Intercessors [94]

Lindstrom and Nie also present a slightly different, but equally systematic, list of external communications techniques to use when the agency's purpose is to be in close touch with public opinion (listed in order of citizen satisfaction, highest to lowest):

1. Video techniques
2. Drop-in center
3. Focus groups
4. Citizen survey
5. Collaborative task force
6. Facilitation
7. Visioning
8. Citizen's advisory committee

9. Brainstorming
10. Telephone techniques
11. Media strategies
12. Charette (an architectural term for a workshop that involves active collaboration on design)
13. Public meetings
14. Fairs
15. Newsletters
16. Open house
17. Booth at exposition/fair
18. Luncheon [95]

Detailed descriptions and explanations of these kinds of standard techniques of public relations are well summarized and easily accessible through several "how-to" publications. [96–98] However, even the two detailed listings of public relations techniques presented here and the other sources the reader is referred to cannot be considered exhaustive. Time, practice, experience, technology and social advances all have the effect of creating new forms of external communications. One's imagination is the only true limitation of the techniques of public relations.

It is important to emphasize the primary benefit of maintaining these lists of public relations techniques for use in planning public relations initiatives. As suggested in this review, the first step in the practice of government public relations is to identify the *purpose* of the external communications effort. Second, based on the particular purpose of the initiative or project, it becomes a relatively straightforward step to then identify the *audience(s)* that would be relevant for the intended purpose. Contrary to the action orientation of American culture, it is only at the third step that one reviews and selects the *techniques* of public relations that would be the most targeted and likely most effective in accomplishing the selected purpose for those selected audiences.

Other Foci

In addition to the importance of focusing on the purposes, audiences and techniques of external relations, six other subjects belong in an overview of this aspect of public administration: crisis management, leadership, structure, performance measurement, conflict management and internal communications.

Crisis Management

The preceding discussion reviewed the important elements of external relations in public administration. These all assume the normal periods of administrative work, with adequate intervals for planning, reviewing, testing and clearing before implementation. Such conventional expectations disappear at times of crisis. External relations during a crisis are fundamentally different from other, more normal time frames. [99–101] As such, external relations education needs to devote separate attention to operations in times of crisis.

Leadership

Training needs to focus on the two distinct meanings of external relations, as a specialized staff function within large organizations as well as an operating concept of administration. [102] The higher a public manager moves up the hierarchy, the more she or he deals with external issues and constituencies. This necessitates a greater need for having and using public relations skills. [103] In the private sector, corporate CEOs are now estimated to spend 25–75% of their time on external relations. [104] For example, during the early years of Social Security, the agency's highest levels of political and administrative leaders used public relations "with great skill" to establish the new program with the public at large and assure its long-term future. [105] On the other hand, a review of three agencies in Michigan in the 1950s concluded that "most managers were, in fact, neglecting minimal outside information and education activities" due to the press of daily business, legislative antagonism to spending money on external relations and hostile special interest groups. [106]

Structure

Grunig and Dozier have outlined the characteristics of an ideal public relations program in a large governmental or business organization as follows:

    I. Micro Level: Strategic management
   II. Managerial (Meso) Level:
      1. A single or integrated public relations department
      2. Separate function from marketing
      3. Direct reporting relationship to senior management
      4. Two-way symmetrical model
      5. Senior public relations person in the managerial role
      6. Potential for excellent public relations, as indicated by:
        a. Knowledge of symmetrical model
        b. Knowledge of managerial role
        c. Academic training in public relations
        d. Professionalism
      7. Schema for public relations in the organization reflects the two-way symmetrical model
      8. Equal opportunity for women and minorities in public relations
  III. Macro Level:
      1. Organic rather than mechanical organizational structure
      2. Symmetrical system of internal communication
      3. Turbulent, complex environment with pressure from activist groups
      4. Sufficient power for public relations director in or with the dominant coalition
      5. Participative rather than authoritarian organizational culture
  IV. Effects of Excellent Public Relations:
      1. Micro-level programs meet communication objectives
      2. Job satisfaction is high among employees
      3. Reduced cost of regulation, pressure and litigation [107,108]

Each of these sub-topics needs to be explored so that public administrators will have an understanding of what factors contribute to an effective external relations program, whether they are directing it, utilizing its services or over it.

Performance Measurement

The increasing emphasis in public administration on performance measurement [109,110] can and should be expected of an agency's external relations just like other sub-units of an agency. Ehling and Dozier have developed several different quantitative, as well as qualitative, approaches that can be used in the public sector as well as the private and the nonprofit sectors. [111,112]

Conflict Management

Administrative organizations face inevitable tugs and pulls in different directions from their multiple external constituencies. For example, a classic situation has clients clamoring for more services while elected officials are seeking to cut budgets, or at least freeze them. According to Cohen and Eimicke, "managing relations with outside organizations is a delicate balancing act between protecting your organization's interests and catering to theirs." [113] Luke, as well, observed that "conflict naturally exists" when a leader tries to convene a group that consists of internal and external stakeholders. [114] Given the permanent presence of friction when conducting external relations, government managers need to possess skills in mediation, negotiation and conflict management. He suggests that a leader must possess advanced conflict management competencies so that he or she is "conceiving ingenious solutions to conflicting interests." [115]

Internal Communications

Public administrators involved in external relations can only be as good as the information they possess. That's why a strong internal communication system is essential to under-gird an effective external relations program. For example, an agency spokesperson must be well informed about policy discussions occurring within an agency. According to Hess, "press secretaries know that it is the sine qua non of spokesmanship to be in the loop" of an agency's inner circle. [116] Similarly, the external communications specialist should not only be well informed, but should also be a participant in internal policy deliberations by assessing probable external reactions to different policy scenarios. According to Linsky, "research and experience" confirm the value of utilizing the expertise of public affairs professionals to gauge the external relations implications of various policy options. [117]

Summary

Public relations in public administration is the use of information outside the boundaries of a government agency. It is integral to the conduct of public administration, whether as a specialized activity or as an approach held by the agency's leadership. External relations can accomplish many different management goals and can be planned to reach specific audiences. Once a government manager has analyzed an external relations challenge and identified the purpose and audience involved, then the techniques for such an effort can be selected from standard menus available to the practitioner.

However, the contemporary curriculum in public administration education pays little attention to external relations. With the rapid expansion of the digital age and the information explosion, the importance of managing informational relationships in the 21st century is certain to increase. It turns out that Simon was premature when he observed in the 1939 *Municipal Year Book* that public relations was "no longer a stepchild" of public administration and instead "is being increasingly recognized as an indispensable element in effective administration." [118] Public administration practitioners and educators need to broaden their scope of attention to embrace external relations. It is a useful, helpful and important aspect of managing government agencies.

Note: *This is an abridged, revised and updated version of Lee, M., Public information in government organizations: A review and curriculum outline of external relations in public administration,* Public Administration and Management: An Interactive Journal, *5, 183, 2000. http://www.pamij.com/5_4/5_4_4_pubinfo.pdf (accessed 2007).*

Endnotes

1. Lee, M., Public relations *is* public administration, *The Public Manager*, 27(4), 49, 1998–99.
2. White, L.D., *Introduction to the Study of Public Administration*, Macmillan, New York, 1926, 476.
3. Herring, E.P., Official publicity under the New Deal, *Annals of the American Academy of Political and Social Science*, 179, 170, 1935.
4. Herring, E.P., *Public Administration and the Public Interest*, Russell & Russell, New York, 1967 [1936], 368.
5. Woolpert, E.D., *Municipal Public Relations: A Suggested Program for Improving Relations with the Public*, International City Managers' Association, Chicago, 1940, 45.
6. Hummel, R.P. and Stivers C., Government isn't us: The possibility of democratic knowledge in representative government, in *Government is Us: Public Administration in an Anti-Government Era*, King, C.S. and Stivers, C., Eds., Sage, Thousand Oaks, CA, 1998, chap. 3, 54.
7. Lee, M., Public relations in public administration: A disappearing act in public administration education, *Public Relations Review*, 24, 509, 1998.
8. Molitor, A., *The University Teaching of Social Sciences: Public Administration; A Report Prepared for the United Nations Economic, Scientific and Cultural Organization [UNESCO] at the Request of the International Institute of Administrative Sciences*, UNESCO, Geneva, Switzerland, 1959, 158, 170, 174, 189.
9. Cleary, R.E., What do public administration masters programs look like? Do they do what is needed?, *Public Administration Review*, 50, 663, 1990.
10. Cleary, R.E., From the section chair, *SPAE Forum* [newsletter of the Section on Public Administration Education of the American Society for Public Administration], 7(4), 1, 1997.
11. Kell, T.W., Communication: Public administration's forgotten art, *Public Manager*, 21, 60, 1992.
12. Swoboda, D.P., Accuracy and accountability in reporting local government budget activities: Evidence from the newsroom and from newsmakers, *Public Budgeting & Finance*, 15(3), 75, 1995.
13. Waugh, W.L., Jr. and Manns, E.K., Communication skills and outcome assessment in public administration education, in *Teaching Public Policy: Theory, Research and Practice*, Bergerson, P.J., Ed., Greenwood, New York, 1991, chap. 11, 137.
14. Thompson, F. (Chair), Report of the APSA-NASPAA Committee on the Advancement of Public Administration, 1998, 4. http://www2.h-net.msu.edu/~pubadmin/tfreport/intro.pdf (accessed 2007)
15. Garnett, J.L., *Communicating for Results in Government: A Strategic Approach for Public Managers*, Jossey-Bass, San Francisco, 1992, xvi.
16. Waldo, D., Foreword, in *Communicating for Results in Government: A Strategic Approach for Public Managers*, Garnett, J.L., Jossey-Bass, San Francisco, 1992, xi.
17. Garnett, J.L. and Kouzmin, A., Eds., *Handbook of Administrative Communication*, Marcel Dekker, New York, 1997.

18. Garnett, J.L., Epilogue: Directions and agenda for administrative communication, in *Handbook of Administrative Communication*, Garnett, J.L. and Kouzmin, A., Eds., Marcel Dekker, New York, 1997, chap. 33, 764.
19. Grunig, J.E., Public relations management in government and business, in *Handbook of Administrative Communication*, Garnett, J.L. and Kouzmin, A., Eds., Marcel Dekker, New York, 1997, chap. 12, 268. (Editor's Note: see Chapter 2.)
20. See also Grunig, J.E., Ed., *Excellence in Public Relations and Communication Management*, Lawrence Erlbaum, Hillsdale, NJ, 1992.
21. National Association of Schools of Public Affairs and Administration, *Guidelines for Graduate Professional Education in Nonprofit Organizations, Management and Leadership*, 2006, 4. www.naspaa.org/accreditation/document/NASPAAGuidelinesforNP%20Final2006.doc (accessed 2007)
22. Wish, N.B. and Mirabella, R.M., Curricular variations in nonprofit management graduate programs, *Nonprofit Management & Leadership*, 9, 104, 1998.
23. Tschirhart, M., Nonprofit management education: Recommendations drawn from three stakeholder groups, in *Nonprofit Management Education: U.S. and World Perspectives*, O'Neill, M. and Fletcher, K., Eds., Praeger, Westport, CT, 1998, chap. 6, 70.
24. Highsaw, R.B. and Bowen, D.L., Eds., *Communication in Public Administration*, Bureau of Public Administration, University of Alabama, Tuscaloosa, 1965.
25. Schachter, H.L., *Public Agency Communication: Theory and Practice*, Nelson-Hall, Chicago, 1983.
26. Graber, D.A., *Public Sector Communication: How Organizations Manage Information*, CQ Press, Washington, DC, 1992.
27. Garnett and Kouzmin, op. cit.
28. Hailey, A.A., Applications of boundary theory to organizational and inter-organizational culture, *Public Administration and Management: An Interactive Journal*, 3(2), 1998. http://www.pamij.com/halley.html (accessed 2007)
29. McCamy, J.L., *Government Publicity: Its Practice in Federal Administration*, University of Chicago Press, Chicago, 1939.
30. McCamy, J.L., Public relations in public administration, in *Current Issues in Library Administration*, Joeckel, C.B., Ed., University of Chicago Press, Chicago, 1939, 301.
31. Simon, H.A., *Administrative Behavior: A Study in Decision-Making Processes in Administrative Organizations*, 4th ed., Free Press, New York, 1997, 294.
32. Pfiffner, J.M. and Presthus, R., *Public Administration*, 5th ed., Ronald, New York, 1967, 154.
33. Stephens, L.F., Professionalism of army public affairs personnel, *Public Relations Review*, 7(2), 43, 1981.
34. Graber, op. cit., chaps. 7–8.
35. Grunig, 1997, op. cit. (Editor's Note: see Chapter 2.)
36. Heath, R.L., *Management of Corporate Communication: From Interpersonal Contacts to External Affairs*, Lawrence Erlbaum, Hillsdale, NJ, 1994.
37. Ledingham, J.A. and Bruning, S.D., Eds., *Public Relations as Relationship Management: A Relational Approach to the Study and Practice of Public Relations*, Lawrence Erlbaum, Mahwah, NJ, 2000.
38. Rivers, W.L., Susan, M., and Gandy, O., Government and the media, in *Political Communication: Issues and Strategies for Research*, Chaffee, S.H., Ed., Sage, Beverly Hills, CA, 1975, chap. 7, 222.
39. Asante, C.E., Ed., *Press Freedom and Development: A Research Guide and Selected Bibliography*, Greenwood, Westport, CT, 1997, 35.
40. Schedler, P.E., Glastra, F.F., and Katz, E., Public information and field theory, *Political Communication*, 15, 445, 1998.
41. Gordon, A.C. et al., Public information and public access: A sociological interpretation, *Northwestern University Law Review*, 68, 280, 1973.
42. Fitzpatrick, D., Public information activities of government agencies, *Public Opinion Quarterly*, 11, 530, 1947–48.
43. Press, C. and VerBerg, K., *American Politicians and Journalists*, Scott Foresman, Glenview, IL, 1988, 241.

44. Dunwoody, S. and Ryan, M., Public information persons as mediators between scientists and journalists, *Journalism Quarterly*, 60, 647, 1983.

45. Anonymous, Wartime activities of special interest to political scientists: The recording of World War II, *American Political Science Review*, 38, 335, 1944. In order to comply with World War II security guidelines, *APSR* waived for this article its normal requirement that authors of all articles be named.

46. *The Technique of Municipal Administration*, International City Managers' Association, Chicago, 1940, chap. 12.

47. Davis, K.C., Reflections of a law professor on instruction and research in public administration, *American Political Science Review*, 47, 749, 1953.

48. Herman, R.D. and Heimovics, D., Executive leadership, in *The Jossey-Bass Handbook of Nonprofit Leadership and Management*, 2nd ed., Herman, R.D., Ed., Jossey-Bass, San Francisco, 2005, chap. 7, 159.

49. NASPAA, op. cit.

50. National Aeronautics and Space Administration, *NASA Office of External Relations*, homepage. http://www.hq.nasa.gov/office/oer/ (accessed 2007)

51. National Weather Service, Headquarters Structure and New Field Organizations. http://www.nws.noaa.gov/hdqreorg.php (accessed 2007)

52. Spicer, C., *Organizational Public Relations: A Political Perspective*, Lawrence Erlbaum, Mahwah, NJ, 1997, 43–48.

53. Dimock, M.E. and Dimock, G.O., *Public Administration*, 3rd ed., Holt, Rinehart and Winston, New York, 1964, 329.

54. Dimock, M.E. and Dimock, G.O., *Public Administration*, 4th ed., Holt, Rinehart and Winston, New York, 1969, 591.

55. Rosenbloom, D.H., *Public Administration: Understanding Management, Politics, and Law in the Public Sector*, 3rd ed., McGraw-Hill, New York, 1993, 458.

56. Waugh and Manns, op. cit., 135–39.

57. Garnett, J.L., op. cit., 1992, 165–200.

58. Gates, S. and Hill, J., Democratic accountability and governmental innovation in the use of nonprofit organizations, *Policy Studies Review*, 14, 138, 1995.

59. Denning, S., Toward an end to fear and loathing of the news: Making the media work for you, *The Agenda* (newsletter of the Section on Health and Human Services Administration of the American Society for Public Administration), 4(2), 4, 1997.

60. Viteritti, J.P., The environmental context of communication: Public sector organizations, in *Handbook of Administrative Communication*, Garnett, J.L. and Kouzmin, A., Eds., Marcel Dekker, New York, 1997, chap. 4. (Editor's Note: see Chapter 21.)

61. Kirlin, J.J., The big questions of public administration in a democracy, *Public Administration Review*, 56, 416, 1996.

62. Moe, R.C. and Gilmour, R.S., Rediscovering principles of public administration: The neglected foundation of public law, *Public Administration Review*, 55, 135, 1995.

63. Patterson, T.E., Time and news: The media's limitations as an instrument of democracy, *International Political Science Review*, 19, 55, 1998.

64. Hess, S., Media to government: Drop dead, *Brookings Review*, 18(1), 28, 2000. http://www.brook.edu/press/review/winter2000/hess.htm (accessed 2007)

65. Kettl, D.F., Relentless reinvention, *Government Executive* 32(1), 26, 2000. http://www.govexec.com/features/0100/0100s4.htm (accessed 2007)

66. Rubin, J., The truth and nothing but the truth — but sometimes not the whole truth, *Harvard International Journal of Press/Politics*, 5, 110, 2000.

67. Lee, M., Administrators are from Jupiter, reporters are from Mercury, *PA Times*, 24(6), 7, 2001.

68. Cater, D., *The Fourth Branch of Government*, special ed., Random House, New York, 1977 [1959], 17–18.

69. Cohen, S. and Eimicke, W., *The Effective Public Manager: Achieving Success in a Changing Government*, 3rd ed., Jossey-Bass, San Francisco, 2002, 242–43.

70. Lee, M., Reporters and bureaucrats: Public relations counter-strategies by public administrators in an era of media disinterest in government, *Public Relations Review*, 25, 451, 1999.
71. Cooke, M.L., *Our Cities Awake: Notes on Municipal Activities and Administration*, Doubleday Page, Garden City, NY, 1919, 197–204.
72. Government Finance Officers Association, GFOA Awards for Recognition. http://www.gfoa.org/services/awards.shtml#PAFR (accessed 2007)
73. Grunig, L.A., Activism: How it limits the effectiveness of organizations and how excellent public relations departments respond, in *Excellence in Public Relations and Communication Management*, Grunig, J.E., Ed., Lawrence Erlbaum, Hillsdale, NJ, 1992, chap. 19, 525.
74. Kever, J., US Mint tries again with dollar coin, *Houston [TX] Chronicle*, December 2, 1999, 7. See also, Crutsinger, M., Associated Press, For George's birthday, a $1 coin, *Milwaukee [WI] Journal Sentinel*, February 15, 2007, 5A.
75. Neu, C.R., Anderson, R.H., and Bikson, T.K., *Sending Your Government a Message: E-Mail Communication Between Citizens and Government*, Rand, Santa Monica, CA, 1999.
76. Kotler, P.A., Generic concept of marketing, *Marketing Management*, 7(3), 48, 1998 [1972]; Kotler, P., Haider, D., and Rein, I., There's no place like our place!, *PM. Public Management* 76(2), 15, 1994.
77. For example, see paid advertisement by the federal government about the new drug benefit offered as part of Medicare: U.S. Department of Health and Human Services, Watch it. Tape it. Talk about it with family and friends (advertisement), *New York Times*, November 19, 2005, A9.
78. Underhill, P., *Why We Buy: The Science of Shopping*, Simon & Schuster, New York, 1999, 45–91.
79. Weiss, J.A., Public information, in *The Tools of Government: A Guide to the New Governance*, Salamon, L.S., Ed., Oxford University Press, New York, 2002, chap. 7.
80. Rice, R.E. and Atkin, C.K., Eds., *Public Communication Campaigns*, 3rd ed., Sage, Thousand Oaks, CA, 2001.
81. Burnett, J.H., III, Anti-gun program being publicized heavily: Messages on buses, billboards will promote Operation Ceasefire, *Milwaukee [WI] Journal Sentinel*, March 28, 2000. http://www.jsonline.com/news/Metro/mar00/cease28032700a.asp (accessed 2007)
82. Murphy, K., Callers keep watch for drunken drivers, *Milwaukee [WI] Journal Sentinel*, November 24, 1998. http://www.jsonline.com/news/Metro/nov98/981124callerskeepwatchfordr.asp (accessed 2007)
83. Perlman, E., Services online, CIOs on loan, *Governing: The Magazine of States and Localities*, 13(1), 53, 2000. See also Garza, J., It's March and potholes are sprouting, *Milwaukee [WI] Journal Sentinel*, March 13, 2007, 5B.
84. Graham, G.A., Trends in teaching of public administration, *Public Administration Review*, 10, 73, 1950.
85. Simon, H.A., Smithburg, D.W., and Thompson, V.A., *Public Administration*, Transaction, New Brunswick, NJ, 1991 [1958], 385, 415–21. For a contemporary example, see the full page color ad by the Army National Guard in the *New York Times*. This was distinctly not a recruiting ad, but rather one focusing on explaining to the readership what its mission was (U.S. Army National Guard, The National Guard always goes to the same place. Where it's needed [advertisement], *New York Times*, January 17, 2007, A7).
86. Pew Research Center For The People & The Press, *Performance and Purpose: Constituents Rate Government Agencies*, Washington, DC, April 12, 2000. http://people-press.org/reports/display.php3?PageID=225 (accessed 2007)
87. Barr, S., Users mostly rate agencies favorably, *Washington Post*, April 13, 2000, A29.
88. Ryan, T., Luck cinched key submarine shot, *[Minneapolis, MN] Star Tribune*, May 18, 1995, 4E.
89. Hughes, J., Forest Service denies lobbying, *Detroit News*, November 27, 1998, A10.
90. Fulbright, J.W., The Navy public affairs program, *Congressional Record*, 115(27), December 2, 1969, 36344.
91. Elling, R.C., *Public Management in the States: A Comparative Study of Administrative Performance and Politics*, Praeger, Westport, CT, 1992, 196.

92. Linden, R.M., *Seamless Government: A Practical Guide to Re-Engineering in the Public Sector*, Jossey-Bass, San Francisco, 1994, 271.

93. Morgan, D., *The Flacks of Washington: Government Information and the Public Agenda*, Greenwood, New York, 1986, 67, 79.

94. Garnett, 1992, op. cit., chap. 7.

95. Lindstrom, M. and Nie, M.A., Public participation and agency planning, *Public Manager*, 29(1), 34, 2000.

96. Bjornlund, L.D., *Media Relations for Local Governments: Communicating for Results*, International City/County Management Association, Washington, DC, 1996.

97. Wade, J., *Dealing Effectively with the Media*, National League of Cities, Washington, DC, 1993.

98. Helm, L.M. et al., *Informing the People: A Public Affairs Handbook*, Longman, New York, 1981, sec. 3.

99. Berry, S., We have a problem…Call the press!, *PM. Public Management*, 81(4), 4, 1999.

100. Ogrizek, M. and Guillery, J.-M., *Communicating in Crisis: A Theoretical and Practical Guide to Crisis Management*, Aldine de Gruyter, Hawthorne, NY, 1999.

101. Bjornlund, op. cit., 86–94.

102. Ehling, W.P., White, J. and Grunig, J.E., Public relations and marketing practices, in *Excellence in Public Relations and Communication Management*, Grunig, J.E., Ed., Lawrence Erlbaum, Hillsdale, NJ, 1992, chap. 13, 385.

103. Simon, H.A., *Administrative Behavior: A Study in Decision-Making Processes in Administrative Organizations*, 4th ed., Free Press, New York, 1997, 294.

104. Grunig, J.E., What is excellence in management?, in *Excellence in Public Relations and Communication Management*, Grunig, J.E., Ed., Lawrence Erlbaum, Hillsdale, NJ, 1992, chap. 9, 236.

105. Lieberman, R.C., *Shifting the Color Line: Race and the American Welfare State*, Harvard University Press, Cambridge, MA, 1998, 78–79.

106. Janowitz, M., Wright, D., and Delany, W., *Public Administration and the Public — Perspectives Toward Government in a Metropolitan Community*, Michigan Government Studies No. 36, Bureau of Government, Institute of Public Administration, University of Michigan, Ann Arbor, 1958, 96.

107. Grunig, 1997, op. cit. (Editor's Note: see Chapter 2.)

108. Dozier, D.M., *Manager's Guide to Excellence in Public Relations and Communication Management*, Lawrence Erlbaum, Mahwah, NJ, 1995, chap. 6.

109. Hatry, H.P., *Performance Measurement: Getting Results*, Urban Institute Press, Washington, DC, 1999.

110. Epstein, P.D., Coates, P.M., and Wray, L.D., *Results that Matter: Improving Communities by Engaging Citizens, Measuring Performance and Getting Things Done*, Jossey-Bass, San Francisco, 2006.

111. Ehling, W.P., Estimating the value of public relations and communication to an organization, in *Excellence in Public Relations and Communication Management*, Grunig, J.E., Ed., Lawrence Erlbaum, Hillsdale, NJ, 1992, chap. 23.

112. Dozier, op. cit., 218–30.

113. Cohen and Eimicke, op. cit., 2002, 258.

114. Luke, J.S., *Catalytic Leadership: Strategies for an Interconnected World*, Jossey-Bass, San Francisco, 1998, 194.

115. Ibid, 216.

116. Hess, S., *The Government/Press Connection: Press Officers and Their Offices*, Brookings Institution, Washington, DC, 1984, 26.

117. Linsky, M., *Impact: How the Press Affects Federal Policymaking*, W.W. Norton, New York, 1986, 125.

118. Simon, H.A., Municipal reporting, in *The Municipal Year Book 1939*, Ridley, C.E. and Nolting, O.F., Eds., International City Managers' Association, Chicago, 1939, 38.

Chapter 2

Public Relations Management in Government and Business

James E. Grunig

Contents

Introduction

Until recently, public relations was an occupation defined more by its techniques than by its theory. Most public relations practitioners are the masters of a number of techniques. They know how to secure media coverage, prepare press releases, write speeches, write and design brochures, produce video news releases, negotiate with activists, interview community leaders, lobby representatives in Congress, stage a special event, or prepare an annual report. Recently, however, scholars of public relations have developed a body of knowledge that puts public relations on a par with recognized professions. Public relations professionals do not write and design brochures because they think it would be nice for the organization to have one or strive for publicity because the boss likes to see his or her name in the media. Instead, they use such a technique because they decide that it is the most effective way to communicate with a public that is strategic to their organization's success.

Organizations, like people, must communicate with others because they do not exist alone in the world. If people had no relationships with family, neighbors, friends, enemies, or co-workers, they would have no need to communicate with anyone but themselves. But they are not alone, and they must use communication to coordinate their behavior with people who affect them and are affected by them. Organizations also have relationships — within their "family" of employees and with communities, governments, consumers, financiers, supporters, detractors, and other publics. Organizations need *public relations*, in other words, because they have *relationships with publics*. Organizations succeed when they achieve their missions and goals, and most organizations prefer to choose their own missions and set their own goals. Seldom can they do so alone, however. Publics also have a stake in organizations, and they attempt to influence these organizations' missions and goals.

For example, employees want the organization to provide them with satisfying jobs. Environmentalists want the organization to preserve nature. Government agencies insist on safe products. Communities want clean air, less traffic, and donations to community projects. Organizations probably would not choose these goals if they existed alone in their environment. If they do not choose them, however, publics will pressure them to do so — just as children pressure parents to take them to amusement parks, employers pressure people to work late, or neighbors pressure us to keep our yards neat. Life for both people and organizations, therefore, is a constant process of negotiation and compromise. And communication is one of the most effective means we have to negotiate and compromise.

Organizations that communicate well with the publics with whom they have relationships know what to expect from those publics, and the publics know what to expect from them. They may not always agree or have a friendly relationship, but they do *understand* one another — and *understanding* is a major objective of public relations. Although an organization with good public relations may have to incorporate the goals of strategic publics into its mission, in the long run it will be able to pursue its own goals more effectively than it would if it ignored or fought the goals of publics.

As a result, communication and compromise make money for an organization by allowing it to sell products and services to satisfied customers, secure funds from constituents or donors, or expand its operations. Communication and compromise also save the organization money that might be spent on lawsuits, regulations, boycotts, or training of new employees. Communication and compromise, therefore, are the essence of public relations.

Most definitions of public relations — many of which are long and complicated — contain two elements: communication and management. [1] Public relations is the formal way in which organizations communicate with their publics. Public relations, however, is planned — or managed — communication. Although much communication by an organization happens by chance, public relations is communication that professional communication managers plan and coordinate. In essence, then, most administrative communication can be considered to be public relations. Most managers must communicate in the daily course of their work, but few of them are experts in communication. As a result, most organizations need a staff of professional communicators — public relations experts. In many instances, responsibility for communication is delegated to the public relations department. But much public relations (managed communication) is too important to delegate to the public relations department. Thus, in addition to communication on behalf of management, public relations practitioners also should be responsible for training and coaching other managers to be more effective communicators.

I have defined public relations as the management of communication between an organization and its public. [2] I define communication as a behavior — of people, groups, or organizations — that consists of moving symbols to and from other people, groups, or organizations. Thus, we can say that public relations is an organization's managed communication behavior. Public relations professionals plan and execute communication for the entire organization or help parts of the organization to communicate. They manage the movement of messages into the organization, for example, when conducting research on the knowledge, attitudes, and behaviors of publics and then using the information to counsel managers on how to make the organization's policies or actions acceptable to publics. They may manage the movement of messages *out of* the organization when they help management decide how to explain a policy or action to a public and then write a news story or fact sheet to explain it.

Even though public relations is one of the most important management functions for every type of organization, until recently few practitioners around the world have operated with a basic body of knowledge that is unique to the profession. They are what Canadian public relations practitioner, Michel Dumas, called "improvised communicators." [3] In addition, most managers and administrators — and especially the general population — have little understanding of public relations — equating it with publicity, "image making," or outright deception. Bishop [4] and Spicer, [5] for example, have documented the presence of such misunderstandings in the news media; Cline found a similar bias in mass communication textbooks. [6]

In the last 25 years, however, a small, "invisible college" of public relations scholars has developed, first in the United States and now worldwide. In the last five to ten years, this group of researchers has made remarkable progress, and its work has reached the point where a general theory of public relations is in sight. At the beginning, the small, invisible college of public relations researchers borrowed heavily from theories of communication and other social and behavioral sciences. Now, however, they have carved out their own domain of research and theory. That domain can be described best as a sub-domain of communication, but it also is closely related to theories of management and to organizational sociology and psychology.

Since 1985, I have headed a team of six researchers who have conducted research funded by the IABC (International Association of Business Communicators) Research Foundation on the characteristics of excellent public relations departments and on how such departments make their organizations more effective. In constructing a theory to guide that study, we have constructed a general theory of public relations that subsumes many specific theories in the domain. [7] This general theory will be developed and described throughout this chapter. [8]

This chapter, therefore, reviews the development of public relations research and theory and explains the evolution of the general theory of public relations that has emerged from the IABC project. It then discusses the extension of the theory to a global setting. The result is a theory that consists of several generic principles that seem to apply throughout the world, although the theory suggests that these concepts must be applied differently in different cultures and political–economic systems. The theory also applies in different organizational settings such as government agencies, corporations, nonprofit organizations, and associations. In short, the theory offers a conceptual framework for a professional culture of public relations, which, with appropriate applications and revisions in different organizational and national cultures, is a fundamental component of effective management throughout the world.

Development of Public Relations Research and Theory

Until about 1970, research on public relations in the United States consisted mostly of biographies of leading practitioners, case studies of public relations practice, and some highly applied studies — such as research on the factors leading to the acceptance of news releases or the proportion of content in the news media that comes from public relations sources. In addition, public relations educators and practitioners considered much of communication research to be relevant to their problems, although they did little of this research themselves. Relevant communication research was that on public opinion, attitudes and persuasion, effects of the mass media, effects of information campaigns, and — to a lesser extent — interpersonal and organizational communication.

The first research on public relations, then, differed little from other communication research. What sets current research on public relations apart from the rest of communication science, however, is the blending of various organizational theories with communication theories. Public relations now is developing from what philosophers of science call an immature science to a more mature one. [9,10] This evolution has progressed through three levels of public relations problems — the micro, meso, and macro levels of abstraction. Researchers have developed separate theories at each of these levels but now have begun to fit each of these special theories into a general theory of public relations.

The micro level refers to the planning and evaluation of individual public relations programs. The meso level refers to how public relations departments are organized and managed. The macro level refers to explanations of public relations behavior, the relationship of public relations to organizational effectiveness, and critical evaluations of the role of public relations in society.

The Micro Level: Individual Public Relations Programs

From an historical perspective, the micro level was the logical place for researchers to start because this level deals with the ongoing phenomena of greatest concern to public relations practitioners. In particular, practitioners wanted to know whether their programs and campaigns were successful and how to make them more effective. The micro level also was an easy place to borrow theories from other domains of communication. We begin with the most common problem and with borrowed theory.

The Effects of Public Relations

Although public relations practitioners continue to debate whether public relations is more or less than communication, scholars nearly always have agreed that most of what a public relations person does can be described as communication or the management of communication. Some practitioners define communication narrowly as the techniques of publicity and journalism used by practitioners and argue that the research, counseling, and decision-making activities of true professionals make public relations more than a communication function. Most scholars, however, define communication more broadly and consider these activities to be part of communication.

Most scholars, therefore, agree in principle — if not in the exact definition — with the definition in J. Grunig and Hunt cited earlier in this chapter. [11] The consensus that public relations is communication might have developed for logical reasons or simply because most public relations scholars have been trained as communication theorists and researchers, either in a school or department of journalism or speech communication. Whatever the reason, however, most courses and most textbooks in public relations devote time or a chapter to the process and effects of communication.

This discussion almost always includes one or more of the source-message-medium-receiver models of the communication process. It also includes public relations, the diffusion process, attitudes and persuasion, and the effects of communication, especially the effects of the mass media. [12] Of the topics, the two that have attracted the most interest from public relations researchers have been the effects of the media and the effects of persuasive messages on attitudes and behaviors.

As a result, public relations educators and researchers have used or contributed to the research on effects of the media or research on persuasion. Most of the researchers did not think of their research as public relations research, however, preferring instead to think of themselves as more generic communication researchers. Recently, several of the researchers studying the effects of campaigns have begun to consider themselves public relations scholars and have made more of an attempt to apply their work directly to public relations. [13–17] The communication researchers whose work came closest to public relations were those studying the effectiveness of public information campaigns — on such issues as smoking, birth control, forest fires, use of seat belts in automobiles, nutrition, acquired immunodeficiency syndrome (AIDS), prevention of crime, or development projects in third-world countries. [18–21] Most of these campaigns have been sponsored by government agencies, and much of the research on them has been evaluation research funded by the same agencies. In this sense, government public relations has been based on communication theory and research more than has corporate communication.

Many of the researchers studying the effects of individual messages, campaigns, or the mass media still cling to the idea that communication must persuade (change attitudes or behaviors) to be effective. [22] Most of those researchers have been trained in social psychology or rhetoric and are found more often in speech communication units than in journalism. Many others, however, have identified other effects of communication — especially effects on cognition — that occur more often than persuasion. [23–25] Communication scholars also have begun to look at the effects of communication as a dialogue rather than communication as a monologue. [26,27] Public relations scholars who follow their lead, therefore, conceptualize public relations more broadly than as an organization attempting to persuade a public to do want it wants.

Many of this latter group of public relations scholars have based their analyses on the concept of co-orientation, which Chaffee and McLeod introduced to the communication discipline. [28–32] The co-orientation model isolated four effects of public relations: accuracy, understanding, agreement, and complementary behaviors.

The co-orientation model has been especially useful to theorists who prefer to look at public relations as dialogue rather than monologue. I have used those concepts, for example, as the basis of a taxonomy of effects that can be used as objectives to plan and evaluate public relations programs. [33] Broom and Dozier have used them in a similar fashion in their book on research in public relations. [34] Many master's theses and doctoral dissertations on public relations throughout the United States have been based on the co-orientation model. An example can be found in Knodell. [35]

Research on the effects of communication has, therefore, been used widely by public relations educators, scholars, and practitioners to help conceptualize the planning and evaluation of public relations messages, campaigns, and programs — the micro level of public relations. Some public relations scholars have contributed to these theories of effects, especially those who have moved back and forth between public relations and related communication domains — such as those studying information campaigns, persuasion and attitude change, and media effects. Alone, however, theories of communication effects provide only a set of dependent variables, which cannot constitute a genuine theory, even if the theory is restricted to the micro level. Thus, we move to other micro-level theories that are part of the emerging general theory of public relations.

Segmentation of Publics

Because most public relations scholars have connections to the broader field of mass communication, many have accepted that field's assumption that the communication process they are studying is *mass communication*. "Mass communication" implies that public relations practitioners help their organizations communicate with a large, heterogeneous, and undifferentiated mass — as that term was defined by classic sociologists such as Blumer. [36]

Mass communication theorists such as Lowery and DeFleur, C. R. Wright, and McQuail no longer believe that the audiences of the mass media are a "mass" in the classic sense of a mass society. [37–39] Indeed, McQuail suggested that although media audiences may be massive in size, they do not fit the description of a mass in classic theory. Most communication theorists who have studied the effects of public information campaigns have concluded, therefore, that campaigns cannot be effective unless they are aimed at specific segments of the mass population. [40,41]

Most public relations practitioners have remained oblivious to these conclusions from communication research. As a result, they are still preoccupied with publicity in the mass media and continue to believe that they are dealing with a "general public." A "general public" actually is a contradiction because publics arise around shared problems or concerns; therefore, a public always is specific and cannot be general. Communicating with the general public, therefore, means communicating with the general "population"; and communication research shows that is rarely possible.

Despite this penchant for mass communication, some practitioners have borrowed segmentation techniques from marketing research, such as demographics, psychographics, geo-demographics, or VALS (the commercial name for the technique originally called "values and life-styles"). Although these techniques help make a public relations program or campaign more effective than it would be if it were aimed at the general population, these techniques are more useful in marketing than in public relations because they are based on a theory of "markets" rather than a theory of "publics."

In the United States and many other countries, practitioners and scholars are engaged in a heated debate over the difference between public relations and marketing. Several marketing theorists, such as Kotler, [42–44] and especially advertising scholars claim public relations as a marketing technique. [45] Public relations theorists such as Ehling, [46] J. Grunig, [47] and Ehling and colleagues [48] maintain that public relations and marketing serve different functions and communicate with different stakeholders.

These public relations theorists believe that public relations and marketing should operate at both a managerial level and a technical level. When public relations is submerged into marketing, it is reduced to a technical function that provides publicity for marketing efforts. At the management level, marketing helps the organization exchange products and services with consumer markets. Public relations, in contrast, deals with the many publics that respond to the consequences when an organization pursues its mission or that enable the organization to gain support from its environment. These publics may include communities, governments, employees, shareholders, and activist groups as well as consumers. An organization with marketing managers but without public relations managers thus cannot resolve conflict with these publics that can support or constrain the organization's ability to pursue its mission.

Although the distinction between public relations and marketing may seem relevant only to public relations in business, the confusion between the two functions has become equally important in government and nonprofit public relations. For example, Kotler and Andreasen included a chapter on public relations in their book on nonprofit marketing, and Lewton discussed the difference between the two functions in her book on public relations for health care organizations. [49,50] Some U.S. government agencies also have begun to refer to their clientele as "customers," for instance, the U.S. Department of Energy and the U.S. Forest Service. [51,52]

It may seem to make sense to think of the clientele of government agencies as customers when the agency essentially is trying to sell a service to that clientele. However, most agencies are obliged to help their clientele solve problems, such as the Department of Agriculture's serving farmers or the National Park Service's serving users. These "publics" are there to be served, even though the organization might not always want them to be "markets." In fact, a welfare agency, the prison system, or the Social Security Administration may prefer that fewer people use their services, even though they must communicate with and serve these publics. If the agency does not communicate with the publics it affects, these publics will demand the agency's attention — something that "markets" seldom do.

Although there is a place for some marketing activities as well as public relations in government *service* agencies, it makes no sense to think of the clientele as "customers" for agencies that *regulate, penalize,* or *collect revenue.* For example, the U.S. Internal Revenue Service has used the concept of integrated marketing communication and refers to taxpayers as customers. [53] Taxpayers have little choice about using the IRS' services. However, the IRS clearly has consequences on taxpayers, and taxpayers' behavior certainly affects the IRS' ability to accomplish its mission. Thus, it should seem clear that government agencies are much more likely to communicate with publics than markets and that their communication function is much more likely to be public relations than marketing communication.

The concept of a public also is useful for government communication programs because citizens in a democracy are expected to involve themselves — participate — in their government. The concept of a public captures well the active and symmetrical relationship between government agencies and citizen publics assumed in democracies. U.S. President Bill Clinton explained well why public relations is more relevant to government than marketing, as he was quoted in the *Washington Post*:

> "Both parties and all candidates" bear responsibility for treating Americans as if they were "consumers" of politics, not participants, turning them into "political couch potatoes" observing debates over whose political ads are better, who is constructing what political messages, and who is better at answering back his opponent. [54]

The relationship between government agencies and publics, in this sense, is an example of a political system that Charlton said has been called by various political scientists as bargained, liberal, or societal corporatism. [55] Societal corporatism represents a relationship between governments and publics ("interest groups" in the language of comparative politics) that incorporates aspects of pluralism, in which publics compete for government attention, and corporatism, in which governments attempt to co-opt and dominate publics and interest groups attempt to capture government agencies for their own purposes. [56–59]

A corporatist political system can be dangerous to democracy if either government agencies or publics dominate the other or collaborate to achieve their mutual interests at the expense of other groups in society. [60] But in societal corporatism, government agencies collaborate and bargain with publics they are supposed to serve or regulate to balance the interests of those publics and society at large, which is the ideal form of symmetrical public relations as defined in this chapter. [61]

The theoretical concept that is extremely important to public relations, therefore, is the concept of a public, which is different from a market. Organizations can create their own markets by carving up a population into the segments most likely to consume their products and services. [62,63] Publics, in contrast, organize around problems and seek out organizations that create those problems — to seek information, to seek redress of grievances, to pressure the organization, or to seek government regulation. [64] Publics, in other words, make "issues" out of "problems." As publics move from being latent to active, organizations have little choice but to communicate with them, whereas organizations can choose to ignore markets if they wish.

Communication researchers, however, have done little to define and explain publics' behavior. The most extensive research has been of the "adopter categories" in research on the diffusion of innovations. [65–67] Adopter categories resemble markets more than publics, however, and have been more useful in marketing than in public relations. Dewey [68] and Blumer [69] developed classic theories of publics, and Cobb and Elder described types of publics in a theory of public opinion. [70] V. Price, however, is one of the few scholars to apply these concepts of a public to mass communication research. [71,72] In addition, theories of uses and gratifications have defined the characteristics of active audiences, [73,74] which Pavlik and associates used to define employee publics. [75]

A number of strategic management researchers also have used the concept of "stakeholders." Stakeholders are people who are "linked" to an organization because they and the organization affect each other. People linked to an organization have a stake in it, which A. Carroll defined as "an interest or a share in an undertaking." [76] A stakeholder, therefore, is "any individual or group who can affect or is affected by the actions, decisions, policies, practices, or goals of the organization." [77]

All these elements from theories of mass communication, public opinion, and strategic management are relevant to a theory of publics, but none of them constitutes such a theory alone. I have incorporated — or explained — most of these concepts in my "situational theory of publics" that I have been developing for nearly 30 years. [78–90]

In developing that theory, I have conceptualized the crucial distinction for segmenting a population of people into publics as the extent to which people passively or actively communicate about an issue and the extent to which they actively behave in a way that supports or constrains the organization's pursuit of its mission. The theory contains three major concepts that are used to segment people into active and passive publics. The theory states that (a) publics are more likely to be active when the people who make them up perceive that what an organization does *involves them* (*level of involvement*), (b) that the consequences of what an organization does is a *problem* (*problem recognition*), and (c) that they are *not constrained* from doing something about the problem (*constraint recognition*). [91,92]

If none of these conditions fits a group of people, these people constitute a "nonpublic"; they are thus of no concern to an organization. Whenever an organization does something that affects people or people affect the organization, it is likely that they will perceive an involvement and recognize a problem. Thus, consequences produce, at the minimum, a *latent* public — a public that is passive but that can become active. As level of involvement and problem recognition increase and constraint recognition decreases, however, these publics can become *aware* and *active*. [93]

Active publics are important targets for public relations programs because they are most likely to be aware of and concerned with what the organization is doing. In addition, if an organization does not communicate with active publics and attempt to manage conflict, those publics can become activist groups that can limit an organization's ability either directly through protest, boycott, or strike or indirectly through government regulation.

The situational theory of publics has been cited widely by scholars of public relations. [94–103] In addition, many practitioners have begun to use it. It has therefore become an important component of the emerging general theory of public relations because it identifies — at the micro level — those publics most likely to constrain the organization at the macro level and at which specific public relations programs should be aimed. Theories of publics and of effects, then, lead to a comprehensive micro-level theory of public relations — a theory of the strategic management of public relations and its relationship to the overall strategic management of organizations.

Strategic Management and Public Relations

At the point in the development of public relations research and theory described thus far, public relations theories were still much indebted to mainstream communication research. The theory that ties these theories to a more comprehensive theory of micro-level processes of public relations is that of the relationship between public relations and strategic management.

"Strategic public relations" is a loosely defined concept that recently has become popular among public relations practitioners. Both major professional organizations in the United States, the Public Relations Society of America (PRSA) and IABC, for example, regularly hold seminars on the topic and include the topic in their publications. Public relations scholars also have developed strategic theories of public relations. [104–108]

Most of the discussion of "strategic" public relations, however, consists of loose references to the idea that public relations should be planned, managed by objectives, evaluated, and connected in some way to organizational objectives. Thus, in essence, "strategic" public relations refers to managed public relations as opposed to public relations as a set of communication tactics supplied by communication technicians who are subservient to a client organization that dictates what they do.

As part of the Excellence Project funded by the IABC Research Foundation, J. Grunig and Repper reviewed the literature of strategic management in the search for the role of public relations within that overall organizational function. [109] They concluded that a strategic approach to public relations at the micro level is one of 14 characteristics of excellent public relations departments and that involvement in the overall strategic management of the organization is a second of those characteristics. Strategic management is crucial to excellent public relations because it describes how public relations should be practiced if it is to contribute the most to an organization's success. Recently, Vercic, [110] a Slovenian scholar and practitioner who has replicated the IABC study in that country, [111] developed the theory of public relations and strategic management further to show that when public relations is an integral part of strategic management, organizations are more likely to capitalize on strategic externalities in their environment to gain a competitive advantage.

As an academic field, strategic management is as young as public relations. Both disciplines have much in common, but until recently both have been oblivious of the other. Bowman said that business schools offered a capstone course in business policies in their masters of business administration programs before the 1960s, courses in which students were expected to tie together the courses they had taken in different functional areas of management. [112] In the 1960s, however, three books became available that helped strategic management to emerge as a field that was more than a composite of other management functions. [113,114] These books were Chandler's historical study of how the strategic ideas of executives changed the direction of four major corporations, [115] Ansoff's more normative book on the concept of strategy and the process of strategy formulation, [116] and the Harvard textbook *Business Policy: Text and Cases.* [117]

Half of the Harvard book consisted of cases; the other half, which was written largely by Kenneth Andrews, discussed the formulation and implementation of strategy. [118] According to Rumelt and co-workers, [119] Andrews introduced "the notion of an uncertain environment to which management and the firm had to adapt":

> In Andrews's view, the environment, through constant change, gave rise to opportunities and threats, and the organization's strengths and weaknesses were adapted to avoid the threats and take advantage of the opportunities. An internal appraisal of strengths and weaknesses led to identification of distinctive competencies; an external appraisal of environmental threats and opportunities led to identification of potential success factors. [120]

Since Andrews introduced the concept of environment to strategy, the literature has been permeated by two words — *mission* and *environment*. Together, they suggest that organizations must make long-term, strategic choices that are feasible in their environments. Higgins, for example, defined strategic management as "the process of managing the pursuit of the accomplishment of organizational mission coincident with managing the relationship of the organization to its environment." [121] Greene and colleagues similarly defined it as "a process of thinking through the current mission of the organization, thinking through the current environmental conditions, and then combining these elements by setting forth a guide for tomorrow's decisions and results." [122]

According to Steiner and associates, "strategic management" can be distinguished from "operational management" by "the growing significance of environmental impacts on organizations and the need for top managers to react appropriately to them." [123] Managers who manage strategically do so by balancing the organization's mission — what it is, what it wants to be, and what it wants to do — with what the environment will allow or encourage it to do. Pearce and Robinson described this internal–external balancing act as "interactive opportunity analysis." [124]

Although the concept of environment pervades the literature on strategic management, until recently the concept has been conceptualized in "general, even rather vague" terms. [125] Pearce and Robinson, for example, defined environment as "the sum total of all conditions and forces that affect the strategic options of a business but that are typically beyond its ability to control." [126] These writers mention many components of the environment such as customers, suppliers, creditors, and competitors. They also mention economic and cultural conditions. Most also mention the traditional stakeholders with whom public relations manages relationships: governments, communities, stockholders, employees, public and private interest groups, and constituents. [127–129] Pearce and Robinson explained that executives must pay attention to "economic conditions, social change, political priorities, and technological developments." [130] Wheelen and Hunger distinguished between the task environment and the societal environment. They explained that in accomplishing its mission an organization works in its task environment but that the societal environment may divert its attention from the task environment. [131]

In a comprehensive overview of theories of an organization's environment, Ring pointed out that researchers have paid more attention to the task environment than "to the categories and components of the external environment that do not fit within the scope of the task environment." [132] He added that "historians, political scientists, and economists, among others, regularly chronicle changes in these [non-task] components of the external environment. Only rarely, however, ... do they focus on the impact that these changes have on the strategies of specific firms, or on how firms attempt to adapt to these changes." [133] Ring concluded:

> In summarizing this brief sketch of the environment–organization literature, a number of conclusions can be drawn. First, the external environment is now viewed as a critical determinant of organizational effectiveness. Second, the full extent of the role of the environment in determining organization–environment and environment–environment relationships is probably masked by a persistent focus on perceptions of the task environment. Third, while recognizing that environment–environment relationships exist, much of the research ignores these relationships and their implications for strategic choice. In combination, these conclusions lead one to question whether models of the environment that have guided explanations of environment–organization relationships are entirely satisfactory. [134]

To a public relations scholar, Ring's discussion of the inadequacies of strategic management theories in explaining how an organization should relate to the environment clearly suggests the role of public relations in strategic management. Although writers on strategic management discuss the environment and make lists of its components, only a few of these writers have recognized or described the role of public relations in helping the organization to identify the most important components of its environment and in using communication to build relationships with them. The exceptions are Post and co-workers, Gollner, and Marx. [135–137] In general, management scholars seem largely to be unaware of how public relations scholars' work can contribute to theories of strategic management.

Although scholars of strategic management originally conceptualized the environment as a constraint on an organization's mission and choices, Porter turned the relationship around and conceptualized the environment as a source of competitive advantage. [138–141] For example, he found that multinational corporations with strong competitors in their home country were better able to compete in other countries because of the pressure to excel at home. [142] Likewise, he found that government regulation, traditionally seen by corporate managers as an intrusion on their decision making, can stimulate changes in organizational behavior that provide a competitive advantage. Stringent standards for product performance, product safety, and environmental impact contribute to creating and upgrading competitive advantage. They pressure firms to improve quality, upgrade technology, and provide features in areas of important customer (and social) concern. [143]

Vercic extended Porter's idea that an organization can gain competitive advantage from successful relationships with competitors and governments in the environment to relationships with other stakeholder publics. [144] For example, a corporation that successfully solves its environmental problems, usually when pressured by environmental activists, will gain an advantage from relationships with stockholders, consumers, employees, government, and communities that can support or constrain that corporation. Likewise, a government agency that responds well to pressures from its constituents will be more likely to gain support from those publics as it competes for limited public funding.

Out of this framework, the contribution of public relations to strategic management and, as a result, to organizational effectiveness becomes clear. Public relations contributes to strategic management by building relationships with publics that it affects or is affected by — publics that support the organization's mission or that can divert the organization from its mission. Organizations plan public relations programs strategically, therefore, when they identify the publics that are most likely to limit or enhance their ability to pursue their mission and design communication programs that help the organization manage its interdependence with these strategic publics.

Public relations is most effective, in other words, when the publics with whom practitioners communicate are identified within the framework of organizational strategic management and when the function is managed strategically from the public relations department. These two levels of strategic management also are identified in the literature on strategic management. According to Pearce and Robinson, strategic management takes place at three levels: corporate (organizational), business (specialty), and functional. [145] At the corporate or organizational level, the board of directors, chief executive officer, and chief administrative officers set grand strategies and reflect the interests of stockholders and society. Business or specialty levels deal with market segments or provide specialized services. Functional levels are composed of managers of products, geographic areas, or functions such as marketing or public relations.

In addition to these three levels, Bowman added a fourth, the institutional level, which involves "the issues of how a corporation fits itself into the social environment and the body politic." [146] Of the four levels, Bowman said, scholars of strategic management have paid the least attention to the institutional level and must address that level much more: "For instance, problems of hazardous waste in the chemical industry are enormously important to that industry.... This is an institutional problem of the kind that strategy research typically ignores." What Bowman called the institutional level obviously is the substance of public relations and a level at which theories of strategic management would benefit greatly from the work of public relations scholars and practitioners.

However, Brody has pointed out that public relations traditionally has been relegated to the functional level, where it has been responsible for implementing organizational objectives but not for helping scan the environment or formulate organizational objectives. [147] Kotler and Andreasen, for example, concluded that marketing is strategic for an organization but that public relations is not. [148] However, a survey of public relations counselors reported in Nager and Truitt showed that respondents rated strategic planning and in-depth counseling of senior executives as the most important contributions that their firms make to clients. [149] Only half as many counselors responding rated implementation of communication programs as their most important contribution.

In our IABC research project, we asked the chief executive officer and the senior communication manager in 326 organizations in the United States, Canada, and the United Kingdom the extent to which public relations is involved in organization-wide strategic management and the extent to which they practice each step of the strategic process for public relations itself (Table 2.1). The results of that study strongly support the importance of strategic management for excellent public relations programs. [150,151] Both involvement in overall strategic management and practicing public relations strategically were among the strongest indicators of excellent departments.

In the IABC study, the relationship of excellent public relations to the strategic management function was equally likely to occur in governmental and nonprofit organizations as in corporations. In fact, government agencies were somewhat more likely to integrate public relations and strategic management than were corporations. Lapinski, similarly, studied the relationship

Table 2.1   Steps in the Strategic Management of Public Relations

1.	Stakeholder stage: An organization has a relationship with stakeholders when the behavior of the organization or of a stakeholder has consequences on the other. Public Relations should do formative research to scan the environment and the behavior of the organization to identify these consequences. Ongoing communication with these stakeholders helps to build a stable, long-term relationship that manages conflict that may occur in the relationship.
2.	Public stage: Publics form when stakeholders recognize one or more of the consequences as a problem and organize to do something about it or them. Public Relations should do research to identify and segment these publics. At this stage focus groups are particularly helpful. Communication to involve publics in the decision process of the organization helps to manage conflict before communication campaigns become necessary.
3.	Issue stage: Publics organize and create issues. Public Relations should anticipate these issues and manage the organization's response to them. This is known as Issues Management. The media play a major role in the creation and expansion of issues. In particular, their coverage of issues may produce publics other than activist ones — especially "hot-issue" publics. At this stage, research is particularly useful to segment all of the publics. Communication programs at this stage usually use the mass media but should also include interpersonal communication with activist publics to try to resolve the issue through negotiation.
	Public Relations should plan communication programs with different stakeholders or publics at each of the above three stages. In doing so, it should follow steps 4–7.
4.	Public Relations should develop formal objectives, such as communication, accuracy, understanding, agreement, and complementary behavior for its communication programs.
5.	Public Relations should plan formal programs and campaigns to accomplish the objectives.
6.	Public Relations, especially the technicians, should implement the programs and campaigns.
7.	Public Relations should evaluate the effectiveness of programs in meeting their objectives and in reducing the conflict produced by the problems and issues that brought about the programs.

of public affairs and strategic management in 13 agencies in the U.S. federal government. [152] Integration of the two functions, he found, made both functions more effective. Public affairs departments were more likely to be managed strategically when they were integrated into the organizational level of strategic management. Likewise, managers judged strategic planning units more effective when they were integrated with public affairs because they "paid more attention to critical constituents." [153]

A theory of strategic management used in a government agency should not differ from theory developed for corporations. However, the specific applications of that theory will differ; in particular, there will be more stakeholders and there will be conflicting stakeholders for a government agency to take into account. In addition, the leaders who provide strategic direction for a government agency are not only the "managers" of that agency but also legislators and the chief executive of the nation, state, or locality. Bingman and Kee described the challenge for strategic management in the public sector as follows:

While strategic management never works like textbook examples, even in the private sector, there are greater uncertainty, more actors, and significant external influences in strategic management in the public sector.

Strategic management in the federal government involves constant accommodations between the politician/policymaker and the administrator/manager. Very often the manager must follow a vision set by others, with limited ability to influence its design. Even where the manager helps to establish the vision, it is subject to annual change and validation in the legislative budget process. [154]

Because strategic management in government is so complicated, the public relations process is even more important there than in business or nonprofit organizations. There are more constituencies with which to establish relationships and more communication needed between the agency, legislative bodies, and other agencies. In fact, most government agencies have public affairs specialists to communicate with the legislature as well as specialists to communicate with external groups.

It is crucial, therefore, for public relations to be involved in strategic management in all kinds of organizations; in reality, however, the two functions often have no connection. In contrast to the strategic approach to public relations described in Table 2.1, most organizations carry out the same public relations programs year after year without stopping to determine whether they continue to communicate with the most important publics. Dozier and L. Grunig have pointed out that at some point in their history, most organizations probably develop their public relations programs strategically — that is, the presence of a strategic public probably provides the motivation for initiating public relations programs. [155] As time passes, however, organizations forget the initial reason for the programs and continue communication programs for publics that no longer are strategic. Public relations then becomes routine and ineffective because it does little to help organizations adapt to dynamic environments.

The model in Table 2.1 also reflects three other extensive programs of research. The first is the research on the situational theory of publics, which is reflected in the publics stage of the model. The second is Dozier's ten studies of the extent to which organizations use research to scan the environment (the stakeholder stage) and to evaluate programs. [156] The third program consists of research on issues management (the issues stage). The concept of issues management was developed by a public relations practitioner. [157] Since then it has been studied both by management scholars [158–160] and by public relations scholars. Heath has been the most consistent and active researcher of issues management among public relations scholars. [161,162]

Most of the literature on issues management conceptualizes the process as asymmetrical — that is, of anticipating what issues publics or activists will create in the future and then acting proactively to defeat these potential opponents. The process in Table 2.1, however, sees issues management as a more symmetrical process. Table 2.1 states that issues arise because publics create them — that is, publics make issues out of problems. Thus, a public relations manager serves strategic management by identifying management decisions that affect people not involved in the decision — that is, create problems for those people. Publics develop to address the problems and, if the organization does not involve them in the decision, make issues out of the problems. In symmetrical issues management, then, public relations managers attempt to communicate with publics before decisions are made so that problems are resolved collaboratively before publics are forced to make issues out of them.

Issues, then, are strategic to an organization because of what Eadie called his "rough and ready" definition of a strategic issue: "It is a problem or opportunity that, if action is not taken on it now, it is likely to saddle the organization with unbearable future costs." [163] Public relations, as we will see next, helps the organization avoid these unbearable future costs.

From Strategic Management to Public Relations Excellence and Organizational Effectiveness

The theory of public relations and strategic management, therefore, represents the first component of the general theory of public relations produced by the IABC research team. Involvement of public relations in strategic management is perhaps the most crucial element of the general theory because it links micro-level public relations programs to the meso level of management and to the macro level of organizational effectiveness in the environment. Before moving to the meso and macro levels, however, it is important to define the concepts of excellence in management and organizational effectiveness to clarify how the IABC study was conducted and how the general theory of public relations is related to organizational and management theories.

The IABC study began with the research question posed in a request for proposals from the IABC Research Foundation: How, why, and to what extent does communication contribute to the achievement of organizational objectives? In responding to the request for proposals, the research team pointed out that the one question posed by the IABC Foundation — the *effectiveness* question — was not enough. We realized that many organizations do not manage communication programs strategically and that these programs do not make their organizations more effective. Thus, we added what we called the excellence question: How must public relations be practiced and the communication function be organized for it to contribute the most to organizational effectiveness?

In developing a general theory of the relationship of excellent public relations to organizational effectiveness, we began by reviewing studies of excellence in management [164] and the literature on organizational effectiveness. [165] Most of the studies of and books on excellence searched for attributes of excellent management, but they defined and identified excellence in different ways. Most researchers began with a dependent variable, an indicator of organizational effectiveness, to identify organizations for study. They then worked backward to identify management characteristics these "effective" organizations had in common.

Peters and Waterman, for example, used six financial criteria to identify excellent companies for analysis: (1) compound asset growth, (2) compound equity growth, (3) average ratio of market value to book value, (4) average return on total capital, (5) average return on equity, and (6) average return on sales. [166] Hobbs identified his excellent companies by measuring return on sales and return on owner's investment. [167] Paul and Taylor used similar financial measures to identify the 101 best-performing companies in America. [168]

Carroll, [169] in a review of Peters and Waterman, [170] criticized the use of financial measures for identifying excellence in management. He pointed out that several independent variables other than management also affect financial performance: "such factors as proprietary technology, market dominance, control of critical raw materials, and national culture and policy also affect financial performance, regardless of the excellence of management."

Other writers defined excellence in terms of organizational behaviors and outcomes other than financial performance. Kanter and Pinchot defined excellence as innovativeness. [171–173] *Fortune* magazine annually lists the most admired corporations based on (1) quality of management, (2) quality of products and services, (3) innovation, (4) value as a long-term investment, (5) financial soundness, (6) ability to attract, develop, and keep talented people, (7) community and environmental responsibility, and (8) use of corporate assets. Similarly, Lydenberg and colleagues and the Council on Economic Priorities rated corporations on their social conscience; [174] Levering and co-workers on human resources benefits for employees; [175] and Zeitz and Dusky on benefits for women. [176] Hickman and Silva suggested that each organization create its unique criteria for excellence and then suggested how leadership can help the organization meet those criteria. [177] Finally, Nash and Zullo named a "Misfortune 500" on the basis of such criteria as "badvertising" campaigns, unjustified promotions, mismanagement, and poorly conceived products. [178] Although all these lists are of corporations, the Public Broadcasting System (PBS) also aired a program in 1990 in which it named and featured several excellent governmental and nonprofit organizations.

Most of these studies of excellence have had two major problems. The first problem is that most began with a single or limited definition of an *outcome* of organizational behavior that could be used to identify excellent organizations. For example, Peters and Waterman [179] identified 43 excellent corporations using financial criteria that, as Carroll pointed out, [180] are subject to many variables other than the behavior of management. Peters and Waterman's limited definition of the outcome of excellence called the entire study into question within two years, when *Business Week* reported that "at least 14 of the 43 excellent companies ... had lost their luster ... — significant earnings declines that stem from serious business problems, management problems, or both." [181]

The studies of excellence, such as Peters and Waterman's, would have had a more sound theoretical basis if they had been linked to the extensive literature on organizational effectiveness, which shows that no single criterion can identify the best-managed organizations. [182] The second problem with these studies, however, is that they made only an empirical connection between the outcomes they defined as indicators of excellence and management characteristics these excellent companies shared. They did not begin by developing a logical theoretical relationship between management characteristics of excellent companies and the outcomes produced by the characteristics — that is, a theoretical linkage between independent and dependent variables.

In the IABC Excellence Project, we began by reviewing the literature on organizational effectiveness to determine what an effective organization is so that we then could conceptualize how different public relations variables could be linked to organizational effectiveness. [183] Thus, we defined excellence in public relations, not by an arbitrary set of outcomes or of characteristics of management alone, but as the theoretical relationship between a set of independent variables (characteristics of public relations) and a set of dependent variables (indicators of organizational effectiveness) to which they are logically and empirically related. These independent and dependent variables are described in Table 2.2.

The literature on organizational effectiveness is large and contradictory. In fact, some theorists question the value of even trying to define effectiveness. For overviews of the literature, see J. Price, Goodman and Pennings, Robbins, and Hall. [184–187] Robbins and Hall, however, have integrated this literature into a coherent framework that clearly suggests the role of public relations in making organizations more effective. [188,189] They identified four approaches, each of which contributes to a comprehensive theory of organizational effectiveness.

1. The *goal-attainment* approach, which states that organizations are effective when they meet their goals. The goal-attainment approach is limited, however, because it cannot explain effectiveness when an organization has multiple goals and different stakeholders of an organization have conflicting goals. It also cannot explain the role of the environment in organizational effectiveness.

2. The *systems* approach states that organizations are effective when they survive in their environment and successfully bring in resources from the environment necessary for their

Table 2.2   Characteristics of Excellent Public Relations Programs

I. Micro Level	
1.	Managed strategically
II. Managerial (Meso) Level	
2.	A single or integrated public relations department
3.	Separate function from marketing
4.	Direct reporting relationship to senior management
5.	Two-way symmetrical model
6.	Senior public relations person in the managerial role
7.	Potential for excellent public relations, as indicated by:
	a. Knowledge of symmetrical model
	b. Knowledge of managerial role
	c. Academic training in public relations
	d. Professionalism
8.	Schema for public relations in the organization reflects the two-way symmetrical model
9.	Equal opportunity for men and women in public relations
III. Macro Level	
10.	Organic rather than mechanical organizational structure
11.	Symmetrical system of internal communication
12.	Turbulent, complex environment with pressure from activist groups
13.	Public relations director has power in or with the dominant coalition
14.	Participative rather than authoritarian organizational culture
IV. Effects of Excellent Public Relations	
15.	Micro-level programs meet communication objectives
16.	Job satisfaction is high among employees
17.	At the macro level, reduces costs of regulation, pressure, and litigation

survival. The systems approach, therefore, adds the environment to the equation of organizational effectiveness, but it is limited because survival is an extremely weak goal. In government, for example, Cunningham pointed out that "public organizations ... rarely die." [190] The systems approach also defines the environment in vague terms. It does not answer the question of how an organization determines what elements of the environment are important for its success.

3. The *strategic constituencies* approach puts meaning into the term *environment* by specifying the parts of the environment that are crucial for organizational survival and success. Strategic constituencies are the elements of the environment whose opposition or support can threaten the organization's goals or help to attain them. Taken broadly, the environment is both external and internal so that employee groups and management functions can be strategic constituencies as much as can external groups.

4. The fourth piece of the effectiveness puzzle comes from the *competing-values* approach. That approach provides a bridge between strategic constituencies and goals. It states that an organization must incorporate strategic constituencies' values into its goals so that the organization attains the goals of most value to its strategic constituencies. Thus, different organizations with different strategic constituencies in their environments will have different goals and thus their effectiveness will be defined in different ways — what Hall called the contradiction model of effectiveness:

> Put very simply, a contradiction model of effectiveness will consider organizations to be more or less effective in regard to the variety of goals which they pursue, the variety of resources which they attempt to acquire, the variety of constituents inside and outside of the organization, and the variety of time frames by which effectiveness is judged. [191]

A theory of organizational effectiveness that incorporates the competing values of strategic constituencies into the goals chosen to define success fits logically with theories of strategic management that provide a model for organizations to develop missions (sets of goals) that fit with the threats and opportunities provided by strategic constituencies in the environment. Such a theory also makes the role of public relations in organizational effectiveness clear. Robbins described that role well when he discussed the limitations of the strategic constituencies model. The role of public relations is to provide the information about the environment that Robbins said is difficult for other managers to attain:

> The task of separating the strategic constituencies from the larger environment is easy to say but difficult to do in practice. Because the environment changes rapidly, what was critical to the organization yesterday may not be so today. Even if the constituencies in the environment can be identified and are assumed to be relatively stable, what separates the strategic constituencies from the "almost" strategic constituencies? Where do you cut the set? And won't the interests of each member in the dominant coalition strongly affect what he or she perceives as strategic? An executive in the accounting function is unlikely to 'see the world' — or the organization's strategic constituencies — in the same way as an executive in the purchasing function. Finally, identifying the expectations that the strategic constituencies hold for the organization presents a problem. How do you tap that information accurately? [192]

The theory of strategic management and public relations in Table 2.1 and the situational theory of publics incorporated into it provides the mechanisms that Robbins called for in this quote. It states that public relations managers can begin to identify strategic constituencies by identifying stakeholder categories and then by segmenting members of those categories into active and passive publics. Active publics — or potentially active publics — are most strategic for an organization. Thus, their values must be incorporated into organizational goals. To do so means that an organization must build both short- and long-term relationships with strategic publics to be effective.

L. Grunig and colleagues reviewed literature on characteristics of successful relationships with strategic constituencies and concluded that "the following are most important: reciprocity, trust, credibility, mutual legitimacy, openness, mutual satisfaction, and mutual understanding." [193] Vercic went one step further when he related the concept of trust to theories of economics and strategic management and pointed out that trust is the characteristic that allows organizations to exist — trust by stockholders, employees, consumers, governments, and communities, for example. [194] Without trust, stockholders will not buy stock, employees will not work, consumers will not buy products, and governments will interfere with the organization's mission.

If there are more strategic constituencies with which the organization has the resources to build relationships, it must separate the strategic constituencies from the "almost" strategic constituencies, to use Robbins' words. To help make that decision, the excellence research team used theories of cost–benefit analysis to help set such priorities. [195] Likewise, the excellence research also found that excellent public relations managers help to bring the values and goals of different functional managers together by working with them to build relationships with relevant publics and to bring the perspectives of those publics into strategic management [196] — another of Robbins' questions about strategic constituencies.

This integrated theory of organizational effectiveness, therefore, provides the basic integrating premise for a general theory of research. The micro-level theory of public relations discussed to this point specifies that an organization should practice public relations strategically by developing programs to communicate with the publics, both external and internal, that provide the greatest threats to and opportunities for the organization. If communication programs achieve their micro-level objectives of communication accuracy, understanding, agreement, or complementary behavior of the organization and its publics, they help organizations achieve their missions and goals at the macro level.

When public relations helps the organization build relationships with strategic constituencies, it saves the organization money by reducing the costs of litigation, regulation, legislation, pressure campaigns, boycotts, or lost revenue that result from bad relationships with publics — publics that become activist groups when relationships are bad. It also helps the organization make money by cultivating relationships with donors, consumers, shareholders, and legislators that are needed to support organizational goals. Good relationships with employees also increase the likelihood that they will be satisfied with their jobs, which makes them more likely to support and less likely to interfere with the organization's mission. [197]

The general theory, therefore, shows why organizations benefit from public relations. The general theory also integrates the theories developed by several generations of public relations scholars at the micro, meso, and macro levels of analysis. The theory of strategic management and public relations is the essential link between public relations and organizational effectiveness. Many organizations do not practice public relations strategically, however. To understand why some organizations do and others do not practice public relations strategically, researchers have developed theories at the next level of abstraction, the meso level, to explain the characteristics of public relations units most likely to practice the excellent version of public relations.

The Meso (Managerial) Level

Table 2.2 describes all the characteristics of excellent public relations identified by the Excellence research team, including the micro-level characteristics of individual communication programs discussed thus far, the relationship of public relations to strategic management at the meso level, and the outcomes of excellent communication that contribute to organizational effectiveness. This section, therefore, describes the other meso-level variables in Table 2.2.

When public relations researchers began to work at the meso level of abstraction, they totally left the familiar confines of existing communication research to construct original theories of public relations. Instead of communication theory, public relations researchers turned to theories of organizations and management for useful theories. Communication scholars, even those studying organizational communication, had not looked at the consequences of organizational structures and roles on the communication activities of organizations until public relations researchers began to do so. [198]

Of the meso-level characteristics of excellent public relations listed in Table 2.2, the first three relate logically to strategic management of the process. The first characteristic — a single, integrated department — can be contrasted to the situation in many organizations that have multiple public relations departments reporting to other departments such as marketing, human resources, or finance. The second characteristic, a department separate from marketing, highlights the importance of a separate public relations department. The third, a direct reporting relationship to senior management, emphasizes the importance of not sublimating public relations to other organizational functions.

When public relations departments do not have these functions, strategic management becomes basically impossible because the organization has set up separate public relations departments to respond to each public of the organization. When that happens, the organization loses its ability to move resources and programs from one public to another as new publics become strategic. Research from the IABC study has strongly confirmed the importance of these three variables as characteristics of an excellent public relations department. [199,200]

The remaining characteristics of excellent public relations have been developed from two of the most extensive programs of research on public relations in the United States: one on models of public relations and the other on public relations roles.

Models of Public Relations

With the publication of a monograph in 1976, I began a program of research to identify the most typical ways that organizations practice public relations as four "models" of public relations. [201] J. Grunig and Hunt identified these four models of public relations in the history of public relations. [202] Extensive research has shown that one of these models, the two-way symmetrical, is more effective than the others when used alone or combined with a two-way asymmetrical model. Other research suggests that the two-way symmetrical model also is inherently ethical and socially responsible, whereas the other models make ethical and socially responsible behavior extremely difficult.

The first two models see public relations as a monologue. The press agentry model describes public relations programs whose sole purpose is getting favorable publicity for an organization in the mass media. It is common in the work of publicists who promote sports, movie stars, products, politicians, or senior managers.

The public information model is similar to press agentry because it, too, is a one-way model that sees public relations only as the dissemination of information. With the public information model, an organization uses "journalists-in-residence" — public relations practitioners who act as if they are journalists — to disseminate relatively truthful information through the mass media and controlled media such as newsletters, brochures, and direct mail. Although information communicated through this model is truthful, it usually does not reveal the whole truth, only "facts" that the organization chooses to release.

Both the press agentry and public information models describe communication programs that are not based on research and strategic planning. Press agentry and public information also are "asymmetrical" or imbalanced models — that is, they try to change the behavior of publics but not of the organization. They try to make the organization look good either through promotional hype (press agentry) or by disseminating only favorable information (public information).

Public relations practitioners who take a professional approach base their communication programs on more sophisticated and effective models. The two-way asymmetrical model uses research to develop messages that are likely to persuade strategic publics to behave as the organization wants. Two-way asymmetrical public relations uses theories of persuasion and the services of research firms to plan messages most likely to influence the behavior of publics. Thus, the model sees public relations as a dialogue, albeit a dialogue dominated by the organization. Because the two-way asymmetrical model uses research on publics' attitudes, it more often achieves its objectives than do the press agentry or public information models.

Two-way asymmetrical public relations also is a selfish model, however, because the organization that uses it believes it is right (and the public wrong) and that any change needed to resolve a conflict must come from the public and not from the organization. The model seems to work reasonably well when the organization has little conflict with a public and the public stands to benefit from a change in its behavior. For example, even though members of a target public for a health campaign may resist changes in behavior to prevent a heart attack or AIDS, they do benefit from changes advocated by the campaign.

The fourth model, the two-way symmetrical, describes a model of public relations that is based on research and that uses communication to manage conflict and improve understanding with strategic publics. Because the two-way symmetrical model bases public relations on negotiation and compromise, it does not force the organization to choose whether it is right on particular issues. Rather, two-way symmetrical public relations allows the question of what is right to be settled by negotiation, since nearly every side to a conflict — such as nuclear power, abortion, or gun control — believes its position to be right.

J. Grunig and L. Grunig traced the history of research on these models. [203,204] They found that studies based on samples of respondents from all types of organizations consistently have shown press agentry to be the most common form of public relations. [205–208] The means on quantitative scales designed to measure the other three models tend to be similar, although public information generally is the lowest of the three. In studies of specific types of organizations, this pattern also was true in associations, hospitals, and Blue Cross and Blue Shield medical plans. [209–212]

The pattern differed substantially in government agencies, however. In government, public information consistently was the most common model, although press agentry was not far behind. [213–216] The public information model especially was strong in scientific organizations. [217,218]

Although the two-way asymmetrical and two-way symmetrical models did not show up as the dominant form of public relations in any of the studies, the mean scores generally fell at about the middle of the scales used to measure them. This indicates that many organizations within the samples did indeed practice these models. When these models were practiced, the two-way symmetrical model was more common than the asymmetrical in governmental organizations. The two-way asymmetrical was most common in corporations. [219]

When Turk classified 12 agencies in the Louisiana state government by the predominant model practiced, she found that five practiced the two-way symmetrical model, four the press agentry model, two the two-way asymmetrical model, and one the press agentry model. [220] In short, individual government agencies did practice the symmetrical model, even though the public information model had the highest mean score across all the government agencies.

Van Dyke found a similar pattern for 45 U.S. Navy public affairs officers (PAOs). [221] He used a single item to measure each model of public relations and asked the PAOs to select the item that best described Navy public affairs offices: 49 percent selected the two-way symmetrical model, 29 percent the public-information model, 16 percent the two-way asymmetrical model, and 7 percent the press agentry model. Van Dyke also looked at data about the way Navy PAOs performed, however, and concluded that their work corresponded more to the public-information model than the two-way symmetrical model, "disseminating truthful information ... but lacking efforts to evaluate communication effect or efficiency." [222]

Wetherell's study, however, may have produced the most accurate estimates of the practice of the four models — using methods that subsequently were used in the IABC excellence study. [223] She used a fractionation scale to measure the models, an open-end scale that allowed organizations to provide any number from zero to as high as the respondents wanted to go to estimate how well items described their public relations. With the fractionation scale, respondents are told that 100 is the average score for a typical item for a typical organization. Wetherell found a mean for press agentry right at this average, suggesting that it is the typical model in practice. Public information had similar means that were slightly below the average of 100 — high enough to show they are practiced but below what respondents considered to be average for all organizations.

Wetherell also developed an index to measure the extent to which practitioners said they would *like to practice* each of the four models and to measure the extent to which they possessed the knowledge needed to practice each model. [224] These results, too, reveal what seem to be meaningful generalizations about typical public relations practitioners. When respondents reported their preferred model, the two-way symmetrical and asymmetrical models jumped into a virtual tie for first place with scores around 140 on the fractionation scale, while press agentry and public information dropped to 75 and 66, respectively. Bissland and Rentner corroborated this finding when they found that two-thirds of the practitioners in their sample preferred the symmetrical model. [225] In Wetherell's study, however, practitioners reported that they had the most knowledge about how to practice the public information and press agentry models — reflecting, no doubt, their journalistic backgrounds. [226] Practitioners reported that they possess less of the knowledge needed to practice the two-way models.

Gaudino and colleagues researched the question of whether regulated businesses would be most likely to practice the two-way symmetrical model in a study of 27 utilities. [227] They concluded that the utilities did indeed practice public relations in a way similar to the two-way symmetrical model. However, even though the utilities perceived mutual understanding with publics as their goal and had set up mechanisms for dialogue, they generally had asymmetrical results in mind. They believed that if publics were "educated," they would agree with the organization. "If you knew what I knew, you'd make the same decision" was the assumption underlying what on the surface was symmetrical public relations.

Although most of these studies have looked for patterns in the types of organizations that practice the models, two studies suggested that individual public relations programs within an overall public relations function may be a more meaningful place to look for differences in the models.

Cupp found that chemical companies were most likely to practice the two-way symmetrical model during a crisis and an asymmetrical model in pre-crisis public relations programs. [228] Nelson conducted two case studies, one of a bank and another of a telecommunications company. [229] The bank had identified community publics as most strategic and used the two-way symmetrical model to communicate with them. The telecommunications company had identified consumers as most strategic and used two-way asymmetrical public relations and press agentry for its marketing communication program.

Research supports the idea that models of public relations vary among types of organizations and that they vary among programs within organizations. The variation among organizations probably occurs for historical reasons. For example, public information is most common in government because of historical restrictions placed on its practice there. The variation by programs probably is strategic: for some programs (such as communication with activists, during a crisis, or with government), symmetrical communication may be the only choice.

In addition to this research on the practice of the four models, other research provides evidence that the two-way symmetrical model makes organizations more effective in building relationships with their environment and in meeting organizational goals. Two types of research have been done: on the ethics of public relations and on the effectiveness of the models in achieving public relations objectives. Essentially, this research shows that the two-way symmetrical model is the most ethical approach to public relations and that ethical public relations also is the model most effective in meeting organizational goals.

Discussions of the ethics of public relations frequently hinge on the relativism of an issue, an ideology, or a behavior. Is it ethical, for example, to promote guns, smoking, abortion, or alcohol? J. Grunig argued that the models other than the symmetrical one can be used to justify almost any cause. [230] Based on the apparent assumption that all public relations is asymmetrical, Olasky and Gandy did critical research to support the argument that all public relations is unethical. [231,232] Dozier, in contrast, argued that the symmetrical model of public relations is the only model "*inherently* consistent with the concept of social responsibility." [233]

The two-way symmetrical model avoids the problem of ethical relativism because it defines ethics as a *process* of public relations rather than an *outcome*. Symmetrical public relations provides a forum for dialogue, discussion, and discourse on issues for which people with different values generally come to different conclusions. As long as the dialogue is structured according to ethical rules, the outcome should be ethical, although not usually one that fits the value system of any competing party perfectly.

Pearson has produced the best-developed ethical rationale for the symmetrical model, [234–236] based primarily on Habermas's concept of the ideal communication system. [237] Pearson, for example, developed a set of rules for ethical, symmetrical public relations and provided practical advice for evaluating a public relations program by the extent to which those rules have been followed. [238]

Although research supports the idea that the two-way symmetrical model makes public relations more ethical, senior managers of organizations also want to know whether it pays for their organizations to practice the more ethical model. Research suggests that it does. Several studies have shown the ineffectiveness of the press agentry, public information, and two-way asymmetrical models. Although L. Grunig found that none of the 31 organizations she studied had used the two-way symmetrical model to deal with activist groups, she also found that none of the other models reduced conflict with these groups. [239] Lauzen found that franchising organizations that used the two-way symmetrical model combined with the press agentry and two-way asymmetrical models reduced their conflict with franchise holders. [240] Because the franchises combined the three models, however, we cannot conclude whether the symmetrical model alone would have been more effective.

In critical studies of the Nuclear Regulatory Commission and of fund-raising programs in higher education, Childers [aka Hon] and Kelly documented the failure of asymmetrical models to contribute to organizational goals or to the public interest. [241,242] Studies of media relations also have demonstrated the superiority of the symmetrical model or the failure of other models. Turk concluded that public information officers using that model in state agencies had little effect in influencing the "agency picture portrayed by the news media." [243] Habbersett found that science reporters strongly supported a set of symmetrical procedures for media relations. [244] Theus measured the extent to which news reports on a sample of organizations were discrepant from the way the organizations thought the stories should have been reported. [245] She found that the more open and symmetrical an organization's communication system, the less the discrepancy in news coverage.

The IABC research provided strong evidence that excellent public relations departments use the two-way symmetrical model and that as a result they more often meet the objectives of their communication and make the organization more effective. [246,247] However, we also found that excellent public relations departments combine the two-way symmetrical and asymmetrical models in what Murphy called a mixed-motive model. [248] Excellent public relations departments balance attempts to persuade publics with the asymmetrical model with attempts to negotiate with them using the symmetrical model. In doing so, they engage in a form of symmetrical persuasion: they attempt to persuade publics to move closer to the interests of management and management to move its interests closer to those of publics.

In the theoretical model of excellence that guided this research, the two-way symmetrical model appears in five of the characteristics of excellent public relations programs in Table 2.2. First, excellent programs practice the two-way symmetrical model. Second, excellent departments have the potential to practice it — they have practitioners who know how to practice the model, with formal education in public relations (which usually emphasizes that model), and with the characteristics of professionals (such as reading research and professional publications and attending meetings of professional societies). Finally, the schema — or the world view — of the senior managers in the organization (a group we call the dominant coalition) defines public relations in a way similar to the two-way symmetrical model.

Public Relations Roles

The second major program of research on public relations in the United States in the last decade has studied the roles that practitioners occupy in public relations departments. [249,250] Although researchers have identified as many as seven roles that practitioners play, two central roles always emerge — communication technicians and communication managers. Communication managers plan and direct public relations programs. Communication technicians provide technical services such as writing, editing, photography, media contacts, or production of publications. The majority of public relations people are technicians. Without technicians, public relations programs could not be implemented. Without managers, however, public relations programs would resemble a perpetual motion machine that churns out press releases, publications, or special events without stopping to think why they are needed. [251]

The same person may be both a manager and a technician in many organizations, especially small ones. [252] Many practitioners play both roles in their careers, generally beginning as technicians and becoming managers as they are promoted. Many practitioners have satisfying, long-term careers solely as technicians. [253] Many public relations programs, however, have no managers to guide them.

The theory of excellence in public relations states that a public relations program cannot be effective unless it has a manager to manage it strategically — to aim it at the publics in an organization's environment that have the greatest effect on the organization. Other research also shows a strong relationship between the managerial role and the two-way models of public relations — both the asymmetrical and symmetrical. [254] Practitioners who know only the technician role cannot practice those more sophisticated models.

The managerial role, like the two-way symmetrical model, shows up in several of the meso-level characteristics of excellent public relations programs in Table 2.2. First, an excellent public relations department must have the senior person in the managerial role — he or she must be more than a senior technician or technical supervisor who coordinates the work of the department. He or she must be a strategic manager who makes most of the decisions for the organization about public relations strategy. A public relations department also will have greater potential if someone in the department knows how to practice the managerial role. And knowledge will be greater if practitioners have academic training in public relations and have the characteristics of professionals.

Finally, extensive research has shown that female practitioners fill the managerial role less often than males, primarily but not exclusively because of discrimination against women in management. [255] The public relations profession now has a majority of females practicing it in the United States, and over two-thirds of the students studying public relations there now are women. Women, therefore, enhance the potential of the public relations department because they have the knowledge to practice public relations strategically and symmetrically. Keeping them out of the managerial role thus limits the excellence of most public relations departments.

The Macro Level: What Makes Excellent Public Relations Possible?

Thus far, the emerging general theory of public relations has explained how public relations should be practiced at the strategic, micro level to contribute the most to organizational effectiveness and the characteristics that public relations departments must have — at the meso level — to practice public relations in this excellent way. Another program of research, however, has shown that not all organizations — or, more accurately, the people with the most power in them — choose to practice public relations in this way. Research has gradually identified the organizational conditions necessary for excellent public relations.

Macro Conditions for Excellent Public Relations

The research on the macro conditions leading to excellent public relations has progressed from the tenth to the fourteenth characteristic of excellent public relations in Table 2.2. In general, researchers followed the trends in organizational sociology and applied them to public relations. [256] At first, researchers thought that organizational structure would explain how organizations practice public relations: they believed that decentralized structures in which employees at all levels participate in decisions should facilitate excellent public relations. [257] In addition, research demonstrated that symmetrical systems of internal communication are part of these decentralized structures. [258,259]

Structure explained some of the variance in the practice of public relations but left much of it unexplained. Next, then, researchers turned to the organizational environment for an explanation and studied the extent to which the presence of complex, turbulent environments stimulates excellent public relations. [260–262] Again, the nature of the environment was associated only to a limited extent with the practice of public relations.

Most recently, researchers have adopted the power-control perspective now dominant in organizational sociology. [263] That perspective maintains that organizations behave as they do because the people with the most power — the dominant coalition — choose to do so. The results from the IABC study have confirmed the overriding importance of power for public relations. [264–268] Public relations cannot be effective unless the senior public relations person has power to affect organizational decisions, either formally or informally. Our data strongly suggest that public relations departments without power do not practice public relations strategically. Lack of power, therefore, seems to explain why few public relations programs are excellent.

Finally, research suggests that both the characteristics of excellent public relations and the power of the senior public relations person are affected strongly by the organization's culture [269,271] and that organizational culture, in turn, is affected by the culture of a country or region of a country. [272, 273] Our review of the literature suggested that organizational culture varies along a continuum from authoritarian to participative, and a factor analysis of 45 indicators of organizational culture confirmed that those two dimensions do explain a large portion of the variance in those indicators. [274] In our literature review, we hypothesized that excellent public relations departments would exist more often in a participative culture than an authoritarian culture, as would the other macro-level characteristics that bring about excellent public relations departments.

The results showed, however, that a participative culture does correlate positively with excellent public relations but that many excellent departments are found in organizations with authoritarian cultures. Thus, we concluded that a participative culture provides a nurturing environment for excellent public relations but that an excellent public relations function can make incremental changes in an authoritarian culture to make it more participative and therefore more nurturing for further excellence in public relations. The data suggested that such incremental change begins with internal communication — development of a symmetrical system of internal communication begins the process of culture change that in turn stimulates excellence in other facets of public relations.

The excellence study provided less evidence of the effect of societal culture on organizational culture and public relations. We found no differences in any of our variables in the three countries in our study — the United States, Canada, and the United Kingdom. These countries have similar cultures, however — at least as measured by Hofstede's dimensions of culture. [275] A replication of the excellence study in Slovenia produced essentially the same results as in the three Anglo countries, [276] but qualitative research on the work of the major public relations firm in Slovenia suggested that the principles of excellent public relations had to be applied differently there to fit a different culture. [277] The qualitative research also suggested, though, that excellence in public relations can move a societal culture incrementally toward a culture that nurtures further excellence, much as it can move organizational culture toward more participative characteristics.

Critical Research on Public Relations

In addition to the research that has produced the general theory of public relations described in this chapter, public relations scholars with a rhetorical approach also have engaged in a related type of macro-level research — critical research on public relations. Although most academic scholars — and the more professional practitioners of public relations — now seem to be reaching a consensus on this general theory of public relations, some scholars and many practitioners take issue with it because it describes a type of public relations different from that in practice today. [278] As a result, critical scholars have done research to document the poor ethics, negative social consequences, or ineffectiveness of forms of public relations that differ from the general theory of excellent public relations.

Some critics have evaluated public relations from a political perspective. Olasky, a conservative, has maintained that corporations have used public relations to consort with government, thus restricting competition. [279] Gandy, a Marxist, has argued that public relations helps to preserve the dominant power structure in society. [280] Other critical scholars such as Rakow have suggested that the two-way symmetrical model of public relations cannot work in the United States without a radical transformation of its culture and political structure. [281] Mallinson also suggested that the two-way symmetrical model may work better in European cultures than in the United States. [282]

Rhetorical theorists such as Smilowitz and Pearson, [283] Cheney and Dionisopoulos, [284] Cheney, [285] and Pearson [286,287] have examined public relations against the yardstick provided by rhetorical theories such as Habermas's ideal communication situation [288] or Burke's theory of "identification" in persuasion — the co-creation by the persuader and persaudee of a state-of-affairs. [289] Toth has compared rhetorical and critical approaches to what she calls the systems approach represented in the general theory described previously. [290] Heath has explained the rhetorical approach to public relations [291] and the critical approach. [292] The entire volume edited by Toth and Heath contains examples of rhetorical and critical analyses of public relations. [293]

Pearson has developed a theory of public relations ethics based on the two-way symmetrical model and Habermas's ideal communication situation. [294] Several other scholars, including Bivins, [295–298] McElreath, [299] Pratt, [300] Pratt and colleagues, [301] Ryan and Martinson, [302] and D. Wright [303,304] have begun to work on ethics of public relations based on ethical theories in philosophy and psychology, and L. Grunig has begun to develop a complete philosophy of public relations. [305]

Finally, a large and growing community of scholars has begun to use feminist theory to criticize public relations. [306–312] They theorize, in essence, that current public relations practice is based on male models of competition, hierarchy, and dominance. Public relations would be more ethical, responsible, and effective, they add, if instead it were based on female models of cooperation and equity.

The State of Public Relations Research

Only a few years ago, public relations research essentially did not exist except for research on, and narrow theories of, effects borrowed directly from the larger discipline of communication. Recently, public relations research has grown rapidly both in quantity and theoretical quality. Public relations scholars have reached the point where public relations has become a respected domain within both the disciplines of communication and management. This chapter has shown that public relations has drawn from these larger disciplines in constructing its own theories but that the new theories of public relations add dimensions that were lacking in the other disciplines' theoretical structures.

In addition, the body of knowledge public relations scholars have produced is affecting the practice of public relations. In fact, the Public Relations Society of America (PRSA) has codified the emerging body of knowledge into a database of abstracts that can be obtained either in hard copy or on computer disk. Most of the same body of knowledge has been integrated in the first *Excellence* book. [313] This organized body of knowledge has made it possible to educate a new generation of practitioners. It also allows current practitioners, who are willing to take the time and effort necessary, to interpret their current approaches in terms of the theory or to use the theory to develop a new way of practicing.

Although most of the research cited here has been done in the United States, similar advances are being made in other countries throughout the world, [314] and public relations in the 21st century will be practiced globally. This fact leads to the most important trend in the profession and to projections for 2000 and beyond.

The Global Trend in Public Relations

Among public relations practitioners today, the slogan initiated by environmentalist René Dubos, "think globally, act locally," has become nearly axiomatic. [315] Practitioners use the slogan to make the point that all organizations have global relationships. Even a small, seemingly local business may have competition from other countries and purchase supplies from an international supplier. Nevertheless, the "act locally" part of the slogan suggests that most organizations still implement global strategies at the local level.

Jean Farinelli, the chief executive officer of the New York public relations firm Creamer Dickson Basford, Inc., and Joe Epley, a past president of PRSA and owner of Epley Associates, a Charlotte, North Carolina, public relations firm, both emphasized the need to think of the global connections of what might seem to be local decisions. [316,317] According to Farinelli, "today, many of the issues facing even so-called 'local' clients are affected by world economic and political conditions." [318] She added: "The point is, if not today, your next assignment, or your next job, could very well require international understanding and public relations skills." [319]

Epley named four changes that are making global relationships important even to ostensibly local organizations:

1. *Communications technology* that makes it possible to learn global news almost instantaneously and to do business around the world 24 hours a day.
2. *Realignments of economic power* such as those that produced the European Community and the North American Free Trade Agreement, so that business often is conducted continent by continent rather than country by country and multinational corporations are world citizens rather than citizens of only one country.
3. *Major issues know no political boundary.* Organizations may be affected by issues created by publics in many countries, not just the country in which they are headquartered.
4. *The prospect of unprecedented world peace*, which means that communication will be used more than military strength to resolve issues. [320]

Farinelli and Epley both added, however, that U.S. public relations practitioners are losing their leadership in the profession because they do not have enough international knowledge and experience. In Farinelli's words:

Unfortunately, as more U.S. companies and executives shift to an international focus, they find their public relations counselors — both agencies and in-house staff — lacking the background, the understanding, even the interest necessary to be effective.... Moreover, public relations has fewer people with international knowledge and experience than any of the other business sectors such as advertising, financial services, and management consulting. We all service the same clients — but public relations has the worst record of all in keeping pace with international changes. [321]

Farinelli urged practitioners to think of "international" public relations and to stop thinking that "things happening outside the United States are somehow 'foreign' to us and our clients' interests. They are not." [322] She suggested that practitioners should be better informed about world events, have strong educations and diverse interests, be more open to new ideas, and think laterally (from several perspectives at once) rather than linearly (from one central perspective).

Generic Principles and Specific Applications: Between Ethnocentrism and Polycentrism

Given this trend toward global public relations, both practitioners and scholars have begun to ask whether there are or can be global principles of public relations. Can public relations programs in different countries be standardized, or must different, localized programs be developed for each country — or indeed for different regions within a country with different cultures? The question is especially important for multinational organizations — those that work in more than one country or have publics in more than one country. The question also is important for public relations education and for the development of a global public relations profession. Can the same principles be taught in different countries and included in a body of knowledge that can be used throughout the world?

Public relations people have not been alone in asking this question. Marketing experts also debated whether the same products could be marketed and advertised in the same way in different countries or whether different products must be developed and marketed differently. [323] Likewise, management scholars debated whether management practices could be culture-free or culture-specific. [324]

Gavin Anderson, who heads a New York public relations firm that bears his name, used the terms *global* and *international* to distinguish between public relations practiced in the same way throughout the world and public relations customized for each culture:

> *International* public relations practitioners very often implement distinctive programs in multiple markets, with each program tailored to meet the often acute distinctions of the individual geographic market. *Global* public relations superimposes an overall perspective on a program executed in two or more national markets, recognizing the similarities among audiences while necessarily adapting to regional differences. [325]

G. Anderson chose the global model over the international one, saying: "Global, as opposed to multinational, businesses demand that programs in distinctive markets be interrelated. While there will always be local differences and need for customization, the programs will probably share more than they differ." [326] Botan came to the opposite conclusion. He called the global approach the ethnocentric model and concluded that practitioners from Western countries often impose the assumptions of their culture on public relations practice in other countries. [327] Under a polycentric model, in contrast, practitioners in each country in which a multinational organization works have considerable freedom to practice public relations in a way they believe is appropriate for that country.

Emerging out of this debate about the merits of two extreme positions seems to be a consensus that the ideal model for multicultural public relations lies somewhere in the middle — that public relations programs, in Ovaitt's words, can share strategic elements even if these strategies are implemented in different ways in different cultures. [328] Two scholars of international management, Brinkerhoff and Ingle called this middle approach the use of *generic principles* and *specific applications*. They identified five management functions that they said are "generic to good performance." However, how each of these functions is actually applied "can vary from setting to setting":

> For example, a rural development agency in country X may establish a formal goal specification and review procedure, whereas an agency in country Y may accomplish the same function with a more informal arrangement. What matters is that participants develop ways of fulfilling the functions that fit with their organizational and cultural environments. [329]

Stohl provided an example of how a management principle can vary from culture to culture. [330] She asked managers in Denmark, England, France, Germany, and the Netherlands how they implemented the management principle of worker participation in management. Although the managers all based their behavior on the same principle, they implemented that principle differently in each country — in ways that reflected their country's culture.

To understand the concept of a generic theory, however, it is important to distinguish between a normative and positive theory. This global theory is a *normative* theory. It includes concepts that explain how public relations *should* be practiced throughout the world to be most effective. Public relations may be practiced in other ways — as *positive* descriptions of the models of public relations practiced in several countries provided by J. Grunig and associates showed. [331]

A theory of multicultural public relations based on generic principles and specific applications fits more closely with what G. Anderson called the global approach than with the international approach. [332] A global theory, therefore, contains what Sharpe called "principles understood around the world." [333] However, this global theory also spells out differences in the way these principles are applied that make them culturally specific rather than ethnocentric — differences that overcome Botan's reservations about ethnocentric public relations. [334]

A Global and Specific Theory of Public Relations

Scholarly research on a global theory of public relations is only beginning. At this point, most of what we know about the topic comes from short articles in professional publications in which practitioners have described their experiences in many countries. These experiences of practitioners are important in identifying principles and practices of public relations that work in a global setting. However, at this point it is important that scholars systematically translate these practical experiences into theory and test the theoretical principles through research.

Vercic and co-workers and Wakefield have made the first attempts to develop such a global theory. [335,336] They have hypothesized that the 14 characteristics of excellent public relations that make up the general theory of public relations described in this chapter (Table 2.2) also will be generic principles of global public relations. They have hypothesized also that five specific variables must be taken into account when the generic principles are applied in different settings: (1) the political–economic system, (2) culture, including language, (3) the extent of activism, (4) the level of development, and (5) the media system. In essence, this global theory states that when public relations is managed strategically in a global context, these five variables must be taken into account when the public relations manager scans an organization's environment as part of public relations' strategic management.

In the first research on the generic–specific propositions, Vercic and co-workers conducted a case study of a public relations firm in Slovenia that has made the 14 principles of excellence the knowledge base for its practice in this newly democratized country — in essence, providing an experimental test of the normative principles. [337] This case study analyzed, in particular, how the change in the political–economic system from communism to democracy affected public relations practice in Slovenia and how the generic principles were affected by the cultural characteristics identified by Hofstede. [338] In addition, Vercic and co-workers provided nine examples of specific applications of the generic principles used by the public relations firm, and they showed that these principles had indeed been effective in Slovenia. [339]

Implications

For at least 100 years, public relations has been an important communication trade. It has been a trade rather than a profession because the practice of public relations has been based on trial and error and the application of communication techniques rather than being based on the systematic application of theoretical principles. In the 1920s, Bernays applied social science theories of the time to public relations, but few other practitioners followed his lead. [340] In the 1950s, Cutlip and Center wrote the first public relations textbook that used theory and went beyond a description of the techniques used by practitioners. [341] In the 1960s, Robinson wrote a public relations textbook based largely on theories from psychology, although few practitioners read the book and few copies were used in classrooms. [342]

Today, the book *Excellence in Public Relations and Communication Management* has followed in the tradition of these earlier attempts to apply theory to the practice of public relations. Although *Excellence* uses theories from other disciplines, most of the body of knowledge developed in the book has been produced by public relations scholars. In contrast to the earlier books, it also is being read widely and used by practitioners as well as scholars. Sociologists who study the professions have identified five traits that set a profession apart from a trade or occupation: (1) professional values, (2) professional organizations that develop a professional culture, (3) professional norms and ethics, (4) an intellectual body of knowledge, and (5) professional education. [343]

The key one of these traits is the body of knowledge. The body of knowledge provides a base for education, for values and ethics, and for the activities of professional associations. Indeed, the body of knowledge makes it possible for a profession to develop a culture — complete with values, norms, and a process of education. As a profession develops, it also spreads throughout the world so that professionals can interact and learn from one another in different cultural and political settings. As this chapter has demonstrated, public relations scholars have developed a general theory of public relations that now provides a base of knowledge needed for a global professional culture.

Although much public relations practice around the world is improvised, atheoretical, ineffective, and unethical, that kind of practice will be found less often as standards and expectations for public relations practice increase and as more and more practitioners use the general theory of public relations as a basis for their work. When that happens, public relations practice will become more effective, it will contribute more to the well-functioning of global societies, and its reputation will improve worldwide.

Note: *Originally published in Grunig, J.E., Public relations in government and business, in* Handbook of Administrative Communication, *Garnett, J.L. and Kouzmin, A., Eds., Marcel Dekker, New York, 1997, chap. 12.*

Endnotes

1. Grunig, J.E. and Hunt, T., *Managing Public Relations*, Holt, Rinehart and Winston, Fort Worth, TX, 1984, 6–8.
2. Ibid, 6.
3. Dumas, M., Communication in a World Rich with Cultural Differences, paper presented to the International Association of Business Communicators, Washington, DC, 1991, 13.
4. Bishop, R.L., What newspapers say about public relations, *Public Relations Review*, 14(3), 50, 1988.
5. Spicer, C.H., Images of public relations in the print media, *Journal of Public Relations Research*, 5, 47, 1993.
6. Cline, C.G., The image of public relations in mass communication texts, *Public Relations Review*, 8(3), 63, 1982.
7. Grunig, J.E., Ed., *Excellence in Public Relations and Communication Management*, Lawrence Erlbaum, Hillsdale, NJ, 1992.
8. Portions of this chapter were revised from Grunig, J.E., The development of public relations research in the United States and its status in communication science, in *Ist Public Relations Eine Wissenschaft?* (*Is Public Relations a Science?*), Avenarius, H. and Armbrecht, W., Eds., Westdeutscher Verlag, Opladen, Germany, 1992, 103.
9. Grunig, J.E., The status of public relations research, *International Public Relations Association Review*, 3(1), 9, 1979.
10. Grunig, J.E., Symmetrical presuppositions as a framework for public relations theory, in *Public Relations Theory*, Botan, C.H. and Hazleton, Jr., V.T., Eds., Lawrence Erlbaum, Hillsdale, NJ, 1989, 17.
11. Grunig, J.E. and Hunt, T., *Managing Public Relations*, Holt, Rinehart and Winston, Fort Worth, TX, 1984.
12. Cutlip, S.M., Center, A.H., and Broom, G.H., *Effective Public Relations*, 7th ed., Prentice-Hall, Englewood Cliffs, NJ, 1994, chaps. 8, 12.
13. Salmon, C.T., The Role of Involvement in Health-Information Acquisition and Processing, unpublished doctoral dissertation, University of Minnesota, Minneapolis, 1985.
14. Pavlik, J.V., The Effects of Two Health Information Campaigns on the Complexity of Cognitive Structure: An Information Processing Approach, unpublished doctoral dissertation, University of Minnesota, Minneapolis, 1987.
15. Anderson, R.B., Reassessing the odds against finding meaningful behavioral change in mass media health promotion campaigns, *Public Relations Theory*, Botan, C.H. and Hazleton, V.T., Jr., Eds., Lawrence Erlbaum, Hillsdale, NJ, 1989, chap. 18.
16. VanLeuven, J.K., Theoretical models for public relations campaigns, in *Public Relations Theory*, Botan, C.H. and Hazleton, Jr., V.T., Eds., Lawrence Erlbaum, Hillsdale, NJ, 1989, 193.
17. VanLeuven, J.K. and Slater, M.D., How publics, public relations, and the media shape the public opinion process, *Public Relations Research Annual*, 3, 165, 1991.
18. Rice, R.E. and Paisley, W., Eds., *Public Communication Campaigns*, Sage, Newbury Park, CA, 1981.

19. Rice, R.E. and Atkin, C.K., Eds., *Public Communication Campaigns*, 2nd ed., Sage, Newbury Park, CA, 1989.
20. Salmon, C.T., Ed., *Information Campaigns: Balancing Social Values and Social Change*, Sage, Newbury Park, CA, 1989.
21. O'Keefe, G.J. and Reid, K., The uses and effects of public service advertising, *Public Relations Research Annual*, 2, 67, 1990.
22. Miller, G.R., Persuasion and public relations: Two "Ps" in a pod, in *Public Relations Theory*, Botan, C.H. and Hazleton, Jr., V.T., Eds., Lawrence Erlbaum, Hillsdale, NJ, 1989, 45.
23. Grunig, J.E. and Hunt, T., *Managing Public Relations*, Holt, Rinehart and Winston, Fort Worth, TX, 1984, chap. 6.
24. Berger, C.R., Goals, plans, and discourse comprehension, in *Message Effects in Communication Science*, Bradac, J.J., Ed., Sage, Newbury Park, CA, 1989, 75.
25. Kellerman, K. and Lim, T.S., Inference-generating knowledge structures in message processing, in *Message Effects in Communication Science*, Bradac, J.J., Ed., Sage, Newbury Park, CA, 1989, 102.
26. Bradac, J.J., Hopper, R., and Wiemann, J.M., Message effects: Retrospect and prospect, in *Message Effects in Communication Science*, Bradac, J.J., Ed., Sage, Newbury Park, CA, 1989, 294.
27. Grunig, J.E., Symmetrical presuppositions as a framework for public relations theory, in *Public Relations Theory*, Botan, C.H. and Hazleton, Jr., V.T., Eds., Lawrence Erlbaum, Hillsdale, NJ, 1989, 17.
28. Chaffee, S.H. and McLeod, J.M., Sensitization in panel design: A coorientational experiment, *Journalism Quarterly*, 54, 661, 1968.
29. Grunig, J.E. and Stamm, K.R., Communication and the coorientation of collectivities, *American Behavioral Scientist*, 16, 567, 1973.
30. Broom, G.M., Coorientational measurement of public issues, *Public Relations Review*, 3(4), 110, 1977.
31. Culbertson, H.M., Breadth of perspective: An important concept for public relations, *Public Relations Research Annual*, 1, 3, 1989.
32. Pearson, R., Beyond ethical relativism in public relations: Coorientation, rules, and the idea of communication symmetry, *Public Relations Research Annual*, 1, 67, 1989.
33. Grunig, J.E. and Hunt, T., *Managing Public Relations*, Holt, Rinehart and Winston, Fort Worth, TX, 1984, 134.
34. Broom, G.M. and Dozier, D.M., *Using Research in Public Relations: Applications to Program Management*, Prentice-Hall, Englewood Cliffs, NJ, 1990.
35. Knodell, J.E., Matching perceptions of food editors, writers, and readers, *Public Relations Review*, 2(3), 37, 1976.
36. Blumer, H., The mass, the public, and public opinion, in *Reader in Public Opinion and Communication*, 2nd ed., Berelson, B. and Janowitz, M., Eds., Free Press, New York, 1966, 43.
37. Lowery, S. and DeFleur, M.L., *Milestones in Mass Communication Research*, Longman, White Plains, NY, 1983.
38. Wright, C.R., *Mass Communication: A Sociological Perspective*, 3rd ed., Random House, New York, 1986.
39. McQuail, D., *Mass Communication Theory*, 3rd ed., Sage, Newbury Park, CA, 1994.
40. Mendelsohn, H., Some reasons why information campaigns can succeed, *Public Opinion Quarterly*, 37, 50, 1973.
41. Solomon, D.S., A social marketing perspective on communication campaigns, in *Public Communication Campaigns*, 2nd ed., Rice, R.E. and Atkin, C.K., Eds., Sage, Newbury Park, CA, 1989, 87.
42. Kotler, P. and Andreasen, A.R., *Strategic Marketing for Nonprofit Organizations*, 3rd ed., Prentice-Hall, Englewood Cliffs, NJ, 1987, chap. 20.
43. Kotler, P., *Marketing Management*, 7th ed., Prentice-Hall, Englewood Cliffs, NJ, 1991, 643.
44. Kotler, P. and Anderson, G., *Principles of Marketing*, 5th ed., Prentice-Hall, Englewood Cliffs, NJ, 1991, chaps. 16, 17.
45. Schultz, D.E., Tannenbaum, S.I., and Lauterborn, R.F., *Integrated Marketing Communications*, NTC Business Books, Chicago, 1993.

46. Ehling, W.P., Public Relations Management and Marketing Management: Different Paradigms and Different Missions, paper presented at the Public Relations Colloquium 1989, San Diego State University, San Diego, CA, 1989.

47. Grunig, J.E., Publics, audiences, and market segments: Segmentation principles for campaigns, in *Information Campaigns: Balancing Social Values and Social Change*, Salmon, C.T., Ed., Sage, Newbury Park, CA, 1989, 199.

48. Ehling, W.P., White, J., and Grunig, J.E., Public relations and marketing practices, in *Excellence in Public Relations and Communication Management*, Grunig, J.E., Ed., Lawrence Erlbaum, Hillsdale, NJ, 1992, chap. 13.

49. Kotler, P. and Andreasen, A.R., *Strategic Marketing for Nonprofit Organizations*, 3rd ed., Prentice-Hall, Englewood Cliffs, NJ, 1987, chap. 20.

50. Lewton, K.L., *Public Relations in Health Care: A Guide for Professionals*, American Hospital Publishing, Chicago, 1991, 51–55.

51. U.S. Department of Energy, *Communication and Trust Strategic Plan*, Government Printing Office, Washington, DC, 1993, 3.

52. U.S. Forest Service, *Forest Service Reinvention: Executive Summary*, Government Printing Office, Washington, DC, 1994, 1.

53. Schultz, D.E., Tannenbaum, S.I., and Lauterborn, R.F., *Integrated Marketing Communications*, NTC Business Books, Chicago, 1993, 62–63.

54. Devroy, A. and Balz, D., Clinton Tries to Energize Democrats, *Washington Post*, January 22, 1995, A1, A8.

55. Charlton, R., *Comparative Government*, Longman, London, 1986, 112.

56. Ibid, 111–123.

57. Hague, R. and Harrop, M., *Comparative Government and Politics*, 2nd ed., Macmillan, London, 1987, 113–121.

58. Roberts, G.K., *An Introduction to Comparative Politics*, Edward Arnold, London, 1986, 92–95.

59. Needler, M.C., *The Concepts of Comparative Politics*, Praeger, New York, 1991, 104–111.

60. Olasky attacked such collaboration between business and government as an infringement on free markets (Olasky, M.N., *Corporate Public Relations and American Private Enterprise: A New Historical Perspective*, Lawrence Erlbaum, Hillsdale, NJ, 1987). Cunningham identified the dangers of collaboration when he said, "Effectiveness in public-sector agencies deteriorates when clients come to dominate other stakeholders, or new and opposing stakeholders arise. Antipoverty programs of the late 1960s drew heavy criticism from local politicians as poor people began to act like other interest groups in making demands on the political system.... The Legal Services Cooperation in the 1970s aroused opposition primarily not from other lawyers, but from governments and business who were being sued by legal services attorneys" (Cunningham, R.B., Perspectives on public-sector strategic management, in *Handbook of Strategic Management*, Rabin, J., Miller, G.J., and Hildreth, W.B., Eds., Marcel Dekker, New York, 1989, chap. 5, 127).

61. Jim Caplan, public affairs director of the U.S. Forest Service, told the author that government public affairs must be a balancing act between a democratic corporatist process in which (1) an agency builds relationships with key publics who affect and are affected by the agency, with "an opportunity for others to look over your shoulder" as you build these relationships to make sure that vested interests are not served at the expense of society and (2) remaining in an "opportunist mode" for all citizens at all times to come to the agency when new situations make new relationships necessary (telephone interview with the author, January 23, 1995, author's files).

62. Bonoma, T.V. and Shapiro, B.P., *Segmenting the Industrial Market*, Lexington Books, Lexington, MA, 1983, 2.

63. Levitt, T., *The Marketing Imagination*, exp. ed., Free Press, New York, 1986, 5.

64. Grunig, J.E., Publics, audiences, and market segments: Segmentation principles for campaigns, in *Information Campaigns: Balancing Social Values and Social Change*, Salmon, C.T., Ed., Sage, Newbury Park, CA, 1989, 199.

65. Robertson, T.S., *Innovative Behavior and Communication*, Holt, Rinehart and Winston, New York, 1971.
66. Lionberger, H.F. and Gwin, P.H., *Communication Strategies: A Guide for Agricultural Change Agents*, Interstate Printers and Publishers, Danville, IL, 1982.
67. Rogers, E.M., *Diffusion of Innovations*, 3rd ed., Free Press, New York, 1983.
68. Dewey, J., *The Public and Its Problems*, Swallow, Chicago, 1927.
69. Blumer, H., The mass, the public, and public opinion, in *Reader in Public Opinion and Communication*, 2nd ed., Berelson, B. and Janowitz, M., Eds., Free Press, New York, 1966, 43.
70. Cobb, R.W. and Elder, C.D., *Participation in American Politics: The Dynamics of Agenda Building*, Johns Hopkins University Press, Baltimore, 1972.
71. Price, V., On the public aspects of opinion: Linking levels of analysis in public opinion research, *Communication Research*, 15, 659, 1988.
72. Price, V., *Public Opinion*, Sage, Newbury Park, CA, 1992.
73. Palmgreen, P., Uses and gratifications: A theoretical perspective, in *Communication Yearbook 8*, Bostrom, R.N., Ed., Sage, Newbury Park, CA, 1984, 20.
74. Levy, M.R. and Windahl, S., Audience activity and gratification: A conceptual clarification and exploration, *Communication Research*, 11, 51, 1984.
75. Pavlik, J.V., Nwosu, I.E., and Ettel-Gonzalez, D., Why employees read company newsletters, *Public Relations Review*, 8, 23, 1982.
76. Carroll, A.B., *Business and Society: Ethics and Stakeholder Management*, Southwestern, Cincinnati, OH, 1989, 56.
77. Freeman, F.E., *Strategic Management: A Stakeholder Approach*, Pitman, Boston, 1984, 25.
78. Grunig, J.E., Some consistent types of employee publics, *Public Relations Review*, 1(4), 17, 1975.
79. Grunig, J.E., Evaluating employee communication in a research operation, *Public Relations Review*, 3(4), 61, 1977.
80. Grunig, J.E., Defining publics in public relations: The case of a suburban hospital, *Journalism Quarterly*, 55, 109, 1978.
81. Grunig, J.E., A new measure of public opinions on corporate social responsibility, *Academy of Management Journal*, 22, 738, 1979.
82. Grunig, J.E., The message-attitude-behavior relationship: Communication behaviors of organizations, *Communication Research*, 9, 163, 1982.
83. Grunig, J.E., Developing economic education programs for the press, *Public Relations Review*, 8(3), 43, 1982.
84. Grunig, J.E., *Communication Behaviors and Attitudes of Environmental Publics: Two Studies*, Journalism Monograph No. 81, 1983.
85. Grunig, J.E., Washington reporter publics of corporate public affairs programs, *Journalism Quarterly*, 60, 603, 1983.
86. Grunig, J.E., Sierra Club study shows who become activists, *Public Relations Review*, 15(3), 3, 1989.
87. Grunig, J.E., A Situational Theory of Publics: Conceptual History, Recent Challenges, and New Research, paper presented to the International Public Relations Research Symposium, Bled, Slovenia, 1994.
88. Grunig, J.E. and Ipes, D.A., The anatomy of a campaign against drunk driving, *Public Relations Review*, 9(2), 36, 1983.
89. Grunig, J.E. et al., Communication by agricultural publics: internal and external orientations, *Journalism Quarterly*, 65, 26, 1988.
90. Grunig, J.E. and Childers, L., Reconstruction of a Situational Theory of Communication: Internal and External Concepts as Identifiers of Publics for AIDS, paper presented to the Association for Education in Journalism and Mass Communication, Portland, OR, 1988.
91. Grunig, J.E. and Hunt, T., *Managing Public Relations*, Holt, Rinehart and Winston, Fort Worth, TX, 1984, chap. 5.
92. Grunig, J.E., A Situational Theory of Publics: Conceptual History, Recent Challenges, and New Research.

93. For more detail on this theory and its relationship to other segmentation theories, see Grunig, J.E, Publics, audiences, and market segments: Segmentation principles for campaigns, in *Information Campaigns: Balancing Social Values and Social Change*, Salmon, C.T., Ed., Sage, Newbury Park, CA, 1989, 199.

94. Atwood, L.E. and Cheng, P., Public Opinion and Media Use in Hong King: The '1997' Question, Occasional papers no. 15, Centre for Hong Kong Studies, Institute of Social Studies, Chinese University of Hong Kong, 1986.

95. Jeffers, D.W., Putting the "public" first in public relations: An exploratory study of municipal employee public service attitudes, job satisfaction, and communication variables, *Public Relations Research Annual*, 1, 197, 1989.

96. Jeffers, D.W., Using public relations theory to evaluate specialized magazines as communication channels, *Public Relations Research Annual*, 1, 115, 1989.

97. Cameron, G.T. and Yang, J., Refining Grunig's Situational Theory: The Addition of Valence of Support as a Key Variable, paper presented to the Association for Education in Journalism and Mass Communication, Minneapolis, MN, 1990.

98. VanLeuven, J.K. and Slater, M.D., How publics, public relations, and the media shape the public opinion process, *Public Relations Research Annual*, 3, 165, 1991.

99. Cameron, G.T., Memory for investor relations messages: An information-processing study of Grunig's situational theory, *Journal of Public Relations Research*, 4, 45, 1992.

100. Major, A.M., Environmental concern and situational communication theory: Implications for communicating with environmental publics, *Journal of Public Relations Research*, 5, 251, 1993.

101. Major, A.M., A test of situational communication theory: Public response to the 1990 Browning earthquake prediction, *International Journal of Mass Emergencies and Disasters*, 11, 337, 1993.

102. Vasquez, G.M., A homo narrans paradigm for public relations: Combining Bormann's symbolic convergence theory and Grunig's situational theory of publics, *Journal of Public Relations Research*, 5, 201, 1993.

103. Vasquez, G.M., Testing a communication theory-method-message-behavior complex for the investigation of publics, *Journal of Public Relations Research*, 6, 267, 1994.

104. Nager, N.R. and Allen, T.H., *Public Relations Management by Objectives*, Longman, White Plains, NY, 1984.

105. Brody, E.W., *The Business of Public Relations*, Praeger, New York, 1987.

106. Grunig, J.E., Research in the strategic management of public relations, *International Public Relations Review*, 11(3), 28–32, 1987.

107. Nager, N.R. and Truitt, R.H., *Strategic Public Relations Counseling*, Longman, White Plains, NY, 1987.

108. Brody, E.W., *Public Relations Programming and Production*, Praeger, New York, 1988.

109. Grunig, J.E. and Repper, F.C., Strategic management, publics, and issues, in *Excellence in Public Relations and Communication Management*, Grunig, J.E., Ed., Lawrence Erlbaum, Hillsdale, NJ, 1992, chap. 6.

110. Vercic, D., Cultural Biases in U.S. Public Relations: Constraints and Advantages, paper presented to the Research Center in Public Communication and the College of Journalism Graduate Student Association, University of Maryland, College Park, 1994.

111. Gruban, B., Vercic, D., and Zavrl, F., Odnosi Zjavnostmi v. Sloveniji (Public Relations in Slovenia), *Pristop*, special issue, 1994 (January).

112. Bowman, E.H., Strategy changes: Possible worlds and actual minds, in *Perspectives on Strategic Management*, Fredrickson, J.W., Ed., Harper Business, New York, 1990, 9.

113. Ibid, 10–12.

114. Rumelt, R.P., Schendel, D.E., and Teece, D.J., Fundamental issues in strategy, in *Fundamental Issues in Strategy: A Research Agenda*, Rumelt, R.P., Schendel, D., and Teece, D.J., Eds., Harvard Business School Press, Boston, 1994, chap. 1, 16–18.

115. Chandler, Jr., A.D., *Strategy and Structure: Chapters in the History of American Enterprise*, MIT Press, Cambridge, MA, 1962.

116. Ansoff, H.I., *Corporate Strategy: An Analytical Approach to Business Policy for Growth and Expansion*, McGraw-Hill, New York, 1965.

117. Learned, E.A. et al., *Business Policy: Text and Cases*, Richard D. Irwin, Homewood, IL, 1965.
118. Bowman, E.H., Strategy changes, 11.
119. Rumelt, R.P., Schendel, D.E., and Teece, D.J., Fundamental issues in strategy, 17.
120. Ibid, 413.
121. Higgins, H.M., *Organizational Policy and Strategic Management: Texts and Cases*, Dryden, Hinsdale, IL, 1979, 1.
122. Greene, C.N., Adam, E.A., Jr., and Ebert, R.J., *Management for Effective Performance*, Prentice-Hall, Englewood Cliffs, NJ, 1985, 536.
123. Steiner, G.A., Miner, J.B., and Gray, E.R., *Management Policy and Strategy*, 2nd ed., Macmillan, New York, 1982, 6.
124. Pearce, J.A., II and Robinson, R.B., Jr., *Strategic Management: Strategy Formulation and Implementation*, Richard D. Irwin, Homewood, IL, 1982, 65.
125. Rumelt, R.P., Schendel, D.E., and Teece, D.J., Fundamental issues in strategy, 22.
126. Pearce, J.A., II and Robinson, R.B., Jr., *Strategic Management*, 62.
127. Steiner, G.A., Miner, J.B., and Gray, E.R., *Management Policy and Strategy*, 18.
128. Holt, D.H., *Management: Principles and Practices*, Prentice-Hall, Englewood Cliffs, NJ, 1987, 149–151.
129. Ring, P.S., The environment and strategic management, in *Handbook of Strategic Management*, Rabin, J., Miller, G.J., and Hildreth, W.B., Eds., Marcel Dekker, New York, 1989, chap. 3, 59.
130. Pearce, J.A., II and Robinson, R.B., Jr., *Strategic Management*, 3.
131. Wheelen, T. and Hunger, J. *Strategic Management*, 2nd ed., Addison-Wesley, Reading, MA, 1987, 148.
132. Ring, P.S., The environment and strategic management, 56.
133. Ibid, 71.
134. Ibid, 78.
135. Post, J.E. et al., The public affairs function in American corporations: Development and relations with corporate planning, *Long Range Planning*, 12(2), 12, 1982.
136. Gollner, A.B., *Social Change and Corporate Strategy: The Expanding Role of Public Affairs*, Issue Action Press, Stamford, CT, 1983.
137. Marx, T.G., Strategic planning for public affairs, *Long Range Planning*, 23, 9, 1990.
138. Porter, M.E., *Competitive Strategy: Techniques for Analyzing Industries and Competitors*, Free Press, New York, 1980.
139. Porter, M.E., *Competitive Advantage: Creating and Sustaining Superior Performance*, Free Press, New York, 1985.
140. Porter, M.E., *The Competitive Advantage of Nations*, Free Press, New York, 1990.
141. In the introduction to a handbook on strategic management in public administration, Miller also pointed out that managers can use strategic devices "in two basic, complementary ways to eliminate competitive threats to organizational survival, and to exploit opportunities for increasing organization wealth and security ... the notion of strategy as a defensive planning technique, or the notion of strategy as seeking advantage." He added that the concept of strategy came from a war analogy "that considered effort should go toward creating order out of chaos, whether or not it would mean surviving and transcending one's enemies" (Miller, G.J., Introduction, in *Handbook of Strategic Management*, Rabin, J., Miller, G.J., and Hildreth, W.B., Eds., Marcel Dekker, New York, 1989, ix–x).
142. Porter, M.E., Toward a dynamic theory of strategy, in *Fundamental Issues in Strategy*, Rumelt, R.P., Schendel, D.E., and Teece, D.J., Eds., Harvard Business School Press, Boston, 1994, chap. 15, 451.
143. Porter, M.E., *The Competitive Advantage of Nations*, 647.
144. Vercic, D., Cultural Biases in U.S. Public Relations.
145. Pearce, J.A., II and Robinson, R.B., Jr., *Strategic Management*, 6–7.
146. Bowman, E.H., Strategy changes, 30.
147. Brody, E.W., *The Business of Public Relations*, 9.
148. Kotler, P. and Andreasen, A.R., *Strategic Marketing for Nonprofit Organizations*.
149. Nager, N.R. and Truitt, R.H., *Strategic Public Relations Counseling*.

150. Grunig, J.E. et al., *Excellence in Public Relations and Communication Management: Initial Data Report and Practical Guide*, IABC Research Foundation, San Francisco, 1991.

151. Grunig, L.A., Dozier, D.M., and Grunig, J.E., *IABC Excellence in Public Relations and Communication Management, Phase 2: Qualitative Study, Initial Analysis: Cases of Excellence*, IABC Research Foundation, San Francisco, 1994.

152. Lapinski, M.J., An Exploration of the Relationship Between Strategic Management, Public Relations and Organizational Effectiveness in the Federal Government, unpublished master's thesis, University of Maryland, College Park, 1992.

153. Ibid, 228.

154. Bingman, C.F. and Kee, J.E., Strategic management in federal government, in *Handbook of Strategic Management*, Rabin, J., Miller, G.J., and Hildreth, W.B., Eds., Marcel Dekker, New York, 1989, chap. 17, 399–400.

155. Dozier, D.M. and Grunig, L.A., The organization of the public relations function, in *Excellence in Public Relations and Communication Management*, Grunig, J.E., Ed., Lawrence Erlbaum, Hillsdale, NJ, 1992, chap. 14.

156. Dozier, D.M., The innovation of research in public relations practice: Review of a program of studies, *Public Relations Research Annual*, 2, 3, 1990.

157. Chase, W.H., *Issues Management: Origins of the Future*, Issue Action Publications, Stamford, CT, 1984.

158. Buchholz, R.A., Evans, W.D., and Wagley, R.A., *Management Response to Public Issues*, 2nd ed., Prentice-Hall, Englewood Cliffs, NJ, 1989.

159. Carroll, A.B., *Business and Society*.

160. Eadie, D.C., Identifying and managing strategic issues: From design to action, in *Handbook of Strategic Management*, Rabin, J., Miller, G.J., and Hildreth, W.B., Eds., Marcel Dekker, New York, 1989, chap. 7.

161. Heath, R.L. and Nelson, R.A., *Issues Management: Corporate Public Policymaking in an Information Society*, Sage, Newbury Park, CA, 1986.

162. Heath, R.L., Corporate issues management: Theoretical underpinnings and research foundations, *Public Relations Research Annual*, 2, 29, 1990.

163. Eadie, D.C., Identifying and managing strategic issues, 172.

164. Grunig, J.E., What is excellence in management?, in *Excellence in Public Relations and Communication Management*, Grunig, J.E., Ed., Lawrence Erlbaum, Hillsdale, NJ, 1992, chap. 9.

165. Grunig, L.A., Grunig, J.E., and Ehling, W.P., What is an effective organization?, in *Excellence in Public Relations and Communication Management*, Grunig, J.E., Ed., Lawrence Erlbaum, Hillsdale, NJ, 1992, chap. 3.

166. Peters, T.J. and Waterman, Jr., R.H., *In Search of Excellence: Lessons from America's Best-Run Companies*, Warner Books, New York, 1982.

167. Hobbs, J.B., *Corporate Staying Power: How America's Most Consistently Successful Corporations Maintain Exceptional Performance*, Lexington Books, Lexington, MA, 1987.

168. Paul, R.N. and Taylor, J.W., *The 101 Best-Performing Companies in America*, Probus, Chicago, 1986.

169. Carroll, D.T., A disappointing search for excellence, *Harvard Business Review*, 61(6), 79, 1983.

170. Peters, T.J. and Waterman, Jr., R.H., *In Search of Excellence*.

171. Kanter, R.M., *The Change Masters*, Simon and Schuster, New York, 1983.

172. Kanter, R.M., *When Giants Learn to Dance*, Simon and Schuster, New York, 1989.

173. Pinchot, G., III, *Intrapreneuring: Why You Don't have to Leave the Corporation to Become an Entrepreneur*, Harper & Row, New York, 1985.

174. Lydenberg, S.D., Marlin, A.T., and Strub, S.O., *Rating America's Corporate Conscience*, Addison-Wesley, Reading, MA, 1986.

175. Levering, R., Moskowitz, M., and Katz, M., *The 100 Best Companies to Work For in America*, Signet Books, New York, 1985.

176. Zeitz, B. and Dusky, L., The 53 best companies for women, *New Woman*, 1988 (June), 134.

177. Hickman, C.R. and Silva, M.A., *Creating Excellence*, Plume Books, New York, 1984.

178. Nash, B. and Zullo, A., *The Misfortune 500*, Pocket Books, New York, 1988.
179. Peters, T.J. and Waterman, Jr., R.H., *In Search of Excellence*.
180. Carroll, D.T., A disappointing search for excellence.
181. Who's excellent now?, *Business Week*, 76, November 5, 1984.
182. Hall, R.H., *Organizations: Structures, Processes, and Outcomes*, 5th ed., Prentice-Hall, Englewood Cliffs, NJ, 1991, 247.
183. Grunig, L.A., Grunig, J.E., and Ehling, W.P., What is an effective organization?
184. Price, J.L., *Organizational Effectiveness: An Inventory of Propositions*, Richard D. Irwin, Homewood, IL, 1968.
185. Goodman, P.S. and Pennings, J.M., Eds., *New Perspectives on Organizational Effectiveness*, Jossey-Bass, San Francisco, 1977.
186. Robbins, S.P., *Organization Theory: The Structure and Design of Organizations*, Prentice-Hall, Englewood Cliffs, NJ, 1990.
187. Hall, R.H., *Organizations: Structures, Processes, and Outcomes*.
188. Robbins, S.P., *Organization Theory*.
189. Hall, R.H., *Organizations: Structures, Processes, and Outcomes*.
190. Cunningham, R.B., Perspectives on public-sector strategic management, 127.
191. Hall, R.H., *Organizations: Structures, Processes, and Outcomes*, 247.
192. Robbins, S.P., *Organization Theory*, 67.
193. Grunig, L.A., Grunig, J.E., and Ehling, W.P., What is an effective organization?, 83.
194. Vercic, D., Cultural Biases in U.S. Public Relations.
195. Ehling, W.P., Estimating the value of public relations and communication to an organization, in *Excellence in Public Relations and Communication Management*, Grunig, J.E., Ed., Lawrence Erlbaum, Hillsdale, NJ, 1992, chap. 23.
196. Grunig, L.A., Dozier, D.M., and Grunig, J.E., *IABC Excellence in Public Relations and Communication Management, Phase 2: Qualitative Study, Initial Analysis*.
197. For a review on the relationship between employee communication and job satisfaction, see Grunig, J.E., Symmetrical systems of internal communication, in *Excellence in Public Relations and Communication Management*, Grunig, J.E., Ed., Lawrence Erlbaum, Hillsdale, NJ, 1992, chap. 20.
198. Grunig, J.E., *Organizations and Public Relations: Testing a Communication Theory*, Journalism Monograph No. 46, 1976.
199. Grunig, J.E. et al., *Excellence in Public Relations and Communication Management: Initial Data Report and Practical Guide*.
200. Grunig, L.A., Dozier, D.M., and Grunig, J.E., *IABC Excellence in Public Relations and Communication Management, Phase 2: Qualitative Study, Initial Analysis*.
201. Grunig, J.E., *Organizations and Public Relations: Testing a Communication Theory*.
202. Grunig, J.E. and Hunt, T., *Managing Public Relations*.
203. Grunig, J.E. and Grunig, L.A., Toward a theory of the public relations behavior of organizations: Review of a program of research, *Public Relations Research Annual*, 1, 27, 1989.
204. Grunig, J.E. and Grunig, L.A., Models of public relations and communication, in *Excellence in Public Relations and Communication Management*, Grunig, J.E., Ed., Lawrence Erlbaum, Hillsdale, NJ, 1992, chap. 11.
205. Grunig, J.E., Organizations, environments, and models of public relations, *Public Relations Research Education*, 1(1), 6, 1984.
206. Schneider [aka Grunig], L.A., The role of public relations in four organizational types, *Journalism Quarterly*, 62, 567, 1985.
207. Ossareh, J.C., Technology as a Public Relations Tool: Theoretical Perspectives, Practical Applications, and Actual Use, unpublished master's thesis, University of Maryland, College Park, 1987.
208. Wetherell, B.J., The Effect of Gender, Masculinity, and Femininity on the Practice of and Preference for the Models of Public Relations, unpublished master's thesis, University of Maryland, College Park, 1989.

209. McMillan, S.J., Public Relations in Trade and Professional Associations: Location, Model Structure, Environment and Values, unpublished master's thesis, University of Maryland, College Park, 1984.

210. McMillan, S.J., Public relations in trade and professional associations: Location, model, structure, environment, and values, in *Communication Yearbook 10*, McLaughlin, M.L., Ed., Sage, Newbury Park, CA, 1987, 831.

211. Fabiszak, D.L., Public Relations in Hospitals: Testing the Grunig Theory of Organizations, Environments and Models of Public Relations, unpublished master's thesis, University of Maryland, College Park, 1985.

212. Buffington, J., CEO Values and Corporate Culture: Developing a Descriptive Theory of Public Relations, unpublished master's thesis, University of Maryland, College Park, 1988.

213. Habbersett, C.A., An Exploratory Study of Media Relations: The Science Journalist and the Public Relations Practitioner, unpublished master's thesis, University of Maryland, College Park, 1983.

214. Pollack, E.J., An Organizational Analysis of Four Public Relations Models in the Federal Government, unpublished master's thesis, University of Maryland, College Park, 1986.

215. Turk, J.V., Public relations in state government: A typology of management styles, *Journalism Quarterly*, 62, 304, 1985.

216. Pollack, R.A., Testing the Grunig Organizational Theory in Scientific Organizations: Public Relations and the Values of the Dominant Coalition, unpublished master's thesis, University of Maryland, College Park, 1986.

217. Habbersett, C.A., An Exploratory Study of Media Relations.

218. Pollack, R.A., Testing the Grunig Organizational Theory in Scientific Organizations.

219. Ibid.

220. Turk, J.V., Public relations in state government.

221. Van Dyke, M.A., Military Public Affairs: Is it PR Management or Technology? A Study of U.S. Navy Public Affairs Officers, independent study paper, Syracuse University, Syracuse, NY, 1989.

222. Ibid, 52.

223. Wetherell, B.J., The Effect of Gender, Masculinity, and Femininity on the Practice of and Preference for the Models of Public Relations.

224. Ibid.

225. Bissland, J.H. and Rentner, T.L., Goal Conflict and its Implications for Public Relations Practitioners: A National Survey, paper presented to the Public Relations Society of America, Cincinnati, OH, 1988.

226. Wetherell, B.J., The Effect of Gender, Masculinity, and Femininity on the Practice of and Preference for the Models of Public Relations.

227. Gaudino, J.L., Fritch, J., and Haynes, B., "If you knew what I knew, you'd made the same decision": A common misperception underlying public relations campaigns?, *Public Relations Research Annual*, 1, 299, 1989.

228. Cupp, R.L., A Study of Public Relations Crisis Management in West Virginia Chemical Companies, unpublished master's thesis, University of Maryland, College Park, 1985.

229. Nelson, D.G., The Effect of Management Values on the Role and Practice of Public Relations within the Organization, unpublished master's thesis, University of Maryland, College Park, 1986.

230. Grunig, J.E., Symmetrical presuppositions as a framework for public relations theory.

231. Olasky, M.N., The aborted debate within public relations: An approach through Kuhn's paradigms, *Public Relations Research Annual*, 1, 87, 1989.

232. Gandy, O.H., Jr., *Beyond Agenda Setting: Information Subsidies and Public Policy*, Ablex, Norwood, NJ, 1982.

233. Dozier, D.M., Importance of the Concept of Symmetry and its Presence in Public Relations Practice, paper presented to the International Communication Association, San Francisco, 1989, 5.

234. Pearson, R., Beyond ethical relativism in public relations.

235. Pearson, R., Business ethics as communication ethics: Public relations practice and the idea of dialogue, in *Public Relations Theory*, Botan, C.H. and Hazleton, Jr., V.T., Eds., Lawrence Erlbaum, Hillsdale, NJ, 1989, 111.

236. Pearson, R., A Theory of Public Relations Ethics, unpublished doctoral dissertation, Ohio University, Athens, 1989.
237. Habermas, J., *The Theory of Communicative Action*, Vol. 1, Beacon Press, Boston, 1984.
238. Pearson, R., Business ethics as communication ethics.
239. Grunig, L.A., Activism and Organizational Response: Contemporary Cases of Collective Behavior, paper presented to the Association for Education in Journalism and Mass Communication, Norman, OK, 1986.
240. Lauzen, M., Public Relations and Conflict within the Franchise System, unpublished doctoral dissertation, University of Maryland, College Park, 1986.
241. Childers [aka Hon], L., Credibility of public relations at the NRC, *Public Relations Research Annual*, 1, 97, 1989.
242. Kelly, K.S., Shifting the Public Relations Paradigm: A Theory of Donor Relations Developed through a Critical Analysis of Fund Raising and its Effect on Organizational Autonomy, unpublished doctoral dissertation, University of Maryland, College Park, 1989.
243. Turk, J.V., *Information Subsidies and Media Content: A Study of Public Relations Influence on the News*, Journalism Monograph No. 100, 1986, 24–25.
244. Habbersett, C.A., An Exploratory Study of Media Relations.
245. Theus, K.T., Discrepancy: Organizational Response to Media Reporting, unpublished doctoral dissertation, University of Maryland, College Park, 1988.
246. Grunig, J.E. et al., *Excellence in Public Relations and Communication Management: Initial Data Report and Practical Guide*.
247. Grunig, L.A., Dozier, D.M., and Grunig, J.E., *IABC Excellence in Public Relations and Communication Management, Phase 2: Qualitative Study, Initial Analysis*.
248. Murphy, P., The limits of symmetry: A game theory approach to symmetric and asymmetric public relations, *Public Relations Research Annual*, 3, 115, 1991.
249. Broom, G.M. and Smith, G.D., Testing the practitioner's impact on clients, *Public Relations Review*, 5(3), 47, 1979.
250. Dozier, D.M., The organizational roles of communication and public relations practitioners, in *Excellence in Public Relations and Communication Management*, Grunig, J.E., Ed., Lawrence Erlbaum, Hillsdale, NJ, 1992, chap. 12.
251. Broom, G.M. and Dozier, D.M., *Using Research in Public Relations*, 14.
252. Piekos, J.M. and Einsiedel, E.F., Roles and program evaluation techniques among Canadian public relations practitioners, *Public Relations Research Annual*, 2, 95, 1990.
253. Creedon, P.J., Public relations and 'women's work': Toward a feminist analysis of public relations roles, *Public Relations Research Annual*, 3, 67, 1991.
254. Wetherell, B.J., The Effect of Gender, Masculinity, and Femininity on the Practice of and Preference for the Models of Public Relations.
255. Hon, L.C., Grunig, L.A., and Dozier, D.M., Women in public relations: Problems and opportunities, in *Excellence in Public Relations and Communication Management*, Grunig, J.E., Ed., Lawrence Erlbaum, Hillsdale, NJ, 1992, chap. 15.
256. Robbins, S.P., *Organization Theory*.
257. Grunig, J.E., *Organizations and Public Relations: Testing a Communication Theory*.
258. Grunig, J.E., A Structural Reconceptualization of the Organizational Communication Audit, with Application to a State Department of Education, paper presented to the International Communication Association, Honolulu, HI, 1985.
259. Grunig, J.E. and Theus, K.T., Internal Communication Systems and Employee Satisfaction, paper presented to the Association for Education in Journalism and Mass Communication, Norman, OK, 1986.
260. Schneider [aka Grunig], L.A., The role of public relations in four organizational types.
261. Schneider [aka Grunig], L.A., Organizational Structure, Environmental Niches, and Public Relations: The Hage-Hull Typology of Organizations as Predictor of Communication Behavior, unpublished doctoral dissertation, University of Maryland, College Park, 1985.

262. Grunig, J.E., Organizations, environments, and models of public relations.
263. Robbins, S.P., *Organization Theory*.
264. Grunig, J.E., IABC study shows CEOs value PR, *Communication World*, 7(8), 5, 1990.
265. Grunig, L.A., Preliminary Findings on Power and Gender in the Excellence Project, paper presented to the International Association of Business Communicators, Vancouver, 1990.
266. Dozier, D.M., A Tale of Two Corporations, paper presented to the International Association of Business Communicators, Vancouver, 1990.
267. Grunig, J.E. et al., *Excellence in Public Relations and Communication Management: Initial Data Report and Practical Guide*.
268. Grunig, L.A., Dozier, D.M., and Grunig, J.E., *IABC Excellence in Public Relations and Communication Management, Phase 2: Qualitative Study, Initial Analysis*.
269. Sriramesh, K., Grunig, J.E., and Buffington, J., Corporate culture and public relations, in *Excellence in Public Relations and Communication Management*, Grunig, J.E., Ed., Lawrence Erlbaum, Hillsdale, NJ, 1992, chap. 21.
270. Grunig, J.E. et al., Models of Public Relations in an International Setting, paper presented to the Association for the Advancement of Policy, Research, and Development in the Third World, Nassau, Bahamas, 1991.
271. Grunig, L.A., Dozier, D.M., and Grunig, J.E., *IABC Excellence in Public Relations and Communication Management, Phase 2: Qualitative Study, Initial Analysis*.
272. Sriramesh, K. and White, J., Societal culture and public relations, in *Excellence in Public Relations and Communication Management*, Grunig, J.E., Ed., Lawrence Erlbaum, Hillsdale, NJ, 1992, chap. 22.
273. Vercic, D., Grunig, L.A., and Grunig, J.E., Global and Specific Principles of Public Relations: Evidence from Slovenia, paper presented to the Association for the Advancement of Policy, Research, and Development in the Third World, Cairo, Egypt, 1993.
274. Grunig, J.E. et al., *Excellence in Public Relations and Communication Management: Initial Data Report and Practical Guide*.
275. Hofstede, G., *Culture's Consequences: International Differences in Work-Related Values*, Sage, Beverly Hills, CA, 1980.
276. Gruban, B., Vercic, D., and Zavrl, F., Odnosi Zjavnostmi v. Sloveniji (Public Relations in Slovenia).
277. Vercic, D., Grunig, L.A., and Grunig, J.E., Global and Specific Principles of Public Relations.
278. For descriptions of current public relations, see books such as those by Speakes, Wood, and Dilenschneider (Speakes, L., *Speaking Out: Inside the Reagan White House*, Charles Scribner's Sons, New York, 1988; Wood, R.J. and Gunther, M., *Confessions of a PR Man*, North American Library, New York, 1988; Dilenschneider, R.L., *Power and Influence: Mastering the Art of Persuasion*, Prentice-Hall, New York, 1990). These books reveal the continuing dominance of the press agentry model in public relations and the lack of an integrating theory to explain what public relations is about. Essentially, the books show that in practice, public relations often is little more than what public relations people do.
279. Olasky, M.N., *Corporate Public Relations and American Private Enterprise*; Olasky, M.N., The aborted debate within public relations.
280. Gandy, O.H., Jr., *Beyond Agenda Setting*.
281. Rakow, L.F., Information and power: Toward a critical theory of information campaigns, in *Information Campaigns: Balancing Social Values and Social Change*, Salmon, C.T., Ed., Sage, Newbury Park, CA, 1989, 164.
282. Mallinson, B., Bridging the Gap between Theory and Practice in Post-1992 Europe: The Changing Face of Public Relations, paper presented to the International Communication Association, Dublin, Ireland, 1990.
283. Smilowitz, M. and Pearson, R., Traditional, enlightened, and interpretive perspectives on corporate annual giving, in *Public Relations Theory*, Botan, C.H. and Hazleton, Jr., V.T., Eds., Lawrence Erlbaum, Hillsdale, NJ, 1989, 83.

284. Cheney, G. and Dionisopoulos, G.N., Public relations? No, relations with publics: A rhetorical-organizational approach to contemporary corporate communications, in *Public Relations Theory*, Botan, C.H. and Hazleton, Jr., V.T., Eds., Lawrence Erlbaum, Hillsdale, NJ, 1989, 135.

285. Cheney, G., The corporate person (re)presents itself, in *Rhetorical and Critical Approaches to Public Relations*, Toth, E.L. and Heath, R.L., Eds., Lawrence Erlbaum, Hillsdale, NJ, 1992, chap. 8.

286. Pearson, R., Beyond ethical relativism in public relations: Coorientation, rules, and the idea of communication symmetry.

287. Pearson, R., Business ethics as communication ethics.

288. Habermas, J., *The Theory of Communicative Action*.

289. Gusfield, J.R., *Kenneth Burke on Symbols and Society*, University of Chicago Press, Chicago, 1989.

290. Toth, E.L., The case for pluralistic studies of public relations: Rhetorical, critical, and systems perspectives, in *Rhetorical and Critical Approaches to Public Relations*, Toth, E.L. and Heath, R.L., Eds., Lawrence Erlbaum, Hillsdale, NJ, 1992, chap. 1.

291. Heath, R.L., The wrangle in the marketplace: A rhetorical perspective of public relations, in *Rhetorical and Critical Approaches to Public Relations*, Toth, E.L. and Heath, R.L., Eds., Lawrence Erlbaum, Hillsdale, NJ, 1992, chap. 2.

292. Heath, R.L., Critical perspectives on public relations, in *Rhetorical and Critical Approaches to Public Relations*, Toth, E.L. and Heath, R.L., Eds., Lawrence Erlbaum, Hillsdale, NJ, 1992, chap. 3.

293. Toth, E.L. and Heath, R.L., Eds., *Rhetorical and Critical Approaches to Public Relations*, Lawrence Erlbaum, Hillsdale, NJ, 1992.

294. Pearson, R., A Theory of Public Relations Ethics.

295. Bivins, T.H., Applying ethical theory to public relations, *Journal Business Ethics*, 6, 195, 1987.

296. Bivins, T.H., Ethical implications of the relationship of purpose to role and function in public relations, *Journal of Business Ethics*, 8, 65, 1989.

297. Bivins, T.H., A systems model for ethical decision making in public relations, *Public Relations Review*, 18, 365, 1992.

298. Bivins, T.H., Public relations, professionalism, and the public interest, *Journal of Business Ethics*, 12, 117, 1993.

299. McElreath, M.P., *Managing Systematic and Ethical Public Relations*, Brown and Benchmark, Madison, WI, 1993.

300. Pratt, C.A., Gender Implications in Public Relations Ethics: Kohlberg, Gilligan, and the PRSA Code of Professional Standards, paper presented to the Association for Education in Journalism and Mass Communication, Minneapolis, MN, 1990.

301. Pratt, C.B., Im, S.H., and Montague, S.N., Investigating the application of deontology among U.S. public relations practitioners, *Journal of Public Relations Research*, 6, 266, 1994.

302. Ryan, M. and Martinson, D.L., Public relations practitioners, public interest and management, *Journalism Quarterly*, 62, 111, 1985.

303. Wright, D.K., Individual ethics determine public relations practices, *Public Relations Journal*, 41(4), 38, 1985.

304. Wright, D.K., Enforcement dilemma: Voluntary nature of public relations codes, *Public Relations Review*, 19, 13, 1993.

305. Grunig, L.A., Toward the philosophy of public relations, in *Rhetorical and Critical Approaches to Public Relations*, Toth, E.L. and Heath, R.L., Eds., Lawrence Erlbaum, Hillsdale, NJ, 1992, chap. 4.

306. Grunig, L.A., A research agenda for women in public relations, *Public Relations Review*, 14(3), 48, 1988.

307. Grunig, L.A., Applications of Feminist Scholarship to Public Relations: Displacing the Male Models, paper presented to the National Women's Studies Association, Towson, MD, 1989.

308. Grunig, L.A., Toward a Feminist Transformation of Public Relations Education and Practice, paper presented to the Association for Education in Journalism and Mass Communication, Washington, DC, 1989.

309. Toth, E.L., Making peace with gender issues in public relations, *Public Relations Review*, 14(3), 36, 1988.

310. Creedon, P.J., Public relations and 'women's work.'

311. Rakow, L.F., From the feminization of public relations to the promise of feminism, in *Beyond the Velvet Ghetto*, Toth, E.L. and Cline, C.G., Eds., International Association of Business Communicators, San Francisco, 1989, 287.

312. Cline, C.G., Public relations: The $1 million dollar penalty for being a woman, in *Women in Mass Communication: Challenging Gender Values*, Creedon, P.J., Ed., Sage, Newbury Park, CA, 1985, 263.

313. Grunig, J.E., Ed., *Excellence in Public Relations and Communication Management*, Lawrence Erlbaum, Hillsdale, NJ, 1992.

314. Avenarius, H. and Armbrecht, W., Eds., *Ist Public Relations Eine Wissenschaft?* (*Is Public Relations a Science?*), Westdeutscher Verlag, Opladen, Germany, 1992.

315. Piel, G. and Segerberg, Jr., O., Eds., *The World of René Dubos: A Collection of his Writings*, Henry Holt, New York, 1990.

316. Farinelli, J.L., Needed: A new U.S. perspective on global public relations, *Public Relations Journal*, 46(11), 19, 1990.

317. Epley, J.S., Public relations in the global village: An American perspective, *Public Relations Review*, 18, 109, 1992.

318. Farinelli, J.L., Needed: A new U.S. perspective on global public relations, 37.

319. Ibid, 19.

320. Epley, J.S., Public relations in the global village.

321. Farinelli, J.L., Needed: A new U.S. perspective on global public relations, 19, 42.

322. Ibid, 42.

323. Ovaitt, F., Jr., PR without boundaries: Is globalization an option?, *Public Relations Quarterly*, 33(1), 5, 1988.

324. Adler, N.J. and Doktor, R.H., From the Atlantic to the Pacific century: Cross-cultural management reviewed, *Journal of Management*, 12, 295, 1986.

325. Anderson, G., A global look at public relations, in *Experts in Action: Inside Public Relations*, 2nd ed., Cantor, B., Ed., Longman, White Plains, NY, 1989, 413.

326. Ibid.

327. Botan, C., International public relations: Critique and reformulation, *Public Relations Review*, 18, 149, 1992.

328. Ovaitt, F., Jr., PR without boundaries.

329. Brinkerhoff, D.W. and Ingle, M.D., Integrating blueprint and process: A structured flexibility approach to development management, *Public Administration and Development*, 9, 493, 1989.

330. Stohl, C., European managers' interpretations of participation: A semantic network analysis, *Human Communication Research*, 20, 97, 1993.

331. Grunig, J. E. et al., Models of Public Relations in an International Setting.

332. Anderson, G., A global look at public relations.

333. Sharpe, M.L., The impact of social and cultural conditioning on global public relations, *Public Relations Review*, 18, 104, 1992.

334. Botan, C., International public relations.

335. Vercic, D., Grunig, L.A., and Grunig, J.E., Global and Specific Principles of Public Relations.

336. Wakefield, R.I., Excellence in International Public Relations: An Exploratory Delphi Study, unpublished dissertation prospectus, University of Maryland, College Park, 1994.

337. Vercic, D., Grunig, L.A., and Grunig, J.E., Global and Specific Principles of Public Relations.

338. Hofstede, G., *Culture's Consequences*.

339. Vercic, D., Grunig, L.A., and Grunig, J.E., Global and Specific Principles of Public Relations.

340. Bernays, E.L., *Crystallizing Public Opinion*, Boni and Liveright, New York, 1923.

341. Cutlip, S.M. and Center, A.H., *Effective Public Relations*, [1st ed.], Prentice-Hall, Englewood Cliffs, NJ, 1952.

342. Robinson, E.J., *Communication and Public Relations*, Charles E. Merrill, Columbus, OH, 1966.

343. Grunig, J.E. and Hunt, T., *Managing Public Relations*, chap. 4.

Chapter 3

What Do Federal Public Information Officers Do?

U.S. Office of Personnel Management

Contents

Defining the Series of Public Affairs Positions

Employment under the Public Affairs Series includes positions responsible for administering, supervising, or performing work involved in establishing and maintaining mutual communication between federal agencies and the general public and various other pertinent publics including internal or external, foreign or domestic audiences. Positions in this series advise agency management on policy formulation and the potential public reaction to proposed policy, and identify and carry out the public communication requirements inherent in disseminating policy decisions. The work involves identifying communication needs and developing informational materials that inform appropriate publics of the agency's policies, programs, services and activities, and planning, executing, and evaluating the effectiveness of information and communication programs in furthering agency goals. Work in the series requires skills in written and oral communication, analysis, and interpersonal relations.

Scope of Public Affairs

Positions in the Public Affairs Series are primarily concerned with advising management on the formulation and articulation of agency policy and designing, executing, and evaluating the information programs that communicate agency policies, programs, and actions to various pertinent publics.

Public affairs positions work in and contribute to a variety of functional programs. The term *functional program* refers to the basic objectives of a federal agency and its operations and activities in achieving them. A functional program may include the entire mission of an agency or any one of many programs administered by the department or agency. Positions in this series require a practical understanding and knowledge of functional programs to facilitate communication between an agency and its publics on program-related problems, activities, or issues. Much of this program knowledge is obtained from specialists in the functional program areas or through review of agency-developed material, interviewing program specialists, or reading professional and trade publications. This series covers positions involving one or more of the following functions:

1. Design, plan, and direct or advise on the public affairs program in an agency or organization within an agency
2. Develop and disseminate informational materials to the general public or specialized target groups within a domestic or foreign setting
3. Provide information of particular value and interest to agency employees
4. Establish and maintain effective working relationships with all media, both foreign and domestic, and develop and disseminate informational materials to pertinent publics through the media

Many positions in the series involve duties in all of these areas, especially in those organizations where the public affairs staff is small and everyone functions as a generalist. Some positions combine several functions, while others are assigned duties restricted to only one specific area. In addition to the kinds of duties encompassed by the four categories above, some agencies assign other types of duties to public affairs positions. Administration of Freedom of Information Act and Privacy Act concerns, while not requiring communication or information skills, are found in some public affairs positions. Other agencies have placed this function elsewhere.

Occupational Information

One of the important functions of the federal government is to communicate with the public concerning the programs administered and activities engaged in by various federal agencies. This communication serves the dual purpose of: (1) informing the broad spectrum of individuals and groups affected by agency programs of the benefits, services, or requirements of such programs; and (2) assessing the degree of understanding or interest the public has in these programs and activities. In addition to the general public, federal agencies communicate with many specialized segments of the population, e.g., farmers, taxpayers, military personnel, educators, state and local government officials, manufacturers, and so on. Federal agencies communicate with the general public and these other pertinent publics in a variety of ways, for many different purposes, and in countless organizational settings across the country, and around the world.

While many positions within federal agencies are responsible for some aspects of communicating with specialized groups, to facilitate dealings with these publics, federal agencies establish positions primarily concerned with advising, planning, managing, implementing, and evaluating the meaningful interchange of communication between federal agencies and the various publics served or affected by these agencies. Incumbents of these positions use a variety of communication media, methods, and techniques in making known the programs, policies, services, and responsibilities of the agencies and obtaining feedback to agency programs from various groups and individuals. This feedback and advice to top management serve in guiding agency management in developing programs that are more responsive and appropriate in meeting the needs of the pertinent publics they serve while still conforming to the legislative and executive mandates establishing the programs.

Structure of Public Affairs Positions

The public affairs function exists throughout the federal government at all major organizational levels including headquarters, agency, region, command, district, and local installation in both domestic and foreign locations and is staffed by public affairs specialists who support a variety of agency program functions. While public affairs specialists deal with varied fields, they are not necessarily experts in them. However, through on-the-job experience they develop knowledge of the concepts and issues of the subject of agency programs. Although public affairs specialists do acquire a substantial degree of program knowledge, it is their knowledge of the full framework of communication that enables them to facilitate the effective communication between management and various publics.

The diversity of program areas in which public affairs specialists are found and the variety of organizational alignments and structures of the public affairs function among the agencies produces a wide variability among positions in this series. When viewed from the broader perspective of the primary purpose of the job, positions in this series may include one or more of the following four categories:

1. Positions that conduct the public affairs program of an agency or an organization within an agency. Such positions participate with management in policy formulation, advise on the potential public reaction to proposed policies, and plan, organize, and evaluate communication strategies, programs, and materials. Representative duties may include:
   - Formulate and recommend policies, programs, and procedures governing information functions related to the work of the agency
   - Plan, initiate, and implement comprehensive public affairs campaigns to enhance the understanding of the agency's programs among the general public and specialized groups and organizations
   - Evaluate the effectiveness and efficiency of the internal information program, media relations, and community relations programs in achieving greater understanding of the facility's mission and programs
   - Advise agency's top management officials on the possible public and media reactions to proposed policy statements or agency actions
   - Identify to the regional director and other program officials the information needs of the general public and various specialized groups within the region
2. Positions that inform, familiarize, or obtain feedback from an agency's various publics concerning programs, policies, services, and regulations. Such positions develop and disseminate informational material to the general public or specialized target groups and use the full range of communication methods and techniques in analyzing input from the publics for

feedback to the agency's decision makers. These functions are referred to as public information or education. Representative duties may include:

- Develop and disseminate a wide range of information and data concerning the nature and objectives of agency programs, employing all types of media, including radio, television, newspapers, magazines, professional and scientific journals, still and motion pictures, posters, exhibits, and advertisements
- Arrange and conduct workshops, seminars, and other meetings with various organizations in stimulating participation in agency activities, identifying their concerns, and motivating these groups to conduct similar programs for their membership
- Advise and assist personnel at subordinate echelons on carrying out community relations activities, furnishing policy guidance, developing directives for policy procedures, and evaluating program effectiveness
- Collect and summarize input from specialized groups or individuals through surveys, public opinion studies, or group meetings, and prepare reports to management on the public's perception of agency programs
- Arrange and conduct tours of the facility, briefing local, national, and international visitors and officials on the function and operation of the organization

3. Positions that provide informational material to agency employees concerning programs, staff achievements, awards, and news of personal benefit to employees such as pay, benefits, retirement, charity appeals, blood drives, etc. Such positions are found in activities known as internal information, internal relations, employee communication or information, command information, etc. Representative duties include:

- Prepare newsletters or other communications for distribution to field offices to keep them acquainted with programs at agency headquarters
- Conduct a facility's internal information program designed for the benefit of all employees including foreign nationals employed by the organization
- Maintain liaison with subordinate organizations' public affairs personnel to produce ideas or communication materials for use in a headquarters magazine, or develop recommendations on ways the magazine can better serve the total mission
- Plan, design, and conduct information programs for awards and special recognition designed to improve employee morale
- Plan and conduct attitude and opinion surveys among employees in developing recommendations to improve communication

4. Positions that establish and maintain relationships with representatives of the news media in providing information about agency programs, policies, and services. Such operations are referred to as media relations, press relations, etc. Representative duties may include:

- Organize and coordinate news media interviews with staff, and oversee arrangements with media representatives involving organization activities; provide supporting materials as required
- Establish and maintain relations with the news media in enlisting their cooperation in providing the public with information about benefit programs
- Gather information, and produce informational materials concerning departmental policies, programs, and activities for dissemination to the news media, and obtain feedback on the effectiveness of these materials
- Survey mass and specialized media coverage of agency activities and recommend methods and techniques for disseminating information that will increase public awareness of programs and benefits to the public

– Develop and maintain cooperative working relationships with representatives of foreign news media in facilitating communication between the facility and its foreign national neighbors

Communication Methods

Public affairs specialists use a variety of communication methods in carrying out their mission to inform agency publics about the programs, policies, and services that are of interest to or affect various groups or individuals. For examples of communication methods and vehicles, see Table 3.1.

Public Affairs Specialist is the basic title authorized for all positions in this series. Positions which meet or exceed the criteria in the "General Schedule Supervisory Guide" for evaluation as a supervisor are titled *Supervisory Public Affairs Specialist.*

Note: *Originally published in Classification Programs Division, Workforce Compensation and Performance Service, Position Classification Standard for Public Affairs Series, GS-1035, U.S. Office of Personnel Management, Washington, DC, 2002.*

Table 3.1 Methods of Communication and Vehicles

Method	Vehicle
Written	News release, fact sheet, speeches, written response to media or public inquiry, feature articles, pamphlets, newsletters, magazines
Oral	Television, radio, audio tapes
Visual	Photographs, films, slides, video tapes
Personal	Interviews, briefings, seminars, hearings, tours, awards ceremonies, speeches, workshops, news conferences, discussions

Chapter 4

The Campaign of the Committee on Public Information: Its Contributions to the History and Evolution of Public Relations

Bruce Pinkleton

Contents

Abstract: The campaign of the Committee on Public Information (CPI) was an ambitious attempt by the U.S. government to influence public opinion. More importantly, the CPI contributed to the evolution of public relations through its use of basic principles of effective communication including unity of voice, message simplicity, and source credibility. The committee's campaign encouraged citizens to be stakeholders in their government and heightened their sense of community. The work of the CPI followed a period of unrest between industrialists and journalists and was an important link between the recognition of the need for public relations services and an understanding of the means through which public opinion is crystallized.

Introduction

An examination of the historical evolution of public relations provides insights into its role in society and its changing functions. One aspect of public relations history worthy of special attention concerns the work of the Committee on Public Information (CPI) during World War I. Although it is true that there is nothing new in the use of publicity, [1] the work of the CPI was an ambitious attempt by the federal government to mold public opinion on an unprecedented scale. More importantly, the committee contributed to the evolution of public relations through its use of basic principles of effective communication including unity of voice, source credibility, and message simplicity. The CPI encouraged targeted publics to participate in the war effort through a variety of government programs, making them stakeholders in their government and increasing their sense of community.

The success of the CPI is mentioned in many textbooks and articles addressing public relations history. These texts contain little information about the actual work of the CPI, however, and rarely mention its contributions to the evolution of public relations. The purpose of this article is to examine the principal domestic programs used by the Creel Committee between 1917 and 1919 to crystallize public opinion in support of the war effort. The creation and purpose of the CPI is addressed initially. This is followed by a discussion of the most important divisions and bureaus of the Domestic Section of the committee. The chapter concludes with a discussion of the role of the CPI in the history and evolution of public relations.

CPI Creation and Purpose

President Woodrow Wilson created the Committee on Public Information by Executive Order 2594 on April 14, 1917. [2] George Creel, an ardent Wilson supporter and editor of the *Rocky Mountain News*, was appointed civilian chairman. Other members of the committee included Secretary of War Newton D. Baker, Secretary of the Navy Josephus Daniels, and Secretary of State Robert Lansing.

The CPI was composed of two large sections, the Foreign Section and the Domestic Section. The Foreign Section conducted propaganda activities abroad, eventually establishing offices in more than 30 countries. [3,4] The primary job of the Domestic Section was to combine censorship of the press with the dissemination of official government news and facts. [5] The committee actively directed the propaganda efforts of the government in an attempt to influence public opinion. As Creel noted:

Realizing public opinion as a vital part of the national defense ... our task was to devise machinery with which to make the fight for loyalty and unity at home, and for the friendship and understanding of the neutral nations of the world. [6]

The Creel Committee possessed no official censorship authority. Creel advocated voluntary censorship, opposing the severe restrictions favored by U.S. military leaders and already in use in Britain and France. [7] In May 1917, the CPI issued a "Preliminary Statement to the Press of the United States" dividing news into three categories: dangerous, questionable, and routine. [8] The dangerous category contained news items relating to military operations in progress, threats against the life of the president, the movement of official missions, and related sensitive matters. This information was never to be printed. The questionable category included information concerning training-camp routines, technical innovations, and war-related rumors. These stories were to be sent to the CPI for approval before publication. The bulk of news material fell into the routine category and was of no concern to the CPI. [9–11]

Despite the voluntary nature of this arrangement, Creel was a member of the Censorship Board and possessed a high degree of influence. From his position, Creel could suggest that the Department of Justice prosecute an editor, prohibit a newspaper from using the mail, or cut off a newspaper's supply of newsprint. [12,13] Evidence indicates that Creel sought to suppress information that portrayed the United States unfavorably or that contained ideas he felt were too dangerous for the U.S. public. [14]

The usefulness of the CPI ended with the signing of the armistice. Congress legislated the committee out of existence on June 30, 1919, as the liquidation of the offices of the CPI was taking place. [15]

Divisions and Bureaus of the Domestic Section

The internal structure of the Domestic Section of the CPI was complex. [16,17] Bureaus and divisions were created quickly and often divided, merged, or dropped. [18] The divisions and bureaus discussed in this article are based on *The Creel Report: Complete Report of the Committee on Public Information, 1917: 1918: 1919*. [19] These were the primary divisions of the CPI and, because of this, were most actively involved in shaping public opinion.

Division of News

The Division of News was an integral part of the CPI and was created automatically with the committee's formation. [20–22] This division was the sole outlet for official war information from the armed services, the White House, the Department of Labor, the Department of Justice, the National War Labor Board, the War Industries Board, the Council of National Defense, the Alien Property Custodian, and the War Trade Board. [23,24] The division was open 24 hours a day, 7 days a week, acting as a clearinghouse for government news and a service bureau to the press. [25]

The efforts of the Division of News made it possible for the Creel Committee to adopt a policy whereby "the channels of communication were literally choked with official, approved news and opinion." [26] During its 3-year existence, the division issued a total of 6,000 press releases estimated by Creel to have been published to an extent of 20,000 newspaper columns per week. [27]

The division conducted interviews with government officials for release to the press, prepared daily casualty lists, and supplied information and statistics to reporters. To reach rural audiences with timely war information, the division prepared digests of official war news that went to country weeklies, and later country dailies, in galley form. A total of 12,000 newspapers received this service. [28]

The Division of News also published the *Official Bulletin* (later the *Official U.S. Bulletin*) to reach important internal and external audiences with government news and propaganda. The *Bulletin* began daily publication in May 1917 and reached a daily average peak circulation of 118,008 in August 1918. [29] Distribution of the *Bulletin* was free to public officials, newspapers, and public and semipublic agencies. The *Bulletin* was also posted in military camps and post offices, and individual subscriptions were available for $5 per year.

The *Bulletin* printed all types of government news, including the texts of speeches by the president, announcements of important contracts awarded, texts of important laws, proceedings of the Supreme Court, and other official government news. [30] The *Bulletin* ceased publication on April 1, 1919. The preceding month, its daily average circulation had fallen to an all-time low of 33,454. [31]

Advertising Division

The Advertising Division was created by executive order on April 14, 1917. [32] The work of the division consisted primarily of directing patriotic advertising and obtaining contributions of free advertising space. William H. Johns, president of the American Association of Advertising Agencies, served as director of this division and Carl Byoir served as its Washington liaison officer.

The Advertising Division directed some of the most memorable publicity campaigns of the war, contributing to surging national enthusiasm and government support. By encouraging sales of bonds and war savings stamps, for example, the work of the division strengthened national commitment by giving citizens a vested interest in their government. In the same way, participation in food and energy conservation encouraged a greater sense of community among citizens. [33]

The Advertising Division directed campaigns to a variety of audiences including labor, employers, farmers, college students, children, and women. Organizations served by this division included the war savings stamps and Liberty Loan drives of the Treasury Department, the Food Administration, the War Department, the Department of Agriculture, the Council of National Defense, the Department of Labor, the Fuel Administration, and the Red Cross. [34]

The media used by the Advertising Division included space donated by general circulation magazines and trade publications, including farm publications and house organs. Additional space was donated by outdoor media and newspapers, including college newspapers. The division also used less traditional media such as window displays and theater curtains. [35]

Figures from the Advertising Division show that 9,367 insertions were made in various media with a circulation totaling 548,833,148. [36] The value of advertising placements was calculated by Creel to be worth $1,594,814.71, [37] not including 60,000 window displays or outdoor advertising for which figures were not available. Creel estimated the total value of the contributions generated by the Advertising Division at $5 million. [38]

Division of Pictorial Publicity

The Division of Pictorial Publicity, created on April 17, 1917, was closely allied with the Advertising Division. [39] The division was directed by Charles Dana Gibson, one of the United States' most famous illustrators and a regular contributor to *Life* magazine. Gibson believed that Americans were too isolated from the war to understand the conflict in Europe. As a result, he created posters and drawings designed to appeal to the heart and imagination of Americans. [40]

The division often targeted its work to specific audiences for specific purposes, encouraging boys to join the war effort by purchasing war savings stamps, for example. The division's art was used in the campaigns of several agencies, including the War Department, the war savings stamps and Liberty Loan drives of the Treasury Department, the Red Cross, the Young Men's Christian Association, and the Department of Agriculture.

The Division of Pictorial Publicity created a total of 700 poster designs; 122 car, bus, and window cards; 310 drawings for newspapers and advertisements; 287 cartoons; and 19 seals, buttons, and banners. [41]

Bureau of Cartoons

The Bureau of Cartoons was officially established by George J. Hecht on May 28, 1918. [42] The purpose of the bureau was to "mobilize and direct the scattered cartoon power of the country for constructive war work." [43] The work of the Bureau of Cartoons was closely allied with the Division of Pictorial Publicity. The primary activity of the Bureau was the weekly publication of the *Bulletin for Cartoonists*. The *Bulletin*, which had a mailing list of 750 cartoonists, contained ideas and captions for drawings to support ideas that a branch of the government wished emphasized. Thirty-seven different agencies forwarded ideas to cartoonists through the *Bulletin*. [44]

Thrift, conservation, and the Liberty Loan drives comprised nearly one third of the material in each publication. [45] The *Bulletin* also encouraged cartoonists to stimulate recruiting, popularize the draft, and warn against German propaganda. [46] The bureau released 25 bulletins between June 1918 and the end of the war. [47]

Division of Syndicate Features

The Division of Syndicate Features was established in August 1917 and directed by L. Ames Brown. [48] The work of this division was to make government information easier to understand and more interesting for the average citizen to read. The division recruited approximately 100 novelists, short story writers, and essayists to produce feature materials. [49] These materials were distributed through the CPI to the nation's newspapers. Creel estimated that the features reached 12 million people per month. [50] The work of the Features Syndicate was curtailed in June 1918 due to budget reductions.

The Division of the Four Minute Men

The Four Minute Men have likely received more attention than any other aspect of the CPI. [51] As noted in Creel's *Report*, "the Four Minute Men will live in history as one of the most unique and effective agencies developed during the war for the stimulation of public opinion and the promotion of unity." [52]

The Division of the Four Minute Men was created shortly after the establishment of the CPI as a specialized publicity service. [53,54] The name *Four Minute Men* originated from the Minute Men of the Revolutionary War and the time limit imposed on speeches. [55] The original work of the Four Minute Men consisted of 4-minute talks by local volunteers given during the intermission at movie theaters, in accordance with a standard national plan.

Each national plan of the Four Minute Men was established in the *Four Minute Men Bulletin*, which contained information on a predetermined topic. It was up to the individual speaker to develop a speech on the basis of the policy, points of emphasis, lines of argument, and general information contained in each bulletin. [56] The speeches of the Four Minute Men then were presented at theaters between specified dates. A total of 46 *Bulletins* concerning 36 topics were issued. [57]

As the war progressed, the efforts of the Four Minute Men were expanded, often to target specific audiences. Some states organized women's divisions to speak at matinee theater performances and to women's groups and clubs. A Junior Four Minute Men group was established to speak in schools and a special *School Bulletin* was developed. Other special developments included a college Four Minute Men division, Four Minute Men singing, and the publication of an *Army Bulletin* for presentations to soldiers. [58]

The work of the Four Minute Men comprised one of the most successful programs of the CPI. By the end of the war, 75,000 Four Minute Men in 7,629 branches covered every state in the union, as well as the Panama Canal Zone, the District of Columbia, Guam, Hawaii, Alaska, the Philippine Islands, Puerto Rico, and Samoa. [59,60] Estimates from Creel, based on incomplete accounting, put the total number of speeches given at 755,190 and the total audience for those speeches at 314,454,514, although other estimates put these numbers higher. [61]

Speaking Division

The Speaking Division of the CPI was created in September 1917 and restructured a year later as the Speakers' Bureau of the Four Minute Men. [62,63] The division kept a file of more than 10,000 speakers, including a select list of 300 of the most effective speakers. [64] Most of the work of the division involved the arrangement of speaking tours for representatives of the U.S. and allied governments.

In many instances, the CPI enlisted the services of Allied soldiers who had witnessed the fighting in order to lend credibility to speeches. This included, for example, French Lieutenant Paul Perigord, known as the "Warrior Priest"; 100 "Blue Devil" French veterans; and a regiment of Belgian soldiers who fought on the Russian front. [65]

One of the division's most important duties was supplying speakers for state and local war conferences. A total of 45 conferences were held in 37 states having "a profound effect upon public opinion and upon the efficient organization of State [sic] war work." [66] Unfortunately, the total number of speeches given and an estimate of the total audience for these speeches have not been documented, possibly due to the decentralization of the division. [67]

Division of Films

The Division of Films was established on September 25, 1917, and was directed by Charles S. Hart. [68] In the beginning, war material made by the Signal Corps was collected and provided to weekly film services for distribution at a nominal price. At least 23 films were made this way. [69] These films were not featured in movie theaters, unless they were specially engaged for a war benefit or other purpose, and were usually shown for free.

Sensing that these films were not living up to their potential and feeling a financial strain, the division sought to make greater use of Signal Corps material. [70,71] Using the best Signal Corps footage, the committee produced feature films "designed to set before the people a comprehensive record of war progress." [72]

To take greater advantage of the potential exposure offered by films, a Bureau of Distribution was arranged within the Division of Films seeking the widest possible distribution in the shortest possible time. The Bureau of Distribution also provided 500 feet of film each week to the four film news organizations — Gaumont, Universal, Mutual, and Pathe — as the *Official War Review*. [73,74]

In June 1918, the Scenario Department of the Division of Films began operation. [75] This department produced war-related documentaries based on the belief that stories of the government at work and the people at war would appeal to audiences. [76,77] The Scenario Department produced 18 films during the year of its existence. [78]

The CPI actively promoted its films to make sure they were shown. The committee published a biweekly bulletin, the *Official Film News*, describing war films and informing readers of events within the Division of Films. Publicity materials were provided to periodicals and newspapers, and press sheets were provided to film exhibitors, in an attempt to increase bookings in rural communities. [79]

By the end of the war, Signal Corps cameramen had shot nearly 1 million feet of film and the Division of Films had produced over 60 government films ranging from multi-reel features to single newsreels. [80] Although no total movie attendance figures are available, it was not uncommon for feature films to have more than 4,000 bookings. The gross income from the sale or rental of films was $852,744 [81] and the expenditures of the Division of Films totaled $1,077,730. [82]

The Bureau of War Photographs and the Department of Slides were also part of the Division of Films. The Bureau of War Photographs investigated applicants for camera permits and inspected photographs. This bureau also distributed Signal Corps photographs to the press, schools, and libraries.

The Department of Slides was created to supply "a long-felt need for official and authentic photographs in stereopticon form for the use of ministers, lecturers, school teachers, and others." [83] Slides were made available for presentations at 50% to 80% below what they cost to produce. Various experts produced lectures using the slides, which could be ordered by organizations such as churches or schools. The Department of Slides distributed a total of 200,000 slides in the year of its existence. [84]

Division of Civic and Educational Cooperation

One of the primary duties of the CPI was to educate the public. [85] As Creel noted in his *Report*:

> A[n] ... imperative duty of the Committee on Public Information was to put into convincing print America's reasons for entering the war, the meaning of America, the nature of our free institutions, and our war aims, together with a thorough analysis of the Prussian system, as well as an exposure of the enemy's misrepresentations, aggressions, and barbarities. [86]

The Division of Civic and Educational Cooperation (later the Division of Civic and Educational Publications) was formed for this purpose. Directed by historian Guy Stanton Ford, the division enlisted the aid of writers, economists, historians, and political scientists to produce literature ranging from simple pamphlets to elaborate war encyclopedias. [87]

This division was given the task of reaching America's schools, colleges, and universities with the messages of the CPI. Division representatives spoke before teachers' institutes, summer sessions, and educational bodies. The division also produced the *National School Service*, a 16-page paper issued twice a month to 520,000 teachers. [88] The Division of Civic and Educational Cooperation printed more than 75 million pieces of literature, not including reprints in newspapers and magazines. [89]

Division of Women's War Work

The Division of Women's War Work was established on November 1, 1917, "for the purpose of informing and energizing the women of the country." [90] Through the Women's Division, the CPI attempted to keep in touch with women's groups, providing them with material and making them part of the war effort. [91]

The Division of Women's War Work produced between 1,000 and 2,300 news stories. [92] Feature articles were sent to 19,471 newspapers and other publications. [93] In addition, between 250 and 292 pictures were furnished to the press, showing women actively engaged in war work. [94] Cuts in the CPI budget forced the division to close in June 1918. [95]

As an additional note, there were several other divisions and bureaus of the Domestic Section of the CPI that have not been addressed due to space limitations. These included the Division of Work with the Foreign Born, the Bureau of State Fair Exhibits, and the Bureau of War Expositions, among others.

The Role of the CPI in Public Relations History and Evolution

The work of the CPI was significant and is deserving of a prominent position in the early history of public relations. Although the CPI served primarily as a propagandist for the U.S. government, it is important to note that propaganda did not have the same negative connotations in 1917 as it does today. The CPI conducted its work unaware of the abuses of the propagandists and publicists to follow it. Instead, the work of Creel and his committee reflected a naive faith in the integrity of the U.S. government and the power of ideas to transform public opinion. [96]

Irrespective of moral judgments, the work of the CPI was crucial in creating support for the war effort among the American people. This task was especially difficult because the security of the United States was not directly threatened. [97] Given their task, Creel and the CPI demonstrated the ability of propaganda and publicity to shape public opinion more than any other public relations pioneer. [98] Although not well organized initially, the CPI eventually put forth an organized, systematic campaign designed to reach targeted audiences with specific messages, often through specialized media.

The audiences targeted by the Creel Committee included young men of draft age, women including mothers and wives of soldiers, employers, laborers, farmers, children, and college students. These audiences were targeted through advertisements, feature materials, movies, bulletins, newspapers and news stories, posters, pamphlets, books, cartoons, and speeches.

The CPI showed a surprising awareness of basic principles of effective communication in its campaign. The CPI issued uniform information to its nationwide network of speakers, the Four Minute Men, recognizing the need to speak with unity of voice. Unified ideas concerning cartoon captions and themes also were presented to cartoonists. The CPI relied on the Division of Syndicate Features to make its material simple and interesting, recognizing the need to appeal to the average reader. Likewise, understanding the importance of source credibility, the campaigns arranged by the Speaking Division sought out veterans who not only were good communicators but who also enjoyed enhanced credibility because of their war experiences.

In addition, CPI messages encouraged targeted publics to participate in the war effort through conservation efforts, the purchase of war savings stamps and bonds, the planting of victory gardens, and other activities. These activities strengthened the involvement of citizens in the war effort, giving them a vested interest in their government and increasing their sense of community. [99]

Finally, it is significant to recognize the role of the CPI in the evolution of public relations campaign practices. Edward Bernays suggested that the period between 1914 and 1918 was a distinct era in public relations development, dominated by the work of the CPI in its attempts to sell the war aims and ideals of the U.S. government to the U.S. public. [100]

The work of the CPI followed a period of unrest between industrialists and muckraking journalists. The need for public relations counsel was recognized during this period, largely for the first time. In its efforts to crystallize public opinion, the CPI provided a practical introduction to the means through which public opinion is influenced.

The work of the CPI served as a valuable training ground for two of the leading figures in public relations history, Bernays and Carl Byoir. These practitioners were the leaders among a handful of budding public relations experts who were able to take the lessons learned from the CPI and apply them to other areas, including product promotion, constituent and political relations, and fund raising. [101] In this way, the work of the CPI served as an important link between the recognition of the need for public relations services and an understanding of the means through which public opinion is crystallized.

Note: *Originally published in Pinkleton, B., The campaign of the Committee on Public Information: Its contributions to the history and evolution of public relations,* Journal of Public Relations Research, *6, 229, 1994.*

Endnotes

1. Goldman, E.F., Public relations and the progressive surge: 1898–1917, *Public Relations Review*, 4(3), 52, 1978.
2. U.S. Congress, House, Committee on Appropriations, *Sundry Civil Bill, 1919: Committee on Public Information* (Vol. 3), public hearings, 65th Congress, 2nd session, Government Printing Office, Washington, DC, 1918. Creel reported the creation of the CPI as April 4, 1917 (*The Creel Report: Complete Report of the Chairman of the Committee on Public Information, 1917: 1918: 1919*, Da Capo, New York, 1972 [1920]). The Sundry Civil Appropriation Bill for 1919 contains a reading of the executive order creating the CPI, also dated April 14, 1917. Mock and Larson and Vaughn reported the creation date to be April 13, 1917 (Mock, J.R. and Larson, C., *Words That Won the War*, Princeton University Press, Princeton, NJ, 1939; Vaughn, S., *Holding Fast the Inner Lines: Democracy, Nationalism, and the Committee on Public Information*, University of North Carolina Press, Chapel Hill, NC, 1980). April 14 is reported as the creation date of the CPI in this article due to the corroboration of Creel and information contained in the Sundry Civil Appropriation Bill.
3. Creel, G., *The Creel Report: Complete Report of the Chairman of the Committee on Public Information, 1917: 1918: 1919*, Da Capo, New York, 1972 [1920].
4. Vaughn, S., *Holding Fast the Inner Lines: Democracy, Nationalism, and the Committee on Public Information*, University of North Carolina Press, Chapel Hill, NC, 1980.
5. Vaughn, S., First amendment liberties and the Committee on Public Information, *American Journal of Legal History*, 23, 95, 1979.

6. Creel, G., *The Creel Report*, op. cit., 1.
7. Vaughn, S., First amendment liberties and the Committee on Public Information, op. cit.
8. Larson, C. and Mock, J.R., The lost files of the Creel Committee of 1917–19, *Public Opinion Quarterly*, 3, 5, 1939.
9. Ibid.
10. Mock, J.R. and Larson, C., *Words That Won the War*, op. cit.
11. Vaughn, S., First amendment liberties and the Committee on Public Information, op. cit.; Vaughn, S., *Holding Fast the Inner Lines*, op. cit.
12. Mock, J.R. and Larson, C., *Words That Won the War*, op. cit.
13. Vaughn, S., First amendment liberties and the Committee on Public Information, op. cit.
14. Ibid.
15. Larson, C., Found: Records of the Committee on Public Information, *Public Opinion Quarterly*, 1, 116, 1937.
16. Tobin, H. and Bidwell, P., *Mobilizing Civilian America*, Council on Foreign Relations, New York, 1940.
17. Vaughn, S., *Holding Fast the Inner Lines*, op. cit.
18. Mock, J.R. and Larson, C., *Words That Won the War*, op. cit.
19. Creel, G., *The Creel Report*, op. cit.
20. Larson, C. and Mock, J.R., The lost files of the Creel Committee of 1917–19, op. cit.
21. Mock, J.R. and Larson, C., *Words That Won the War*, op. cit.
22. Vaughn, S., *Holding Fast the Inner Lines*, op. cit.
23. Creel, G., *The Creel Report*, op. cit.
24. Vaughn, S., *Holding Fast the Inner Lines*, op. cit.
25. Creel, G., *How We Advertised America*, Arno, New York, 1972 [1920].
26. Mock, J.R. and Larson, C., *Words That Won the War*, op. cit., 11.
27. Creel, G., *The Creel Report*, op. cit.
28. Ibid.
29. Ibid. Mock and Larson reported the highest circulation for the *Official Bulletin* to be 115,000 in October 1918 (Mock, J.R. and Larson, C., *Words That Won the War*, op. cit.). Creel (*The Creel Report*) reported the highest circulation for the *Bulletin* to be 118,008 in August 1918. Creel's figures are used because the *Report* contains more complete information regarding circulation figures than Mock and Larson's book.
30. Creel, G., *How We Advertised America*, op. cit.
31. Creel, G., *The Creel Report*, op. cit.
32. Ibid.
33. Vaughn, S., *Holding Fast the Inner Lines*, op. cit.
34. Mock, J.R. and Larson, C., *Words That Won the War*, op. cit.
35. Creel, G., *The Creel Report*, op. cit.
36. Ibid.
37. Ibid.
38. Ibid.
39. Ibid.
40. Vaughn, S., *Holding Fast the Inner Lines*, op. cit.
41. Creel, G., *The Creel Report*, op. cit.
42. Ibid. George Hecht stated that the Bureau of Cartoons was established in December 1917 under the auspices of the National Committee of Patriotic Societies and moved under the direction of the CPI in June 1918 (Hecht, G.J., *The War in Cartoons*, Garland, New York, 1971 [1919]). Creel (*The Creel Report*) reported that the bureau was formed as part of the CPI on May 28, 1918. This article reports May 28, 1918, as the creation date of the bureau because that is the date reported by Creel in his report. As an additional note, the Bureau of Cartoons was founded by George J. Hecht, who maintained unofficial supervision of the work of the bureau. The bureau was under the direction of the CPI's Executive Division, however, and was officially directed by Alfred M. Saperston, later replaced by Gretchen Leicht.

43. Creel, G., *The Creel Report*, op. cit., 76.
44. Creel, G., *The Creel Report*, op. cit.
45. Vaughn, S., *Holding Fast the Inner Lines*, op. cit.
46. Hecht, op. cit.
47. Vaughn, S., *Holding Fast the Inner Lines*, op. cit.
48. Mock, J.R. and Larson, C., *Words That Won the War*, op. cit.
49. U.S. Congress, op. cit.
50. Creel, G., *The Creel Report*, op. cit.
51. The name "Four Minute Men" contains an adjective pair that is normally hyphenated. The name is both hyphenated and unhyphenated in a number of texts, including official government publications. Creel *did not* hyphenate the name in his *Complete Report* and other publications of the CPI also failed to hyphenate the name. For this reason, the name is not hyphenated in this text.
52. Creel, G., *The Creel Report*, op. cit., 21.
53. Larson, C. and Mock, J.R., The four-minute men, *Quarterly Journal of Speech*, 25, 97, 1939.
54. Oukrop, C., The four minute men became a national network during World War I, *Journalism Quarterly*, 52, 632, 1975.
55. Mock, J.R. and Larson, C., *Words That Won the War*, op. cit.
56. Creel, G., *The Creel Report*, op. cit.
57. Larson, C. and Mock, J.R., The four-minute men, op. cit.
58. Ibid.
59. Creel, G., *The Creel Report*, op. cit.
60. Mock, J.R. and Larson, C., *Words That Won the War*, op. cit.
61. Creel, G., *The Creel Report*, op. cit. Creel placed the number of speeches given at 755,190 and the total audience at 314,454,514. Mock and Larson suggested that Creel reported the total number of speeches given at one million and the total audience at four million (Mock, J.R. and Larson, C., *Words That Won the War*, op. cit.). The figures from Creel (*Creel Report*) are used because Mock and Larson's numbers appear to be approximations.
62. Creel, G., *The Creel Report*, op. cit.
63. Vaughn, S., *Holding Fast the Inner Lines*, op. cit.
64. Creel, G., *The Creel Report*, op. cit.
65. U.S. Congress, op. cit.
66. Creel, G., *The Creel Report*, op. cit., 35.
67. Vaughn, S., *Holding Fast the Inner Lines*, op. cit.
68. Creel, G., *The Creel Report*, op. cit.
69. Ibid.
70. Ibid.
71. Vaughn, S., *Holding Fast the Inner Lines*, op. cit.
72. Creel, G., *How We Advertised America*, op. cit., 120–21.
73. Creel, G., *The Creel Report*, op. cit.
74. Vaughn, S., *Holding Fast the Inner Lines*, op. cit.
75. Creel, G., *The Creel Report*, op. cit.
76. Mock, J.R. and Larson, C., *Words That Won the War*, op. cit.
77. Vaughn, S., *Holding Fast the Inner Lines*, op. cit.
78. Creel, G., *The Creel Report*, op. cit.
79. Vaughn, S., *Holding Fast the Inner Lines*, op. cit.
80. Ward, L.W., *The Motion Picture Goes to War: The U.S. Government Film Effort During World War I*, UMI Research Press, Ann Arbor, MI, 1985.
81. Creel, G., *The Creel Report*, op. cit.
82. Vaughn, S., *Holding Fast the Inner Lines*, op. cit.
83. Creel, G., *The Creel Report*, op. cit., 62.
84. Creel, G., *The Creel Report*, op. cit.

85. Vaughn, S., "To create a nation of noble men": Public education, national unity, and the National School Service, 1918–1919, *The Historian*, 91, 429, 1979.

86. Creel, G., *The Creel Report*, op. cit., 15.

87. Mock, J.R. and Larson, C., *Words That Won the War*, op. cit.

88. Creel, G., *The Creel Report*, op. cit.

89. Ibid.

90. Creel, G., *How We Advertised America*, op. cit., 75.

91. U.S. Congress, op. cit.

92. In *The Creel Report*, Creel presented the total number of news stories and feature articles as 1,000. In *How We Advertised America*, Creel presented the total number of news stories and feature articles as 2,305. A range is used in citing this statistic.

93. Creel, G., *The Creel Report*, op. cit.

94. Ibid. In *The Creel Report*, Creel listed the total number of photographs as 250. In *How We Advertised America*, he listed the total number of photographs at 292. A range is used in citing this statistic.

95. Creel, G., *How We Advertised America*, op. cit.

96. Vaughn, S., *Holding Fast the Inner Lines*, op. cit.

97. Taylor, A.J.P., *The First World War*, Capricorn, New York, 1972.

98. Cutlip, S.M., Center, A.H., and Broom, G.M., *Effective Public Relations*, 6th ed., Prentice-Hall, Englewood Cliffs, NJ, 1985.

99. Vaughn, S., *Holding Fast the Inner Lines*, op. cit.

100. Cited in Harlow, R.F. and Black, M.M., *Practical Public Relations*, Harper & Brothers, New York, 1952.

101. Cutlip, Center, and Broom, op. cit.

Appendix I

Questions for Review and Discussion

1. What are the eight *purposes* of government public relations?
2. What are the four *models* of public relations, what are the differences among them, and why is the two-way symmetrical model recommended?
3. The head of a large U.S. federal agency has hired you as a consultant. She is convinced that her agency could do a better job at public relations. You, in turn, hire a research assistant to investigate the agency's current public relations activities. Write a memo to the research assistant describing what you want investigated and why.

Additional Reading

Arnette, S.U., Improving your agency's image, *Journal of Housing and Community Development*, 52(2), 38, 1995.

Avery, G.D. et al., Public affairs in the public sector, in *Practical Public Affairs in an Era of Change: A Communications Guide for Business, Government and College*, Dennis, L.B., Ed., Public Relations Society of America and University Press of America, Lanham, MD, 1996, chap. 13.

Baker, B., Public relations in government, in *Handbook of Strategic Public Relations and Integrated Communication*, Caywood, C.L., Ed., McGraw-Hill, New York, 1997, chap. 31.

Édes, B.W., The role of government information officers, *Journal of Government Information*, 27, 455, 2000.

Harding, T.S., Genesis of one "government propaganda mill," *Public Opinion Quarterly*, 11, 227, 1947. [Reviews the 19th century origins of U.S. Department of Agriculture's extensive public information program, mostly geared to disseminating helpful information to its clients.]

Herring, E.P., Publicizing administrative activities, in *Public Administration and the Public Interest*, Russell & Russell, New York, 1967 [1936], chap. 22. [Early effort to theorize about the need for, and roles of, public relations in public administration in response to the enormous growth in the scope of federal operations during the New Deal.]

Lee, M., Public relations is public administration, *The Public Manager*, 27(4), 49, 1998–1999.

McCamy, J.L., *Government Publicity: Its Practice in Federal Administration*, University of Chicago Press, Chicago, 1939. [Definitive and first academic study of government public relations, as practiced during the New Deal.]

Motschall, M. and Cao, L., An analysis of the public relations role of the police public information officer, *Police Quarterly*, 5, 152, 2002.

PURPOSES OF GOVERNMENT PUBLIC RELATIONS: MEDIA RELATIONS

Introduction to Section II

Media relations tend to dominate the common view of what government public relations comprises. This is understandable, as it is the most traditional and most visible aspect of the practice of public relations in the public sector. When we think about an agency's public information officer or of a governmental spokesperson, we tend to visualize someone dealing with reporters.

Furthermore, the omnipresence and enormous impact of the media in the early 21st century indicates the importance of media relations in public administration. Reporters and editors decide what to cover and what not. Once they've identified a subject as news, they then decide how to cover the topics they've selected. These decisions essentially define the public agenda. Through the media's selection and framing of issues, the citizenry is informed not only regarding the specifics of a particular story, but also what to think *about*.

Certainly, in the 1980s, the American media was much more monolithic: three national over-the-air TV networks, daily newspapers, and assorted radio news services. By the second decade of the 21st century, the 'old media' was being largely replaced by a new paradigm: cable news networks ascending over traditional news networks, online and real-time news Web sites over print newspapers, and talk radio over radio news. Finally, blogging gave individual citizens a megaphone almost as powerful as that of a news medium. Still, regardless of its composition, it is the news media (as a whole) that continues to define the public agenda. It decides what is important and what isn't. It is in this live-or-die environment that government agencies struggle to survive. Being noticed, hopefully favorably, carries enormous impacts. No wonder media relations is so important in the practice of government public relations.

The first chapter in this section (Chapter 5) is an overview of the current state of the relationship between public sector agencies and the media. Then, the next chapter provides specifics about the conditions necessary for governments to have effective media relations. The role of a spokesperson is a complex one, requiring allegiance both to the mother agency but, simultaneously, also to the values of the news media, such as honesty and full disclosure. Public administrators need to recognize these conflicting loyalties and learn to accept their importance to maintaining the credibility of the agency's spokesperson. Chapter 7 is a more in-depth discussion of the trends that have contributed to the contemporary relationship between reporters and public administration. These trends have been a long time in coming and continue to evolve to the present.

The last chapter in this section (Chapter 8) presents the results of empirical research regarding press secretaries for members of Congress. Admittedly, the topic of the chapter is, at first glance, beyond the scope of this volume, which focuses on public administration in government and not on elected officials. However, the chapter has much to add to our understanding of government media relations. Even discounting for the differences between politicians and managers, the research provides tangible data and a vivid depiction of how government staff that specialize in media relations operate, what their environment is like, and the culture of the reporters with whom they deal. That's why, despite its slightly off-target subject, the chapter is included in this book. It is quite relevant to government managers. Media relations practitioners in public administration can learn much for the agility of press secretaries on Capitol Hill. The working conventions and fleet-footedness shown by these media relations specialists for legislators are nearly fully applicable to government agencies.

While Chapter 21 is included in the section dealing with the external environment of government public relations, it includes a discussion that is relevant to the practice of media relations. In the section on "Channels of Interaction," Viteritti writes about the *techniques* of dealing with the mass media. He identifies and describes the media relations methods of press advisories, media releases, briefings for reporters, news conferences, interviews, and editorial board meetings. His discussion of the techniques of media relations can be used as a supplement to the readings in this section, providing more tangible detail on some of the tools available to the media relations specialist in government.

Chapter 5

The Media versus the Bureaucracy

Mordecai Lee

Contents

Abstract: News media hostility to bureaucracy is a fixed field in American political culture that has its roots in the 18th century anti-government motive of the founding of the republic. Contemporary negative coverage must be understood as deeply embedded. All responses to it must be based on that premise. While some public administrators in occasional situations may receive positive coverage, that is the exception, rather than the rule. Civil servants need to accept this harsh media environment rather than bemoan it. Constructive responses can include professionalizing agency public information activities, being sensitive to public relations implications during the policy development process and, with the development of more sophisticated E-government technologies, bypassing the media to reach the public directly.

Introduction

This chapter reviews media coverage of public administration in the United States. First, it discusses the history of such coverage and ties it to an element of American political culture which is consistently negative towards government. Second, the contemporary state of news coverage of American bureaucracy in the early 21st century is examined. It identifies elements that contribute to and exacerbate such negative coverage, including an anti-bureaucracy meta-narrative that tends to be embedded in journalism, the difficulty of making public administration interesting in a visual medium, the emergence of attack journalism, and the reduction in original reporting versus the rise in punditing.

Third, possible responses by civil servants are presented. Public administrators have little influence to attenuate the anti-bureaucracy tilt of news coverage. However, government managers have some modest options regarding softening the hard edges of this coverage. They can professionalize relations with reporters, take advantage of opportunities to present positive stories, and utilize new digital technologies to communicate directly with the public instead of relying on the traditional intermediary role of the news media.

History

The negative view of government in American journalism is as old as America itself. The American revolutionary war was justified as a reaction to tyranny, depicted as the abusive use of government power by Great Britain against the colonists. The 1776 Declaration of Independence comprised little more than a litany of complaints about the British government. A primary vehicle for the revolution was circulars and pamphlets denouncing uncaring and distant government by Committees of Correspondence, early versions of American journalism.

With the founding of the United States, the First Amendment to the federal Constitution guaranteed freedom of the press in order to facilitate journalism's role as an instrument of democracy. The duty of an independent press was to report what government did and did not do, so that an informed public could exercise its will, whether through formal mechanisms (elections) or informal ones (public opinion). Therefore, the ethos of American journalism was that its *raison d'être* was to cover government critically. Freed of government regulation, American newspapers were presumed to take an adversarial attitude towards government, helping guarantee democracy and the other constitutional freedoms possessed by the citizenry.

The anti-government strain of U.S. journalistic and civic culture has been a permanent phenomenon since then. While the emergence of a merit-based and professionalized civil service in the late 19th century was a new element in the public sector, public administration was still part of government, the presumed heavy in the given narrative of American society. While muckraking was viewed as a new form of journalism at the beginning of the 20th century, it shared a world view that was not novel: government was one of the bad guys, even though Progressive reformers often turned to government to solve problems. The exposé of problems in Chicago's meat packing plants was as much a condemnation of corrupt or ineffective government inspections as it was of the mendacity of big business. One staple of journalism of that era was exposing the malfeasance or corruption of urban political machines, how they misused government agencies to line their own pockets, whether with rigged bidding for purchase of goods and services or the corruption of law enforcement to protect organized crime. Reporters often called for reform, sometimes with government as the problem, sometimes as the solution, sometimes both. It was in that context that public administration emerged in the U.S. Separating politics from administration through civil service reform was viewed then as a solution (although, in retrospect, a chimera).

The so-called 'golden age' of media coverage of the bureaucracy began with Franklin Roosevelt's New Deal, when an alphabet soup of administrative agencies sprouted up to rid the country of the Great Depression and the power of the economic royalists. Suddenly, public administration was not only the solution, but also the possessor of nearly inexplicable expertise. That made reporters more than ever dependent on the public relations staffs of the new agencies. Journalists needed help to understand and interpret bureaucratic actions into terms meaningful and understandable to their lay readers. [1] The intense coverage of the bureaucracy — and deference to its innate fairness, wisdom, and patriotism — largely continued through World War II and the first decades of the Cold War. Kurtz described media coverage of that era as "page after page of gray type and boring stories about bureaucracy." [2] However, those mid-century decades of extensive and largely informative coverage of public administration need to be seen now as an aberration, not the normal state of affairs.

The return to journalistic normalcy, of negative coverage of the bureaucracy (in contradistinction to how reporters covered politicians in general and presidents in particular) was triggered by the coalescing of several trends. In part, reporters fell out of love with public administration, after such high profile events as the failure of Defense Secretary Robert McNamara's bureaucratic approach to win the Viet Nam war, the domestic bureaucracy's inability to win the War on Poverty, and the seeming failure of the economic policy bureaucracy to tame inflation in the 1970s. News reporting of government, especially after Watergate, became increasingly negative. Not just the traditional skeptical and adversarial stance, but of barely-disguised cynicism, disbelief, and outright hostility. All of government, whether elected or civil service, bore the brunt of that. But, most importantly, then came television.

By the 1970s, television had fully eclipsed print as the dominant news media. This had several key consequences for coverage of the bureaucracy, mostly dictated by the medium's technological parameters. First, TV was a visual medium and public administration was hard to cover when pictures were needed. Most developments from government departments were long-running policy issues, mind-numbing in detail and took too long to explain. Sure, efforts at securities regulation were an important story, but the subject was inherently detail oriented and lacking in dramatic pictures. Second, even more than print journalism, television was best at telling short stories, which required a beginning, middle, and end, all wrapped up in the same report. Again, disadvantage bureaucracy. TV was especially good at telling dramatic and emotion-laden stories about a person, a suffering victim, with whom the viewers could empathize. This kind of storytelling was conducive to covering the bureaucracy, but only when it was the bad guy, insensitively victimizing a poor innocent citizen.

By the end of the 20th century, admitted a senior reporter for the *New York Times*, "newspapers cover governmental *process* less than they used to. Television hardly covers it at all." [3] And public administration is all about *process*. The trend accelerated during the first decade of the 21st century. Kettl observed that "'waste-fraud-and-abuse' has become a single word in the media." [4] Also, there was more and more news, but less original reporting and, of that reporting, even less of it was about departments and agencies. And what little there was almost always was negative. [5] "Television newsmagazines regularly alternated 'give me a break!' features about government gone amuck with plaintive stories of citizens in need" who were being ignored by bureaucrats. [6]

The impact of these trends in media coverage of the bureaucracy meant that citizens increasingly considered government as "something that may be watched, and even viewed with disgust, but nonetheless regarded as a series of events with which the individual citizen is not directly involved." [7] This further separated the citizenry from experiencing or exercising its ownership role in democratic government, especially public administration.

As Seen on Your TV Screen: Contemporary Media Coverage of American Bureaucracy

The technical requirements for TV storytelling greatly exacerbated the pre-existing secular trends in American journalism: a general distrust of government and pervasively negative spin to coverage. Public administration was a made-for-TV heavy. As TV news sought to be increasingly entertaining and outrage-promoting, a new mutation of reporting, called attack journalism, had the daily effect of depicting the bureaucracy as deviant and arousing public indignation about these transgressors of goodness. [8] Public administrators faced a lose–lose world of a "court of public opinion in which media is the prosecutor, judge, and decision maker." [9] (Somewhat similar trends have begun occurring in media coverage of the nonprofit sector. [10])

Zoonen sought to identify a typology of contemporary news coverage. He suggested there were four meta-narratives that reporters consciously or unconsciously used to craft their stories: quest, bureaucracy, conspiracy, and soap. Bureaucracy stories were ones dominated by motifs of incompetence, waste, and "as a force beyond the individual's control." Zoonen also suggested that the four meta-narrative categories were not mutually exclusive, with the story line of news coverage often invoking several simultaneously. Hence, bureaucracy stories were also a good fit for the running themes of quest (bureaucracy as the evil obstacle to a successful quest to do right), conspiracy (deliberate and secretive efforts to harm society), and soap (dramatic tale of an individual up against an institution that inherently suppresses individual choice). [11] The anti-bureaucracy meta-narrative can be embedded in many kinds of stories, even those not specifically about the bureaucracy, rather tossed in for good measure.

For news coverage that is explicitly about government agencies, Vermeer identified three categories for such coverage: stories about failure and conflict; stories about high profile agencies (such as EPA and Social Security) rather than obscure ones; and stories about the particular civic interest in a local media market. [12] An example of the latter would be the interest in southwestern states in water decisions by the U.S. Bureau of Reclamation, which is part of the Interior Department. As with meta-narratives, these kinds of stories were not mutually exclusive. Continuing with the same example, a story about a new Bureau of Reclamation water policy might not only fit in the third category of local interest, but also the first category, regarding conflict. Water distribution decisions can be very controversial. Different categories of users would criticize the Bureau for proposing policies that go against their particular parochial interests.

Then television begat cable TV, which begat 24-hour cable news networks, which begat punditry as an industry. The right-of-center tilt of talk TV (and talk radio) meant commentary was inherently anti-government, even when the right-of-center party controlled all elected institutions in Washington. In a parallel, but decreasingly separate, reality the Internet begat real-time news sites (often of newspapers seeking to adapt and survive), which begat the blogosphere, which made every American a pundit. Blogging is not, strictly speaking, journalism, but in the first decade of the 21st century it began influencing and driving the media's agenda for coverage.

Bureaucratic Responses to Media Coverage

As the Darth Vader of early 21st century America, it would seem that U.S. bureaucrats have few options regarding their media image. To paraphrase the 1990s bestseller, administrators are from Jupiter and reporters are from Mercury. In Imperial Rome, Jupiter was the god of the state, while Mercury was the bearer of messages, often eloquent, but cunning and unpredictable. Can Jovian managers and mercurial reporters co-exist? The adaptations required of public administration to survive necessitate some traditional as well as innovative responses. Most of all, government managers need to be philosophical about the perennial journalistic hostility to their work. This is little different from the persistence of a baseball pitcher at striking out each batter. As batters, public administrators need to be satisfied with a .300 average, even .250, since that's about as good as it'll ever get. [13]

Media Relations and Public Information

Love 'em or hate 'em, because of the essential difference between public administration and of management in the business and nonprofit sectors, the constitutional, legal, and professional duty of the civil servant is to cooperate with the media. The government manager is part of the public sector and, therefore, must be a participant in the democratic system. Given the First Amendment and the federal Freedom of Information Act (or its state counterparts, sometimes called open records or sunshine laws), public agencies must answer reporters' inquiries, whether the answers are in the best interest of the agency or not.

However, this necessity to cooperate with the media can sometimes be converted into a virtue. Beyond passively answering unsolicited requests for information from the media, public administration can view media relations and public information as a tool of governance, which may be used to advance the mission of the agency. [14] Its various purposes could include informing citizens of eligibility for new services; informing the public of new laws that may affect them personally; seeking to promote socially desired behavior ("Only you can prevent forest fires"); and promoting voluntary cooperation with laws and regulations rather than relying on expensive regulatory and enforcement approaches. [15] Also, there are circumstances when the media seeks and disseminates agency information. For example, in times of crisis and disaster, relevant departments are given virtually unlimited access to media channels to provide instructions, advice, and updates to affected populations. [16]

In-House Staffing and Planning

Good (or, at least, occasionally decent) public relations doesn't just happen. It requires the agency having professional staff in its public information bureau, training all employees in the basics of handling unsolicited media inquiries, having top managers who are attuned to public relations, involving senior public information officials in decision making, and engaging in planning for foreseeable scenarios as well as unforeseeable crises.

Bypassing the Media

Other bureaucratic counter-strategies can aim at changing the context of media coverage or bypassing the media altogether. For example, through policy entrepreneurship the administrator can gradually build support for the 'do something!' dynamic of American society. By working behind the scenes to help define a problem with various attentive audiences, the government manager can create a frame of reference that invariably puts the agency in a good light, as responding to a social need. [17] Similarly, the traditional duty of a public administrator to report to the citizenry on agency activities can be transformed in this digital era to E-reporting, using the Internet to reach citizens directly with information about agency performance. [18]

Conclusion

A natural human tendency is to complain about a situation that one is dissatisfied with. Like most Americans, reporters complain through their journalism about bureaucracy, and then bureaucrats complain about hostile media coverage. The difference between the two is that reporters have the power to frame events for news consumers while public administrators don't. This asymmetry of power is at the heart of the problem of media coverage of American bureaucracy. For the foreseeable future, Mercury always trumps Jupiter. The negativity of American political culture to government is permanent and is the root cause that leads to the harshness of media coverage of bureaucracy in the U.S. Developments in the news industry in the first decade of the 21st century made press coverage even more negative. There are more profit-oriented media outlets, which leads to hyper-competition for audiences, less original reporting, more punditing, more spin, and an obsession with scandal and outrage.

However, with the emergence of digital and Internet-based technologies for E-government and E-democracy in the 21st century, public sector agencies have, for the first time in American history, the potential of bypassing the media and reaching the citizenry directly. Also, occasional policy openings or crisis situations provide opportunities for agencies to present a countervailing picture to the citizenry through a cooperative news media. Still, public administrators have little choice but to be philosophical about this national tendency to bureaucracy bashing. Most have experienced such negative media coverage to prove it. And, with the Americanization of global media patterns, this is becoming an international tendency as well. [19]

Note: *Originally published in Lee, M., Media and bureaucracy in the United States, in* Encyclopedia of Public Administration and Public Policy, *2nd ed., Taylor & Francis, Boca Raton, FL, 2008.*

Endnotes

1. McCamy, J.L., *Government Publicity: Its Practice in Federal Administration,* University of Chicago Press, Chicago, 1939.
2. Kurtz, H., *Media Circus: The Trouble with America's Newspapers,* Times Books, New York, 1994, 357.
3. Clymer, A., *Edward M. Kennedy: A Biography,* William Morrow, New York, 1999, 607, emphasis added.
4. Kettl, D.F., Relentless reinvention, *Government Executive,* 32(1), 26, 2000.
5. Lichter, S.R. and McGinnis, P., Government in and out of the news, *Public Manager,* 32(3), 47, 2003.
6. Kettl, D.F., *The Transformation of Governance: Public Administration for Twenty-First Century America,* Johns Hopkins University Press, Baltimore, 2002, 63.
7. Roberts, A., *Blacked Out: Government Secrecy in the Information Age,* Cambridge University Press, New York, 2006, 236.
8. Patterson, T. and Seib, P., Informing the public, in *The Press,* Overholser, G. and Jamieson, K.H., Eds., Oxford University Press, New York, 2005, 192–196.
9. Kalantari, B., Media and the bureaucracy in the United States, in *Handbook of Comparative and Development Public Administration,* 2nd ed., Farazmand, A., Ed., Marcel Dekker, New York, 2001, 881. (*Editor's Note:* See Chapter 7.)
10. Stephenson, M., Jr. and Chaves, E., The Nature Conservancy, the press, and accountability, *Nonprofit and Voluntary Sector Quarterly,* 35, 345, 2006.
11. Zoonen, L.V., *Entertaining the Citizen: When Politics and Popular Culture Converge,* Rowman & Littlefield, Lanham, MD, 2005, chap. 7.

12. Vermeer, J., Bureaucracy and the media, in *Media Power, Media Politics,* Rozell, M.J., Ed., Rowman & Littlefield, Lanham, MD, 2003, 102.
13. Lee, M. Administrators are from Jupiter, reporters are from Mercury, *PA Times,* 24(6), 7, 2001.
14. Weiss, J.A., Public information, in *The Tools of Government: A Guide to the New Governance,* Salamon, L.S., Ed., Oxford University Press, New York, 2002, chap. 7.
15. Lee, M., Public information in government organizations: A review and curriculum outline of external relations in public administration, *Public Administration and Management: An Interactive Journal,* 5, 183, 2000. http://www.pamij.com/5_4/5_4_4_pubinfo.pdf (accessed 2007) (*Editor's Note:* See Chapter 1.)
16. Lee, M., Media relations and external communications during a disaster, in *Disaster Management Handbook,* Pinkowski, J., Ed., Taylor & Francis, Boca Raton, FL, 2008, chap. 19. (*Editor's Note:* See Chapter 17.)
17. Lee, M., Reporters and bureaucrats: Public relations counter-strategies by public administrators in an era of media disinterest in government, *Public Relations Review,* 25, 456–457, 1999.
18. Lee, M., E-Reporting: Using managing-for-results data to strengthen democratic accountability, in *Managing for Results 2005,* Kamensky, J.M. and Morales, A., Eds., Rowman & Littlefield, Lanham, MD, 2005, chap. 4. Also published as a monograph and available online: http://www.businessofgovernment.org/pdfs/Lee_Report.pdf (accessed 2007). (*Editor's Note:* See Chapter 25.)
19. Lee, M., Globalization and media coverage of public administration, in *Handbook of Globalization, Governance, and Public Administration,* Farazmand, A. and Pinkowski, J., Eds., Taylor & Francis, Boca Raton, FL, 2007, chap. 8. (*Editor's Note:* See Chapter 24.)

Chapter 6

The Effective Agency Spokesperson

Mordecai Lee

Contents

Context

At the close of the first decade of the 21st century, bureaucracy found itself in what could be called a geometrical dilemma. Bureaucracy is an inherently hierarchical and pyramidal entity that needs to adapt to what Friedman calls a flat world. [1] This contemporary paradox can be seen as the modern manifestation of the traditional problem of democracy relying on an inherently non-democratic bureaucracy to organize the delivery of public goods and services. [2]

Bureaucracy's placement in the public sector has always meant that it operates in a fishbowl. Yet, the 21st century has redesigned the fishbowl to put unprecedented pressures on public administration. [3] Demands by the news media, advocacy organizations, politicians, legislative auditors and reformers constantly push the envelope for greater transparency, increased freedom of information, more openness in drafting of policies and regulations, enhanced whistle-blower protections (and, subtly, encouragement of it), and expanded citizen involvement in agency decision making. Simultaneously — if not hypocritically — those same social forces often push for greater privacy protections regarding agency data and personal information.

A bureaucracy has many different ways it can respond to these contemporary pressures for increased external communications, including specialized training for its staff, development of policies, pursuit of alternative channels to reach the public, use of E-government technology to interact with the citizenry directly, public reporting and specialized operations during crises and disasters. [4]

Still, the in-house professional who faces the greatest pressures to communicate on a daily basis is the agency's spokesperson. This person is the voice and face of the agency on a daily, even hourly, basis in dealing with the news media in all of its variegated 21st century manifestations: daily newspapers, wire services, specialized publications and magazines, cable news channels, TV networks and radio reporters along with the new media of bloggers and websites. The agency spokesperson is at the crucial and important intersection of bureaucracy and democracy, trying to serve several clamoring and, sometimes, contradictory stakeholders. But, surprisingly, "few positions in government are as misunderstood as the public information official." [5]

Overview

Bureaucracy's antecedents extend to the early Middle Eastern and Mediterranean societies. By Biblical times, bureaucracy was an essential component of advanced civilizations. [6] Yet it was not until the 19th and 20th centuries, with the parallel emergence of mass democracy and the independent daily newspaper, that a new reality of public administration set in. [7] Government agencies were expected to engage in symmetrical two-way communications with the citizenry-at-large. [8] Outwards, they needed to be explaining, advertising, reporting, promoting, encouraging and interpreting. Simultaneously, inwards, they sought to be initiating, listening, responding, adjusting, changing and terminating. This was public relations in the plainest and best meaning of the term, before the initials PR took on the manipulative, insincere and superficial meaning of contemporary usage. Such public relations programs were sometimes conducted indirectly via the news media and sometimes through direct contact with the public-at-large. Either way, modern bureaucracy needed to learn how to engage in public relations. The nexus for bureaucratic PR is the agency spokesperson and his or her home base in the agency's public information office.

The subtlety and nuance involved in the practice of the public information profession is illustrated by a story told of Robert McCloskey, the near legendary spokesman for the U.S. State Department in the 1970s:

> McCloskey has three distinct ways of saying, "I would not speculate": spoken without accent, it means the department doesn't know for sure; emphasis on the "I" means "I wouldn't but you may — and with some assurance"; accent on "speculate" indicates that the questioner's premise is probably wrong. [9]

McCloskey himself, after retirement, acknowledged one technique of his mastery of the profession: "After a while, an official's *gesture* may be all that a reporter needs to confirm a lead." [10]

This chapter presents the role of, and best practices for, government public information officers (PIOs) as identified from research by academicians and practitioners. This has been a somewhat neglected subject in public administration, an odd omission given that the central tenet of the discipline is that management in the public sector is inherently different from the business sector. One key aspect of that difference is a news media that is a constitutionally based instrument of democracy with government managers having an absolute obligation to cooperate with it. Virtually total transparency is the premise imposed on American public administration. This is a wholly different dynamic than that faced by executives in the corporate or nonprofit sectors. [11] Furthermore, using the prism of bureaucratic politics, the conduct of external communications is a vital aspect of any public agency's struggle for survival, stability and security.

(*Note to the reader:* If only for variety in the text, the terms spokesperson and PIO are used as synonyms in this chapter, even though they are slightly different.)

Effectiveness as a Performance Standard

As academic disciplines, public administration and public relations have paid attention to the role of government public relations (in contradistinction to media relations by *elected* officials) sporadically. [12] Book-length and major contributions from academicians and independent researchers that focused in whole or in part on the broad subject of external communications in the public sector have included (in chronological order) McCamy, [13] Mosher, [14] Pimlott, [15] Lindsey, [16] Rubin, [17] Rourke, [18] Nimmo, [19] Hiebert and Spitzer, [20] Dunn, [21] Chittick, [22] Sigal, [23] Helm et al., [24] Schachter, [25] Hess, [26] Morgan, [27] Garnett, [28] and Graber. [29] This broader literature naturally includes some attention to the work of PIOs.

Academic literature that focuses more directly on spokespersons in public administration is sparser, largely limited to articles in refereed journals. Some of it is quite dated. Major examples include (in chronological order) Stephens, [30] Dunwoody and Ryan, [31] Fletcher and Soucy, [32] Swartz, [33] and Motschall and Cao. [34] This author has surveyed spokespersons for local governments to document their roles and work, [35] examined the film image of government PIOs, [36] identified strategies by government agencies for dealing with new trends in media coverage, [37] and presented a comprehensive typology of the purposes of public relations in public administration. [38]

Paralleling the academic literature, personal memoirs by PIOs working for administrative (rather than elected) officials constitute a significant, if anecdotal, ground-level view of the difficulties of speaking for a bureaucracy. While there is a relatively plentiful literature of spokespersons for elected officials, such as from former White House press secretaries, that category of spokespersonship must necessarily be excluded from this inquiry. The extant literature of senior PIOs in public administration has included books by two former Assistant Secretaries of State for Public Affairs, [39,40] former Assistant Secretary of Defense for Public Affairs, [41] the U.S. government spokesman in Saigon during the early years of the Vietnam war, [42] an Army PIO, [43] the Deputy Commissioner for Public Affairs at the New York City Police Department, [44] and a guidebook from a PIO association. [45] A non-U.S. source is the memoir of the Chief Information Officer of the British Ministry of Supply. [46] Some contemporary examples of articles by practitioners published since 1990 have been authored by (in chronological order) the official State Department spokesman (a position sometimes separated from the role of assistant secretary for public affairs), [47] a housing agency spokeswoman, [48] a health and human services PIO, [49] the PIO for the Los Angeles Fire Department, [50] the spokesman for the Maryland Fire

Marshall, [51] an FBI communications trainer, [52] the PIO of a California city, [53] and a public affairs officer for the American reconstruction agency in Iraq. [54] A non-U.S. source was written by the PIO for an international organization in post-Communist Eastern Europe. [55] Earlier articles and published lectures by practitioners before 1990, now mostly of historical value, include a Marine Corps publicity specialist, [56] two more Assistant Secretaries of State for Public Affairs, [57,58] a Foreign Service officer, [59] PIOs of two state social service agencies, [60,61] and the head of an association of federal PIOs. [62]

What lessons can be learned from this relatively modest academic and practitioner literature? A consistent theme is the contemporary focus of public administration and public relations on organizational effectiveness. [63] The performance standard of effectiveness helps identify the Holy Grail of successfully connecting bureaucracy with democracy in general and to the news media in particular. The components of effectiveness are those that relate to the multiple — and usually conflicting — perspectives of the news media, the agency head, the agency's staff and, finally, the profession's own code of standards.

Defining the effectiveness of the spokesperson for a bureaucracy, of course, is a reflection of who is making the observation. Certainly, where you stand depends on where you sit. Reporters want to see a spokesperson who is well informed, truthful, volunteers information, helpful, willing to act as a fact-finder, and has unlimited access to the highest level of officials in the agency. On the other hand, the head of the agency may want the spokesperson to advance his or her short-term career interests, such as providing positive publicity and suppressing negative coverage. Meanwhile, the careerists in the agency may want the PIO to emphasize or downgrade issues that will advance the long-term interests of the agency itself, which may or may not correlate with the short-term interests of the appointed head of the agency. Finally, the spokesperson has his or her own professional standards and ethics, derived from a conception of an accountable public administration that serves the citizenry, the public interest and democracy. Yet this professional code of conduct may at times conflict with the tugs and pulls of other constituencies.

These cross-cutting currents suggest that a PIO works in an unusually precarious environment in public administration. They also raise the question of what or where spokespersons consider themselves to be. Are they loyal members of a bureaucracy? Paid by a bureaucracy, but loyal to the professional standards of journalism? Or somewhere in-between?

Effectiveness from the Media's Perspective

Reflecting on his two years as the State Department's spokesman and acting Assistant Secretary for Public Affairs, Nicholas Burns identified three key factors that the media used to measure the effectiveness of a bureaucracy's spokesman:

- Credibility: "He or she must speak, and be seen to speak, clearly and authoritatively" for the agency.
- Knowledge: "Always try to be better prepared than the press corps."
- Responsiveness: "Understand the often Byzantine nature of the modern press corps." [64]

When possessing this trifecta, a bureaucracy's PIO can be effective in the eyes of the news media. If Burns had lacked even one of the three, it would have been fatal because reporters would quickly turn against him. For example, if Burns had been credible and informed, but he didn't cater to the technical needs of reporters (such as deadlines and connectivity) to do their jobs, then his effectiveness would have sharply dropped.

More crucially, in a different incomplete combination of the trifecta, Burns could have been well informed and responsive, but he would not have the respect of journalists covering the agency if they perceived a lack of credibility when speaking on behalf of the Department's senior leadership. In this kind of situation, it was not enough for reporters to know that Burns was fully informed of developments within the State Department. For them to trust him, they needed to have the confidence that the information he was dispensing was not only technically accurate, but credible. For example, if Burns had said, "The Secretary has no plans to meet today with the Governor of California," but then the two met the next day as perhaps had been previously arranged, then Burns would have lost his credibility. While he had been literally correct in what he said, he was misleading by parsing the meaning of his words to be misleading. If he claimed that he was providing all the information that had been given to him, then he'd be implicitly confessing to not being truly in the know. The prompt response from reporters would be, "In that case, give us someone who is."

Even though the professional role the spokesperson is playing is, strictly speaking, only that of an amplifier and conveyer of information, but because it was coming from Burns the reporters gauged the credibility of the information on Burns' own authority and reputation. The press corps wants someone who is an objective conveyer of information and doesn't add spin; doesn't withhold information, lie, deceive or mislead; withstands intra-agency pressures to withhold information; and, when needed, acts as a reporter and fact-finder within the agency to be sure he or she knows what's really going on.

Credibility and knowledge are gained when the spokesperson has the confidence and trust of the senior leaders of the agency. When that happens, then the PIO knows what the agency head is thinking about or leaning toward, long before a matter is ready to become public. He or she is included in preliminary policy decisions and trusted to be discrete about such information. The spokesperson is well informed of the agency head's activities and preferences, even if that information cannot be released to the media. The PIO is always kept in the know, if only for background purposes, and is trusted to use his or her best judgment and skills not to share such information inadvertently with the press. There are several indicators of credibility and knowledgeableness, measures used by reporters and outside observers to identify how close the spokesperson actually is to the head of the agency, and in turn, how 'in the know' the spokesperson is.

Access

How much personal and direct access does the spokesperson have to the boss? How frequently do they see each other? Can the PIO see the agency head on very short notice, leaving it up to the spokesperson to decide whether the topic is important enough to bring up, even interrupt a meeting?

Physical Proximity

How close is the PIO's office to that of the agency head? Is it within earshot, at least on the same floor? Or, is it outside hailing distance, even on a different floor of the agency's headquarters building? For example, during the Nixon administration, State Department spokesman Robert McCloskey had the title of Deputy Assistant Secretary for Public Affairs, clearly hierarchically a subordinate to the Assistant Secretary for Public Affairs. However, McCloskey's office was on the seventh floor of Foggy Bottom (a nickname for the State Department's headquarters in Washington, DC, in a low-lying neighborhood near the Potomac River that often was shrouded in fog), near the office of the Secretary, while McCloskey's bureaucratic superior, the Assistant Secretary, was one floor below with all the other assistant secretaries.

Invited to Daily Senior Staff Meetings

Is the spokesperson a regular attendee of the start-of-the-day senior staff meeting? Or perhaps only invited during media crises? While these sessions cover mostly routine business, they are vital for keeping the PIO aware of the diurnal agenda that all subunits of the agency are working on.

Participates in Policy Discussions

Besides the morning staff meeting, is the spokesperson routinely invited to major policy-making meetings? At a minimum, such participation should be as an observer, so that the PIO will be well informed about agency developments. Signals of stronger standing in the agency would be if at such meetings the spokesperson would be asked to evaluate the potential public relations and media relations aspects of the idea or invited to suggest revisions to the nascent policy to improve probable external reaction.

Title

In a bureaucracy, a person's power is not constant. Rather, it depends on exactly how much power the superior wants the staffer to have. The successful spokesperson needs to have the full backing and support of the agency head, which can only emanate from a personal relationship of trust. No formal title can obscure or overcome the lack of this personal relationship. Formal titles cannot confer power in organizations the way a personal relationship can.

Certainly, a formal title has some importance in any bureaucracy, especially in hierarchy-sensitive organizations, such as the military. The title can confer some amount of bureaucratic clout to the spokesperson when he or she engages in in-house politics. For example, there have been proposals that all federal cabinet departments have an assistant secretary for public affairs, a position that at the time of writing (2007) was in only half the departments. The argument is that the title strengthens the hand of the spokesperson in occasional battles with lower ranked program officials for releasing information. However, this emphasis on titles can be misguided. An assistant secretary is not automatically a powerful person, rather only as powerful as the secretary would want.

When a PIO has, and is also perceived to have, credibility and knowledge, then the journalists covering the agency can themselves develop a relationship of trust with the spokesperson. They would concede to themselves that even if they were to prowl the corridors of the agency headquarters building or pound the pavement for external sources they would not be likely to get any more key information than already provided by the spokesperson. When that perception is achieved, then the phrase used by all cautious PIOs, "to the best of my knowledge," becomes synonymous with "here's the maximum amount of information you'll be able to get one way or the other." (McCloskey used the phrase, "I am informed," to signal to the press the opposite meaning.)

The third factor that Burns listed for an effective PIO was responsiveness to the media. This means that the spokesperson can see the world through the eyes of the press corps and thereby know what reporters need to be able to do their jobs. Whether a former journalist or not, the PIO can identify enough with the journalistic profession to be understanding of the sine qua non of being a media correspondent. Some components of responsiveness overlap with the preceding discussion of credibility and knowledge, while others relate more to the technical, physical and professional needs of the news media to be able to do its work. Regarding the latter category, from journalists' perspective, the ideal PIO demonstrates responsiveness by being helpful and of assistance to them; understanding and acting on their different needs, interests, deadlines, timing, technical infrastructure and span of attention of the disparate press corps; and by not taking personally the adversarial tone of reporters' inquiries, not becoming defensive or insulted, and not carrying a grudge.

As soon as the media senses that the spokesperson is no longer fulfilling Burns' three factors of credibility, knowledge and responsiveness, they will then treat the PIO in an increasingly hostile manner and demand access to someone who *is* effective and has the power to fulfill Burns' typology. This usually means the head of the agency. Hence, the rational and pragmatic agency head does well to evaluate the consequences of keeping the agency's spokesperson uninformed and ineffective, for this inevitably leads to having to cope directly with the press which can be, among other things, an extremely time-consuming activity.

Conflicting Constituency: The Agency

Based on the preceding discussion, the PIO would simply need to have a self-identification with the press and work at accomplishing effectiveness from its perspective. Some press officers indeed have the philosophy that their role is exclusively to serve the press, even though they are on the organization's payroll.

However, the difficulties inherent in being an effective spokesperson immediately become clear when identifying the other constituencies with which the PIO must work. While reporters might be the most vocal publicly about what they want, the interests of internal stakeholders often conflict with, or are diametrically opposed to, those of the press corps. In-house constituencies include the agency head and the agency staff. They have their own conflicting interests that can lead them to wonder about the spokesperson, "Whose side are you on?" In this multi-player game, all participants are trying to decide who is friend and who is foe — for today's policy issue.

What the media wants to know might be precisely what the agency doesn't want it to know. Conversely, a press release extolling the successes of the agency or activities of its CEO might prompt a ho-hum reaction from the media. Reporters want to focus on what's new, controversial and unprecedented. They want to pry the secrets of the organization out of it. Simultaneously, public administrators often want to focus on such matters as the agency's performance, the continuity and expansion of its programs, indicators of accomplishment, and lowering expectations from modest experiments with alternate approaches. Journalists want to talk about people, whether victims or heroes, and who gets the credit or the blame. On the other hand, the agency wants to talk about the organization, its teamwork and cooperation. Reporters and bureaucrats can be ships passing in the night.

In some circumstances, an agency official might leak some confidential information on a proposed policy as a trial balloon or as a way to generate opposition. Whatever the motive, the leaking official has interests at odds with the agency's PIO. State Department spokesman Robert

McCloskey, in criticizing leaking, articulated the benefits of relying on the PIO to present policy developments. Official spokespersons, he wrote,

> work hard to prevent leaks, partly out of self-interest (because they want to be the recognized authoritative voice) but, more important, also because they believe that the public interest is best served on-the-record, where policy can gain the respect that comes with clarity and consistency. [65]

The inherent conflict-filled environment of the PIO had been identified early by researchers. Beginning in the 1960s, the academic and practitioner literature has been consistent and replete with efforts to describe the conflicting constituencies of the spokesperson, including (in chronological order):

- An intermediary and go-between who tries to balance conflicting needs and requirements [66]
- "In an administrative no-man's land … not quite trusted by either the public or the agency" [67]
- "A stepchild of the bureaucracy" [68]
- In a relationship with reporters as "allies and adversaries" simultaneously [69]
- A mediator between the media and the agency [70]
- On the margin, between journalist and agency [71]
- A boundary spanner [72]
- "In the bureaucracy but not truly of it" [73]
- "…expected to be all things to all people" [74]

Therefore, hypothetically, an alternative scenario to the PIO who chooses to concentrate solely on being effective with the media could be to resolve the issue of trust by focusing exclusively on loyalty to the agency head or to the agency as an organization. After all, the citizenry pays his or her salary. If selecting this path, the PIO is a promoter, advocate and publicist for the organization. But a spokesperson cannot simply resolve any dilemmas regarding a proper role by asserting loyalty solely to the organization whose name appears on the monthly pay stub (let alone deal with the concomitant loss of effectiveness with reporters). Since the PIO deals constantly with the press, it is inevitable that people within the agency view him or her as being tainted by this. When trying to respond to a request for information held by an agency staffer, the reflexive answer might be, "You and *your* press corps can go to hell."

These kinds of conflicts can arise in the daily work of a bureaucracy. The agency head, probably a political appointee, is there for only a few years and may have career ambitions that are different from the careerists in the agency. [75] Coverage that benefits the agency head may not be welcome by the civil servants. When the PIO successfully blunts the impact of negative coverage, the benefits might accrue only to the agency head, not to the careerists. The conflicting interests of the CEO and organizational staff can manifest themselves when the latter want to hold information closely and when asked by the PIO for information might respond, "*Why* do you want to know?" In those situations information is, indeed, power. Yet when the agency head has to intervene too often with staff to release information to the spokesperson, then the CEO's own political capital can become depleted, leading the agency head to wonder if the PIO is more trouble than he or she is worth.

Hence, the spokesperson must accept the inevitable tugs and pulls of being a person with a foot in two (or three) different camps, each sometimes the adversary of the other(s). This adversarial relationship is often described in combat metaphors, such as entering a battle zone, being on the firing line, or 'surviving' a media gaggle. These, of course, are extreme examples that occur only in some situations. They are useful because they help identify the important elements of the environment in which a PIO works, whether those factors are on the surface at any given moment or not. However, it is also important to emphasize that many of the daily contacts with the press on the outside and agency staff on the inside are routine and without conflicting pressures. Cooperation is more common in day-to-day interactions that the spokesperson has with the media, on one hand, and agency staff on the other.

Resolving Constituency Conflicts: PIO Professionalism

Given the built-in conflicts of public spokespersonship, the literature has identified some best practices for navigating the minefield located at the intersection of bureaucracy, democracy and the news media. Most important, one needs to transcend the parochial demands for loyalty, whether coming from the media, the agency head or the agency staff. A spokesperson can define his or her loyalty to the public interest and democracy itself. Using this as a permanent professional North Star, the actions and decisions of the PIO might in any particular instance be viewed as pro-media and anti-agency or the opposite.

How can a spokesperson's commitment to professional standards as the resolution to constituency conflicts be operationalized? Research has identified several practices that strengthen the professionalism of public agency spokespersons:

- Has full responsibility and authority for all public communications of the agency
- Has budget control over all information activities
- Views self as an agent of the public
- Depending on circumstances, is a direct source of information to the media or the facilitator of information, by connecting a reporter to the appropriate agency official
- Willingness to act as the conscience of the agency, an ever-present goad and reminder of the agency's public role and civic responsibilities
- Willingness to act as a gadfly, calling managerial attention to sources of actual and potential criticism affecting the agency
- Serves as a feedback loop from the public to the agency, making sure that important outside information is brought to the attention and consideration of the decision makers

A great deal of empirical research still needs to be done regarding the work of public information officers. As is clear from this synthesis, the literature has too few contemporary contributions, whether from academic or practitioner authors. In the meantime, until additional theoretical and applied research is published, the last word appropriately belongs to a statement of professional values developed by six practitioners in the 1990s. They zeroed in on the conflicting constituencies and pressures that face the public spokesperson. In that context, they suggested a professional's orientation as a way out of the morass of contradictory loyalties that occurs at the intersection of bureaucracy, democracy and the news media:

While they [PIOs] must satisfy their current masters, they also are duty bound to always keep the public interest, however defined, as their overriding obligation and concern. In the final analysis, allegiance to the national or public interest is the full measure of their performance and professionalism. [76]

Note: *Originally published in Lee, M., At the intersection of bureaucracy, democracy and the media: The effective agency spokesperson, in* Handbook of Bureaucracy, *2nd ed., Farazmand, A., Ed., Taylor & Francis, Boca Raton, FL, 2008, chap. 24.*

Endnotes

1. Friedman, T.L., *The World Is Flat: A Brief History of the Twenty-First Century*, updated and expanded ed., Farrar, Straus and Giroux, New York, 2006.
2. Blau, P.M. and Meyer, M.W., *Bureaucracy in Modern Society*, 3rd ed., McGraw-Hill, New York, 1993 [1987].
3. Roberts, A., *Blacked Out: Government Secrecy in the Information Age*, Cambridge University Press, New York, 2006.
4. Lee, M., Media relations and external communications during a disaster, in Pinkowski, J., Ed., *Disaster Management Handbook*, Taylor & Francis, Boca Raton, FL, 2008, chap. 19. (*Editor's Note:* See Chapter 17.)
5. Willis-Kistler, P., The public information professional increases public awareness and understanding, *Western City*, 79(9), 15, 2003.
6. Lee, M., Bureaucracy in the Hebrew Bible: A neglected source of public administration history, *Public Voices*, 5(1–2), 79, 2002.
7. Starr, P., *The Creation of the Media: Political Origins of Modern Communications*, Basic Books, New York, 2004, 395–402.
8. Grunig, J.E., Public relations management in government and business, in *Handbook of Administrative Communication*, Garnett, J.L. and Kouzmin, A., Eds., Marcel Dekker, New York, 1997, chap. 12. (*Editor's Note:* See Chapter 2.)
9. Crisis spokesman, *Newsweek*, 76(14), October 5, 1970, 106.
10. McCloskey, R.J., The care and handling of leaks, in *The Media and Foreign Policy*, Serfaty, S., Ed., St. Martin's, New York, 1990, 117, emphasis added.
11. Lee, M., Intersectoral differences in public affairs: The duty of public reporting in public administration, *Journal of Public Affairs*, 2(2), 33, 2002.
12. Lee, M., Public relations in public administration: A disappearing act in public administration education, *Public Relations Review*, 24, 509, 1998.
13. McCamy, J.L., *Government Publicity: Its Practice in Federal Administration*, University of Chicago Press, Chicago, 1939.
14. Mosher, W.E., Chairman, *Public Relations of Public Personnel Agencies: A Report Submitted to the Civil Service Assembly by the Committee on Public Relations of Public Personnel Agencies*, Civil Service Assembly of the United States and Canada, Chicago, 1941.
15. Pimlott, J.A.R., *Public Relations and American Democracy*, Kennikat, Port Washington, NY, 1972 [1951].
16. Lindsey, R., *This HIGH Name: Public Relations and the U.S. Marine Corps*, University of Wisconsin Press, Madison, 1956.
17. Rubin, B., *Public Relations and the Empire State: A Case Study of New York State Administration, 1943–1954*, Rutgers University Press, New Brunswick, NJ, 1958.
18. Rourke, F.E., *Secrecy and Publicity: Dilemmas of Democracy*, Johns Hopkins University Press, Baltimore, 1961.

19. Nimmo, D.D., *Newsgathering in Washington: A Study in Political Communication*, Atherton, New York, 1964.
20. Hiebert, R.E. and Spitzer, C.E., Eds., *The Voice of Government*, John Wiley, New York, 1968.
21. Dunn, D.D., *Public Officials and the Press*, Addison-Wesley, Reading, MA, 1969.
22. Chittick, W.O., *State Department, Press, and Pressure Groups: A Role Analysis*, Wiley-Interscience, New York, 1970.
23. Sigal, L.V., *Reporters and Officials: The Organization and Politics of Newsmaking*, D.C. Heath, Lexington, MA, 1973.
24. Helm, L.M. et al., Eds., *Informing the Public: A Public Affairs Handbook*, Longman, New York, 1981.
25. Schachter, H.L., *Public Agency Communication: Theory and Practice*, Nelson-Hall, Chicago, 1983.
26. Hess, S., *The Government/Press Connection: Press Officers and Their Offices*, Brookings Institution, Washington, DC, 1984.
27. Morgan, D., *The Flacks of Washington: Government Information and the Public Agenda*, Greenwood, New York, 1986.
28. Garnett, J.L., *Communicating for Results in Government: A Strategic Approach for Public Managers*, Jossey-Bass, San Francisco, 1992.
29. Graber, D.A., *The Power of Communication: Managing Information in Public Organizations*, CQ Press, Washington, DC, 2003.
30. Stephens, L.F., Professionalism of Army public affairs personnel, *Public Relations Review*, 7(2), 43, 1981.
31. Dunwoody, S. and Ryan, M., Public information persons as mediators between scientists and journalists, *Journalism Quarterly*, 60, 647, 1983.
32. Fletcher, J.E. and Soucy, P.E., Army public affairs officer as perceived by press and by military colleagues, *Journalism Quarterly*, 60, 93, 1983.
33. Swartz, J.E., On the margin: Between journalist and publicist, *Public Relations Review*, 9(3), 11, 1983.
34. Motschall, M. and Cao, L., An analysis of the public relations role of the police public information officer, *Police Quarterly*, 5, 152, 2002.
35. Lee, M., The agency spokesperson: Connecting public administration and the media, *Public Administration Quarterly*, 25, 101, 2001.
36. Lee, M., The image of the government flack: Movie depictions of public relations in public administration, *Public Relations Review*, 27, 297, 2001.
37. Lee, M., Reporters and bureaucrats: Public relations counter-strategies by public administrators in an era of media disinterest in government, *Public Relations Review*, 25, 451, 1999.
38. Lee, M., Public information in government organizations: A review and curriculum outline of external relations in public administration, *Public Administration and Management: An Interactive Journal*, 5, 183, 2000. http://www.pamij.com/5_4/5_4_4_pubinfo.pdf (accessed 2007) (*Editor's Note:* see Chapter 1.)
39. Barrett, E.W., *Truth Is Our Weapon*, Funk & Wagnalls, New York, 1953.
40. Berding, A., *Foreign Affairs and You! How American Foreign Policy Is Made and What It Means to You*, Doubleday, Garden City, NY, 1962.
41. Goulding, P.G., *Confirm or Deny: Informing the People on National Security*, Harper & Row, New York, 1970.
42. Mecklin, J., *Mission in Torment: An Intimate Account of the U.S. Role in Vietnam*, Doubleday, Garden City, NY, 1965.
43. Oldfield, B., *Never a Shot in Anger*, Duell, Sloan and Pearce, New York, 1956.
44. Daley, R., *Target Blue: An Insider's View of the N.Y.P.D.*, Dell, New York, 1978 [1973].
45. Krey, D., Ed., *Delivering the Message: A Resource Guide for Public Information Officials*, 2nd ed., California Association of Public Information Officials, Sacramento, 2000.
46. Williams-Thompson, R., *Was I Really Necessary?*, World's Press News, London, 1951.
47. McCloskey, op. cit., 109.

48. Arnette, S.U., Improving your agency's image, *Journal of Housing and Community Development*, 52(2), 38, 1995.
49. Denning, S., Toward an end to fear and loathing of the news: Making the media work for you, *The Agenda* (newsletter of the Section on Health and Human Services Administration of the American Society for Public Administration), 4(2), 4, 1997.
50. Ruda, S.J., The PIO: A position with infinite boundaries, *Fire Engineering*, 151(12), 61, 1998.
51. Gosnell, A.R., Maximizing media coverage, *Fire Engineering*, 153(5), 93, 2000.
52. Staszak, D., Media trends and the public information officer, *FBI Law Enforcement Bulletin*, 70(3), 10, 2001.
53. Willis-Kistler, op. cit.
54. Krohn, C.A., Confessions of a P.A.O., *Columbia Journalism Review*, 42(6), 35, 2004.
55. Édes, B.W., The role of government information officers, *Journal of Government Information*, 23, 455, 2000.
56. Proctor, C.B., First Marine Corps publicity bureau, *Recruiters' Bulletin*, 6(8), 5, 1920.
57. Manning, R.J., Journalism and foreign affairs, in Gross, G., Ed., *The Responsibility of the Press*, Fleet Publishing, New York, 1966, 184.
58. Carter, Hodding, III, *Whose News Is It?*, Kansas State University, Manhattan, 1984.
59. Zorthian, B., A press relations doctrine for the foreign service, *Foreign Service Journal*, 48(2), 20, 1971.
60. Courter, E.M., Putting the resident Pollyanna to work, *Public Welfare*, 32(2), 53, 1974.
61. Goldstein, S., 'Hi, I'm from government and I want to help you', *Public Relations Journal*, 37(10), 22, 1981.
62. Brown, D.H., Information officers and reporters: Friends or foes?, *Public Relations Review*, 2(2), 29, 1976.
63. Wise, K., Linking public relations processes and organizational effectiveness at a state health department, *Journal of Health and Human Services Administration*, 25, 497, 2002–2003.
64. Burns, N., Talking to the world about American foreign policy, *Harvard International Journal of Press/Politics*, 1(4), 10, 1996.
65. McCloskey, op. cit., 119.
66. Nimmo, op. cit., 24–25.
67. Moss, J.E., Future problems and prospects, in *The Voice of Government*, Hiebert, R.E. and Spitzer, C.E., Eds., John Wiley, New York, 1968, chap. 2, 30.
68. Cutlip, S.M., Public relations in the government, *Public Relations Review*, 2(2), 15, 1976.
69. Morgan, D., *The Capitol Press Corps: Newsman and the Governing of New York State*, Greenwood, Westport, CT, 1978, 34.
70. Dunwoody and Ryan, op. cit.
71. Swartz, op. cit.
72. Fletcher and Soucy, op. cit.
73. Hess, op. cit., 37.
74. Willis-Kistler, op. cit., 15.
75. Peters, B.G., *Comparing Public Bureaucracies: Problems of Theory and Method*, University of Alabama Press, Tuscaloosa, 1988, 147.
76. Avery, G.D. et al., Public affairs in the public sector, in *Practical Public Affairs in an Era of Change: A Communications Guide for Business, Government and College*, Dennis, L.B., Ed., Public Relations Society of America and University Press of America, Lanham, MD, 1996, chap. 13, 175.

Chapter 7

Media and the Bureaucracy in the United States

Behrooz Kalantari

Contents

Introduction

The main objective of this chapter is to highlight certain characteristics about the dominant entertainment media and their relation to society, culture, politics, and bureaucracy in the United States. Other considerations, including differences among various media outlets, citizens' own predispositions and perceptions on certain issues, and other factors which can influence the relations among the media, public, and political institutions are not given attention. Therefore, the focus of attention is on the role of media in society.

The role of media in society and its impact on politics has been an important topic in the study of political communication. It is crucial to concentrate on the ways and means by which the mass media use their capabilities and opportunities to influence the formation and implementation of public policy in the United States. Although it is difficult to assume a great degree of uniformity among different media networks, there are some characteristics which can be attributed to the most dominant media. Some members of the media are more even-handed than others in dissemination of information to the public (public radio and television fall within this category). The emphasis of this study is on entertainment media.

Due to the nature of the media and the mechanism of its operation, the most effective way for the media to affect the political decision-making process is through influencing the public. This is accomplished through altering and shaping the public's perception of politics or political organizations. Individual citizens usually receive their information about public affairs from two major sources: the mass media and interpersonal communication. However, the importance of media is prevalent because "the content of most politically relevant information, as well as of conversation about politics, is dependent on information obtained from the media." [1] Therefore, the media have become the single most important source for disseminating information in society.

It can be argued that the national media networks developed and evolved into an entity which independently shapes the reality inside and outside the United States. Although there is considerable difference among different communications media in their relationship with the environment and the public, they all share several important attributes. They create, demonstrate, and portray reality through "the use of symbols or interpretation of the most abstract form of concepts in society." [2]

Newspapers were the first mass medium to reach many people. They started during the 1830s and were followed by the mass circulation of national magazines by the turn of the 20th century. Shortly after that, in the beginning of the 20th century, movies reached the public; and in 1906 voice communication was sent through the radio signals and captured the imagination of millions of people. [3] Television effectively entered the race in the 1950s.

The most important attribute of the mass media is its ability to create images which contribute to better understanding of reality and enhancement of its scope. It can

> enlighten, comfort, uplift, and inspire. They are the basic coinage of all culture, the essential units on which civilization rests. Respect for words are two sides of the same coin, and that coin is the currency that will enable the media to make a decisive contribution to world culture. [4]

Studies on the behavior of American voters indicate that most voters receive their information on political events from the mass media. [5]

Among the communications media, studies show that "television news and newspapers are major sources of information" for the voters. [6] Particularly, television uses "verbal and nonverbal symbols, sound, and visual imagery" to communicate its messages. [7] The television medium has an advantage of being more accessible to the public than other media. Therefore, television has turned into the most powerful tool to influence and shape the people's attitude and beliefs concerning political and social events. [8]

Media and Creation of Images

Many criticisms have been launched against the media concerning the way they carry their functions as an institution which is trusted to convey political and social events in a value-free and neutral manner. The media have often been condemned for their bias in creating negative images of reality and even working against the social fabric of society. For example, the media are held responsible for the deterioration of family values in the United States.

As opposed to the ideal world, in which the media are only a medium of transmitting information, the media are not value-free agents; they play and advocate certain social and political values and priorities in society. [9] Regardless of its rise and fall in the public's perception, the media still remain the major force in shaping the attitudes and perceptions of the people and their political leaders. This is often accomplished through the exploitation and manipulation of the dominant political culture of society.

Significance of Political Culture

Political culture is not a new concept and has been used by ancient civilizations. According to Kincaid, "Greeks believed that...regimes are basically products of character, chance, and circumstance." [10] Modern usage of the concept is very common in the literature under different terms such as national character, tradition, ideological orientation, etc. [11] Some political science scholars refer to the concept of political culture as a "common belief" among the people in a community. They believe that it provides the citizens with a perception of their role in society and "how the government ought to be conducted and what it should try to do." [12] Gabriel Almond used the concept of "political culture" for the first time and believed that "every political system is embedded in a particular pattern of orientations to political action." [13] The collective orientations are referred to each society's political culture. The orientations can be cognitive (knowledge of the system), affective (feeling toward the system), and evaluative (opinion and judgment about the political system). [14]

Lucian Pye argues that "political systems are held together by a sense of collective identity and thus are based upon sentiments of loyalty which evoke parochial attachment to unique historical experience." [15] He perceives the political culture as a "subjective understanding on behalf of the individuals." [16] According to Hunt, political culture reflects "the values, expectations, and implicit rules that expressed and shaped collective intentions and actions." [17] Therefore, it can be argued that political culture as an important concept is deeply rooted in the human political history and plays a significant role in determining the success or failure of a polity. [18]

One of the main characteristics of political culture is its changing nature, which is due to the change of citizens' perception and expectations about government and politics. These changes in perception take place mostly through the exchange of information between the citizens and their environment. In this process of change and exchange of information, the mass media play the most prominent role in creating new images and expectations:

> The images conjured up and projected by the media help to shape and reshape the images held by the audiences. In other words, the public imagination is in part the imaginary experiences afforded by the popular media. [19]

Although the pattern of change is usually slow and differs from one society to another, acquisition of information is vital to the images that they hold and expectations that they develop concerning the proper role of their political systems. There is no preconceived agenda or code of conduct for interpreting the news or information by the media; they usually interpret the events according to their own personal beliefs and for the benefit of their sponsor organizations. Perhaps the profit motive is the strongest force that shapes the way information is processed and presented to the public. Therefore, in some instances, media can easily overlook the most important part of the news and present the public with a sensational view of the events. [20]

Media's Motives and Characteristics

People with different political orientations have blamed the media for its bias. [21] In reality, the underlying purpose of the media is to attract more audiences and increase its popularity and profit. It is widely believed that "the product of the news media, the content of which is not designed primarily to serve the purchaser ... is to please a third party — the advertiser." [22] On the other hand, it is important to realize that in production and presentation of political events many individuals are involved, which makes it a very complex process. This is due to the fact that almost everyone in the production process tries to mold and shape the reality according to his or her own value system and present it to the public. Therefore, a piece or information can be interpreted differently from one person to another, depending on who has been producing and reporting it. Consequently, the media are not neutral observers or reporters of the news and information, but participants in and interpreters of the information. Members of the media see themselves not only as representing the public interest but also as the determinant of what the public should hear, think, and decide concerning an issue, with their own interests in mind. [23]

Entertainment has become the major focus for the media by giving priority to those pieces of information which can amuse the public regardless of its quality. Therefore, in order to make the news more presentable to the public, they trivialize it and, in some instances, undermine important aspects of its content. [24] For example, analysis of the media's treatment of the 1996 presidential election indicate that they "trivialized and cheapened the campaign" and ignored the issues of the election. [25] Therefore, most of the mass media treated the presidential election as a race between opposing groups rather than how politics affects the public. [26] For the media, the most important aspect is "selectivity" of information to match their own standards of newsworthiness, which determines what kinds of information should be disseminated to the public. Members of media

> not only are more subjective in determining whether a story will make it into the news, but in deciding what sort of 'slant' it will be given and how much coverage it will receive. Even the wire services have succumbed, running (or not running) stories that, in the past, would have gotten the reporters and editors responsible fired. The worst examples of bias and selectivity are seen on network television programs, which have come to value entertainment more than the news. [27]

As a result, the public cannot grasp the magnitude of many important issues because it gets cluttered and wrapped up with unrelated but amusing information. This phenomenon is often called "entertainmentization" of information. Consequently, the "lines between politics, news, and entertainment" eventually get blurred and it is hard to separate news from entertainment. [28]

The other characteristic of the media which is often investigated is its negative and cynical approach in interpreting the issues and information. [29] In other words, mass media have a tendency to portray the negative aspects of reality and news and overlook the positive. The underlying reason for media's negativity is its obsession with its profit motive. Therefore, since negativity sells, there is no reason to be positive about things. [30] They see themselves as agents of public sensationalism and arousal rather than just neutral channels of information for the people. Media reporters want to make the public listen and pay attention by emotionalizing the issues in order to attract more customers, more advertisers, higher ratings, and higher profits.

In order for the media to justify its negativity and cynicism, it is important to find a villain on whom to put the blame and maximize its profit-making objective. The most logical choice and often used potential villains in society are public institutions and politics in general. Perhaps the underlying reason for media's choice is the United States' political culture, which is generally cynical about politics. Therefore, the media effectively seize the opportunity and materialize on that. For example, "media coverage of political corruption confirms public's belief in the fallibility of politicians." [31] However, for the media establishment, this negativity and cynicism is usually perceived differently. They call it "adversarial journalism," which is often praised by its practitioners and promoted through the profession. [32]

Setting the Public Agenda

It is difficult to investigate the media's ultimate effects on an individual citizen's behavior. However, as was indicated earlier, the media are an important source of political socialization in every society. Therefore, it has a powerful effect on people's perception of reality in evaluating and processing the relevant facts and information about political events. In practice, the popular or entertainment media constantly send messages that tell us "who we are — or ought to be — within the context of the larger community and what values and institutions we should adhere to, as members of that community." [33] In other words, the media set the public's agenda by determining what is important and what is not relevant to their everyday life. [34]

Perhaps the issue of agenda setting by the media is the most critical issue concerning the political decision-making process. In the political arena, there are many agendas that can be followed and "just as there are many more issues, concerns, and conflicts than government can address, there are many more potential stories that the media can report." [35] Media influences the political agenda by emphasizing certain issues while ignoring others, which gives prominence to some issues at the expense of others. [36] Therefore, policy makers have to watch for the negative effects of the media coverage on the public concerning their policies. [37] Moreover, they have to be cognizant of the fact that negative media coverage can also influence some undecided legislators as well. [38] Consequently, in the final analysis, the media determine the outcome of political decisions and the direction of political issues. [39]

Media, Politics, and Bureaucracy

The media's negativity and self-centered view of social and political events have caused profound distrust by the public toward their political institutions and have severely questioned their legitimacy. [40] The ultimate result of this popular distrust and doubt about government's conduct is a sense of national despair and lack of confidence in political institutions and political leaders, which in the final analysis are the guardians of public trust. [41]

In this court of public opinion in which media is the prosecutor, judge, and decision maker, politicians are in an awkward situation. On the one hand, they are part of the political establishment which has been blamed for all societal faults. On the other hand, they understand the power of the media and their need to influence and shape public opinion in their favor. [42] Therefore, they try to gain access to the media by making themselves presentable and disassociate themselves from political institutions and political establishment. [43] They project the image of being outsiders, and have nothing to do with real politics in Washington and political organizations. Consequently, politicians, in order to please the media and win their favor, instead of defending the government and politics which are constantly under attack, point at bureaucracy and other government institutions as real villains.

Although in the long run politicians themselves will be hurt for bashing the government, their immediate concern is getting as much popularity as they can and get elected to a political office. Ultimately, the bureaucracy and other institutions of government, with little influence and access to the media, get victimized and condemned without proper investigation of their operation. Ideally, no person or institution should be assumed guilty or innocent for its conduct, and there should be a balanced and fair treatment in reaching any verdict, but in reality this does not take place. [44] The main problem with the media game is to legitimize its position on issues which usually are not fully analyzed; ultimately, the public is left misinformed and misguided. Due to the constitutional guarantees and importance of freedom of expression in society, it is hard to conceive of much legal restriction on the media's behavior. However, consideration of imposition of some ethical standards on the media's conduct and behavior could be a major improvement. [45]

Conclusion

Everyone in the media and in the political arena is striving to influence the public for his own personal or organizational gain. Therefore, in this competitive game for the public's attention, the gatekeepers, who are the media persons, have the upper hand. They are able to influence the political culture, determine the life and career of politicians, change national priorities, and provide support for their choices. [46] Consequently, the media have gained a great deal of power in determining the outcome of political decisions and the public's perception of bureaucracy.

In this game of power and influence, the real losers are those who do not have adequate access to the media and are the targets of media attacks. The most obvious victim is the government in general, and the bureaucracy in particular. It only makes sense that the media, with such power and influence, be held responsible for their behavior in dealing with the public's political life.

It is hard to impose any specific value and responsibility on the media. However, there are standards of fairness and morality, which are compatible with the democratic values in society and can provide guidance in determining the behavior of the media. Considering the fact that 80% of the media is controlled by 50 major corporations in the United States, perhaps corporate values should loosen their grip on those institutions that are supposed to serve the public interest. [47]

Note: *Originally published in Kalantari, B., Media and the bureaucracy in the United States, in* Handbook of Comparative and Development Public Administration, *2nd ed., Farazmand, A., Ed., Marcel Dekker, New York, 2001, chap. 61.*

Endnotes

1. Silva, L., *Shaping Political Attitude: The Impact of Interpersonal Communication and Mass Media*, Sage, Thousand Oaks, CA, 1994, 4.
2. Edelman, M., *The Symbolic Use of Politics*, University of Illinois Press, Urbana, 1967, 5.
3. Swanson, D.L., Popular art as political communication, in *Politics in Familiar Contexts: Projecting Politics Through Popular Media*, Savage, R.L. and Nimmo, D.D., Eds., Ablex, Norwood, NJ, 1990.
4. Johnson, P., The media and truth: Is there a moral duty?, *Current*, December, 1992, 4.

5. Weaver, D.H., What voters learn from media, *Annals of the American Academy of Political and Social Science,* 546, 34, 1996.

6. Chaffee, S. and Frank, S., How Americans get political information: Print versus broadcast news, *Annals of the American Academy of Political and Social Science,* 546, 48, 1996.

7. Nimmo, D.D. and Combs, J.E., *Mediated Political Realities,* Longman, New York, 1990, 27.

8. Schwelien, M., CNN: Television for the global village, *World Press Review,* 37(12), 34, 1990.

9. Weaver, P., Newspaper news and television news, in *Television as a Social Force: New Approaches to TV Criticism,* Cater, D. and Adler, R., Eds., Praeger, New York, 1975, 81.

10. Kincaid, J., Ed., *Political Culture, Public Policy and American States,* Institute for the Study of Human Issues, Philadelphia, 1982, 2.

11. Martindale, D., The sociology of national character, *Annals of the American Academy of Political and Social Studies,* 370, 30, 1967.

12. Beer, S.H., The analysis of political system, in *Patterns of Government: The Major Political Systems of Europe,* 2nd ed., Beer, S.H. and Ulam, A.B., Eds., Random House, New York, 1962, part 1, 32.

13. Almond, G.A., Comparative political systems, *Journal of Politics,* 18, 396, 1956.

14. Parsons, T. et al., Some fundamental categories of the theory of action: A general statement, in *Toward a General Theory of Action,* Parsons, T. and Shills, E., Eds., Harvard University Press, Cambridge, MA, 1954, chap. 1, 13.

15. Pye, L.W. and Pye, M.W., *Asian Power and Politics: The Cultural Dimensions of Authority,* Belknap Press, Cambridge, MA, 1985, 125.

16. Pye, L.W., *Politics, Personality, and Nation Building: Burma's Search for Identity,* Yale University Press, New Haven, CT, 1962, 12.

17. Hunt, L., *Politics, Culture and Class in the French Revolution,* University of California Press, Berkeley, 1984, 610.

18. Almond, G.A., The intellectual history of the civic culture concept, in *Civic Culture Revisited,* Almond, G.A. and Verba, S., Eds., Little Brown, Boston, 1980, chap. 1.

19. Savage, R.L. and Nimmo, D.D., Eds., *Politics in Familiar Contexts: Projecting Politics Through Popular Media,* Ablex, Norwood, NJ, 1990, 6.

20. Jamieson, K., *Atlanta Constitution,* September 15, 1994, A13.

21. Newcomb, H. and Alley, R., Eds., *The Producer's Medium,* Oxford University Press, New York, 1983; Parenti, M., *Make-Believe Media,* St. Martin's, New York, 1992; Rusher, W., *The Coming Battle for the Media,* Morrow, New York, 1988; Robinson, M.J., Just how liberal is the news? 1980 revisited, *Public Opinion,* 7, 55, 1983.

22. Bagdikian, B.H., *The Media Monopoly,* 4th ed., Beacon, Boston, 1992, 207.

23. Lester, E., Manufactured silence and the politics of media research: A consideration of the propaganda model, *Journal of Communication Inquiry,* 16, 45, 1992.

24. Parenti, op. cit., 1992, 178.

25. Grossberger, L., Cutting on the bias, *Media Week,* 6(43), 46, 1996.

26. McCarthy, A., The media vs. the people: Please tell us what we need to know, *Commonweal,* 123(4), 8, 1996.

27. Novak, R., Political correctness has no place in the newsroom, *USA Today Magazine,* 123, 45, March 1995.

28. Dennis, E.E., *The Homestretch: New Politics, New Media, New Voters?,* Freedom Forum Media Studies Center, New York, 1992, 99–100.

29. Weaver, P.H., Selling the story (op ed column), *New York Times,* July 29, 1994, A27.

30. Robinson, M.J., op. cit.

31. Wines, M., Corruption lite, democracy's junk food, *New York Times,* January 12, 1997, E1, E5.

32. Ansolabehere, S., Behr, R., and Iyengar, S., *The Media Game: American Politics in the Television Age,* Macmillan, New York, 1983, 221.

33. Savage and Nimmo, op. cit., 1990, 3.

34. Page, B.I., Shapiro, R.Y., and Dempsey, P.R., What moves public opinion?, *American Political Science Review,* 81, 40, 1987.

35. Nelson, B.J., The agenda-setting function of the media: Child abuse, in *Media Power in Politics,* 2nd ed., Garber, D.A., Ed., CQ Press, Washington, DC, 1990, 84.

36. Trumbo, C., *Longitudinal Modeling of Public Issues: An Application of the Agenda-Setting Process to the Issue of Global Warming,* Journalism and Mass Communication Monograph No. 152, Association for Education in Journalism and Mass Communication, Columbia, SC, 1995, 50.

37. Adams, W.C., Marrying the functions: The importance of media relations in public affairs, *Public Relations Quarterly,* 40, 10, 1995.

38. Iyengar, S. and Kinder, D.R., *News That Matters: Television and American Opinion,* University of Chicago Press, Chicago, 1987.

39. Roberts, D.F. and Bachen, C.M., Mass communication effects, *Annual Review of Psychology,* 31, 350, 1981; Schmuhl, R., Putting a national spin on politics, *Chicago Tribune,* December 18, 1994, 4.

40. Robinson, M.J., Public affairs television and the growth of political malaise, *American Political Science Review,* 70, 425, 1976.

41. Lipset, S.M. and Schneider, W., *The Confidence Gap: Business, Labor, and Government in the Public Mind,* Free Press, New York, 1983.

42. Nimmo, D.D. and Combs, J.E., *The Political Pundits,* Praeger, New York, 1992.

43. Hattersley, R., Society that bites off less than it can chew, *Guardian,* 21(1), 3, 1994.

44. Davis, R., *The Press and American Politics: The New Mediator,* Longman, New York, 1992, 45.

45. Kennamer, J.D., Ed., *Public Opinion, the Press, and Public Policy,* Praeger, New York, 1992.

46. Linsky, M., *Impact: How the Press Affects Federal Policymaking,* W.W. Norton, New York, 1986.

47. Purenti, M., The myth of a liberal media, *Humanist,* 55(1), 7, 1995.

Chapter 8

Hacks, Flacks, and Spin Doctors Meet the Media: An Examination of the Congressional Press Secretary as a (Potential) Public Relations Professional

Edward J. Downes

Contents

Abstract: In this study, I examine the "theories in the heads" of the Congressional press secretaries, a group of professional communication managers, who, to date, have been neglected in the literature. The data — generated via a focus group, semi-structured interviews, and a survey — suggest that the press secretaries, as they mature in their position, gradually (a) become members of the dominant coalition, (b) have a relationship with the media based on "guarded honesty," and (c) tend to practice a press agentry model of public relations. I conclude by suggesting that these individuals, although they share characteristics of many public relations professionals, ought not be automatically labeled as such until additional studies (in which the press secretaries serve as units of analysis) are conducted.

"I have to consider, about every other day on my job, that I work for someone who's been elected to office — who the people have put a trust in. Moreover, that someone is working for a federal government that, for better or worse, is the government that has been established by the people and our Constitution. And, uhh, it's a weighty responsibility" (38-year-old male press secretary with six years of experience).

Introduction

Although a great deal of research has been devoted to understanding the motivations and practices of the media, especially in the political area, far fewer studies have examined those public relations professionals who supply information to them. In the study detailed in this chapter, I address that imbalance by developing lines of research and theory related to one such supplier: the Congressional press secretary.

Capitol Hill's press secretaries play a significant role in the shaping of America's messages and consequent public policies. In their role as proxy for individual Members of Congress, the press secretaries act as gatekeepers, determining what information to share with, and to hold from, the media; thus, they have command over news shared with the citizenry. [1,2]

The press secretaries, however, remain unexplored in the public relations literature. Although, for example, there is a body of public relations analyses in roles research and a growing body of knowledge in specialized areas such as issues management, there remains a dearth of studies examining the work of Capitol Hill's communication managers. This is despite the fact that the press secretaries have become invaluable assets to Members of Congress: Their numbers have grown exponentially in the last few decades, and their expertise is present in virtually every Congressional office. [3–6] In fact, the Congressional press secretary position is today a fully designated post on Capitol Hill.

Unlike those Members serving only 10 to 15 years ago, today's representative and senators are watched daily through televised proceedings of their debates, evaluated through call-in talk shows, and must respond (through their staffs) to thousands of "just sent" email notes. Hence, these national legislators are increasingly called to task for the choices they make, and they rely on their press secretaries' continuing guidance when constructing their responses and justifying their decisions to the media.

To date, only two published studies have used the Congressional press secretaries as units of analysis. [7,8] Collectively, these works total fewer than 50 pages, and their findings are largely descriptive. This is unfortunate because, if we are going to elevate the credibility of those public relations professionals associated with press secretary work in general, and Congressional press secretary work specifically, we must build a body of research examining the roles these individuals play. With this in mind, I asked three questions in this study:

1. Do the press secretaries serve in the Congressional office's inner circle of decision makers?
2. Do they view their relationships with the media as adversarial or as mutually beneficial?
3. Do they practice effective models of public relations?

These three inquiries examine collectively — for the first time — issues related to the professionalism of Capitol Hill's communication managers.

Literature Review

Hesse predicted, quite accurately, that, as the media became more intrusive and sophisticated, political public relations, as an occupation, would take on significantly more importance. In regard to political press secretaries, he argued that as "legislators turn their attention to the business of drafting legislation, the business of communication becomes the main concern of the staff or communication consultant, and the legislators normally abide by the 'communication strategies' designed by [these] experts." [9] The "experts" to whom Hesse referred are, today, the press secretaries.

Studies made in the roughly 20 years since Hesse's work have supported his belief. Numerous analyses, for example, have described how information provided to the media by individuals such as the press secretaries influences political decisions. [10–18] Furthermore, many works in this category speak directly to the ability of a communication manager to frame issues in a manner most suitable to the legislator — a skill pertinent for the Congressional press secretary. Shapiro and Williams, and Iorio and Huxman, for example, pointed out the impact framing has had on public perceptions, [19,20] and Dorman explored the effects of framing on media exposure and opinion change. [21] In addition, the literature has described how media images created by information suppliers such as the press secretaries impact political decisions. Graber, for example, pointed out the importance visuals have on viewers, [22,23] and Wicks examined the effects of media images on information-processing strategies. [24]

This press-politics-public relations nexus is particularly well illustrated in Graber's edited book, *Media Power in Politics*, which illustrates the codependent partnership between the press and the politician. [25] Miller's essay, "Reporters and Congressmen: Living in Symbiosis," for instance, sheds light on this symbiotic relationship by pointing out that the Members of Congress and the reporters who cover them share a unique partnership; namely, that reporters are eager to receive tips from Members on provocative news stories, which, in turn, allow the reporters to uncover news of a sensational or scandalous nature. [26] Other essays in Graber's work universally stress the imperative partnership, for which the press secretary serves as ever-present liaison, between the politician and the press.

Perhaps no theoretical consideration more clearly illustrates the symbiotic partnership between a press secretary (as information supplier) and a reporter (as information receiver) than the little-explored notion of agenda subsidies. This view suggests that those with the potential to subsidize the media (by providing press releases, speech transcripts, access to the decision makers such as a Member of Congress, etc.) with information have the power to influence the media's agenda. Turk argued that institutions seek, through their symbiotic relationships with the media, to use the press as liaisons between themselves and key constituencies (or publics). [27] Gandy argued that news costs less when subsidies are provided. [28] Hence, those Members of Congress with the ability, through the relationship that their press secretaries build with the media, to provide subsidies to the media increase the chances that the messages inherent in those subsidies will influence the news that reaches the Congressional district's voters.

Furthermore, the agenda subsidies' literature implies that the job of the press secretary (i.e., the information "subsidizer") is to successfully subsidize the media. When done effectively, the stories, views, and policy positions espoused by the Member the press secretary represents are printed or broadcast. The result is a healthy symbiotic relationship between the press secretary and the media.

What characterizes a healthy symbiotic relationship? That is, what does the literature suggest are the elements of a sound, even robust, partnership between the press secretary and the reporters with whom he or she works? J. E. Grunig's *Excellence in Public Relations and Communication Management* provided the answer. In the over 600-page *Excellence Study* — a definitive work in the public relations literature — are suggested new paradigms for analyzing the field. The book lists the characteristics of excellent public relations programs and the types of communication systems inherent to such programs. To illustrate the assertions, he suggested that four distinct models of public relations are practiced within the United States: the press agentry model, the public information model, the two-way asymmetrical model, and the two-way symmetrical model.

> The press agentry model applies when a communication program strives for favorable publicity, especially in the mass media. A program based on the public information model uses "journalists in residence" ... to disseminate relatively objective information through the mass media and controlled media. ... Both press agentry and public information are one-way models of public relations. ... The third model, the two-way asymmetrical model, is a more sophisticated approach in that it uses research to develop messages that are most likely to persuade strategic publics to behave as the organization wants. ... Two-way symmetrical describes a model of public relations that is based on research and that uses communication to manage conflict and improve understanding with strategic publics. [29]

Grunig argued further that only one model of the four — the two-way symmetrical model — was found in organizations that practiced excellent public relations. [30]

How would a Congressional press secretary, through a symbiotic relationship shared with a reporter, practice the two-way symmetrical model? First, the press secretary would seek to provide a balance between his or her Congressional office and its environment by promoting accuracy and truth in information flow with reporters. Second, the press secretary would use research when formulating truthful communication objectives. Finally, the press secretary would stress bargaining and negotiation with the media to bring symbiotic changes in knowledge, attitudes, and beliefs.

What would a press secretary practicing the two-way symmetrical model avoid doing? First, the press secretary would not attempt to give only partial truths, as someone practicing the press agentry model might. Second, the press secretary would not rely on propaganda, as someone practicing a public information model might. Finally, the press secretary would not manipulate the media via focused research attempts, as someone practicing the one-way asymmetrical model might.

Thus, the symbiotic relationship between the press secretary and the media would be most healthy (i.e., most effective) if the press secretary were to practice the two-way symmetrical model. By sincerely conversing with the media via the practice of the two-way model, reporters would benefit by receiving straightforward information, and the Congressional office would benefit by being able to operate with greater autonomy and freedom while, simultaneously, earning the trust and confidence of this important public. Thus, the aforementioned healthy symbiotic relationship between the press secretary and the media would be one built from the characteristics inherent in the two-way symmetrical model.

A Place in the Congressional Office's Dominant Coalition

In addition to providing information on the notion of a two-way symmetrical model, Grunig's work offers a second component that also sheds light on the symbiotic nature of the press secretary and the reporter. [31] Here, the suggestion is that an organization's culture — such as the culture of a Congressional office — is heavily influenced by what Thompson referred to as the "dominant coalition." [32] To illustrate such a coalition — which exists in some form in the vast majority of organizations — would be comprised of the top decision makers, policy makers, or inner circle within an organization. The choice as to whether to practice the two-way symmetrical (or some other) model of communication is determined by this coalition. Thus, if the press secretary is a member of his or her office's dominant coalition, he or she will have a substantially better chance of determining the Congressional office's policies and direction and, hence, that office's model of public relations.

Although the Congressional office's dominant coalition is called on to deal with a handful of publics — interest groups, federal agencies, office staff, Congressional coalitions, and others — clearly, among the most strategic would be that public on which the press secretary concentrates his or her activities: the media. In fact, the media are essential to communications with all other publics. Stories about responses to a group of organized constituents (such as an anti-death-penalty interest group), stories about a single federal agency's policy (such as the decision to promote "work fare" over welfare), stories about a Member's staff (such as those examining the degree to which that staff is diverse), or stories about a Member's work on a Congressional coalition (such as the Black Caucus) are disseminated to the media and, then, to the Member's half-million constituents from the symbiotic base the press secretary has built with reporters.

References throughout the *Excellence Study* reinforce the notion that, if an organization's public relations efforts are represented in its dominant coalition, that organization holds a stronger likelihood of being excellent. In turn, the mutually beneficial relationships between the individual overseeing media relations (i.e., the press secretary) and the media with whom that individual works would share what I have described as a healthy symbiotic relationship.

Thus, a healthy symbiotic base is directly related to the practice of the two-way symmetrical model, and the two-way symmetrical model is directly related to the world view of the Congressional office's dominant coalition.

Method: The Qualitative Data

In this study, I utilized a mixed-method approach, in which focus group and interview data built the foundation from which a survey instrument was constructed.

The focus group data were gathered in April 1994 when my research partner [33] and I brought together a sample of eight current and former Congressional press secretaries and conducted a group interview in Alexandria, Virginia. Collectively, the participants in the theoretical sample represented approximately 75 years of experience as Capitol Hill press secretaries. They worked for both Republicans and Democrats and represented a geographically diverse set of states and Congressional districts. Three of the eight worked for high-profile Members with extensive national exposure, and I worked for an individual who was in the House leadership at the time. Respondents were perceptive, voluble, and articulate.

The interview data were gathered in May 1996 through 17 one-on-one interviews with practicing press secretaries; they were conducted in House Congressional offices. The interview script, developed from an analysis of the focus group data, was significantly more structured (i.e., less exploratory) than the one used for the focus group. In turn, a handful of themes developed from the focus group were refined and further explored via the interviews.

The collection and analysis of these focus group and interview datasets is rooted in a phenomenological paradigm that holds that reality (here, the reality of the press secretaries) is socially constructed through individual or collective definitions of the situations under investigation. [34] It supports the preposition that the press secretaries are the best source to tell the story of "what's really going on" while simultaneously opening the door for serendipitous insights. The affirmatives that emerged from these data sets provided rich insights into the feelings, personal experiences, empathies, emotions, intuitions, subjective judgments, imaginations, and diverse forms of creativity [35] held by the press secretaries; that is, they allowed, for the first time, an exploration of how these individuals see their world — to discover and probe untapped processes, categories, and topologies as dictated by the press secretaries — to, in essence, get closer to them than anyone had before. Every effort was made when compiling the results to allow the press secretaries, through their own words, to tell their story. Who better could do so?

Finally, a survey instrument was built from the contextual and clarifying data generated by the study's qualitative (i.e., focus group and interview) findings. The instrument's Likert scale ratings ranged from 1 (strongly agree) to 5 (strongly disagree).

The questionnaires were distributed, by hand, door-to-door, to the 435 Member offices and to the five delegate offices. [36] I approached the receptionist in each, requested the press secretary's name, and on the envelope containing a cover letter, questionnaire, and self-addressed return envelope, wrote each potential respondent a handwritten note requesting his or her participation in the research. When possible, the note contained a sentence relevant to the district the office represented (e.g., "I recently visited your state and especially enjoyed ...," "My sister lives in ...," "I attended school at ...," etc.) A research assistant mapped our route through the House of Representatives' three office buildings and compiled an up-to-date listing of press secretaries' names. In the week following, I made approximately 320 follow-up phone calls and faxes. The purpose was to thank those press secretaries who may have already returned their questionnaire and to encourage those who had not filled out the questionnaire to do so.

A total of 440 questionnaires were distributed: one to each of the House's 435 Representatives' offices and one to each of its five Delegate offices. Within ten days of their distribution, 142 had been completed and returned; within 25 days, 175. Approximately 20 press secretaries informed me in person or over the phone that their office had a policy against responding to surveys, and people in two additional offices wrote personal notes saying the same. Interest groups had, with increased frequency, been contacting the press secretaries and asking them to respond to bogus or slanted surveys. Because of the onslaught of requests to participate in surveys, this policy was implemented in many offices. Thus, although approximately 25 offices informed me that they had a policy against participating in surveys, there is a strong likelihood that perhaps another 25 did not return completed questionnaires for the same reason. Also, individuals in three offices told me that, at present, they had a vacancy in their press secretary position and, thus, did not have an individual to fill out the questionnaire. Finally, I received one letter from a Congressman informing me that he, not a press secretary, handled all media matters.

In total, 204 offices (46%) contacted me after receiving my questionnaire, 175 (40%) of which completed it. The response rate of this study, relative to others that have used a self-administered questionnaire, was significantly higher. [37–39] Of these three previous studies, the Bruce and Downes analysis had collected the most responses — 132 (30%) — which is 43 fewer than this study. All survey data were keyed into a statistical package within two weeks of their receipt. When frequencies were examined, the qualitative data's themes, on which the survey instrument's questions were built, were generally supported.

Results

The results spoke to two meaningful notions generated from the *Excellence Study*. The first spoke to notions of the dominant coalition as they related to the press secretaries' place in the Congressional office; the second, to the press secretaries relationships' with the media as measured by the models of public relations practiced.

The Press Secretaries and Their Role in the Dominant Coalition

Although younger press secretaries, such as those who have recently graduated from college, are occasionally overseen in their activities by a more senior staff member (such as the Chief of Staff), the more mature ones find themselves in the Congressional office's inner circle. One accomplished press secretary, with 11 years of press secretary and media experience told me how he gets "deeply involved" in his Congressional office's legislative strategies and in building campaigns to dissuade public opinion: "I mean, you take for granted what you know how to do."

Another experienced respondent indicated he simply could not do his job if he were not part of the office's "decision making body":

> Don't have me in for the splashdown if I'm not in for the takeoff. I can't do my job that way. ... I'm not some nosy person who has to know everything that's going on, but I need to be in at the ground level — and I told the Senator this during my second interview with him. I said: "I'm just curious how you view your press operation. Is it a part of your shop or something you think of later?" And the Senator said: "I very much feel our press operation is an integral part of the job."

> I have to be in every meeting [laughs] — you know, like I don't have enough time in the day to get everything done because he [the Senator] has made me part of the senior staff! ... I have a beeper, and he [the Senator] has my home number. But it's important

to him and he sees [the press operation] as a vital part of what he does to communicate his message. ... For example, we [the respondent, Chief of Staff, Legislative Director, and the Director of State Operations] sat down in January and plotted out what [the Senator's] going to do this next year.

Another long-term press secretary — even though his job remains one dedicated primarily to the Member's press duties — is also involved with communications efforts for his boss's committee work and with several high-visibility projects in the district. He said: "The press role I often find myself in is one more toward determining policy."

As press secretaries gained experience in their craft or gained communication management experience off Capitol Hill (often as newspaper reporters, sometimes as public relations practitioners, occasionally in the broadcast media), they moved toward involvement in policy discussions and strategic communication planning of that office. Furthermore, these experienced press secretaries are also less nervous to speak on the record and are given more leeway in what they say to the media. [40] Thus, the qualitative data suggested that more experienced press secretaries were more inclined to be members of the Congressional office's dominant coalitions.

Two indexes were developed as a means to quantify questions related to the press secretaries' place as members of the dominant coalition:

- The first (the Dominant Coalition Index — General) tested the hypothesis (H), suggested by the qualitative data, that "the press secretaries, as they mature in their positions, are more inclined to be part of the dominant coalition."
- The second (the Dominant Coalition Index — Campaign) tested the H, also suggested by the qualitative data, that "the press secretaries, as they mature in their position, are more involved in designing campaign strategies."

To test the expected but unconfirmed relationships inherent in these two Hs, the survey contained the following questions for which respondents were asked to indicate their level of agreement on a scale from 1 (strongly agree) to 5 (strongly disagree).

Dominant Coalition Index — General

H1: The press secretaries, as they mature in their position, are more inclined to be a part of the dominant coalition.

Questions:
1. "I consistently and often advise the Member on how our communication strategies fit in with our office's overall strategies — legislative and otherwise" (M = 2.1).
2. "When the Member and Chief of Staff/AA [Administrative Assistant] hold policy-related meetings, I am always a part of those" (M = 2.3).
3. "While I am primarily a press secretary, I am also involved with a series of non-media-related special projects and/or take a good chunk of time planning our legislative strategy" (M = 2.3).

Index: Dominant Coalition — General
Index Mean: 2.20
Alpha: .63

Discussion: The index mean of 2.20 indicates that most press secretaries agree that they are part of their offices' dominant coalition. In addition, the alpha appears to be strong enough (i.e., it is only .02 short of reaching the conservatively acceptable .65 level) to hold its own. The H, however, suggested not only that the respondents were members of the dominant coalition but also that those press secretaries who had matured in their position were more inclined to be members of that coalition. Therefore, a correlation matrix was developed to test the research question.

The separate variable, "years in current position," was correlated with this index (p = .001). This datum strongly supports the notion that the longer a press secretary has served in a Member's office, the more likely it is that the individual is part of the office's dominant coalition. The somewhat wide standard deviation of 1.13, however, indicates that, although a fair number of press secretaries see themselves as definite members of the dominant coalition, a fair number also do not.

Dominant Coalition Index — Campaign

H2: The press secretaries, as they mature in their position, are more involved in designing campaign strategies.

Questions:
1. "I am intricately involved, with the campaign staff, in planning our reelection strategy" (M = 3.1).
2. "As the campaign gets closer I am consulted, with increased frequency, on strategies related to it" (M = 3.6).
3. "At reelection time, my 'gears switch' toward the campaign strategy and away from my normal activities" (M = 3.5).

Index: Dominant Coalition — Campaign
Index Mean: 3.40
Alpha: .65

Discussion: Here, the index mean of 3.40 suggests that the majority of press secretaries do not play a role in organizing the Member's campaign. A handful of respondents informed me that the reason they were not allowed to work on the campaign was because funding for campaign staff and Capitol Hill staff must, by law, remain separate. This is not to suggest, however, that advising or otherwise being involved with a campaign — even if serving full-time on the Member's staff — is in itself illegal. Rather, the H suggested that those press secretaries who had matured in their position were more likely to be involved in the campaign.

To explore this further, a separate variable, "years in current position," was correlated with the index just described (p = .03). This datum, as did the datum in the previous question, suggests that, as the press secretaries mature, they are more involved in designing campaign strategies.

Most interesting, however, is the finding generated when Dominant Coalition Index — General results are compared with the Dominant Coalition Index — Campaign results. Here, besides discovering that both met conservatively acceptable alpha levels (and thus could be used with confidence in future surveys), the data strongly suggest that those press secretaries who are members of the office's dominant coalition are also involved with designing campaign strategies.

The Press Secretaries and the Models of Public Relations Practiced

Although the press secretaries are conciliatory and universally respectful toward the wishes of the Member for whom they work, the same does not appear to hold true in their relationships with the media. One press secretary described these relationships as "confrontational"; another, as "antagonistic." When asked how the media would describe them, one participant during the focus group responded: "as flacks, barriers, the ones that won't let you get to the Member." Another simply said: "as spin doctors."

One focus group participant suggested a possible explanation for the group's inimical relationships with the media: "One of the problems with the press nowadays is they're always looking [for a scandal]; too many want to be like Bob Woodward. ... They're always writing the worst things instead of writing the good stories."

Although several respondents stressed that they needed the media to communicate with constituents, one forcefully said that "they [the media] need us too — don't forget that!" The focus group and survey data from the Bruce and Downes study support this adversarial theme. [41] For example, two thirds of the adjectives the press secretaries chose to describe how the media perceive them were negative ones, such as *hack*, *flack*, and *spin doctor*. [42]

As the data from the follow-up interviews came in, however, they suggested my initial perception (which indicated the press secretaries have an adversarial relationship with the media) should be revisited. Although adversarial might be a correct interpretation for some, a more accurate adjective, based on the follow-up interview data, would be *managed*. That is, the press secretaries manage the media with whom they work, and they do so not with a mean-spirited attitude toward the press but, rather, with the recognition that the media, like they, have "a job to do." The following interview excerpt highlights this recognition:

> Interviewer: How would you describe your relationship with the media? Is it adversarial, symbiotic, mutually beneficial...?
>
> Respondent: I call the press [when they get a story wrong] and sometimes that's tense, but the reporter understands as well as I do that it can't remain a problem. We get over it. ... I've had some confrontations, but for the most part I've had some really good experiences. ... I really personally like the reporters.
>
> Interviewer: You like the reporters?
>
> Respondent: Yeah. ... Maybe I'm just naive, but I understand that it's not personal. They're doing their job and you have to play it that way.

To examine whether these relationships were best described as adversarial — or would be better viewed as ones based on mutual respect — two indexes (an Adversarial Index and a Mutual Respect Index) were developed.

Adversarial Index

H3: The press secretary and the media have an adversarial relationship.

Questions:
1. "The media are interested in 'worst-case scenarios' — they want scandal and conflict, not truth and facts" (M = 2.68).
2. "To reporters, I'm viewed largely as a 'hack,' 'flack,' or 'spin doctor'" (M = 3.45).
3. "The media see me not as a conduit but as an obstacle between the Member and them" (M = 4.01).

Index: Adversarial
Index Mean: 3.39
Alpha: .37

Discussion: Here, the survey data suggested that the average press secretary did not agree that he or she had an adversarial relationship with the media; yet, much of my qualitative data suggested just the opposite. To explore this disparity, I revisited the sources from the qualitative data that suggested the questions for this index: Questions 1 and 3 were taken directly from notions with which most press secretaries heartily agreed, and the terms used in Question 2 (hack, flack, and spin doctor) paralleled those provided by two thirds of respondents in the Bruce and Downes study. [43]

I was baffled — until I reexamined the survey instrument utilized in the Bruce and Downes study [44] — and was reminded that press secretaries responded to an open-ended question, and thus, the press secretaries themselves chose those terms (used as the foundation for these three questions) to describe how they were perceived. This open-ended question gave them the opportunity to both label themselves as such or to temper the two-thirds majority of negative terms they provided with some positive ones as well. This study's survey instrument, however, did not utilize an open-ended question to explore the concept of an adversarial relationship with the media. Rather, it utilized a Likert scale and, thus, presented to respondents terms I seemed to have chosen. It may have appeared to the respondents, therefore, that I (the researcher) had imposed a label such as "hacks, flacks, and spin doctors" on them (without any positive terms). Similarly, it may have appeared that I (the researcher) viewed them as obstacles and not as conduits. [45] The respondents, quite simply, may not have wanted to be labeled (by me) with such terms. Thus, they disagreed with the emphases of the index's three questions. [46] Finally, although the data from the responses to the three individual questions that relate to this H may be instructive, the alpha alone is not strong enough to be acceptable.

Mutual Respect Index

H4: The press secretaries and media share a mutual respect.

Questions:
1. "In general, I respect the reporters with whom I work" (M = 2.09).
2. "In general, the reporters with whom I work respect me" (M = 2.04).
3. "The media know I have job to do; I know they have a job to do and, with that mutual recognition, we get along" (M = 1.86).

Index: Mutual Respect
Index Mean: 2.00
Alpha: .51

Discussion: The means between Questions 1 and 2 are almost identical. This suggests that the press secretaries are as respectful of the media as they perceive the media are respectful of them — and would, therefore, describe a relationship with the media as one based on mutual respect rather than one described as adversarial. The question remains, however, why Question 1 showed a slightly higher level of agreement than the two previous questions.

Perhaps the essential notion in Question 3 is that of mutuality. The press secretaries may believe that a mutual understanding between them and the media — an understanding that will allow both parties (through their symbiotic relationships) to meet their first priority of getting the job done — is of the highest importance, regardless of considerations of the respect one group holds for the other.

When the Adversarial Index was compared to the Mutual Respect Index, the latter showed a lower index mean (2.00) than the former (3.39). These data suggest that the press secretaries view their relationships with the media as ones based on mutual respect significantly more than as ones based on adversarial exchanges.

To examine more fully the concept of mutual respect, I probed the notion of one hand (the press secretary's) washing the other (the reporter's). The qualitative data strongly supported this notion, indicating, for example, that if a press secretary helped a reporter at one point, it would not be uncommon for the reporter, at a later date, to help out the press secretary. To illustrate, one respondent summarized how, once the reporter's constraints are recognized, it can prove beneficial for the press secretary if he or she can proactively provide information to a member of the media:

> You anticipate the press's needs. Be one step ahead and they are very grateful. These people [the media] work on a crazy deadline that breathes down their necks. ... If the reporter doesn't have access, he's not going to get anywhere — and I understand that so I try and accommodate it. ... I think empathy goes a long way. ... So we stay in touch — sometimes I call them just to say "Hey, we've got this potential story coming up." ... You always want to be as hospitable as you can. I consider myself as a conduit of information — and it goes both ways.

One former press secretary, reinforcing the same theme, shared this illustrative quote:

> There was one particular reporter who I had a great relationship with and I knew that anything that I told him, off-record, deep-background was not going to get attributed or come back to our office. And I would call him sometimes and I would tell him: "Hey, just a heads up; I know you're very interested in this one issue and these particular Members aren't going to vote for it because of thus-and-such. ..." It kind of angled him and gave him a story.

Involuntary paybacks for favors or tips generated by the press secretary and provided to a reporter may enhance the relationship between the press secretary and the media with whom he or she deals most often. One long-term Democrat described these informal you-wash-my-hand-I'll-wash-yours arrangements as characteristic of the mutually beneficial relationship he shares with the media:

> I don't wait for them [the press] to come to me. I pass on a lot of things to them — especially things that don't involve my boss ... that gives them a leg up on the competition and they, in turn, feel favorably disposed to me.

I think my actions, in many instances, have saved [my boss] from bad publicity. ... There have, for example, been instances when the press could have very easily mentioned my boss in a bad light but left her out of the stories. I think the service that I provide, giving them tips on other stories, pays dividends. Therefore, I keep them informed about what's going on. Because of this relationship ... they might have the chance, down the road, to give a favorable mention to the Congresswoman, so they'll call her up, they'll ask for a quote. ...

It's just understood in the relationship between press secretaries and the media that if you can help them, they may help you. ... [It's] kind of a symbiotic relationship.

While examining these results, it is paramount to remember that a one-hand-washes-the-other relationship (or one described as mutually beneficial or symbiotic) is not the same as a relationship between friends. To this point, several respondents stressed that, although their relationships with reporters may be cordial, they were generally not friendly. To illustrate, one relatively new press secretary said:

While you want to maintain a relationship, at the same time you pretty much can't count on the media to be your friend — especially if you're a Republican, conservative, and freshman. [47] ... It's a working relationship — they're never going to be your friend.

The cordial nature of the relationship between press secretary and reporter, however, thrives on truths shared between parties. To illustrate, the press secretaries were asked: "If you were teaching a group of undergraduates 'Media Relations 101' from the perspective of a Congressional press secretary, what would you tell them?" These individuals stressed, first and foremost, that a press secretary must never lie to a reporter. Over a dozen respondents believed this principle to be paramount. Four illustrative quotations follow:

- You just simply cannot lie to a reporter. I've seen people do it for short-term gain, and it turns out to be a disaster. You never win a reporter's trust again.
- Look, you're only as good as your last phone call. ... The first rule that any press secretary has to learn, regardless, is two words: never lie. Period.
- Be honest; be direct; never be deceitful or never lie to a reporter.
- First rule: never lie. If you lie and you're caught, you're done — and you're going to get caught. The second rule follows: never be afraid to say, "I don't know, I'll have to get back to you." If you aren't one-hundred percent sure, don't say it because either you're going to be perceived as a liar, or you're going to be perceived as a person who has to be fact-checked. ... Reporters develop certain sources and they'll trust you or they won't.

However, although these individuals were adamantly against lying, they did not consider telling an untruth to be the same as "putting one's best side forward," or "being sure the reporter knows our side of the story," or answering questions asked without volunteering additional information that could put the Member in a bad light. Thus, the press secretaries are honest with reporters and, to an equal degree, guarded with them.

Several, for example, stressed that it was the reporter's responsibility not only to ask relevant questions but to ask the right relevant questions. As one self-assured respondent noted: "We control a great deal of information. If we don't want people to know something, we don't tell them unless the reporter knows what to ask." An experienced press secretary, during a discussion of how much information she shared, said: "Some reporters are better than others at asking point-blank questions — others just kind of skim the surface." Her implication, like those of her colleagues, was that the press secretary provides truthful information that is intended to benefit the Member he or she serves — and, often, provides nothing additional. Hence, these individuals are careful not to expand beyond what the reporters asks — thus, the guarded honesty theme.

One respondent, in discussing the notion of guarded honesty, addressed the concept of spinning. He first defined it: "You've heard the term 'spin.' That means that right from the start we're able to put a certain angle on what we say — to push it one way or another." He then described how a reporter might react to his spin:

> I mean most reporters do their job fairly well, but a lot of reporters will take a couple sources that they hear quite often and they trust them — so they'll take whatever angle you put on it and that's the angle they'll base their stories on.

Although this interviewee used the term *spin* to describe what he does, several respondents expressed discomfort with the word — it put a bad taste in their mouths. However, seconds after noting this discomfort, they offered accounts of what they do — and, interestingly, these met the previous respondent's description of a spin. One such example follows. In the first two sentences, the respondent indicates that he does not think of himself as someone who spins messages. The later sentences, however, describe someone who meets the previous respondent's description of an individual who spins a message, that is, an individual who puts the best angle on a story without regard for objectivity or balance:

> The trait I hate is when they call me a "spinner." ... I don't think of myself as a spinner. I mean, you know, I certainly sell a story to a reporter but I'm not out there trying to put some funky aspect to it. The Congressman I work for is a straight shooter and, as his press secretary, I have to basically mirror his ideology. ... So I think of myself more as a provider of factual information — as a provider of the Congressman's view to the press.

Another press secretary discussed the same discomfort with the concept of spinning and, as was the pattern, first said she did not spin, then noted that she did:

> I can't try to spin reporters in some direction. ... I have to level with them and I have to show them the numbers and I have to tell them how it is. Now, having said that, we do try to put a positive spin on certain things we do.

Later, in discussing the same topic, she said: "You try to put a positive approach on what you're doing and downplay the other guy, and criticize the other guy. ... You try to put your best foot forward — that's what we all try to do up here."

To explore the concept of spin as it relates to what the press secretaries described as putting the best angle on a story, an index was developed and incorporated into the questionnaire that examined the notion of spin.

Spin Index

H5: The press secretary, through spinning a story, puts his or her Member's point of view before any other.

Questions:
1. "To 'spin' a story means I put the Member's best foot forward" (M = 1.83).
2. "'Spinning' isn't lying at all; rather, it's a means to get my Member's message 'out there' in the best light possible" (M = 1.90).

Index: Spin
Index Mean: 1.87
Alpha: 64

Discussion: Implicit in this finding is the suggestion that the press secretaries view truth as a spin toward the best and most positive angle of a story. It is not a means to tell the whole story, a means to tell the objective story, or a means to inform the media of all facets of a story. Rather, the data both reinforced and synthesized what the qualitative data suggested: that a spin is a statement to the press that, although it is not based on half truths, is one that is based on selective angles to the truth.

This tension between providing whole versus partial truths to reporters is perpetuated by the media as well as the press secretaries. When the press secretaries give the media their angle to a story, the media, in turn, have several choices: they may accept that angle, they may research that angle further, they may contrast that angle with opposite angles provided by other press secretaries, or they may put their own interpretation on the angle (i.e., their spin) on that story.

Some press secretaries described their frustration when a reporter, over time, simply refused to report his or her boss's interpretation of a story. As a response, the press secretary occasionally chose to cut off such a reporter. This excerpt from the focus group data illustrates how a press secretary (only occasionally it seems) might respond to a particularly bothersome or supposedly biased reporter:

Participant 1: [Describing a certain reporter with whom many of the participants had interacted] He was so antagonistic! He was so obnoxious!
Moderator: What does that mean, to be "obnoxious"?
Participant 2: He liked to ask real provocative questions to see if he could crack you.
Participant 1: Crack you. Yeah, yeah.
Participant 3: If he had something [some dirt on the Member], then he was even a little bit more obnoxious.
Participant 1: We dealt with him though. ... We cut him off for over a year and would not even return his calls.
Moderator: But this is jeopardizing this man's career here, his job, right?
Participant 2: Right. ... And he wouldn't get first crack at the story either.

Models of Public Relations

The aforementioned participants suggested that a relationship exists between the press secretary and the media that is based on guarded honesty and is characterized by suppositions of mistrust, spun statements, and an occasional decision to shut off a reporter. These results suggest that the press secretaries practice a model of public relations that more closely parallels that of the one-way, more than the more preferable two-way, model. As a means to test this assertion, three survey questions were derived to measure characteristics of each of the *Excellence Study*'s four models of public relations. Wording taken verbatim from the survey instruments used in the original *Excellence Study* provided the foundation on which all 12 questions were built. Some variation was present, however, to make the questions more applicable to the work of the press secretaries. The following is a synopsis of findings related to each model. [48]

Press Agentry Model Survey Questions

- "In my work, 'media relations,' 'public relations,' and 'publicity' mean essentially the same thing" (M = 2.81, SD = 1.35).
- "I mostly attempt to get favorable publicity into the media and to keep unfavorable publicity out" (M = 1.89, SD = 1.01).
- "My success can be gauged by the number of positive media 'hits' I generate, or the number of reporters I get to attend an event" (M = 2.44, SD = 1.05).
  Mean of the means: 2.38
  Mean of the standard deviations: 1.14

Public Information Model Survey Questions

- "I view myself more as a neutral disseminator of information than as an advocate for my office" (M = 3.97, SD = 0.96).
- "When speaking with the media, I always disseminate accurate information but do not volunteer any other" (M = 2.54, SD = 1.15).
- "Broadly stated, my goal is to persuade constituents who don't agree with the Member to see things as he or she does" (M = 2.98. SD = 1.12).
  Mean of the means: 3.16
  Mean of the standard deviations: 1.07

Two-Way Asymmetrical Model Survey Questions

- "We keep meticulous numbers and statistics on the makeup of our constituents and gear our messages accordingly" (M = 3.32, SD = 1.18).
- "When thinking about a media strategy, it is important to do a survey or informal research in order to know how to gear my message" (M = 3.31, SD = 1.22).
- "After concentrating on getting a particular angle on an issue 'out there' to the media, we do research to determine if we were effective" (M = 3.78, SD = 1.03).
  Mean of the means: 3.47
  Mean of the standard deviations: 1.14

Two-Way Symmetrical Model Survey Questions

- "It is paramount to sincerely 'converse' with the media, in the same manner you would with a trusted friend" (M = 3.19, SD = 1.31).
- "The purpose of my study is to develop an understanding between the media and our office" (M = 2.40, SD = 1.12).

- "My job is to provide mediation for my office to help us to better negotiate conflicts with the media" (M = 2.92, SD = 1.12).
  Mean of the means: 2.84
  Mean of the standard deviations: 1.18

The standard deviations for these four sets of questions was similar (range = 0.11), suggesting an even spread of opinion among and between the respondents. When means were examined, however, the cluster of opinions was wide (range = 1.09). This suggests that the press secretaries favored some models over others. The results in Table 8.1 indicate that the press agentry model (M = 2.38) was the most popular, followed by the two-way symmetrical model (M = 2.84), the public information model (M = 3.16), and the two-way asymmetrical model (M = 3.47). The most commonly practiced, although the least desirable, model (the press agentry model) was the most popular with the press secretaries, whereas the most desirable model (the two-way symmetrical model) was the second most popular.

Table 8.1   Models of Public Relations Practiced by Congressional Press Secretaries

Model	M	SD
Press agentry	2.38	1.14
Two-way symmetrical	2.84	1.18
Public information	3.16	1.07
Two-way asymmetrical	3.47	1.14

The press secretaries' practice of the press agentry model, although telling, should be noted with caution. Consider, for example, that the House of Representatives is — relative to other organizations in the private, nonprofit, and public sectors — unique: (a) Its "CEOs" risk being kicked out every two years; (b) it is more closely scrutinized than perhaps any other entity worldwide; (c) multiple actors, over which the press secretaries have little or no control or contact, try to influence its daily activities; (d) neither a board of directors nor a chairperson appoints their bosses, rather, a half-million constituents do; (e) their "place of work" receives more national news coverage than any other organization; (f) their bosses' decisions, with those of their boss's colleagues (i.e., the other Members of Congress), impact every citizen; and (g) "office politics" find themselves in a strange mix with "national politics."

This is not to suggest, however, that the data showing the press secretaries to be practitioners primarily of the press agentry model are meaningless. They are not. Rather, we must recognize that this is the first time the relationship between the *Excellence Study*'s models and the work of the press secretaries has been explored. Although it is revealing to find that they practice a press agentry model of public relations — and although the *Excellence Study*'s public relations models have found applicability across a wide range of organizational types — the uniqueness of the environment in which the press secretaries practice must also be considered.

Conclusions

We can conclude the following from this study:

1. Press secretaries who bring substantive communication management to Capitol Hill, who develop that experience while serving as press secretaries, or who do both are more inclined to be — and, in fact, do serve as — members of a Congressional office's dominant coalition.
2. Press secretaries build relationships with the media that are based on guarded honesty. Although these individuals do not have friendly relationships with the press, they recognize (albeit reluctantly at times) the irony that they need the media to be successful.
3. Press secretaries spin messages but do not like the negative connotations attached to the concept.
4. Press secretaries prefer the press agentry model — although not universally.

In addition, three generally reliable indexes were developed and are available for use in future survey research: the Dominant Coalition Index — General (α = .63), the Dominant Coalition Index — Campaign (α = .65), and the Spin Index (α = .64). There was also one liberally acceptable index that was developed: the Mutual Respect Index (α = .53).

Future Study

An opportunity exists to explore the phenomenon of the Congressional press secretary further. Until additional studies take place, however, it is difficult to confirm whether the Congressional press secretaries consider themselves to be (or truly are) public relations professionals. There are tempting parallels. Both groups act as communication managers, analyzing, stimulating, and evaluating the relationship of their organization to its environment; both are involved with task identification, task analysis, and task performance [49]; both are commonly drawn from the ranks within the media; and both experience the increased demands, if they desire to perform at their highest level, to bring management and perhaps research skills to their position. Thus, a timely and significant research track has been opened via this initial effort at better understanding the theories in the heads of Capitol Hill's communication managers.

Acknowledgments

My sincere thanks to Dennis Kinsey for his guidance and to Syracuse University for the grant that provided funding for this study. I also thank Stephanie Flores for her work as a research assistant.

Note: *Originally published in Downes, E.J., Hacks, flacks, and spin doctors meet the media: An examination of the Congressional press secretary as a (potential) public relations professional,* Journal of Public Relations Research, *10, 263, 1998.*

Endnotes

1. Bruce, I. and Downes, E., The theories in the heads of Capitol Hill's press secretaries, paper presented at the meeting of the Association for Education in Journalism and Mass Communication, Syracuse, NY, 1995.
2. Downes, E.J., Messages from the Hill: A conceptual framework for understanding the Congressional press secretary, unpublished doctoral dissertation, Syracuse University, Syracuse, NY, 1997.

3. Bruce and Downes, op. cit.
4. Cook, T.E., *Making Laws and Making News: Media Strategies in the U.S. House of Representatives*, Brookings Institution, Washington, DC, 1989.
5. Downes, op. cit.
6. Hess, S., *Live from Capitol Hill! Studies of Congress and the Media*, Brookings Institution, Washington, DC, 1991.
7. Cook, op. cit.
8. Hess, op. cit.
9. Hesse, M.B., Strategies of the political communication process, *Public Relations Review*, 7(1), 33, 1981.
10. Baker, B., Public relations in government, in *Handbook of Strategic Public Relations and Integrated Communication*, Caywood, C.L., Ed., McGraw-Hill, New York, 1997, chap. 31.
11. Bartels, L.M., Messages received: The political impact of media exposure, *American Political Science Review*, 87, 267, 1993.
12. Graber, D.A., Seeing is remembering: How visuals contribute to learning from television news, *Journal of Communication*, 40, 134, 1990.
13. Hess, S., *The Washington Reporters*, Brookings Institution, Washington, DC, 1981.
14. Hess, S., *The Government/Press Connection: Press Officers and their Offices*, Brookings Institution, Washington, DC, 1984.
15. Hess. S., *The Ultimate Insiders: U.S. Senators in the National Media*, Brookings Institution, Washington, DC, 1986.
16. Howard, C. and Mathews, W., *On Deadline: Managing Media Relations*, 2nd ed., Waveland, Prospect Heights, IL, 1994.
17. Patterson, T.E., *Out of Order*, New York, 1993.
18. Ornstein, N.J., The open Congress meets the President, in *Both Ends of the Avenue: The Presidency, the Executive Branch, and Congress in the 1980s*, King, A., Ed., American Enterprise Institute, Washington, DC, 1983, chap. 7.
19. Shapiro, M.E. and Williams, W., Jr., Agenda-setting and political framing in the 1982 Illinois Gubernatorial Campaign, paper presented at the annual meeting of the International Communication Association, Dallas, TX, 1983.
20. Iorio, S.H. and Huxman, S.S., Media coverage of political issues and the framing of personal concerns, *Journal of Communication*, 46(4), 97, 1996.
21. Dorman, W.A., Beyond reason: The media, politics, and public discourse, paper presented at the annual International Conference for Critical Thinking and Moral Critique, Rohnert Park, CA, 1992.
22. Graber, op. cit.
23. Graber, D.A., Ed., *Media Power in Politics*, CQ Press, Washington, DC, 1984.
24. Wicks, R.H., Applying schema theory in mass media information processing: Moving toward a formal model, paper presented at the annual meeting of the International Communication Association, Chicago, 1986.
25. Graber, *Media Power in Politics*, op. cit.
26. Miller, S.H., Reporters and Congressmen: Living in symbiosis, in *Media Power in Politics*, Graber, D.A., Ed., CQ Press, Washington, DC, 1978, 274.
27. Turk, J., Information subsidies and media content: A study of public relations influence on the news, paper presented at the meeting of the Association for Education in Journalism and Mass Communication, 1986.
28. Gandy, O.H., *Beyond Agenda Setting: Information Subsidies and Public Policy*, Ablex, Norwood, NJ, 1982.
29. Grunig, J.E., Communication, public relations, and effective organizations: An overview of the book, in *Excellence in Public Relations and Communication Management*, Grunig, J.E., Ed., Lawrence Erlbaum, Hillsdale, NJ, 1992, chap. 1, 18.

30. "Murphy (1991) thus suggested that the two-way symmetrical model might be described as the mixed-motive model because it incorporates both asymmetrical and symmetrical tactics. She then argued that a mixed-motive model does a better job of describing the behavior of public relations practitioners in the real world than does a purely symmetrical model" (Grunig, J.E. and Grunig, L.A., Models of public relations and communication, in *Excellence in Public Relations and Communication Management*, Grunig, J.E., Ed., Lawrence Erlbaum, Hillsdale, NJ, 1992, chap. 11, 311–312).

31. Grunig, *Excellence in Public Relations and Communication Management*, op. cit.

32. Thompson, J.D., *Organizations in Action: Social Science Bases of Administrative Theory*, McGraw-Hill, New York, 1967.

33. Ian Bruce, a doctoral candidate at Syracuse University's Newhouse School of Public Communications, worked with me on the focus group.

34. Firestone, W.A., *Meaning in Method: The Rhetoric of Quantitative and Qualitative Research*, Research for Better Schools, Philadelphia, 1987.

35. Rosenau, P.M., *Post-Modernism and the Social Sciences: Insights, Inroads, and Intrusions*, Princeton University Press, Princeton, NJ, 1992.

36. Delegates are Members who, because they do not represent a Congressional district, do not vote on the floor of the House. They may, however, vote in committee and may also publicly address the House during floor debate. They represent Guam, Puerto Rico, the Virgin Islands, American Samoa, and the District of Columbia. In the current Congress, all are Democrats.

37. Bruce and Downes, op. cit.

38. Cook, op. cit.

39. Hess, *Live from Capitol Hill*, op. cit.

40. While exploring this concept, I occasionally used the phrase, "putting words in the Member's mouth." One press secretary warned me, however, to use the phrase with caution. She said: "You're never, if you're a good press secretary, putting words or thoughts out there that haven't been espoused by the Member. You may be making up the sentence that espouses their views and giving their thoughts. ... But still it's their thought and that's important."

41. Bruce and Downes, op. cit.

42. The survey question was, "In your opinion, what words would a typical journalist or reporter use to describe the typical press secretary?"

43. Bruce and Downes, op. cit.

44. Ibid.

45. Although the respondents may have believed otherwise, they — not I — provided the terminology for, and precise focus of, these questions through their responses during the focus group and interview.

46. Perhaps the high disagreement score in Question 3 again supports the notion that, although the press secretaries may put their ego on hold when dealing with the Member, they house a strong ego themselves; for example, they disagreed with the notion that they are not a conduit to the media but, rather, are an obstacle to them. In addition, because the interview data suggested the press secretaries have a guarded honesty rather than an adversarial relationship with the media, the former rather than the latter should have been probed in this index.

47. Although the Bruce and Downes (op. cit.) study indicated no significant difference in media coverage of Republican and Democrats, four respondents, at different points in their interviews, brought up the notion of a liberal bias in the media. All were Republicans. One conservative Republican, on his questionnaire, wrote a note summarizing his frustrations: "The national media establishment (networks, *The Washington Post*, *NY Times*, *Newsweek*, *Time*, etc.) are cynical, biased, way left, lazy, and fundamentally dishonest." Another wrote: "As a former member of the press, and having been in this town for ten years, I am astonished at the repulsion that most reporters have for the GOP."

48. When examining findings reviewed in this section, note that, unlike in the indexes described earlier in the study, concepts such as those surrounding a dominant coalition, adversarial relationship, mutually beneficial relationship, and so forth were not examined. Rather, the quantitative data described in this section measured specific characteristics inherent to already established, predetermined, broadly stated models of public relations. Thus, although the aforementioned indexes examined concepts that will form the foundation on which new models will be built, the data discussed in this section examined models — and the degree to which they were practiced — which have already been established and which have been shown to be reliable.
49. Crable, E. and Vibbert, S.L., *Public Relations as Communications Management*, Bellweather Press, Edina, MN, 1986.

Appendix II

Questions for Review and Discussion

1. Why is media relations a difficult task for the modern-day public administrator?
2. What are some factors that contribute to successful media relations by a government agency?
3. Is Chapter 8 fully applicable to public administration? If yes, how so? If not, which of the research results are relevant to the practice of media relations by both politicians and bureaucrats, and which do not apply to government managers?

Additional Reading

Lee, M., Reporters and bureaucrats: Public relations counter-strategies by public administrators in an era of media disinterest in government, *Public Relations Review*, 25, 451, 1999.

Lee, M., Administrators are from Jupiter, reporters are from Mercury, *PA Times*, 24(6), 7, 2001.

Lee, M. The agency spokesperson: Connecting public administration and the media, *Public Administration Quarterly*, 25, 101, 2001. [How public information officers at the local level of government in the United States spend their time, their views of media coverage, training, and experience, etc.]

Mead, T.D., The daily newspaper as political agenda setter: *The Charlotte Observer* and metropolitan reform, *State and Local Government Review*, 26, 27, 1994.

Roberts, A., Style or substance? Media perceptions of Clinton's economic and timber summits, *Public Administration Quarterly*, 21, 227, 1997.

Swoboda, D.P., Accuracy and accountability in reporting local government budget activities: Evidence from the newsroom and from newsmakers, *Public Budgeting & Finance*, 15(3), 74, 1995.

See also the annotated bibliography of historical sources relating to public administration and the news media in the Appendix at the end of the book.

PURPOSES OF GOVERNMENT PUBLIC RELATIONS: PUBLIC REPORTING

Introduction to Section III

Public reporting is one discrete activity within a government agency's overall obligation in a democracy to make information available and transparent. Reporting consists of communications from the agency to the public-at-large with the primary purpose of disseminating general information about the agency's record and being open to subsequent interactive relationships. From that point on, there occurs an opaque process by which public opinion coalesces and communicates itself into the democratic process and back to government.

Based on this description of public reporting, what agency external communications activities would 'count' and which ones wouldn't? Public reporting activities are those that are intended to fulfill the manager's obligation to democracy by providing information about agency performance to the public-at-large, such as:

- Annual reports, whether hard copy or digital, which provide overall information about the agency's performance in a way that is understandable and meaningful to a lay citizen.
- Periodic reports (for periods shorter or longer than a year) that are intended to give a 'big picture' overview of governmental activities and programs.
- Special reports on specific topics about which the agency wants to inform the public.
- Capsule and brief reports that are inserted in other media (such as agency mailings, agency magazines, local newspapers, etc.) that provide condensed summary information for the citizenry.

On the other hand, these programs would not automatically be considered public reporting because they have purposes and functions other than the goals of public reporting:

- Reports fulfilling legal and other professional requirements for financial, budgetary, and accounting purposes, such as those mandated by the Governmental Accounting Standards Board (GASB), which covers state and local government.
- Reports required by elected and other political oversight institutions, such as regular reports that federal agencies must file with Congress on their progress in implementing the Clinger–Cohen Act of 1996 (CCA) regarding use of information technology.
- Reports for purpose of *internal* management control, such as using performance measurement information systems to hold lower-level managers accountable.
- Specialized reports and other communications to attentive publics and tangible stakeholders, such as clients and customers, special interest groups, and legislative liaison with committees having jurisdiction over the agency.
- Marketing and public relations efforts to accomplish the core goals and mission of the agency, such as marketing efforts to increase utilization of existing programs and inform people of new laws they would be affected by or services for which they may be eligible.
- Efforts to *listen* to the public through public opinion surveys, market research, focus groups, etc.
- Efforts aimed exclusively to accomplish public participation in decision making regarding future agency policies and programs, such as through advisory committees, public hearings, invitations for comments on proposed rules, and customer referenda.

Certainly this long list of exclusions is not intended to minimize or belittle the value of these other communications and external relations programs. They are equally important to the functioning of a government agency. Rather, a targeted focus of public reporting helps zero in on this distinct obligation that public managers have to democracy. Also, public reporting has a 'cheek-by-jowl' relationship to many of these other agency activities. As such, they can often be implemented and delivered in a coordinated and interlocking fashion.

There are three chapters in this section. Chapter 9 presents a concise introduction to the concept of public reporting, its history, practices, and current trends. The next chapter focuses on how the profession of government finance officers has tried to create an accounting product that is meaningful to the lay public. Called 'popular reporting,' this is an effort to use the information contained in traditionally obtuse financial reports that are created and used by accountants in a format that the citizenry can read and understand. Chapter 11, the last chapter in this section, presents a comprehensive history of municipal reporting in the United States. While many historical studies have little relevance to current practice, the reading is included in this volume because it provides tangible examples of how city government had, earlier in the 20th century, conducted very robust reporting programs. The chapter includes examples of the different formats and venues for the reports, the multiplicity of media used, and the variety of distribution methods that were employed to reach the citizenry. These examples continue to be relevant in the 21st century, whether replicated exactly or modified to reflect contemporary technology and standards. Modern-day public administration has a way to go before it re-establishes the full potential — and importance — of public reporting.

For those interested in reinvigorating their agencies' public reporting program, the Organisation for Economic Co-operation and Development (OECD) conducted an international survey of government practices and identified nine initial principles for doing effective public reporting:

1. Take it seriously.
2. Start from the citizen's perspective.

3. Deliver what you promise.
4. Settle in for the long-term.
5. Be creative, explore the ever-expanding options of E-government technology.
6. Be prepared for criticism — that's democracy.
7. Involve all staff in reporting efforts, don't exile the project to an isolated outpost.
8. Develop a coherent policy.
9. Start! (Adapted from Gramberger, M.R., *Citizens as Partners: OECD Handbook on Information, Consultation and Public Participation in Policy-Making*, Organisation for Economic Co-operation and Development, Paris, 2001, 92–100.)

Finally, while not included in this section, Chapter 25 is very relevant to the practice of public reporting in government. It discusses the future of public reporting by suggesting that the development of digital technologies can permit its evolution into E-reporting. This can have a revolutionary impact on the relationship between a government agency and the public by permitting direct reporting to the citizenry in lieu of indirect reporting through the news media.

Note

Portions of this introduction were adapted from Lee, M., E-reporting: Using managing-for-results data to strengthen democratic accountability, in *Managing for Results 2005*, Kamensky, J.M. and Morales, A., Eds., Rowman & Littlefield, Lanham, MD, 2005, chap. 4. Also published by the IBM Center for the Business of Government as a monograph and available online: http://www.businessofgovernment.org/pdfs/Lee_Report.pdf (accessed 2007). However, none of the material in this introduction duplicates the text of Chapter 25.

Chapter 9

An Overview of Public Reporting

Mordecai Lee

Contents

Introduction

Public reporting refers to the actions of a government agency to account to the citizenry for its activities in the recent past, including its record of performance and its stewardship of public funds. The term refers both to the normative obligation of public entities in a democracy to perform such activities and to the internal management activities necessary to accomplish this external communications goal.

Public reporting was developed by public administration theorists in the first half of the 20th century in an effort to harmonize the emergence of the administrative state with democracy. Since permanent and professionalized bureaucracies were not subject to elections, there was a need to define the role of public administration in democracy. By assigning to senior civil servants the duty to report directly to the citizenry on agency activities, theorists sought to make government departments accountable to the public-at-large, not just to elected officials. Public reporting would contribute to an informed citizenry, the ultimate source of power and decision making in democracy.

Origins

With the emergence of the administrative state in advanced Western societies in the late 19th and early 20th centuries, a natural concern arose regarding the need to harmonize democracy with the inherently undemocratic nature of bureaucracy. Political, legal and constitutional responses were the understandable initial solutions. Administrative agencies would be formally accountable to the elected and appointed oversight institutions of democracy, such as through budget and policy controls possessed by the chief elected executive officer, oversight activities by legislative bodies and the jurisdiction of the courts to rule on agency policies and procedures. These elected and appointed constitutional branches of government would be able to assure that democracy would reach into bureaucracy through external controls and interventions. Yet these approaches all assumed that bureaucracies were only *indirectly* accountable to the citizenry — the source of democratic sovereignty and power.

However, another line of thinking suggested that bureaucracies also needed to be *directly* accountable to the voters. It was not enough, this theorizing went, to be accountable to the citizenry through other democratic institutions. Instead, agencies should also be directly responsible to the electorate. Thus was born public reporting.

As it gradually developed in the 1920s and 1930s in the United States, public reporting referred to the duty of the public administrator to report regularly to the public-at-large on the activities of the agency. Since an informed public was the *sine qua non* of democracy, [1] then government agencies should be one of the sources of information for the citizenry about the operations of the public sector. For public opinion to be the central engine of decision making in a democracy, the voters needed to have basic information upon which to construct their opinions. In the administrative state, information should come not only from traditional sources such as newspapers, civic groups and elected officials, but also from the newest component of the public sector, government departments. That meant government managers had the obligation of preparing and releasing reports on a regular schedule, helping to assure that the public would become familiar with agency activities. [2–4]

Public reporting first emerged as part of the efforts by reformers to 'clean up' American city governments in the early 20th century. A knowledgeable citizenry would become a bulwark against patronage, waste and corruption in city halls. One of the first references to public reporting was in 1912, when Bruère argued that the concept of 'efficient citizenship' required regular reporting by city government to the public. [5] In the 1930s, the International City Management Association sponsored contests to promote improved public reporting [6] and through the 1950s continued actively encouraging municipalities to conduct robust reporting programs. [7]

The public reporting imperative of the government manager is one of the activities that operationalizes the difference between business and public administration. Given the public-sector environment in which it operates, government management is a qualitatively different activity from business administration. The duty of public reporting is one of the components of public administration that reflects this inherent intersectorial difference. [8]

Definition

Public reporting is only one element of the array of interactions that government agencies have with the public-at-large. In that respect, it needs to be delineated in a way that clearly separates it from other related, but distinctly different, activities.

In the context of agency external communication programs, public reporting is an activity that is not related to the efficient implementation of the agency's core mission. Many public relations programs are aimed at furthering the *raison d'être* of an agency, such as informing the public of new programs and services, using publicity as a substitute for regulation and encouraging the public to serve as the 'eyes and ears' of the agency. [9] In that respect, public reporting is a communication activity that doesn't 'do' anything in context of the pragmatic get-the-job-done pressures of daily management and communications. Rather, reporting simply provides information for information's sake.

Similarly, public reporting focuses on efforts to contribute to an informed public. In that sense, reporting contributes to the functioning of democracy. However, public reporting focuses only on the transmission of information from the administrative agency to the public and not on the subsequent developments that it triggers. So, public reporting is different from citizen participation in agency decision making or agency 'listening' to customers and clients in an effort to improve the quality of consumer interactions.

Given that the modern definition of communication is a two-way flow of information, then public reporting focuses solely on the first half and front end of the entire communications loop and only on communication intended to inform for democratic purposes. Therefore, public reporting is defined as

> the management activity intended to convey systematically and regularly information about government operations, in order to promote an informed citizenry in a democracy and accountability to public opinion. It consists of direct and indirect reporting of the government's record of accomplishments and stewardship of the taxpayers' money. Public reporting is presented in many different communication formats, but always uses vocabulary that is understandable and meaningful to lay citizens. [10]

Public reporting occurs when an agency conveys information about its performance to the citizenry, rather than to political and elected oversight institutions. Certainly, public opinion gains information about the operations of the government from elected officials, whether those from the executive or the legislative branches. However, the central concept of reporting focuses on government agencies communicating with the public *besides* the formal, legal and constitutional channels they are subject to.

Generally, a bureaucracy can report to the public in two ways, directly and indirectly. Indirect reporting refers to communication efforts *through* the intermediary institution of the news media. Direct reporting focuses on non-mediated communications from the agency to the public-at-large for the purpose of conveying summary and performance information.

Indirect Reporting

One way for an agency to inform the public is by facilitating media coverage of its operations. As an instrument of democracy, the news media can provide the public with ongoing information about the activities and performance of the government. Given this constitutional role of the press in contributing to an informed citizenry, agencies have a counterpart obligation to assist the press in its efforts to report about agency operations. This perspective is the underlying rationale for public sector agencies to maintain media liaison offices, staffed with specialists trained in dealing with reporters.

Some news coverage of an agency is headline driven. In those situations, the agency is passively reacting to inquiries from the press. This form of interaction rarely leads to providing the public with a more systematic and comprehensive understanding of agency performance. Instead, it provides highly selective — and often negative — snapshots driven by the media's need for controversy. Therefore, a better opportunity for indirect reporting occurs when an agency is able to initiate and generate coverage. Events such as observing a milestone in a program's operations, the ribbon cutting at a new site and the kick-off of a new service all provide an opportunity to report indirectly to the public about the general and overall activities of an agency. While, by necessity, an incomplete snapshot of the entire agency's operations, this category of news coverage nonetheless is a channel for reporting to the citizenry on the more routine and daily aspects of government, in contradistinction to news coverage that is crisis and controversy driven.

One of the advantages of indirect reporting is that it is free. The agency incurs no additional cost when the media reports to the public about it. Yet, while agencies should make efforts to 'tell their story' to the citizenry via the news media, indirect reporting — by itself — rarely is adequate to accomplish the broad democratic goals intended for public reporting.

Direct Reporting

The more prominent and effective approach to public reporting is through direct contact with the citizenry. In the pre-digital era when public reporting first began, direct reporting often focused on printed materials. Items such as annual and quarterly reports were viewed as one of the basic ways that agencies could inform the public about their accomplishments. Two key elements have been identified as necessary for effective printed reports: contents and distribution.

First, printed reports should be prepared with the audience of the lay public in mind. Reports need to be in plain English and must focus on the key items that represent the agency's accomplishments. Long and detailed descriptions, use of technical jargon and impenetrable statistical presentations are examples of what a good report should not contain. Besides use of plain language, effective public reports extensively rely on graphics, photos and other visual techniques to make the documents user-friendly. Similarly, linking agency information to comparisons that are understandable to average citizens ("for the cost of an average breakfast, our agency delivers to each of our clients...") is another way to contribute to an effective public report. This focus on content and presentation also helps highlight the difference between public reporting and financial reporting. Annual reports prepared by accountants and auditors to satisfy various legal and constitutional requirements rarely qualify as public reporting. The density of numerical information in financial reports generally precludes creating a product that is meaningful to a lay reader.

Second, effective reporting also requires significant efforts to disseminate reports as broadly as possible. Some agencies indeed prepare annual reports, but their dissemination efforts are half-hearted and incomplete. Certainly, copies should be sent to elected officials, key civic leaders, the media, public libraries and major civic groups. However, the concept of public reporting calls for efforts to put the report directly in the hands of the citizenry. In the middle of the 20th century, municipalities experimented with a wide variety of dissemination channels. Some examples included inserting the annual report in the annual property tax bill or in quarterly bills from municipal utilities, inserting the report in the daily newspaper, having sanitation workers distribute the reports while on their rounds and recruiting Boy and Girl Scout troops to adopt, as their civic project, the distribution of the report door-to-door.

However, annual reports and other regularly issued publications (such as quarterly ones) are not the only way that government agencies can engage in direct public reporting. Referring again to examples from the mid-20th century, other efforts included open houses, speakers bureaus, billboards, signs on subways and buses, annual exhibits keyed to the budget adoption process, movie shorts, public service advertising, regular radio programs and film versions of annual reports. Like other marketing and advertising efforts, multiple products and channels need to be utilized to maximize the potential of reaching as much of the citizenry as possible.

Roosevelt's Office of Government Reports

In the federal government, the high water mark of traditional public reporting was the Office of Government Reports (OGR), which President Roosevelt established in 1939. In the Executive Order creating it, one of its central missions was to "distribute information concerning the purposes and activities of executive departments and agencies." [11] Roosevelt viewed OGR as the executive branch-wide agency that would report to the public on the activities of the federal government. In a national radio address, he explained that once informed factually of the record of the Administration, public opinion could then express its will to Congress regarding the continuation or cessation of those federal programs. [11] As a reflection of the importance he assigned to OGR, Roosevelt made it one of the five original agencies comprising the Executive Office of the President (EOP), which he also established in 1939. However, OGR was a very controversial agency, especially with the conservative coalition in Congress. Overcoming strong resistance on Capitol Hill to the concept of such a federal reporting agency, in 1941 Roosevelt succeeded in shepherding through Congress a law authorizing permanent appropriations for OGR. [12] However, continued opposition to OGR by legislators forced Roosevelt in 1942 to merge it for the duration of World War II into the temporary Office of War Information (OWI). When President Truman tried to reestablish OGR after the war, as Roosevelt had intended, the Republican 80th Congress refused to appropriate any additional funding for it. OGR went out of existence in 1948. [12]

The political blowout relating to OGR presented a high profile case of how easily public reporting can become politically controversial. Whether an accurate assessment or not, the lesson learned was that for public reporting to occur, it needed to be blander and less engaging. In fact, for the second half of the 20th century, public reporting gradually ossified into boring annual reports at most levels of government. Those half-hearted reports were given limited circulation and triggered even less interest.

21st Century Transformation: E-Reporting

While the rationale for public reporting retained its validity, in the post-OGR era of the second half of the 20th century, as a concrete activity it gradually faded from prominence in both public administration theory and practice. However, the emergence of the communications age and the digital era has provided an opportunity to revive and reestablish the value of public reporting in the 21st century. New communications technologies now permit government agencies to communicate quickly, efficiently and inexpensively directly to the citizenry. Annual and special reports posted on agency websites and distributed by email provide an opportunity to perform public reporting in ways that could not have been envisioned a century earlier.

Similarly, the increased attention in public administration to performance measurement has provided a new format by which agencies can report on their operations to the public-at-large. While performance measurement was originally developed largely for management control purposes — whether for the senior management of the agency or for oversight by the executive and by the legislative branch — it has much potential and value to the lay citizenry as well.

Therefore, the combination of digital technology with the focus on performance measurement has provided an opportunity to reformulate and reinvigorate the original conception of public reporting. Now called E-reporting, it consists of:

> the administrative activity that uses electronic government technology for digital delivery of public reports that are largely based on performance information. E-reporting is a tool of e-democracy that conveys systematically and regularly information about government operations that is valuable to the public-at-large, in order to promote an informed citizenry in a democracy and accountability to public opinion. E-reports are planned to be citizen-friendly, by being understandable and meaningful to the lay public. [10]

Conclusion

Public reporting has been making a comeback in public administration. Herzlinger has suggested that one of the ways to restore public trust in government is through improved reporting. That would include an increase in the amount of important information disclosed to the citizenry as well as better and broader dissemination of such regular reports. [13] The Organisation for Economic Co-operation and Development (OECD), an association of the most developed Western countries, issued two reports in 2001 calling for improved public reporting and providing guidelines for such efforts. [14,15]

Whether widely or well practiced, public reporting is a permanent and inherent element of public administration in a democracy. Civil servants are expected to engage in systematic efforts to report to the citizenry on their agencies' activities, performance and stewardship of taxpayer funds. The profession of public management entails more than effectively running an agency. It also involves contributing to the working of democracy. Public reporting is the vehicle for such efforts. For more information see References [16–20].

Note: *Originally published in Lee, M., Public reporting, in* Encyclopedia of Public Administration and Public Policy: First Update Supplement, *Taylor & Francis, Boca Raton, FL, 2005, 239.*

Endnotes

1. Brown, R.D., *The Strength of a People: The Idea of an Informed Citizenry in America, 1650–1870*, University of North Carolina Press, Chapel Hill, 1996.
2. Beyle, H.C., *Governmental Reporting in Chicago*, University of Chicago Press, Chicago, 1928.

3. National Committee on Municipal Reporting, *Public Reporting, with Special Reference to Annual, Departmental, and Current Reports of Municipalities*, Municipal Administration Service, New York, 1931.

4. Ridley, C.E. and Simon, H.A., *Specifications for the Annual Municipal Report*, International City Managers' Association, Chicago, 1948.

5. Bruère, H., Efficiency in city government, *Annals of the American Academy of Political and Social Science*, 41, 3, 1912.

6. Simon, H.A., Inter-city contests, in *Municipal Year Book, 1937*, Ridley, C.E. and Nolting, O.F., Eds., International City Managers' Association, Chicago, 1937, 137.

7. Snyder, R.W., Municipal reporting in 1953, in *Municipal Year Book, 1954*, Ridley, C.E. and Nolting, O.F., Eds., International City Managers' Association, Chicago, 1954, 269.

8. Lee, M., Intersectoral differences in public affairs: The duty of public reporting in public administration, *Journal of Public Affairs*, 2(2), 33, 2002.

9. Lee, M., Public information in government organizations: A review and curriculum outline of external relations in public administration, *Public Administration and Management: An Interactive Journal*, 5, 183, 2000. http://www.pamij.com/5_4/5_4_4_pubinfo.pdf (accessed 2007) (*Editor's Note:* See Chapter 1.)

10. Lee, M., E-Reporting: Using managing-for-results data to strengthen democratic accountability, in *Managing for Results 2005*, Kamensky, J.M. and Morales, A., Eds., Rowman & Littlefield, Lanham, MD, 2005, chap. 4. Also published as a monograph and available online: http://www.businessofgovernment.org/pdfs/Lee_Report.pdf (accessed 2007). (*Editor's Note*: See Chapter 25.)

11. Roosevelt, F.D., *The Public Papers and Addresses of Franklin D. Roosevelt, 1939*, Macmillan, New York, 1941, 305-10, 494.

12. Lee, M., *The First Presidential Communications Agency: FDR's Office of Government Reports*, State University of New York Press, Albany, 2005.

13. Herzlinger, R.E., Can public trust in nonprofits and government be restored?, *Harvard Business Review*, 74(2), 97, 1996.

14. Caddy, J. and Vergez, C., *Citizens as Partners: Information, Consultation and Public Participation in Policy-Making*, Organisation for Economic Co-operation and Development, Paris, 2001.

15. Gramberger, M.R., *Citizens as Partners: OECD Handbook on Information, Consultation and Public Participation in Policy-Making*, Organisation for Economic Co-operation and Development, Paris, 2001.

16. Campbell, O. W., San Diego's 1951 annual report, *Public Administration Review*, 13, 30, 1953.

17. Graves, W.B., Public reporting in the American states, *Public Opinion Quarterly*, 2, 211, 1938.

18. Lee, M., Is there anything new under the sun? Herbert Simon's contributions in the 1930s to performance measurement and public reporting of performance results, *Public Voices*, 6(2-3), 73, 2003.

19. Scott, J.D., Local government publications, in *Effective Communication: A Local Government Guide*, Wheeler, K.M., Ed., International City Management Association, Washington, DC, 1994, chap. 10.

20. Wall, N.L., *Municipal Reporting to the Public*, International City Managers' Association, Chicago, 1963.

Chapter 10

Popular Reporting

Joy A. Clay

Contents

Introduction

Professional bodies concerned with assuring and promoting high-quality government accounting and financial reporting practices, such as the Governmental Accounting Standards Board (GASB) and Government Finance Officers Association (GFOA), view quality financial reporting as an important facet of assuring government accountability. [1,2] Accordingly, state and local governments are encouraged to issue a high quality, comprehensive annual financial report (CAFR) in conformance with generally accepted accounting principles (GAAP). This annual financial report, the CAFR, is increasingly being supplemented with a more stylish and simpler report, the popular annual financial report (PAFR), aimed at general, "popular" audiences.

Although the simpler report has less technical language and provides less detailed information than the CAFR, the PAFR is expected to be credible and present an accurate, objective picture of governmental activity. PAFRs are generally aimed at lay audiences such as citizens, activists, business leaders, civic organizations, etc. who are more interested in gaining a broad understanding of a government's activities and who often are not versed in, or want to take the time to understand, governmental accounting and bureaucratic language.

Context for the Report: Government Accountability

Underlying democratic government is an expectation that those in power are held accountable for their decisions and actions. Public reaction to the recent financial and governance scandals in the private sector, such as Enron, and continued public concern about government spending have added increased energy to the public management reform efforts started in the 1980s. A growing consensus on the part of public administration professional groups, including the International City/County Management Association (ICMA), GFOA, GASB, and the American Society for Public Administration (ASPA), has led these groups to place pressure on governments to expand vehicles and processes of accountability. Consequently, public agencies and governments are encouraged not just to improve formal evaluation or auditing processes but to assure the transparency of governmental actions; that is, not just to evaluate programmatic results but to regularly report on them to citizens in a way that assures reliable, useful, understandable, and accurate information is being provided to a broad audience. Thus, governments are expected to generate consistent performance data and report it regularly and publicly. [3] The PAFR is one of the vehicles for governments to report on performance results. The underlying assumption is that regular governmental attention to public accountability will in the short and long term further public trust in and credibility of government as it reduces information asymmetry. [3]

Characteristics of the Popular Report

The most specific guidance available on PAFR characteristics is offered by GFOA. In summary, GFOA recognizes that PAFRs can be presented in a variety of formats. Specifically, GFOA strongly encourages governments to produce a summary financial report that successfully attends to the following five characteristics:

1. Presents timely information (no later than six months after the close of the fiscal year)
2. Clearly describes scope (defines what is included in the report), providing an explicit link to the CAFR to facilitate further research if desired by the reader
3. Thoughtfully presents helpful comparative data, for example, trends or benchmarks
4. Presents a report design/layout that is attractive, engaging, clear, and concise, with a format that avoids technical jargon and includes supportive and summative graphic material such as charts and photographs or narrative material that enhances reader understanding
5. Implements an appropriate dissemination strategy (that is, the distribution approach actually gets the report to the target audience/stakeholders)

An important challenge for governments is this last characteristic, the appropriate distribution of the report. The distribution strategy must balance cost, including production and distribution costs, as well as predict volume, based on estimated readership interest. Increasingly governments make these reports available on their websites. [4,5] Electronic posting of the PAFR not only saves distribution costs but broadens accessibility.

Recognition for Excellence

The Outstanding Achievement in Popular Annual Financial Reporting Award was established by GFOA in 1991. [6] This award recognizes those governments that develop a high quality PAFR. Judging by the history of success that GFOA has had with the CAFR award, over 3,000 governments annually apply for the CAFR award, [7] this is a successful means of encouraging innovation and adoption of a high quality financial reporting practice. As with CAFR award winners, governments, specifically the finance and budget offices, winning the PAFR award tend to advertise receiving the award as a prestigious measure of their performance.

GFOA asks judges to assess PAFRs on their overall quality and usefulness, specifically evaluating the report's reader appeal, understandability, distribution methods, and degree of creativity/innovation. A slowly increasing number of governments are applying for the award. For fiscal year end 1996, only 29 governments applied for the award but 55 applied for 1997. More recently, the number of applicants for the award has increased approximately 6% annually. [6] GFOA reports that in 2006, 130 governments submitted reports to the program, and 134 are expected to submit reports in 2007. [8] The growing list of state and local governments seeking this relatively recent award attests to the number of governments producing this new financial report.

Implementation Considerations

Leadership Responsibility

Before deciding to undertake creation of a PAFR, government executives need to make several key decisions, including assignment of responsibility for preparing the report and coordinating data collection, scope of the report content, dissemination guidelines, and cost parameters. Executive leaders will also need to take into consideration the political ramifications associated with such a report, including degree of involvement of legislative leaders, capacity to continue with the report once started, willingness to receive public feedback, and the ability to present balanced and objective information. Inherently, the PAFR is to be a public and accessible document. Thus, both successes and challenges will need to be presented. GFOA states very clearly that "most important, the popular report should establish its credibility with its intended readers by presenting information in a balanced and objective manner." [7]

Report Tasks

Once the broad framework has been decided upon by government leaders, the work can be delegated to the appropriate unit and staff member(s) and responsibility for collecting the data and preparing the report can proceed. A critical decision rests on the assessment of staff capacity, that is, budget analysts may not have the requisite graphic or stylistic creativity needed to produce a highly styled report. Consequently, leaders may need to seek outside assistance, especially to create the cover design and layout, decisions which may add to the overhead cost of the report as the design becomes more sophisticated. If the governmental entity wishes to seek the GFOA excellence award, the report also needs to reflect innovative and creative practice. Consequently, leaders will need to commit time and attention to the project. This may present a challenge because these same leaders generally have the responsibility for producing the CAFR. All of these managerial decisions rest within budget constraints and feasibility considerations.

As with any report, the lead narrative and graphic information should capture the essence of the governmental unit. With the PAFR, this approach must be pleasing to the eye. Key content decisions include finalizing the scope of the report (what will be included, breadth and depth), how best to link to the CAFR, appropriate inclusion of insightful trend and/or benchmark information as well as graphic/photo illustrations add to the attractiveness and understandability features of the report but also to the cost of the report. [9–11] The use of color enhances the presentation quality of the report but adds to production costs.

A significant feature of the PAFR also can be the inclusion of results of citizen satisfaction information. Integrating an assessment of citizen satisfaction with programmatic performance reporting will more comprehensively address various issues related to public accountability. [12]

The PAFR, especially if available on the government website, offers the opportunity for place marketing. [13] This makes the section that introduces the community context and strategic visioning of the community of particular value. The PAFR, thus, can serve as a promotional vehicle that communicates the government's assets and the essence of the community to readers. Achieving a balance between substance and presentation is a measure of a government's ability to present policy, performance, and programmatic information in a manner that encourages readers to actually read the report and, thus, better understand their government.

Conclusions

As with all government reports, public administrators need to attend to data quality issues including any problems with reliability and validity of data, and objectivity. Although in "popular" format, the PAFR is an official government financial report.

The decision to broaden the availability of government financial reporting recognizes that citizens are stakeholders in their community, not just customers of services, and should be able to expect a return on their tax dollars. [14] The PAFR presents an opportunity for governments to proactively provide information that addresses policy, program, and performance accountability. The value of the PAFR lies in the nature of the report, that is, governments must present this information in human terms, not shrouded in technical and complex financial or programmatic language. To engage in the PAFR process encourages creativity on the part of budget and finance officials and reinforces the need to be able to articulate a community context, the vision of the community, achievements to date, and artfully position challenges.

Note: *Originally published in Clay, J.A., Popular reporting, in* Encyclopedia of Public Administration and Public Policy, *2nd ed., Taylor & Francis, Boca Raton, FL, 2008.*

Endnotes

1. Government Accounting Standards Board, *Reporting Performance Information: Suggested Criteria for Effective Communication*, Special Report, Norwalk, CT, August 2003.
2. See www.seagov.org and www.gfoa.org, respectively (accessed 2007).
3. Coe, C.K., A report card on report cards, *Public Performance and Management Review*, 27, 53, 2003.
4. For the fifth annual popular report of the City of Memphis for fiscal year 2004, see http://www.cityofmemphis.org/pdf_forms/2004_citizensReport.pdf (accessed 2007).

5. For hotlinks to the winners of the PAFR award, see GFOA, Award Winners for Fiscal Periods Ending in 2004: http://www.gfoa.org/services/awards.shtml#PAFR (accessed 2007).

6. Phillips, J., Personal communication with author, September 14, 2004.

7. Government Finance Officers Association, *Criteria for Popular Annual Financial Reporting Awards Program*, GFOA Technical Services Center: http://www.gfoa.org/. (*Editor's Note:* Not accessible in 2007.)

8. Government Finance Offices Association, Popular annual financial reporting award (PAFR program): http://www.gfoa.org/services/awards.shtml#PAFR (accessed 2007).

9. Ammons, D.N., *Municipal Benchmarks: Assessing Local Performance and Establishing Community Standards*, 2nd ed., Sage, Thousand Oaks, CA, 2001.

10. Morley, E., Bryant, S.P., and Hatry, H.P., *Comparative Performance Measurement*, Urban Institute, Washington, DC, 2001.

11. Hatry, H., *Performance Measurement: Getting Results*, Urban Institute, Washington, DC, 1999.

12. Van Ryzin, G.G. et al., Drivers and consequences of citizen satisfaction: An application of the American customer satisfaction index model to New York City, *Public Administration Review*, 64, 331, 2004.

13. Kotler, P., Haider, D.H., and Rein, I.J., *Marketing Places: Attracting Investment, Industry, and Tourism to Cities, States, and Nations*, Free Press, New York, 1993.

14. Smith, G.E. and Huntsman, C.A., Reframing the metaphor of the citizen-government relationship: A value centered perspective, *Public Administration Review*, 57, 309, 1997.

Chapter 11

A History of Municipal Public Reporting: Examples of Robust Reporting in the 20th Century

Mordecai Lee

Contents

Abstract: In the first half of the 20th century, municipal administration included emphasizing that municipal officials in a democracy must contribute to the maintenance of an informed citizenry by reporting to the public, using such techniques as annual reports. Municipal reporting was at its heyday from the 1920s to the 1940s. Then, by the end of the 20th century, it gradually disappeared from the municipal administrator's agenda. Nonetheless, based on its theory and rationale, municipal reporting remains a duty of the public manager in a democracy. While not part of the E-government agenda yet, the new technologies of the digital era have the capacity to transform the traditional 20th century concept of municipal reporting into E-reporting for the 21st century.

Introduction, Research Questions and Methodology

Since the earliest writings about municipal administration, theorists have emphasized that municipal officials in a democracy must report to the public about their agencies' activities in order to contribute to an informed citizenry, the basis for both democracy and republican government. Public reporting received great attention from theorists and practitioners at the early part of the 20th century, peaking from the 1920s to the 1940s. Theorists suggested reporting had great promise and would bring benefits to urban democracy, public administration and governance. But, based on the historical record, reporting never lived up to its potential.

Then, municipal reporting slowly faded from the literature and practice to the point of practically disappearing from the municipal administrator's agenda by the end of the 20th century. Generally, it became a minor activity for contemporary urban public managers. Little writing about municipal reporting occurred after the 1960s. By the turn of the century, it was a largely forgotten and neglected element of municipal management.

Nonetheless, based on its theory and rationale, municipal reporting theoretically remains a duty of the public manager in a democracy. Specifically, public reporting is integral to Kirlin's final 'big question' of public administration in a democracy, namely "How can processes of society learning be improved, including knowledge of choices available, of consequences of alternatives, and of how to achieve desired goals, most importantly, the nurturing and development of a democratic polity?" [1] This chapter reviews and analyzes the history of the concept and practice of municipal reporting. This is a topic that in contemporary times has largely been ignored and unexplored by academics as well as practitioners.

Research design calls for research questions to be developed and posed at the beginning of an inquiry, rather than inductively at the end. [2] Therefore, based on the preceding introduction, the research questions for this inquiry about municipal reporting are:

- Is the theory and practice of public reporting a 20th-century anachronism or is it still valid in the 21st century?
- What is the source(s) of the decline of public reporting during the second half of the 20th century?
- Is the decline of public reporting evidence of public administration's shirking those topics that are not closely related to internal management issues?
- If municipal reporting is still relevant to the contemporary urban manager, what, if anything, is needed to update it?

Historical analysis is a common qualitative methodology in social science. [3–5] According to Gladden's overview in the 1970s, historians of government had up until then generally focused on power and leaders, giving less attention to public administration. [6] Since then, historical reviews and analyses have become more common in public administration. [7–14] One of the standard themes in historically based research is the attempt to identify and analyze trends. [15]

Given the dearth of attention to municipal reporting in contemporary literature (documented in a later section of this chapter) this is an exploratory study, a common methodology of public administration research techniques. [16] As such, it is intended, in part, to catalyze resumed attention by public administration academics and more empirically based research on specific aspects of municipal reporting.

Defining Municipal Public Reporting

Municipal corporations engage in external communications for many different reasons. In some cases, they seek to increase the utilization of their services by engaging in a marketing effort of informing potential clients about the availability of such services. Sometimes, agencies seek to maximize public compliance with laws and regulations by broadly disseminating information about those requirements. At other times, the dissemination of information is an end in itself, since the information is the 'product' of the agency, such as public libraries or a city assessor. Another purpose of external relations includes public service campaigns intended to modify mass behavior (e.g., 'Don't be a litter bug: Help keep ____ [name of city] clean'). Similarly, a local 911 emergency system seeks to obtain the assistance of citizens as the 'eyes and ears' of emergency services departments. All these external communications purposes are integrally tied to implementing the particular missions of city departments. By using multiple communications strategies, each agency is able to increase its efficiency at accomplishing its goals. The common thread shared by all these external communications programs is that they have a useful purpose. They are a tool of governance intended to facilitate the delivery of municipal goods and services, comparable to the many other techniques found in the municipal administrator's toolbox. [17,18]

However, beyond these practical communications programs, the municipal administrator also has an obligation to conduct one other external communication effort. Different from all the other ones, this has no benefit to the efficiency of the administrative process. Called municipal reporting or public reporting, it entails enhancing democracy by helping maintain an informed citizenry, the *sine qua non* of democracy. [19] The reporting imperative does not accomplish a pragmatic managerial purpose. Unlike the informational activities that contribute to the efficacy of agency operations, public reporting is information for information's sake. It doesn't 'do' anything. Rather, it is inherent in the *raison d'être* of public administration. Therefore, due to its underpinnings in democratic theory, public reporting is unique to the public sector, and does not exist as such in the business and nonprofit sectors. While some private and nonprofit agencies engage in external communication activities that are comparable to public reporting, these efforts are voluntary and goodwill-oriented, rather than an absolute requirement. [20]

Therefore, municipal public reporting is defined here as *the management activity intended to convey systematically and regularly information about government operations to the public-at-large, in order to promote an informed citizenry in a democracy and accountability to public opinion. It consists of direct and indirect reporting of the government's record of accomplishments and stewardship of the taxpayers' money. Public reporting is presented in many different communication formats, but always uses vocabulary that is understandable and meaningful to lay citizens.*

Municipal reporting is intended to provide an accounting to the voters of what the city had done in the recent past and how it has spent the public's tax dollars. Often focusing on annual reports, municipal reporting can be as varied as the methods and channels of communication that exist. Examples of reporting activities of cities have included, besides annual reports, monthly or quarterly reports, newspaper inserts, regular radio or TV programs, inserts in tax and utility bills, open houses, exhibits, parades, billboards and posters, movies, kiosks, videotapes and internet web pages.

This form of municipal reporting is to be distinguished from financial reports routinely generated by accountants and auditors. These reports, generally dense with financial information, are an integral part of a city's internal and external financial controls. Such reports are intended for the finance professionals and cannot be understood by the average resident of the city. For example, recent new financial reporting requirements associated with GASB 34 are mandating significant changes in municipal financial reporting. [21–23] Generally, these financial reports are intended to move public sector accounting toward full accrual accounting methods and to make them more similar to financial statements issued by private sector corporations. However, two aspects of GASB 34 statements are more closely tied to the concept of municipal public reporting. First, all statements will include a section entitled 'Management Discussion and Analysis' which is likely to contain information on general municipal activities and operations that would be closely akin to public reports. Second, GASB has been supporting efforts to assure that the performance measurement information contained in the new format of financial statements be understandable and useful to lay citizens. [24]

In an effort to connect the highly specialized uses of financial reports and the concept of municipal reporting to the public-at-large, the GASB and the Government Finance Officers Association have developed a by-product of financial reports called 'popular reports.' These are attempts to make financial reports understandable to non-specialized readers. The popular reporting approach seeks to bridge the gap between financial reporting and public reporting. [25–27] However, this form of popular reporting is also generally oriented to financial information and is not structured to guarantee the inclusion of other operational information important for democratic accountability.

Similarly, the contemporary focus on performance measurement in urban areas has largely concentrated on internal uses of data generated by local managers. Hatry emphasized that performance measurement is a system "used to help improve programs." [28] While he provides guidelines for releasing results to the public, he nonetheless focuses on the major purpose for the data to "use performance information to make program improvements that would not have been made in its absence." [29] Also, when refining his concepts two years later, he and his co-authors noted, "the persons likely to have the greatest interest in the report are the managers of the agencies being compared. They have the most at stake." [30] When identifying the uses of comparative performance information, communicating with the public is listed as tenth in priority and importance. [31]

Municipal reporting is also different from citizen participation in government decision making, sometimes called 'deliberative government.' Both, of course, relate to the uses of information by citizens interested in their municipal government. However, reporting focuses on retrospective knowledge 'for your information.' It is the feedback loop of the information cycle. Citizen participation, on the other hand, focuses on citizens using information prospectively to help local governments make decisions on future actions. Thus, reporting occurs at the back end of the process (such as end-of-year reports), while citizen participation is the initial stage at the front end of the policy process. In reporting, information is provided for its own sake, knowledge as a desirable civic goal. It is an end, in and of itself. In contradistinction, citizens participating in the policy development process use information as a means to an end, as a component of informed decision making. [32–34]

The Theory and Birth of Municipal Reporting: 1880s–1925

Since the earliest writings on public administration, theorists had emphasized that municipal administrators must report to the public about their agencies' activities. According to these writers, democratic accountability is accomplished not only by agency reports to the common council and other elected officials such as comptrollers and treasurers, but also through direct reporting to the public-at-large.

The theory and profession of public administration had emerged as part of the progressive movement in the late 19th and early 20th centuries. It sought to reform government, especially city government, to improve its efficiency and professionalism and to strengthen the democratic accountability of government agencies. [35] As reformers sought to free cities from corrupt machines, they realized that they needed to accomplish two goals in tandem. First, the delivery of municipal services needed to be professionalized through the development of civil service systems of trained, nonpolitical, insulated managers. Second, with elections no longer controlled by party machines, citizens needed to gain the skills to cast informed judgments in free elections. Previously habituated to following the instructions of the ward boss, voters would need to be 'retooled' to learn how to make decisions for themselves.

Reformers sought to define the basis for such decision making as frugality in government, businesslike methods in running cities and financial responsibility. The focus on the limited inherent skills of voters was partly because the intellectual roots of the good government reform movement included the reaction to perceived failures of post-Civil War Reconstruction, viewed by Northern urban elites (not just Southern racists) as a failure largely due to the expansion of suffrage to those who weren't capable of exercising intelligently their right to vote. [36] For example, in 1897 Goodnow stated as fact that "the existence of a large ignorant negro population" in the South was a valid justification for extra-legal limits on universal suffrage there. [37] He saw a rough parallel to lower class whites in large Northern cities. In 1910, he stated flatly, "the social qualities that are developed by urban life are not the qualities that favor good government." [38] Universal suffrage for city voting was not an appealing concept to him. Yet, the reformers could not openly call for anti-democratic municipal government. Campaigns for such reforms as new city charters, civil service protections, short ballots and the commission form of governance were intended in part to insulate city government from mass democracy.

Given that reformers could not openly advocate anti-democratic changes to city government, they needed to harmonize their publicly stated good-government goals with whatever form of mass democracy already existed at that time. (Note that women didn't get the right to vote until 1920. For African-Americans, limitations on their political participation in Northern cities were not as absolute as in the South, but there were significant barriers nonetheless.)

Wilson was seeking a way to rationalize America's traditional commitment to popular will and public opinion with a need for modern, professionalized public administration: "The problem is to make public opinion efficient without suffering it to be meddlesome ... Let administrative study find the best means for giving public criticism this control and for shutting it out from all other interference." [39] Clearly, he saw the separation of public administration from public opinion as a key element in successful government management. Nearly two decades later, Harvard's Munro was more explicit about the limits of democracy in city government:

> The most serious indictment against the American municipal system is ... its failure to interest and instruct the people in public affairs. Whoever is bent upon steady improvement in civic administration must begin by recognizing the normal impulses and shortcomings of the ordinary voter ... If we spent half as much on the instruction of the voter as we waste every year through inadequate fire-prevention measures, there would soon be an end to the political supremacy of the wrong sort of men. [40]

In a later volume Munro elaborated on the limitations of the voters:

> There is a common impression that real democracy can be established by merely giving voting rights to everybody and letting things take their course. As well might we try to

make the world righteous by putting a copy of the Ten Commandments in everyone's hand and calling the job complete ... And it [democracy] will not achieve this end unless the people have been schooled to a reasonable aptitude in seeing things clearly and thinking straight. [41]

It was at this point that early public administration theorists began suggesting that one way to accomplish an educated citizenry was by cities considering that they had the duty to keep the public routinely informed about their activities. This educational orientation for public administration fit well into John Dewey's philosophy that the *raison d'être* for public education was the creation of citizens for a democracy. [42] For example, regarding law enforcement, Woods emphasized the connection between an informed public and good government:

The public should know what is going on. It has a right to know in detail what its guardians are doing in order that it may intelligently conclude as to whether they should be discharged, or slapped on the back with approval and have their pay raised. [43]

Another initiative connected municipal reporting and education to the annual budget process. Between 1908 and 1911, reformers in New York City experimented with popular budget exhibits that explained the choices and decisions that needed to be made as part of the process of adopting the city's budget for the next year; a similar effort in Spokane, Washington was visited by one third of the city's voting population. [44]

In general, organized and planful municipal reporting would become the basis for creating, maintaining and advancing an informed electorate. According to Bruère, such reports would "equip the people 'to rule' with intelligence." [45] Similarly, Munro called for annual city reports as the way to educate the electorate. [46] Bradford suggested that reports were the key to the success of the commission form of city government — one of the key elements of the 'goo-goo' reform agenda. He recommended not only annual reports be given wide circulation to the citizenry, but also quarterly and even monthly reports. [47]

Municipal reporting could be accomplished in two ways. First, reporting could occur indirectly through press coverage, with citizens gaining ongoing information about the operation of government. Second, direct reporting could be accomplished through publications published by municipalities and distributed directly to the citizens.

One major leader in the development of municipal reporting during this period was Morris Cooke. According to White (who had just authored the first textbook on American public administration in 1926), [48] "the golden age of public reporting [was] inaugurated by Mr. Morris L. Cooke of Philadelphia." [49] Cooke, who had served as Director of Public Works for the City of Philadelphia, later became a consulting engineer and wrote extensively about municipal reform. He was an admirer of Taylor's 'scientific management' approach and corresponded with him for 30 years. [50,51] One of the municipal management concepts Cooke focused on was the duty of city governments to engage in publicity in order to educate the voters, especially through annual and other regular reports. He described municipal reports as having "the greatest room for improvement" of all aspects of government publicity. [52] In particular, he lauded New York City's 1915 annual report as "a neat volume printed in good type filled with many easily grasped facts and altogether enjoyable reading. It is in reality a citizen's handbook." [53]

The public reporting obligation of municipalities transformed the administrative apparatus of American city government from being a passive instrument implementing decisions to that of a public educator, a civics instructor, even a molder of public opinion. City government had to take an activist role in making democracy work. Through the device of municipal reporting, reformers could envision a mass electorate that rose above its baser instincts and exercised its popular will for a government that was to the socio-cultural liking of the reformers themselves.

Good stewardship by the new class of city managers would not be enough. City managers would also need to call attention to their accomplishments and take the initiative to put their record before the electorate. Public administrators needed to think of themselves as directly accountable to the citizenry through reports in order to strengthen democracy in the administrative state. This led to the emergence of municipal reporting as a feature of the new profession of public administration.

Zenith of Municipal Reporting: 1925–1950

By the late 1920s, municipal reporting was becoming institutionalized as one of the standard activities that theorists were including in the scope of municipal administration. For example, White's 1927 volume on *The City Manager* included a half-page discussion of the respective roles of the city manager and the city council — and possible role conflicts — regarding issuance of public reports. [54] A substantial body of literature was published during this period. In particular, two major publications in 1928 helped organize and formalize attention to the subject, Beyle's *Governmental Reporting in Chicago* [55] and Kilpatrick's *Reporting Municipal Government*. [56]

Beyle's 303-page volume was an academic analysis of the contents and format of every lay report issued by local government agencies operating in the City of Chicago in 1923, which totalled more than five feet of shelf space. His theme was that "official reports of governmental authorities submitted or made available to the public as an accounting of official conduct might be made a more effective agency for the promotion of good government and an essential foundation of popular rule." [57] After an exhaustive critical review of those reports, his conclusions included "what constitutes good reporting practice." Notwithstanding the academic orientation of the study (which was his dissertation at the University of Chicago), these conclusions were as useful to a practitioner as to future academic researchers. Best practices in municipal reporting, he suggested, would consist of 23 recommendations for reportorial activities, 3 recommendations regarding the substance of reports and 21 recommendations for presentation issues. [58] Beyle's final statement at the end of the book focused on the connection between improving municipal reporting and democracy:

> Improvement of governmental reporting must go hand in hand with other developments making for increased intelligence, good will, and efficiency on the part of democratic citizenry ... Here, the theme is that one very important instrumentality of democratic political life which is worthy and in much need of improvement is governmental reporting — potentially a system of vital communication between governmental servants and those whom government serves. [59]

That same year, University of Virginia professor Wylie Kilpatrick wrote the other major report on municipal reporting for the Municipal Administration Service. Even though an academic wrote it, the 77-page booklet was intended as a how-to manual for municipal officials. He emphasized that "reporting must be conceived as part of administration," [60] good reporting entailed two-way communication including city officials listening to the public and that reporting can occur through many instrumentalities besides the municipality itself, including citizens' associations, other levels of government, state municipal leagues, the press and radio. In particular, reports should have the same liveliness as headline stories in daily newspapers: "The report must be designed to tie in with the personal experience of the reader or listener. It has achieved its object when it has stirred to expression an opinion on the same or a related subject." [61]

Clarence Ridley of the International City Managers' Association (ICMA) and the University of Chicago began writing about municipal reporting in 1927 and continued through 1940. He also assigned his research assistant to work with him on the project, first-year University of Chicago graduate student Herbert A. Simon. [62,63] Ridley's first article on the topic appeared in the *National Municipal Review* in 1927. The theme of the article challenged the readers with the question, "How we can improve the art of municipal reporting to citizens and taxpayers?" [64] The next year, he began evaluating and grading the municipal reports from various cities based on 20 criteria he had developed for exemplary reports. His evaluation criteria included prompt publication, physical attractiveness to encourage readership, illustrative material to enhance presentation, clear and concise literary style, maximum length of 50 pages, use of comparative data for previous years and no more than three to four financial statements in the report. [65]

In 1937, Ridley reviewed developments in reporting from a more academic perspective. His perspective was that "the philosophy of governmental reporting has cleared many of the obstacles to general acceptance by the men who run cities." In his definition of the subject, government reporting was an active mode of communication intended to persuade, not merely to inform passively:

> It is clearly recognized in some cities that effective governmental and social progress do not proceed by automatic stages and that the community must be convinced at every step that the governmental program is worthy of support. [66]

He summarized various techniques of reporting that he had documented, such as annual printed reports, movies, radio programs, billboards, newspaper columns, open houses at municipal buildings, leaflets included in tax and water bills, budget hearings, regular newspaper columns and routine press coverage. By 1940, he reported that 89 municipalities were issuing periodic reports for the lay public (thus excluding purely financial reports). Newer reporting methods he discovered included a municipal parade that included 200 posters explaining city activities and exhibits on all aspects of city programs and departments at the municipal museum. [67] Other interesting details in the evolution of municipal reporting in the late 1940s and early 1950s included:

- Sanitation workers distributing the annual report to the homes on their routes [68]
- A political science class at a local college preparing the report [69]
- Newspapers publishing the annual report in serial form [70]
- Girl and Boy Scouts delivering the reports to homes [71]
- Posters on subways, buses and streetcars with reporting information [72]
- Early experiments in using the new medium of television for purposes of ongoing reporting [73,74]

Throughout the 1930s, municipal reporting had become a standard item in the training curriculum for municipal administrators. For example, the first edition of Pfiffner's long-running textbook in 1935 included a 16-page chapter entitled, 'Reporting to the Public' [75] and in the 1946 second edition it was half of a chapter on 'Publicity and Reports.' [76] Similarly, the subject was covered in Munro's 1934 text [77] and by White in his 1933 volume *Trends in Public Administration*. [78]

The definitive codification and formalization of municipal reporting occurred in 1931, with the publication of the final recommendations of the National Committee on Municipal Reporting. [79] The American Municipal Association (now the National League of Cities), the Governmental Research Association, ICMA and the National Municipal League (now the National Civic League) had created the committee in 1929. It spent two years preparing recommendations for a definitive and standard municipal report format. The four sponsoring organizations hoped the Committee's publication would be the founding document of what it called "public reporting administration." [80] From their perspective, public reporting was so important and integral a part of public administration that it should be recognized as one of the major components of the profession, along with such other standard rubrics as public personnel administration and public budgeting.

The cumulative effect of all these efforts clearly had an impact on practice. When Ridley began ICMA's annual survey of municipal annual reports in 1927, 12 cities had submitted their reports for review. [81] That number had grown to 188 in 1953. [82]

Yet, it was one thing for the subject to be part of a training curriculum, and another for the practice to be institutionalized and done so with a quality that achieved the intended goal of a product that is informative and understandable to a lay citizen reader for purposes of democratic accountability. While more and more cities were issuing annual reports and engaging in other forms of public reporting, the issue of lack of improvement in the 'real world' quality of this reporting was a running theme through much of the published research in the 1930s and 1940s:

1933: "Highly unsatisfactory" [83]
1934: "The preparation of municipal reports has been regarded as mere incident, not as an essential operation in the process of government" [84]
1938: "Has the City Lost Its Voice?" [85]
1939: "Municipal Reports or Museum Pieces?" [86]
1946: "These reports, though conscientious and accurate, have always been dry statements of facts and columns of figures, so deadly dull that not one in a hundred male voters ever took the trouble to read them through, and probably not one woman in a thousand" [87]
1948: "How Good Is Your Annual Report?" [88]

An exception to this trend was Price's observation in 1946 that, "in general, the quality of purely factual reporting has unquestionably improved. Cities have competed with each other to issue the most informative and interesting annual reports." [89] Nonetheless, this preponderance of comments in the literature signaled a lack of progress in the improvement of municipal reports and a lack of institutionalization of the activity in practice.

Atrophying of Municipal Reporting: 1950–2000

In the 1950s, practitioner and academic publications continued giving some attention to municipal reporting. The premier journal in the discipline, *Public Administration Review*, carried a three-page article on San Diego's 1951 Annual Report. [90] The monthly journal of the League of California Cities reported on innovative reporting efforts by state cities including movies, bulletins, tours, monthly reports, annual reports, radio coverage and TV coverage. [91] Yet, these were more the exceptions than the rule. For example, a bibliography of municipal public relations between 1960 and 1974 contained 70 entries, with only six about reporting and three of these citations coming from the same volume. [92]

The International City Managers' Association also continued its now two-decade-plus commitment to promoting the importance of municipal public relations in general and reporting in particular. Its monthly journal *Public Management* initiated in its January 1949 issue a regular monthly feature on municipal public relations. [93] It almost always included a review of current practices in reporting, not only of the traditional focus on annual reports, but also many other approaches and techniques including leaflets, newsletters, brochures, films and regular press releases. However, the section was discontinued with the November 1956 issue. [94] Similarly, ICMA's annual *Municipal Year Book* had always included a separate article on municipal reporting beginning with the 1938 volume [95] and continuing through the 1954 volume, when it was discontinued. [96] The annual article on reporting was replaced by one on municipal public relations beginning with the 1955 volume, [97] but it, too, was discontinued with the 1967 volume. [98] These developments indicated ICMA's perception that public reporting had not become a permanent and important feature in the practice of municipal management.

The same disappearance occurred with the leading long-running multi-edition public administration textbooks. A new textbook in 1953 by Dimock and Dimock included instruction in public reporting, [99] a topic that continued to be covered in subsequent editions in 1958 [100] and 1964. [101] However, the topic was reduced to a seven-line paragraph in the 1969 edition. In it, the authors briefly discussed the early history of municipal reporting with 1941 as their most recent citation. [102]

Similarly, reporting disappeared from the Pfiffner and Presthus textbook. While the 1935 and 1946 editions had detailed discussions of reporting (see above), the topic disappeared from the 1953 third edition [103] and all subsequent editions through the sixth and final edition in 1975. [104–106] Notwithstanding White's early writings on the importance of municipal reporting, his own textbook demonstrated the same trend as the others. While reporting is discussed in a two-page section of the 1949 edition, [107] it is absent from the last version in 1955. [108]

By the 1960s and on, not only was less attention paid to municipal reporting, but also the scope of the concept had largely shrunk from multiple methods and channels of reporting to, solely, the annual municipal report. At an international conference on local government public relations, reporting was discussed in only one of six papers of the conference proceedings. The speaker recommended translating the municipal annual report to other media, including slides with a synchronized tape. He lauded examples of more frequent reports, sometimes as newspaper inserts. [109] One of the rare discussions of municipal reporting at the end of the century was Schachter's suggestion of strengthening the role of citizens in government by having cities generate a three-step reporting system consisting of an annual city report, monthly agency presentations and digital access to daily operational reports of individual bureaus. [110]

ICMA did not totally abandon its commitment to municipal reporting. It published a 71-page booklet in 1963 that provided 'how to' instructions on annual reports as well as other forms of reporting. [111] While pleased that 431 cities were now issuing annual municipal reports, [112] the booklet conceded, "current municipal reporting may have fallen into a rut and may be on a lean diet of resources." [113] Increasingly, municipal reporting was limited to annual reports, which were printed as cheaply as possible and thus becoming less and less attractive to readers. This was not what Ridley and the early pioneers had originally had in mind for municipal reporting.

ICMA's 1966 volume *Municipal Public Relations* included a limited discussion of the value of reporting:

In most state, county, and local governments public reporting is a legal requirement, particularly in fiscal matters. Public relations requirements of providing information to the public transcend this legal duty; however, it is imperative of both common sense and morality. Nor does the provision for making information public through such vehicles as the annual report fulfill the entire obligation of government. [114]

Again in 1975, ICMA's handbook on *Public Relations in Local Government* included a chapter on Special Reports and Events including a discussion of reporting. [115] It urged "techniques of reporting through every vehicle possible and at every opportunity possible" including publications, annual reports, special reports, newsletters and reporting in person. [116]

The fading importance of, and interest in, public reporting in general, and municipal reporting in particular, was made clear with the publication in 1998 and 2003 of de novo encyclopedias of public policy and administration. They contained no entries on reporting, whether by municipalities or by any other level of government. [117] Even ICMA's traditional interest in the subject seemed to have diminished. Its 1994 handbook *Effective Communication* contained no stand-alone discussion of the specific role and importance of municipal reporting. Instead, discussions of annual reports, newsletters, etc. were meshed within other chapters, such as on planning, external communications and publications. [118]

Analysis

This inquiry has used the printed record to create a comprehensive history of municipal reporting in theory and practice. At this stage, an analysis of the results of the review is to be used to address the original research questions.

First, is the theory and practice of public reporting an anachronism of the 20th century or is it still valid in the 21st century? In a preceding section, the rationale for municipal reporting provided in the theoretical literature was examined. The writings of public administration theoreticians who originally created and refined the concept demonstrated the connection of reporting to the accountability of modern public administration in a democracy. As such, the rationale for public reporting continues to be relevant to government management in the 21st century as it was when originally conceived in the first half of the 20th century. As an indication of this, in 2001, an international organization of First World and developed countries called for increased public reporting at all levels of government as a first step in increasing citizen participation in policy making. [119]

Second, what has caused the decline of public reporting during the second half of the 20th century? As a result of this in-depth historical review, no single source or cause has presented itself to explain the decline of public reporting. Some of the issues that were identified in this historical record as weaknesses in robust and effective public reporting included:

■ The narrow scope of reporting focusing on management efficiency as opposed to policy choices, i.e., process, not substance. This obsession with management information may not be responsive to information the citizenry either wants or finds interesting.
■ The persistent problem of creating reports that were visually interesting to readers.
■ Municipal reporting didn't 'do' anything. Unlike other management and communication activities, this was information for information's sake, rather than for the purpose

of administrative efficiency. As such, it would naturally be lower on the urban manager's agenda than other 'real' projects.

■ When seeking to be vigorous protectors of the public purse, elected officials at all levels have been quick to cut the public relations spending in agency budget proposals. [120–127] A manifestation of this occurred when ICMA surveyed its members in 1966 about their public relations activities. Forty-three cities responded that they didn't have any public relations programs or expenditures and didn't have any staff that engaged in it. One clerk wrote back on the survey form, "We spend our time building new sewers, water systems, and repaving streets. No time for anything else." [128]

■ The diminishing attention given to the subject by ICMA, perhaps related to the passing of long-time executive director Clarence Ridley and the successors he had personally trained and influenced.

■ The diminishing attention given to the subject by public administration educators, as demonstrated by the content of successive editions of some of the major textbooks.

While not specifically identified in the historical record, another possible and logical explanation for the decline in public reporting could be tied to 'demand side' issues. In other words, has there been a lack of expressed interest by the public-at-large for reporting? Are municipal managers merely reflecting a civic apathy? This is certainly possible, especially since it had been reformers — supposedly speaking on behalf of the public or, at least, the public interest — who had prompted the original emergence of municipal reporting. These advocates were based in academe, practitioner organizations or good-government advocacy associations. Perhaps there had been no authentic citizen interest in receiving and reviewing reports, notwithstanding the arguments of the reformers. Shifting the direction of this potential demand-side explanation from the past to the present and the future, it is possible that a reinvigorated citizen-based demand for municipal reporting could be caused by the rise of attention to civil society, public concerns prompted by the Enron Corporation bankruptcy and other private-sector scandals caused by false reporting, and the general increase in public advocacy. Survey research, especially public opinion polling, could help examine this hypothesis.

Regarding the third research question, is the decline of public reporting evidence of public administration's shirking topics that are not closely related to internal management issues? The 'hot' subjects of the 1990s focused predominantly on management issues. Such topics as the new public management, reinventing government, performance measurement, IT, strategic planning, and service delivery innovations such as contracting out and public–private partnerships have the inevitable effect of drawing the profession's attention (whether of academicians or practitioners) to management efficiency issues rather than to democratic governance issues. In this sense, public administration's recent trends have focused on the 'administration' rather than the 'public' in its title. Municipal reporting is one of the concepts at the core of what makes public administration different from business administration, namely its unique placement within the public sector, within democratic government. As long as public administration remains preoccupied with increasing efficiency, it will give little attention to the various democratic obligations of the public administrator.

Fourth, if municipal reporting is still relevant to the contemporary urban manager, what, if anything, is needed to update it? The digital age has spawned new approaches to governance, sometimes called e-government. As a new technology for conducting external relations, government agencies have focused on using the tools of e-government to 'get things done.' The primary focus of e-government's growth until now has been on transactions, such as renewing a driver's license online, or on access to information such as property appraisal data. Academe's attention has also been relatively limited. According to Fountain, "a review of the first-tier journals in organization theory and political science yields an almost imperceptible nod to the Internet." [129]

When e-government has focused on governance instead of transactions, such studies have concentrated largely on deliberative democracy and tools of governing. For example, using the Internet for enhancing citizen participation in government for specific activities and purposes is often discussed, but not using it to accomplish traditional reporting through new means and technologies. [130–134]

Nonetheless, the same technology is available for use as e-reporting. [135] Benefits from using these technologies could include reaching individual citizens on a 24/7 basis, bypassing dependence on coverage by the news media, the ability to tailor information based on depth of detail desired by various attentive publics, savings in printing costs, environmental friendliness of reduced paper consumption and elimination of maintenance of mailing lists.

Future Research

Based upon this analysis of the historical record and the original early 20th century rationale for municipal reporting, this researcher concludes that public reporting needs to be revived and revitalized by the profession. While so much of the managerial work of the urban public administrator has changed over the last 100 years, the manager's democratic responsibilities have not. For public administration to fulfill its original and continuing commitment to efficient management in the public sector, it must not abandon its simultaneous focus on democracy as well as on management.

Exploratory research inevitably generates additional questions for subsequent research. It is only the first step in a systematic and comprehensive research agenda. Some of the possible future research questions that arise from this historical analysis include:

- Empirical research: What, if any, reporting are municipalities currently undertaking? What is the frequency, content, format and delivery technology of contemporary reporting?
- Comparative empirical research: What are the reporting activities of municipal governments in other developed democratic countries? What differences, trends and innovative approaches are apparent?
- Survey research: Is there a demand-side push for reporting from the citizenry?
- Theory development: Based on societal and technological changes, should the theoretical premise of reporting be revised? What should be the normative expectations and benchmarks for 21st century e-reporting?
- Practitioner oriented research: What are 'best practices' in e-reporting? What should be the content, format and delivery technology of municipal reporting?

Note: *Originally published in Lee, M., The history of municipal public reporting,* International Journal of Public Administration, *29, 453, 2006.*

Endnotes

1. Kirlin, J.J., The big questions of public administration in a democracy, *Public Administration Review*, 56, 421, 1996.

2. Brower, R.S., Abolafia, M.Y., and Carr, J.B., On improving qualitative methods in public administration research, *Administration & Society*, 32, 386, 2000.

3. Gabrielian, V., Qualitative research methods: An overview, in *Handbook of Research Methods in Public Administration*, Miller, G.J. and Whicker, M.L., Eds., Marcel Dekker, New York, 1999, chap. 10.

4. Denzin, N.K. and Lincoln, Y.S., Eds., *Handbook of Qualitative Research*, 2nd ed., Sage, Thousand Oaks, CA, 2000, 375.

5. Williamson, J.B. et al., *The Research Craft: An Introduction to Social Research Methods*, 2nd ed., Little Brown, Boston, 1982, chap. 10.

6. Gladden, E.N., *A History of Public Administration*, Vol. I, Frank Cass, London, 1972, vii.

7. Raadschelders, J.C.N., *Handbook of Administrative History*, Transaction, New Brunswick, NJ, 1989.

8. Schachter, H.L., *Frederick Taylor and the Public Administration Community: A Reevaluation*, State University of New York Press, Albany, 1989.

9. Stivers, C., *Bureau Men, Settlement Women: Constructing Public Administration in the Progressive Era*, University Press of Kansas, Lawrence, 2000.

10. Farazmand, A., Ed., *Handbook of Comparative and Development Public Administration*, 2nd ed., Marcel Dekker, New York, 2001. The second part of the volume is entitled *Historical Bases of Public Administration and Bureaucracy*.

11. Pfiffner, J.M., *Research Methods in Public Administration*, Ronald, New York, 1940, chap. 10.

12. McNabb, D.E., *Research Methods in Public Administration and Nonprofit Management: Quantitative and Qualitative Approaches*, M.E. Sharpe, Armonk, NY, 2002, chap. 23.

13. Wrege, C.D., Greenwood, R.A., and Hata, S., What we do not know about management history: Some categories of research and methods to uncover management history mysteries, *Journal of Management History*, 5, 414, 1999.

14. Tuchman, G., Historical social science: Methodologies, methods, and meanings, in *Handbook of Qualitative Research*, Denzin, N.K. and Lincoln, Y.S., Eds., Sage, Thousand Oaks, CA, 1994, chap. 19.

15. Williamson, op. cit., 246.

16. Gabrielian, op. cit.

17. Weiss, J.A., Public information, in *The Tools of Government: A Guide to the New Governance*, Salamon, L.M., Ed., Oxford University Press, New York, 2002, chap. 7.

18. Lee, M., Public information in government organizations: A review and curriculum outline of external relations in public administration, *Public Administration and Management: An Interactive Journal*, 5, 183, 2000. http://www.pamij.com/5_4/5_4_4_pubinfo.pdf (accessed 2007) (*Editor's Note:* See Chapter 1.)

19. Brown, R.D., *The Strength of a People: The Idea of an Informed Citizenry in America, 1650–1870*, University of North Carolina Press, Chapel Hill, 1996.

20. Lee, M., Intersectoral differences in public affairs: The duty of public reporting in public administration, *Journal of Public Affairs*, 2(2), 33, 2002.

21. Chaney, B.A., Mead, D.M., and Schermann, K.R., The new governmental financial reporting model, *Journal of Government Financial Management*, 51, 26, 2002.

22. Schermann, K., NAIPFA conference: GASB 34 — What it says, *Municipal Finance Journal*, 22(2), 35, 2001.

23. Allen, T.L., Improving governmental financial reporting, *Municipal Finance Review*, 21(4), 69, 2001.

24. Fountain, J. et al., *Report on the GASB Citizen Discussion Groups on Performance Reporting*, Governmental Accounting Standards Board, Norwalk, CT, 2002.

25. Carpenter, F.H. and Sharp, F.C., *Popular Reporting: Local Government Financial Reports to the Citizenry*, Governmental Accounting Standards Board, Norwalk, CT, 1992.

26. Allison, G.S., GFOA's popular reporting awards program: Revised and improved, *Government Finance Review*, 11(3), 36, 1995.

27. Kravchuk, R.S. and Voorhees, W.R., The new governmental financial reporting model under GASB Statement No. 34: An emphasis on accountability, *Public Budgeting and Finance*, 21(3), 1, 2001.

28. Hatry, H.P., *Performance Measurement: Getting Results*, Urban Institute Press, Washington, DC, 1999, 151, emphasis in original.

29. Ibid, 157.

30. Morley, E., Bryant, S.P., and Hatry, H.P., *Comparative Performance Measurement*, Urban Institute Press, Washington, DC, 2001, 77.

31. Ibid, 96.

32. Sanoff, H., *Community Participation Methods in Design and Planning*, Wiley, New York, 2000.

33. Forester, J., *The Deliberative Practitioner: Encouraging Participatory Planning Processes*, MIT Press, Cambridge, MA, 1999.

34. King, C.S., Stivers, C., and Box, R.C., *Government Is Us: Public Administration in an Anti-Government Era*, Sage, Thousand Oaks, CA, 1998.

35. Schachter, H.L., Ed., The importance of the progressive era in public administration today, *Administrative Theory and Praxis*, 24(3), 437, 2002.

36. Foner, E., *Reconstruction: America's Unfinished Revolution, 1863–1877*, Harper & Row, New York, 1988, 492–494.

37. Goodnow, F.J., *Municipal Problems*, Macmillan, New York, 1897, 147. This racist statement is appalling to a contemporary reader, yet it accurately reflects the shared values of the country's elite at that time. Goodnow, of course, made a major contribution to the intellectual basis for American public administration with his 1900 book *Politics and Administration: A Study in Government*.

38. Goodnow, F.J., *City Government in the United States*, Century Company, New York, 1910, 110.

39. Wilson, W., The study of administration, *Political Science Quarterly*, 2, 215, 1887.

40. Munro, W.B., *Principles and Methods of Municipal Administration*, Macmillan, New York, 1916, 8.

41. Munro, W.B., *Municipal Government and Administration*, Vol. I, Macmillan, New York, 1925, 253.

42. Hawley, E.W., *The Great War and the Search for a Modern Order: A History of the American People and Their Institutions, 1917–1933*, St. Martin's Press, New York, 1979, 142–144.

43. Woods, A., *Policeman and Public*, Yale University Press, New Haven, CT, 1919, 178.

44. Kahn, J. *Budgeting Democracy: State Building and Citizenship in America, 1890–1928*, Cornell University Press, Ithaca, NY, 1997, chap. 4; and George, R.E., Increased efficiency as a result of increased governmental functions, *Annals of the American Academy of Political and Social Science*, 64, 82, 1916. Despite their success, the budget exhibits in New York City were discontinued, partly due to differences of opinion among the leadership of the New York Bureau of Municipal Research and partly due to conditions attached to continued Rockefeller funding of the Bureau.

45. Bruère, H., *The New City Government*, D. Appleton, New York, 1916, 130.

46. Munro, W.B., *Principles and Methods of Municipal Administration*, op. cit., 7.

47. Bradford, E.S., *Commission Government in American Cities*, Macmillan, New York, 1915, 218.

48. White, L.D., *Introduction to the Study of Public Administration*, Macmillan, New York, 1926.

49. White, L.D., Public administration, 1928, *American Political Science Review*, 23, 437, 1929.

50. Taylor, F.W., Cooke, M.L., and Smith, O., *Correspondence Collection on Frederick W. Taylor*, Vol. 3, Social Science Institute, Osaka, Japan, 1992. See also Schachter, H.L., *Frederick Taylor and the Public Administration Community: A Reevaluation*, State University of New York Press, Albany, 1989, chap. 6; Kanigel, R., *The One Best Way: Frederick Winslow Taylor and the Enigma of Efficiency*, Viking, New York, 1997.

51. Cooke had an extraordinary career in Public Administration, extending from Taylor to the 1950s. During the New Deal and World War II, he served in the Roosevelt Administration in several major positions, including Administrator of the Rural Electrification Administration from 1935 to 1937. He concluded his career as Chairman of the President's Water Resources Policy Commission during the Truman Administration. He died in 1960 at age 88 (Seligman, L.G. and Cornwell, E.E., Jr., Eds., *New Deal Mosaic: President Roosevelt Confers with his National Emergency Council, 1933–1936*, University of Oregon Books, Eugene, 1965, 555; Caro, R.A., *The Years of Lyndon Johnson [Vol. 3]: Master of the Senate*, Alfred A. Knopf, New York, 2002, 252, 289, 300).

52. Cooke, M.L., *Our Cities Awake: Notes on Municipal Activities and Administration*, Doubleday, Page, Garden City, NY, 1919, 197.

53. Ibid, 204.

54. White, L.D., *The City Manager*, University of Chicago Press, Chicago, 1927, 216.

55. Beyle, H.C., *Governmental Reporting in Chicago*, University of Chicago Press, Chicago, 1928.

56. Kilpatrick, W., *Reporting Municipal Government*, Municipal Administration Service, New York, 1928.

57. Beyle, op. cit., 6–7.

58. Ibid, 241–249.

59. Ibid, 254.

60. Kilpatrick, op. cit., 61.

61. Ibid, 58.

62. Simon, H.A., *Models of My Life*, HarperCollins, New York, 1991, 70–72.

63. For a detailed examination of Simon's contributions to municipal reporting, see Lee, M., Is there anything new under the sun? Herbert Simon's contributions in the 1930s to performance measurement and public reporting of performance results, *Public Voices*, 6(2–3), 73, 2003.

64. Ridley, C.E., Municipal reports, *National Municipal Review*, 16, 243, 1927.

65. Ridley, C.E., Appraising municipal reports: Some essentials of a good municipal report, *National Municipal Review*, 17, 150, 1928.

66. Ridley, C.E., Municipal reporting taken seriously, *Public Opinion Quarterly*, 1(1), 112, 1937.

67. Ridley, C.E., Municipal reporting, in *The Municipal Year Book, 1940*, Ridley, C.E. and Nolting, O.F., Eds., International City Managers' Association, Chicago, 1940, 248.

68. Ridley, C.E., Municipal reporting, in *The Municipal Year Book, 1941*, Ridley, C.E. and Nolting, O.F., Eds., International City Managers' Association, Chicago, 1941, 253.

69. Ridley, C.E., Municipal reporting, in *The Municipal Year Book, 1942*, Ridley, C.E. and Nolting, O.F., Eds., International City Managers' Association, Chicago, 1942, 348.

70. Rippy, J.F., Jr., Municipal reporting, in *The Municipal Year Book, 1943*, Ridley, C.E. and Nolting, O.F., Eds., International City Managers' Association, Chicago, 1943, 323.

71. Snyder, R.W., Municipal reporting in 1953, in *The Municipal Year Book, 1954*, Ridley, C.E. and Nolting, O.F., Eds., International City Managers' Association, Chicago, 1954, 271.

72. Rinn, F.J., Municipal public relations in 1954, in *The Municipal Year Book, 1955*, Ridley, C.E. and Nolting, O.F., Eds., International City Managers' Association, Chicago, 1955, 256.

73. Snyder, op. cit., 273.

74. Rinn, op. cit., 260.

75. Pfiffner, J.M., *Public Administration*, Ronald, New York, 1935, 472–487.

76. Pfiffner, J. M., *Public Administration*, Revised Edition, Ronald, New York, 1946, 589–611.

77. Munro, W.B., *Municipal Administration*, Macmillan, New York, 1934, 196–199.

78. White, L.D., *Trends in Public Administration*, McGraw-Hill, New York, 1933, 319–320.

79. National Committee on Municipal Reporting, *Public Reporting, with special reference to annual, departmental, and current reports of municipalities*, Municipal Administration Service, New York, 1931.

80. Ibid, 3.

81. Ridley, C.E., Appraising municipal reports: Some essentials of a good municipal report, *National Municipal Review*, 17, 150, 1928.

82. Snyder, op. cit., 269.

83. White, L.D., *Trends in Public Administration*, McGraw-Hill, New York, 1933, 319.

84. Munro, W.B., *Municipal Administration*, Macmillan, New York, 1934, 197.

85. Hazelrigg, H., Has the city lost its voice?, *Public Opinion Quarterly*, 2, 457, 1938.

86. Clark, W.C., Municipal reports or museum pieces?, *Public Opinion Quarterly*, 3, 292, 1939.

87. Mead Corporation Research Division, Ed., *Planning the Modern Municipal Report*, Mead Corporation, New York, 1946, 5. The book, published by a papermaking company, was compiled largely from an exhibit at the New York Public Library that had been organized by the American Institute of Graphic Arts. The overt sexism of the quote, a reflection of 1940s values, is striking, yet routine in those days.

88. Toner, J.S., How good is your annual report?, *Public Management*, 30, 318, 1948.

89. Price, D. K., Democratic administration, in *Elements of Public Administration*, 2nd ed., Morstein Marx, F., Ed., Prentice-Hall, Englewood Cliffs, NJ, 1959, 73.

90. Campbell, O.W., San Diego's 1951 annual report, *Public Administration Review*, 13, 30, 1953.

91. Public relations — How 40 California cities supplement the local press, *Western City*, 28(2), 41, 1952.

92. White, A.G., *Municipal Public Relations: A Selected Bibliography 1960–1974*, Council of Planning Librarians, Monticello, IL, 1977.

93. Municipal public relations, *Public Management*, 31(1), 13, 1949.

94. Municipal public relations, *Public Management*, 38(11), 252, 1956.

95. Simon, H.A., Municipal reporting, in *The Municipal Year Book, 1938*, Ridley, C.E. and Nolting, O.F., Eds., International City Managers' Association, Chicago, 1938, 47.

96. Snyder, op. cit., 269.

97. Rinn, op. cit., 256.

98. Tureck, M.C., Municipal public relations in 1966, in *The Municipal Year Book, 1967*, Nolting, O.F. and Arnold, D.S., Eds., International City Managers' Association, Chicago, 1967, 242.

99. Dimock, M.E. and Dimock, G.O., *Public Administration*, Rinehart, New York, 1953, 420–423.

100. Dimock, M.E., Dimock, G.O., and Koenig, L.W., *Public Administration*, rev. ed., Rinehart, New York, 1958, 496–499.

101. Dimock, M.E. and Dimock, G.O., *Public Administration*, 3rd ed., Holt, Rinehart and Winston, New York, 1964, 343–346.

102. Dimock, M.E. and Dimock, G.O., *Public Administration*, 4th ed., Holt, Rinehart and Winston, New York, 1969, 592.

103. Pfiffner, J.M. and Presthus, R.V., *Public Administration*, 3rd ed., Ronald, New York, 1953.

104. Pfiffner, J.M. and Presthus, R.V., *Public Administration*, 4th ed., Ronald, New York, 1960.

105. Pfiffner, J.M. and Presthus, R., *Public Administration*, 5th ed., Ronald, New York, 1967.

106. Presthus, R., *Public Administration*, 6th ed., Ronald, New York, 1975.

107. White, L.D., *Introduction to the Study of Public Administration*, 3rd ed., Macmillan, New York, 1949, 230–231.

108. White, L.D., *Introduction to the Study of Public Administration*, 4th ed., Macmillan, New York, 1955.

109. Rosen, A.S., Public relations: Activities and means, in *The Public Relations of Local Governments; Papers Presented at the World Conference of Local Governments, June 15–20, 1961*, M. Nijhoff for the International Union of Local Authorities, The Hague, Netherlands, 1962, 36.

110. Schachter, H.L., *Reinventing Government or Reinventing Ourselves: The Role of Citizen Owners in Making Better Government*, State University of New York Press, Albany, 1997, 85–89.

111. Wall, N.L., *Municipal Reporting to the Public*, International City Managers' Association, Chicago, 1963.

112. Ibid, 2.

113. Ibid, 4.

114. Anderson, D.L., Public relations and the administrative process, in *Municipal Public Relations*, Anderson, D.L., Ed., International City Managers' Association, Chicago, 1966, 28.

115. Gilbert, W.H., Special reports and events, in *Public Relations in Local Government*, Gilbert, W.H., Ed., International City Management Association, Washington, DC, 1975, 164.

116. Ibid, 184.

117. Shafritz, J.M., Ed., *International Encyclopedia of Public Policy and Administration*, HarperCollins, Boulder, CO, 1998; Rabin, J., Ed., *Encyclopedia of Public Administration and Public Policy*, Marcel Dekker, New York, 2003.

118. Wheeler, K.M., Ed., *Effective Communication: A Local Government Guide*, International City/County Management Association, Washington, DC, 1994.

119. Caddy, J. and Vergez, C., *Citizens as Partners: Information, Consultation and Public Participation in Policy-Making*, Organisation for Economic Co-operation and Development, Paris, France, 2001.

120. Yarwood, D.L. and Enis, B.M., Problems in regulating federal executive branch publicity and advertising programs, *American Review of Public Administration*, 18, 29, 1988.

121. Yarwood, D.L. and Enis, B.J., Advertising and publicity programs in the executive branch of the federal government: Hustling or helping the people?, *Public Administration Review*, 42, 37, 1982.

122. Pimlott, J.A.R., *Public Relations and American Democracy*, Kennikat, Port Washington, NY, 1972 [1951].

123. Fulbright, J.W., *The Pentagon Propaganda Machine*, Random House, New York, 1971. The author was a U.S. Senator (D-AR) and chair of the Foreign Relations Committee.

124. McCamy, J.L., *Government Publicity: Its Practice in Federal Administration*, University of Chicago Press, Chicago, 1939.

125. Price, op. cit., 73.

126. Lee, M., When Congress tried to cut Pentagon public relations: A lesson from history, *Public Relations Review*, 26, 131, 2000.

127. Lee, M., President Nixon sees a 'cover up': Public relations in federal agencies, *Public Relations Review*, 23, 301, 1997.

128. Tureck, op. cit., 242.

129. Fountain, J.E., *Building the Virtual State: Information Technology and Institutional Change*, Brookings Institution, Washington, DC, 2001, 16.

130. Kamarck, E.C. and Nye, J.S., Jr., Eds., *Governance.com: Democracy in the Information Age*, Brookings Institution, Washington, DC, 2002.

131. Salamon, L.M., Ed., *The Tools of Government: A Guide to the New Governance*, Oxford University Press, New York, 2002.

132. Moon, M.J., The evolution of e-government among municipalities: Rhetoric or reality?, *Public Administration Review*, 62, 426 and Table 1, 2002.

133. Ho, A.T.-K., Reinventing local governments and the e-government initiative, *Public Administration Review*, 62, 434, 2002.

134. Hague, B.N. and Loader, B.D., Eds., *Digital Democracy: Discourse and Decision Making in the Information Age*, Routledge, London, 1999.

135. Lee, M., E-Reporting: Using managing-for-results data to strengthen democratic accountability, in *Managing for Results 2005*, Kamensky, J.M. and Morales, A., Eds., Rowman & Littlefield, Lanham, MD, 2005, chap. 4. Also published as a monograph and available online: http://www.businessofgovernment.org/pdfs/Lee_Report.pdf (accessed 2007). (*Editor's Note:* See Chapter 25.)

Appendix III

Questions for Review and Discussion

1. Why are government agencies expected to engage in public reporting? What is public reporting intended to accomplish?
2. If you are currently employed in public administration, investigate and summarize the public reporting activities of your agency. If you are not at present working in the public sector, select a governmental agency that is based in your locality (such as the municipality's public works department, the county's social services department, etc.) and research its reporting activities. Then, based on the readings in this section, what — if anything — would you propose to improve that organization's reporting programs?

Additional Reading

Hassett, W.L., Citizen newsletters: Are they worth the trouble?, *PM: Public Management,* 84(3), 20, 2002.

Lee, M., Intersectoral differences in public affairs: The duty of public reporting in public administration, *Journal of Public Affairs,* 2(2), 33, 2002.

Lee, M., *The First Presidential Communications Agency: FDR's Office of Government Reports,* State University of New York Press, Albany, 2005.

Lee, M., Empirical experiments in public reporting: Reconstructing the results of survey research in 1941–42, *Public Administration Review,* 66, 252, 2006.

Mack, J. and Ryan, C., Is there an audience for public sector annual reports? Australian evidence, *International Journal of Public Service Management,* 20, 134, 2007.

Roberts, A., *Blacked Out: Government Secrecy in the Information Age,* Cambridge University Press, New York, 2006.

PURPOSES OF GOVERNMENT PUBLIC RELATIONS: RESPONSIVENESS TO THE PUBLIC

Introduction to Section IV

In Chapter 2, Grunig emphasized that a fully developed public relations program entails two-way symmetrical communications. Therefore, good public relations is more than outgoing communication, which he calls the press agentry and public information models. Rather, a government agency also needs to focus on receiving messages from the public, to hear what the citizenry is saying. This closes the circle of communications and reflects a comprehensive approach to public relations.

This aspect of government public relations focuses on the specific purpose of being responsive to the public. By being responsive to citizens' needs, an agency is perforce doing a better job at implementing its mission. This means it is improving its performance as a service provider as well as having the indirect effect of increasing public support for the agency, the latter being the eighth purpose for government public relations. Happy customers and clients make for successful public administration and strong organizations. Being responsive to the public can have many manifestations. Generally, it involves developing successful relationships with the public on the front end of the policy process — i.e., before major decisions are made — and at the back end of public administration, after a program has been implemented and services have been provided.

Whether occurring at the beginning or the end of the administrative process, responsiveness to the public extends to many aspects of agency activity, some not normally included in the rubric of public relations. For example, the importance of citizen participation in governmental decision making, holding public hearings, and naming advisory bodies tends to be a distinct and free-standing topic within political science, public administration, and even (public sector) marketing.

However, as government public relations has been defined in this volume, it can be considered an aspect of a comprehensive public relations program as well.

The first chapter in this section (Chapter 12) is a detailed examination of how to conduct — and how *not* to conduct — public participation programs. The authors review the different methods of involving the citizenry in decision making and identify some important criteria that need to be fulfilled for participation to be meaningful. The chapter identifies some techniques that seem to be more effective and more authentic than others, but they are time consuming and necessitate involving individuals who can help make the process successful. Perhaps a shorthand summary of the message of the chapter is that citizen participation is easier said than done.

Chapter 13 is also largely about the front end of public administration. It presents a summary of the various approaches to engaging with citizens, listing many different techniques and methods. Written from the perspective of the United Kingdom, the chapter helps give the reader an understanding of the importance of this subject on an international level. Responsiveness is not limited to any particularity of U.S. political culture. Rather, the need for — and difficulty of implementing — citizen participation is a universal one for democracies.

Chapter 14 and Chapter 15 discuss responsiveness to the public at the back end of the public administration process. The city of Taipei in Taiwan had created a citizen complaint process and, in Hong Kong, an ombudsman position was established to investigate public complaints. Both are similar in that they are intended to provide a feedback loop to government agencies. In some cases, these are issues that entail an individual, virtually case work. Someone feels he or she wasn't treated right, was given incorrect information, was shortchanged by a program officer, etc. This is customer service at the retail level, one client at a time. An ombudsman can also be a venue for such matters. However, unlike the complaint system, the ombudsman usually has some investigatory powers, akin to inspectors general in federal departments and agencies. This permits the ombudsman to look into issues that are larger than one person's inadequate service. So, besides the retail approach, the ombudsman can be involved in wholesale matters as well, i.e., general matters of government policy and operations that affect more than one individual. Chapter 15 includes a discussion of the Hong Kong Ombudsman's inquiry into three major matters and then evaluates the ability of the office to deal with such larger issues.

In general, this aspect of government public relations is intended to make the government manager more sensitive to *listening* to the public. Whether this involves the front end or back end of the administrative process or it involves retail or wholesale issues, the key for the successful practitioner is to know the importance of communications coming into the agency from the outside, not just sending messages from the agency to the public. Good public relations is a two-way street. An awareness of the importance of responsiveness to the public is the first step to successfully implementing this distinct purpose of government public relations.

Chapter 12

Encouraging Community Dialogue: Approach, Promise, and Tensions

Amy Helling and John Clayton Thomas

Contents

Abstract: There has been growing interest in recent years in what might be termed "community dialogues," or techniques for engaging broad-based discussions of issues within particular communities. The purpose of this article is to survey and assess this movement based on prior research. We first contrast traditional citizen involvement in public planning as a method of pursuing community dialogues with the newer, collaborative public decision-making approaches. The article then examines the benefits of community dialogues and the tensions that arise from their pursuit. We conclude by offering an assessment of how we might think about these techniques in the future.

Introduction

There has been a growing interest in recent years in what might be termed "community dialogues," that is, techniques for engaging broad-based discussions of issues within particular communities of interest. Falling under this rubric are both traditional public planning processes designed to allow citizen input and collaborative public decision making, including such specific techniques as visioning and search conferences.

The purpose of this chapter is to attempt a preliminary assessment of community dialogue as an approach to public decision making. The assessment is divided into four parts. First, traditional citizen involvement in planning and newer collaborative approaches to public participation are described in an effort to identify the commonalities and important differences between the two approaches. Second, the potential benefits — or promise — of the newer approach are examined. Third, several tensions that arise in using the newer techniques are explored. Finally, in light of both the potential benefits and the tensions, a concluding section considers how we should think about community dialogue in the future. Can it, for example, contribute to rebuilding the seemingly eroded social capital of U.S. cities? And, relative to the subject of this section, can community dialogues be an effective vehicle for transformational change?

The New Community Dialogue Movement

A thesaurus offers these synonyms for dialogue: "formal discussion, conference, talk, exchange of viewpoints, parley, conclave, personal meeting." What we here term the "new community dialogue movement" encompasses a variety of means for exchanging information and opinion within and among the communities that share interest in and/or influence over what Gray calls a "problem domain." [1] The presumed goal of all of these techniques is to define issues and then to address them in a manner that the whole community of interest can support. Local, state and federal agencies may use the techniques to help them plan, make decisions or manage. Citizens may also use some of these techniques to organize themselves and influence outcomes.

There are multiple means of pursuing these ends. Some approaches are top-down, used primarily as tools to improve formal decision making and to increase the likelihood that decisions will be implemented successfully. Others are bottom-up, serving as means to harness perceived common interests or concerns to achieve mutually beneficial results without any formal charge, constraint or support from official powers. All promote dialogue as a means of achieving consensus on problem definition and action to be taken, and generally "argue for new directions in governance modes which are more sensitive to the 'consumers' of public policy rather than the government 'producers' of policy." [2]

Traditional Citizen Participation in Planning

The oldest form of community dialogue in widespread use in the U.S., traditional citizen participation or public involvement, is required for certain types of public decision making, particularly local and regional comprehensive planning. This derives from the tradition of "openness" of public deliberations and records as a safeguard against abuse of government power, and is American rather than originating from British common law. [3] Public participation in the U.S. grows out of our history of administrative law and federal and state constitutional guarantees of individual rights.

Many administrative decisions affect citizens directly. A local decision to rezone a parcel of land is officially recognized to affect the interests of owners of adjoining property, for example. However, who must be notified and how, how long notice must be given in advance of the decision, and how citizen feedback is to be incorporated into decision making are established by law in only a small subset of all decisions that affect the public. Spicer has argued that elected officials have insufficient control over the bureaucracy to protect citizen interests on many matters; hence, public involvement may be an essential part of our constitutional system of checks and balances. [4]

Most planners are familiar with the due process requirements associated with regulating local land use, and their professional ethics include a strong commitment to broader public participation. [5] Thus, local public planning has been in the forefront of involving average citizens since the Great Society programs of the 1960s. Roberts has argued that citizen participation serves bureaucratic self-interest by legitimating officials' exercise of discretion. [6] This motive does in fact appear (in more positive language) in arguments for involving the general public more broadly in planning, where it is said to generate more information, more ideas, more public trust and support, and less conflict and delay. [7]

However, these benefits are not guaranteed to result from broad public involvement, and may come at substantial cost in time and effort, given that "opportunities for involvement sometimes fuel opposition rather than result in cooperation." [8] Professional judgment and substantive planning expertise also often conflict with public opinion expressed in an open process. Charles Hoch identifies this as the central paradox of professional planning:

> When planning professionals in the United States do their jobs ... they search for ways to straddle the dilemma between professional freedom and social justice. The professional protocol promises that expert knowledge will produce advice that serves the public interest and will therefore obtain public consent. Research studies through the decades on professional planning practice, however, ... have found evidence of persistent tension between the authority of the professional and the politics of the public good. [9]

This conflict can be at least partly avoided in top-down citizen involvement in a traditional public planning process. Although some goals may have already been determined by legislative requirements or other means, interested citizens are invited to help define the goals for the planning effort. Formal and informal budget and other constraints are likely already in place as well. Technical alternatives are then developed by professional planning staff to address the goals without violating the constraints. The staff conducts a preliminary screening of these alternatives and makes information on one or more preferred alternatives available to the public. Public comments are accepted, but in most cases how they are used is left to the discretion of the staff preparing the plan. The staff makes public a final recommendation, and citizens are invited to comment before the recommendation is formally adopted by the appropriate official body. Conflicts which arise between experts and the public do not necessarily delay the process, unless one party goes to court, because there are typically no requirements for consensus. The pressure to address public comments and criticisms is indirect, created by planners' professional norms, and the sensitivity of the adopting body to citizen reaction.

Clearly citizens play a circumscribed role in such a process — one which has oversight and avoidance of gross error or injustice as its major purpose. It has been sharply criticized over the years for giving citizens too little real influence [10] and marginalizing their real concerns. [11] Yet this limited role for citizens still involves dialogue.

A fairly recent innovation which has become widespread in otherwise traditional, top-down planning processes involves "visioning." A vision presents "a clear and succinct description of what the ... community should look like after it ... achieves its full potential." [12] Like a traditional master plan, a vision is an ideal future state, and many communities now call their comprehensive plans "visions" to keep up with the latest phraseology. [13] Yet the term is used in a variety of ways. Visions commonly rely on visual images, as the name implies, and thus often focus on physical design. However, several Midwestern states have programs to foster "community strategic visioning" which focus primarily on rural development. [14] The unifying idea is that the future vision should be made as specific and concrete as possible to stimulate public engagement and interest. Accurate though they may be, when goals identified at the outset of creating or updating a community plan are abstract, they are often similar from one community to the next, [15] and may thus appear obvious or uninteresting to citizens. Visioning is thus used as a technique to stimulate involvement in both top-down and bottom-up processes.

Godschalk and Stiftel long ago proposed an ambitious evaluation standard for citizen involvement called the exchange model, which would consider the degree to which participation programs promoted what we here term community dialogue. According to this model, "if participation is to be effective, there must be a quid pro quo." [16] But for a traditional citizen participation process to achieve the purpose of checking excessive administrative discretion, it need only have been properly carried out. Thus, evaluating public involvement against this objective is much simpler and the objective itself is far easier to achieve. The evaluator has only to observe whether public records were made adequately available, whether proper notice of public meetings was provided, how many members of the public attended, and what comments they made. This simpler standard has prevailed.

And many public decisions, for planning and other purposes, are still made with little or no citizen input. Even when formal voter approval is required, as with referenda on tax increases or bond issues, "public involvement" may mean only publicity techniques and public education to convince voters, and no significant opportunities for two-way communication on defining the needs and alternative ways of meeting them.

Traditional citizen participation in planning thus is a community dialogue in a real, but limited, sense. In such a process citizens are largely expected to react rather than initiate; thus, they are constrained to alternatives developed by others. This form of dialogue does establish an explicit standard, yet many agree that the standard is inadequate. It occupies only the fourth rung on Arnstein's classic eight-rung ladder of citizen participation ("consultation," the lower of two "degrees of tokenism"), where the rungs measure degrees of citizens' power. [17] The question is, can newer approaches to community dialogues do better?

Collaborative Public Decision Making

Examples of approaches more typical of the new community dialogue movement are "collaborative decision making" [18] and "public deliberation." [19] The two are combined here into a single term, "collaborative public decision making," to describe an approach that (1) involves a broad public, (2) focuses on decision making, and (3) emphasizes collaboration among the different parts of the public in that decision making.

Here citizens originate most of the ideas, with public managers and other leaders mostly facilitating discussion. Central to this approach is the idea of collaboration, which Gray defines this way:

> Collaboration is a process through which parties who see different aspects of a problem can constructively explore their differences and search for solutions that go beyond their own limited vision of what is possible ... Those parties with an interest in the problem are termed stakeholders. Stakeholders include all individuals, groups, or organizations that are directly influenced by actions others take to solve the problem. [20]

> [C]ollaboration creates a temporary forum within which consensus about the problem can be sought, mutually agreeable solutions can be invented, and collective actions to implement the solutions can be taken. [21]

Chrislip and Larson offer a detailed description of what the process of a successful collaboration looks like. [22] It differs from traditional citizen participation by being a bottom-up process, in which the stakeholders themselves as a group create both the impetus and select a method of proceeding, rather than responding individually to public entities' requests for input.

For Roberts, who writes about public deliberation, the crucial element of such a process is "generative learning." According to her, those who facilitate an effective public deliberation should promote

> generative learning — learning that develops people's capacity to create new solutions to old problems — rather than settling for adaptive learning, which only prepares them for coping. Generative learning opens up new ways of looking at the world and encourages a deeper understanding of a system and its underlying dynamics. Such learning becomes possible through an open, deliberative process when people are invited to help craft policy and set organizational direction... [23]

Advocates of collaboration often reject the idea of measuring success in terms of achieving predetermined outcomes. This keeps the process flexible and allows the participants the greatest possible number of opportunities for achieving positive results.

> [E]valuation of consensus processes must recognize not only that the processes we use may produce different results than originally were intended or desired. The journey itself and the evaluation and feedback process may help to change those intentions and desires. Evaluation must also take into account that in the meantime the participants and their social, intellectual and political reality have changed. Thus the most fundamental criterion is whether what was produced or resulted was of adequate value to

the community and whether it had positive effects on the system by making it more adaptable and responsive. [24]

Such objectives are likely different from those of the public officials in a top-down process, who need to demonstrate that public involvement meets legal requirements and professional ethical standards. Public officials are also often bound by standards of decision quality, desires to diffuse antagonisms and legitimate their own decisions and the need to demonstrate results.

One technique sometimes used to encourage a group to seek creative alternatives is the search conference. As defined by Purser and Emery, search conferences examine systemic problems from multiple perspectives. They require broad-based participation, plan for the long-term future, and can be expected to work only if supported by the relevant formal authorities. [25] Although the search conference technique is appropriately used by organizations, including private companies, non-profits and public agencies, our interest is in its usefulness for "communities and regions that need to bring together people with diverse and often conflicting perspectives on complex social issues..." [26] Thus, search conferences can be a technique for achieving community dialogue through collaborative public decision making. Such "community-based search conferences" have been used to tackle a variety of issues [27] including:

- Developing a long-term community plan for the Macatawa region in southwestern Michigan
- Formulating goals for water quality decision making in the upper Colorado River basin
- Planning for school reform in the municipality of Wheeling, Illinois

Community-based search conferences begin with a planning process to determine, first, if a search conference is an appropriate approach. For example, is there a true systemic problem to be tackled? Will the appropriate formal authorities commit to the search conference approach, including the need for broad participation? If a search conference does appear to be appropriate, planners select the conference participants using "a referral process for identifying and selecting participants that results in a genuine microcosm of the larger community or region." [28] The method begins with identification of key interest groups and institutions, progresses to generation of the names of possible representatives, and concludes with selection of representatives from among those names. The actual conference will ideally involve 20 to 35 people chosen on the basis of

> such criteria as their knowledge of the system and their potential for taking responsibility for implementation. Participants are also selected to reflect a full range of perspectives on the system, but they attend in their own right, not as representatives of stakeholder groups. [29]

The conference itself begins with broad consideration of the external environment for the relevant system, moving to consideration of the internal system, and eventually narrowing to the formulation of action plans. In the words of Purser and Emery:

> Participants ... work on planning tasks in a mixture of large-group plenary sessions and small groups. As a whole community, participants scan their external environments, review their history, and analyze the strengths and weaknesses of their current

system. This provides a shared context for their most important task: the development of strategic goals and action plans. [30]

The final step in the search conference approach is implementation and diffusion, putting the action plan into operation. In an oversight not uncommon with community dialogue techniques, however, Purser and Emery give relatively little attention to implementation.

The Promise of Community Dialogues

In general, community dialogues promise movement toward consensus on goals or issues, more and better alternatives to address those goals, a greater diversity of views heard before making a decision and broad commitment to taking the chosen action. Each of these components warrants brief discussion.

First, community dialogues may lead to agreement on issues and on possible solutions to them. Advocates of collaborative processes maintain that, if facilitated effectively, such processes have high potential for producing consensus — or something approaching consensus. By contrast, traditional citizen involvement in a top-down planning or decision-making process may polarize communities.

Second, community dialogues may produce more and potentially better alternatives. Roberts has argued that if generative learning occurs in a bottom-up dialogue, it can produce and evaluate good ideas which might never be taken seriously in a top-down process. [31] Although citizens may offer alternatives in traditional public involvement processes, this is not the contribution they are invited to make. Thus if this promise were regularly fulfilled, community dialogues could yield innovative and effective ways of approaching problems.

Third, community dialogues may allow more diverse views to be heard, which would be particularly valuable when the issues involve multiple interests, at least some of which are unorganized and poorly informed. This would be especially important if none of the parties had sufficient power to impose a satisfactory solution unilaterally, [32] as appears to be increasingly the case in the late 20th-century U.S. [33]

Fourth, by virtue of involving many different stakeholders, the process may produce outcomes that these stakeholders will support. This is based on the logic that if more people are involved in making a decision, more will be satisfied with it and can be expected to support it. And, broad support for decisions can be crucial in ensuring that implementation actually occurs. [34]

The following are examples of purportedly successful collaborative public decision-making processes, where success was defined in terms of outcomes:

- The Baltimore Commonwealth: A partnership between community groups, the business community, and government, focused on keeping students in school and then moving them into productive jobs. [35]
- The Newark Collaboration Group: An effort "to bring together key leaders from all the city's sectors — business, government, nonprofit, neighborhood, academic, and religious" to develop solutions to the city's many problems. [36]
- The convening of a Minnesota school district as a community, involving principals, other administrators, teachers, and citizens, to formulate recommendations for necessary budget cuts that were later unanimously approved by the Board of Education. [37]
- Deliberations by the educational community across Minnesota to develop recommendations for the governor on the future of education in the state. These recommendations were eventually passed by the State legislature. [38]

Most broadly, community dialogues may offer a means for building or rebuilding the social capital which some believe has deteriorated in the U.S. since the 1960s. Social capital, as defined by Putnam, [39] refers to features of social organization, such as networks, norms, and trust, that facilitate coordination and cooperation for mutual benefit. Social capital enhances the benefits of investment in physical and human capital, and thus can also contribute to economic development. [40] Although there are conflicting views on whether social capital in the U.S. is declining, [41] if community dialogues could move some citizens toward increasing involvement with community and greater feelings of efficacy, this would be a benefit.

The Difficult Tensions within Community Dialogues

As these discussions indicate, public managers and planners pursue community dialogues to obtain more information and ideas, public trust, support and good will, and possibly legitimacy for their own exercise of discretion. Citizen stakeholders hope community dialogues will provide a check on official power and an opportunity to influence decisions they care about for various reasons. Pursuing these goals simultaneously creates the "exchange" which Godschalk and Stiftel observed, with benefits to both groups. [42]

Yet community dialogues also introduce tensions around a number of goals, including:

- **Representativeness.** What Godschalk and Mills wrote more than 30 years ago still holds today: "A successful democratic planning process, like a successful democratic government, must allow for the representation of the interests and identities of its subcommunities." [43] Any process of community dialogue must be representative in some meaningful sense if the results of the process are to have legitimacy for the larger public, and provide an effective check on inappropriate bureaucratic decisions.
- **Decision quality.** Public employees must meet scientific or technical quality standards in resolving most public issues. [44] To achieve such standards, decision-making processes must take good advantage of specialized expertise.
- **Support from influential elites.** Community dialogues must also have the support of influential elites, especially elected policy makers and civic leaders, if the products of the dialogue are to become policy for the community.
- **Efficiency.** How much time and money the process consumes are important to participating citizens and elites as well as decision makers. All public decisions must consider efficiency as well as equity and effectiveness.
- **Community consensus.** When there is communitywide agreement on goals and perhaps policies, much can be accomplished.
- **Action on solving problems.** Agreement on goals or process attributes may not be sufficient. Participants often expect movement toward solving the problems that prompted the dialogue in the first place. Without it, community dialogues could be criticized as only talk.

Tensions arise because the pursuit of each of these goals competes with achieving others. In the contemporary enthusiasm for community dialogues, challenges posed by these tensions often seem to be underestimated or overlooked entirely. Yet, these tensions must be recognized and addressed if community dialogues are to be considered effective. In the remainder of this section we examine some of the most important of the tensions, and consider possible means for reducing them.

Representativeness

Beatley, Brower and Lucy define three types of representation: representation of citizens' attributes (such as gender, race, ethnicity, residence location, etc.); representation of citizens' opinions on issues; and representation by "trustees" whose individual judgments resemble those their constituency would have made under the same circumstances. [45] The last can only be evaluated by the constituents themselves, and so is most appropriate for elected representatives. Lack of representativeness weakens the perceived legitimacy of the process, causing both citizens and policy makers to take it less seriously, and creating a vicious circle that further reduces participation. Yet, representativeness is difficult to obtain. In Healy's words, "The inclusionary challenge is to prevent those 'not [physically] present' from being 'absent' from the discussion." [46]

Research on representativeness in public dialogues indicates that participating citizens tend to differ in predictable ways from the larger population. Generally, participants are better educated and of higher socioeconomic status than the larger public. [47] Minority groups, those without sponsorship from their employers, and those with less compelling ties to the community, including renters, all tend to be under-represented. [48] These problems are inherent, independent of tensions with other goals, but likely to be exacerbated by tensions between representativeness and other desirable attributes of community dialogues.

Listening to Both Citizens and Experts

Broad representation is likely to increase conflict with expert opinion, and so imperil decision quality. At the extreme, scientific critics contend that some issues "are so highly specialized that only experts are qualified to make competent judgments." [49] In particular cases of community dialogue, slighting the opinions of municipal administrators — the municipal experts — can undermine the entire value of having a dialogue. [50] But claims for expertise can be overstated as well, as Manring has reported. [51] In negotiating resolutions of appeals of their forest plans, Forest Service staff recognized that they had confused "conventional management practice" with science-based quality standards until challenged by citizen groups.

Fostering community dialogue sets the stage for conflict with the older, rational paradigm because the philosophies of community dialogue and rational planning and policy analysis diverge. The rational paradigm constrains decision making with objectives and policy criteria and relies on deduction and scientific logic to draw conclusions. The role of the expert is central in such an approach. Communicative approaches, by contrast, reject claims that strategies and policies can be selected objectively based solely on technical criteria, and instead treat science and academic knowledge as "thoughtworlds" which are "carefully constructed social products." [52] This relativistic view recognizes personal values arising from a variety of individual cultural communities and social networks, and gives no special influence or status to the expert whose perspective conflicts with stakeholders' culturally constructed understandings.

Although in their purest forms these two models are irreconcilable, the older rational paradigm has been around long enough to have been modified by pragmatists into something which can enrich communicative approaches like those discussed here. Lindblom and Cohen argued that analysis by experts and interactive social problem solving by non-experts are and ought to be complementary. [53] And there is a growing body of evidence that expert opinions and citizen opinions can be effectively combined in processes of community dialogue. Innes recounted how experts serving as paid staff or consultants responsible to a collaborative group assisted with interactive problem solving, without controlling it. [54] Wheeland described how presentations by experts provided a useful introduction to a citywide citizens' strategic planning effort in Rock Hill, South Carolina. [55] Practically, since volunteer stakeholders sometimes feel ill equipped to produce or evaluate extensive substantive proposals for change, they may be grateful for expert assistance to assure decision quality, as long as the experts assist rather than dictate. [56]

Involving Both the Public and Influential Elites

There is a similar tension between representativeness and the support of influential elites. Involving the broad public can reduce the willingness of elites to participate because the process of discussion, education and arriving at a group consensus is time consuming, unlikely to mirror their values, and uncontrollable. [57] These elites may become dissatisfied and unwilling to continue, thereby threatening the successful conversion of the results of the dialogue to community policy. Alternatively, too much deference to the opinions of elites can undermine citizens' belief that the planning process is truly representative.

There are at least two ways to reduce this tension. First, the support of influential elites may be sought before any process of community dialogue begins. It may be challenging to convince elites to accept such a process based on its promise, but this support is more likely in advance than after the collaboration has come to its conclusions. Second, elites too have a place at the table, and should be given the opportunity to participate as stakeholders. Like experts, elites should be involved, but not allowed to control.

Representativeness versus Efficiency

There is often a tradeoff between representativeness and decision-making efficiency in that a more inclusive process takes more time because more voices must be heard in the debate. The additional time might be warranted if it brought the compensating advantages of greater inclusiveness: limiting the power of government and special interests to use the political process for their own ends, and distributing knowledge of policies and their potential consequences to raise the level of debate and the quality of policy. [58]

But taking the additional time necessary to be more inclusive could, ironically, prove counterproductive. The need for substantial time commitments could eventually eliminate many participants who cannot or will not devote this amount of time or who find the schedule or location for the dialogue inconvenient or impossible. The resulting attrition would mean poor attendance at later meetings, compromising representativeness. [59]

Organizers should be sensitive to the value of participants' time, and plan for the most efficient use of that time. Such planning should reflect stakeholders' desires, for example, in the mix of large- and small-group discussions, the time and location of meetings, and telecommunication and mail alternatives to meeting attendance. They may also consider subsidizing costs and providing special incentives to encourage continued participation, especially by likely drop-outs.

Representativeness versus Consensus

The philosophy underlying community dialogue places a high value on achieving consensus. A principal reason for initiating these dialogues is to achieve communitywide agreement on key issues. Requiring consensus can also be a way of bolstering the influence of the less powerful participants and checking others' power. Yet, since stakeholder opinion is diverse on many matters of public policy, broader involvement might appear unlikely to lead to agreement. [60] Any consensus that can be reached across a community as a whole might have to be so general and inoffensive as to be meaningless.

But prior research does not suggest that representativeness and consensus are necessarily mutually exclusive goals for community dialogues. Kathlene and Martin describe input into a transportation plan in Boulder, Colorado, obtained from a panel of citizens who each answered one telephone survey, four mail surveys and participated in two in-depth interviews. [61] Because this group was perceived by decision makers to be legitimately representative of the community, and because the feedback from the survey was timely, there was much higher congruence between the citizen survey panel's responses and the policy options incorporated in the plan by the Transportation Advisory Committee to the Boulder City Council than between the plan and citizens who attended public hearings on the plan.

Nonetheless, there is substantial disagreement about whether a representative community dialogue can promote movement toward consensus, reconciling differing interests. The ability to reach consensus is affected by other attributes of the process and the setting in which it takes place, like the number and characteristics of stakeholders, and the way the process is managed, for example. In addition, pressure to reach consensus is increased when problems are urgent and stakeholders expect significant adverse consequences from inaction.

Consensus versus Action

Achieving consensus also frequently competes with taking action. Sometimes community dialogues are not results-oriented to begin with. "Specifying defined output criteria a priori ... denies the process of creative invention in response to a changed frame of reference." [62] According to this view, to identify goals of a truly collaborative community dialogue would be to constrain and stifle it.

The kind of consensus which may result from a representative dialogue can also retard the prospects for action. A consensus that everyone can accept could well imply little change from the status quo. As a result, requiring consensus as the basis for action may inhibit action, especially if action implies change. Requiring consensus for action thus may be impractical. [63]

Finally, the considerable energy which is spent on achieving consensus may leave little energy for seeing that the consensus is advanced to action. Or, there simply may have been too little thought given to how the consensus might be implemented, as happened in Corpus Christi, for example, when the necessary implementers were entirely excluded from the consensus-building effort. [64]

Giving up on action is a high price to pay for consensus, however. In practice, achieving results tends to be very important to participants in community dialogues; and those participants sometimes see these efforts as insufficiently action-oriented. [65] Participants are likely to feel used by the process of community dialogue if their input languishes in a report unread and unheeded by decision makers. As Healy says, "[G]overnance activity should be seen to work and deliver noticeable material result." [66]

Perhaps the strongest counsel this tension implies for organizers of community dialogues is to consider in advance how the products of a dialogue can be translated to action. Certainly, the involvement of influential elites can be helpful; their support can pave the way to action. More may be necessary, however, given the obstacles.

The Need for More Systematic Evaluation

Having identified these various tensions, much remains unknown about how effective contemporary efforts at community dialogues have been. Unfortunately, there have been too few efforts at comprehensive and systematic evaluation of these techniques. This lack of evaluation may be due to two very different factors. On one hand, much of the writing on community dialogues comes from advocates. Instead of attempting rigorous, balanced assessments, some advocates seem more interested in publicizing and marketing techniques, limiting their evaluative efforts to "how to" advice for making the techniques work better. On the other hand, the sheer enormity of such an evaluation may discourage the effort.

Consider that a comprehensive evaluation should at least: (1) compare participant characteristics to population characteristics and track changes in participation over the duration of the dialogue, (2) analyze expert and elite participation in and influence on the dialogue, (3) assess the quality of the recommendations, (4) assess the dialogue's long-term impact, and (5) evaluate the efficiency with which these recommendations and results were achieved. Any one of these components by itself could be a major research undertaking; all of them together represent a daunting task. And the best evaluations of such complex processes are not initiated after the fact. Instead, they are conceived at the same time as the dialogue itself, so that relevant data and opinions can be collected from primary sources, and a true before-and-after picture can be constructed.

In spite of these challenges, such evaluations are essential to understanding when, why and how community dialogues work or do not work. Future research on community dialogues must consequently give a high priority to more and better evaluations.

Conclusions: How Can Community Dialogues Deliver on Their Promise?

The key to community dialogues delivering on their promise seems to be to adapt a bottom-up method, collaboration, for use in a public decision-making structure which is inherently top-down. To achieve this, community dialogues need to be hybrids of the traditional citizen involvement process in comprehensive planning and citizen-organized collaborative processes. This will be difficult, but if achieved, might be an effective vehicle for transformational change.

In earlier work, one of us suggested guidelines for how to address these dilemmas in public involvement generally. [67] This advice includes defining governmental quality requirements in advance, assessing the likely agreement of the public with governmental preferences, and gauging the likely disagreement within the public itself. This information can then be used to determine how to involve the public in making a particular decision. Similar guidelines might usefully be explored for determining when community dialogues would be the most appropriate method for involving the citizenry.

It is already evident that successful community dialogues require changes from traditional top-down decision making. There is a need to remove constraints from traditional citizen involvement processes to the extent possible, allowing stakeholders to set the meeting agendas, times, and places, to purchase analyses and evidence from outside sources, and to communicate freely with one another without staff interference. Equally important, public officials who would invite these dialogues should be clear at the outset on the role of community participants, even if that role is modest. The public entity pursuing a dialogue takes a big risk if it permits or encourages participants to think their influence will be greater than that actually planned.

These public officials must understand, too, that successful dialogues require resources. When citizens donate their time, and experts and public servants are paid to participate, they should be supported with what they need to carry out their collaborative responsibilities well. Even a traditional citizen involvement process is costly in time and money. A more collaborative community dialogue is likely to cost more. But advocates maintain that such community dialogues will also deliver more: more agreement, more ideas and alternatives, more representativeness and more widespread support leading to results, including possibly transformational change.

In addition, successful community dialogues require an even more difficult change of mind-set among public officials. Planners, other public administrators, and elected officials should function less as leaders or directors of such processes, and more as facilitators and consensus-builders. Yet they must continue to uphold the representativeness of the process and the quality and implementability of the decisions. This is a tall order. It requires moving from the top-down approach of formulating and then announcing solutions to a bottom-up approach of listening, and then contributing to an emerging consensus that they as professional public servants can responsibly endorse. But change of this kind may be essential if community dialogues are to bring real results.

Other keys to the success of community dialogues may be discovered through further research. If particular efforts at community dialogue are thoughtfully and honestly evaluated in the future, in spite of the difficulties this poses, it will eventually be possible to conduct a meta-analysis of these dialogues, and draw more general conclusions than are evident from any single effort. Such an analysis should examine the similarities among the efforts that succeeded as well as among those that failed.

Even in the absence of such an analysis, the anecdotal reports of community dialogues are sufficiently positive to indicate that they have potential value for transformational change of communities. True community dialogues, those that involve a broad range of stakeholders in discussing problems and defining solutions, offer the unique promise of uniting a community behind a goal of changing itself. This promise deserves further exploration.

Note: *Originally published in Helling, A. and Thomas, J.C., Encouraging community dialog: Approach, promise, and tensions, International Journal of Public Administration, 24, 749, 2001.*

Endnotes

1. Gray, B., *Collaborating: Finding Common Ground for Multiparty Problems,* Jossey-Bass, San Francisco, 1989.
2. Healy, P., *Collaborative Planning: Shaping Places in Fragmented Societies,* University of British Columbia Press, Vancouver, 1997, 205.
3. Linde, H.A. and Bunn, G., *Legislative and Administrative Processes,* Foundation Press, Mineola, NY, 1976.
4. Spicer, M.W., *The Founders, the Constitution and Public Administration: A Conflict in Worldviews,* Georgetown University Press, Washington, DC, 1995.
5. American Institute of Certified Planners, AICP/APA ethical principles in planning, and AICP code of ethics and professional conduct (adopted in 1992), in *AICP 1996/1997 Roster,* American Institute of Certified Planners, Washington, DC, 1996.
6. Roberts, A., "Civic discovery" as a rhetorical strategy, *Journal of Policy Analysis and Management,* 14, 291, 1995.

7. Cogan, A., Sharpe, S., and Hertzberg, J., Citizen participation, in *The Practice of State and Regional Planning*, So, F.S., Hand, I., and McDowell, B.D., Eds., International City Management Association and American Planning Association, Chicago, 1986, chap. 12.

8. Ibid, 290.

9. Hoch, C., *What Planners Do: Power, Politics and Persuasion*, Planners Press, American Planning Association, Chicago, 1994, 7.

10. Arnstein, S.R., A ladder of citizen participation, *Journal of the American Institute of Planners*, 35, 216, 1969.

11. Tauxe, C.S., Marginalizing public participation in local planning: An ethnographic account, *Journal of the American Planning Association*, 61, 471, 1995.

12. Bryson, J.M., *Strategic Planning for Public and Nonprofit Organizations: A Guide to Strengthening and Sustaining Organizational Achievement*, rev. ed., Jossey-Bass, San Francisco, 1995, 155.

13. Kennedy, C., Comprehensive plans: Making the vision come true, PAS Memo (Planning Advisory Service of the American Planning Association), July, 1, 1992.

14. Walzer, N., Ed., *Community Strategic Visioning Programs*, Praeger, Westport, CT, 1996.

15. Moore, T. and Thorsnes, P., *The Transportation/Land Use Connection* (Planning Advisory Service Report No. 448/449), American Planning Association, Chicago, 1994.

16. Godschalk, D.R. and Stiftel, B., Making waves: Public participation in state water planning, *Journal of Applied Behavioral Science*, 17, 599, 1981.

17. Arnstein, S.R., op. cit.

18. For example, see Chrislip, D.D. and Larson, C.E., *Collaborative Leadership: How Citizens and Civic Leaders Can Make a Difference*, Jossey-Bass, San Francisco, 1994.

19. For example, see Roberts, N., Public deliberation: An alternative approach to crafting policy and setting direction, *Public Administration Review*, 57, 124, 1997.

20. Gray, B., *Collaborating: Finding Common Ground for Multiparty Problems*, Jossey-Bass, San Francisco, 1989, 5.

21. Gray, B., op. cit., 16.

22. Chrislip, D.D. and Larson, C.E., op. cit., 52–54.

23. Roberts, N., op. cit., 125.

24. Innes, J.E., Evaluating Consensus Building: Making Dreams into Realities, unpublished paper prepared for delivery at the annual conference of the Association of Collegiate Schools of Planning, Fort Lauderdale, FL, November 6–9, 1997, 8.

25. Emery, M. and Purser, R.E., *The Search Conference: A Powerful Method for Planning Organizational Change and Community Action*, Jossey-Bass, San Francisco, 1996, 151.

26. Ibid, 9.

27. Ibid., 21–32.

28. Ibid., 157.

29. Ibid, 10.

30. Ibid.

31. Roberts, N., op. cit., 125.

32. Gray, B., op. cit.; Innes, J.E. et al., Coordinating growth and environmental management through consensus building, *CPS Brief*, 6(4), California Policy Seminar, Berkeley, CA, 1994.

33. Thomas, J.C., *Public Participation in Public Decisions: New Skills and Strategies for Public Managers*, Jossey-Bass, San Francisco, 1995.

34. Ibid.

35. Chrislip, D.D. and Larson, C.E, op. cit., 52–54.

36. Ibid.

37. Roberts, N., op. cit., 125.

38. Ibid.

39. Putnam, R.D., The prosperous community: Social capital and public life, *American Prospect*, 13, 35, 1993.

40. Ibid, 38.
41. Ibid; Tarrow, S., Making social science work across space and time: A critical reflection on Robert Putnam's *Making Democracy Work, American Political Science Review,* 90, 397, 1996.
42. Godschalk, D.R. and Stiftel, B., op. cit., 599.
43. Godschalk, D.R. and Mills, W.E., A collaborative approach to planning through urban activities, *Journal of the American Institute of Planners,* 32, 86, 1996.
44. Thomas, J.C., Public involvement in public management: Adapting and testing a borrowed theory, *Public Administration Review,* 50, 435, 1990.
45. Beatley, T., Brower, D.J., and Lucy, W.H., Representation in comprehensive planning: An analysis of the Austinplan process, *Journal of the American Planning Association,* 60, 185, 1994.
46. Healy, P., op. cit., 275.
47. Beatley, T., Brower, D.J., and Lucy, W.H., op. cit.; Kathlene, L. and Martin, J.A., Enhancing citizen participation: Panel designs, perspectives and policy formulation, *Journal of Policy Analysis and Management,* 10, 46, 1991.
48. Helling, A., Differences in employer-sponsored and self-sponsored participation in collaborative visioning: Theory, evidence and implications, *Journal of Applied Behavioral Science,* 34, 222, 1998; Kathlene, L. and Martin, J.A., ibid.
49. Dutton, D., The impact of public participation in biomedical policy: Evidence from four case studies, in *Citizen Participation in Science Policy,* Petersen, J.C., Ed., University of Massachusetts Press, Amherst, 1984, chap. 9, 170.
50. McClendon, B.W. and Lewis, J.A., Goals for Corpus Christi: Citizen participation in planning, *National Civic Review,* 74, 72, 1985.
51. Manring, N.J., Reconciling science and politics in Forest Service decision making: New tools for public administration, *American Review of Public Administration,* 23, 343, 1993.
52. Healy, P., op. cit., 36.
53. Lindblom, C.E. and Cohen, D.K., *Usable Knowledge: Social Science and Social Problem Solving,* Yale University Press, New Haven, CT, 1979.
54. Innes, J.E., Group processes and the social construction of growth management: Florida, Vermont and New Jersey, *Journal of the American Planning Association,* 58, 440, 1992.
55. Wheeland, C.M., Citywide strategic planning: An evaluation of Rock Hill's 'Empowering the Vision,' *Public Administration Review,* 53, 68, 1993.
56. Helling, A., Collaborative visioning: Proceed with caution! Results from evaluating Atlanta's Vision 2020 project, *Journal of the American Planning Association,* 64, 335, 1998.
57. Ibid; McCoy, W.J., Building coalitions for the future in Charlotte-Mecklenburg, *National Civic Review,* 80, 120, 1991.
58. Spicer, M.W., op. cit.
59. Helling, A., Differences in employer-sponsored and self-sponsored participation in collaborative visioning, op. cit.; McCoy, W.J., op. cit.
60. O'Toole, L. and Mountjoy, R.S., Interorganizational policy implementation: A theoretical perspective, *Public Administration Review,* 44, 491, 1984; Roberts, A., op. cit.
61. Kathlene, L. and Martin, J.A., op. cit.
62. Healy, P., op. cit., 69.
63. Buchanan, J. and Tullock, G., *The Calculus of Consent,* University of Michigan Press, Ann Arbor, 1962.
64. McClendon, B.W.; Lewis, J.A., op. cit.
65. Helling, A., Collaborative visioning, op. cit.; McCoy, W.J., op. cit.
66. Healy, P., op. cit., 69.
67. Thomas, J.C., *Public Participation in Public Decisions,* op. cit.

Chapter 13

Engaging with Citizens and Other Stakeholders

Steve Martin

Contents

Introduction

Public participation is not new. There were attempts to promote local involvement in planning decisions in the United Kingdom (UK) as long ago as the 1960s. User involvement has long been a feature of some social services, and community involvement is a pre-condition of funding from most UK and European Union (EU) regeneration programs. Until relatively recently, though, many mainstream services remained under the control of expert professionals who, it was assumed, acted in the best interests of service users and the public at large. Voters could remove unpopular politicians through the ballot-box, but they were not expected to take much of a direct interest in policy debates or the management of public services between elections.

Current attempts to improve services and modernize governance systems have, however, placed public engagement center stage. Policy makers in Western democracies appear united in the belief that it offers an important means of rebuilding trust in government and ensuring that services are responsive to users' needs and aspirations. Local politicians have seen engagement with the public as a means of substantiating their claim to be close to the citizen. Meanwhile, in the age of spin, ministers and their advisers have turned to assorted panels, opinion polls and focus groups to help inform political priorities, policy development and presentation.

Why Engage with the Public?

The Organisation for Economic Co-operation and Development (OECD) argues that engaging with citizens is "a core element of good governance." It claims that the benefits include:

- Improving the quality of policy-making by allowing government to tap wider sources of information, perspectives and potential solutions
- Facilitating greater and faster interaction between citizens and governments
- Increased accountability and transparency which increases representativeness and public confidence [1]

The current UK government also sees engagement with the public as vital. The assumption is that increased participation will act as a force for service improvement, bringing pressure to bear on otherwise unresponsive and inefficient public bureaucracies. It is believed that this will increase the perceived legitimacy of government by encouraging more effective community leadership.

> *At its heart the* **Best Value** *program seeks to reshape the relationship between government and the electorate.*
>
> **— Hilary Armstrong, former UK Minister for Local Government and the Regions**

Pressure for increased engagement has been fueled by low, and falling, levels of turnout in local elections in the UK (see Table 13.1). In contrast, there has been a rapid growth in *direct* participation at the local level. [2] In particular, Agenda 21 has proved an important trigger, as have regeneration initiatives, such as the New Deal for Communities program, which has spawned a plethora of local community-based partnerships (see Case Example 13.1).

Table 13.1   Turn-Out in Local Elections (%)

	Pre-1995	*Post-1995*	*% Change*
Italy	85	80	−5
Sweden	85	79	−6
Germany	72	70	−2
France	68	72	+4
Netherlands	54	47	−7
UK	40	35	−5

Case Example 13.1
The New Deal for Communities Program

The New Deal for Communities program, run by the Neighborhood Renewal Unit, provides more than £800 million over a 10-year period to 39 of the most deprived areas of England. Ministers have insisted that funding is given directly to community groups "who have not traditionally led regeneration programs." They have also relaxed detailed monitoring requirements of the kind previously placed on local authority-led partnerships for fear that these may inhibit community involvement. Further details are available at: http://www.neighbourhood.gov.uk/ (accessed 2007).

There has also been a much greater emphasis in recent years on direct public involvement in planning and delivering services. Clause 3.1 of the 1999 Local Government Act requires local councils, police and fire authorities and a range of other statutory agencies to consult not only service users and taxpayers (both individuals and businesses) but also anyone else who they deem to have legitimate interest in the area (which might, for example, include commuters, tourists and representatives of voluntary and community organizations). In addition, councils must ensure that their "staff are involved in any plans to change the way in which services are provided." [3]

Councils must involve the public in reviewing current services and setting targets for future improvement. They must publish annual performance plans giving details of current service standards, targets for year-on-year improvement and action plans to achieve them. They also have to gauge resident satisfaction using performance indicators imposed by central government. Failure to fulfill any of these requirements can lead to censure by auditors and inspectors, and direct intervention in the running of an authority's services by the Secretary of State.

The early signs are that these new requirements have increased both the scale and scope of engagement by local authorities with local people. Most councils have introduced consultation in services that previously have not had much direct contact with the public. Many have adopted new, more interactive approaches and sought to reach communities and groups with which they previously had only limited contact. [4]

Case Example 13.2:
The People's Panel

The People's Panel was set up by the UK Cabinet Office in 1998 to provide feedback on levels of public satisfaction with public services. It was wound up in 2001 but ministers claim other departments have now developed their own mechanisms for public engagement.

An independent evaluation of the panel concluded that it had provided a useful 'high-level feel' for public opinion, stimulated new consumer research and demonstrated the government's intention to better engage citizens. However, it found weaknesses in the design of the panel and criticized the newsletter produced by the Cabinet Office for being unduly self-serving.

At the national level, there has been a strong emphasis on listening to the public. The People's Panel, consisting of a representative sample of 5,000 people, was used as an important sounding board, and ministers toured the country attending so-called listening events at which ordinary people could air their views (see Case Example 13.2).

Forms of Public Engagement

The rhetoric of public service modernization and improvement, including many of the initiatives outlined above, frequently conflates very different kinds of public participation. Recent government statements in the UK have, for example, referred to the importance of consultation, listening, being in touch with the people, involving users, and strengthening accountability to local people, almost as if these very different activities were synonymous or interchangeable. In fact, they represent a wide spectrum of different types of interaction.

One of the most widely quoted typologies of public participation is the hierarchy of approaches developed by Sherry Arnstein (see Figure 13.1). [5] On the lower rungs of a ladder of participation she placed manipulation of the public. What she saw as tokenistic activities — informing and consultation — came in the middle section. At the upper end were approaches that empower the public. This typology is misleading, however, in that it implies that some forms of engagement are inherently superior. In practice what matters most is that the form of participation used is fit for the purpose. A more useful typology is perhaps that shown in Figure 13.2.

All three of these activities in Figure 13.2 are likely to be important components of an organization's strategy for engaging with its service users and other stakeholders.

Communication

Some commentators have echoed Arnstein's skepticism about insincerely motivated forms of participation. Pollitt, for example, dismisses what he dubs the "charm school and better wallpaper end of the spectrum." [6] However, honest and effective communication with the public is a legitimate

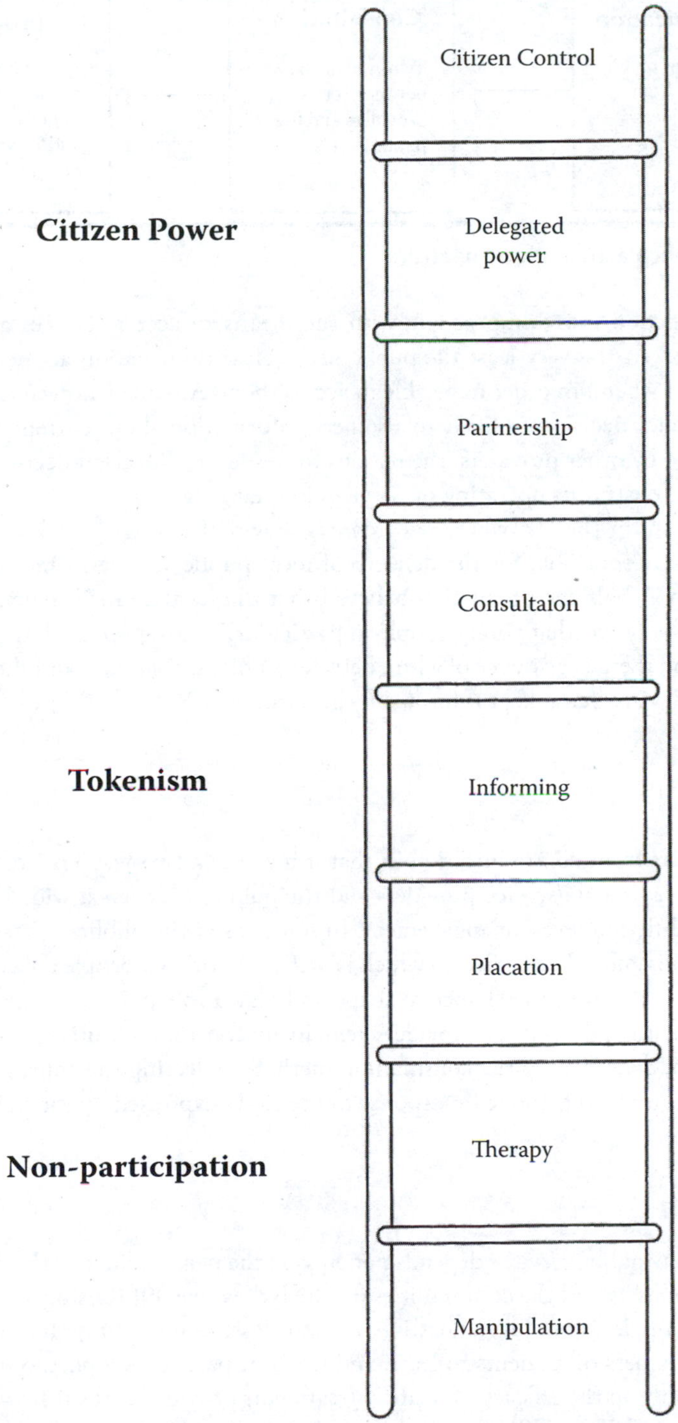

Citizen Power

Citizen Control

Delegated power

Partnership

Consultaion

Tokenism

Informing

Placation

Non-participation

Therapy

Manipulation

Figure 13.1 Arnstein's Ladder of Participation [5]

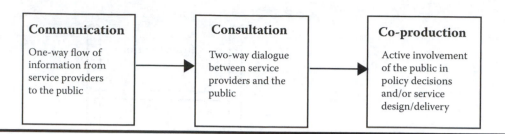

Figure 13.2 Public Participation Spectrum

and necessary function, providing people with the means to access services and engage in an informed dialogue. At the very least the public needs clear information about what services are on offer, when and where, in order to be able to access them. Anyone who wants a greater level of involvement in policy decisions is likely to also need information about current service standards, standards achieved by other providers, the reasons for resource allocation decisions made by their provider, and any constraints operating on services in their area.

This is important in the UK where research has shown alarmingly low levels of awareness of which agencies are responsible for the delivery of local public services. One survey found that in some areas almost half the population believed that the local council managed hospitals. [7] Opinion polls have shown that young people in particular feel they lack information about their local authority, and there is evidence of a link between public satisfaction and the degree to which people feel that they are being kept informed by government. [8]

Consultation

Consultation differs from communication in that it involves a two-way flow of information and views between governments/service providers and the public. It covers a wide range of activities involving widely differing levels of engagement. In some cases, the public is presented with a narrow range of options and asked to decide which it prefers. In others, people are consulted at a very early stage and may be given the chance to shape and play a role in conducting the consultation exercise. Typically, though, service providers remain in control — initiating the consultation, setting the agenda, determining the consultation methods, selecting the consultees and deciding what, if anything, needs to be done in response to the views expressed by the public.

Co-Production

The efficacy of many public services depends not only on the performance of the providers but also on the responses of users and the communities in which they live. [9] Raising levels of educational attainment, for example, is not just a question of good classroom teaching. It also depends on the capacity and willingness of students to learn and levels of parental support. Similarly, mortality rates depend not only on the efficacy of medical treatments provided by health services but also on the lifestyle choices of the public (including diet, exercise, smoking and so forth). Many services therefore benefit from the active involvement of users in design and production. This can help to increase the chances that services meet users' needs. It can also play an important part in the social role valorization of, for example, people with learning disabilities. Co-production therefore seeks to go beyond an attempt to attune public services to the wishes of passive recipients. Its aim is to empower users to take greater control over, and responsibility for, their lives.

Participation by Whom?

Another important issue is with whom governments and service providers need to engage:

- Customers: In some cases the input of users/clients will be the most valuable form of engagement; for example, in informing detailed operational issues relating to the delivery of particular services.
- Citizens: In others, the citizenry as a whole has an important stake in the decision-making process. For example, taxpayers who do not use a service may have a legitimate interest in the relative costs of alternative approaches to service delivery (and their preferences may well be at odds with those of service users).
- Communities: In the case of initiatives designed to benefit particular neighborhoods or sections of the population, it may be important to engage with specific communities of place, identity or interest. [10]

Combining the three levels of interaction identified in Figure 13.2 with this threefold categorization of the main stakeholder groups provides a useful typology of different modes of engagement (see Figure 13.3).

Experience suggests that it is important to be clear from the outset about what the objectives of each exercise in public participation are. This helps to ensure that the right tools and techniques are used. It can also help to clarify what level of influence is being offered to the public, thus

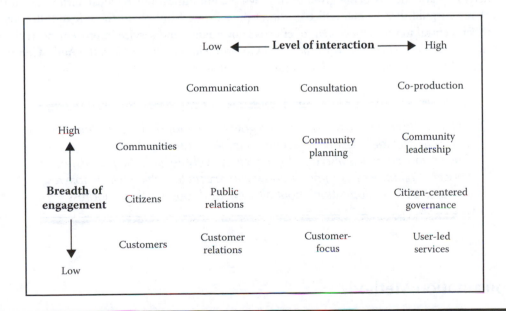

Figure 13.3   Modes of Public Participation. *Source:* Adapted from Martin and Boaz [11].

reducing the risk of disillusionment among consultees who come to believe that engagement has delivered less than they expected.

Practical Approaches to Public Engagement

There is a plethora of good toolkits and consultation manuals for practitioners wishing to engage with the public. The aim of this section therefore is not to give a comprehensive guide but to provide a flavor of the range of techniques currently in use.

Communication Tools

Governments at local and national levels use a wide variety of media to provide information to the public. Traditional approaches include notice boards, council newspapers, service directories, videos, road shows, exhibitions and public awareness campaigns. In recent years electronic information and communications technologies have provided new ways of disseminating information — including websites, community information points (e.g., in libraries) and CD-ROMs. Some rural local authorities see the Internet as an important new means of serving the needs of sparsely populated areas.

Bristol City Council is one of many local councils to have set up multimedia kiosks around the city which provide free access to its website and other sources of information.

Increasing attention is being given to improving communications by local authorities in the UK. A report published by the Office of the Deputy Prime Minister in the UK in 2002 stated that this is central to the achievement of effective governance and service improvement, [12] and central government has worked with the Local Government Association and the Audit Commission to produce a *Communications Toolkit* for use by all authorities. [13]

"Herefordshire in Touch" aims to use government-funded regeneration programs to provide broadband access to information about council services. The county council is also developing a joint website with the police, health service, Chamber of Commerce and voluntary sector which will enable residents to access information about all services through a single address.

Consultation Methods

Lowndes et al. found that the vast majority of British local authorities used traditional consultative mechanisms. [14] Nine out of ten held public meetings, ran complaints/suggestions schemes and

---

Case Example 13.3
Major Surveys in the UK

The Home Office commissions an annual British Crime Survey of 40,000 people to assess attitudes to and experiences of crime, the police and the courts.

The Department of Health's "Through the Patient's Eyes" survey assesses hospital in-patients' views on the way they were treated in the hospital.

The Strategic Rail Authority runs a twice-yearly National Passenger Survey which analyzes the views of train passengers about the punctuality and frequency of trains and the level of ticket prices.

---

undertook written consultations. Two-thirds organized service user forums, 62% had area forums and half had forums focused on particular issues or services. Many were developing more deliberative methods. Half reported using focus groups, a quarter had involved the public in visioning exercises or community appraisals and 5% had held citizens' juries.

Some councils have arranged listening days during which senior managers and councilors have gone out into the streets to talk to shoppers and householders. Others have opened up council meetings to local people and scheduled regular public question times. Some have begun to broadcast committee meetings on the Web. Free phone lines to enable citizens to record comments and suggestions are now widespread, and at least one UK council has installed video booths in the town so that residents can record video messages.

Although they were relatively rare ten years ago, almost all local councils, and many other local service providers, now conduct residents' surveys regularly to gauge public satisfaction with existing services. Central government has also invested heavily in recent years in surveys of the general public (see Case Example 13.3).

Many local councils, police forces and health authorities in the UK have used citizens' panels (representative samples, typically of 1,000–2,000 local people) as sounding boards whose views are sought regularly about key policy issues. Panels of service users and particular communities are also now commonplace.

Citizens' juries bring together a small group of laypeople (selected as a representative sample of the population as a whole) to consider evidence from experts on a specific policy or service issue and to produce recommendations. Juries have been used in the U.S. and Germany for some years [15] and have recently been used by health authorities and local authorities in the UK (see below).

Some agencies have also developed what are in effect larger citizens' juries, often called public scrutiny workshops or consensus conferences, to explore key policy issues.

The City Councils of Milton Keynes and Bristol have both held referenda on the level of council tax offering residents a range of options and spelling out the implications for service budgets.

Interactive information and communications technologies are being used to consult individual local people; for example, through message boards and online discussions with policy makers, and an increasing number of local councils are consulting the public about budget decisions. Some have held referenda on the level of council tax. Others have sought the public's view about allocations between services.

Co-Production

Co-production is less common than consultation but can take a number of different forms — including public involvement in formulating strategies (e.g., planning for real, visioning exercises and community appraisals), designing services, co-managing them and monitoring performance. User groups can have roles in providing services, working in partnership in developing services and campaigning for more resources and policy change. [16]

Obstacles to Effective Engagement

Power to the People?

Increased public participation does not enjoy unqualified support among public officials and politicians. Not surprisingly, some see it as a threat to their professional judgment or democratic legitimacy, fearing governance by referendum in which their role is reduced to that of rubber-stamping decisions made by the public.

> Unraveling the interests of different groups in our services will be one of the key roles of councilors; their job will be to act as community leaders and to act as brokers, balancing the different interests of different groups and developing integrated policies which meet local needs best.
>
> — City of York Council

However, in practice, engagement with users and citizens does not obviate the need for service experts or for political judgment. In most cases, it simply provides more information about the range of, often conflicting, views among the public. Politicians and senior managers still need to decide how best to reconcile competing interests and to allocate resources accordingly.

Have We Got the Right Approach?

Many public sector organizations focus a great deal of effort on choosing the 'right' approach to public participation. In practice, however, there is rarely one correct method. Some of the approaches described above, for example, public meetings, citizens' juries and focus groups, offer high levels of interaction but reach only a small proportion of the population. They are also relatively costly, time-consuming and require skilled facilitation. Other methods, such as citizens' and users' panels and resident's surveys, offer breadth of coverage and are relatively cheap, but they provide less in-depth interaction.

Most organizations therefore need to have a balanced portfolio of approaches that are tailored to the objectives of engaging with users and citizens, the resources available to those managing the process, the timescale and the capacity of respondents.

Let's Work Together

It is quite common for several local agencies, or even several service departments within the same agency, to pursue their own individual consultation exercises in isolation from each other and unaware that effort is being duplicated. This is problematic for two reasons. First, it is a waste of resources. Second, it increases the risk of consultation fatigue among the public.

> *We usually ask a question ten times and use the information once. We must learn to ask once and use the answer ten times in different settings.*
>
> — Local authority chief executive

In order to avoid duplication and bring together disparate initiatives, some organizations have developed databases of previous consultations. In some areas joint consultation strategies are being developed by local councils, health authorities, the police and other agencies to ensure that they coordinate their initiatives.

Overcoming Apathy

Another problem is that many members of the public are unwilling to engage in the ways and to the degree that governments wish. Research suggests, for example, that only one in five citizens in the UK wants to engage more closely with their local authority (see Box 13.1).

Box 13.1
Public Attitudes to Participation

- I'm not interested in what the Council does, or whether it does its job: 1%
- I'm not interested in what the Council does as long as it does its job: 16%
- I like to know what the Council is doing, but I'm happy to let it get on with its job: 57%
- I would like to have more of a say in what the Council does and the services it provides: 21%
- I already work for/am involved with the Council: 3%
- Don't know: 1%

By definition the minority who do get involved are therefore unlikely to be representative of the community as a whole, particularly because the most vulnerable groups, those on lower incomes, young people, older people, members of households with a disabled person and members of ethnic minority communities, are usually the least inclined to be involved. Moreover, most people express a strong preference for relatively passive forms of engagement. In a recent survey in the UK the public strongly favored one-off consultations via postal surveys and face-to-face interviews. Very few were prepared to participate in in-depth consultations — only 13% said they would be willing to go to public meetings, just 6% said they would participate in a citizens' panel and only 3% would take part in a citizens' jury. [17]

One way of alleviating this problem is to focus on those policies and issues which citizens say they care most about — typically services such as community safety, street cleaning, and leisure facilities for young people. Another is to use the consultation methods that members of the public say they are most comfortable with. It is also vital to give feedback on how results were used, what decisions were taken and why, so that people can see that their views were taken seriously and made a real difference. Finally, some public service providers that have made important strides in engaging with the public have been less adept at consulting their own staff. This is a missed opportunity because many front-line staff live locally and use local services. They are therefore in a position to provide valuable feedback on their own and their families' experiences.

Ensuring It Makes a Difference

One of the major reasons for citizens' unwillingness to engage is widespread skepticism about whether governments and public service providers are willing to respond to public opinion. In many cases the scope for action will be constrained by the fact that an agency has only limited control over a policy area. Local authorities in the UK, for example, have little or no direct influence over many of the key issues about which local people feel most strongly including health, community safety and employment, and often have limited room for maneuver in terms of the services they do provide directly due to centrally determined performance targets and ring-fenced budgets.

If voting changed anything, they'd abolish it.

— Ken Livingstone, Mayor of London

It is therefore important to make clear at the outset what the parameters of engagement are, what issues are up for negotiation, what changes are possible and what is off-limits. It is also crucial that there is effective communication with users and citizens throughout the process and, where possible, that some early wins are achieved and celebrated — communities often complain that decision-making processes are too slow, and lose interest if improvements do not materialize fairly rapidly.

Evaluating Participation

There is now a strong body of knowledge about public participation, its potential and pitfalls — both in the UK and in many other Western countries. For example, Coote and Lenaghan [18] and McIver [19] evaluate the use of citizens' juries in the health service. Hall and Stewart provide a detailed account of early experiments with juries in six local authorities in England covering subjects as diverse as library services, waste management, drugs in the community, community facilities in rural areas and regeneration. [20]

However, public service providers often fail to tap this reservoir of knowledge or to reflect on their own experiences of public participation. The result is that they risk re-inventing the wheel and repeating mistakes made elsewhere.

It is therefore important to take time to evaluate the results of previous attempts to engage with users and citizens, assessing what is already known about what the public wants, how people wish to be involved in decisions and which approaches work best. It is also important for policy makers and practitioners to consider carefully the scope for coordinating their actions with those of other local agencies and to look further afield to gain new ideas about engagement from other service settings and other countries.

Summary

Engaging service users and citizens in policy making and the design and delivery of services is not new, but it is being seen increasingly as a key to good governance in most Western democracies. As a result there has been a plethora of new programs and initiatives designed to ensure greater public participation.

Engagement can take many forms. Less interactive approaches involve communication — the one-way flow of information from policy makers and managers to the public. More interactive approaches include consultation — a two-way flow of information, views and perspectives between policy makers/managers and users/citizens, and co-production — involving active partnership between providers and the public to develop strategies, design and deliver services and monitor standards.

Participation may include a range of different stakeholder groups. In some circumstances it is appropriate to engage first and foremost with service users. In others it is necessary to involve the public as a whole. In some cases it is important to work with particular communities of place or specific groups.

There is a vast array of techniques for public engagement. What matters most is that the tools used by an organization are fit for the purpose and are appropriate to its own capacity and that of the groups with which it is seeking to engage.

Public participation offers a range of potential benefits but also entails formidable challenges. There is a lot of experience that can be tapped from across a range of services and different national settings. It is important that policy makers, politicians and public service managers draw upon this growing body of evidence in developing their own organizations' approaches to public engagement.

Note: *Originally published in Martin, S., Engaging with citizens and other stakeholders, in* Public Management and Governance, *Bovaird, T. and Löffler, E., Eds., Routledge, London, 2003, chap. 15.*

Endnotes

1. Public Management Service, Organisation for Economic Co-operation and Development, *Engaging Citizens in Policy-Making: Information, Consultation and Public Participation*, PUMA Policy Briefing No. 10, Organisation for Economic Co-operation and Development, Paris, 2001. http://www.oecd.org/dataoecd/24/34/2384040.pdf (accessed 2007).

2. Lowndes, V. et al., Enhancing Public Participation in Local Government: A Research Report to the Department of the Environment, Transport and the Regions, UK Department of the Environment, Transport and the Regions, London, 1998.

3. UK Department of the Environment, Transport and the Regions, Modernising Local Government: Improving Services through Best Value, UK Department of the Environment, Transport and the Regions, London, 1998.

4. Martin, S. et al., Improving Public Services: Evaluation of the Best Value Pilot Programme: Final Report, UK Department of the Environment, Transport and the Regions, London, 2001.

5. Arnstein, S., The ladder of citizen participation, *Journal of the Royal Town Planning Institute,* 57(1), 176, 1971.

6. Pollitt, C., Bringing consumers into performance measurement: Concepts, consequences and constraints, *Policy & Politics,* 16(2), 77, 1988.

7. Bromley, C., Stratford, N., and Rao, N., Revisiting Public Perceptions of Local Government: A Decade of Change: Finance and Services, Information Provision, Consultation and Participation, UK Department of the Environment, Transport and the Regions, London, 2000.

8. UK Office of the Deputy Prime Minister, Connecting with Communities: Improving Communications in Local Government, Office of the Deputy Prime Minister, London, 2002. *Editor's Note:* For the 2006 update report on the same project, see: http://www.idea.gov.uk/idk/core/page.do?pageId=5452193 (accessed 2007).

9. Bovaird, T., Public management and governance: Emerging trends and potential future directions, in *Public Administration: An Interdisciplinary Critical Analysis,* Vigoda, E., Ed., Marcel Dekker, New York, 2002, chap. 16.

10. *Editor's Note:* See also Chapter 16 in this volume, which had been originally published in 2003 in the same book as this chapter.

11. Martin, S.J. and Boaz, A., Public participation and citizen-centred local government, *Public Money & Management,* 20(2), 47, 2000.

12. UK Office of the Deputy Prime Minister, op. cit.

13. For details see: http://www.idea.gov.uk/idk/core/page.do?pageId=1 (accessed 2007).

14. Lowndes, V. et al., op. cit.

15. Renn, O., Webler, T., and Wiedemann, P.M., Eds., *Fairness and Competence in Citizen Participation: Evaluating Models for Environmental Discourse,* Kluwer Academic, Dordrecht, The Netherlands, 1995.

16. Barnes, M. et al., The new management of community care: User groups, citizenship and co-production, in *The New Management of British Local Governance,* Stoker, G., Ed., Macmillan, Basingstoke, UK, 1999.

17. Martin et al., op. cit.

18. Coote, A. and Lenaghan, J., *Citizens' Juries: Theory into Practice,* Institute for Public Policy Research, London, 1997.

19. McIver, S., An Evaluation of the King's Fund Citizens' Juries Programme, Health Services Management Centre, Birmingham, UK, 1997.

20. Hall, D. and Stewart, J., Citizens' Juries in Local Government: Report for the LGMB on the Pilot Projects, UK Local Government Management Board, London, 1997.

Chapter 14

The Management of Citizen Participation in Taiwan: A Case Study of Taipei City Government's Citizen Complaints System

Don-yun Chen, Tong-yi Huang, and Naiyi Hsaio

Contents

Abstract: Citizen participation is one of the core values of democracy. Democratization means an increase in citizen participation in public affairs. However, the issue of democratization is rarely studied in the field of public administration. In this article, we use the Taipei City Government (TCG) Citizen Complaints System to illustrate some tensions relating to citizen participation in a newly democratizing country. We interviewed the TCG officials to piece together the puzzle of how the citizen complaints system works. Furthermore, we conducted a survey on how each channel and media are used by citizens to file their complaints. Then, we focused on the development of the Taipei City Mayor's email box to see how the tension between participation and cost is handled by utilizing newly emerging information technology. We then evaluate these developments in terms of publicity, accessibility, and accountability suggested by Seneviratne and Cracknell. [1] Accordingly, we propose suggestions for improvement from these three aspects for the TCG and other governments as well to establish a citizen complaints system that substantiates democracy.

Introduction

Citizen participation is one of the core values of democracy. However, critics of the democratic way of governing can easily raise problems concerning its practical aspect. [2] For one part, participation is costly to the individual citizen as well as the government. [3] As a result, to require citizen participation in the governing process can mean that the government is unable to act swiftly and decisively. This is because efficiency is one of the most important aspects of good governance from a popular viewpoint. Simple addition can tell us that the decision cost for a group can increase drastically as the group size increases. [4] Even the recently popular arguments for "deliberative democracy" or "reinventing government" to strengthen democratic governance cannot ignore this practical problem. [5] This undeniable problem creates a tension between the public's right to participate and the government official's role to act efficiently in the process of democratization. [6]

For example, for the past decade, citizen participation in meaningful elections in Taiwan (Republic of China, R.O.C.) has created a truly democratic state on the small island. [7] However, because of the rapid change, the government of Taiwan has not been able to catch up with the growing need of its citizenry to participate in the public policy process. Under increasing budgetary limitations in recent years and with increasing popular demands on quality service from the government, the bureaucrats are asked to have a customer-oriented mentality. [8] Elected executives throughout the island have invested a lot of effort to establish various citizen complaints procedures to ensure "customers' satisfaction" with governmental services. As a result, the public sector in Taiwan after the democratic transition is no longer purely a public goods production factory, but a service industry whose main goal is to figure out ways to gain customer satisfaction in order to keep their elected officials in power.

From a resource allocation viewpoint, without relieving bureaucrats' daily operations in producing public goods, they are burdened with replying to citizens' complaints and inquiries in a genial and efficient manner. This burden becomes a managerial problem with calculating costs and benefits of managing increased participation. [9] As a result, government agencies are forced to find more efficient ways to handle these time-consuming affairs.

In this chapter, we use the Taipei City Government (TCG) as an example to illustrate the described managerial problem in a newly democratizing country. We especially focus on the development of the Citizen Complaints System to see how this problem is handled by using traditional means as well as newly emerged information technology. Finally, we evaluate these developments by a set of criteria established by Seneviratne and Cracknell and suggest reform measures for the system in the future. [10]

The Dilemma of Citizen Participation: A Managerial Problem with Political Implications

Political scientist Robert A. Dahl defined the term "democracy" as "to be responsive to the preference of its citizens." [11] As long as one of the major differences between democratic and non-democratic regimes is governmental responsiveness to citizen's preference, democratization will be defined as a process where a ruling system is transforming from a non-responsive to a responsive one. Generally, there are two ways to ensure governmental responsiveness to citizens in a democratic polity — passive and active ways.

Citizen Participation: Passive and Active Role in a Democratic Polity

The first way is a passive one. That is, in every democratic regime there exists a system of periodic elections intended to remove unpopular politicians. Usually, this way of participation is defined as a group of "legal acts by private citizens that are more or less directly aimed at influencing the selection of governmental personnel and/or the actions that they take." [12] Political scientists have long been treating this method as the major channel of citizen participation.

The second way is an active one whose core is to involve the citizen in the planning, implementing, and monitoring of governmental activities. [13] Experts from the field of public administration have long been proposing a "participatory state" or a "deliberative planning procedure" as major methods to reinvent the government's efforts of running the constitution. [14] However, the efforts of involving the public in the policy process are not always effective. [15] Some have suggested that the reason behind this failure in citizen participation is the general decline of public trust or social capital in Western governments. [16] Others have questioned the lack of a concept of "citizenship" in modern public administration. [17] King, Feltey, and Susel use interviews and focus-group discussions and find that a more dynamic role-playing relationship between administrators and citizens is needed to improve the general ineffectiveness of citizen participation. [18]

The Costs of Participation: The Problem of "Sovereign Transactions"

One way of thinking about citizen participation is through the lens of transaction cost economics. [19] From this viewpoint, the persuasion, learning, negotiation, decision-making or deliberative activities in the public arena can be seen as the "sovereign transactions" parallel to market trans-actions in the economic arena. [20] The costs of both kinds of transactions do not equal zero. As a result, under the principle of resources scarcity, to encourage citizen participation is by nature to increase individual as well as collective costs of running the political system. Sometimes, this encouragement might have the opposite effect and cause instability in the political system. This is one of the reasons why some political scientists, such as Berelson, think that the efficiency and stability of a political system can only be reached by a small group of able and willing elites and the majority of citizens' non-involvement for most of the time. [21]

Through this viewpoint, any normative proposal to encourage citizen participation should be balanced with efficient accounts of ways to minimize sovereign transactions. Otherwise, the proposal will be seen as unrealistic. [22] From a public manager's perspective, although promot-ing citizen participation is normatively desirable and politically feasible, public managers still have to take the "costs" factor into account in order to evaluate the organizational feasibility of related reform efforts to encourage citizen participation. This evaluation can be best expressed in Harlan Cleveland's words, "how do you get everybody in on the act and still get some action?" [23]

In this chapter, we select the TCG's efforts to handle citizen complaints as an example to show public managers' efforts to deal with increasing citizen participation in a democratizing polity. As we will see, the recurrent theme in these efforts is to create new ways to reduce "sov-ereign transactions" in order to cope with the increasing citizen participation after democratiza-tion in Taiwan. [24]

Democratization, Participation, and the Taipei City Government's Citizen Complaints System

The 1980s was a crucial period in Taiwan's democratization. As the authoritarian state was moving from a "hard" to "soft" one, [25] the quasi-Leninist regime dominated by the ruling Nationalist Party (Kuomintang; KMT) began to launch reform measures to overcome challenges from various external and domestic sources. [26] In 1986, after former president Chiang Ching-kuo announced his intention to lift 37-year-old emergency decrees adopted after the KMT fled from mainland China in the late 1940s, Taiwan was on a one-way track to democratization whose central idea was for citizen participation in the policy-making process. Although scholars still argue about the motivation behind Chiang's decision to reform, [27] his message to open up the political arena to the public was clear. The mentioned news report had quoted a foreign observer saying that:

> Chiang wants in his final years in office to bequeath some kind of stable, lasting sys-tem, and has concluded that the only way he can do this is to invite broader participa-tion in the political process. [28]

During the same period of time, the rise of various social movements had begun to form a participatory civil society in Taiwan. As a local scholar observed:

> A new kind of political culture is gradually appearing in Taiwan — a participatory one — emerging, slowing but surely, from the mobilization of its civil society in the 1980s. Taiwan's civil society is no longer a passive recipient of the state's domination. [29]

Indeed, "the road to openness" is the key phrase to describe Taiwan in the 1980s. During and after the democratic transition, people in Taiwan were more and more getting used to not only participating in local and nation-wide elections, but also organizing and involving community-building and other public policy-related activities to express their preferences to the government. This change has created an environment for public managers to have a chance as well as a pressure to establish a democratic relationship with the general public in Taiwan. For many observers of Taiwan's fate in the process of democratic consolidation, building a meaningful and collaborative relationship with the revived civil society is the key to having a quality democratic system in the future. [30] The road to openness is a road of no return. The best response that government can take is to figure out ways to handle citizen participation more effectively. To illustrate one example of the response, we introduce and review the TCG's Citizen Complaints System in the remainder of this chapter. [31]

The Development of the Taipei City Government's Citizen Complaints System

Taipei is the capital city of Taiwan. It is also the most modernized city and has been the political and economic center of the small island country since the late 1940s. Most importantly, the TCG always pioneers in various government reform measures, which includes efforts to redesign procedures to facilitate citizen participation.

Long before the authoritarian regime started to democratize in the late 1980s, the central government of Taiwan and the TCG set up different channels for citizens to appeal. The TCG also set up the Commission of Administrative Appeals to review citizens' petitions and appeals when they are wronged by certain measures or actions of the TCG. Although the government expanded channels for citizen complaints, citizens in general were not satisfied with the system. [32]

The TCG Citizen Complaints System, just as the complaints system of other government agencies, served as a democratic facade without much substantive meaning for years until 1994, when reform-minded Mayor Chen took office. Being the first popularly elected mayor after the Kuomintang's 37-years-long dominance, Mayor Chen took two important steps to strengthen the TCG's responsiveness and effectiveness in handling citizens' complaints.

First, in 1994, shortly after Chen's electoral victory, he launched a program called "Meeting with Citizens." Every Wednesday, Mayor Chen met with citizens to listen to their complaints or suggestions on specific city policies or administrative issues. The mayor tried to solve the citizens' problems in the meetings. The issues that couldn't be solved by the mayor were left to relevant agencies of the TCG and were tracked down by the TCG's Commission of Research, Development, and Evaluation. This system is still in operation but with a little twist.

Aside from riding on the tides of democratization and populism, Mayor Chen also took good advantage of new technology to facilitate communication between the TCG and its citizens. On October 12, 1995, Mayor Chen launched an electronic mailbox called the "A-Bian Mailbox." [33] It was the very first citizen-participation initiative in Taiwan's government agencies. The A-Bian Mailbox was first implemented in text-mode in an electronic Bulletin Board System (BBS), and was revised to a Web-based edition on March 24, 1998. In November 2001, the Mayor's Box was still in operation and receiving more and more letters. Most bureau chiefs/deputy directors also have set up their own email boxes for citizens to file complaints.

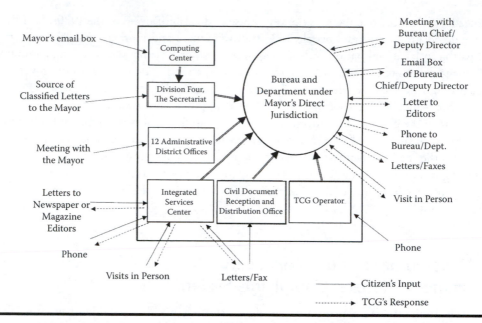

Figure 14.1   The Taipei City Government Citizen Complaints Systems

Before Mayor Chen stepped down in 1998, the TCG provided a variety of channels for citizens to communicate with its agencies, as will be illustrated in the next section. No matter how convenient and easily accessible the system was, however, it could have been drastically altered or even abolished by another elected mayor because the system was set up according to guidelines rather than as enacted laws. Only in 1999 did the Legislative Yuan pass the Administrative Procedure Act that obligates government agencies to make operational rules to handle citizen complaints and dispatch officials to deal with them speedily and properly. [34] By this law, citizens' rights to present their appeals to the government are better protected. Government agencies are now required by law to provide citizens' complaints channels and to manage them. Inappropriate management of citizens' complaints are now subject to more severe legal penalties. This was another step toward a more responsive government.

In sum, the TCG's citizen complaints mechanism has become more complete as a result of democratization in Taiwan. Under authoritarianism, the TCG provided channels for citizens to express complaints, but the government generally responded passively. The first party turnover involved initiatives to communicate more proactively with citizens and to be more responsive. Recently, citizens' rights to comment on governmental actions or inactions are better protected by the passage of the Administrative Procedure Act in 1999.

The Operation of the Current Citizen Complaints System

Citizen Complaints Procedures

As Figure 14.1 illustrates, there are a variety of ways citizens can reach the city government. For those who know the specific bureau/department that may be related to their grievance, direct contact will be made with these units or even specific officials. Citizens can make telephone calls, or send letters, faxes, or emails to the bureau/department or the bureau chief/deputy director. They can also make their appeals in person or make appointments with the bureau chief/deputy director through other procedures.

Complainants may write letters to newspaper/magazine editors, who would forward the letters to the TCG, in addition to publishing these letters. Complainants also can reach the TCG through several channels that function as a "one-stop" service, if they have no idea which bureau/department to contact. The least costly way among these channels is probably phone calls to the TCG operators who will direct the call to the relevant units. The TCG provides a separate, special number (1999) [35] for citizens to reach the TCG, in addition to several lines that can be found through a directory service line (104) provided by the telephone company. A more official and traditional alternative is to mail or fax letters to the TCG. The advantage of this channel is that it enables complainants to attach documents or other supporting materials to make their case.

Citizens can also easily get access to the Internet; a similar, but less costly way is to send an email directly to the Taipei City Mayor's email box. Once citizens direct their Web browser (such as Internet Explorer or Netscape Navigator) to the address, they are instructed to fill in their email address, the subject of their complaint, and the contents of the complaint. After the "submit" button has been pressed, an automatic email response will be sent to the specified email address. People will receive confirmation of the complaints they just sent to the City. This re-confirmation design is to guarantee that the complaining citizens are using authentic email addresses. A valid email address also implies that the efforts of the City agencies to process the complaints will not be a waste of taxpayers' resources.

In addition to the TCG operator and the Taipei City Mayor's email box, citizens can make phone calls or send letters/faxes to the Integrated Service Center which functions as a "one-stop" service for citizens to search consultancy or to file complaints. The Integrated Service Center is located near the entrance of the TCG Building and it has 24 counters to provide various services. Citizens can visit the Center in person to seek help if they don't know where to start to make their complaints. The Center also serves as a bridge between the media and the TCG on citizen complaints handling. For example, the *United Daily News* provides a hotline for citizens' opinions. Those opinions/complaints toward the TCG expressed through this hotline as well as those sent to the editors of other media are passed on to the Integrated Service Center.

Complainants may not be satisfied with contacting the bureaus/departments only and may want to reach the mayor himself. Two approaches can be taken. First, the citizen can seek to pass a message through political or social networks, such as a city councilor, interest group leaders, or affiliated party officials, to the mayor's office or the mayor himself. These messages (most of them are in letters) would be passed to the Secretariat and become classified. Division Four of the Secretariat reviews the case and distributes it to the related TCG unit. Second, citizens can also take advantage of "Meeting with the Mayor" and file the application through the administrative district offices. But the application and review process takes at least four weeks and may not be accepted if the problem can be solved by other bureaus/departments. [36]

The review process for Meeting with the Mayor is more tedious and time consuming than other procedures. One week prior to the meeting, an official from the Commission of Research, Development, and Evaluation, the District office, and the related bureau/department hold a meeting and integrate their responses for the mayor's meeting with the applicant. Within four days of the meeting, the District office is then requested to submit the minutes of the meeting to the mayor for his signature after which the minutes are sent to the related bureau/department. Upon receiving the minutes, the bureau/department has to reply to the complainant and at the same time send the reply to the Commission of Research, Development, and Evaluation for further monitoring. After each session, the Commission submits a monitoring report to the Executive Meeting on City Affairs (chaired by the mayor).

Usage of Procedures and Media

Table 14.1 illustrates the frequency distribution of the procedures and media which citizens used to file their cases in June 2001. The total complaints numbered 12,242 cases. On average, there are 400 complaints sent to the TCG each workday. Among all the procedures listed in Table 14.1, the Taipei City Mayor's email box was the most frequently used channel by citizens. The Taipei City Mayor's email box, classified letters to the mayor's office, and meeting with the mayor account for 53% of the total complaints received in June 2001. Such results are consistent with Lin Shoei-po's findings that while hesitating to trust government agencies as a whole, complainants tend to believe that their grievance would be likely to be lessened by the heads of the government agencies. [37] Aside from complaints directed to the ISC and the mayor, more sophisticated citizens contacted specific bureaus and departments. One-third of these complaints are to the chiefs and directors and the other two-thirds are to the agencies. Altogether letters to the agencies or their heads amount to one-third of the total.

In terms of media usage, about one-third of the complainants sent emails to the mayor, 11% sent emails to bureau chiefs or deputy directors. Table 14.2 and Figure 14.2 summarize the growing use of the Taipei City Mayor's email box since its inception dating back to the second quarter of 1996. It is worth noting that the number seems to stay around 8,000 since the first quarter of 2000. That is, the City agencies have to respond to around 2,600 emails a month, which has caused serious work overload.

The Taipei City Mayor's email box provides a low-cost and convenient tool for citizens to voice their day-to-day problems and ask for an immediate resolution from the city agencies. Meanwhile, however, the low "entering cost" at which the city agencies are informed of citizen complaints also leads to competing use of the limited working hours of the agencies' staff members. According to the previous summary, for instance, some agencies even invest more than half of their human resources to deal with citizen complaints. The result also indicates increasing use of the Internet among Taipei citizens. The popularity of Internet usage among Taipei citizens may be attributed to the current and former mayors' advocacy to construct a Cyber City.

Post and facsimile letters account for one-quarter of all the TCG complaints media usage in June 2001. In this category, classified letters to the mayor or his office occupies more than one-third and letters to the bureau/departments are almost equal. Although written letters in post mail or facsimile are considered more formal and confidential and may be taken seriously, they count for less than half of the amount of email usage. The third largest category of media usage is telephone and it covers 20% of the complainants. Among citizen complaints to the TCG by telephone, about half of them reached the bureaus and departments. However, whether these calls were directed by the hotline operator or made directly to the TCG units is unknown. The last two categories, personal visits and letters to the editors of news media to express complaints, constitute 7.6% and 3.65% respectively, with Meeting with the Mayor a bit over half of the first categories.

In addition to the complaints classified by channels and media illustrated by Table 14.1, Table 14.3 demonstrates the ratio of cases under monitoring for each item. Some cases are closely monitored by the respective department head or by the Commission of Research, Development, and Evaluation. But other cases are processed through ordinary document handling procedures. Among the 15 items, complaints through the Taipei City Mayor's email box has the highest ratio

Table 14.1 Citizen Complaints Procedure and Media, Taipei City Government (June 2001)

	Letter/ fax	Phone	Visit in person	Email	Letter to newspaper	Total (monitored)	Total, % (monitored, %)
BD	1,156	1,236	111		82	2,585	21.12
	(1,034)	(51)	(5)		(5)	(1,095)	(15.11)
APPBD			113			113	0.92
			(33)			(33)	(0.46)
EBDMX				1,290		1,290	10.54
				(605)		(605)	(8.35)
EMMX				4,080		4,048	33.33
				(3,879)		(3,879)	(53.54)
CL	1,169	571	94		77	1,911	15.61
	(740)	(113)	(18)		(1)	(872)	(12.04)
MM			483			483	3.95
			(32)			(32)	(0.44)
ISC	680	691	136		273	1,780	14.54
	(246)	(243)	(60)		(180)	(729)	(10.06)
Total (monitored)	3,005	2,498	937	5,370	432	12,242	100
Total (monitored)	(2,020)	(407)	(148)	(4,484)	(186)	(7,245)	(100)
Total, %	24.55	20.41	7.65	43.87	3.53	100	Ratio of monitored
Total (monitored, %)	(27.88)	(5.62)	(2.04)	(61.89)	(2.57)	(100)	59.18

Key: BD: Bureau/Department; APPBD: Meeting with Bureau Chiefs/Deputy Director; BDBM: Bureau Chief/Deputy Directors' email box; TCME: Taipei City Mayor's email box; CL: Classified Letters of the Mayor's office; MM: Meeting with the Mayor; ISC: Integrated Services Center.

Table 14.2   Taipei City Mayor's Email Box Processed Emails

Time	Type I and II	Type III	Sum	Type III Ratio, %
Q2/1996	594	133	594	22
Q3/1996	868	212	868	24
Q4/1996	1,116	227	1,116	20
Q1/1997	1,074	251	1,074	23
Q2/1997	1,534	327	1,534	21
July–August/1997	1,095	213	1,095	19
September–November/1997	1,891	642	1,891	34
December/1997–February/1998	1,492	597	1,492	40
March–May/1998	3,546	1,341	3,546	38
June–August/1998	3,706	1,505	3,706	41
September–November/1999	3,424	2,219	3,424	65
December/1998–March/1999	5,014	1,105	5,014	22
Q2/1999	6,258	1,817	6,258	29
Q3/1999	6,887	2,076	6,887	30
Q4/1999	5,867	2,212	5,867	38
Q1/2000	7,032	1,303	7,032	19
Q2/2000	8,406	827	8,406	10
Q3/2000	10,217	567	10,217	6
Q4/2000	9,342	668	9,342	7
Q1/2001	7,632	562	7,632	7
Q2/2001	10,863	1,645	10,863	15

under monitoring, post and fax letters to bureau/department second highest, and post and fax letters to the mayor or his office in the third position. In terms of channels and media, the Taipei City Mayor's email box outnumbered other alternatives. Overall, about 59% of all the complaints are under monitoring.

Complaints Handling Mechanism

Since the TCG citizen complaints system has existed for almost 30 years, the TCG has developed a routine to handle citizen complaints it receives. According to our interviews with different bureaus and departments, a typical complaint goes through the following steps.

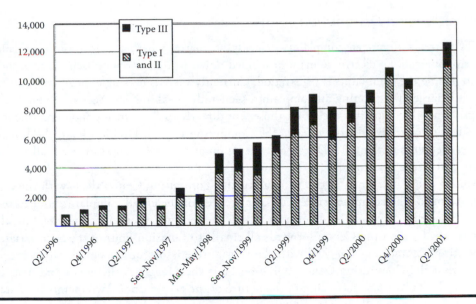

Figure 14.2   Taipei City Mayor's Email Box Processed Email

Table 14.3   Monitored Complaints as Percentage of All Complaints for Each Procedure/Media

	%					
	Letter/fax	Phone	Visit in person	Email	Letter to newspaper	Total (monitored)
BD	89.4	4.7	4.5		6.1	42.4
APPBD			29.2			29.2
EBDMX				46.9		46.9
EMMX				95.1		
CL	63.3	19.8	19.1		1.3	45.6
MM			6.6			6.6
ISC	36.2	35.2	44.1		65.9	41
Total (monitored)	67.2	16.3	15.8	83.5	43.1	59.2

Key: BD: Bureau/Department; APPBD: Meeting with Bureau Chiefs/Deputy Director; BDBM: Bureau Chief/Deputy Directors' email box; TCME: Taipei City Mayor's email box; CL: Classified Letters of the Mayor's Office; MM: Meeting with the Mayor; ISC: Integrated Services Center.

Registration and Distribution

The TCG treats all citizen complaints officially no matter whether they are input through a simple phone call, an electronic mail, or handed down to the mayor himself. Hence, the first step to handle the complaints is registration. Currently there is no single integrated unit in the TCG in charge of registering all complaints. Generally speaking, the Secretariat takes charge of registering all complaints except for those sent directly to the bureaus and departments and through administrative district offices. The Computing Center, Division Four, the Integrated Services Center, and the Civil Document Reception and Distribution Office are all under the jurisdiction of the Secretariat.

Among these four units of the Secretariat, the Computing Center deals with the technical problems of the computer system to keep records of the email complaints and to receive and screen redundant emails. After it cleans up the redundant emails from a technical perspective, the Computing Center forwards all emails to Division Four of the Secretariat. The Computing Center does not deal with the substantive issues of the email. Upon receiving letters from the Computing Center, Division Four then registers the email and distributes letters to the TCG units according to the nature of the complaints. Two members of staff in the Secretariat work full-time to read all emails through a Web-based interface and initially assign the agencies that will be responsible for responding to the emails. Both of the two Secretariat staff members have been working on the dispatching duty for a long time (almost since the establishment of the Taipei City Mayor's email box) and hence have accumulated rich, relevant knowledge.

While the units under the Secretariat register and distribute complaints, the bureaus/departments tackle the substantive issues raised by complainants. Upon receiving complaints from citizens directly or indirectly, a person in charge registers the complaint in the unit's record system and goes through the Commission of Research, Development, and Evaluation personnel for monitoring. After the registration procedure, the person in charge distributes complaints to sections or divisions under its direction. The section chief further appoints officials to deal with the substantive issues the complainant specifies.

Review and Action

According to the "Guidelines to Handle Citizen Complaints," the TCG officials don't need to process a complaint without any substance. [38] However, the TCG has to respond to anonymous complaints with specific evidence. The process takes several days before the citizen complaints reach the exact official(s) in charge of the complainant's issues. However, officials are required to complete a case within 15 days and within seven days for cases under monitoring. [39] In general, most cases can be completed within the time requested by the Monitoring System.

Within the required time limit some units, such as the Building Standards Department of the Bureau of Public Works, are unable to follow the time line. Citizens' complaints to the Bureau mostly concerned with illegal building, which demands investigation on-site and may involve other TCG units, demands cross-departmental actions. These are always time consuming.

To meet the time line, officials have to deal with the cases effectively. There are many ways to gain necessary knowledge for solving problems. More than 90% of our interviewees consult their colleagues or review similar old cases. Only five out of the 43 surveyed units have development manuals.

Reply and Evaluation

After the official from the specific bureau reviews the case or takes any actions, he or she has to reply to the complainant. The TCG units take three different approaches in responding to citizens. In 28 out of the 43 TCG units we surveyed, the administrators double-check the content of the reply letter before it is sent. In 11 out of the 43 units, the official who deals with the substantive issues drafts and sends the reply letter directly without its being double-checked.

A complainant may receive different letters from several bureaus or departments if a subject matter involves cross-departmental coordination. [40] Generally, a reply is sent to the complainant through the very channel and media the citizen used. For example, the TCG uses email to reply to citizens who wrote to the mayor's email box unless other media is needed (for example, postal mail).

The complaints handling procedure doesn't end with the reply letter to the complainant. Internally, the official who replies has to inform related units and the Commission of Research, Development, and Evaluation personnel to clear the case from the monitoring system. The Commission personnel then delete the case and compile it into the monthly statistics. To better understand the complainants' appraisal of the system, a survey is attached to show how satisfied the complainants are with the system.

Evaluations and Suggestions

In a study that investigated consumer complaints in a public sector service in local authorities in England, Mary Seneviratne and Sarah Cracknell proposed that complaints procedure must be considered not only efficient but also fair. [41] They must be available to the socially disadvantaged who do not know how to express their complaints or are afraid to do so. In practice, the procedures must be published and must ensure that everyone should be able to use them. Fair and accessible procedures alone do not necessarily bring about citizen satisfaction without a good management system. To have an effective management system at the operational level, Seneviratne and Cracknell further suggested one specialist authority-wide officer for logging and monitoring complaints. *Publicity*, *accessibility*, and *accountability* are the criteria for evaluating a citizen complaints system.

In terms of publicity, the TCG specifies all channels and media of the complaints system in a brochure distributed to every household of Taipei City. This information is also available on the Internet. As most information about the complaints system is in written form, we suspect that citizens may still be ill-informed about the purpose and function of the whole system, because the 161-page brochure is only a massive collection of channels and media to reach certain bureaus. Although the TCG had established a serve-all telephone number "1999" in the year 2001 with a highly publicized campaign to inform the citizens of Taipei, the telephone line, according to our interviews, leads only to the general operator of the TCG. With regard to the Taipei City Mayor's email box, people who connect to the TCG's official Website can easily find the Taipei City Mayor's email box to click into it.

We suggest that the TCG should do more in publicity by establishing an easy-to-remember, unified, and clearly promoted citizen complaints system entry point such as the 1-800 number of many businesses to handle customers' complaints. The person who serves at the entry point should not simply be a general operator to connect to different bureaus, but a well-trained expert in customer relations to help a citizen to file his or her complaint and gain satisfaction from the TCG.

The second aspect is whether every citizen is able to use the procedure, i.e., the accessibility of the citizen complaints system. As discussed previously, the TCG has provided different procedures and media for citizens to file complaints. Citizens are not required to express their complaints in a written document supported by strong evidence. As shown previously, the ratio of telephone complaints under monitoring is much lower than other media; whether the emphasis on more formal media is a critical issue demands further studies. Also, as citizen complaints through the Taipei City Mayor's email box continue to grow, this trend shows its worth as an effective citizen complaints channel because of its relatively lower cost. On the other hand, the problem of the so-called "digital divide" might block some strata of our society from using this tool to connect with the TCG. [42]

We suggest that the TCG should invest more to promote not only the existence of media or channels to file complaints, but it should educate the general public about their rights to complain and provide step-by-step instruction about the procedure to file a complaint through different media and channels.

A third and equally important criterion is accountability. The TCG has set up a computerized system to monitor the processing and handling of all complaints through the Taipei City Mayor's email box to ensure accountability. Also, letters to the mayor are also closely monitored by the Commission of Research, Development, and Evaluation. Complaints from other channels and those cleared on-site or on the phone are also registered and recorded in written form. To prevent complaints from drifting aimlessly and to ensure every single complaint is taken seriously, the Third Section of the Commission of Research, Development, and Evaluation sends the Commission personnel to each bureau/department to monitor the complaints handling process. These personnel report to the Commission monthly. The reports only summarize a total number of complaints and record the content of each complaint. However, as we collected the June 2001 data from the TCG, we found that the data from our survey and the monthly report could not be matched. Also, the information in written form has never been used for any analysis.

As a result, we suggest that the Commission of Research, Development, and Evaluation set up a Website to allow the Commission personnel in various departments to file their monthly reports through the Internet. It is by no means a cheaper way to enhance accountability of the system. We also suggest that certain variables be added to the monthly report, such as the media and channel of the complaints used in this research for the purpose of a better analysis of the pattern and behavior of citizen complaints. Also, using a Website to collect complaint data can allow us to do the job of so-called "data mining" in citizen relationship management to assemble useful knowledge to help the TCG to dig out recurrent problems in the daily operation.

Conclusion

Democratization means a regime is transforming from a non-responsive to a responsive one. Citizens in a democratizing polity will begin to expect bureaucrats to be responsive to their requests and demands. However, difficulties arise when citizens expect too much responsiveness. From the transaction cost economics perspective, one of the difficulties might be that it is too costly to run the nation when there is "too much" participation. Excessive participation might paralyze the administrative capacity of the regime. Obviously, elected politicians will not take steps to hinder participation's transaction costs to the civil servant if such steps would impede their re-election. As a result, the bureaucracy must continuously search for more efficient ways to handle increasing requests and demands from the public. This tension forms a managerial problem with political implications in a democratizing polity.

After examining the TCG's system of handling citizen complaints, we found that email has become the most popular media to file complaints. On average, the TCG has to process about 2600 email complaints each month. The monitoring system of the Taipei City Mayor's email box is the most established one compared with those of other media and channels. The reason behind this development is the increased presence of the Internet in Taiwanese society. We can see that the Internet is a valuable tool for both citizens and civil servants to reduce the sovereign transaction costs of participation.

In the end, after we evaluated the citizen complaints system of the TCG from three criteria, publicity, accessibility, and accountability, we suggest the following three reform measures to improve the TCG's citizen complaints system:

1. The TCG should do more publicity by establishing an easy-to-remember, unified, and clearly promoted citizen complaints system entry point such as the 1-800 number of many businesses to handle customers' complaints.
2. The TCG should invest more to promote not only the existence of certain media or channels to file complaints, but it should also educate the general public about their rights to complain.
3. The TCG's Commission of Research, Development, and Evaluation should set up a Website to allow Commission personnel in various departments to file their monthly reports and reduce the cost of monitoring.

Acknowledgments

The authors would like to acknowledge the research grant from the Taipei City Government's Commission of Research, Development, and Evaluation.

Note: *Originally published in Chen, D.-y., Huang, T.-y., and Hsaio, N., The management of citizen participation in Taiwan: A case study of Taipei City Government's Citizen Complaints System,* International Journal of Public Administration, *26, 525, 2003.*

Endnotes

1. Seneviratne, M. and Cracknell, S., Consumer complaints in public sector services, *Public Administration*, 66, 181, 1988.
2. One important practical aspect of participation, which will not be discussed in this chapter, is the problem of citizen competence. For related works, see Elkin, S.L. and Soltan, K.E., Eds., *Citizen Competence and Democratic Institutions*, Pennsylvania State University Press, University Park, 1999, 1–20.
3. Costly participation to the individual citizen can be described best by Anthony Downs' famous theory of "rational ignorance." It declares that the information cost to participate is high for any individual. As a result, the individual will weigh the benefit and cost of information gathering while in the public arena. Usually the individual will prefer to remain ignorant on public issues for financial reasons (Downs, A., *An Economic Theory of Democracy*, Harper & Row, New York, 1957, 207–78).
4. Dahl, R.A., *On Democracy*, Yale University Press, New Haven, CT, 1999, 107 and Table 1.

5. Barber, B., *Strong Democracy: Participatory Politics for a New Age*, University of California Press, Berkeley, 1984; Dryzek, J.S., *Deliberative Democracy and Beyond: Liberals, Critics, Contestations*, Oxford University Press, Oxford, UK, 2000; Osborne, D. and Gaebler, T., *Reinventing Government: How the Entrepreneurial Spirit Is Transforming the Public Sector*, Addison-Wesley, Reading, MA, 1992; Osborne, D. and Plastrik, P., *Banishing Bureaucracy: The Five Strategies for Reinventing Government*, Addison-Wesley, Reading, MA, 1997.

6. Simonsen, W. and Robbins, M.D., *Citizen Participation in Resource Allocation*, Westview, Boulder, CO, 2000, 1–20. They have categorized the tension into three general parts: politics vs. administration, expertise vs. access, and representation vs. participation.

7. Tsang, S.Y.-s. and Tien, H.-m., Eds., *Democratization in Taiwan: Implications for China*, St. Martin's, NY, 1999; Wu, J.J., *Taiwan's Democratization: Forces Behind the New Momentum*, Oxford University Press, Oxford, UK, 1995, 33–71.

8. Kuo, Y.-y., New public management in Taiwan: Government reinvention, in *Learning from International Public Management Reform*, Part B, Jones, L.R., Guthrie, J., and Steane, P., Eds., JAI, New York, 2001, 337.

9. Benjamin, C., *Participation Revisited: A Managerial Perspective*, Monographs No. 6, Center for Democracy and Governance, U.S. Agency for International Development, Washington, DC, 2000. http://www.usaid.gov/our_work/democracy_and_governance/publications/ipc/mn-6-ms.pdf (accessed 2007)

10. See endnote 1.

11. Dahl, R.A., *Polyarchy: Participation and Opposition*, Yale University Press, New Haven, CT, 1971, 2.

12. Verba, S., Nie, N.H., and Kim, J.-o., *Participation and Political Equality: A Seven-Nation Comparison*, University of Chicago Press, Chicago, 1978, 1.

13. Seargeant, J. and Steele, J., *Consulting the Public: Guidelines and Good Practice*, Policy Studies Institute, London, UK, 1998; Thomas, J.C., *Public Participation in Public Decisions*, Jossey-Bass, San Francisco, 1995; Whitaker, G.P., Coproduction: Citizen participation in service delivery, *Public Administration Review*, 40, 240, 1980.

14. Peters, B.G., *The Future of Governing: Four Emerging Models*, University Press of Kansas, Lawrence, 1996, 47–71; Foster, J.F., *The Deliberative Practitioner: Encouraging Participatory Planning Process*, MIT Press, Cambridge, MA, 1999.

15. Crosby, N., Kelly, J.M., and Schaefer, P., Citizen panels: A new approach to citizen participation, *Public Administration Review*, 46, 170, 1986; Parsons, G.A., Defining the public interest: Citizen participation in metropolitan and state policy making, *National Civic Review*, 79, 118, 1990.

16. Pharr, S.J. and Putnam, R.D., Eds., *Disaffected Democracies: What's Troubling the Trilateral Countries?*, Princeton University Press, Princeton, NJ, 2000; Putnam, R.D., Bowling alone: America's declining social capital, *Journal of Democracy*, 6, 65, 1995.

17. Cooper, T.L., *An Ethic of Citizenship for Public Administration*, Prentice-Hall, Englewood Cliffs, NJ, 1991.

18. King, C.S., Feltey, K.M., and Susel, B.O., The question of participation: Toward authentic public participation in public administration, *Public Administration Review*, 58, 317, 1998.

19. For the idea of transaction costs, see Coase, R., The nature of the firm, *Economica*, 4, 386, 1937.

20. Williamson, O.E., Public and private bureaucracies: A transaction cost economics perspective, *Journal of Law, Economics & Organization*, 15, 306, 1999.

21. Berelson, B.R., Democratic theory and democratic practice, in *Voting*, Berelson, B.R., Lazarsfeld, P.F., and McPhee, W.N., Eds., University of Chicago Press, Chicago, 1954.

22. That is, the constraint on participation is one of economy. See Dryzek, J., Deliberative Economy and Discursive Legitimacy, paper presented at the Conference on Deliberating about Deliberative Democracy, University of Texas, Austin, 2000.

23. Cleveland, H., How do you get everybody in on the act and still get some action?, *Public Management*, 57(6), 3, 1975.

24. The effort to handle citizen complaints has an analogy with so-called "customer relationship management" (CRM) which focuses on finding out more efficient ways to manage customer complaints in the area of business administration. More and more public managers are utilizing CRM to help them to deal with anxious citizens. See Epstein, J., *Public Services: Working for the Customer*, European Foundation for the Improvement of Living and Working Conditions, Luxembourg, 1990; Barton, A., Good complaint resolution = good government, *Public Management*, 79(6), 14, 1997; McClendon, B., Complaint-free customer service, *Public Management*, 79(3), 21, 1997.

25. Winckler, E., Institutionalization and participation in Taiwan: From hard to soft authoritarianism?, *China Quarterly*, 99, 481, 1984.

26. Cheng, T.-j., Democratizing the quasi-Leninist regime in Taiwan, *World Politics*, 41, 471, 1989.

27. Nathan, A.J. and Ho, J.V.S., Chiang Ching-Kuo's decision for political reform, in *Chiang Ching-Kuo's Leadership in the Development of the Republic of China on Taiwan*, Leng, S.C., Ed., University Press of America, Lanham, MD, 1993, 31.

28. Southerland, D., Taiwan president to propose end to island's martial law: Action would mean the lifting of restrictions after 37 years, *Washington Post*, October, 8, 1986, A18.

29. Hsaio, H.-h.M., Emerging social movements and the rise of a demanding civil society in Taiwan, *Australian Journal of Chinese Affairs*, 24, 163, 1990.

30. Shiau, C.-j., Civil society and democratization, in *Democratization in Taiwan: Implications for China*, Tsang, S.y.-s. and Tien, H.-m., Eds., St. Martin's, New York, 1999.

31. We selected the TCG as our case because the TCG has been the pioneer in the citizen complaints procedure and management. In this study, we conducted interviews with 15 officials of seven relevant TCG units in May 2001. We further conducted a survey of the 43 bureaus/departments under the direct jurisdiction of the mayor. All 43 agencies surveyed answered the questionnaire.

32. Lin, S.-p., The cognition, evaluation, and trust of complainants towards complaints system, *Chinese Political Science Review* (in Chinese), 9 (December), 297, 1981. Similar studies by Du Bao-zhang and Guo Dong-yao also demonstrate that citizens are either ignorant of the complaints system or have negative attitudes toward the system (Du, B.-z., *Study on Managing Peoples' Complaints* [in Chinese], Research Report for Taiwan Provincial Government, 1986; Guo, D.-y., *Analysis on People's Complaint Cases* [in Chinese], Research Report for Taiwan Provincial Government, 1979).

33. "A-Bian" is the nickname of Mayor Chen, the current president of Taiwan. See the following section for details about the development of the "A-Bian Mailbox."

34. The Legislative Yuan is the National Parliament of Taiwan.

35. Rather than dialing an eight-digit number, the special number is shortened to four digits for easy memorization. In pronunciation, it connotes lucky meaning for Mayor Ma that is "long live Ying-jiu."

36. Applicants are required to fill out a form specifying the reason for meeting four weeks before the designated meeting date. The District office faxes the form to the related bureau/department that would review the form and reply to the office.

37. See endnote 2 for reference.

38. The *Guidelines* are an administrative order issued by the TCG according to the Administrative Procedure Act of 1999.

39. According to the *Guidelines to Handle Citizen Complaints* for the TCG and the agencies under its jurisdiction, the citizen complaint cases handled by the mayor, vice mayor, bureau chief or deputy director, and the Commission of Research, Development, and Evaluation should be classified under monitoring.

40. TCG is now designing a system to cope with this problem.

41. See endnote 1 for reference.

42. Norris, P., *Digital Divide? Civic Engagement, Information Poverty, and the Internet Worldwide*, Cambridge University Press, New York, 2001.

Chapter 15

Toward an Accountable and Quality Public Administration in Hong Kong: Redressing Administrative Grievances through the Ombudsman

Carlos Wing-Hung Lo and Robert J. Wickins

Contents

Abstract: Following considerable public pressure, in 1989, the Hong Kong government followed many other countries and established an Ombudsman. The establishment of the post has to be seen in the context of the political awakening of Hong Kong and demands for a more accountable and client-oriented public service. Previously, complaints of maladministration in Hong Kong were dealt with under a diffuse and fragmentary system which lacked effective powers. Effective legal action against the government for maladministration is also severely constrained by a number of factors. This chapter traces the growth of the Ombudsman concept and jurisdiction in Western countries over the last few decades and outlines the structure and jurisdiction of the Ombudsman's office in Hong Kong by way of comparison. The effectiveness of the Hong Kong Ombudsman is then evaluated by a detailed analysis of his achievements over the last ten years in combating maladministration, and his role in three high profile cases. These cases also elucidate some of the limitations inherent in the Ombudsman's role. Lastly the future of the Ombudsman in Hong Kong is explored. It is concluded that the Office of the Ombudsman has scored initial success in Hong Kong public administration, and has enhanced government efficiency as well as satisfying public needs and filling a major gap in the system of public redress. However, problems of continuing resources and mapping out a sustainable ethos remain.

Introduction

Political democratization and public sector reform, commenced in 1985 and 1989 respectively, have given rise to the concepts of an accountable and quality public administration in Hong Kong. A political awakening has also taken place among Hong Kong people as a result of the 1997 issue and democratization, and this has made them more critical of the way they are treated and served by government departments. Public administration is increasingly seen as being service orientated, and there is mounting pressure for it to be responsive to public concerns on a wide range of issues. This contrasts with the more authoritarian rule, bureaucratic style of administration and submissive public attitudes of the past. It was within this changing context that an Ombudsman institution (the Commission for Administrative Complaints [COMAC], which was renamed as the Office of the Ombudsman in December 1996) was established in 1989 to redress administrative grievances. [1]

There are three major categories of complaints against the administration in Hong Kong. The first one is complaints against public servants' graft and corruption in performing their duties. The Independent Commission Against Corruption was formed in 1973 to clean up the administration and has successfully proved that it is an effective and credible institution in combating corruption. [2] The second one is complaints against the police in the course of enforcing law and order. The Complaints Against Police Office (CAPO), a special section of the Royal Hong Kong Police Force, was put in charge of investigations of all complaints by the public against the police in 1974. However, CAPO has failed to fully alleviate public concerns in this area, and there are calls from time to time by Legislative Council members and other public figures for a more accountable or independent investigating body. [3] The third one is complaints against the administrative decisions and operational performance of government departments. This is the most diverse group, with the great bulk of the cases being non-criminal in nature. [4] In the past the complaints system for this type of problem was fragmented and unreliable because of the absence of a distinct and independent office which could provide a focus and the necessary driving force to resolve administrative complaints.

The purpose of this chapter is to examine in detail the government's initiative in establishing a formal administrative complaint institution to redress popular administrative grievances. It is divided into five sections. It starts with a review of the growth of the Ombudsman concept in other countries. It then identifies the contextual changes which have made local people more articulate in cases of real or perceived mistreatment by government departments, and elucidates the pre-existing system for the handling of administrative grievances. The third section is an institutional analysis of the Office of the Ombudsman. In the fourth section, the effectiveness of the Ombudsman is evaluated in the light of the administrative complaints it has handled since its inception. The last section discusses the future of the Office of the Ombudsman.

The Growth of the Ombudsman Concept

The modern Ombudsman concept, originated in Scandinavia, generally referrs to an officer appointed by the legislature to handle complaints against administrative and judicial action. [5] With a vision of improving their fragmented and ineffective system of dealing with administrative grievances, most democratic countries have shown an interest in the concept as a simple and effective means of providing citizens with redress against the increasing power and pervasive scope of modern government in a fair and reasonable manner after the Second World War. [6] Thus, New Zealand established an Ombudsman in 1962, and Britain followed suit in 1967, although preferring to call the office the Parliamentary Commissioner. France, despite having a well-developed system of administrative law, introduced the concept of an Ombudsman (Mediateur) in 1973. Most of the countries of Western Europe and the British Commonwealth have followed the trend and established Ombudsmen. [7] The idea has even spread to a number of Latin American states such as Argentina and Guatemala, and some Asian nations such as Japan, South Korea, and Thailand. Quite a few individual states of the United States, such as Alaska and Hawaii, also have Ombudsmen. In fact, the concept has proved so popular that some countries now have more than one Ombudsman to handle special areas of administration. Thus, Britain has introduced separate Commissioners for local government and the health service to supplement the Parliamentary Commissioner. Germany has a separate Ombudsman for the armed forces. The concept has also proved attractive to private industry, and in Britain the insurance and financial services sectors as well as the legal profession have voluntarily established Ombudsmen to deal with complaints from clients. In Australia the leading banks have established a banking Ombudsman to fulfill a similar function in the banking sector.

Although established in a wide range of countries with diverse social and cultural backgrounds, the basic concept of the Ombudsman shows a remarkable degree of uniformity, especially in the British Commonwealth. An Ombudsman was defined by the International Bar Association in 1974 as follows:

> An office provided for by the constitution or by an action of the legislature or parliament and headed by an independent, high-level public official who is responsible to the legislature or parliament, who receives complaints from aggrieved persons against government agencies, officials, and employees or who acts on his own motion, and who has the power to investigate, recommend corrective action, and issue reports. [8]

The wide adoption of the Citizen's Chapter in the Commonwealth countries has enhanced the role of Ombudsman as safeguarding the right of the citizen "as a consumer to expect proper standards of public services and to be compensated in the event of a failure." [9] Critical of its middle-class orientation, it was urged that the Ombudsman should add a significant "citizens' defender" to its dimension of work to play a substantial role in human rights or defense of the underprivileged. [10] At the same time, there is an increasing demand that the Ombudsman should play the active role of improving public administration to prevent future injustice and maladministration, apart from the remedial role of redressing individual grievances against maladministration. [11]

As a grievance resolution institution, the Ombudsman generally has power to investigate maladministration by government departments and statutory bodies on the receipt of a complaint from a person affected by it, and in some countries he can also investigate of his own motion without waiting for a complaint. [12] Maladministration has been described in the British Parliament as covering bias, neglect, inattention, delay, incompetence, and arbitrariness in administration. [13] It has been given a very wide meaning in legislation dealing with the Ombudsman. For example, in Hong Kong it has been defined in the Commissioner for Administrative Complaints Ordinance (the Ombudsman Ordinance after 1996) as including inefficient, bad, or improper administration; unreasonable conduct such as delay, discourtesy, and lack of consideration; abuse of power such as unjust, unreasonable, oppressive, or improperly discriminatory practices or procedures; and mistakes of law or fact. [14] Thus, the Ombudsman generally cannot investigate whether statutory laws or government policies themselves are unfair, harsh, or excessive. The emphasis is on whether these things lead to bad administration of some kind. After all, the Ombudsman is not an elected official responsible to the voters, and in a democracy the appropriateness of laws and general social policies should be largely in the hands of the legislature. One of the major limitations on the jurisdiction of the Ombudsman in most countries is that he is not to investigate the conduct or decision in any civil or criminal court case or tribunal hearing. This is to avoid compromising the independence of the judiciary. [15]

In handling citizens' complaints, the Ombudsman has extremely wide powers of investigation. He may obtain any information or documents and make such inquiries as he thinks fit. He may adopt such procedures as he thinks fit. Investigations are conducted in private, and generally there is no right to legal counsel when appearing as a witness or a party before the Ombudsman. Generally, government officials cannot refuse to produce information or documents to the Ombudsman on the grounds of confidentiality or crown immunity in the public interest. Again, the fact that an administrative decision is declared by legislation to be final or not open to legal challenge does not prevent the Ombudsman from investigating it. The Ombudsman can even enter government premises to further his investigations. It is a criminal offense to obstruct or hinder an investigation, or to fail to comply with the Ombudsman's requirements with regard to information or documentation. [16] These wide powers mean that the Ombudsman can get to the heart of a complaint quickly and informally, and is in a position to reach an objective and independent overview of a problem. In contrast, the Ombudsman can only recommend a solution to an administrative grievance, and his only weapon is adverse publicity if government officials refuse to accept his recommendations. However, this has generally proved to be a very effective deterrent, and examples of situations where Commonwealth governments have refused to carry out such recommendations are rather rare. Despite this limited authority, it has been strongly agreed that the presence of the Ombudsman "has increased public confidence in public administration, provided a means of rectifying administrative errors and succeeded to some extent in humanizing the bureaucracy." [17]

There is an emerging consensus that an effective Ombudsman institution should meet the following set of criteria. First is independence, which requires the Ombudsman institution to be independent of government administration in the exercise of its grievance resolution functions. Second is visibility, which refers to the high degree of awareness of the public about the existence and functions of Ombudsman as a complaint handling mechanism. Third is accessibility, which asks the provision of Ombudsman service to the public free in terms of the cost and simple in terms of the procedures for lodging a complaint. Fourth is jurisdiction, which demands the Ombudsman to put all kinds of administrative actions and decisions under its scrutiny. Fifth is powers of investigation, which demands the equipment of Ombudsman with adequate powers of investigation. Sixth is remedial action, which means that the Ombudsman should have the ability to ensure a proper course of action for any identified administrative shortcomings. Seventh is impact, which means that the Ombudsman should have the ability to arouse actions from the administrative agencies under investigation to improve service quality and delivery procedures. [18]

The following sections will examine the case of Hong Kong, a latecomer in the use of the Ombudsman as a grievance resolution institution, with a view to assess its effectiveness.

The Rise of the Notion of an Accountable and Quality Public Administration in Hong Kong

Political Democratization and the Emergence of an Open and Accountable Public Administration

After a few years of indirect elections through functional constituencies, which deepened public debate, introduction on a limited scale of direct election of legislators (18 out of 60) in 1991 and the ensuing emergence of clear party politics within the Legislative Council marked the inaugural era of political pluralism in Hong Kong. The former Governor Patten's move to abolish the traditional practice of appointment of Legislative Councillors to sit in the Executive Council, and his retirement from the role of Legislative Council Chairman, have formally institutionalized the separation of power between the administration and the legislature. These new political and constitutional adjustments have inevitably led to confrontation between the executive and the legislature, while at the same time emphasizing that the former should be accountable to the latter. Hence, a mechanism of checks and balances in the administrative state has been constituted which has tempered considerably the aloofness of the traditional executive-led government in Hong Kong. The momentum for an open and accountable public administration has gathered force. [19]

The democratic basis for the political system in Hong Kong has been consolidated, with all the Legislative Councillors being either directly or indirectly elected since the 1995 election. The old system of government-appointed members has thus finally come to an end. The pluralist trends have become more explicit as most elected councillors have clear party affiliations. [20] With a mandate from the people, the Legislative Council can now perform its watchdog function more comfortably and competently, and ensure a responsive and responsible government and public administration. Indeed, the bureaucracy in Hong Kong has already found that it has to operate with a prototype of a multi-party political system. Government officials now have to conduct public sector management in a more transparent manner, and are made more answerable to the democratically constituted Legislative Council. Indeed, considerable pressure has been exerted on the administration to respond to public concerns on various issues by the threat of private members' bills and the use of powers to formally examine public officials. All of this has resulted in widespread public debate on major issues. The democratic trends have been reinforced by elections for District Board membership and for the Regional and Urban Councils. [21]

Public Sector Reform as a Service Quality Reform

Public sector reform in Hong Kong is a move to align with international trends which seek to transform public administration into public sector management. [22] Adopting a managerial perspective, it centers its themes on improving the productivity and quality of public services. [23] This leads to a clear division of work between policy branches and administrative departments. The former take care of management effectiveness through policy formulation, program development, and resource allocation. The latter deal exclusively with operational efficiency and service quality in program implementation and service delivery. In order to maximize the utilization of financial and human resources, greater delegation of authority at a lower operational level is practiced. Privatization, corporatization (such as the establishment of the Hospital Authority), contracting out (such as tunnel management and street cleaning), and trading fund arrangements (such as the one set up in the Electrical and Mechanical Service Department) are among the major policy options in this reform endeavor. [24] At the operational level, performance pledges have been widely adopted and business centers have been established by service departments (e.g., Inland Revenue Department and Hospital Authority). Measurement of performance in terms of efficiency and service quality has now formed an important part of management control within the public sector. [25]

Public sector reform indicates a change of administrative philosophy from that of bureaucratic control of resource utilization to that of management efficiency and service quality. [26] Attention has now been shifted from the input dimension to both the process (efficiency) and output dimension (quality) in the administration of government policies and the delivery of public services. "Value for money" becomes the watchword of public sector management. As a result, this reform movement has created a new administrative ethos by introducing a client-oriented management culture of taking care of public needs. This erodes the traditional administrative approach of bureaucratic domination over the society and the general public. Government's commitment to the cause of "higher efficiency and better services" has put the entire public sector management under public evaluation. The expectation on the part of the general public for equity and fair treatment in the provision of public services has been effectively enhanced. Information is now seen as a public resource rather than government property. Transparency in administration is now an important objective, which leads to an increasing need to provide the public with reasons and explanations for administrative decisions.

Public Political Consciousness: From Apathy to Participation

Hong Kong people's past passivity in political and public affairs has been largely ascribed to the lack of channels for genuine political participation and administrative supervision. The 1997 issue has jolted the Hong Kong people from their political apathy. With the government's endeavor to democratize the political system since the 1980s as a catalyst, Hong Kong people have experienced a political awakening. [27] Through the 1991, 1995, and 1997 direct elections of legislators, as well as the District Board elections, they have acquired the experience of democratic politics and came to realize that they should have greater control over their lives. They have begun to ask for an open and responsible government, and have become more articulate than ever, particularly on social issues such as housing, environmental protection, and health services. The rapid increase in the volume of petitions, protests, and complaints against the administration in the last few years is an indicator of the public's growing political awareness. Hence, a participatory type of political culture has begun to develop.

Indeed, the emergence of party politics has provided people with a channel for active political participation and for exercising their democratic rights. The adoption of a Bill of Rights and the resulting public debate and discussion on this issue have helped people to identify the civil liberties they can enjoy. [28] The enactment of the Basic Law has further sharpened debate on human rights issues. [29] Consequently, people have developed a clearer idea of the proper relationship between the public and the government, namely, that the government should serve the people and public administration should be placed under public scrutiny. In short, the entire political and administrative orientation of the Hong Kong people has been redefined, and a passive mentality has been gradually replaced by a more active, participatory one. [30]

As indicated by the "Serving the Community" initiative launched by the former Governor Patten, the community has the right to demand "greater openness and accountability from the public sector which it pays for." [31] This progressive notion of an accountable, responsive, and quality management has triggered popular demands against government departments for more sensitive administration. The rise of party politics and citizens' increasing active participation in public affairs has forced the government to handle administrative complaints in a more serious manner.

The Pre-Existing System for the Handling of Administrative Grievances

The system for the handling of administrative grievances against government departments prior to the creation of the Ombudsman institution was fragmented and generally ineffective. Citizens could approach members of the Legislative or Executive Councils (the OMELCO Complaints Office), District Board or Urban Council members, or Heung Yee Kuk members to obtain help in the redress of administrative grievances. [32] However, such persons might have limited knowledge, expertise, or time to deal with administrative complaints. In any event, such persons individually did not have any real legal power to demand information or explanations directly from public officials or to inspect government files. All they could do was request cooperation from government departments in resolving citizen's grievances, and give issues a public airing in the Legislative Council or some other forum. The government was thus in a position to release as much or as little information as it desired, and to regulate such cooperation in its own interests. Even a Legislative Council resolution or the result of a motion debate was not usually binding on the government. Furthermore, private member's bills seeking to change the law to redress public grievances have been rare in the past and constrained by procedural difficulties. [33]

Another possibility was for citizens to petition the Governor or the Parliament in England. Again, these avenues were of limited effectiveness. In the case of non-statutory petitions, the Governor had an absolute discretion in how he handled the matter, and whether he encouraged government departments to provide any remedy. Even in petitions based on the provisions of a particular ordinance, such as those relating to New Territories lease cancellation, the Governor or the Executive Council often had wide and unfettered discretion, and judicial review of decisions of the Governor in Council was specifically excluded. [34] Petitions to the Parliament in England might attract the sympathy of a few members who might arrange a debate or make inquiries of a Minister, but would rarely obtain a reversal of firm government policy. Furthermore, they would rarely persuade the British government or Parliament to breach the constitutional convention that the Hong Kong government and legislature be allowed a large measure of self-rule on local issues without outside interference.

The last major avenue of redress was through the judicial system. However, this approach has numerous constraints. It is a very time-consuming, complex, and expensive process. Furthermore, judicial remedies in the area of administrative grievances are quite limited in scope. Judicial review of administrative decisions is not a full rehearing of the dispute, and the courts generally only intervene if there is some serious defect in procedure or abuse of statutory power. Even then, the courts do not substitute their own views or decisions for that of the official; they only declare the original decision void. The government is thus often free to reinstate the original decision by using the correct procedure or the proper statutory provision. Another constraint is that there is no general and independent right to damages at common law for the breach of constitutional rights, although the courts in New Zealand have recently tried to establish such a right. [35] Citizens must bring themselves within existing torts when seeking redress or monetary compensation for administrative grievances, and these may be of very limited application. For example, the courts in Hong Kong and England have been very reluctant to apply the tort of negligence to the higher levels of government activity, such as the supervision of deposit-taking companies and banks or the implementation of policies concerning investment by foreign companies. [36] Thus, investors or depositors may be left without any remedy against the government if they suffer through serious failures of government supervision. Again, the tort of misfeasance in a public office only applies where government officials knowingly exceed statutory powers and cause loss to citizens. Lastly, it is not unusual for public officials to be given full or partial statutory immunity against being sued for actions done in the execution of their duties. Examples in Hong Kong include the post office, squatter clearance officials, bank supervisors, and building inspectors. [37]

The Establishment of an Ombudsman in Hong Kong

The Institutional Framework of the Ombudsman

Following considerable pressure from interested public groups, the Hong Kong government followed the international trends and established an Ombudsman in 1989. In Hong Kong he or she was referred to in the legislation as the Commissioner for Administrative Complaints (COMAC) until this title was changed to the Ombudsman in December 1996. However, the Ombudsman in Hong Kong is given all the powers commonly given to the Ombudsman in other jurisdictions, and the Hong Kong legislation on this topic is in no way inferior to that in other Commonwealth countries. [38] The Ombudsman was established as an independent office generally standing outside the government administrative framework. In order to perform a watchdog role, the Ombudsman is appointed by the Chief Executive (by the Governor before the handover in 1997) to hold office for five years.

The Ombudsman is required to make an annual report to the Chief Executive on his or her activities and investigations, and the Chief Executive must lay a copy before the Legislative Council. The Ombudsman can also refer individual reports to the Chief Executive if he thinks fit, or if he feels government officials have not acted adequately on his recommendations. [39]

The structural arrangements of the administrative complaints system are both simple and plain, given its initial small establishment of 27 staff members. [40] Currently, the Office of the Ombudsman has three functional divisions. The Administration and Development Division, led by a Principal Executive Officer, maintains in-house administrative order and takes care of public relations between the Office of the Ombudsman and the society on one hand and the government departments on the other hand. These functions are performed by the Community Relations Section, the Administration Section, and the Translation Section. The Assessment Team in this Division receives and processes complaints lodged by the public. The two Investigation Divisions, led by an Assistant Ombudsman, are responsible for the investigation of complaints. [41]

The policy source of the Office of the Ombudsman is the Directorate, which is composed of the Ombudsman, the Deputy Ombudsman, the two Assistant Ombudsmen, and the Principal Executive Officer. Professional and expert advice concerning issues arising in the handling of administrative complaints comes from three independent panels of legal, medical, and engineering advisors. These advisors are nominated by the Ombudsman. [42]

Organizational Capacity and Independence

Organizational capacity and independence are the two major concerns that arise in regard to the current structure of the administrative complaints system.

The Directorate arguably appears somewhat thin as it is the top management which initiates plans, makes policies, conducts reviews, and supervises reports. Unlike most government departments, where top-level administrators are seldom involved in daily operations, the Ombudsman (formerly the Commissioner) himself has to spend most of his time in handling complaints. Despite the fact that the establishment has been strengthened significantly in the last few years, the Ombudsman remains a small office of 90 staff and its ability to handle effectively complaints against a government establishment of 62 departments with approximately 180,000 public servants is constantly open to considerable doubt (see Table 15.1). Moreover, the workload of the Office of the Ombudsman (formerly the COMAC) has increased dramatically [43] since the extension of its jurisdiction to cover the Mass Transit Railway Corporation, Kowloon-Canton Railway Corporation, the Securities and Futures Commission, and the Regional and Urban Councils, the abolition of the referral system in favor of a direct access arrangement for the receipt of complaints, and the empowerment of the Ombudsman institution to initiate investigations itself in 1994 (see Table 15.2). [44] The number of cases to be handled by the Office of the Ombudsman is anticipated to increase further. [45]

The independence of the Office of the Ombudsman can be considered in relation to the three aspects of staffing, funding, and accountability. Considerable use has been made of seconded government staff, and the Office of the Ombudsman has yet to acquire complete independence in staffing, which means that its recruitment and staffing policies are indirectly under the control of the government which is the subject of its oversight. Although there is no explicit evidence that

Table 15.1   The Establishment and Annual Budget of the Ombudsman, 1989–1999

Year[a]	1989	1989–90	1990–91	1991–92	1992–93	1994–95	1995–96	1996–97	1997–98	1998–99
No. of staff	27	17	26	26	26	45	55	81	88	90
Annual budget (million HK$)	5.82	6.67	7.5	8.8	13	16.1	28.9	42.3	48.48	NA

[a] Reporting period stretches from June to May of that year.

Source: Annual Report of the Commissioner for Administrative Complaints, Hong Kong, 1989–1996; Annual Report of the Ombudsman, Hong Kong, 1997–1999, The Government Printer, Hong Kong.

Table 15.2   The Workload of the Ombudsman, 1989–1999

Year[a]	1989	1989–90	1990–91	1991–92	1992–93	1994–95	1995–96	1996–97	1997–98	1998–99
No. of complaints received	71	167	150	162	173	1,211	2,784	2,844	3,073	4,125
No. (%) of complaints concluded[b]	18	156	188	169	159 (74%)	801 (63%)	2,603 (80%)	2,961 (85%)	3,010 (84%)	3,828 (81%)
No. of inquiries received	117	177	394	908	1,054	3,348	6,493	5,922	7,578	10,192

[a] Reporting period stretches from June to May of that year.
[b] Included those carried forward from previous year.

Source: Annual Report of the Commissioner for Administrative Complaints, Hong Kong, 1989–1996; Annual Report of the Ombudsman, Hong Kong, 1997–1999, The Government Printer, Hong Kong.

such a staffing arrangement has undermined the independent status of the Office of the Ombudsman, the possibility of conflicting assumptions and potential conflicts of interest cannot be completely ruled out. Staff stability, continuity, and commitment are called into question as a majority of its staff has to transfer back to individual administrative departments upon the completion of their secondments. The Office of the Ombudsman thus has to spend resources to train new staff from time to time, and is deprived of the chance to build its own team of staff, with advanced training, a clear career orientation, and a long-term vision. This should be contrasted with the ICAC, which as an independent office has been given complete autonomy in staffing.

The expenditure of the Office of the Ombudsman is currently part of the government's annual budget. Such a financial arrangement is not conducive to the healthy growth of the Ombudsman Office in the long term as it gives rise to the suspicion that the administration may have a vested interest in keeping the resources allocated to the Ombudsman Office at a minimal level. Indeed, an aggressive Ombudsman may not be welcome by the Establishment which might feel that a larger, more resourceful, and powerful Ombudsman Office may pose a serious threat to its traditional status of executive supremacy. For example, there was a widely held belief that one of the major reasons for Andrew So, the former Ombudsman, to fail to get another term was due to the government's resentment of his initiation to investigate into the administrative confusion of the new airport at Chek Lap Kok in 1998 despite there was already a special working group appointed by the government to look into this case. An arrangement of financial autonomy subject to legislative approval may be a feasible alternative to take the Ombudsman Office out of the government's direct financial control.

The current accountability arrangements for the Ombudsman are also controversial as far as its independence is concerned. Being accountable directly to the Chief Executive (formerly the Hong Kong Governor), the impression given is that the Office is the Chief Executive's watchdog over the administration instead of an impartial mechanism of administrative oversight for the general public. It is part of the government establishment in a sense. Such a sentiment was frankly expressed by Andrew So, the Ombudsman between 1993–1998, who stated that "there is a certain element of conflict of interest for the Government to be directly involved in reviewing the financial and staffing needs of this (COMAC) office." [46] To provide a fair and credible administrative redress system for the public, it is arguable that the Ombudsman Office should be detached from the Chief Executive and should report only to and be accountable to the elected Legislative Council. This would bring Hong Kong more into line with other countries on this issue. However, Hong Kong is rather peculiar in that the legislature does not have as much control over the government as in a ministerial system. This may be an argument for continuing to allow the Chief Executive to have a role in enforcing the Ombudsman's recommendations.

The Jurisdiction of the Office of the Ombudsman

The Ombudsman has jurisdiction over maladministration committed by government departments, and a limited number of statutory bodies. It is clear from the legislation establishing the Ombudsman institution that maladministration can arise from omissions and recommendations as well as from firm decisions. However, some matters are specifically exempted from investigation by the Ombudsman. The main ones are matters certified by the Chief Executive as affecting security, defense, or international relations: the pay, conditions of service, and discipline of the civil service; any decisions concerning the grant or renewal of interests in government land; any action taken by government departments or statutory bodies in relation to contractual or commercial transactions other than tender exercises; any action taken by the Securities and Futures Commission in relation to the Hong Kong Codes on Takeovers and Mergers and Share Repurchases; any action taken personally by the Chief Executive in administering Hong Kong; and the conduct of any criminal or civil proceedings before any court or tribunal. Most of these exceptions are not of any great consequence, and do not affect the mainstream of administrative grievances. [47] The only one which could give rise to concern is that relating to commercial transactions, especially if the government engages in increasing privatization, contracting out, and commercialization of government services.

The Ombudsman has also been given no power over complaints against the police and the ICAC. However, this can be justified on the basis that such complaints usually involve allegations of criminal misconduct. These require investigation by specially trained investigators, and it is not appropriate for the informal methods of the Ombudsman to be applied to criminal cases when the consequences can be so serious. Criminal cases should be decided in accordance with the strict and formal procedures of the criminal courts, which provide due protection for the rights of the accused. It should be noted that the exemption of police authorities from the Ombudsman's jurisdiction is not that unusual, and is not limited to Hong Kong. Exceptionally, the Australian State of Victoria did establish a special police Ombudsman to hear complaints from the public against the police, but this was abolished after a few years because of the inherent difficulties involved. In Hong Kong, the Ombudsman is a member of the Police Complaints Committee and the ICAC Complaints Committee which oversee CAPO and the ICAC, so he or she has some input into those areas in any event.

The Ombudsman has wide powers of investigation. If, after investigation, the Ombudsman finds evidence of maladministration he or she can recommend to the head of a department or statutory body or ultimately the Governor, that a matter or view of the law be reconsidered; that an omission be rectified or an action be cancelled or varied; that an administrative practice be altered; that reasons be given; or that any other step be taken. [48] It can thus be seen that the Ombudsman has in one sense far wider powers than a court. Whereas courts do not substitute their views for a wrongful government decision but only order in effect that the decision be made again in accordance with proper procedures, the Ombudsman can recommend a particular solution which he regards as fair or reasonable. Furthermore, it is clear that the Ombudsman is not bound by the limitations of legal concepts and doctrines, but has a very wide discretion to recommend any remedy which he or she feels is morally fair. Thus, the Ombudsman can recommend an apology or that detailed reasons be given within a fixed time period, as well as ex gratia compensation.

The Effectiveness of the Office of the Ombudsman

It could be argued that in the first few years of its existence the Ombudsman institution in Hong Kong was of limited effectiveness because it received less than 200 complaints a year. This was far below the level of other Western countries such as Australia, Canada, and New Zealand, although not of Great Britain. Commentators wondered whether the low rate reflected cultural differences, with Hong Kong people being more loathe to complain compared with the public in Western countries. However, it seemed more probable that the difference was mainly due to the indirect access requirement of referral by a Legislative Council member, and the fact that the public tended to regard the newly established Ombudsman institution as only an optional last resort after other traditional and more familiar channels had been exhausted. In fact, the provision of an indirect access system has never fulfilled its primary justification of filtering out claims that are trivial, unjustified, or not within the Commissioner's jurisdiction. This has proved to be so in Hong Kong and in Britain.

The first Commissioner in Hong Kong, Arthur Garcia, pressed strongly and repeatedly for a direct access system. The government had taken the position when the COMAC (the title of the Ombudsman institution at that time) was first set up that it should begin as a supplement to the existing avenues of complaint, and once it had firmly established itself the question of wider access would be reconsidered. After public consultation, the government legislated a system of direct access in 1994. Since then complaints have risen dramatically to the point where the Ombudsman Office has almost been overwhelmed by the flood. The number of complaints lodged by the public in 1998–1999 was three times more than in 1994–1995. The Ombudsman has consistently requested substantially more staff to deal with the increase, and has decided to refer simple complaints back to the departments concerned with the consent of complainants as a temporary means of coping with the overwhelming workload. Thus, the problem now seems to be whether the Ombudsman Office can mobilize sufficient resources to deal effectively with the rapidly rising level of administrative complaints. The need for the Ombudsman could not be more clearly emphasized as Alice Tai, the current Ombudsman, pinpointed that "the workload of the Office has increased seventeen-fold since 1994 but the establishment has only increased in three-fold." [49]

Even before direct access was introduced, it is clear useful work was done in firmly establishing the Ombudsman institution as an impartial, popular, and effective agency for the resolution of administrative grievances. The first Commissioner firmly established the Ombudsman institution as an impartial, independent, and committed institution which was quite prepared to criticize even the most senior government officials when it was felt the occasion warranted it. Undoubtedly, he was helped in achieving these aims by his previous long and distinguished career in the Hong Kong judiciary. The second Commissioner, Andrew So, has made determined efforts since his appointment in February 1994 to build on the actions of his predecessor. Considerable effort has been expended in popularizing the institution, and increasing its public recognition. The second Commissioner has begun to criticize major government policies in areas such as housing. His past background as an appointed legislator and his service on various government committees and boards has provided useful expertise for his attempt to give the Ombudsman institution a broader and more populist role. Certainly, both of them have received praise from Legislative Council members of all political parties for their efforts in upholding the integrity and effectiveness of the administrative complaints system. However, doubts have been cast over Alice Tai, who took up the office of Ombudsman in April 1999, for her ability to keep up this critical and popular approach given her strong civil servant background.

The Work of the Office of the Ombudsman

A detailed perusal of the Commissioner's (and the Ombudsman's) Annual Reports since 1989 is necessary before the scope and effectiveness of his work can be accurately gauged. It is clear from the reports that nearly every department of the Hong Kong government is the subject of legitimate administrative complaints, meaning ones which have been fully or partially substantiated. The number of complaints against some departments is much higher than others, but this merely reflects the fact that some departments such as those dealing with housing, tax, or immigration have far more contact with the public than others. [50]

Problems of maladministration range across the whole spectrum of governmental activity, from birth registration, immigration, tax collection, and legal aid to hospital treatment, postal services, and control of hawkers and swimming pools. It is clear that most of the complaints relate to matters which by their nature would not justify legal proceedings, but which are often deeply frustrating to the citizen and undermine confidence in the system of government in Hong Kong. Again, in many quite serious cases it is hard for the citizen to identify or quantify any obvious financial loss arising from the maladministration, which would be recognized by the rules of law. Thus, the Ombudsman institution in Hong Kong does provide a very useful adjunct to the judicial system, while not duplicating it. Common types of maladministration identified by this office as a result of its investigations are unreasonable delays of all kinds; unclear or unnecessarily complex procedures or forms; poor staff attitudes involving rudeness; lack of consideration, over-zealousness, incompetence, or lack of effort; inadequate records or loss of records or property; lack of effective communication or coordination between sections or departments; failure to enforce laws adequately and ineffective control procedures; lack of clear policies or laws to deal with problems; unnecessary, inefficient, or inadequate inspections; failure to anticipate problems or to plan effective responses; failure to regularly review policies or procedures to meet changing public needs; failure to consult the public or interested parties fully or at all on major issues and policy changes; sudden changes of policies or procedures which confuse the public; the provision of incorrect information or advice, or the failure to provide adequate or meaningful information or reasons for decisions; and failure to obtain proper legal or expert advice which would speedily resolve problems. It is quite clear from these Annual Reports that even a simple delay by government organizations is sometimes excessive, and can lead to serious consequences for citizens. The Ombudsman has drawn attention to cases where the simple refund of fees has taken up to five months to reach fruition, and where disputed matters have dragged on for up to ten years of ineffective correspondence and meetings to the frustration of individual citizens. In some instances, government delays have led or contributed to the loss of an effective right of appeal, the right to licenses, or to statutory compensation.

It is also clear from the reports that the Ombudsman in some instances has persuaded government departments to make major changes or improvements in important policies of benefit to citizens. Thus, the Ombudsman was instrumental in obtaining a clearer, fairer, and more transparent set of guidelines for kidney transplants, and a change of policy with regard to color blindness tests for drivers of government vehicles.

The activities of the Ombudsman Office have been useful in furthering the drive for a management-orientated civil service, as well as in helping the citizen. Thus, the Ombudsman Office has identified the need in particular situations for more effective coordination between sections and departments; for new and clearer laws and regulations to fill gaps and loopholes; for detailed training and briefing of staff in new and complex policies and procedures; for complaints registers and other records to enable effective management of problem cases; for formal mechanisms to enable senior staff to intervene regularly in difficult or protracted disputes; for working groups and action teams to carry out regular policy reviews and formulate new strategies to deal with changing public needs; and for continuing efforts to streamline and simplify procedures. The benefit to the government can thus be seen to be considerable, as the Ombudsman Office in effect acts as an independent consultancy service with the potential to greatly improve government efficiency and thereby save public funds. The Ombudsman Office also helps to improve the political image and legitimacy of the government by making it more responsive to public needs and grievances. Thus, the Ombudsman Office benefits the government as much as the public, and should not be seen as being in an antagonistic role to the Hong Kong style of executive-led government.

Major Cases Handled by the Ombudsman Institution in Hong Kong

We now review three major cases handled by the Ombudsman Office (during the COMAC era) which have received considerable airing in the press, in order to gain a further perspective on the effectiveness of the Ombudsman institution in Hong Kong.

Maladministration in Connection with the Closure of the BCC Bank

This case arose from the collapse of the international financial operations of the Bank of Credit and Commerce, amid allegations of widespread fraud and money laundering. The Hong Kong Banking Commissioner made public statements to reassure depositors on July 5, 1991 that the Hong Kong subsidiary of the Bank of Credit and Commerce was sound and viable, and that the Exchange Fund was ready to provide backing for the Hong Kong subsidiary on commercial terms. To the surprise of depositors, the subsidiary closed its doors for good on July 8, after only opening for half a day after the Banking Commissioner's statement. It was then put into liquidation. [51]

Several depositors later complained to COMAC about the government's handling of the whole affair. After a long and thorough investigation, the Commissioner for Administrative Complaints issued a report which criticized the Commissioner of Banking and the Secretary for Monetary Affairs.

The Commissioner found that although the Commissioner of Banking had acted out of good intentions in what he believed to be the best interests of depositors, his public statements were overconfident and unintentionally misleading to ordinary depositors. His statement that the subsidiary was sound and viable did not reveal that this largely depended on confirmation of a guarantee of financial support by the government of Abu Dhabi, which was being urgently sought by the Hong Kong authorities. Again, his statement about the backing from the Exchange Fund, although technically correct, was liable to give ordinary depositors the impression that the support was substantial and long term, when in fact it was only a very limited and temporary emergency line of credit. The Secretary for Monetary Affairs was also criticized for making a public statement that implied some of the depositors might be conspiring to create a run on the bank for their own purposes, when there was no real evidence that this was happening.

The case demonstrates that COMAC had the determination and fortitude to criticize very senior officials in a high-profile controversy, and to persist in an investigation despite strong arguments by the government that COMAC had no jurisdiction in such a case.

However, the case also demonstrates the limitations of the Ombudsman system. The Financial Secretary rejected calls for a public inquiry to further investigate all aspects of the matter, following the criticisms by COMAC. Although it may be true that a further inquiry would be unlikely to add anything useful to the criticisms already made of the two officials' conduct, it may have highlighted deeper issues. According to sources at the time, the bank collapse revealed a lack of overall strategy by the government in dealing with such matters, and differences of approach between the Exchange Fund Office and other departments. [52] So despite the criticisms leveled by COMAC there is no guarantee that any future bank collapse will be handled any more effectively. In fact, COMAC did point out weaknesses in banking supervision in a previous case referred to it in connection with another bank collapse.

Although the government has tightened bank supervision, partly perhaps as a result of COMAC criticisms, it is clearly beyond the capacity of COMAC to mandate and enforce the implementation of coordinated strategies by government, or to resolve policy differences between departments. The impact of COMAC on maladministration is thus limited.

Maladministration in the Case of the Proposed Shalotung Golf Course Development

Shalotung is adjacent to the Pak Sin Leng Country Park (Country Park) in the Northeast New Territories. The Shalotung Development Company (SDC), a developer, expanded a proposal for a nine-hole golf course in its government-supported development project for private housing in Shalotung to an eighteen-hole course in 1983. This required the excision of thirty-one hectares of government land from the Country Park. The application for allowing SDC to use the Country Park land, prepared by the Lands Department, was formally approved by the Country Parks Authority (CPA) on the advice of the Country Parks Board in March 1990. After an approval-in-principle was given by the Country Park Committee in 1986 and the revised plan approved in 1989, [53] SDC was required by the Environmental Protection Department (EPD) to conduct a comprehensive Environmental Impact Assessment (EIA) of the project after a simple Environmental Review Report was regarded as inadequate in October 1990.

In view of the project's damaging impact on the ecological environment and the allocation of Country Park land for private development purposes, six environmental groups, namely, the Conservancy Association, Friends of the Earth (FoE), the Green Lantau Association, Green Power, the Lamma Island Conservation Society, and the World Wide Fund for Natural Hong Kong, formed a crusade against the Administration's decision to allow SDC to use the designated Country Park land for private development. Arguing that golf is an elitist sport and that the golf course had restricted access for the general public, they rejected the official view that the proposed project was in the public interest. [54] As the project was supported by both the District Board and the Rural Committee in Tai Po, the Lands Department confirmed the proposal in principle in January 1991, while setting the condition that all the environmental issues raised by the EIA study be satisfactorily resolved. [55]

Judging that CPA had acted beyond its legal powers in purporting to use the Country Parks Ordinance in approving the proposed project, FoE applied for judicial review of CPA's decision. The High Court ruled that the CPA approval under section 10 of the Ordinance was invalid and hence quashed in April 1992. The Administration defended itself publicly by saying that the CPA's approval was merely technically incorrect, and that the development could be validly approved under another section of the Country Parks Ordinance. However, the developer revised the project by reducing its scope to prevent it from occupying Country Park lands, and resubmitted the application which had undergone a full EIA study. The final draft EIA report was later sent to concerned government departments and interest groups for comment in August 1993. [56]

In 1993 Mary Riley, the former Chairperson of the FoE, filed a complaint of maladministration with the Legislative Council complaints division against the CPA for approving the Shalotung project. This case was later referred to COMAC. After a nine-month investigation, Arthur Garcia, the Commissioner for Administrative Complaints, upheld the complaint and concluded in December 1993 that the CPA had acted improperly in approving the golf project on land legally designated as country park. [57] Apart from confirming that their approval was ultra vires, the Commissioner also pinpointed the fact that the CPA approval was premature in the absence of an EIA study and adequate public consultation.

A number of recommendations were made by the Commissioner for consideration by the Administration. First, proper procedures for considering development proposals in country parks should be devised. Second, all proposed projects that involve the use of country parks land should be required to undertake an EIA study. Third, in cases of a controversial nature, public consultation should be widely conducted before making a final decision. Fourth, the process of reviewing the Country Parks Ordinance should be speeded up in order to make appropriate amendments in the near future. Fifth, approval in principle for development projects affecting park boundaries should be granted only after all the important matters of principle, e.g., valid objections, EIA study, etc., have been resolved. [58]

COMAC's conclusions were disputed by the Administration. The Administration disagreed that it had not acted lawfully within its powers, regarding the matter as a technical error rather than one of real substance. The administration also disagreed that it had a general obligation to consult the public stating that "CPA's duty of public consultation ends with CPB and any other consultation is a matter of judgment."

While the Administration has never fully accepted COMAC's recommendations, nor fully complied with those it did accept, it is worth noting that when the Administration proposed encroaching on country parks in later developments (Shek O Quarry in Shek O Country Park and Route 3 in Tai Lam Country Park), it chose to adopt the proper procedures under the Ordinance, and also invited objections from the public.

Although COMAC once again did not shrink from criticizing the government in a major high-profile case, and did persuade the government to at least review its procedures, the result is not encouraging in a broader sense. COMAC clearly has no real power to stop development of country parks, and it is doubtful if the government will change deep-seated policies in this area because of COMAC criticism, as distinct from merely reviewing procedures.

Maladministration in the Case of Hong Kong Stadium

The Hong Kong Stadium, a public sporting playground, was built in 1955 under the management of the Urban Council (UC). It is situated in the District of So Kon Po on Hong Kong Island, with mostly upper-middle class residential areas in its vicinity. It was redeveloped into a modern multi-purpose venue for both sporting and recreational activities in 1992. At the same time the redeveloped stadium, while still under the jurisdiction of the UC, was made self-financing in its operation. This redevelopment project was entirely funded, managed, and constructed by the Royal Hong Kong Jockey Club (RHKJC). In order to commercialize its operation and hence to bring in more revenue, UC contracted out the management of the stadium to Wembley International Limited (Wembley), a British sport facilities management firm, in February 1993. [59] Holding pop concerts was considered by the UC and Wembley to be the biggest source of potential income, based on the successful experience of the Hong Kong Coliseum in generating handsome profits by converting itself from a sports arena to almost exclusively a pop concert venue. Therefore, it was planned that around six or seven pop concerts would be held in the stadium every year.

The inaugural concert celebrating the official re-opening of the stadium in March 1993 indicated that the stadium was poorly equipped for pop concerts. With the noise level well above the prescribed ceiling of 70 decibels throughout the evening event, the stadium's lack of effective noise abatement facilities was revealed. Despite warnings from the Environmental Protection Department (EPD) and protest from local residents, the UC approved seven pop concerts to take place in the following months. All of them were heavily monitored by the EPD and environmental groups. Noise nuisance for local residences was recorded. Wembley was later brought to court by the EPD for breaching noise control regulations, and this resulted in a fine of HK$150,000. Until May 1994, 687 complaints were received from residents. [60] The UC finally succumbed to social pressure and agreed that there should be no more pop concerts until the noise problem had been effectively resolved. Because of structural constraints, all remedial noise reduction measures adopted by the UC were proved to be of limited effectiveness.

The excessive noise being generated from pop concerts staged at the Hong Kong Stadium gave rise to heated debates as to the parties responsible, both in society and inside the Administration. [61] The public blamed the EPD for its inability to stop concerts from being staged, while also attacking the Chairman of the UC for giving the green light to pop concerts. They also questioned the stadium's lack of effective noise abatement facilities. The EPD defended itself by pointing out that it had notified the project designer of the potential noise problem at the Hong Kong Stadium in September 1991, and also warned the Urban Services Department (USD) of it in May 1992. Urban Councillors accused the USD of concealing information concerning the stadium's noise problem from them for more than one and a half years. [62] The USD argued that it was the management responsibility of Wembley to handle this technical matter. [63] The HOK Sports Facilities Group, the consultancy firm commissioned by the RHKJC, claimed that they were allowed by the government in May 1990 to skip the step of an environmental impact assessment in the design of the stadium, a step prescribed in the government's internal directive for commercial construction and development projects. The Secretary for Recreation and Culture contended that the stadium as a venue for sport activities did not require any such assessment. [64]

A group of residents later lodged a formal complaint at the Office of Members of the Legislative Council against the government and the UC for maladministration in this case, and the complaint was eventually referred to COMAC. The complaint centered on two issues. First, whether both the Administration and UC had failed to consider adequately the noise problems in the design and redevelopment stages of the stadium. Second, whether the UC had allowed pop concerts to be staged in the stadium without sufficient noise reduction measures. [65]

COMAC completed the investigation in March 1995, and the inquiry report was made public. It concluded that the complaint against the Administration and UC as a whole was substantiated. [66] It was pointed out that there was impropriety on the part of Recreation and Culture Branch (RCB), USD, EPD, and UC. Both the RCB and the USD, being members of the Stadium Project Steering Committee, should bear a major responsibility for the stadium's eventual noise problem. The former had performed the role of project initiator and coordinator badly by failing to address and handle the noise issue properly, while the latter had adopted a passive attitude throughout the entire process. EPD had been too slow giving timely feedback on the noise assessment report submitted by the RHKJC's noise consultant in February 1992, and had failed to draw RCB's attention to the problem. The UC was found at fault in giving approval for concerts to be held in the stadium, despite being aware of the stadium's insufficient noise reduction facilities. Finally Andrew So, the Commissioner of Administrative Complaints, suggested that the major planning steps of both public sector and government projects should strictly follow the established government procedures for commercial projects and be properly coordinated. [67]

The parties involved reacted differently to the critical comments of COMAC. The Secretary for RCB was defensive, although he admitted that the RCB had conceded that it had not done a good job with regard to the stadium project. He strongly rebutted the charge of not having taken the noise problem seriously, arguing that ensuring the construction work for the stadium was completed on time was also a major concern on this project. The USD accepted the criticism leveled at it, and was receptive to COMAC's suggestions. The EPD responded by admitting that the EIA arrangements for construction projects needed further improvement. [68] The members of the Democratic Party later petitioned former Governor Patten, urging him to reprimand or take disciplinary action against the top-ranking government officials who had been involved in the case. [69]

In the wake of a full discussion of COMAC's report with RCB, USD, EPD, and the Planning, Environment, and Land Branch, the Chief Secretary concluded that the government had committed errors in handling the noise issue. There had been poor coordination between policy branches and administrative departments in the stadium project. In light of this experience, the Chief Secretary reached the conclusion that a policy branch should be appointed to coordinate public projects of this nature in the future. [70]

Meanwhile, the stadium's noise problems have not been fully resolved. The UC has continued to hold concerts with noise control measures which have not proved fully satisfactory to residents. Complaints have been lodged and the EPD has threatened to prosecute Wembley should the latter fail to control the level of noise emission at the end of a grace period which was granted. The Vice-Chairman of the UC has criticized the EPD's tough approach as being unnecessary. [71] Approximately 300 residents are still unhappy about concert noise, but the UC is still proposing to hold concerts by seeking approval from the EPD to waive legal noise limits on concert days. Attempts are also being made by the UC to reach some satisfactory compromise with the residents. [72]

Once again, the case shows the limitations of the Ombudsman Office. Maladministration has been identified, and future projects may be more effectively handled. However, the noise problem at the stadium has not been fully resolved to the satisfaction of a considerable number of residents.

The Future of the Office of the Ombudsman

It is clear that the Ombudsman institution in Hong Kong has been firmly established through the efforts of the first two Commissioners as an impartial and effective office for the redress of administrative grievances. A direct access system has been achieved, and the jurisdiction expanded to cover some major statutory bodies. The office has been popularized, and currently enjoys a good reputation with the public and the legislature. At the same time, the Ombudsman has not antagonized the government to a degree that its effectiveness in dealing with government departments is undermined. This is important because effective investigation depends to a considerable degree on trust and cooperation by government departments.

The main difficulty for the immediate future seems to be whether the Ombudsman can mobilize the financial and staff resources to deal with the significantly higher level of complaints arising from a direct access system. It is clear from the experience in Western countries that the level of complaints, once established under a direct access system, rarely falls significantly. Certainly, Ombudsmen in Western countries have often had to battle forcefully with governments to obtain the level of funding that they feel is necessary to maintain an adequate standard of service. Obviously, if the Ombudsman Office finds it impossible to deal with complaints quickly, the level of popular support for the office is likely to fall dramatically. So the issue of adequate financial support is likely to be a continuing concern, especially if Hong Kong enters a period of financial stringency in the public sector in the wake of the Asian financial crisis.

Another concern is the impartial image of the Ombudsman Office. The appointment of Alice Tai, who was a civil servant for 25 years, as the successor of Andrew So in April 1999 has aroused a lot of public suspicion. First, it was more desirable to appoint a public figure without any civil service background as an Ombudsman. [73] Second, it was widely considered that her strong tie with the civil service would make it difficult for her to uphold administrative justice, particularly because her husband is currently serving as the Commissioner of Transport in the government. Third, Tai was not a very prominent figure in the government establishment, which would make it difficult for her to command public and civil servants' respect. As a whole, the status of the Ombudsman Office as an impartial and highly respected institution has been undermined to a considerable extent. Tai's appointment should not make it a conventional practice of having civil servants as Ombudsman which would accord the Ombudsman Office a pro-government image. To maintain public confidence in the Ombudsman Office, future appointments should be reserved to either elected legislators or independent prominent public figures.

One problem with the whole concept of the Ombudsman Office is that a great deal depends on the character and personality of the Ombudsman. He or she is the prime mover in the whole process, and much depends on his or her personal style of operation and general beliefs as to the role of the office. Because of the very flexibility and generality of the concept, the office can be very effective or totally ineffective to a large extent because of nothing more than the personality of the Ombudsman. This is in contrast to many government departments, where firmly entrenched and clear policies may continue to be effectively administered under a wide range of personalities. The first Commissioner has stated that the holder of the office needs to possess impartiality, integrity, thoroughness, speed, reasonableness, and tenacity. These are qualities which are surely not easy to find, especially in one person. Although the first two holders of the office have received praise from the press and legislators for possessing the necessary personal qualities to do the job fairly and effectively, it may be more difficult to sustain a continuous flow of such personalities in the long term. Again, the fact that the Ombudsman is appointed for a five-year term is a cause for some concern. This hardly gives the Ombudsman much security of tenure compared with judges of the higher courts, although it could be argued his work is likely to be even more politically sensitive than that of a judicial post. It might be more advisable to consider lengthening the term of office, and having the appointment confirmed by the legislature.

A last concern is over the continuing role and ethos of the office. It is suggested that on the one hand the Ombudsman Office must steadily evolve to meet changing needs and to retain public support, otherwise it is likely to become just another government department handling mundane matters according to a mechanistic formula. On the other hand, it is not clear how further evolution can take place, or to identify its general thrust. The Ombudsmen to date have firmly established the office with a reputation for integrity, fairness, and efficiency, and have popularized the office with the public and legislators. In one sense little remains to be done as the office has established itself as a major force in dealing with maladministration. However, lack of further development may lead to stagnation. Yet, it is not easy to see how the Ombudsman Office can develop its role further to meet public expectations. Andrew So, the former Ombudsman, had once sought to address the broader policy issues which lie behind individual instances of maladministration. This obviously makes sense, as correction of a faulty or unfair policy may save a great deal of time and effort as compared with continually correcting the results of the policy in a large number of individual cases. However, the government has shown resistance to this approach, at least where major policies involve important social, political, or financial factors. Thus, the government has refused to accept criticisms and recommendations of change from the Ombudsman Office with regard to general policies concerning building signs and illegal structures. Despite COMAC sending a report to the Governor for the first time to underline the seriousness of the issue, the matter was delegated to the Secretary for Planning, Environment, and Lands. He replied that lack of resources and questions of cost and social justice required the government to continue to implement existing policies. [74] This general issue has surfaced in other countries as well. Governments and other elected bodies such as local councils in Western countries are often very reluctant to allow the Ombudsman a role in policy formulation, as they regard this as their exclusive domain as representatives of the voters. So any future evolution of the Ombudsman Office faces some major obstacles, and may not be as easy as the establishment of the office in the mainstream of administrative complaints.

Conclusion

The need to provide a quick, simple, and inexpensive avenue for the redress of administrative complaints has led to the establishment of an Ombudsman in many countries with diverse social and cultural systems. Hong Kong followed this trend in 1989 when the Ombudsman institution in Hong Kong was established. The establishment of the Ombudsman institution was also part of a wider movement for a more open and accountable style of government, brought about by political and social changes in Hong Kong. Despite the initial handicap of an indirect access system, the Ombudsman Office has proved a success, and has built up a reputation for integrity and effectiveness in dealing with complaints of maladministration, without duplicating existing avenues of redress. The jurisdiction of the Ombudsman Office has been expanded to include a number of statutory bodies, and the Ombudsman Office has even been given power to investigate maladministration without a formal complaint from the public.

The Ombudsman Office has successfully investigated a number of high-profile cases involving senior government officials. However, these cases do tend to show some of the limitations of the Ombudsman's jurisdiction. The Ombudsman Office cannot easily reverse major government policies, enforce effective cooperation between government departments, or cancel all the effects of individual instances of maladministration.

Difficulties facing the Ombudsman Office include obtaining sufficient resources to deal with the vast increase in complaints following the abolition of the indirect access system; entrenching its impartial image by severing the close link with civil service; and the need to identify an evolving role and ethos to sustain public support. It is suggested that the basic concept of the Ombudsman is flexible enough to surmount future problems, although a great deal depends on the personal characteristics of individual Ombudsmen. It is certainly true that the Ombudsman Office has firmly established itself as an important public guardian of open and accountable government in Hong Kong, as well as performing a valuable role in identifying management weaknesses in the process of administration.

Acknowledgments

This article was prepared under the project "Alternative Delivery Systems for Public Services in Hong Kong," funded by the Research Grants Council of the Hong Kong Special Administrative Region (project no. HKP 8/95). We would like to thank the constructive comments from the two anonymous readers.

Note: *Originally published in Lo, C.W.-H. and Wickins, R.J., Towards an accountable and quality public administration in Hong Kong: Redressing administrative grievances through the Ombudsman,* International Journal of Public Administration, *25, 737, 2002.*

Endnotes

1. Established by the Commissioner for Administrative Complaints Ordinance Cap 397 of the Laws of Hong Kong.
2. Miners, N., *The Government and Politics of Hong Kong*, 5th ed., Oxford University Press, Hong Kong, 1995, 95–97. For later developments of the ICAC, see Lo, S.H., Anti-corruption and crime, in *The Other Hong Kong Report 1996*, Nyaw, M.-k. and Li, S.-m., Eds., Chinese University Press, Hong Kong, 1996, 153.
3. Ibid.
4. Ibid. See also So, A.K.W., Bringing COMAC to the people, *Hong Kong Public Administration*, 4, 145, 1995.
5. Seneviratne, M., *Ombudsmen in the Public Sector*, Open University Press, Buckingham, UK, 1994, 2.
6. Ibid, 2–4; Gregory, R. et al., Eds., *Practice and Prospects of the Ombudsmen in the United Kingdom*, Edwin Mellen Press, Lewiston, NY, 1995; Calden, G.E., Ed., *International Handbook of the Ombudsman: Evolution and Present Function*, Greenwood, Westport, CT, 1983.
7. For a brief account of the growth of the Ombudsman system, see Wade, H.W.R., *Administrative Law*, 5th ed., Oxford University Press, New York, 1982, 74–77.
8. Quoted in Haller, W., The place of the Ombudsman in the world community, in *Fourth International Ombudsman Conference Papers*, Canberra, Australia, 1988, 40.
9. Hayes, M., Emerging issues for Ombudsmen, *United Kingdom Ombudsman Conference Paper*, Meriden, 1991, 14.
10. Harlow, C., The issues, in *Practice and Prospects of the Ombudsmen in the United Kingdom*, Gregory, R. et al., Eds., Edwin Mellen Press, Lewiston, NY, 1995, 51.
11. Ibid; Seneviratne, op. cit.
12. Ombudsmen in most of the Commonwealth countries can only handle cases of administrative complaints referred by the legislature, while those in most European countries and non-Commonwealth nations can also take up a case on their own initiative (Seneviratne, op. cit.; Matscher, F., Ed., *Ombudsman in Europe: The Institution*, N.P. Engel, Arlington, VA, 1994).
13. Hayes, op. cit., 81–82.
14. Section 2, Commissioner for Administrative Complaints Ordinance Cap 397.
15. See, for example, Section 2, Commissioner for Administrative Complaints Ordinance Cap 397, Schedule 2. Note also that under section 10(l)(e) the Commissioner is not to investigate a complaint if the complainant has a remedy by proceedings in any court or a right of appeal or review on the merits under any ordinance to the Governor, the Governor in Council or any board or tribunal, unless the Commissioner is satisfied that it is not reasonable in the circumstances to expect the complainant to use such remedy or right.
16. See, for example, sections 12, 13(1), 14, 20, and 23 of the Ordinance for these powers and offenses.
17. Seneviratne, op. cit., 132.
18. Seneviratne, op. cit., 13–15; Gregory, R. et al., op. cit., 12–37; Gregory, R. and Pearson, J., The parliamentary Ombudsman after twenty-five years, in *The Ombudsman: Twenty Five Years On: A Series of Conference Papers Presented at Leicester Polytechnic, March 1992*, Hawke, N., Ed., Cavendish, London, 1993, chap. 1.
19. Lo, C.W.H. and Yuen, P.P., Hong Kong public administration in transition: An overview, *Hong Kong Public Administration*, 3, 1, 1994; Burns, J., Administrative reform in a changing political environment: The case of Hong Kong, *Public Administration and Development*, 14, 241, 1994.
20. Miners, N., The transformation of the Hong Kong Legislative Council 1970–1994, *Asian Journal of Public Administration*, 16, 224, 1998.
21. Tang, S.-y., Perry, J.L., and Lam, W.-f., Changing institutional contexts and administrative reform in Hong Kong, *Hong Kong Public Administration*, 3, 31, 1994; Chan, H.S. and Huque, A.S., Hong Kong facing China: The changing political and administrative contexts, *Hong Kong Public Administration*, 3, 15, 1994.

22. Scott, I., Changing concepts of decentralization: Old public administration and new public sector management in the Asian context, *Asian Journal of Public Administration*, 18, 3, 1996; Tang, S.Y., Perry, J.L., and Lam, W.F., The politics of structural reform in Hong Kong: An institutional perspective, *International Review of Administrative Sciences*, 60, 447, 1994; Huque, A.S., The changing nature of public administration in Hong Kong: Past, present, future, *Issues & Studies*, 32(6), 113, 1996.

23. Tsang, D., Public sector reform: Key issues and future, in *Public Sector Reform in Hong Kong*, Lee, J.C.Y. and Cheung, A.B.L., Eds., Chinese University Press, Hong Kong, 1995, 5–6.

24. Ibid, 7–8.

25. Cheung, A.B.L., The civil service in transition, in *The Other Hong Kong Report 1996*, Nyaw, M.-k. and Li, S.-m., Eds., Chinese University Press, Hong Kong, 1996, 67.

26. Sankey, C., Public sector reform: Past developments and recent trends, in *Public Sector Reform in Hong Kong*, Lee, J.C.Y. and Cheung, A.B.L., Eds., Chinese University Press, Hong Kong, 1995, 21–22.

27. Kwok, R., Leung, J., and Scott, I., Eds., *Votes Without Power: The Hong Kong Legislative Council Elections 1991*, Hong Kong University Press, Hong Kong, 1992.

28. Hong Kong people's active pursuit of a Bill of Rights is a vivid example of increasing public awareness. Responding to public pressure, the government enacted the Hong Kong Bill of Rights Ordinance Cap 383 in 1991 (Chan. J.M.M., The legal system, in *The Other Hong Kong Report 1992*, Cheng, J.Y.S. and Kwong, P.C.K., Chinese University Press, Hong Kong, 1992, 16; Wacks, R., Ed., *Human Rights in Hong Kong*, Oxford University Press, Hong Kong, 1992).

29. The Basic Law was adopted by the Seventh National People's Congress of the People's Republic of China on April 4, 1990 as the Constitution of the Hong Kong Special Administrative Region after public consultation in Hong Kong. It also contains an extensive Bill of Rights.

30. Cheng, J.Y.S., Political participation in Hong Kong in the mid-1990s, in *The 1995 Legislative Council Elections in Hong Kong*, Kuan, H.-c. et al., Eds., Hong Kong Institute of Asian-Pacific Studies, Chinese University of Hong Kong, Hong Kong, 1996, 13.

31. Patten, C., *Our Next Five Years: The Agenda for Hong Kong*, The Government Printer, Hong Kong, 1992, 26.

32. The Heung Yee Kuk is a government advisory and consultative body for the New Territories given statutory recognition by the Heung Yee Kuk Ordinance Cap 1097.

33. It should be noted that there is a Private Bills Ordinance Cap 69, and Orders 23 and 39 of the Standing Orders of the Legislative Council provided that a private member's bill which changed the revenue or public moneys of Hong Kong required the recommendation of the Governor before introduction into the Legislative Council. There was a substantial increase in private members bills shortly before the 1997 transition. Note that Article 74 of the Basic Law also allows for private members bills, subject to certain restrictions.

34. Section 9 of the Crown Rights (Re-entry and Vesting Remedies) Ordinance Cap 126 provides that the Governor or the Governor in Council can cancel any memorial of re-entry on such terms as he in his discretion may think fit. Note that section 64 of the Interpretation and General Clauses Ordinance Cap 1 provides that the Governor in Council when considering any appeal or objection shall act in an administrative or executive capacity and not in a judicial or quasi-judicial capacity and shall be entitled to consider any information or advice in his absolute discretion and may make any decision he shall think fit, and no court proceedings by way of judicial review may be taken against the Governor in Council in respect of any such proceedings.

35. *Simpson v. Attorney General [1994] 3NZLR 667*. However, in *Northern Territory of Australia v. Mengel [1995] 129 ALRI,* the High Court of Australia refused to extend the law of tort to provide a remedy to a citizen for economic loss caused by the unauthorized actions of government officials.

36. See, for example, *Rowling v. Takaro Properties Ltd [1988] 1 AIIER 163*; *Ngao To-ki v. Attorney General [1981] HKLR 259*; *Yuen Kun-yeu v. Attorney General [1987] HKLR 1154*; *Davis v. Radcliffe [1990] 2 AIIER 536*.

37. Section 7 of the Post Office Ordinance Cap 98, section 18 of the Crown Land Ordinance Cap 28, section 123 of the Banking Ordinance Cap 155, and section 37 of the Buildings Ordinance Cap 123.

38. For a comparison of the provisions of the Ordinance with those in other Commonwealth countries, see Clarke, D., Commissioner for administrative complaints ordinance, *Hong Kong Law Journal*, 19, 69, 1989.

39. See sections 16(3) and 22 of the Ordinance.

40. Garcia, A., *The First Annual Report of the Commissioner for Administrative Complaints Hong Kong*, The Government Printer, Hong Kong, 1989, 22.

41. Tai, A., *The Eleventh Annual Report of the Commissioner for Administrative Complaints Hong Kong*, The Government Printer, Hong Kong, 1999, Annex 11.

42. So, A., *The Eighth Annual Report of the Commissioner for Administrative Complaints Hong Kong*, The Government Printer, Hong Kong, 1996, 40–41.

43. Tai, A., *The Eleventh Annual Report of the Commissioner for Administrative Complaints Hong Kong*, The Government Printer, Hong Kong, 1999, 27.

44. So, A., *The Eighth Annual Report of the Commissioner for Administrative Complaints Hong Kong*, The Government Printer, Hong Kong, 1996, 6.

45. Ibid, 40–41 and Annex 1; Tai, A., *The Eleventh Annual Report of the Commissioner for Administrative Complaints Hong Kong*, The Government Printer, Hong Kong, 1999, 27.

46. So, A., *The Eighth Annual Report of the Commissioner for Administrative Complaints Hong Kong*, The Government Printer, Hong Kong, 1996, 40–41 and Annex 1; Tai, A., *The Eleventh Annual Report of the Commissioner for Administrative Complaints Hong Kong*, The Government Printer, Hong Kong, 1999, 11.

47. See schedules 1 and 2 of the Ordinance.

48. See section 16 of the Ordinance.

49. Tai, A., *The Eleventh Annual Report of the Commissioner for Administrative Complaints Hong Kong*, The Government Printer, Hong Kong, 1999, 27.

50. See, first through eighth *Annual Report(s) of the Commissioner for Administrative Complaints*, The Government Printer, Hong Kong, 1989–96; ninth and tenth *Annual Report(s) of The Ombudsman, Hong Kong*, The Government Printer, Hong Kong, 1997–1999.

51. *South China Morning Post*, March 15, 1992.

52. *South China Morning Post*, March 15, 1996.

53. So, A., *The Sixth Annual Report of the Commissioner for Administrative Complaints Hong Kong*, The Government Printer, Hong Kong, 1994, 95; *Hong Kong Standard*, 1990.

54. Friends of the Earth, 1995, 6.

55. Ibid.

56. Ibid.

57. *South China Morning Post*, February 25, 1994.

58. So, A., *The Sixth Annual Report of the Commissioner for Administrative Complaints Hong Kong*, The Government Printer, Hong Kong, 1994, 98.

59. *South China Morning Post*, January 16, 1995.

60. *South China Morning Post*, May 11, 1994.

61. *South China Morning Post*, April 25, 1995.

62. *South China Morning Post*, April 30, 1994.

63. *South China Morning Post*, May 4, 1994.

64. *South China Morning Post*, May 11, 1994.

65. So, A., *The Sixth Annual Report of the Commissioner for Administrative Complaints Hong Kong*, The Government Printer, Hong Kong, 1995, 211.

66. Ibid, 215.

67. Ibid, 217.

68. *Ming Pao Daily*, March 16, 1995.

69. *Ming Pao Daily*, March 19, 1995.

70. *Ming Pao Daily*, February 5, 1995.
71. *Ming Pao Daily*, November 4, 1995.
72. *South China Morning Post*, February 5, 1996.
73. Alice Tai joined the government as Administrative Officer in 1974. In 1990, she was appointed as the Director of Intellectual Property. In 1994, she acted as the Judiciary Administrator to assist the Chief Justice in the administration of the Judiciary.
74. *Hong Kong Standard*, October 6, 1995.

Appendix IV

Questions for Review and Discussion

1. Think of your own experience as a user of public services. What services or issues would you like to have more influence over? How might the organization(s) responsible for these services engage most effectively with you?
2. What are the benefits of representative democracy? How can these be reconciled with increasing direct public participation in policy decisions?
3. Pick a government agency with which you have some familiarity. Then, imagine that you have been hired to prepare an action plan for addressing any weaknesses it has in how it is responsive to the public. How would you go about investigating the answers? What issues would you look at? What might be some likely recommendations you'd have?
4. What are the necessary ingredients for a successful citizen complaints or ombudsman program?

Additional Reading

Lee, M., The astronaut and foggy bottom PR: Assistant Secretary of State for Public Affairs Michael Collins, 1969–1971, *Public Relations Review*, 33, 184, 2007.

Lindstrom, M. and Nie, M.A., Public participation and agency planning, *Public Manager*, 29(1), 33, 2000.

Local Government Association, *Democratic Practice: A Guide*, Local Government Association, London, 1998.

Martin, S. and Boaz, A., Public participation and citizen-centered local government: Lessons from the Best Value and Better Government for Older People pilot programs, *Public Money & Management*, 20(2), 47, 2000.

Public Management Service, Organisation for Economic Co-operation and Development, *Engaging Citizens in Policy-Making: Information, Consultation and Public Participation*, PUMA Policy Briefing No. 10, Organisation for Economic Co-operation and Development, Paris, 2001. http://www.oecd.org/dataoecd/24/34/2384040.pdf (accessed 2007)

Truman, D.B., Public opinion research as a tool of public administration, *Public Administration Review*, 5, 62, 1945. [Path-breaking essay on using the tools of empirical social science to improve an agency's ability to listen to the public.]

Worthen, J., The public and the foreign policymaker, *Public Manager*, 22(3), 17, 1993.

PURPOSES OF GOVERNMENT PUBLIC RELATIONS: OUTREACH

Introduction to Section V

In the preceding section, Chapter 14 had identified *publicity* is one of the three key factors in contributing to the effectiveness of a program intended to increase governmental responsiveness to the public, in this case through a citizen complaints system. Here, then, was a reference to the importance of outreach, of *informing* the public of the availability of a service. In other words, one purpose of government public relations (responsiveness) needed another purpose (outreach) to be successful. This is a neat way of indicating not only the vital role of government public relations, but also of the pervasiveness of the need for a public relations perspective when practicing public administration.

In this context of public outreach, public relations and marketing overlap. It is difficult to draw a clear line differentiating them. After all, both have the underlying purpose of helping accomplish the goals of an organization by improving its delivery of goods and services. Perhaps one way to distinguish between them is that marketing, ultimately, is about successfully providing a tangible good or service. Marketing is *commodity* oriented, often defined as focusing on the four Ps: product, pricing, promotion, and place. This is a comprehensive approach that encompasses just about everything an organization does to disseminate its product successfully.

On the other hand, public relations focuses only on using *information* as a way of furthering the agency's mission, not necessarily the same as the bottom-line, transaction-oriented, and commodity focus of marketing. As used in this reader, one of the *purposes* of government public relations is outreach. This encompasses informational efforts that improve the operations of the agency by, for example, replacing expensive regulatory efforts with less expensive informational programming. As an aspect of government public relations, these activities are quite different from some elements of marketing, such as pricing, but are similar regarding promotion. Government outreach activities can be oriented to accomplishing four identifiably distinct purposes:

1. Increasing the utilization of services and products
2. Public education and public service campaigns

3. Seeking voluntary public compliance with laws and regulations
4. Using the public as the eyes and ears of an agency

The first purpose, of using public relations to increase the utilization of goods and services, is the most similar to the concept of marketing. When elected officials decide to enact a new program, the responsibility for delivering the goods or services that the new program entails usually falls to the public administrator. In this context, it is not enough for politicians to *create* a new governmental program. The newly available goods or services need clients and customers to utilize them. For example, when the federal government occasionally has surplus food to give away, the program would be a flop if all the implementing agency did was unlock its doors in the morning. Citizens who would potentially be eligible to receive the free food have to *know* about its availability. This is a public-sector application of the saying "if a tree falls in a forest and no one is there to hear it, does it make a sound?" Similarly, if government offers a program and no one comes to use it, has it really provided a new service? Therefore, the tools of information dissemination are inherently part of the strategy of marketing: reaching potential customers and clients so they know about it, know they might be eligible, and then step forward to obtain it.

The remaining three purposes of informational outreach (public education and public service campaigns, seeking voluntary public compliance with laws and regulations, and using the public as the eyes and ears of an agency) are much easier to differentiate from marketing. All three share the same premise, namely that public relations can be used as a substitute for the traditional public administration approach to regulation and enforcement.

Public education and public service campaigns tend to focus on free advertising. In that sense, they are different from governmental *paid* advertising, such as the recruiting programs of the military services. Efforts to influence civic behavior through public education campaigns can significantly reduce agency staffing and spending. For example, an assessment of the U.S. Forest Service's Smokey the Bear campaign ("Only you can prevent forest fires") needs to be judged in the context of 'compared to what?' To answer that question one would have to calculate the costs of fighting forest fires that would have occurred had forest users not been sensitized to putting out camp fires. It can be tricky to measure in precise quantities something that didn't happen. Still, through research one can develop reasonable assumptions about the general effect of the public service campaign on bending the trend line of forest fire statistics. In this respect, public education can replace more expensive administrative responses. In fact, one could probably argue that in some cases even *paid* advertising is still cheaper than traditional public administration. This is an alternative that many government managers omit from their traditional list of implementation options.

A related, but still distinctly different, outreach activity is for a government agency to use information dissemination as a way to maximize voluntary public compliance with laws and regulations. Again, the traditional approach of public administrators when assigned an enforcement or regulatory duty is to hire a staff of field inspectors. While this is always necessary for dealing with the predictable 'bad actors,' it is not necessary for the entire target population. Generally speaking, citizens, corporations, and the like will adhere to new laws and regulations *if they know about them*. This is not an argument with the legal principle that ignorance of the law is no defense. That relates to courtroom situations. Rather, it is unreasonable of a government agency to assume that all affected populations should, on their own, know about changes in laws and regulations. Rather than taking a passive stance ('our only job is to enforce the law'), a government agency is acting in its own best interest if it proactively disseminates information about the new requirements ('just wanted to be sure you knew'). It is not only performing a helpful service to the public, but it is also being pragmatic about reducing its own regulatory and enforcement costs. The more people know, the more likely they are to abide by the law. The broader the voluntary compliance, the lower the administrative costs in terms of a field inspection service. Again, this public relations approach to public administration is often overlooked by government managers.

The final identifiably separate outreach activity of government public relations is using the public as the eyes and ears of an agency. This gets to the heart of the difference between government and business, between citizens and customers. As members of a democracy, citizens have a sense of ownership of government, but in a relationship very different from that of a stockholder to a for-profit corporation. In general, the public wants government to be successful, whether the common good affects them personally or not. For example, regarding the 911 call-in system, a citizen may be driving by a property and notice a fire. That property is perhaps neither in the neighborhood where the citizen lives nor works. The individual would not be personally affected by the fire. Still, as a citizen, he or she feels protective about the city as a whole and wants to safeguard other citizens (even though they are strangers) from harm. The fire and police departments, through their 911 system, have created an informational network that makes it easy for citizens to be the departments' eyes and ears. Short of that, the departments would, theoretically, have to post lookouts on just about every block of the city.

The key is to identify that the underlying premise of a 911 system is common rather than rare. Many government agencies have missions that can be enhanced when the citizenry is willing to act as their eyes and ears. This can relate to a wide variety of governmental functions, whether locating potholes, being alerted to child abuse, protecting rare species, helping find missing persons, or adherence to lawn watering guidelines. Few public administrators consider using this public relations purpose for their agency, thinking that it is only relevant to fire and police departments. With the communications revolution of cell phones, handhelds, and WiFi, the potential of citizens serving as the eyes and ears of a broad panoply of government agencies has barely scratched the surface.

In a sense, the eyes and ears purpose of government public relations is the obverse of public service campaigns and seeking voluntary compliance with laws. For the latter two, the public administrator is trying to *change* civic behavior. This is outgoing communications, from the agency to the public, with a goal of persuasion. On the other hand, the eyes and ears function has communications going in the other direction, from the public to the agency, with citizens actively helping the agency be more effective in accomplishing its mission.

Notwithstanding these valuable uses of public relations to enhance government management, most of the writing about it has been under the rubric of marketing. Therefore, Chapter 16 provides an overview of the topic, albeit using the marketing nomenclature rather than that of public relations. But that's merely an issue of titles. The underlying purposes are quite relevant to government PR. It's merely a rose by another name…

Chapter 16

Marketing in Public Sector Organizations

Tony Bovaird

Contents

Introduction

For many years in the 1970s and 1980s, lectures on marketing in the public sector began apologetically with an explanation of why marketing might be important — and generally they adopted a rather defensive standpoint, assuming that many in the audience would be predisposed to be hostile to the concept. This is no longer the case, as the growing literature on public sector marketing attests. However, the suspicion remains that public sector marketing has to demonstrate its role carefully and has to demarcate itself clearly from private sector marketing. This chapter looks at how marketing can contribute to the more efficient and effective operation of public sector organizations and services.

Box 16.1
Definitions of Marketing

- "The role of marketing is to make selling superfluous." (Michael Baker)
- "Marketing means making products that don't come back for customers who do." (Peter Drucker)
- "Identifying the needs of your target audience and satisfying them according to your organizational objectives." (Institute of Marketing)

The Role of Marketing in a Public Sector Context

Marketing is often thought of as essentially commercial — that is, oriented toward making profits. This clearly is not relevant to most aspects of public services and public sector organizations.

Again, marketing often has rather negative connotations associated with selling, even high-pressure selling or of promotion of goods or services perhaps through hype or of advertising, perhaps through subliminal influencing. Clearly, if marketing is to play a valuable role in a public sector context, these negative aspects will have to be transcended.

Fortunately, there is no reason to believe that marketing must be viewed only in these pejorative terms. It is quite possible to define marketing in ways which suggest that it could be highly valuable to public sector organizations (Box 16.1). After all, markets are only the contexts in which those needing a service are able to use alternative providers, either in the public, private or voluntary sectors. Using markets is therefore not inherently contrary to the public interest. The role of marketing, then, is to mediate between those needing the service and the organization hoping to provide the service. Clearly this can be done either efficiently or inefficiently, fairly or unfairly, ethically or unethically, respectfully or insultingly to the potential service user. In all these respects, marketing is no different from other service functions such as production, HR management or financial management, in terms of the potential for abuse of stakeholders involved in the activity. Perhaps the sensitivity about the potential for abuse of the marketing role comes from the widespread belief that marketing is the most dishonest and unethical of business functions in the private sector. Whether or not this belief is soundly based need not concern us here (although we might say in passing that private sector marketing has a number of competitors for this distinction — including tricky lawyers, creative accountants and captured auditors, all of whom are regularly in the public eye as a result of major corporate scandals).

To make this clearer, we can contrast the two polar extremes — a product orientation, as might typically be evidenced by professionals working in the field who are convinced that they know better than anyone else what service should be provided, and a market orientation, such as would be advocated by marketing specialists (Box 16.2).

Clearly, customers in a public sector context include many different stakeholders, all of whose needs require to be considered in public sector marketing. Here we need to refer to the types of value added in the public sector: value added for users, for wider social groups, for society as a whole ('social value added'), for the polity ('political value added') and for the environment. Mar-

Box 16.2
Product Orientation vs. Market Orientation

Product Orientation

- Emphasis on getting the 'product' right in professional terms.
- Product is developed first, then there is an attempt to attract customers.
- Organization is inward-looking; its production needs come first. Success is measured primarily in terms of professional esteem, with a secondary emphasis on the number of customers attracted.
- And if the service fails? "We did our best, we produced a really good service — but the market didn't appreciate it."

Market Orientation

- Emphasis on doing what the customer wants.
- Services are developed to meet expressed wants and potential wants in a coordinated way.
- Organization is outward-looking — the customers' needs come first.
- Success is measured primarily both by the number and satisfaction level of customers (i.e., quality as well as quantity).
- Customers are central to everything the organization does (i.e., there is a culture of customer obsession).

keting can be employed to explore how to increase value added for all the stakeholders involved in each of these ways.

However, there are a number of very different modes in which marketing may be used (Box 16.3). Some of these modes seek fundamentally to serve the user's interest (positive marketing and some variants of anti-marketing), while some seek to serve society's interest (social marketing) and some seek to serve the interests of target users at the expense of non-target users (de-marketing).

One of the key issues which emerges from this discussion is: Who is the customer? There are many potential customers for the public sector, including:

- People currently receiving the service
- People waiting for the service
- People needing the service but not seeking it actively
- People who may need the service in the future
- People who refused the service
- Carers of people needing the service (both those receiving it and those not receiving it)
- Taxpayers
- Citizens
- Referrers of potential clients of the service

Box 16.3
Modes of Marketing

- Positive Marketing: Encouraging target groups to use particular goods, services or organizations because it will meet their needs.
- Social Marketing: Advancing a social, environmental or political viewpoint or cause because it will meet society's needs.
- Anti-Marketing: Encouraging target groups to cease using particular goods, services or organizations, either because it is against their interest or because it is against society's interest.
- De-Marketing: Deterring non-target groups from service uptake.

Source: Adapted from Sheaff. [1]

In the rest of this chapter, we speak of all of these as customers. But, a proper marketing strategy and marketing plan will normally try to identify the particular needs of each of these different customers and tailor the service to those needs.

Preparing a Marketing Strategy and Marketing Plans

In this section, we will consider how marketing strategies and marketing plans can be constructed in public sector organizations.

There is clearly a very strong connection between strategic management and marketing strategy. Indeed, a marketing strategy will always be an integral part of the overall strategy for any organization (or organizational unit such as a service department). The corporate marketing strategy will consist of that part of the strategy in which the organization decides:

■ Which sectors to work in
■ Which portfolio of services to provide
■ Which target groups to provide with these services
■ What objectives and targets may be set to show whether the target groups have received the benefits expected from the services

Clearly, this relates very closely to Mintzberg's concept of strategy as positioning. The corporate marketing strategy responds to what the environment wants. It will complement the service production and delivery strategy (to make best use of internal capabilities) and the financial strategy (to make best use of all resources).

Typically, each constituent unit of the organization is expected to prepare a business plan for its part of the overall organization, nested within and aligned to the corporate strategy. Similarly, each business unit is likely to prepare a marketing strategy, which starts from the decisions in the corporate marketing strategy on which markets that business is expected to serve and goes

Table 16.1   Stakeholder Power/Interest Matrix

	Stakeholder Interest: High	Stakeholder Interest: Low
Stakeholder Power: Low	Low priority	Keep informed
Stakeholder Power: High	Keep satisfied	Work together to achieve common goals

Source: Adapted from Mendelow. [2]

into greater detail on which services it should produce and what are the target markets for those services. Finally, the marketing strategy at the business-unit level needs to be developed into a marketing plan, considering the detailed elements of the marketing mix.

In order to prepare this suite of plans, three sets of analyses are necessary:

1. Analysis of the external environment of the organization
2. Analysis of the market segments which the organization might serve
3. Analysis of the market options available and their relative merits

We will now look at each of these in turn, before discussing how these analyses may be used in formulating the corporate marketing strategy and business marketing plans.

Analyzing the External Environment

In analyzing the external environment, we seek to understand the factors influencing external stakeholders and the consequent opportunities and threats which face the organization. There are three main elements to this analysis: stakeholder mapping, PESTEL analysis and risk assessment, and Five Forces analysis.

Stakeholder mapping involves identifying the most important stakeholders in the organization and prioritizing them. This is typically done by drawing up a stakeholder power/interest matrix (see Table 16.1). Stakeholders with high power over the organization and high interest in it are clearly crucially important — they should be given central roles in the organization's decision making and activities. At the other extreme, stakeholders with neither power over nor interest in the organization can be largely neglected (subject to giving them the level of information which is required by law — and perhaps rather more than that, just to be on the safe side).

However, the lesson from Table 16.1 is clear — not all stakeholder groups are equal and a public sector organization must decide how to allocate its resources to work most closely with those stakeholder groups which it considers to have priority. Other forms of mapping may be used to help in setting these priorities — but the need for some set of priorities is unavoidable.

PESTEL analysis sets out a statement of the main factors which are likely to impact on external stakeholders in the future, separated out into:

■ Political factors
■ Economic factors
■ Social factors
■ Technological factors
■ Environmental and ecological factors
■ Legal and legislative factors

This analysis is notoriously simple to do, to the extent that one can very easily end up with a document which is ludicrously large, detailing all potentially relevant factors. This is clearly of no practical use, so some sort of filter must be applied to ensure that only the most relevant factors are included in any final document. (However, this still implies that the organization must attempt a very wide and imaginative search for all potentially relevant factors, so that the filter can be applied to them. Of course, in practice we must expect that organizations — and individuals within them — will display blind spots, prejudices and plain ignorance in making this search, so that PESTEL analysis cannot ever pretend to be fully comprehensive.) Risk assessment, the filter applied to the factors, is clearly a crucially important part of PESTEL analysis. There are many different ways of doing this, but typically factors are more likely to be included in the PESTEL statement if they score highly on at least one of the following criteria:

- Is the factor high impact at the moment?
- Will the factor have increasing impact over time?
- Is the factor likely to have a positive or negative effect on external stakeholders? (This takes account of the fact that many stakeholders are risk averse, placing more importance on potential costs and losses than on potential benefits and gains.)
- Is there a high probability that the factor will indeed occur as forecast?
- Will the factor affect our organization more than other similar organizations which are involved in the same type of activity? (This takes account of the fact that an organization will typically be sensitive to changes in its potential competitive advantage in relation to its stakeholders.)

The final piece in the external environment jigsaw is the *Five Forces analysis* of Michael Porter, whereby an organization can consider how attractive the prospects are in a specific sector — and which sectors are therefore unattractive. The Five Forces are:

1. The *threat of new entrants,* which would compete away profit margins
2. The *threat of substitutes,* which puts a ceiling on the prices that can be charged
3. The *bargaining power of suppliers* (including the distribution channels), which puts pressure on costs
4. The *bargaining power of customers,* which puts a ceiling on prices
5. The *level of competitive rivalry,* which drives down prices

This approach was originally applied by Porter to analyze which sectors would be regarded by a private firm as the most competitive — with the implication that these would be the least attractive. Such a model may be relevant for some service-providing organizations in the public sector, where they are driven by the need to make target levels of profit (or not to exceed target levels of subsidy). However, it needs to be adapted to a public sector context.

In particular, we need to take account of two facts: (1) public sector organizations do not always have a choice of which sector they work in (so that this analysis is irrelevant for some organizations, which can only work in certain named sectors, and cannot be applied to some sectors where a particular public sector organization is prohibited from working — and the model is clearly not relevant to service-commissioning organizations); and (2) public sector organizations are not always competitive in their intent, and there are other stakeholders impacting on their choice of sector (particularly government).

Consequently, the Five Forces analysis has a different role in the external environmental analysis undertaken by public sector organizations. First, it helps providing organizations to highlight the sectors in which they are likely to meet strong competitive rivalry. As with private organizations, this is likely to be interpreted as a danger signal: sectors where competitive rivalry is weak will be more attractive.

Second, public sector organizations also need to consider the bargaining power of other stakeholders (which might either increase costs or lower revenue) and the likelihood of interference by other levels of government (which again might affect costs or prices, or might even rule out any work in the sector). Both of these extra forces may make a sector less attractive. (These two factors now mean working with a Seven Forces model, but it is highly unlikely that it will become known as anything other than the Five Forces model.)

Third — and rather differently from many private sector providers — public sector providers need to consider the collaborative potential of the sector. Since so much of their success will depend on working closely with other bodies — groups representing customers, voluntary organizations filling in gaps in public provision, universities evaluating the cost-effectiveness of alternative service designs — it is important that these different bodies are collaborative in nature and prepared to form effective partnerships. [3] We will consider this in more depth in the next section, but for the moment it is important to note that public sector use of the Five Forces can — and should — reject using it purely to explore the competitive rivalry of the sector. It is important to ask, in relation to each of the Five Forces: How does it affect the sector's ability to work in collaboration?

Analyzing Market Segments

Different market segments will normally prefer different services or different designs of a given service. The most typical criteria for drawing up market segments in the public sector are:

- Demographic (e.g., age, household composition)
- Socio-economic (e.g., class, socio-economic group, income)
- Membership of economically or socially disadvantaged group (e.g., pensioners, unemployed, low income, disability groups, women, ethnic minorities, isolated people)
- Geographic (e.g., neighborhood, ward, town, region)

However, more recently there has been greater interest in using such criteria as lifestyle and tastes (often using psychographics). Each of these approaches naturally tends to miss some of the important differences between individuals, while trying to allow a move away from treating all customers as a mass market. Another form of market segmentation looks at the customer's attitude to the service being provided (unaware, hostile, aware, interested, wavering towards action, trialing, occasional user, loyal). Each of these approaches is useful for a particular form of marketing initiative but the crucially important issue is to prioritize between these market segments in order to determine which segments should form the target or priority groups for the public agency. This is one of the fundamental political tasks in any public sector organization.

Analyzing Market Options

The analyses of external factors allow an OT (opportunities and threats) analysis to be compiled for the organization, which can help to identify future market options, and can in turn be combined with internal analysis of the organization to feed into a full strengths-weaknesses-opportunities-threats (SWOT) analysis, which may be used to produce a series of integrated strategic options for the organization. These strategic market options should form coherent statements of a market position — a market to be served, a service to be provided and a target market segment for that service. However, it may well be unproductive to try to evaluate these market options on their own. The evaluation of strategy is most likely to make sense when it considers full strategic options, which combine market options with internal capabilities and financial/resource options. Otherwise, the evaluation is likely to come up with a ranking of market options which is blind to the organization's strengths and weaknesses and resource constraints — this is very likely to lead to the choice of a suboptimal strategy.

Evaluation of market options need not simply be a cognitive exercise, based on a desk study. It is also possible to do market testing of options, either by conducting trials or by analyzing the offers made by alternative suppliers.

From Marketing Strategy to Marketing Plans

The analysis and evaluation of strategic options should help a public sector organization to select its preferred strategic option, including its marketing strategy, with the following key elements:

- A decision on which sectors to work in
- A portfolio of services which will be provided to users
- A description of the target groups for whom these services will be provided
- A set of objectives and targets which can be monitored to show whether the target groups have received the benefits expected from the services

How can this marketing strategy be put into practice? Typically, a marketing plan is prepared which allows the key issues (the marketing mix) to be considered and coordinated in detail (Figure 16.1).

These elements of the marketing mix are closely interrelated and therefore need to be planned together, so that they are aligned with each other and support the chosen strategy:

- The *product* (or *service*) needs to be designed with the needs of the customer in mind. Design features need to include not only the core features of the service itself but also the way in which it is delivered, including such customer care aspects as the availability of the service (e.g., opening hours), reliability (e.g., how often is the service defective?), responsiveness to customers' needs (e.g., does the service take account of differences in gender, age, ethnicity, [dis]ability, etc?), and the empathy with which staff treat service users. A key element of service design is market research, which is becoming much more central to public services management, whether conducted by surveys, focus groups or other methods.
- The *promotion* of the service has to be suitable for the target group, so that over time the users become aware of the service, interested in it, keen to use it and then take action to try it out. The mix of promotional methods needs to be thought out carefully, including advertising, special sales promotions, sponsorship deals and public relations campaigns.
- The *place* in which the service is available has to be suitable for the target service user (so that it is comfortable to use and appropriate transport is available) or services can be made available in e-government initiatives (e.g., over the Internet or through a call center).

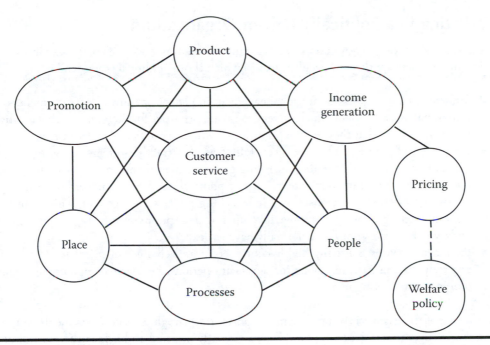

Figure 16.1   The Expanded Marketing Mix for Public Services. *Source:* Adapted from Christopher, Payne, and Ballantyne. [4]

- The *processes* which are used to assess eligibility and to provide the service have to be clear and understandable to the target group (which includes clear and easy-to-use forms, with availability of translation if required) and should be designed to minimize time taken and hassle.

- The *people* who supply the service have to be welcoming and sympathetic to the target group and well trained in giving the service.

- The *income generation* activities of the organization have to be consistent with its principles and organized efficiently so that the net income is maximized. Sources of income might include fund-raising by volunteers, donations, sponsorship, sales of associated services (e.g., from a charity shop), merchandising, sales of advertising space or pricing.

- The *prices* which are charged have to be appropriate to the target group's means (which will be determined partly by the overall national welfare policy to which the organization must conform and to which it contributes), proportionate to the benefits given and consistent with the organization's income generation plan. This will sometimes entail a concessions system (which may require income assessment procedures, with the consequent problems of stigma, deterrence of potential users and high transaction costs).

Clearly, there will be considerable overlap between marketing strategies and marketing plans — for example, the decision on the portfolio of services to be offered figures in both, although it is handled at a finer level of detail in marketing plans. Again, promotion is just one branch of marketing communications, by means of which the organization seeks to keep in touch with its various customers. [5] Moreover, marketing plans and service delivery plans will often overlap (e.g., making sure that proper transport arrangements are in place is part of the place factor in the marketing plan, but also part of the logistics factor in the service delivery plan).

Marketing in a Politically Driven Organization

Marketing is never easy in any context but it assumes extra dimensions of complexity in a political environment. There are three particular areas in which thorny political issues tend to arise:

- Strategic marketing, like strategic management in general, requires clear statements of priorities, particularly about which target groups are priorities for each policy. This means telling many groups that they are not priorities — which is politically embarrassing.
- Promotion of policies and services generally tries to attract customers to use them — but this can be interpreted as selling the ruling group's achievements to the population. Consequently, promotion can often take on a strong political resonance. Furthermore, the political opposition often feels unconstrained in attacking policies and services, which can undermine marketing efforts to improve take-up and perceptions of quality — not something with which private companies normally have to deal.
- Pricing of services is usually highly controversial and changes of prices tend to be made relatively infrequently, removing for significant periods the use of one potentially valuable tool in the marketing mix.

The first of these issues is by far the most important. We might expect, given the rhetoric of the public sector over recent decades, that it has particularly targeted and helped the most disadvantaged groups in society. However, as Le Grand pointed out 20 years ago, "Almost all public expenditure in social services in Britain benefits the better off to a greater degree than the poor … [even in] services whose aims are at least in part egalitarian, such as the NHS, higher education, public transport, and the aggregate complex of housing policies." [6] He went on to suggest that substantial inequalities persist in public expenditure per user, in use (standardized by level of need), in opportunity, in access (including cost of access and time taken to gain access), and in outcomes. He also suggested that, in many policy areas, public policies have probably even failed significantly to reduce inequality. These conclusions are likely to have been reinforced by the events of the past 20 years. [7] If politicians cannot or will not address the need to target public expenditure and public services at the most disadvantaged, while claiming to take the disadvantage seriously, then it seems likely that marketing will remain a relatively weak tool for achieving the purposes of public sector organizations — and those purposes will be much harder to achieve.

Limitations of Marketing

While marketing can help public sector organizations to work more effectively to please their customers, there remain significant limitations to its use in the public sector.

First, it is clear that it is often artificial to regard all those who come into contact with the public sector as its customers — certainly prisoners and parents who abuse their children do not fit this description easily. In some cases, the relationship between the state and its subjects is — and is likely to remain — characterized by relations of dominance and punishment rather than exchange and mutual reward. Marketing is less relevant in these circumstances.

Second, the manipulation of public tastes and preferences to make the public sector's services more desirable is questionable in the public sector. This largely rules out some of the approaches of private sector marketing, such as the encouragement of the "conspicuous consumption of the leisure classes," [8] or the use of the *Hidden Persuaders* which create demand for unnecessary services and encourage motives based on base desires such as power, greed and sex, [9] or the resort to built-in obsolescence and emphasis on style rather than performance. [10]

Third, there are areas where individuals making their own choice will not contribute to the highest good of the society in which they live — whether because of spill-over effects of their decisions, the poor quality of information on which they act, their lack of understanding of their own (long-term) best interest, or for other reasons. Where this is the case — and it seems likely that there are significant areas of such decision making in human behavior — then collective decisions based on political processes will remain superior to individual decisions aided by marketing processes.

In general, then, the balance between marketing as a way of mediating between service users, citizens and service producers is one which will always be hard to find and is likely to shift over time. While marketing may have played too small a role in traditional public administration up to the 1980s, it has perhaps been in danger of encroaching too far in some areas of public policy in the past two decades.

Summary

This chapter has considered a range of techniques for understanding the external environment of organizations and for identifying and evaluating strategic market options. It has also linked these strategies to the marketing plans needed to ensure that they are implemented. It has argued that marketing in a political environment can help to force political decision making to be more open about its underlying purposes, especially in relation to priority target groups, but marketing also has to be sensitive to its limitations when applied in the public domain.

Note: *Originally published in Bovaird, T., Marketing in public sector organizations, in* Public Management and Governance, *Bovaird, T. and Löffler, E., Eds., Routledge, London, 2003, chap. 6.*

Endnotes

1. Sheaff, R., *Marketing for Health Services: A Framework for Communications, Evaluation, and Total Quality Management,* Open University Press, Buckingham, UK, 1991.
2. Mendelow, A.L., Environmental scanning: The impact of the stakeholder concept, in *Proceedings of the Second International Conference on Information Systems,* December 7–9, 1981, Cambridge, MA, Ross, C.A., Ed., 1982, chap. 24.
3. Kooiman, J., *Governing as Governance,* Sage, London, 2003.
4. Christopher, M., Payne, A., and Ballantyne, D., *Relationship Marketing: Bringing Quality, Customer Service, and Marketing Together,* Butterworth-Heinemann, Oxford, UK, 1991.
5. *Editor's Note:* Stakeholder engagement is considered in more detail in Chapter 13 of this volume, which had been originally published in 2003 in the same book as this chapter.
6. Le Grand, J., *The Strategy of Equality: Redistribution and the Social Services,* Allen & Unwin, London, 1982.
7. Percy-Smith, J., Ed., *Policy Responses to Social Exclusion: Towards Inclusion?,* Open University Press, Maidenhead, UK, 2000.
8. Veblen, T., *The Theory of the Leisure Class,* Prometheus, Amherst, NY, 1998 [1899].
9. Packard, V., *The Hidden Persuaders,* D. McKay, New York, 1957.
10. Nader, R., *Unsafe at Any Speed: The Designed-In Dangers of the American Automobile,* Grossman, New York, 1965.

APPENDIX V

Questions for Review and Discussion

1. What does 'marketing' mean? What relationship does it have to 'markets'? Why does the term 'marketing' often appear to have a pejorative meaning? Is this justified?
2. What is the relationship between marketing strategy and the marketing mix? When would changes in the marketing mix be so significant that they would amount to changes in the marketing strategy?
3. Can you think of an example, not mentioned in the introduction to the section or the chapter, of a contemporary government public relations program that has the purpose of:
   - Increasing the utilization of services and products?
   - Public education and public service campaigns?
   - Voluntary public compliance with laws and regulations?
   - Using the public as the eyes and ears of an agency?

Additional Reading

Andreason, A.R. and Kotler, P., *Strategic Marketing for Nonprofit Organizations*, 6th ed., Prentice Hall, Upper Saddle River, NJ, 2003.

Compton, J.L. and Lamb, C.W., *Marketing Government and Social Services*, Wiley, New York, 1986.

Kotler, P., Haider, D., and Rein, I., There's no place like our place!, *PM. Public Management*, 76(2), 15, 1994.

Lawless, D.R., The US general store, *Public Manager*, 28(2), 49, 1999. [Exploration of the contemporary citizen/customer wanting one-stop shopping from government, a centralization of all information about public programs.]

Lee, M., A public relations program even Congress could love: Federal Information Centers, *Public Relations Review*, 30, 61, 2004.

Martinelli, D.K., Strategic public information: Engaging audiences in government agencies' work, *Public Relations Quarterly*, 51(1), 37, 2006.

Sargeant, A., *Marketing Management for Nonprofit Organizations*, Oxford University Press, Oxford, UK, 1999.

Sheaff, R., *Responsive Healthcare: Marketing for a Public Service*, Open University Press, Buckingham, UK, 2002.

Walsh, K., *Marketing in Local Government*, Financial Times Prentice Hall, London, 1995.

Weiss, J.A., Public information, in *The Tools of Government: A Guide to the New Governance*, Salamon, L.M., Ed., Oxford University Press, New York, 2002, chap. 7.

CRISIS MANAGEMENT AS GOVERNMENT PUBLIC RELATIONS

VI

Introduction to Section VI

Nowadays, we often use terms such as *crisis* and *emergency* relatively easily and glibly. It seems that the cable news networks discover a crisis on a weekly basis to help draw and keep viewers. In the world of government, the word *crisis* passes easily from the lips of elected officials who are looking for opportunities to hype their pet issues by grabbing the attention of reporters and voters with such alarmist rhetoric.

However, despite this era of spin and hype, students and practitioners of public administration intuitively understand the difference between such fake crises and real ones. In the public sector, a crisis is a true emergency, a brief moment when a large number of lives are in danger unless action is taken quickly, within the hour, the day, certainly no more than a week. A crisis is when everyone in the agency puts aside their quotidian work, rolls up their sleeves, and pitches in to help the agency provide the vital services that are necessary. Then, after a period of intense activity and emotion, organizational life gradually resumes a more normal and routine status.

One of the key elements of an authentic crisis, often overlooked, is that nearly the totality of public administration is briefly transformed into government public relations. To communicate effectively with large numbers of people, organizations, and partners, the techniques of external communication become the key channel for transmitting information, plans, decisions, and directives. This almost always involves media relations, but not just that. During an emergency, other techniques of government public relations, such as outreach and responsiveness to the public, can be equally important for successful remediation.

Chapter 17 provides a comprehensive overview of the role of government public relations as part of crisis management. 'Getting information out' is the organizational mantra at those times and advance planning is equally essential for success when the time comes. The professionalization of crisis and emergency management is reflected in Chapter 18. Relying almost exclusively on government planning documents, directives, and learning materials, Radvanovsky demonstrates the intricate structure that is expected to be set up — nearly instantaneously — at such moments. Long in advance, plans are finalized that determine who makes what decisions, who's in charge, and what to do. It is within this highly formalized approach that the central role of the public information officer is demonstrated and confirmed. Successful response to an emergency requires the effective involvement and participation of a public information officer in whatever crisis center or headquarters are hastily established. This vital role for public relations is fully recognized in the government planning documents reviewed in Chapter 18.

While placed in the first section of the volume, Chapter 4 also is relevant to the consideration of public relations as an aspect of crisis management in government. By their inherent nature, wars are crisis and emergency times. (However, in many circumstances a wartime mobilization may last several years, as opposed to the days/weeks/months of the more routine kinds of civilian emergencies.) In that context, the work of the Committee on Public Information (CPI) during World War I is another example of government public relations in times of crisis, when the normal 'rules of the game' are suspended due to exceptional circumstances. Indeed, the scope and nature of CPI's work would not be permitted in the regular course of events, only during a wartime emergency.

Chapter 17

Public Relations as Crisis Management

Mordecai Lee

Contents

Overview

In many respects, strategies and policies for disaster public relations by government can be separated into two categories, those that came before and those that came after the three seminal mega-disasters that occurred during the first half-decade of the 21st century: 9/11, the 2004 tsunami in south Asia and Hurricane Katrina in 2005. While 9/11 was, of course, a matter of homeland security, it should also be considered a disaster and, therefore, is applicable to this discussion as well. These three cataclysmic events not only have greatly influenced how practitioners and faculty view public administration in general, but also have significant bearing on their implications for external communications in a crisis.

Parallel to the before and after perspectives on crisis communications as a result of those three disasters, there has also been a great divide in communications technologies, the two sides of the divide being pre- and post-digital technology. Roughly, the decade between 1995 and 2005 (overlapping with these three global disasters) reflected a transformation in government-to-citizen

275

(G2C) communications, including the emergence of the Internet, handhelds, laptops, Wi-Fi, cell phones and so many other new forms of instant communications. However, for all that these three über-disasters and technological developments have transformed our view of crisis communications, the advice from practitioners and specialists about government public relations during a disaster has remained remarkably stable. This suggests that the normative and applied literature, seeking to give guidance to practitioners, has provided real world principles and guidelines that are not only tried-and-true, but also on the mark irrespective of the march of time or the evolution of technology.

Disaster Communications vs. Normal Communications: What's Different?

Crisis management is more than hurry-up public administration. Rather it is a condition when many of the regular rules of operation no longer apply. Therefore, while some of the literature about normal government public relations may be helpful and relevant, [1] there is much about a crisis that involves exceptional circumstances and, therefore, exceptional actions. Conventional expectations disappear at times of crisis. External relations during a crisis is fundamentally different from other, more routine, time frames. [2] Furthermore, successful communications is indispensable to resolving the substantive impacts of the disaster itself. According to Garnett's review of the international literature, "effective crisis communication is crucial to handling crises successfully." [3]

There are two key factors that differentiate crisis communications from normal public relations in the public sector. First, public relations programs by government agencies (or other organizations, for that matter) cover a panoply of activities, audiences and forms of communication. [4] However, in times of crisis, all these forms of external communication are compressed to a single medium: instant communication, such as news media relations and other instantaneous means of communications that were previously nontraditional, such as websites, official blogs and emails. There is no time to prepare magazine articles, publish brochures, send pamphlets through the mail, conduct briefings for neighborhood groups, maintain a lecture bureau or write reports. Therefore, in a time of crisis the public manager and the entire staff of the agency need to change mentality to *instant information only*. In other words, dealing with the news media (along with digital channels of communication) is the only useful and usable outlet. Media relations becomes the only game in town. It is the sole medium for transmitting information. The media rely heavily on official and governmental sources for their ongoing coverage. [5]

Second, at the beginning of an emergency, external communication is sometimes the only or fastest way to communicate *internally*, whether within an organization or throughout a network of agencies. At those moments, external communication is functioning as an exoskeleton of public administration, replacing the traditional internal flow of information that is not in the public realm. According to Radvanovsky, one of the key roles of the public information officer during a crisis includes communicating to an internal audience. [6] Crisis managers should not hesitate to use the news media to convey important information to colleagues, allies and team members. [7] In sum, at the peak of a disaster, it is accurate to state that crisis communications *is* public administration. It cannot be considered secondary to other activities or as an ancillary project. Rather, it is so integral to disaster management that it, at times, becomes the essence of coping with a crisis.

These highly unusual aspects of governmental external communications in a crisis jibe well with the crisis mentality of the news media itself. Given the emergency, reporters have an insatiable desire for information. This is, of course, radically different from the normal routines of media coverage, when reporters and their editors have little interest in government news, which they (often rightly) consider boring and self-serving. The changed stance of the news media welcomes nearly unlimited amounts of official information and doesn't discriminate between information useful to the victims, aimed at residents in the nearby geographical area, or intended for unaffected news consumers worldwide. They want any information they can get and they want it now. Without in any way viewing a disaster as an opportunity for media manipulation, the public administrator has an ally in the news media. Both sides of the normally adversarial relationship need to (and usually do) set aside their usual inhibitions and self-imposed limitations.

Crisis communications is a prevalent theme regarding the practice of public relations in the private sector. To some degree, that business-oriented perspective can be helpful to public sector practitioners as well. [8–12] Lessons regarding nonprofit sector emergency communications can be helpful, too. [13] A pan-sectoral theme that recurs in the literature generally zeroes in on different aspects of organizational effectiveness at dealing with disaster communications. Reporters are seeking a spokesperson who is well informed, truthful, helpful, volunteers information, willing to act as a fact-finder, and has unlimited access to the highest level of officials in the agency. But the most important element of crisis communications is the Golden Rule.

Golden Rule: One Voice Providing a Niagara of Information

The Golden Rule of disaster public relations is to have a sole spokesperson who releases as much information as soon as possible all the time. [14] The goal is to give the public "accurate, coordinated, timely and easy to understand" information. [15] The focus on releasing a Niagara of information should trump all other considerations, such as whether it makes the agency look good or bad in the short run or whether the timing of the release is convenient or inconvenient. *Get it out, get it all out and get it out as fast as possible.* Then, do it all over again with the latest updated information. Disaster communications is the governmental analog to contemporary cable news networks, with a new rolling deadline every half hour, or even more frequently if the situation calls for it.

The lesson of having a public face for crisis communications during 9/11 paralleled the unlessons of Hurricane Katrina. Only one spokesperson should be designated to release all information and make all official announcements. When New York Mayor Giuliani emerged as the sole spokesperson after 9/11, he was providing updates that related not only to the municipal level of government which he headed. (In New York, city and county governments are merged.) He also became briefly the de facto spokesperson for all other relevant activities of regional, state and federal governments. He was *it* for all major matters. [16] This is not to imply that other officials were not also functioning occasionally as spokespersons as well in the post-9/11 period. But they were subsidiary and supportive of Giuliani's role. The opposite happened in the aftermath of Hurricane Katrina. Within the federal government, there was confusion whether the public affairs staff from the Federal Emergency Management Agency or their (theoretical) superiors from the Departmental public affairs office were in charge. Further, the federal government and Louisiana's state government had their own spokespersons, sometimes releasing contradictory information or directives. This multiple spokesperson approach conveyed not only the appearance of lack of cooperation, but also the reality underlying that perception. It *was* disorganized.

[17] Thus, symbolism is very important in crisis communication (as well as during non-crises) because symbols convey realities, whether intended or not. The goal is to project the image of the 'fearless leader.' [18]

The differences regarding spokespersons during these two disasters were not the only key features regarding success or failure in crisis communications. 9/11 and Katrina also were mirror images of lessons about *what* was being released. New York City Mayor Giuliani tried to convey that he was informing the audience of everything that he knew *at that time*. A few hours later, if he had to amend what he had previously said, there was little complaint about his earlier mistake or, worse, an accusation of deliberately misleading the media and the public. Rather, he said what was known and then restated it when more was known. Conversely, the multiple spokespersons of Katrina seemed at times to be ill informed, misinformed or withholding information. This was a recipe for a communications disaster overlaying a natural disaster, as indeed occurred in the days, weeks and even months in the aftermath of Katrina.

Permanent Principles: Media Savvy, Credibility, Access and Monitoring

A longitudinal study of the literature by and for public sector practitioners regarding crisis communications reveals several fixed principles. [19–24] While society and technology have changed considerably over the years, these principles recur on such a consistent basis that they can be identified as constants of governmental communication. These maxims are media savvy, credibility, access and monitoring.

First, all forms of crisis communications need to be sensitive to the professional and technical needs of the news media. Therefore, the government must "understand the often Byzantine nature of the modern press corps." [25] The fastest way for a government agency to assure that coverage shifts to a negative tone is to be ignorant of the modus operandi and expectations of working reporters. For example, notifications of an upcoming announcement need to be disseminated to everyone. The technical prerequisites for television versus radio coverage are inherently different and both need to be accommodated. Print copies and digital versions of major information releases need to be made available as quickly as possible. Similarly, the physical location of a media center needs to be announced and that site needs to provide the essential prerequisites to allow reporters to do their jobs. Also, this is not the time to try to track down news leaks, to ignore leak-based questions from the media or to say 'no comment.' [26]

Second, all government news during a disaster needs to be credible and trustworthy. [27] The spokesperson "must speak, and be seen to speak, clearly and authoritatively" for the agency. [28] A single attempt to mislead the media (and, by extension, the public), withhold information or deliberately release incorrect information is enough to transform the atmosphere of the room from welcoming to accusatory. Unfortunately, the principle of credibility contradicts the "Goulding rule." Phil Goulding had been the spokesman for the Pentagon during the Vietnam war and other assorted crises. He developed the rule that "first reports are always wrong." [29] The essential accuracy of his rule was still valid at the beginning of the next millennium. In 2000, a conference at the University of Virginia concluded that "a major challenge of covering a critical incident, especially in the first minutes and hours, is to avoid repeating inaccurate or exaggerated reports — an easy policy to state but often a difficult one to follow, given the pressure for speed and the insatiable demand for new details." [30]

Certainly, Goulding's rule can be misperceived as a justification for not releasing information until everything can be fully confirmed. But, that would be a misapplication of his key insight. Rather, during disasters governments should release information about important developments as fast as possible, but with the explicitly stated caveat that the first report was sketchy and that the spokesperson is in the midst of fleshing out, confirming or disproving such initial reports. There is a major difference between telling a partial story because that's all you know and not telling what you know because it hasn't yet been confirmed. Therefore, concluded Graber, "the principle challenge facing public affairs officials during crises is to obtain and release accurate information without causing unwarranted panic or complicating recovery efforts." [31] It's not easy to find the right balance, but nonetheless releasing information should almost always be the path chosen.

Third, whoever becomes the 'face' of the government during a disaster has to be more than 'merely' a mouthpiece or martinet. She or he needs to be present at the highest operational levels of the government's crisis headquarters and must be viewed by the top decision makers as an integral part of the command staff. [32] This obtains two key benefits. First, the spokesperson is well-informed and can provide information to the fullest extent that it is available. Second, the spokesperson can contribute to major policy decisions that are made behind the scenes and at the highest levels. He or she might advise for or against doing something that is being considered because of how that decision might play out once it is in the public realm. Spokespersons tend to be sensitive to certain factors that other decision makers might otherwise not bring into consideration. Savvy public administrators know to keep their communications adviser nearby at all times and in the room when decisions are being made. [33]

Finally, notwithstanding the frenetic pace of disaster management, it is crucial to monitor media reports of one's own announcements. This function was pioneered by Commerce Secretary Herbert Hoover when he was the on-site coordinator of the federal response to the Mississippi River floods in 1927. He instructed his staff back in Washington to monitor newspaper coverage of his work and to wire summaries of those clippings to him. Two or three times a week he would personally review the summaries. [34] By knowing the tone of coverage, Hoover was able to instantly adapt what he was doing and saying in reaction to problems in the federal response that the media was covering. This gave him an instant feedback loop that increased his sensitivity to potential issues he should address. The same principle holds true nearly a century later. Notwithstanding the revolution in communications technology, it is vital that the headquarters continuously monitor what the media covers and *how* it covers those subjects. This helps improve disaster communications for several reasons. For example, the spokesperson may realize that there is an unintentional gap between what was intended to be communicated and what the media is saying. So, perhaps using a different vocabulary, explaining intent and other techniques can then instantly correct such problems.

Conversely, the headquarters staff can learn from media coverage. Journalists become the de facto eyes and ears of the government, essentially an intelligence service of the latest developments. Two much recounted communications failures occurred during Hurricane Katrina in 2005. The head of the federal response team claimed he didn't know for several crucial days that evacuees were being sheltered in New Orleans' Superdome stadium, even though it was being reported on TV. [35] Also, key officials didn't know for 24 hours that the levees had been breached. [36]

It might be a slight misnomer to term this monitoring function as feedback. More correctly, given the fluidity of events during a disaster, it should be considered a feed-forward loop. From that perspective, monitoring helps affect upcoming crisis communications activities and decisions, not just as a documentation of what has already occurred. Feed-forward monitoring is a way to engage in instant mid-course corrections of crisis communication strategies.

Planning and Preparedness

Knowing these ingredients of successful government public relations in a crisis, what needs to be done before that disaster occurs? Is it possible to plan for the unknown? To some, perhaps the very concept of planning for a crisis may appear to be an oxymoron. Yet, time after time, it has been demonstrated that it *is* possible for governments to engage in crisis communications planning. Perhaps the most helpful perspective is an axiom that has been attributed to President Eisenhower, planner of D-Day in World War II: "Plans are useless, but planning is indispensable." [37] That saying captures both the benefits and limits of disaster planning. Yes, some aspects of a crisis cannot be foreseen and, therefore, are unplannable. However, other elements of crisis communication are relatively consistent and recurring, making it useful to have gone through a planning process.

A report on bioterrorism in 2001 emphasized the connection between planning and operational success: "Establishing credibility with the public and with the news media before an event occurs is the best way to avoid inaccurate, panicky, irresponsible reporting when the crisis comes. The process of developing a plan should be conducted as openly as possible and a special effort should be made not only to inform the public and media as a plan takes shape, but also to include media representatives in realistic training exercises." [38] For example, the federal Centers for Disease Control and Prevention were unprepared for the media aspects of the anthrax crisis of 2001. [39] In other words, planning can be a key contributor to having credibility and obtaining media cooperation when disasters eventually occur. It is possible to prepare for media relations in a disaster.

Several practitioner sources have developed checklists and guidelines for the elements that should be considered for inclusion in a crisis communications plan. [40–42] For example, they include the need to involve all possible partners in developing the plan, having the support of the top officials of the agencies involved, engaging in practice and mock simulations to test the operational relevance of the plans, preparing stand-by media centers and designating on a rotating basis a go-team of staffers who are on duty 24 hours a day. These generic templates can be easily adapted to the particularistic needs of government agencies at different levels of government and with different areas of responsibility. Also, just as emergency service and first responder departments often sign mutual aid agreements with their nearby counterparts, so public information offices can develop emergency mutual aid agreements with colleagues in other localities. This helps provide an instant method of expanding staff capabilities with supplemental and temporary expertise of other trained and trusted government communications professionals. [43]

In part, disaster communication planning is an activity that is undertaken by information specialists as they try to foresee operational problems that might occur during an unforeseeable crisis. However, it is important that planning not be ghetto-ized to the public information office or to the emergency management office. Senior level officials need to have a basic awareness of such plans and — crucially — agree with them. For example, it is one thing for a crisis communication plan to be disseminated to a newly appointed departmental head. But it is quite another for that new director to explicitly agree, for example, that he or she will not be the spokesperson and face of the agency during a crisis.

This raises the basic issue of generalist public administrators having a core understanding of the role of external communications in government management, whether in times of disaster or not. Training programs in public administration, especially MPA programs, used to include components about public relations, but that subject gradually got squeezed out of the core curriculum. [44] However, in the post-9/11 world, the recognition of the importance of communications training has somewhat increased in public administration and it is slowly being re-established as an important competency that should be part of an overall training program. Raphael and Nesbary focused on the crisis communications aspects of the 2003 fatal explosion of the space shuttle Columbia as a demonstration of the importance of restoring communications to the standard public administration curriculum. [45] Government's reaction to disasters will undoubtedly improve when senior agency officials have the background and training in communications to understand what needs to be done at a time of crisis.

Disaster communications planning does not need to be limited to in-house activities. The public-at-large can be involved as well. For example, helpful planning and stand-by information can be widely disseminated so that individuals can feel that they are prepared and well-informed. Techniques can include, for example, refrigerator magnets with URLs and hotlines to use in times of emergency, checklists of items to have on hand in family disaster kits, and lists of important information that should be duplicated and stored off-site for use by family members if separated. For example, in 2004, the Sunday issue of a widely circulated daily newspaper in Wisconsin included an insert entitled "Public Health Emergencies: Your Preparedness Guide." [46] The ten-page booklet contained helpful information for citizens to be prepared for a disaster and what to do when a disaster occurs.

Finally, Garnett and Kouzmin identify another important stage in disaster communications, namely the learning and feedback phase. [47] This can sometimes be dismissed as an activity that is mostly part of the 'blame game' that politicians love to engage in [48] or that academics are attracted to, often analyzing post hoc events in terms that are largely irrelevant to the real world of the practitioner. While both these concerns have some validity, it is important for the disaster communications planner to understand that the learning and feedback phase is an integral part of the planning process. In fact, the learning and feedback phase needs to be conceived as the first step in the planning process. Only by learning from past mistakes can future plans improve on previous organizational behaviors and increase the effectiveness of disaster communications.

The Future of Crisis Communications: Focusing on Reaching the Public

The preoccupation with communicating through the news media during disasters is both understandable and worthwhile. However, it is important to remember that it is possible to reach the public-at-large through the intermediary of the mass media *and* directly. [49] For example, as we approach the beginning of the second decade of the 21st century, a large percentage of the population will have personalized access to the Internet through land-line connections, broadband cable and Wi-Fi. Similarly, access is not only through PCs, but also through cell phones, handhelds, laptops, ThinkPads and all manner of small personal appliances. It is imperative that disaster communications convey information through traditional dissemination means as well as by using the latest technological advances in communications that are in public use. Gradually, greater and greater portions of the audience will not be obtaining information by watching TV. Instead, they'll be getting the same information by watching a live videostreaming of a press conference, accessing emergency websites and receiving email notifications.

Therefore, part of disaster communications needs to attend to this growing audience that is reachable directly. [50] It is absolutely necessary to be sure that press conferences and other in-person events are videostreamed on the Web, that the front of the podium used for announcements lists a URL for further information, that the central emergency information site is immediately and continuously updated with the latest announcements and information, and that all hotlinks to related sites are working properly. As technology improves, the 20th century concept of the news media and of broadcasting might largely atrophy, even become an anachronism. Even the shift from over-the-air broadcasting to cable narrowcasting (such as niche cable channels) may have only been a transitional stage. It could well be that the traditional intermediary role of the news media will significantly decline as society shifts from broadcasting to webcasting as the central means of G2C communication. When the tipping point of that trend eventually occurs, the traditional approach to crisis communication will have been upended. Instead of the primary focus on reaching the public through the news media and a secondary focus on reaching them directly, direct communication with the citizenry will become the main venue for disseminating information, and the indirect method of communication through the news media will become minor, even negligible.

When that revolution occurs, probably by the second quarter of the 21st century, then the principles of crisis communication will continue unaffected, but the methods and technologies for implementing those principles will be vastly different.

Note: *Originally published in Lee, M., Media relations and external communications during a disaster, in* Disaster Management Handbook, *Pinkowski, J., Ed., Taylor & Francis, Boca Raton, FL, 2008.*

Endnotes

1. Lee, M., Globalization and media coverage of public administration, in *Handbook of Globalization, Governance, and Public Administration*, Farazmand, A. and Pinkowski, J., Eds., Taylor & Francis, Boca Raton, FL, 2006, chap. 8. (*Editor's Note:* See Chapter 24.)
2. For example, during a lingering disaster, there is a temptation to view it as a gradual resumption of normalcy. This understandable inclination needs to be avoided. For a case study of a lingering crisis, see DeVries, D.S. and Fitzpatrick, K.R., Defining the characteristics of a lingering crisis: Lessons from the National Zoo, *Public Relations Review* 32, 160, 2006.
3. Garnett, J.L., Epilog: Directions and agendas for administrative communication, in *Handbook of Administrative Communication*, Garnett, J.L. and Kouzmin, A., Eds., Marcel Dekker, New York, 1997, chap. 33, 759.
4. Lee, M., Public information in government organizations: A review and curriculum outline of external relations in public administration, *Public Administration and Management: An Interactive Journal*, 5, 214, 2000. http://www.pamij.com/5_4/5_4_4_pubinfo.pdf (accessed 2007) (*Editor's Note:* See Chapter 1.)
5. Hutcheson, J. et al., U.S. national identify, political elites, and a patriotic press following September 11, *Political Communication*, 21, 46, 2004.
6. Radvanovsky, R., *Critical Infrastructure: Homeland Security and Emergency Preparedness*, Taylor & Francis, Boca Raton, FL, 2006, 105. (*Editor's Note:* See Chapter 18.)
7. For a more general discussion of inter-organizational communications during a crisis, see Garnett, J. and Kouzmin, A., Communicating during crises: From bullhorn to mass media to high technology to organizational networking, in *Essays in Economic Globalization, Transnational Policies and Vulnerability*, Kouzmin, A. and Hayne, A., Eds., IOS Press, Amsterdam, 1999, 194–195.
8. Mitroff, I.M., *Why Some Companies Emerge Stronger and Better from a Crisis: 7 Essential Lessons for Surviving Disaster*, American Management Association, New York, 2005.

9. Arpan, L.M. and Roskos-Ewoldsen, D.R., Stealing thunder: Analysis of the effects of proactive disclosure of crisis information, *Public Relations Review,* 31, 425, 2005.

10. Pinsdorf, M.K., *All Crises Are Global: Managing to Escape Chaos,* Fordham University Press, New York, 2004.

11. Englehardt, K.J., Sallot, L.M., and Springston, J.K., Compassion without blame: Testing the accident decision flow chart with the crash of ValuJet flight 592, *Journal of Public Relations Research,* 16, 127, 2004.

12. Heath, R.L. and Vasquez, G., Eds., *Handbook of Public Relations,* Sage, Thousand Oaks, CA, 2001, chap. 12, 40–43.

13. Thompson, R.L., Contingency and emergency public affairs, in *The Nonprofit Handbook: Management,* 3rd ed., Connors, T.D., Ed., John Wiley, New York, 2001, chap. 13.

14. For a discussion of the work of local government spokespersons during non-crisis periods, see Lee, M., The agency spokesperson: Connecting public administration and the media, *Public Administration Quarterly,* 25, 101, 2001.

15. Radvanovsky, R., op. cit., 75. (*Editor's Note:* See Chapter 18.)

16. Mortlock, M., Hurricanes and learning organization obsolescence, *The Public Manager,* 34(3), 10, 2005.

17. U.S. Government Accountability Office, Preliminary Observations on Hurricane Response, GAO-06-365R, February 1, 2006; and U.S. Department of Homeland Security, Office of Inspector General, A Performance Review of FEMA's Disaster Management Activities in Response to Hurricane Katrina, OIG-06-32, March 2006, 56–62. http://www.dhs.gov/xoig/assets/mgmtrpts/OIG_06-32_Mar06.pdf (accessed 2007)

18. Brown, L., *Your Public Best: The Complete Guide to Making Successful Public Appearances in the Meeting Room, on the Platform, and on TV,* 2nd ed., Newmarket Press, New York, 2002, 165.

19. Three case studies of media relations by government agencies in times of disaster or crisis were published in volume 31 of *Public Relations Review* in 2005: Martin, R.A. and Boynton, L.A., From liftoff to landing: NASA's crisis communications and resulting media coverage following the Challenger and Columbia tragedies, 253; Kaufmann, J., Lost in space: A critique of NASA's crisis communications in the Columbia disaster, 263; Kersten, A. and Sidky, M., Re-aligning rationality: Crisis management and prisoner abuses in Iraq, 471.

20. Berry, S., We have a problem… Call the press!, *PM. Public Management,* 81(4), 4, 1999.

21. Kellar, E.K., Communicating with elected officials, in *Effective Communication: A Local Government Guide,* Wheeler, K.M., Ed., International City/County Management Association, Washington, DC, 1994, 63.

22. Helm, L.M., Meeting the problems of crises; Agnes: The politics of a flood; and Sunshine mine: Handling the media in a disaster, in *Informing the Public: A Public Affairs Handbook,* Helm, L.M. et al., Eds., Longman, New York, 1981, chaps. 22–24.

23. Spitzer, C.E., Information and policy, in *The Voice of Government,* Hiebert, R.E. and Spitzer, C.E., Eds., John Wiley, New York, 1968, chap. 4, 58.

24. Ratzan, S.C. and Meltzer, W., State of the art in crisis communication: Past lessons and principles of practice, in *Global Public Health Communication: Challenges, Perspectives, and Strategies,* Haider, M., Ed., Jones and Bartlett, Sudbury, MA, 2005, chap. 20, 321.

25. Burns, N., Talking to the world about American foreign policy, *Harvard International Journal of Press/Politics,* 1(4), 10, 1996.

26. Craig, M. et al., Crisis communication in public arenas, *Public Relations Review,* 32, 172, 2006.

27. Federal Communicators Network, *Communicators Guide: For Federal, State, Regional, and Local Communicators,* rev. ed., University of Florida IFAS/Extension, Gainesville, FL, 2001, 27.

28. Burns, N., op. cit.

29. Goulding, P.G., *Confirm or Deny: Informing the People on National Security,* Harper & Row, New York, 1970, 103.

30. Critical Incident Analysis Group, University of Virginia Health System, Threats to Symbols of American Democracy: The Media's Changing Role [Part 5], 19. http://www.healthsystem.virginia.edu/internet/ciag/publications/report_threats_to_symbols_c2000.pdf (accessed 2007)

31. Graber, D.A., *The Power of Communication: Managing Information in Public Organizations*, CQ Press, Washington, DC, 2003, 244–245.

32. Radvanovsky, R., op. cit., 104. (*Editor's Note:* See Chapter 18.)

33. Trattner, J.H., Working with the media, in *Learning the Ropes: Insights for Political Appointees*, Abramson, M.A. and Lawrence, P.R., Eds., Rowman & Littlefield, Lanham, MD, 2005, 98.

34. Barry, J.M., *Rising Tide: The Great Mississippi Flood of 1927 and How It Changed America*, Simon & Schuster, New York, 1997, 273, 288-89.

35. Kranish, M., Bush vows probe of 'what went wrong,' *Boston Globe*, September 7, 2005.

36. U.S. Department of Homeland Security, Office of Inspector General, A Performance Review of FEMA's Disaster Management Activities in Response to Hurricane Katrina, OIG-06-32, March 2006, 33. http://www.dhs.gov/xoig/assets/mgmtrpts/OIG_06-32_Mar06.pdf (accessed 2007)

37. Andrews, R., Ed., *The New Penguin Dictionary of Modern Quotations*, Penguin Books, London, 2003, 162.

38. Critical Incident Analysis Group, University of Virginia Health System, Preliminary Report: Public Responsibility and Mass Destruction: The Bioterrorism Threat, 4. http://www.healthsystem.virginia.edu/internet/ciag/publications/report_bioterrorism_threat_c2001.pdf (accessed 2007)

39. Winett, L.B. and Lawrence, R.G., The rest of the story: Public health, the news, and the 2001 anthrax attacks, *Harvard International Journal of Press/Politics*, 10(3), 3, 2005.

40. Federal Communicators Network, op. cit., 26.

41. Bjornlund, L.D., *Media Relations for Local Governments: Communicating for Results*, International City/County Management Association, Washington, DC, 1996, chap. 7.

42. Wise, K., Pre-crisis relationships, in *Global Public Health Communication: Challenges, Perspectives, and Strategies*, Haider, M., Ed., Jones and Bartlett, Sudbury, MA, 2005, chap. 9.

43. Alsop, R., PIO emergency mutual aid, in *Delivering the Message: A Resource Guide for Public Information Officials*, 2nd ed., Krey, D., Ed., California Association of Public Information Officials, Sacramento, CA, 2000, 71.

44. Lee, M., Public relations in public administration: A disappearing act in public administration education, *Public Relations Review* 24, 509, 1998.

45. Raphael, D.M. and Nesbary, D., Getting the message across: Rationale for a strategic communications course in the public administration curriculum, *Journal of Public Affairs Education*, 11, 133, 2005.

46. Division of Public Health, Wisconsin Department of Health and Family Services, *Public Health Emergencies: Your Preparedness Guide*, 2004. http://dhfs.wisconsin.gov/preparedness/pdf_files/PublicHealthGuide.pdf (accessed 2007)

47. Garnett, J. and Kouzmin, A., Communicating during crises, op. cit., 188-89.

48. See, for example, A Failure of Initiative: The Final Report of the Select Bipartisan Committee to Investigate the Preparation for and Response to Hurricane Katrina. http://a257.g.akamaitech.net/7/257/2422/15feb20061230/www.gpoaccess.gov/katrinareport/mainreport.pdf (accessed 2007)

49. Taylor, M. and Perry, D.C., Diffusion of traditional and new media tactics in crisis communication, *Public Relations Review*, 31, 209, 2005.

50. Haider, M. and Aravindakshan, N.P., Content analysis of Anthrax in the media, in *Global Public Health Communication: Challenges, Perspectives, and Strategies*, Haider, M., Ed., Jones and Bartlett, Sudbury, MA, 2005, chap. 24, 403.

Chapter 18

Public Information for Homeland Security and Emergency Preparedness

Robert Radvanovsky

Contents

Public Information Systems

Because public information is critical to domestic incident management, it is imperative to establish Public Information Systems and protocols for communicating timely and accurate information to the public during emergency situations, as well as principles needed to support effective emergency Public Information Systems. [1]

Under the Incident Command System (ICS), the Public Information Officer (PIO) is a member of the command staff. The PIO advises the Incident Command on all public information matters, including media and public inquiries, emergency public information and warnings, rumor monitoring and control, media monitoring, and other functions required to coordinate, clear with proper authorities, and disseminate accurate and timely information related to the incident. The PIO establishes and operates within the parameters established for the Joint Information System (JIS). [2]

Joint Information Systems (JIS)

The JIS provides an organized, integrated, and coordinated mechanism for providing information to the public during an emergency. The JIS includes plans, protocols, and structures used to provide information to the public. It encompasses all public information related to the incident. [3]

Key elements of a JIS include interagency coordination and integration, developing and delivering coordinated messages, and support for decision makers. The PIO, using the JIS, ensures that decision-makers, as well as the general public, are fully informed throughout a domestic incident response. [4]

Joint Information Centers (JIC)

During emergencies, the public may receive information from a variety of sources. Part of the PIO's job is ensuring that the information the public receives is accurate, coordinated, timely, and easy to understand. [5] One way to ensure the coordination of public information is by establishing a Joint Information Center (JIC). The JIC is designed to help emergency responders get accurate, complete, timely, understandable, and appropriate information to the public and to the news media throughout the emergency. [6]

To make sure information is received quickly, a JIC often is established. The JIC helps different jurisdictions and agencies get accurate, complete, timely, understandable, and appropriate information to the public and media during an emergency. Trained specialists, such as PIOs, from all the groups involved can work in the same facility to gather, share, and process information. This approach means that abilities and resources of each responding organization are maximized during what some might consider an often confusing and emotional time, especially during a regional-wide crisis, emergency or situation; the JIC's primary focus is protecting health and safety. [7] Using the JIC as a central location, information can be coordinated and integrated across jurisdictions and agencies, and between all government partners, the private sector, and nongovernmental agencies. The JIC is the physical location where public information staff involved in incident management activities can co-locate to perform critical emergency information, crisis communications, and public affairs functions. The JIC provides the organizational structure for coordinating and disseminating critical information. [8]

Incident Commanders and Multi-agency Coordination Entities are responsible for establishing and overseeing JICs, including processes for coordinating and clearing public communications. With the case of a Unified Command control structure, those contributing to joint public information management do not lose their individual identities or responsibilities. Essentially, each participating group or organization contributes to the overall unified message. [9]

JIC Levels

JICs may be established at various levels of government. When the JIC is activated, the JIC management team, which includes the JIC manager, a PIO, department/agency spokesperson, and outside agency representatives, should be located where it can most effectively share and coordinate information. These position titles may vary slightly from site to site, but the functions of information coordination, production, dissemination, and monitoring and analysis of media coverage and public perceptions should be incorporated into the JIC organization. Internal and external organizational relationships should be depicted with a defined emergency plan. [10]

All JICs must communicate and coordinate with each other on an ongoing basis using established JIS protocols. When multiple JICs are established, information must be coordinated among them to ensure that a consistent message is disseminated to the public. [11]

JICs have several characteristics in common:

- The JIC includes representatives of just about every member type for managing the incident's response. This may include different jurisdictions, other organizations, private organizations, and other nongovernmental organizations.
- Each JIC must have procedures and protocols for communicating and coordinating effectively with other JICs, and with the appropriate components that are representative of the ICS organizational structure.

In most circumstances, a single JIC location is preferable, but the JIS should be flexible enough to accommodate multiple JICs when the circumstances of the incident require larger-scaled responses. [12] The commander is responsible for overall management of the JIC, the timely release of clear and accurate information to the public and media; oversight of the JIC facility and JIC staff; and remains in direct communication with any representative from a public affairs affiliation, ensures coordination with, and among, local, state, tribal, and federal designated representatives at the JIC and other locations, and accommodates JIC administrative support needs. [13]

JIC Organizational Structure

The typical JIC structure is outlined as follows:

Level I:
   JIC
Level II:
   Press Secretary (jurisdiction)
   JIC Liaison (as needed)
Level III:
   Research Team
   Media Team
   Logistics Team [14]

Command Staff

Command comprises the Incident Commander (IC) and Command Staff (CS). Command staff positions are established to assign responsibility for key activities not specifically identified in the General Staff functional elements. These positions may include the PIO, Safety Officer (SO), and the Liaison Officer (LNO), in addition to others, as required and assigned by the IC.

Depending upon the size and type of the incident or event, it may be necessary for the IC to designate personnel to provide information, safety, and liaison services for the entire organization. The ICS command positions are outlined as:

PIO: Serves as the conduit for information to internal and external stakeholders, including the news media or other organization seeking information directly from the incident or event.

SO: Monitors safety conditions and develops measures for assuring the safety of all assigned personnel.

LNO: Serves as the primary contact for supporting departments and agencies assisting at an incident or event. [15]

Command Staff: Public Information Officer

Some of the responsibilities of the PIO include:

- Advising the IC on issues related to information dissemination and news media relations.
- Serving as the primary contact for anyone who wants information about the incident and the response for it.
- Serving both an external audience through the news media and an internal audience, including both incident staff and agency personnel. Coordinating with other public information staff to ensure that confusing or conflicting information is not issued.
- Obtaining information from the Planning Section, since the Planning Section is gathering intelligence and other information pertinent to the incident.
- Obtaining information from the community, the news media, and others, and providing that information to the Planning Section Chief and the IC. [16]

Note: *Excerpted from Radvanovsky, R.,* Critical Infrastructure: Homeland Security and Emergency Preparedness, *Taylor & Francis, Boca Raton, FL, 2006, 74–76, 104–105. Editor's Note: Some text has been moved from endnotes to the body of the chapter.*

Endnotes

1. Federal Emergency Management Agency, An Introduction to the National Incident Management Systems (NIMS) (IS-700), Self-Study Guide (August, 2004). http://www.training.fema.gov/EMI-Web/IS/is700.asp (accessed 2007).
2. Ibid.
3. Ibid.
4. Ibid.
5. Federal Emergency Management Agency, Public Information Training Curriculum: Basic Public Information Officers (G-290).
6. See: http://des.utah.gov/pdf/csepp/fs_Jic.pdf (accessed 2007).
7. See: http://www.dis.anl.gov/ep/riskcomm/piopao/jic_reference.html (accessed 2007).
8. Federal Emergency Management Agency, An Introduction to the National Incident Management Systems (NIMS) (IS-700), Self-Study Guide (August, 2004).
9. Ibid.
10. See: http://www.directives.doe.gov/pdfs/doe/doetext/neword/151/g1511-1v4-4.pdf (accessed 2007).

11. Federal Emergency Management Agency, An Introduction to the National Incident Management Systems (NIMS) (IS-700), Self-Study Guide (August, 2004).

12. Ibid.

13. See: http://www.directives.doe.gov/pdfs/doe/doetext/neword/151/g1511-1v4-4.pdf (accessed 2007).

14. Federal Emergency Management Agency, Public Information Training Curriculum: Basic Public Information Officers (G-290).

15. Federal Emergency Management Agency, Introduction to the Incident Command System for Federal Workers (IS-100), Student Manual (August, 2004). http://www.training.fema.gov/EMIWeb/IS/is100.asp (accessed 2007).

16. Ibid.

APPENDIX VI

Questions for Review and Discussion

1. In what ways is public relations during a crisis different from public relations in normal day-to-day public administration?
2. If you were asked to write a new crisis management plan for the public relations office of a government agency, what are the five most important components of that plan? Why are those particular five points so important?

Additional Reading

Berry, S., We have a problem … Call the press!, *PM. Public Management*, 81(4), 4, 1999.
Gosnell, A.R., Maximizing media coverage, *Fire Engineering*, 153(5), 93, 2000.

Questions for Review and Discussion

Additional Readings

THE EXTERNAL ENVIRONMENT OF GOVERNMENT PUBLIC RELATIONS

Introduction to Section VII

Up to this point, all the readings in this volume have focused on the practical uses of government public relations. It is simply another tool in the toolbox of government managers, just one that is rarely turned to. The preceding chapters have provided details on the application of public relations to accomplish the core missions of a government agency. Following the listing of the basic purposes of external communications described in the first chapter, public relations can be used for purposes of furthering: (1) media relations, (2) public reporting, and (3) responsiveness to the public, followed by four separate and distinct purposes involving outreach activities, namely, (4) increasing the utilization of services and products, (5) public education and public service campaigns, (6) seeking voluntary public compliance with laws and regulations, (7) using the public as the eyes and ears of an agency, and, finally, (8) increasing public support.

The preceding sections have provided details on most of these applications, with readings that focused on seven of the eight purposes. Therefore, the logical question that a reader might have at this point is: If public relations is so helpful to the government manager, why isn't it more widely practiced? The answer is provided in this section. It relates to the final purpose of government public relations, namely of mobilizing citizen support for the agency. This is the most controversial and contentious use of public relations and the reason that government managers shy away from relying too much on public relations. Let's say that an agency does a really good job of media relations, public reporting, increasing its responsiveness to the public and outreach for purposes of public education and for purposes of notifying the citizenry about new programs and laws. As a *result* of these activities, public support for an agency can increase. So, continuing with our example, let's say that the U.S. Forest Service has earned a positive public image as a result of its Smokey the Bear campaign, public utilization of national forests for recreational reasons, and so on. A consequence of these public relations programs — all specifically furthering the mission of the agency — the Forest Service becomes a popular federal agency, with citizens expressing their approval of its activities to members of Congress. Suddenly, the U.S. senator who is critical of the Forest Service feels constrained from criticizing it too overtly, or the members of the House Appropriations Committee are reluctant to cut its budget. Conversely, in this scenario, a politician who would want to be popular with his or her constituents (the way to win re-election) might issue a press release supporting *increasing* the agency's budget. The politician could then bask in popular approval for such a move. In this way, positive public relations has mobilized public support for the Forest Service, making it less susceptible to political oversight and control.

It is this scenario that elected officials fear from an *institutional* perspective. Regardless of party and ideology, legislators and chief executives do not want an agency so popular with the citizenry that they cannot exercise effective control over it. Therefore, to *prevent* these scenarios from occurring, politicians have a generic hostility to agency public relations. No matter that it might be for furthering the core mission of the agency — such as public reporting, responsiveness to the citizenry or outreach — these politicians understand that a consequence of a robust public relations program can lead to popular support for the agency. Elected officials are therefore quick to accuse public administrators of 'wasting' scarce tax dollars by funding a public information program, of trying to propagandize the public, of using public relations for self-serving reasons and trying to manipulate public opinion. That is why many government managers shy away from using public relations for 'legitimate' reasons for fear of triggering a legislative backlash. Better to have peace with politicians than to use public relations to a degree that gives the agency undue attention from politicians.

This logic has seeped deeply into the culture of American public administration. It has led to a reversal of the show business cliché that there's no such thing as bad publicity. In government, it's almost as though there's no such thing as *good* publicity. It wasn't always that way. Much earlier in the development of public administration as a profession, especially in the 1930s and 1940s, some of its leading theorists suggested that one of the *obligations* of the government manager was to mobilize support for his agency. (In those days, all senior public administrators were men.) Even then, this was a radical approach. It suggested that government managers were political players, who had the right to actively seek public support for the programs the agency administered. This kind of thinking was quickly snuffed out by the conservative coalition in Congress, which opposed much of the rise of the administrative state during the presidencies of Franklin D. Roosevelt and Harry S Truman. As a consequence, in the early 1950s, Congress enacted a series of laws that tried to corral, even neuter, the use of public relations by federal agencies. No propaganda, no publicity for purposes of influencing Congress by trying to influence the public and so on. These enactments (and earlier ones) are described in more detail in the first reading in this section (Chapter 19), Kosar's overview of Congressional restrictions on federal public relations.

Besides those prohibition-oriented restrictions presented in Chapter 19, Congress has also imposed another very different legal condition on the operations of federal agencies, that of documentary transparency. Since it was first enacted in 1966, the federal Freedom of Information Act has created a legal expectation that public administration at the federal level will be open to external review. This law is an important component of the environment in which federal agencies conduct their public relations. It means that the sine qua non of public administration in Washington is a basic openness to the public. This is public relations at its most elemental and democratic level. Public *means* public. Yet, the lofty ideals of the Act have the effect of pitting the public against federal agencies in a perpetual adversarial relationship of openness versus professional discretion. In Chapter 20, Piotrowski summarizes the details relating to the federal Freedom of Information

Act, its scope and operational impacts. As an addendum to her chapter, I have included a 2007 report from the U.S. Government Accountability Office (GAO) — an agency of Congress, not the executive branch — with contemporary information on how federal agencies have been implementing the law. It documents the ongoing problems with accomplishing the goals of the law, even so many years after it was first enacted.

Next, besides the antagonism of elected officials, public relations often — oddly — is criticized by the news media. This, of course, is a situation of biting the hand that feeds it. Still, deep in American journalistic culture is the perspective that agency PR staff are hacks and spin-control experts, rather than facilitators of reporting by the media. Recall, for example, the argot used by the media in Chapter 8 to describe public-sector information staffers. While placed in the media relations section of this volume, that chapter is also a good depiction of the touchy relationships that governmental press secretaries have with the media (albeit using the example of public sector PR staff working for elected officials rather than public administrators).

One of the important points in Viteritti's Chapter 21 is that he depicts the news media as an independent player in the environment of agency communications, not just as the partner in media relations. His chapter also identifies other players in an agency's public environment, as well as various methods of communication. While some may be potential friends, all are potential foes. (Note that Chapter 21 covers not just external communications, but internal communications as well.)

Finally, Chapter 22 discusses how the openness that is expected of public sector organizations in a democratic society can sometimes be in conflict with productivity in public administration. Of four distinct categories when such value conflicts occur, as identified by Garnett and Sigler, three relate to public relations. First, public information activities involve the flow of information from the agency to its external environment, largely through the media. This, therefore, is linked to media relations (Section II). Second, external feedback from stakeholders to the agency involves an inward flow of information. In this volume, this aspect of government public relations is presented in Section IV, regarding responsiveness. Third, Garnett and Sigler identify the problems that can occur with external stakeholders communicating with each other *about* the agency. This puts the government manager in a passive stance, rather than as an actor.

In general, the chapter demonstrates that the environment of government public relations is a dynamic one, reflecting the inherent tensions between the expectations of a democratic society (openness) and the imperatives of a professionalized public administration (productivity). Conflict and problems are built into the situation, a permanent phenomenon. This puts public relations at the crucible of such problems, another indication of its importance. This confirms that the practice of government public relations is a tricky one, not for amateurs. (By 'tricky,' I don't mean misleading; rather that it's like a tightrope walk.) One of the purposes of this volume is to help current and future public administrators master this difficult environment.

The overall intent of the readings included in this section is to serve as a counterweight to the previous sections. The goal is to indicate how touchy the subject of government public relations really is. 'Proceed with caution' is the message. However, it would be a misreading of this section to conclude that public relations is so controversial in government that it should not be practiced. Rather, the overall message of this reader is that *notwithstanding* politicians' dislike of aggressive public relations by government agencies, the tools of public relations remain extremely helpful to the government manager. The purposes of media liaison, public reporting, responsiveness, and outreach are important to accomplishing the purposes of the agency and, if done well, have the simultaneous *effect* of improving an agency's public image. Certainly, a government agency can create a public relations program that is designed with the purpose of mobilizing public support.

But, such activities tend to attract especial political hostility. Therefore, increasing the popularity of an agency tends more often to be a consequence of activities intended to promote other — more acceptable — public relations programs.

Chapter 19

Public Information or Propaganda? Congressional Restrictions on Federal Public Relations

Kevin R. Kosar

Contents

Summary

Controversies recently have arisen over certain executive branch agencies' expenditures of appropriated funds on public relations activities, some of which have been characterized as propagandistic. Generally speaking, there are two legal restrictions on agency public relations activities and propaganda. 5 U.S.C. 3107 prohibits the use of appropriated funds to hire publicity experts. Appropriations law "publicity and propaganda" clauses restrict the use of funds for puffery of an agency, purely partisan communications, and covert propaganda. No federal agency monitors federal public relations activities, but a Member or Committee of Congress may ask the Government Accountability Office (GAO) to examine an agency's expenditures on public relations activities with a view to their legality. Any effort to reform current statutory restrictions on agency public relations activities will face three challenges: tracking public relations activities by agencies, defining "propaganda," and enforcing laws against agency use of funds for publicity experts and propaganda.

On January 26, 2005, H.R. 373 was introduced in the House of Representatives. The bill would require a federal agency to notify Congress no later than 30 days after entering into a public relations contract, codify the publicity and propaganda clause and provide penalties for violations of it, and require federal agencies to label their communications as having been paid for with appropriated funds.

On February 2, 2005, S. 266 was introduced in the Senate. The bill would define "publicity and propaganda," codify the types of communications that constitute publicity and propaganda, provide financial penalties for executive agency officials who authorize the use of appropriated funds for publicity and propaganda, empower both the Attorney General and private citizens to bring civil actions against agency officials who authorize the use of appropriated funds for publicity and propaganda, and provide "whistleblower protection" from agency retribution for employees who take actions in support of this law. This report will be updated as events warrant.

Recent Controversies

Recently, a number of promotional and public outreach actions by executive branch agencies have provoked controversy. [1] Some salient examples follow:

- The Department of Education hired Armstrong Williams, a television commentator and syndicated columnist, to promote the No Child Left Behind Act on his television program. [2]
- The Federal Communications Commission (FCC) launched a high profile public relations campaign (DTV — Get It!) to encourage consumers to purchase digital television sets. As part of this effort, former Chairman Michael K. Powell appeared on *Monday Night Football*, and the FCC created a website [http://www.dtv.gov] that promotes digital television (DTV) and includes hyperlinks to the websites of a number of large corporations with significant financial interests in DTV. [3]
- The Division for Human Resources Products and Services of the Office of Personnel Management (OPM) reportedly issued guidelines to OPM staff who were preparing presentations and promotional materials for a conference. Staff were instructed to include a "picture" of President George W. Bush in slide shows and to make the President's presence "prevalent." [4]
- The White House has reportedly expended public funds to create and maintain Barney.gov, a child-friendly website that celebrates the President's Scottish Terriers, Barney and Miss Beazley. The site features photographs and videos of the dogs, along with their biographies and "answers" letters from children. [5]
- As part of a $1 million public education campaign, the Environmental Protection Agency hired a public relations firm to produce a public service announcement (PSA) urging homeowners to help reduce pollution. [6] The PSA, which came in video format, spoofed one

man's effort to reduce pollution by decreasing the quantity of gasoline required to run his automobile. The video told viewers that a home "can cause twice the greenhouse gases of a car," and directed consumers to a webpage, available online at http://www.energystar.gov/, that listed energy-efficient household appliances; it did not provide information on the varying levels of emissions produced by different automobiles. [7]

- In early April 2004, the Internal Revenue Service issued four press releases to remind taxpayers of the looming filing deadline. The press releases also included a policy assertion: "America has a choice: It can continue to grow the economy and create new jobs as the president's policies are doing, or it can raise taxes on American families and small businesses, hurting economic recovery and future job creation." [8]
- The Forest Service hired a public relations firm to produce a brochure which promoted increased logging in the Sierra Nevada forest. [9] The brochure argued that the forest had grown too dense and that tree removal was a tool in the "campaign against catastrophic wildfires" that would be beneficial to the forest and its fauna. The brochure included photographs that purported to show that the forest had become overgrown in the past century. However, the photograph showing low forest density in 1909 was taken after the forest had been logged. [10]
- The Social Security Administration (SSA) has reportedly drawn up a "strategic communications plan" that urges SSA employees to disseminate the message that "Social Security's long-term financing problems are serious and need to be addressed soon" through speeches, public events, and mass media, and by other means. [11]

In other cases, public relations activities have been judged to have been illegal, as the following examples illustrate.

- The Office of National Drug Control Policy produced video news releases (VNRs) that looked like evening news segments and discouraged the use of illegal drugs. These VNRs were distributed to local news stations which, mistakenly, aired them as actual news. GAO reviewed the videos and judged that they violated appropriations laws. [12]
- Home Front Communications, a public relations firm, produced VNRs for the Department of Health and Human Services' (HHS) Centers for Medicare & Medicaid Services (CMMS). A GAO opinion on the VNRs — which contained newscast-like interviews and reports — found them to be a violation of the publicity or propaganda prohibition of the Consolidated Appropriations Resolution of 2003 (P.L. 108-199) and the Anti-Deficiency Act (31 U.S.C. 1341). [13]

Generally, critics have complained that these public relations activities are inappropriate, are a waste of taxpayers' dollars, and constitute a form of propaganda aimed at selling the policies of President George W. Bush. Critics also have complained that federal dollars are being used to influence media coverage. [14] Proponents of these activities argue that there is nothing wrong with agencies educating the public about their programs, activities, and positions on policies. Moreover, proponents argue that utilizing communications techniques and media commonly found in the private sector, such as video news releases, direct mail, and advertisements, makes sense because they are effective communications tools. [15]

In part, the division between these viewpoints is rooted in longstanding competing notions over the nature of federal executive agencies: should agencies be apolitical and semi-autonomous, or should they be politically responsive? Should they serve first the President, Congress, the public, or the law? And, should federal agencies behave cautiously, taking their cues for action from federal law, regulations, and rules, or should they be entrepreneurial and risk-taking like private sector companies? [16]

Legal Restrictions

The diverse activities described above share one basic feature; they involve the expenditure of federal funds on agency communications with the public. Article I, Section 7, clause 7 of the U.S. Constitution requires that "No Money shall be drawn from the Treasury, but in Consequence of Appropriations made by Law." Statutory restrictions on agency communications with the public are limited to one nearly century-old statute and prohibitions in annual appropriations laws. [17]

- ■ 5 U.S.C. 3107 — passed in 1913 — prohibits the use of appropriated funds "to pay a publicity expert unless specifically appropriated for that purpose."
- ■ Annual appropriations laws, such as the 2004 omnibus statute, usually provide a standard prohibition that funds may not be used "for publicity or propaganda purposes within the United States not heretofore authorized by Congress." [18] These restrictions have appeared in appropriations laws for over a half-century, and are little commented on by Congress in the accompanying reports. [19]

It would appear that agency freedom to expend appropriated funds for public relations and propaganda is quite limited. However, this is not the case, for the following two reasons.

1. No federal entity is required to monitor agency compliance with the publicity and propaganda statutes. At present, the federal government has what has been termed "fire alarm oversight" of agency expenditures on communications. [20] Scrutiny typically occurs when a Member of Congress is alerted by the media or some other source that an agency's spending on communications may be cause for concern. A Member then sends a written request to the Government Accountability Office asking for a legal opinion on the activities in question.
2. The terms "publicity," "propaganda," and "publicity expert" have been interpreted to forbid a very limited number of activities. Congress has not defined the terms "publicity," "propaganda," and "publicity expert." Thus, to GAO has gone the task of delineating what these terms encompass. GAO has done this on a case-by-case basis over the past half-century. [21] Generally speaking, GAO has narrowly defined these terms. It has held that the "publicity or propaganda" prohibition in appropriations laws forbids any public relations activity that:

- ■ involves "self-aggrandizement" or "puffery" of the agency, its personnel, or activities;
- ■ is "purely partisan in nature" (i.e., it is "designed to aid a political party or candidate"); or,
- ■ is "covert propaganda" (i.e., the communication does not reveal that government appropriations were expended to produce it). [22]

GAO has interpreted "publicity agent" to mean someone who "extols or advertises" an agency, "an activity quite different from disseminating information to the citizenry about the agency, its policies, practices, and products." [23]

Thus construed, the laws prohibiting the hiring of publicity experts and the expenditure of appropriated funds on publicity and propaganda place very few limits on agency public relations activities. GAO findings of agency wrongdoing have been infrequent. It has said that the public relations and propaganda laws did not forbid, to cite three examples, the hiring of public relations companies or the expenditure of appropriated funds on:

- Promotional materials that did "not present both the negative and positive consequences" of increased logging of forests and that contained inaccuracies that might have deceived the public; [24]
- CMMS brochures that included "several noteworthy omissions [of fact]" and that "overstate[d] the access beneficiaries will have to the prescription drug program"; [25] or
- Office of Personnel Management (OPM) press release denouncing some Members of Congress who desired to delay a civil service policy that OPM favored. [26]

Additionally, GAO's definition of "propaganda" — as government communications that fail to disclose that they are paid for with appropriated funds (i.e., "covert propaganda") — only prohibits executive agencies from attempting to persuade or deceive the public through surreptitious means. It does not prevent executive agencies from propagandizing in obviously public communications. Executive agencies remain free to use appropriated funds to issue communications that are impossible to verify (e.g., "this policy promotes liberty") and engage in activities that attempt to manipulate the emotions of the public (e.g., placing a revered symbol, such as the United States flag, behind a government spokesperson delivering a speech).

The Challenges of Reform

Tracking Expenditures

There is nothing inherently inappropriate in an agency expending appropriated funds to communicate with the public. [27] As one of the Hoover Commission task forces wrote a half-century ago:

> Apart from his responsibility as spokesman, the department head has another obligation in a democracy: to keep the public informed about the activities of his agency. How far to go and what media to use in this effort present touchy issues of personal and administrative integrity. But of the basic obligation [to inform the public] there can be little doubt. [28]

Even government communications which attempt to persuade members of the public to behave differently may not necessarily be inappropriate. For example, few would likely criticize government-sponsored advertising that encourages citizens to wear their seatbelts while driving motor vehicles or urges hikers and campers to avoid inadvertently setting forest fires.

Any effort to curb agency expenditures on allegedly inappropriate communications with the public will face two challenges: (1) tracking government expenditures on communications, and (2) drafting language that distinguishes legitimate agency communications with the public from puffery and propaganda.

At present, the federal government has little knowledge of the extent of agency expenditures on public communications. [29] According to a minority staff report, the federal government awarded over $88 million in public relations contracts in 2004. Of course, this measure of public relations activities captures only those activities that were contracted out — not those done in-house. [30] Agencies' budgets do not line-item list public relations expenditures, and any effort to do so must grapple with the question of what activities and costs are to be included. A seemingly simple and not unusual example illustrates this point:

> An agency employee (GS-12) spends one hour drafting a one-page press release; two other agency employees (one GS-14, one appointee) spend 45 minutes each editing and proofreading the piece. Another employee, a GS-8, is asked to make 200 copies of the press release. These copies are to be handed out to members of the press at a 30-minute press conference, where another agency employee (an appointee) is to issue the release and take questions. The room used for the press conference is prepared by three agency employees (GS-9), who must bring in chairs, set up the podium and sound system, and so forth. The agency's webmaster (GS-12) spends 15 minutes uploading a copy of the press release to the agency's website. After the press conference, two agency employees (GS-11), over the course of a few days, field occasional calls from reporters seeking further information.

All of these diverse activities were part of this single, modest public relations effort. Which ones should be counted? Who is to do the counting? And how are these activities to be tracked?

Defining "Propaganda"

Beyond accounting for public relations activities is the challenge of distinguishing propaganda from appropriate agency communications with any precision. The *Oxford English Dictionary* gives one definition of "propaganda" as "the systematic propagation of information or ideas by an interested party, especially in a tendentious way in order to encourage or instill a particular attitude or response." [31] This definition is quite broad and not especially helpful in the present context, since it captures any coordinated activity aimed at persuading others of the wisdom and veracity of one's ideas and positions, something that is part and parcel of politics and governance. [32]

Some might suggest that agencies should be permitted to convey only factual information. This instruction, though, would not solve the problem. For example, one can mislead another by communicating just facts but not all the facts. An agency spokesperson might announce that thanks to his agency's tireless efforts, public policy problem X has been eradicated. On hearing this, the listener might think highly of the agency and believe it to be effective. However, his opinion might be less sanguine if he were informed that in the pursuit of eradicating this one public policy problem, the agency had grossly exceeded its budget and neglected its statutorily required duty to attend to a dozen other public policy problems. [33]

Furthermore, even the conveyance of pure facts can have persuasive effects on an audience, depending on how the facts are presented. For example, a government official might state, "5,000 persons are killed by lightning each year." On hearing this, a listener might become wary of venturing outside on cloudy days. If, on the other hand, the same government official said, "On average, you have only a one-twentieth of one-percent chance of being killed by lightning this year," the same listener might feel the risk is so small as not to be worth changing his behavior. However, assuming a population of 100 million, both of these statements are true. The facts are the same; the inference drawn is quite different. [34]

Enforcement and the Separation of Powers

The enforcement of restrictions against agency use of funds to employ publicity agents or to produce propaganda faces hurdles rooted in the separate branches of government established by the U.S. Constitution. In great part, the legislative branch makes the law, but the executive branch administers and enforces it.

In this instance, the power to enforce the statutory restriction against the employment of publicity experts rests with the Department of Justice (DOJ), an executive agency. If DOJ does not find fault with an executive agency's actions, Congress has limited tools available to change the behavior of DOJ or the agency in question. (See below for further discussion.)

But what of the enforcement of publicity and propaganda restrictions in appropriations laws? In March 2005, the DOJ and the Office of Management and Budget (OMB) issued memoranda that stated that executive branch agencies need not heed GAO's interpretations of appropriations law. [35] The DOJ and the OMB memoranda were issued in response to a GAO memorandum circulated to executive branch departments and agencies providing guidance on the use of VNRs for publicity purposes. [36] The OMB memorandum agrees that executive agencies must comply with applicable laws; however, it states, it is the "OLC [Office of Legislative Counsel] ... not the GAO, that provides the controlling interpretations of the law for the Executive Branch." [37] Those in the executive branch with questions about the interpretation of appropriations laws are directed to contact the general counsel of their respective departments or agencies.

The DOJ memorandum takes the same position. "Because GAO is part of the Legislative Branch, Executive Branch agencies are not bound by GAO's legal advice." The DOJ memorandum also contests GAO's interpretation of what constitutes propaganda. DOJ argues, against GAO, that it is not enough for an executive branch communication to be covert as to the source. It also must contain advocacy of a particular viewpoint. DOJ states that government communications that are "purely informational" — even if they do not inform the audience that they are government-produced — are not propaganda and, hence, are "legitimate." [38] DOJ then states that agencies "are responsible for reviewing their VNRs to ensure that they do not cross the line between legitimate governmental information and improper government-funded advocacy." [39]

Thus, the enforcement of restrictions on executive agency spending on publicity experts and propaganda encounters a separation of powers impediment. Congress, however, does possess tools to compel changes in agency behavior. Congress may threaten to reduce an agency's appropriation or powers in order to encourage an agency to follow congressional interpretation of the law. Alternatively, Congress may pass new legislation that more sharply delineates its definition of legal and illegal activities — an effort, as noted above, not without its own challenges — which, then, would increase the probability that executive agencies — and DOJ, especially — would agree with Congress's interpretation of the law. [40]

Recent Legislation

On January 26, 2005, H.R. 373 was introduced in the House of Representatives. The bill would make four major changes to present law. It would:

■ Require a federal agency to notify the House Committee on Government Reform, the Senate Committee on Homeland Security and Governmental Affairs, and the Appropriations Committees of both the House and the Senate no later than 30 days after entering into a contract for public relations activities (Section 3[a]);

■ Codify the publicity and propaganda clause so that "[a]n officer or employee of the United States Government may not make or authorize an expenditure or obligation of funds for publicity or propaganda purposes within the United States unless authorized by law" (Section 4[a]);

■ Provide penalties for violations of the publicity and propaganda clause by an officer or employee of the government (Section 4[b][1]-[2]); and

■ Require federal agencies to label their communications as having been paid for with funds from the respective agencies (Section 5[a]).

H.R. 373 was referred to the House Committee on Government Reform.

On February 2, 2005, a second bill was introduced. S. 266 would:

■ Codify the types of communications that constitute "publicity and propaganda" (Section 3);

■ Provide financial penalties for executive agency officials who authorize the use of appropriated funds for publicity and propaganda (Section 4[a]);

■ Require the Attorney General to investigate "diligently" the use of appropriated funds for publicity and propaganda (Section 4[b]);

■ Permit both the Attorney General and private citizens to bring civil actions against agency officials found to have violated the law;

■ Allow private citizens to collect financial damages against executive agency officials found guilty of appropriating funds for publicity and propaganda (Section 4[e][1]); and

■ Provide "whistleblower protection" from agency retribution for employees who take actions in support of this law (Section 4[h]).

S. 266 was referred to the Senate Committee on the Judiciary.

In the 108th Congress, S. 2416 was introduced in the Senate on May 13, 2004; its companion bill, H.R. 4639, was introduced in the House on June 22, 2004. Both bills would have required GAO to review any advertisement costing more than $10 million. Agencies would not have been allowed to expend appropriated funds on advertisements deemed false, deceptive, or political. Both pieces of legislation expired at the end of the 108th Congress.

Note: *Originally published in Kosar, K.R., Public Relations and Propaganda: Restrictions on Executive Agency Activities, CRS Report for Congress RL32750, Congressional Research Service, Library of Congress, Washington, DC, 2005.*

Endnotes

1. Of course, the current administration is not the only one that has engaged in public relations activities that provoke criticism. For example, the Department of Health and Human Services during the Presidency of William J. Clinton produced video news releases (VNRs) to promote its Medicare reform proposal. Indeed, government public relations activities have raised concerns for at least a century. See, respectively, Kosar, K.R., Medicare Advertising: Current Controversies, CRS Report RS21811; McCamy, J.L., *Government Publicity: Its Practice in Federal Administration,* University of Chicago Press, Chicago, 1939.

2. The Department of Education (ED) contracted with Ketchum Communications, which then subcontracted with a public relations firm co-owned by Williams. The subcontract specified the promotional activities Williams was to provide, and ED signed this contract (Davis, M.R., Department's PR activities scrutinized, *Education Week,* January 19, 2005, 1). The Department of Health and Human Services paid columnist Maggie Gallagher to write brochures on the benefits of marriage, to ghostwrite an essay — for publication in a magazine — for an HHS assistant director, and to produce a training presentation on the benefits of marriage. Reportedly, while under contract, she promoted the Bush Administration's marriage initiative in some of her columns (Kurtz, H., Writer backing Bush plan had gotten federal contract, *Washington Post,* January 26, 2005, C1).

3. Squeo, A.M., FCC tries to sell consumers on digital TVs, *Wall Street Journal,* October 5, 2004, D10.

4. As quoted in Kamen, A., The electric slide: OPM style, *Washington Post,* September 10, 2004, A27.

5. Froomkin, D., White House launches Barney.gov, WashingtonPost.com, May 14, 2004.

6. U.S. Environmental Protection Agency, Five-step energy star campaign can save energy, money, environment, press release, June 16, 2004; Not a laughing matter: The new EPA TV ad is neither funny nor effective (editorial), *Miami Herald,* July 2, 2004, A18.

7. The difference between vehicles can be dramatic: the 2005 Ford Explorer SUV releases 11.5 tons of "greenhouse gas emissions" each year; the 2005 Toyota Prius, just 3.5 tons. Automobile emission rates can be found at http://www.fueleconomy.gov (accessed 2007).

8. Aversa, J., Treasury news releases on taxes attacked, Associated Press, April 9, 2004. Critics were especially incensed because these same words were reportedly found on a fact sheet issued two days earlier by the Republican National Committee (Kamen, A., A week too late, *Washington Post*, April 26, 2004, A21).

9. OneWorld Communications also created a video, which generated less controversy.

10. U.S. Government Accountability Office, Forest Service — Sierra Nevada Forest Plan Amendment Brochure and Video Materials, B-302992, September 10, 2004.

11. Pear, R., Social Security is enlisted to push its own revision, *New York Times,* January 16, 2005.

12. U.S. Government Accountability Office, Office of National Drug Control Policy — Video News Release, B-303495, January 4, 2005.

13. HHS contracted with Ketchum, Inc., which hired Home Front Communications. The VNRs were then distributed by CMMS (Kosar, K.R., Medicare Advertising: Current Controversies, CRS Report RS21811).

14. Some argue that reporters, columnists, and editors and government employees should maintain a professional distance from one another. Historically, though, this has not always occurred. See, for example, Stacks, J.F., *Scotty: James B. Reston and the Rise and Fall of American Journalism,* Little Brown, Boston, 2002.

15. A Department of Education (ED) spokeswoman, Susan Aspey, said the congressional request for a GAO examination of VNRs produced for ED was just "politics and an attempt to distract attention from President Bush's great record on improving education" (Feller, B., Two Democrats request probe of spending as propaganda, Associated Press, October 14, 2004). On government advertising and its controversial aspects, see Kosar, K.R., Government Advertising Expenditures: An Overview, CRS Report RS21746.

16. See, for example, Fisher, L., *The Politics of Shared Power: Congress and the Executive*, 4th ed., Texas A&M University Press, College Station, 1998, chap. 4; West, W.F. and Cooper, J., Legislative influence v. presidential dominance: Competing models of bureaucratic control, *Political Science Quarterly*, 104, 581, 1989-90; Moe, R.C., The importance of public law: New and old paradigms of governmental management, in *Handbook of Public Law and Management*, Cooper, P.J. and Newland, C.A., Eds., Jossey-Bass, San Francisco, 1997, chap. 3.

17. Two addenda are warranted. First, the Hatch Act prohibits employees from engaging in partisan campaign activity on federal property on official duty time (Maskell, J., "Hatch Act" and Other Restrictions in Federal Law on Political Activities of Government Employees, CRS Report 98-885). Second, the Anti-Deficiency Act (31 U.S.C. §1341[a]) also limits these activities, but only as a consequence of violating the publicity and propaganda restrictions — which forbid expenditures that exceed available budget authority (Brass, C.T., Coordinator, General Management Laws: A Compendium, CRS Report RL30795, 93-97).

18. P.L. 108-447, Div. H, Sec. 624. Note also that these restrictions apply only to agency communications directed at a U.S. audience. Thus, for example, the Department of State may legally publish and distribute *Hi*, a glossy magazine aimed at improving the image of the United States in Middle Eastern states.

19. For example, House Report 108-671 on the 2005 appropriation for the Departments of Transportation and Treasury and Independent Agencies (P.L. 108-447, Div. H, Sec. 624) states, "Section 624. The Committee continues the provision prohibiting the use of funds for propaganda and publicity purposes not authorized by Congress."

20. McCubbins, M.D. and Schwartz, T., Congressional oversight overlooked: Police patrols versus fire alarms, *American Journal of Political Science*, 28, 165, 1984.

21. For a dated, but useful, introduction to this topic, see U.S. General Accounting Office, Principles of Federal Appropriations Law, Volume 1, GAO/OGC-91-5, 1991, 4-161–4-166.

22. See U.S. General Accounting Office, Decision of the Comptroller General, B-223098, October 10, 1986, 8-9; GAO, Application of Anti-Lobbying Laws to the Office of National Drug Control Policy's Open Letter to State Level Prosecutors, B-301022, March 10, 2004.

23. U.S. Government Accountability Office, Forest Service, B-302992, 12. Apparently, only once has GAO judged that an agency illegally hired a publicity expert (GAO, Principles of Federal Appropriations Law, Volume 1, 4-191–4-192).

24. U.S. Government Accountability Office, Forest Service, B-302992, 13.

25. U.S. Government Accountability Office, Medicare Prescription Drug, Improvement, and Modernization Act of 2003 — Use of Appropriated Funds for Flyer and Print and Television Advertisements, B-302504, March 10, 2004. For more information on the Medicare advertising controversies, see Kosar, K.R., Medicare Advertising: Current Controversies, CRS Report RS21811.

26. U.S. Government Accountability Office, Principles of Federal Appropriations Law, 4-167.

27. Indeed, the federal courts have "indicated that it is not illegal for government agencies to spend money advocating their positions, even on controversial issues" (ibid, 4-163).

28. The Commission on Organization of the Executive Branch of the Government, Report of the Task Force on Departmental Management: Prepared for the Commission on Organization of the Executive Branch of the Government, Government Printing Office, Washington, DC, 1949, Appendix E, 57.

29. A rough estimate of government expenditures on advertising, a subset of public relations and communications, puts annual spending at over $1 billion (Kosar, K.R., Government Advertising Expenditures: An Overview, CRS Report RS21746).

30. Moreover, the methodology used by the authors of this report involved searching for contracts in the Federal Procurement Data System (FPDS), which contains only records of those contracts of $25,000 or more (U.S. Congress, House, Committee on Government Reform, Minority Staff, Federal Public Relations Spending, 2005 [http://www.democrats.reform.house.gov/Documents/20050126124833-88792.pdf, accessed 2007]). On FPDS, see Riehl, J.R., Federal Funds: Tracking Their Geographic Distribution, CRS Report 98-79.

31. *Oxford English Dictionary* online.
32. And persuasion has been institutionalized; nearly all federal agencies along with Members of Congress and the President have public relations offices or employees who issue communications that provide, usually, positive reports on their activities.
33. The spokesperson also might have deceived the listener by defining the public policy problem differently.
34. These are not the only forms of deception by conveyance of facts (Stone, D., *Policy Paradox: The Art of Political Decisionmaking,* W.W. Norton, New York, 2001).
35. Bradbury, S.G., Principal Deputy Assistant Attorney General, Memorandum for the General Counsels of the Executive Branch, Re: Whether Appropriations May Be Used for Informational Video News Releases, March 1, 2005; Bolten, J., Director, Office of Management and Budget, Memorandum for Heads of Departments and Agencies, Use of Government Funds for Video News Releases, M-05-10, March 11, 2005.
36. Walker, D.W., Comptroller General, Memorandum for Heads of Departments, Agencies, and Others Concerned, Re: Prepackaged News Stories, B-304272, February 17, 2005.
37. Bolten, Use of Government Funds for Video News Releases, 1.
38. In its own opinion on the controversial Medicare VNRs, DOJ found "[t]he VNRs ... did not advocate a particular policy or position of HHS and CMS, but rather provided accurate (even if not comprehensive) information about the benefits provided under" the new Medicare program (Bradbury, S.G., Principal Deputy Assistant Attorney General, Office of Legal Counsel, Memorandum for Alex M. Azar II, General Counsel, Department of Health and Human Services, Re: Whether Appropriations May Be Used for Informational Video News Releases, July 30, 2004). *Nota bene:* The DOJ memorandum of March 1, 2005, refers to the DOJ memorandum of July 30, 2004, by the title Re: Whether Appropriations May Be Used for Informational Video News Releases, which is identical to the title of the March 11, 2005, memorandum. However, the memorandum of July 30, 2004 — as found on the DOJ website at http://www.usdoj.gov/olc/opfinal.htm [accessed 2007] — carries the title Expenditure of Appropriated Funds for Informational Video News Releases.
39. Bradbury, S.G., Re: Whether Appropriations May Be Used for Informational Video News Releases, March 11, 2005, 1–2.
40. These clarifications of the law might also be included in appropriations reports. On the tools of oversight, see Fisher, L., *The Politics of Shared Power: Congress and the Executive,* 4th ed., Texas A&M University Press, College Station, 1998, 68–105.

Chapter 20

Freedom of Information: A Duty of Public Agencies

Suzanne J. Piotrowski

Contents

Introduction

The Freedom of Information Act (FOIA) is the premier open government statute in the U.S. federal government. FOIA works to ensure a more transparent federal administration. The openness afforded by FOIA has become a central aspect of federal administration. After a long debate, FOIA was passed by Congress in 1966 and has been amended periodically. FOIA allows individuals or organizations to request documents from a federal agency. While not all documents are releasable, many are. Federal agencies may withhold documents that fall into nine broad exemption categories. Included within this chapter is an overview of the theoretical underpinnings of the act, a legislative history of FOIA, and a short description of the major provisions of the act.

What is FOIA?

The FOIA is one federal law that deals with open government. Other open government federal laws include the Privacy Act (1974), the Government in the Sunshine Act (1976), and the Federal Advisory Committee Act (1972). Implementation of FOIA is a major administrative function which cost over $270 million in fiscal year 2001. Open government laws are not unique to the federal government. All 50 states have laws governing the release of government documents. Freedom of information and the free exchange of information is a global concern. Over 50 countries ranging from Albania to Zimbabwe have laws facilitating access to government documents. Over half of these international freedom of information laws were passed within the last ten years. [1]

Governmental transparency and democratic accountability are the underlying tenets behind FOIA. Governmental transparency refers to the ability to find out what is going on inside of government. Democratic accountability is holding elected and unelected government officials responsible for their actions. While the initial FOIA was passed in 1966, [2] the debate surrounding transparency in government long predates the act. James Madison wrote in a personal correspondence:

> A popular Government, without popular information, or the means of acquiring it, is but a Prologue to a Farce or a Tragedy; or, perhaps, both. Knowledge will forever govern ignorance: And a people who mean to be their own Governors must arm themselves with the power which knowledge gives. [3]

Madison's sentiments were included in the *Senate Report*, which accompanied the initial FOIA. [4]

The idea of opening up the government and holding officials accountable is an essential aspect of democracy. Francis Rourke made this point eloquently: "Nothing could be more axiomatic for a democracy than the principle of exposing the processes of government to relentless public criticism and scrutiny." [5] Policies which work toward a more transparent government combat administrative and executive secrecy. As explained later in the section "How Does FOIA Work?" not all types of documents are releasable through FOIA requests; however, at its core, FOIA is a disclosure statute.

FOIA also has two other provisions. The first requires agencies to disclose information automatically by publishing it in the *Federal Register*. Information that must be disclosed includes descriptions of agency organizations, functions, and procedures; substantive agency rules; and statements of general agency policy. The second requirement is the reading room provision of FOIA. Final agency opinions and orders rendered in the adjudication of cases, specific policy statements, certain administrative staff manuals, and some records previously processed for disclosure must be made available in agency reading rooms. Some of these disclosed documents must also be posted in an agency's electronic reading room. Failure to disclose some types of information precludes agencies from enforcing or relying on them.

Legislative History

Varying proposed pieces of freedom of information legislation were prepared and debated in Congress for over a decade before the final bill was passed. An early advocate of freedom of information laws, Senator Thomas C. Hennings, Jr. (D-MO), referring to a proposed freedom of information legislation, noted that "The aim ... of this bill ... is to make it clear beyond any doubt that the basic purpose of this section is to ensure the dissemination of the maximum amount of information reasonably possible." [6] FOIA, which amended the Administrative Procedure Act of 1946, was passed on July 4, 1966 and went into affect in 1967.

Since the initial law was passed, a series of amendments have modified the statute. Some changes strengthened the statute while others weakened the reach of the law with regard to access to government. The first series of major amendments came in 1974 in the wake of the presidential Watergate scandal. These amendments significantly strengthen the reach of FOIA disclosures. A little more than a decade later in 1986, another series of amendments were passed by Congress during the Reagan administration. These changes weakened access to government afforded through FOIA by expanding the exemption for law-enforcement documents.

The last major set of amendments came in 1996 and are referred to, collectively, as the Electronic Freedom of Information Act or E-FOIA. These amendments brought FOIA into the Internet age. Electronic documents are now accessible through FOIA requests, and agencies are obligated to proactively post their most frequently requested documents in their electronic reading rooms. In 2002, the Homeland Security Act was passed which also included an amendment to FOIA. Senator Patrick Leahy (D-VT) called this amendment the "most severe weakening of the Freedom of Information Act in its 36-year history." [7] The Homeland Security Act amendment exempts all information deemed related to homeland security which corporations voluntarily disclose to the Department of Homeland Security. This is a very broad exemption that ensures the department will keep the disclosed information secret and allows companies to be free of potential civil liability and antitrust lawsuits if the information indicates wrongdoing.

How Does FOIA Work?

Essentially, FOIA is a disclosure statute. All agency records are accessible to the public unless specifically exempt from disclosure. Documents, not information, are requested and released under FOIA. This is a meaningful distinction. One cannot request the federal government to make a report or compile and summarize information. Under FOIA, one can only request preexisting agency records. There is no clear definition of what is an agency record. Typically, documents must be in control of the agency from which they are requested. After the 1996 E-FOIA amendment, electronic files may be requested and will be released in electronic form. Prior to the 1996 amendments, databases released to requesters would usually have been printed and sent in hard-copy form. Currently, requesters may receive data sets electronically in the electronic format of their choosing. Generally, emails are considered agency records although the line between agency and personal records is at times blurred. For a comprehensive discussion of relevant case law, see *Litigation Under the Federal Open Government Laws 2002: Covering the Freedom of Information Act, the Privacy Act, and the Government in the Sunshine Act, and the Federal Advisory Committee Act.* [8]

Virtually, anyone can make a FOIA request including U.S. citizens, foreign citizens, corporations, and governments. FOIA is a disclosure statute, meaning it opens up documents in the federal government for release. With that said, there are nine exemptions written into FOIA:

1. National security information
2. Internal agency rules
3. Information exempted by other statutes
4. Business information

5. Inter- and intra-agency memoranda
6. Personal privacy
7. Law-enforcement records
8. Records of financial institutions
9. Oil well data

Most of these exemptions are discretionary; that is, if a document falls under one of the exemption categories, then the federal agency has the option whether to release the document or not. However, the first exemption is not discretionary. Documents that have been classified for national defense or foreign policy are not releasable. Documents that are properly classified are not appropriate for a discretionary disclosure. The second exemption refers to documents which relate to internal personnel rules and practices. Documents falling under exemption #2 may be discretionarily disclosed. The third exemption is one of the broadest. If documents are exempt from disclosure through another statute, then they are also exempt under FOIA and cannot be discretionarily disclosed. Examples of statutes that exempt the release of material include the Department of Homeland Security Act, the Immigration and Naturalization Act, the Federal Aviation Act of 1958, and the Ethics in Government Act.

Trade secrets and business information are exempt from release through FOIA by the fourth exemption and rarely are discretionarily disclosed. At times, corporations or businesses seek to prevent the release of information gathered by an agency to a third party. These challenges are referred to as "reverse" FOIA litigation. Documents such as inter- or intra-agency memos regarding pre-decisional policy formation are covered under exemption #5. Documents falling under exemption #5 may be discretionarily disclosed. Individuals' personnel or medical files are not releasable because of the privacy exemption, #6, and generally not deemed appropriate for discretionary disclosures. The law-enforcement provisions, which were strengthened by the 1986 amendment, are covered under exemption #7. Records dealing with financial institutions and oil wells are covered by exemptions #8 and #9, respectively. Documents falling under exemptions #7 through #9 may be discretionarily disclosed.

To make a FOIA request, one must send a written request to the individual agency you would like to release the documents. This can be carried out either by the mail or, increasingly, by fax or email. It is essential that you write to the correct agency and you are as specific as possible about your request. There is a wealth of good references on how to write a FOIA request. The U.S. House of Representative Committee on Government Reforms published *A Citizen's Guide to Using the Freedom of Information Act and the Privacy Act of 1974 to Request Government Records*. [9] A summary of the steps a FOIA office takes to fill a request is presented in Figure 20.1.

However, not all requests are filled. If a request is denied, either in full or in part, the requester has the right to appeal. Frequently, appeals are settled informally by the agency and never make their way to court. Judicial remedy is the last recourse, however.

By law, agencies are required to make a determination on a FOIA request within 20 working days. Agencies are also required to make a determination on administrative appeals within 20 working days of receipt of the appeal. Many agencies do not meet these requirements and some have construed the 20 days as the time frame within which the request needs to be acknowledged. This was not the intent of the law. Agencies frequently do not meet the statutorily prescribed time lines and subsequently have large backlogs of unfulfilled requests. Some agencies have requests that are years old. The 1996 E-FOIA amendments attempted to address this issue by setting up a multi-track processing system. Instead of a first-come first-served basis, they now have a system where simple requests are filled within the order they are received and complex requests are put into a different queue.

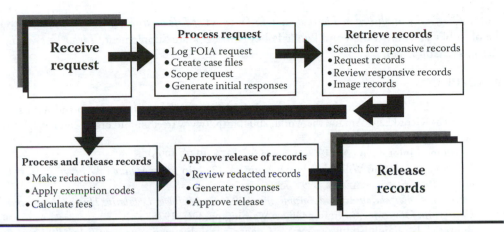

Figure 20.1   Overview of Generic FOIA Process. (U.S. General Accounting Office [2002]. Information Management: Update on Implementation of the Information Act Amendments [GAO-02-493]. Washington, DC: U.S. General Accounting Office, p. 5.)

Agencies can charge requesters for the direct costs associated with searching for documents, the direct costs associated with reviewing documents to determine which portions are releasable, and the duplication costs. Depending on the category of requester, all, some, or none of these fees may be charged. Review, search, and copy charges are set by the Office of Management and Budget (OMB). Certain categories of requesters can apply and receive fee waivers. Individuals or organizations that fall under the category of public interest groups, representatives of the news media, or educational or noncommercial scientific organizations may receive these waivers. Fee waivers are also granted to any requester who can show that the disclosure of the information is in the public interest and will likely contribute to public understanding of governmental operations and activities.

Conclusion

Implementation of the FOIA is a complex process. Inherent in this process are multiple tensions. The first tension is between efficiency and transparency. FOIA is expensive and FOIA offices are periodically under-funded. FOIA functions are not associated with the missions of most federal agencies. When budgets are tight, it is essential to continue funding non-mission-based functions such as FOIA. [10] Budgetary constraints are a major impediment to FOIA implementation. Statutorily, FOIA requests must be filled and lack of funding does not absolve this responsibility. Most agencies have significant backlogs of unfilled requests and requests may take years to be filled. Requesters have little recourse for delayed filling of requests other than litigation.

The tension between privacy and transparency is perennial. Privacy advocates consistently want to decrease the amount of information that can be released with regard to personal privacy, while other groups of people, such as journalists, may push for greater release of personal information. Other areas of tension include national security, homeland security, and business information. These tensions are inherent in any freedom of information law and are most likely never going to be resolved. The need to periodically strike new balances among FOIA's major concerns is not necessarily a problem. Competing interests will help shape the nature of future FOIA amendments.

Note: *Originally published as Piotrowski, S.J., Freedom of Information Act–Federal, in* Encyclopedia of Public Administration and Public Policy: First Update Supplement, *Taylor & Francis, Boca Raton, FL, 2005, 114.*

References

1. Banisar, D., The www.freedominfo.org Global Survey: Freedom of Information and Access to Government Record Laws Around the World, 2004. http://www.freedominfo.org/documents/global_survey2004.pdf (accessed 2007)
2. Freedom of Information Act 1966 (as amended 1974, 1986, 1996).
3. Madison, J., Letter to William T. Barry, August 4, 1822, in *James Madison: Writings, Literary Classics of the United States*, New York, 1999, 790.
4. *Freedom of Information Act and Amendment of 1974 Source Book: Legislative History, Texts, and Other Documents*, Government Printing Office, Washington, DC, 1975.
5. Rourke, F.E., Administrative secrecy: A Congressional dilemma, *American Political Science Review*, 54, 691, 1960.
6. Braverman, B.A. and Chetwynd, F.J., *Information Law: Freedom of Information, Privacy, Open Meetings, Other Access Law* (Books 1 and 2), Practicing Law Institute, New York, 1985, 12.
7. Dalgish, L.A., LaFleur, J., and Leslie, G.P., Eds., *Homefront Confidential: How the War on Terrorism Affects Access to Information and the Public's Right to Know,* 4th ed., Reporters Committee for Freedom of the Press, Arlington, VA, 2003, 67.
8. Hammitt, H.A., Sobel, D.L., and Zaid, M.S., Eds., *Litigation Under the Federal Open Government Laws 2002: Covering the Freedom of Information Act, the Privacy Act, and the Government in the Sunshine Act, and the Federal Advisory Committee Act,* Epic Publications, Washington, DC, 2002.
9. See: http://www.fas.org/sgp/foia/citizen.pdf (accessed 2007)
10. Piotrowski, S.J. and Rosenbloom, D.H., Nonmission-based values in results-oriented public management: The case of freedom of information, *Public Administration Review*, 62, 643, 2002.

Chapter 20 Addendum

Ongoing Problems in the Implementation of the Freedom of Information Act

U.S. Government Accountability Office*

Contents

Editor's Note: In 2007, the US Government Accountability Office (GAO) released an evaluation of the implementation of the Freedom of Information Act by executive branch agencies. This report is tantamount to an update to Piotrowski's chapter.

Why GAO Did This Study

The Freedom of Information Act (FOIA) establishes that federal agencies must provide the public with access to government information, thus enabling them to learn about government operations and decisions. Specific requests by the public for information through the act have led to disclosure of waste, fraud, abuse, and wrongdoing in the government, as well as the identification of unsafe consumer products, harmful drugs, and serious health hazards.

* Originally published as US Government Accountability Office, Freedom of Information Act: Processing Trends Show Importance of Improvement Plans, GAO-07-441, March 30, 2007. The text provided here is an abridgement of the GAO report. For the complete report, see: http://www.gao.gov/new.items/d07441.pdf.

To help ensure appropriate implementation, the act requires that agencies provide annual reports on their FOIA operations to the Attorney General; these reports include information as specified in the act, such as how many requests were received and processed in the previous fiscal year, how many requests were pending at the end of the year, and the median times that agencies or their components took to process requests. Since 2001, we have provided the Congress with periodic analyses of the contents of these annual reports.

On December 14, 2005, the President issued Executive Order 13392 aimed at improving agencies' disclosure of information consistent with FOIA. Among other things, this order required each agency to review its FOIA operations and develop improvement plans; by June 14, 2006 each agency was to submit a report to the Attorney General and the Director of the Office of Management and Budget (OMB) summarizing the results of the agency's review and including a copy of its improvement plan. These plans were to include specific outcome-oriented goals and timetables, by which the agency head is to evaluate the agency's success in implementing the plan.

The Executive Order directs agencies in their FOIA improvement plans to focus on ways to:

- eliminate or reduce any backlog of requests;
- increase reliance on public dissemination of records including through Web sites;
- improve communications with requesters about the status of their requests; and:
- increase public awareness of FOIA processing.

For this study, GAO was asked to examine the status and trends of FOIA processing at 25 major agencies as reflected in annual reports, as well as the extent to which improvement plans contain the elements emphasized by the Executive Order. To do so, GAO analyzed the 25 agencies' annual reports and improvement plans.

What GAO Found

Based on data reported by 24 major agencies in annual FOIA reports from 2002 to 2005, the public continued to submit more requests for information from the federal government through FOIA. Despite increasing the numbers of requests processed, many agencies did not keep pace with the volume of requests that they received. As a result, the number of pending requests carried over from year to year has been steadily increasing. According to agency reports:

- Recently the rate of increase in requests received and processed has flattened. Except for one agency – the Social Security Administration (SSA) – these increases were only about 3% and 2% from 2004 to 2005 (compared to 29% and 27% from 2002 to 2005).
- For most requests processed in fiscal year 2005, responsive records were provided in full. The percentage (87%) is about the same as in previous years.
- Median times to process requests varied greatly. These ranged from less than 10 days for some agency components to more than 100 days at others (sometimes much more than 100).
- Numbers of pending requests carried over from year to year continue to increase. Also, the rate of increase is growing.

Our ability to generalize in one of these areas – FOIA processing times – is limited by the form in which the statistics are reported: that is, as required by the act, agencies report median processing times, not averages. Working with median data only, it is not statistically possible to combine results from different agencies to develop broader generalizations (such as a governmentwide statistic based on all agency reports, or an agencywide statistic based on separate reports from all components of the agency). This limitation on aggregating data impedes the development of broader pictures of FOIA operations, which would be helpful both for public accountability and for effectively managing agency FOIA programs. Further, we omitted from our statistical analysis data from the Department of Agriculture (USDA) because of the unreliability of data reported by a major component (the Farm Service Agency, which appeared to account for about 80% of the department's data). Providing annual report data that are generalizable and accurate is important to meeting the act's goal of providing visibility into government FOIA operations. Finally, in the absence of a requirement that data from the annual reports be summarized or aggregated (a function that the Department of Justice, in its FOIA oversight role, has performed in the past), the public and the Congress have no consistent means of obtaining a governmentwide picture of FOIA processing.

The 25 agencies submitted improvement plans that mostly included goals and timetables addressing the four areas of improvement emphasized by the Executive Order. Based on the results of agencies' reviews of their FOIA operations, the plans also included other improvement activities (such as improving automation and increasing staff training) that are expected to contribute to achieving the goals of the Executive Order. Out of 25 plans, 20 provided goals and timetables in all four areas. In some cases, agencies did not set goals for a given area because they determined that they were already strong in that area. All agencies with reported backlog developed plans to reduce backlog, and (with minor exceptions) all included both measurable goals and milestones.

Except for one department, agencies also generally set milestones for the other areas of improvement emphasized by the Executive Order (that is, increasing public dissemination, improving status communications, and increasing public awareness of FOIA processing); for example, to increase public awareness, agencies generally planned to ensure that their FOIA reference guides were comprehensive and up to date. The exception was the Department of the Treasury, whose review and plan was focused on backlog reduction and omitted the other three areas of improvement. If the department does not review these areas and, as appropriate, establish and report on goals and timetables for them, it will not have assurance that it has taken appropriate steps to address increasing public dissemination, improving status communications, and increasing public awareness of FOIA processing.

Although we agree that the Executive Order and Justice guidance placed great emphasis on backlog reduction, we do not agree that the plan and the other actions described fully address all the areas emphasized in the order. For example, although the improvements to automation described by the department may contribute to (for example) improved communication with requesters, without goals and milestones tying these automation improvements to that objective, neither Treasury management nor the public will be well placed to judge whether the department has succeeded in achieving the objective. We note, however, that Treasury in its comments indicates that it does plan to continue to reevaluate its improvement plan and modify it to accommodate changing circumstances. If future modifications specifically address external communications, particularly with requesters, the goal of our recommendation may be achieved.

What GAO Recommends

To improve the usefulness of the statistics in agency annual FOIA reports, the Congress should consider amending the act to require agencies to report additional statistics on processing time, which at a minimum should include average times and ranges.

To provide a clearer picture of FOIA processing both in a given year and over time, we recommend that the Attorney General direct Justice's Office of Information and Privacy to use data from annual reports to develop summaries and aggregate statistics (as appropriate) for categories of agencies (such as major departments), as well as governmentwide.

To ensure that the USDA's data in FOIA annual reports are accurate and complete, we recommend that the Secretary of Agriculture direct the Chief FOIA Officer for the department to revise the department's FOIA improvement plan to include activities, goals, and milestones to improve data reliability for the Farm Service Agency and to monitor results.

To ensure that its plan includes an appropriate focus on communicating with requesters and the public, we recommend that the Secretary of the Treasury direct the department's Chief FOIA Officer to review its FOIA operations in the other areas emphasized in the Executive Order (increasing reliance on public dissemination of records, improving communications with FOIA requesters about the status of their requests, and increasing public awareness of FOIA processing) and, as appropriate, revise the improvement plan to include goals and milestones in these areas.

Chapter 21

The Environmental Context of Communication: Public Sector Organizations

Joseph P. Viteritti

Contents

Introduction

It happened in the first six months of his administration. President Clinton had nominated someone for high public office whose name he would subsequently have to withdraw. This time it was Lani Guinier. What an embarrassment, a political blunder of the first order! How could a president and his staff recruit a well-known law professor and personal friend to a sensitive position in the Justice Department without knowing her position on key issues? Had they not read her widely disseminated articles from prestigious law reviews? Had they ever bothered to speak with her? Perhaps they had just miscalculated the receptivity of the U.S. Senate.

Apparently nobody had tested the proposal with any key congressional leaders. But it was already too late. The problem now was to explain the ordeal to a wide and diverse array of individuals who would view the episode differently. How could that be accomplished without appearing incompetent to the average citizen, without offending civil rights advocates who felt betrayed, without compromising the middle-of-the-road political ground the President had set out to chart, without jeopardizing the viability of future nominees? One factor figures in all these questions. It helps us in trying to sort out what went wrong, and it must be integrated into any White House strategy to control the political damage. It is called *communication*.

This chapter explains how the environmental context of public organizations shapes the terms of communication between governmental actors and those with whom they interact on the outside. The chapter will begin with an overview of the literature on organizational environment, tracing the evolution of key analytic concepts. Here I will also point to some recognized distinctions between public sector research and more generic organization theory.

The second section will focus more specifically on the ecology of the public organization, identifying major categories of actors who directly or indirectly participate in the life of the enterprise and who receive or transmit communications. The next part describes the channels of interaction that shape the communicative networks between internal members and various outside participants. The final section will explain how the terms of transaction have begun to change over the last quarter century from a conflictual relationship to a more cooperative one. Much of this last section will focus on the local level of government, since it is here that "the rubber meets the road," where the citizen and the state have the most regular and direct contact with each other.

The Environment: Public versus Private

Students of complex organizations have long recognized the importance of investigating the relationship between bureaucratic institutions and their environments. Even Max Weber, who is usually associated with a "closed-system" approach, examined the impact of the social structure of organizations in the course of his comparative historical studies. [1] In early work on the executive role in organizations, Barnard brought attention to the influence of social variables on the decision structures of organizations. [2] In a refinement of Barnard's equilibrium theory of the economy of incentives, Simon observed the need for organizations to maintain the support of clients and suppliers to remain viable. [3] With James March, Simon later demonstrated how a scarcity of resources in the external environment influences the level of internal conflict. [4]

As the "open-systems" approach grew popular in the professional literature, it became more common for scholars to view organizations as organisms that naturally respond to changes in their environments. [5] Thompson and McEwen wrote that goal setting is a process of defining desired relationships between an organization and its environment, [6] anticipating the focus that strategic management would assume in the 1970s and 1980s. [7] Gouldner described the new theoretical orientation in terms of a "natural" as opposed to a "rationalist" approach. [8] Burns and Stalker distinguished between an "organic" and "mechanistic" approach. [9]

Behavioral scientists had been reacting to a once commonly held notion that organizations could (or even should) be held separate and apart from the larger social setting — a boundary that was assumed to maximize managerial control and efficiency. In a landmark work, James D. Thompson integrated the "closed" and "open" approaches. [10] Although recognizing that organizations are constantly subject to the uncertain influences of a changing environment, he also found that they achieve rationality through closedness, and he assigned managerial leaders the role of mediating the boundary of external interference. His work gave rise to the notion of environmental scanning.

From the late 1960s through the 1970s, a substantial literature emerged concerned with the description, classification, and significance of various types of organizational environments. For example, Emery and Trist developed a four-class typology of environments, ranging from "placid randomized" to "turbulent," designed to assess whether particular settings had a stabilizing or disruptive influence on organizational life. [11] This model would later be refined to develop frameworks allowing scholars to understand better the complexity of organizational environments. [12] Lawrence and Lorsch established an empirical connection between organizational environments and structure. [13] According to Aldrich, the definitive characteristics in an organizational environment included resources, homogeneity/heterogeneity, stability/instability, concentration/dispersion, and consensus/dissensus. [14]

A "resource-dependence" model grew out of an understanding that organizations cannot generate the resources they need for goal attainment or survival; it focused on the strategies leaders adopt to enhance their independence and positions with other organizations. [15] A "natural-selection" model would apply biological concepts to explain how organizational survival is a function of the ability to learn and perform according to environmental changes. [16,17]

The organization theory literature that has emerged over the last two decades has enriched our understanding of organizational environments and has also contributed to the generation of prescriptive theory that enables practitioners to negotiate more successfully complex environments. [18–20] However, most of the existing literature has focused on the private sector, and although adapting private-sector models to public-sector research has been useful, it has been inadequate.

For example, drawing from the natural-selection model, a good deal of the private-sector research has focused on the strategies organizations employ to adapt to changes in the environment to survive. [21,22] Although survival is a relevant concept for motivating and evaluating actors in the private sector, it is not of equal significance in the governmental sector. Public organizations, especially those in a liberal democratic society, can and should operate according to criteria determined from more fundamental principles of governance, such as representativeness, responsiveness, and equity. [23]

Some scholars have convincingly warned against oversimplification or exaggerating the differences between public and private organizations. [24–26] Others, however, have pointed to real distinctions. Referring to a quip Wallace Sayre made, Graham Allison noted that public- and private-sector management really are alike in all unimportant respects. [27] Wamsley and Zald have focused on funding and ownership as definitive variables. [28] In their earlier book on the political economy, Dahl and Lindblom distinguished between enterprises and agencies. [29] In the former, the price system links revenues to products and services that are sold, and there is a strong motivation to curtail costs. In the latter, agencies pursue intangible and diverse objectives where costs are less conspicuous and important. Blau and Scott enunciated a four-part taxonomy of organizations based on a determination of whom they benefit, relating this determination to the process of goal formation. The categories include commonweal, business, service, and mutual benefit organizations. [30]

Rainey and his colleagues have been studying and writing on the public/private distinction for nearly two decades. In an original collaboration, they identified a variety of environmental factors peculiar to the public sector, including the absence of an economic market, formal legal oversight, and political influence. [31] These external variables greatly influence the terms of transaction in the governmental sphere where outputs are not measured by price, where activity is both monopolistic and coercive, and where there is greater public scrutiny. To state it another way, government is expected to be open, fair, responsive, and accountable. In a later essay, Perry and Rainey recommend strategies for future research that would integrate the work of management and organizational theorists with scholarship from the fields of political economy and public policy. [32]

The single most important characteristic that distinguishes public-sector organizations from others is a normative dimension. [33,34] As public institutions, governmental organizations must reach beyond managerial notions of accountability measured in terms of efficiency and effectiveness. In a democratic state, public institutions must be politically responsive in a way that allows them to represent the diverse interests of the communities they are supposed to serve. Meaningful communication between government and the people is not merely a managerial practicality. It is a political, albeit moral, obligation that originates from the basic covenant that exists between the government and the people. The structure of the environment, in terms of the population of actors and their relationship to the organization, significantly affects organizations' capacity to be politically responsive.

In my own work on the public-sector environment, I have focused on the analytic distinction between organizational constituents and organizational clients. [35,36] I found analytic confusion between the two concepts, mainly because researchers tend to adapt inappropriately the private-sector notion of client to governmental organizations. This practice compromised the public-sector researchers' ability to deal effectively with normative issues such as responsiveness and representativeness. This confusion will be explained in the following section.

The Ecology of Actors

Although James D. Thompson developed the concept of environmental scanning in the late 1960s, it would be considerably later when public administration scholars took a close look at the organizational environment to identify and categorize the cast of relevant actors. [37] A systematic application of environmental scanning first appeared in the governmental sector as students of public policy began to advance from an analysis of policy outcomes to a prescriptive definition of the key variables for determining successful implementation. [38,39] It was here that the literature on management and policy analysis started to converge. It was considerably later when a strategic approach to public management eventually came into full play, forcing researchers to come to terms with the complexity of the public environment in a conscious way. [40–44]

The actors found that the ecology of the public organizations can be classified into seven categories: clients, constituents, citizens, authorities, network organizations, competitor organizations, and the press. Some are active participants in the life of the organization; others are more passive. Among those who are active, some advance their claims on the organization by exercising formal authority or sheer political power; others depend on the moral claims of accountability that emanate from the principles of democratic governance. External actors who interact with organizational members may have a cooperative or conflictual relationship with their counterparts.

Clients

The term *client* comes to us from the sociological literature on organizations. [45–47] It refers to customers or service recipients. Clients are those institutional members who are most oriented toward organizational outputs. They play a particularly essential role among private organizations because they are usually the major source of resources or income. Simply stated, clients pay the organization directly for the goods and services they choose to consume, be they automobiles, medical service, or electrical power.

In the public sector, clients might include students in a local public school system, patients in a county hospital, recipients of public assistance in a state social service system, or residents in a federal housing project. They are significant actors in the ecology of the government agency. However, their relationship to the acquisition of organizational resources is more complex and indirect than that of clients in the private sector. In most cases, except where user fees are involved, public clients do not pay an agency directly for services rendered. And even in cases where user fees are involved, they rarely pay for the entire cost of the service provided. As I will explain later, the level of funding in public organizations is a function of client support, constituent intervention, and decisions by authorities.

Although the service provider–customer relationship suggests regular interaction, and public servants have a normative responsibility to provide services efficiently and effectively, do not assume that all governmental clients are politically active. Quite the contrary, most clients are not motivated to play a politically active role with the public organizations that serve them. They tend, on the whole, to accept services in a passive way and, when dissatisfied, express it individually rather than through organized political action.

Let us consider, for example, the patient in the local health clinic who becomes dissatisfied with the quality of care. Before taking political action, she is more likely to voice her dissatisfaction to those administrators or providers with whom she comes in direct contact. If she remains dissatisfied after expressing a personal complaint, she might choose to accommodate her health care need elsewhere, perhaps at another clinic, at the emergency room of the county hospital, or, if finances permit, at a private provider's office. Or, it is very likely that even after her complaints have gone unheeded, she will remain a client of the same facility. Such "loyalty" in the latter case might be a function of habit, personal inertia, or lack of information regarding the other options.

There is evidence of a growing pattern in recent years, especially at the local level of government, where clients have become more involved with the actual delivery of service. The purpose in such cases is to take a direct hand at improving the service's quality and effectiveness. As I will explain later, the relationship between service provider and client in the latter type of situation is less political or adversarial and more cooperative.

Constituents

The term *constituents* is derived from the political science literature on legislative bodies. [48,49] It originally referred to those individuals or groups who elect a lawmaker to office and to whom he or she is directly accountable. Constituents are active participants in the political process because they retain the power to exact what they want from governmental actors and they choose to exercise their influence in a deliberate way. [50–52]

Under the traditional or classic notion of public administration, a distinction was made between policy making and administration. [53] Policy making, the determination of governmental objectives, was understood to be the responsibility of elected officials such as legislators or chief executives; administration, a neutral process for carrying out the expressed priorities of policy makers, was seen as the function of the bureaucracy. Later research on implementation indicated that there is a significant degree of discretion inherent in the administrative process and that bureaucrats do indeed make policy throughout the process. [54,55] References to administrative or agency constituents reflected an understanding in political science that public bureaucracies are governmental institutions that make policy, allocate resources, and require public support to stay in existence. [56,57]

Organizational constituents might include a special-purpose interest group that focuses on the activities of a certain government organization, as farmers do the United States Department of Agriculture; or a professional organization like the American Medical Association that is active in health policy; or a labor union that represents the organization's employees such as the American Federation of Teachers or a local Patrolmen's Benevolent Association. Or it might include a less specialized organization like a political party or taxpayers' association that has an interest in or claim on the organization.

At some point the concepts of organizational client and organizational constituent were merged analytically. It happened with the discovery of the mutually beneficial subsystems that exist among government bureaucracies, legislative committees, and organized interest groups. [58–61] The mingling of the two concepts was useful to the extent that the constituencies to which legislators and agencies were accountable happened to be organizational clients. The analytic union of the two terms is not always a legitimate one, however. [62] As the examples above illustrate, not all constituents are clients. Conversely, not all clients are constituents because not all those who depend on an agency for benefits or service possess the political means to get what they want. Thus, one might find policies in the health care organization geared to the interests of physicians rather than patients, or school practices made to accommodate the needs of teachers rather than students.

The dichotomy between constituent and client in public organizations sometimes indicates a serious normative dilemma, especially in agencies that deliver redistributive services to poor, politically ineffective clienteles. Most often the key variable in practically determining whether clients are constituents is power. And, as we shall see, this variable greatly influences the terms of communication between clients and administrative organizations.

Citizens

According to Aristotle, a citizen is "one who enjoys the right of sharing in deliberative or judicial office." [63] Aristotle recognized that the true nature of citizenship in any state depends on the nature of its constitution, or form of government. In a democracy a citizen, therefore, is one who either is eligible for office or who participates in choosing those who are in office. Unfortunately, in modern American democracy relatively few people who are eligible to participate in either way actually exercise that right. Thus, although conceivably citizens may function as either clients or constituents, as a separate analytic category citizenship represents a different sort of actor.

Citizens have a legitimate claim on the benefits and services of the state. Because citizens pay taxes to support the public business, they have a vested interest in the way matters are conducted. Because most adult citizens are enfranchised, they possess the means, although indirect and infrequent, to register their satisfaction or dissatisfaction with governmental officials' performance. A public official who is out of touch with the temperament of the citizenry is often voted out of office. Nevertheless, as an unorganized group without the sense of purpose characteristic of constituents, citizens are a latent force. The conventional wisdom in behavioral political science tells us in clear terms that on the whole, the American citizenry is apathetic when it comes to serious political activity. [64,65]

Citizens resemble clients in the sense that they are not by nature mobilized for political action. However, their stake in the performance of a service organization is not necessarily the same as that of a client who receives the service. For example, the senior citizen who lives on a fixed income has a strong interest in the local school budget, but it is not derived from the same position as that of parents or students who are the direct consumers of educational service. If senior citizens choose to organize in a community to curb educational spending, they become constituents of the school system.

For analytic purposes here, citizens represent the mass of potential voters who are neither direct-service clients nor active political constituents of a particular administrative agency under discussion. Nonetheless, government organizations have a responsibility to keep citizens informed on policies and practices that affect them. In a later section we will see how some public administration scholars have attempted to alter citizens' behavior toward governmental organizations (and vice versa) by advocating a more activist model of citizenship.

Authorities

In his systems analysis of political life, David Easton defines *authorities* according to three basic characteristics: (1) they engage in the daily affairs of the political system, (2) they are recognized by most members as having responsibility for those matters, and (3) their actions are accepted as binding most of the time by most members as long as they act within the limits of the rules. [66] From a service organization's perspective, authorities may include an elected chief executive, a legislative body, or the courts. They may also encompass other administrative organizations, but we will deal with that possibility in a later section.

Authorities can hold administrators accountable for their actions on the basis of a legally defined relationship. The manner in which various authorities exercise influence over an administrative entity is directly a function of their respective constitutional roles. The elected executive does so through the power of appointment, [67] the setting of budget priorities, and the exercise of political support; the legislature does so through the ultimate control over funds and holding investigative hearings; [68,69] and the courts do so by their prerogative not only to interpret laws but, more recently, to help implement them. [70–72]

In practice, for example, a state corrections commissioner is formally accountable to the governor who appoints him or her, the chair of the criminal justice committee in the state legislature, and the state or federal judge who handles litigation that challenges living conditions in prisons. Note, however, that legal accountability does not always determine the ultimate power that an "authority" holds over an agency official.

Power is often defined on the basis of interpersonal relationships and individual leadership qualities. The significance of personality is most apparent on a national level, where gifted figures such as Churchill, De Gaulle, and Mao exercised unusual influence over their nation states. But it is also relevant in less dramatic and profound ways in an administrative context. For instance, FBI Director J. Edgar Hoover and New York planner Robert Moses are dramatic illustrations of appointed officials who acted with relatively little accountability to their executive and legislative overseers. [73] Notwithstanding these noteworthy examples, however, it is foolhardy for most administrators to underestimate the significance of authority figures in the government. And those administrators who disregard the will of elected officials who appoint or oversee them seriously undermine the legitimacy of the organizational roles they play.

Network Organizations

We have already noted the policy subsystems, sometimes referred to as an "iron triangle," that exist among government bureaucracies, legislative committees, and interest groups. Similarly defined "issue networks" exist among agencies that find themselves in constant regularized interaction with each other. [74] The relationships among these organizations may resemble those associated with other environmental actors described above. For example, one governmental organization might be another organization's client. A general services department that provides housekeeping and maintenance services for other agencies may have relatively little interaction with the general public but has many organizational clients within government.

A public organization might act as a constituent of another, enjoying no formal authority over the agency but being a stakeholder in its activities. For example, a local housing agency may lobby a state environmental control board for a building variance or permit that would allow the former to proceed with a desired project. The housing agency's power would derive from its ability to mobilize the support of other stakeholders with an interest in the project. To carry the analogy further, the local housing organization in this case may view the environmental control board as an authority, since the state agency possesses legal discretion that affects its capacity to perform its functions.

Within the overall range of possibilities, one characteristic that more frequently defines the relationship between and among public organizations within the same policy network is interdependence. [75,76] The regularized interaction that connects organizations in a particular network is often a function of a mutual interest in successfully implementing a set of policies for which each is partially responsible. Such organizations would ordinarily perceive themselves as ultimately serving the same client. [77,78]

Thus, the general services agency that delivers truck parts to the highway department garage is part of the same mayoral administration that strives toward effective service delivery. The governor who appoints the environmental control board may be accountable to the same builders' coalition as the mayor who chooses the housing administrator. The fact is, no government organization can effectively carry out its duties without other agencies' help and cooperation. This is how and why relationships are formed and networks are built to the mutual benefit of all parties involved.

Competitor Organizations

As explained above, it was once part of the conventional wisdom in management to distinguish private organizations from public by the absence of competition in the latter sector. Today, no inventory of the public-sector environment is complete without recognizing that it is populated with private organizations that are getting into service areas once reserved for government. Driven by the need to reduce the cost of government, demands for privatization [79,80] and contracting out [81] are significantly changing the structure of "public service."

Beyond those traditional services such as education, health, and transportation that were always commonly found in both sectors, private entrepreneurship is breaking into new areas like policing, parks, corrections, and even tax collection. And in those areas where a private component always existed, there is a more recent emphasis on the role of a competitive market in providing an incentive for more effective performance. Chubb and Moe, for example, have argued that providing students and parents with real choices between public and private schools is good not just for clients, but because it will ultimately improve the quality of public education. [82]

Chubb and Moe's position is highly debatable. Hirschman and proponents of public education, for example, might argue that reform is more probable if clients remain within the school system and become more vocal advocates for change. [83] Regardless of how one stands in this particular debate on the merits of the public and private sectors, its growing significance in education and health care indicates a changing climate; constituents have become more critical and the competition for clients has grown keener in the public sector.

Historically there has been a somewhat cooperative relationship between public and private organizations in the same service area. One reason for this is that they often functioned side by side, serving distinct clienteles. Thus, public schools did not perceive themselves as competing for students who typically attended parochial or private schools, where parental choices were made on the basis of religion, culture, or class. In fact, one finds a sense of cooperation among the two sectors, almost functioning as the network organizations described above. Thus, public school districts provide transportation or meal services to parochial schools as part of their general organizational mission.

This relationship, if Chubb and Moe have their way, may be on the verge of undergoing significant alteration. Private schools will begin to target a larger part of the "market share" among the same client groups of students currently attending public school. More important, they will vie for the limited public funds that are now within local school districts' domain. This will force public educators to think more strategically about their private school colleagues, continually assessing their relative strengths, weaknesses, opportunities, and threats.

As private organizations compete more aggressively with government agencies within the same service areas — whether it be in education, criminal justice, social services, or health — the professional network of relationships once defined as cooperative will change both in spirit and in practice. To put it another way, public-sector organizations will need to function more like private enterprises, with a more immediate stake in survival and growth.

The Press

No institution other than government itself has a more profound influence over public affairs than the media. [84,85] It has changed the face of American politics, to the point of replacing political parties as the ruling force in the electoral process. [86,87] It plays a major role in defining the public policy agenda. [88] It not only reports on events that emerge from Washington, the state capital, and city hall, it also serves to filter, interpret, and even distort what citizens are likely to know. And when there is no news that is really fit to print, the media has a wondrous capacity to produce some. [89,90]

In his provocative book on "attack journalism," Larry Sabato traces three periods in American journalism that portray its evolution from a more passive political actor to an aggressive center-stage role. According to his analysis, "lapdog" journalism prevailed from 1941 to 1966. Here mainstream journalists accepted what politicians told them at face value, rarely challenging the dominant political orthodoxy and serving to reinforce the establishment. In response to the Vietnam War and Watergate, "watchdog" journalism came into more prominent play between 1966 to 1974, where reporters became more inclined to challenge the information made available to them and to conduct their own independent investigations. Since 1974, we have experienced what Sabato calls "junkyard-dog" journalism, where reporting is "harsh, aggressive and intrusive." The preoccupation with gossip and private lives gives rise to the "feeding frenzy," where substantive information takes a back page to titillation and scandal. [91] If Sabato's generalizations are slightly overstated, they point to the realization of a genuine phenomenon in which the media must be recognized as active players in the lives of public organizations.

Entitled to constitutional protection as a fourth estate, this powerful institution is no objective player. It has a serious point of view that often borders on bias, and it frequently loses its balance on the precarious wire-thin line between reporting and editorializing. [92–94] No high-level public manager can survive the cross fire of public discourse without learning how to deal with the press from a strategic perspective. In today's world of government, press relations is no random process of catch as catch can; rather, it is the work of experienced trained professionals. If managing the press is a form of manipulation, it is also a survival skill that assists the public administrator in transmitting information without distortion.

Media relations for the public manager proceed through several different forums. Television and radio make it possible to produce news almost immediately. Sometimes, however, a network's rush to break a story first makes it more likely that the information is treated in a superficial or misleading manner. It used to be that the print media were better able to deal with complex issues more comprehensively than television or radio. The assent of cable television, "independent" broadcasting, and news talk shows has allowed the audio and video media to handle topics more broadly. Unfortunately, the inclination to entertain rather than inform has affected both the selection and treatment of subjects.

In the end, what the media decides to cover and how they do so has a significant impact on the viewpoints and actions of the clients, constituents, citizens, and authorities that populate the public organization. The media is a potential player in every governmental transaction and the ultimate arbiter in determining what issues become part of the public consciousness. The media becomes involved wherever and whenever it chooses and must therefore be taken into consideration with regard to every transaction or communication with the outside world of the public manager.

Channels of Interaction

The actors that populate the public organization environment are many and diverse. Notwithstanding the complexity, turbulence, and uncertainty of the ecology, most administrative agencies develop regularized patterns of interaction with their external actors. The channels of communication that evolve over time become so predictable that they take on the form of an operable system. [95] Such predictability allows communications between executives and their publics to be somewhat manageable. In fact, in the high-technology world today of rapid communication and feedback, no executive can succeed or survive without thinking strategically about communication. [96]

As Garnett explains it, a strategic approach to communication involves planning, deliberate choices, and a firm understanding of the organizational environment. Strategy must begin with a clear sense of purpose. Did President Clinton have a particular goal in mind when he announced his health care plan to the American people? Garnett points out that there are three possible objectives for public communication in government: to inform, to influence attitudes, and to affect behavior. [97] Very often a governmental strategy involves more than one of these purposes. For example, in revealing a health care plan during the early months of his administration, President Clinton wanted to inform the American people of the direction he would take the nation. But he was also trying to get the citizenry to think favorably about his intentions and attempting to persuade powerful interest groups like labor unions and the American Medical Association to lend him support.

In designing a communication strategy, one must always be aware of his or her audiences. Garnett refers to three types of audience — immediate, primary, and secondary. [98] The immediate audience consists of those who transmit or revise a message. The primary audience includes the principal users of the information transmitted. The secondary audience includes others who might use the message, influence it, or be affected by it. Secondary audiences are particularly important in the governmental sector, where public action and communication have such significant symbolic value. [99] And given the fact that the press is always intricately involved in filtering, interpreting, and transmitting public information, it is sometimes difficult to distinguish between primary and secondary audiences.

This section will focus on describing the various channels through which government executives communicate with their publics. Channels, the tools of communication, are also an essential part of the organizational environment. The selection of one channel over another to convey a message influences both the message's content and its impact. Therefore, among more astute organizational actors, such choices are self-consciously strategic. Each channel has its own set of qualities, which may serve as an advantage or a disadvantage, depending on what an actor is trying to achieve.

In reviewing the respective alternatives, attention will be given to the quality referred to by some scholars as "media richness." This concept suggests that communication channels are not equal in their capacity to reduce equivocality or ambiguity. [100] Organizational media can be classified in terms of a richness hierarchy, where richness measures the capacity to change understanding among the target groups. [101] Research indicates that media selection by executives is a function of the amount of equivocality they face in a given situation or may choose to foster. [102] For example, if the President is unsure about the details of a new health care plan, he may want to maintain a level of ambiguity about its content during his early communications on the subject so that he can assess the responses as he works toward a greater certainty on the issue.

Daft and Huber define information capacity on the basis of four variables: (1) opportunity for timely feedback, (2) ability to convey multiple cues, (3) tailoring of messages to personal circumstances, and (4) language variety. [103] According to their hierarchy, face-to-face discussion is the richest medium because it allows for immediate feedback. Unaddressed documents such as flyers or bulletins are the weakest because they are impersonal and do not allow for easy feedback.

In the public sector, selecting a medium for dealing with an outside actor is often a function of power. Administrators tend to rely on richer media for communicating with those who have power over them or their organization, because the need to influence thinking or garner support among powerful outside players cannot be left to chance or pursued haphazardly. Communicating with the powerful must be accomplished strategically and consciously.

A number of scholars have developed their own lists of communication media in organizations. [104–106] In this section we will divide the media into the following categories: (1) face to face, (2) telephonic, (3) the written word, and (4) mass media.

Face to Face

There is no substitute for face-to-face contact. The richest of all media, it is fast, it allows for immediate feedback, and it involves both oral and visual communication. [107,108] Face-to-face contact is also time-consuming. Travel is always involved on the part of one or both parties, and, because few executives travel alone, it can consume many hours. But it is also highly personal; such encounters not only make it possible for parties to transmit information to each other, it is also the most efficient and effective way to negotiate differences.

There are numerous types of forums for the face-to-face transaction. The *one-on-one* meeting between principals is the most intimate. When trying to persuade or work out differences with an influential authority or client, this forum, more than all others, engenders frank, confidential discussion that gets to the heart of a problem. For example, although the Chair of the Judiciary Committee may personally support the President's nominee for a particular position in the Justice Department, he may not be able to produce enough votes on the Committee to ensure confirmation. The communication of such information could save many people from embarrassment. The one-on-one encounter does not have to take place in a business setting. It can occur over lunch or dinner or on the tennis court, where people feel more relaxed.

The *group meeting* does not offer the intimacy or confidentiality of the one-on-one meeting, but it is commonly used to exchange information, negotiate differences, and plan for cooperative action. Such meetings are a regular part of administrative life for managers and their respective authorities, constituents, and network organizations. It is virtually impossible, for example, for network organizations to coordinate activities without such regularized interaction. Could one imagine a district attorney's office functioning effectively without the opportunity to meet with police department personnel on a regular basis?

Some group meetings, when they are conducted in a highly *public forum*, take on a formalistic, almost symbolic nature. In fact, although the parties involved may be speaking directly to each other, the real audience for the dialogue is found among the spectators. A congressional hearing on a highly controversial matter is a case in point. Congressional members who interrogate government bureaucrats are often playing to the folks back home or, more likely, to powerful interest groups watching the hearing. The conversation between the parties present may be incidental to the actual event.

Although most face-to-face meetings involve two-way communication, some allow for less interaction than others. An agency representative may give *a presentation or formal report* to a group of citizens or clients. Although this forum might leave room for questions and comments, the basic function of such meetings is to present information or, more specifically, the government agent's point of view. On occasion, agency members might elicit feedback at such forums to refine policies. However, these formal occasions are not as effective for resolving differences as the group meetings mentioned above.

Telephonic

As Mintzberg pointed out long ago, the spoken word is the preferred means of communication for the busy executive. [109] The telephone is the most convenient way to convey it. Like the face-to-face meeting, the telephone allows the administrator to send information and receive immediate feedback. Although it, for the most part, is limited to audio stimuli, the telephone is an effective means to personal confidential interaction among principals. It is used to negotiate deals, reconcile differences, and curry favor. The regional administrator in the state environmental department can rely on it to communicate with a key authority in the legislature or the governor's office. He or she can use it to keep key constituents informed on policy or administrative developments. Among street-level bureaucrats, the telephone is essential to working with clients and network organizations where regularized interaction is required.

Technology has expanded the use of telephonic communication and has actually overcome some of its original handicaps. *Conference calling* enables individuals in different locations to hold a meeting. The *video phone* has introduced a capacity to send visual messages during such meetings. *Voice mail* makes it possible to send a message to someone instantaneously. Telephonic communication may not be as rich as in-person interaction, but it compensates for time and distance that must be accommodated to orchestrate a meeting. [110]

The Written Word

There are a number of channels through which the written word might be communicated by a government agency. They include the formal report, the agency memorandum, personal correspondence in the form of a letter, or something as informal as a newsletter. Recently government agencies have begun to employ more sophisticated techniques such as public surveys to elicit feedback on issues and services.

Written documents do not provide the opportunity for rapid feedback and response afforded by face-to-face communication, but this is not always perceived as a disadvantage. Putting one's message in writing permits careful planning and consideration; it is not so spontaneous. Moreover, the sender generally does not have to react to an immediate response from the receiver. The entire process of stimulus/response/counter-response is slowed down. One might hope from this that the entire transaction proves to be more thoughtful.

Of course, putting something in writing also subjects it to close scrutiny. It becomes part of the public record and can be evaluated over time, when the circumstances under which it was written no longer exist. Once a document is released it becomes the object of attention by the immediate, primary, or secondary audience — all of whom will review it with different perspectives and priorities. Therefore, before releasing a written document, it is always important to anticipate how different groups and individuals will receive it. Sometimes the same words mean different things to different audiences, depending on their particular experiences. For example, if the newly appointed police chief in Los Angeles releases a report promising to expand the police presence in the city to step up the war on crime, it might be received differently in the black community than among whites.

The Formal Report

On the whole, the formal report is the most comprehensive and sophisticated form of information released by a government organization. It usually comes about under special circumstances, when an issue or problem is of major public concern. It generally involves a relatively high volume of research and data gathering. Formal reports are often written at the request of a particular principal, for instance, the agency head, the chief executive, a legislative leader, or a special commission. Given their importance, however, these documents are widely read and commented on by other parties.

For example, at the end of his first term as governor of New York, Mario Cuomo and the state legislature appointed a blue ribbon panel, headed by a retired judge, to study and evaluate the compensation levels of employees in the three branches of state government. Legally the commission was to prepare its report for the governor, legislative leaders, and chief judge of the state courts. Nevertheless, the document stimulated widespread public interest, not only among state workers who had a direct stake in the results but also among unions, taxpayer organizations, citizen groups, and even civil servants outside of New York state.

The Memorandum

The memorandum is the major currency of written communication in government. A principal vehicle for intra-agency information, it is also the glue that ties together organizational networks over time. Here we find the record of past practices, current activities, and future plans. Here is where roles are assigned, procedures defined, and expectations articulated. Because network organizations are weaved together through a mutuality of needs and interests, all members have a stake in keeping a written record. The advent of personal computers in the workplace has facilitated the production, transmittal, and storage of such records. In an age ruled by freedom of information, these voluminous files of data and communication are no longer solely within the domain of a single bureaucracy or network of organizations. Although tempered by formidable procedural requirements, news reporters and the public at large now have a more clearly defined legal right to request access to such information.

Letter Writing

Letter writing remains a key mechanism for personalized communication between government officials and their publics. Among principals, the personal letter is often used to confirm the contents of a telephone conversation or meeting between an administrator and constituent or authority. It provides a written record of terms agreed on in less formal settings. It is also a vehicle for maintaining contact in a less demanding, unobtrusive way.

Individual correspondence is also a channel of two-way communication with clients and citizens. It can be initiated from either direction. It is more personalized than many of the transactions people have with government, and it is not as time-consuming as a face-to-face meeting. Nor is it as spontaneous, demanding, or potentially adversarial. Although other media have a greater capacity for conflict resolution or persuasion, the letter can be useful to transmit information or correct minor grievances. Personal computers make it possible to send these individualized messages in bulk. When a public organization must circulate routine information, such as the time or place of a meeting, or hours of business, the newsletter, flyer, or poster will usually do the job.

Survey Techniques

In the late 1970s, the Urban Institute, long a pioneer in the art of service measurement and monitoring, began to refine survey techniques for assessing citizen satisfaction. [111] Although few professional analysts would hold that such surveys by themselves are a scientific barometer for evaluating service quality, they do tell us what clients like and dislike about the service. Such information can be useful to the administrator seeking to improve the service. And in cases where it is not possible to do so, then it is at least possible to engage in a dialogue with the client to explain why.

Mass Media

We have already dealt with the press as a significant actor in the public organization environment. Here we cover it as a channel of communication to be used by governmental officials to convey a message. Because the mass media is a vital actor in the political process, it must be approached cautiously, as a player with opinions, biases, and even its own policy agenda. Therefore in many large agencies, trained, experienced professionals handle press relations. Press relations is a two-way road built on an interdependency. Public officials, whether elected or appointed, cannot survive without press support. Conversely, reporters rely on agency personnel and political leaders for information and news.

The mass media plays a crucial role in a democratic society, serving as an intermediary between the government and the people. It is largely through this channel that the vast majority of citizens and clients, who are neither active nor aggressive in public affairs, get their information. When we say in a democracy that the public has a right to know, it is usually by way of the mass media that this right is exercised.

The media can be a severe source of pressure for the public administrator, but if used correctly, it can be a strong asset. Here we will examine techniques for dealing with the press. They include the press advisory, the press release, the press briefing, the press conference, the interview, and the editorial board meeting.

The Press Advisory and the Press Release

The press advisory is a relatively short notification designed to transmit basic non-controversial information to media organizations. It is not meant to have any persuasive value, and it appears almost as a service or reminder to members of the press. For example, an agency might post an advisory to alert reporters to an upcoming public event that they might be interested in covering. A press release, to the contrary, is more substantive. It is generally written from a point of view designed to influence the way reporters treat a topic. For example, if President Clinton wanted to offer a public explanation for withdrawing the nomination of Lani Guinier, but was not ready to subject himself to a full news conference, he might choose to issue a press release explaining the administration's position on the matter.

The Press Briefing

A press briefing is a meeting with reporters designed to give information or respond to questions about a particular matter of interest. It is usually conducted by a representative of an official. It is not normally meant for direct public consumption, which generally means that no cameras are present. Like an advisory, it seeks to facilitate reporters covering a story. However, because the subject of a briefing has a higher potency for conflict, the event is crafted in a way that is sympathetic to the official for which it is held.

The Press Conference

The press conference is a highly staged media production that may be on one or more topics. It requires extraordinary preparation, but it is an effective vehicle for communicating a point of view. It is an opportunity to convince those who are writing the news or observing the event that a particular position is worthy of support.

The Public Interview

A public interview carries many of the advantages of a press conference and in addition allows an official to take his or her case directly to the public. It is nothing less than an art form. Past presidents such as Franklin D. Roosevelt and John F. Kennedy exploited this medium with great skill. For the public administrator, it can be instrumental in reaching that vast population of citizens and clients who remain on the fringe of political life but whose support is crucial to govern.

The Editorial Board Meeting

An editorial board meeting is an attempt to come to terms with the power structure within the mass media. It has all the richness of a face-to-face encounter, the demands of a press conference, and the potential impact of a public interview. Editorial boards set news policies and influence public opinion. When a public leader meets with an editorial board, it is not only listening to the words being said, it is getting a general reading on the person. Is he sincere? Does she speak with conviction? Is he well informed? Can she deliver? Perhaps there is nothing more demanding on a public administrator than the battery of questions from a powerful editorial board. Meeting with editorial boards is an essential ingredient of the job when public support is needed for a key policy or program.

The Changing Environment

The relationship between government agencies and their publics (broadly defined) has always been a topic of great interest among scholars. These organizations have been assailed from different parts of the political spectrum as being both dangerously intimate or too remote from interested actors in their respective environments. Part of the problem in setting normative standards for the relationship between administrative institutions and their publics is a stubborn ambivalence — albeit disagreement — on what should be expected. We just are not sure if these institutions have constitutional standing in our system of government, so we are not quite comfortable with settling on a standard that resembles our expectations for the other branches of government. Recent scholarship has begun to respond to this anxiety, both in addressing the legitimacy of these institutions [112,113] and in structuring more meaningful relationships with the citizenry. [114]

An assessment of the current climate in both the theory and practice of public administration suggests that the relationship between agencies and their publics is being redefined. Notably, it is a relationship that is changing from one discussed primarily in terms of conflict to one more commonly defined by cooperation. This pattern is most apparent at the local level of government, where the interaction between citizen and administrator is intimate and frequent. It is more easily understood by viewing the public participation phenomenon from a historical perspective.

If one looks back at the public participation literature of the 1960s and 1970s, one finds a dialogue cast primarily in terms of adversarial political relationships. [115,116] Conceived at a time when public confidence in governmental institutions and leaders was at a low ebb, it proceeded on the assumption that local service bureaucracies were not being responsive to their service clients' needs. Among reformers, the answer to this dilemma was twofold. On the one hand, they called for an overhaul of bureaucratic structures so that clients would be allowed to participate directly in administrative decision making. [117] On the other hand, they urged citizens to become more actively involved in politics so that their demands might be better articulated, heard, and responded to within the public bureaucracy. [118] To use our own terminology, the overarching goal was to transform clients and citizens who played a relatively passive role in the political and administrative processes into effective constituents who could advance their own interests.

The recent appeal for increased civic involvement also seeks to achieve a more active public within the context of administrative institutions. [119] The ends are quite different from those sought a generation earlier, however. The contemporary notion of civic involvement is cast in classic terms. Public involvement is not to be undertaken merely to satisfy one's parochial self-interest; it is designed to promote the broader public agenda. Moreover, the relationship between citizen and administrator is less adversarial and more cooperative, aligned in a concerted effort to accomplish a public good, namely, the improvement of government services.

Once again, using our own terminology to explain the current phenomenon, contemporary scholars strive to redefine the meaning of citizenship in more activist terms, but public activity remains anchored in larger societal goals, not the narrow agenda of constituent politics. [120] Citizens are depicted as contributors rather than consumers or adversaries. Recognizing the practical dimension of administrative life, citizens are urged to become involved in enhancing service delivery. In other words, they would actually become part of the service network, interacting with workers in a regular and frequent fashion.

An illustrative example of the new thinking is found in the field of criminal justice with the advent of community policing. [121,122] Under the traditional model of policing, the public would define its relationship with departments in one of two ways: (1) either as clients who would request and receive service in the form of radio responses or (2) as constituents who would make their demands and dissatisfaction known to officials through political channels. Among other things, community policing attempts to involve local residents and merchants in designing and implementing safety programs through planning councils, block watches, anticrime initiatives, and other efforts. The goal is for the community and professionals to perceive each other as a mutual resource.

One can find similar cooperative models, sometimes referred to as coproduction in education, emergency health care, and recreation services, to mention a few. [123] One net effect of this approach will, one hopes, be a more effective provision of services. However, as a by-product, or perhaps a precondition, the new arrangement will require a different level of interaction between agencies and their publics. As I described the phenomenon with regard to public education, the concept of a "service community" came to mind. [124] Simply stated, a service community is a collection of individuals brought together by a common set of objectives that operate according to agreed-on norms. In a school, for example, it might include teachers, parents, students, local merchants, and even service providers from municipal agencies.

It is rather instructive that the early manifestations of the most recent participatory impulses were identified in central cities like Chicago, Miami, Houston, Newark, and New York. As the activism of the 1960s and 1970s was a response to the political alienation of the poor, the present-day urge toward civic involvement is a response to the social alienation that is endemic to cities.

Specifically, it is a reaction to the large, impersonal, bureaucratic government that denies one of a sense of belonging. Inherent in the search for community is the desire to foster more personalized social structures and the need for richer forms of interaction and communication.

One of the notable bureaucratic concessions of the 1960s was the community affairs meeting held by local service administrators. The neighborhood precinct captain, for example, would arrive in a sea of blue uniforms, reciting data and displaying multicolored charts. He would patiently listen to complaints, cordially respond to questions, and occasionally volunteer a guarded pledge to improve the local condition. He would then disappear for another month, leaving residents to wonder what would come of the carefully staged ritual. Given a rising level of expectation, evident at least in some more progressive cities, such encounters are found to be even less satisfying by today's standards.

In a functioning service community the interaction between residents and government would be more regular and interactive. Not only would the precinct captain be expected to follow up on a promise, but residents would be given a chance to work directly with service providers (in this case police officers) to address local concerns. Residents' role would no longer be limited to the mere registering of a complaint, but they would actually have a part in crafting a solution. The goal here is to make the relationship between people and government a regular face-to-face interaction that brings tangible results. The new relationship is not only more rewarding for the client, but it is also more meaningful for the service provider. Before community policing, for example, interactions between police officers and the public tended to occur within the context of negative events such as the commission of a crime or some form of infraction against the community. Now there is a vehicle for positive interaction that can lead to a desirable set of outcomes, which is gratifying for all involved.

If the last generation's participatory agenda was to transform citizens and clients into constituents, the order for today is to allow all these actors to become part of a functioning organizational network. And added to the pleas for political empowerment would be the opportunity for richer forms of communication that promote better understanding between government organizations and their publics.

Note: *Originally published in Viteritti, J.P., The environmental context of communications: Public sector organizations, in* Handbook of Administrative Communication, *Garnett, J.L. and Kouzmin, A., Eds., Marcel Dekker, New York, 1997, chap. 4.*

Endnotes

1. Weber, M., *The Theory of Social and Economic Organization,* Free Press, New York, 1947.
2. Barnard, C.I., *The Functions of the Executive,* Harvard University Press, Cambridge, MA, 1938.
3. Simon, H.A., *Administrative Behavior: A Study of Decision-Making Processes in Administrative Organization,* Collier-Macmillan, New York, 1945.
4. March, J.G. and Simon, H.A., *Organizations,* Wiley, New York, 1958.
5. Katz, D. and Kahn, R.L., *The Social Psychology of Organizations,* Wiley, New York, 1966.
6. Thompson, J.D. and McEwen, W.J., Organizational goals and environment, *American Sociological Review,* 26, 23, 1958.
7. Bryson, J.M., *Strategic Planning for Public and Nonprofit Organizations,* Jossey-Bass, San Francisco, 1988.
8. Gouldner, A.W., *Patterns of Industrial Bureaucracy,* Free Press, Glencoe, IL, 1954.
9. Burns, T. and Stalker, G.M., *The Management of Innovation,* Tavistock, London, 1961.

10. Thompson, J.D., *Organizations in Action: Social Science Bases of Administrative Theory*, McGraw-Hill, New York, 1967.

11. Emery, F.E. and Trist, E.L., The causal texture of organizational environments, *Human Relations*, 18, 21, 1965.

12. Milliken, F.J., Three types of perceived uncertainty about the environment, *Academy of Management Review*, 12, 133, 1987.

13. Lawrence, P. and Lorsch, J., *Organization and Environment: Managing Differentiation and Integration*, Harvard University Press, Cambridge, MA, 1967.

14. Aldrich, H., *Organizations and Environments*, Prentice Hall, Englewood Cliffs, NJ, 1979.

15. Pfeffer, J. and Salancik, G.R., *The External Control of Organizations: A Resource Dependence Perspective*, Harper & Row, New York, 1978.

16. Kaufman, H., *Time, Chance and Organization: Natural Selection in a Perilous Environment*, Chatham House, Chatham, NJ, 1985.

17. Hannan, M.T. and Freeman, J., *Organizational Ecology*, Harvard University Press, Cambridge, MA, 1989.

18. Andrews, A., *The Concept of Corporate Strategy*, Irwin, Homewood, IL, 1980.

19. Porter, M.E., *Competitive Strategy: Techniques for Analyzing Industries and Competitors*, Free Press, New York, 1985.

20. Quinn, J.B., Mintzberg, H., and James, R.M., *The Strategy Process: Concepts, Contexts, and Cases*, Prentice-Hall, Englewood Cliffs, NJ, 1988.

21. Freeman, J., Organizational life cycles and natural selection processes, in *Research in Organizational Behavior: An Annual Series of Analytical Essays and Critical Reviews*, 4, Cummings, L.L. and Staw, B.M., Eds., JAI Press, Greenwich, CT, 1982.

22. Hannan, M.T., The ecology of organizational mortality: American labor unions, 1836-1985, *American Journal of Sociology*, 94, 25, 1988.

23. Viteritti, J.P., *Bureaucracy and Social Justice*, Kennikat Press, Port Washington, NY, 1979.

24. Murray, M.A., Comparing public and private management: An exploratory essay, *Public Administration Review*, 35, 364, 1975.

25. Weinberg, M.W., Public management and private management, *Journal of Policy Analysis and Management*, 3, 107, 1983.

26. Bozeman, B., *All Organizations Are Public: Bridging Public and Private Organizational Theories*, Jossey-Bass, San Francisco, 1987.

27. Allison, G.T., Public and private management: Are they fundamentally alike in all unimportant respects?, in *Public Management: Public and Private Perspectives*, Perry, J.L. and Kraemer, K.L., Eds., Mayfield, Palo Alto, CA, 1983.

28. Wamsley, G.L. and Zald, M.N., *The Political Economy of Public Organizations*, Heath, Lexington, MA, 1973.

29. Dahl, R.A. and Lindblom, C.E., *Politics, Economics and Welfare: Planning and Politico-Economic Systems Resolved into Basic Social Processes*, Harper & Row, New York, 1953.

30. Blau, P.M. and Scott, W.R., *Formal Organizations: A Comparative Approach*, Chandler, San Francisco, 1962.

31. Rainey, H.G., Backoff, R.W., and Levine, C.L., Comparing public and private organizations, *Public Administration Review*, 36, 233, 1976.

32. Perry, J.L. and Rainey, H.G., The public-private distinction in organization theory: A critique and research strategy, *Academy of Management Review*, 13, 182, 1988.

33. Wamsley, G.L. et al., Public administration and the governance process: Shifting the political dialogue, in *A Centennial History of the American Administrative State*, Chandler, R.C., Ed., Free Press, New York, 1987, chap. 1.

34. Terry, L.D., Leadership in the administrative state, *Administration & Society*, 21, 395, 1990.

35. Viteritti, J.P., *Across the River: Politics and Education in the City*, Holmes & Meier, New York, 1983.

36. Viteritti, J.P., Public organization environments: Constituents, clients and urban governance, *Administration & Society*, 21, 425, 1990.

37. Thompson, J.D., *Organizations in Action: Social Science Bases of Administrative Theory*, McGraw-Hill, New York, 1967.

38. Van Meter, D.S. and Van Horn, C.E., The policy implementation process: A conceptual framework, *Administration & Society*, 6, 445, 1975.

39. Sabatier, P.A. and Mazmanian, D.A., The implementation of public policy: A framework for analysis, *Policy Studies Journal*, 8, 538, 1980.

40. Backoff, R.W. and Nutt, P.C., A process of strategic planning with specific application for the nonprofit organization, in *Strategic Planning: Threats and Opportunities for Planners*, Bryson, J.M. and Einsweiler, R.C., Eds., Planners Press, Chicago, 1988, chap. 8.

41. Bryson, J.M., *Strategic Planning for Public and Nonprofit Organizations*, Jossey-Bass, San Francisco, 1988.

42. Ring, P.S., Strategic issues: What are they and from where do they come?, in *Strategic Planning: Threats and Opportunities for Planners*, Bryson, J.M. and Einsweiler, R.C., Eds., Planners Press, Chicago, 1988, chap. 5.

43. Nutt, P.C. and Backoff, R.W., *Strategic Management in Public and Third Sector Organizations*, Jossey-Bass, San Francisco, 1992.

44. Wechsler, B. and Backoff, R.W., The dynamics of strategy in public organizations, in *Strategic Planning: Threats and Opportunities for Planners*, Bryson, J.M. and Einsweiler, R.C., Eds., Planners Press, Chicago, 1988, chap. 7.

45. Lefton, M. and Rosengren, W.R., Organizations and clients: Lateral and longitudinal dimensions, *American Sociology Review*, 31, 802, 1966.

46. Parsons, T., How are clients integrated into service organizations?, in *Organizations and Clients: Essays in the Sociology of Service*, Rosengren, W.R., Lefton, M., and Bidwell, C.E., Eds., Charles Merrill, Chicago, 1970, chap. 1.

47. Rosengren, W.R., The careers of clients and organizations, in *Organizations and Clients: Essays in the Sociology of Service*, Rosengren, W.R., Lefton, M., and Bidwell, C.E., Eds., Charles Merrill, Chicago, 1970, chap. 6.

48. Turner, J., *Party and Constituency: Pressures on Congress*, Johns Hopkins University Press, Baltimore, 1951.

49. Miller, W.E. and Stokes, D.E., Constituency influence in Congress, *American Political Science Review*, 62, 45, 1963.

50. Mayhew, D.R., *Congress: The Electoral Connection*, Yale University Press, New Haven, CT, 1974.

51. Eulau, H. and Karps, P.D., The puzzle of representation: Specifying the components of responsiveness, *Legal Studies Quarterly*, 2, 233, 1977.

52. Fenno, R.F., *Home Style: House Members in their Districts*, Little Brown, Boston, 1978.

53. Wilson, W., The study of administration, *Political Science Quarterly*, 2, 197, 1887.

54. Pressman, J.L. and Wildavsky, A., *Implementation*, University of California Press, Berkeley, 1973.

55. Bardach, E., *The Implementation Game: What Happens After a Bill Becomes a Law*, MIT Press, Cambridge, MA, 1977.

56. Rourke, F.E., *Bureaucracy, Politics and Public Policy*, Little Brown, Boston, 1969.

57. Meier, K.J., *Politics and the Bureaucracy: Policymaking in the Fourth Branch of Government*, Brooks/Cole, Pacific Grove, CA, 1987.

58. Leiserson, A., *Administrative Regulation: A Study in Representation of Interests*, University of Chicago Press, Chicago, 1942.

59. Truman, D.B., *The Governmental Process: Political Interests and Public Opinion*, Alfred A. Knopf, New York, 1951.

60. Freeman, J.L., *The Political Process: Executive Bureau — Legislative Committee Relations*, Random House, New York, 1955.

61. Wildavsky, A., *The Politics of the Budgetary Process*, Little Brown, Boston, 1964.

62. Viteritti, J.P., Public organization environments: Constituents, clients and urban governance, *Administration & Society,* 21, 425, 1990.
63. Barker, E., Ed., *The Politics of Aristotle,* Oxford University Press, New York, 1962, 95.
64. Milbrath, L.M. and Goel, M.L., *Political Participation: How and Why Do People Get Involved in Politics?,* 2nd ed., Rand McNally, Chicago, 1977.
65. Conway, M.M., *Political Participation in the United States,* CQ Press, Washington, DC, 1991.
66. Easton, D., *A Systems Analysis of Political Life,* Wiley, New York, 1965, 212.
67. Seidman, H. and Gilmour, R., *Politics, Position and Power: From the Positive to the Regulatory State,* 4th ed., Little Brown, Boston, 1986.
68. Rosen, B., *Holding Bureaucracies Accountable,* Praeger, New York, 1989.
69. Aberbach, J.D., *Keeping a Watchful Eye: The Politics of Congressional Oversight,* Brookings Institution, Washington, DC, 1990.
70. Horowitz, D., *The Courts and Social Policy,* Brookings Institution, Washington, DC, 1977.
71. Viteritti, J.P., *Across the River: Politics and Education in the City,* Holmes & Meier, New York, 1983, 99–156.
72. Flicker, B., Ed., *Justice and School Systems: The Role of the Courts in Education Litigation,* Temple University Press, Philadelphia, 1990.
73. Lewis, E., *Public Entrepreneurship: Toward a Theory of Bureaucratic Political Power,* Indiana University Press, Bloomington, 1984.
74. Heclo, H., Issue networks and the executive establishment, in *The New American Political System,* Beer, S.H. and King, A.S., Eds., American Enterprise Institute, Washington, DC, 1978.
75. Milward, H.B., Interorganizational policy systems and research on public organizations, *Administration & Society,* 13, 457, 1982.
76. Keller, L.F., The political economy of public management: An interorganizational network perspective, *Administration & Society,* 15, 455, 1984.
77. Dahl, R.A. and Lindblom, C.E., *Politics, Economics and Welfare: Planning and Politico-Economic Systems Resolved into Basic Social Processes,* Harper & Row, New York, 1953.
78. Benson, J.K., The interorganizational network as a political economy, *Administrative Science Quarterly,* 20, 229, 1975.
79. Savas, E.S., *Privatizing the Public Sector: How to Shrink Government,* Chatham House, Chatham, NJ, 1982.
80. Donahue, J.D., *The Privatization Decision: Public Ends, Private Means,* Basic Books, New York, 1989.
81. Osborne, D. and Gaebler, T.A., *Reinventing Government: How the Entrepreneurial Spirit is Transforming the Public Sector,* Addison-Wesley, Reading, MA, 1992.
82. Chubb, J.E. and Moe, T.M., *Politics, Markets and America's Schools,* Brookings Institution, Washington, DC, 1990.
83. Hirschman, A.O., *Exit, Voice and Loyalty: Responses to Decline in Firms, Organizations, and States,* Harvard University Press, Cambridge, MA, 1970.
84. Leonard, T.C., *The Power of the Press: The Birth of American Political Reporting,* Oxford University Press, New York, 1986.
85. Stephens, M., *A History of News: From the Drum to the Satellite,* Viking, New York, 1989.
86. Ranney, A., *Channels of Power: The Impact of Television on American Politics,* Basic Books, New York, 1983.
87. Entman, R.M., *Democracy Without Citizens: Media and the Decay of American Politics,* Oxford University Press, New York, 1989.
88. Iyengar, S. and Kinder, D.R., *News that Matters: Television and American Opinion,* University of Chicago Press, Chicago, 1987.
89. Epstein, E.J., *Between Fact and Fiction: The Problem of Journalism,* Random House, New York, 1975.
90. Bates, S., *If No News, Send Rumors: Anecdotes of American Journalism,* St. Martin's, New York, 1989.
91. Sabato, L.J., *Feeding Frenzy: How Attack Journalism has Transformed American Politics,* Free Press, New York, 1991, 25–26.

92. Altheide, D.L., *Creating Reality: How TV News Distorts Events,* Sage, Beverly Hills, CA, 1976.

93. Bennett, L., *News: The Politics of Illusion,* Longman, White Plains, NY, 1988.

94. Lee, M.A. and Solomon, N., *Unreliable Sources: A Guide to Detecting Bias in the News Media,* Lyle Stuart, New York, 1990.

95. Krone, K.J., Jablin, F.M., and Putnam, L.L., Communication theory and organizational communication: Multiple perspectives, in *Handbook of Organizational Communication: An Interdisciplinary Perspective,* Jablin, F.M. et al., Eds., Sage, Beverly Hills, CA, 1987, chap. 1, 30–32.

96. Grunig, J.E. and Repper, F.C., Strategic management, publics, and issues, in *Excellence in Public Relations and Communications Management,* Grunig, J.E., Ed., Lawrence Erlbaum, Hillsdale, NJ, 1992, chap. 6.

97. Garnett, J.L., *Communicating for Results in Government: A Strategic Approach for Public Managers,* Jossey-Bass, San Francisco, 1992, 36.

98. Ibid, 43.

99. Edelman, M., *The Symbolic Uses of Politics,* University of Illinois Press, Urbana, 1964.

100. Huber, G.P. and Daft, R.D., The information environments of organizations, in *Handbook of Organizational Communication: An Interdisciplinary Perspective,* Jablin, F.M. et al., Eds., Sage, Beverley Hills, CA, 1987, chap. 5.

101. Daft, R.L. and Langel, R.H., Organizational information requirements, media richness and structural design, *Management Science,* 32, 554, 1986.

102. Daft, R.L. and Langel, R.H., Information richness: A new approach to managerial information processing and organizational design, in *Research in Organizational Behavior: An Annual Series of Analytical Essays and Critical Reviews,* 6, Staw, B.M. and Cummings, L.L., Eds., JAI Press, Greenwich, CT, 1984.

103. Daft, R.L. and Huber, G.P., How organizations learn: A communication framework, in *Research in the Sociology of Organizations,* Bacharach, S. and Tomasso, N., Eds., JAI Press, Greenwich, CT, 1986.

104. Ibid.

105. Lewis, P.V., *Organizational Communication: The Essence of Effective Management,* Wiley, New York, 1987.

106. Garnett, J.L., *Communicating for Results in Government: A Strategic Approach for Public Managers,* Jossey-Bass, San Francisco, 1992.

107. Meherabian, A., *Silent Messages,* Wadsworth, Belmont, CA, 1971.

108. Argyle, M. and Cook, M., *Gaze and Mutual Gaze,* Cambridge University Press, New York, 1976.

109. Mintzberg, H., *The Nature of Managerial Work,* Harper & Row, New York, 1973.

110. Williams, E., Teleconferencing: Social and psychological factors, *Journal of Communication,* 28, 125, 1978.

111. Hatry, H.P. et al., *How Effective are Your Community Services: Procedures for Monitoring the Effectiveness of Municipal Services,* Urban Institute, Washington, DC, 1977.

112. Rohr, J.A., *To Run a Constitution: The Legitimacy of the Administrative State,* University Press of Kansas, Lawrence, 1986.

113. Wamsley, G.L. et al., Public administration and the governance process: Shifting the political dialogue, in *A Centennial History of the American Administrative State,* Chandler, R.C., Ed., Free Press, New York, 1987, chap. 1.

114. Frederickson, H.G. and Chandler, R.C., Eds., Symposium on citizenship and public administration, *Public Administration Review,* 44, 99, 1984.

115. Altshuler, A., *Community Control,* Pegasus, New York, 1970.

116. Kotler, M., *Neighborhood Government: The Local Foundations of Political Life,* Bobbs-Merrill, Indianapolis, IN, 1969.

117. Marini, F., Ed., *Toward a New Public Administration: The Minnowbrook Perspective,* Chandler, New York, 1973.

118. Moynihan, D.P., *Maximum Feasible Misunderstanding: Community Action in the War on Poverty,* Free Press, New York, 1969.

119. Gawthrop, L.C., Civis, civitas, civititas: A new focus for the year 2000, *Public Administration Review,* 44, 101, 1984.
120. Stivers, C., The public agency as polis: Active citizenship in the administrative state, *Administration & Society,* 22, 86, 1990.
121. Goldstein, H., *Problem-Oriented Policing,* Temple University Press, Philadelphia, 1990.
122. Sparrow, M.K., Moore, M.H., and Kennedy, D.M., *Beyond 911: A New Era of Policing,* Basic Books, New York, 1990.
123. Brudney, J.L. and England, R.E., Toward a definition of the coproduction concept, *Public Administration Review,* 43, 59, 1983.
124. Viteritti, J.P., Urban governance and the idea of a service community, *Proceedings of the Academy of Political Science,* 37(2), 110, 1989.

Chapter 22

When Productivity and Communication Clash: Ethical Issues for Government Managers

James L. Garnett and Jay A. Sigler

Contents

Abstract: Productivity and communication are two administrative ideals that have received substantial emphasis in public management theory and practice. A major, although not adequately tested, assumption in government is that improved intra- and inter-organizational communication among government officials, managers, and employees; and closer contact among provider agencies, their service clienteles, and other non-client public will improve service productivity. More open and more accurate information flow among key participants in the service delivery process is assumed to result in greater productivity and better feedback on performance.

Without denigrating the importance of sound communication, this chapter examines situations where the need to communicate with elected officials, voters, and service clients jeopardizes efforts to improve productivity and service delivery. It explores the ethical implications for managers when the right-to-know in a democratic society conflicts with government's efforts to improve productivity and performance by identifying four types of productivity and communication conflict and noting some of the legal, administrative, and political causes of such conflict. By using a trifocal conceptual lens involving productivity–communication–ethics, public managers can gain a more realistic, accurate understanding of some key issues and value choices they must resolve.

Productivity and Communication: Ideal and Reality
Productivity and Communication: The Administrative Ideal

According to the traditional administrative ideal and to conventional wisdom, productivity and communication are both administrative values managers should pursue. Productivity has long been articulated as a core value of business and public management. Productivity has been defined in different ways and has often been understood differently by public managers and scholars. [1] Brudney and Morgan hold that "in the public sector, productivity has normally been defined to encompass both efficiency (output per unit of input) and effectiveness, the extent to which program objectives are met." [2] If this conceptualization is used, productivity encompasses a significant part of government performance, even if an agency's stated goals exclude notions of quality, equity, and other administrative values. The homages to productivity and its roots of efficiency and effectiveness are too numerous to capture fully. There are several useful attempts to do this. [3] The god of efficiency in particular has been so revered that it has even been articulated to accomplish other administrative aims. [4]

Even though *communication* has not held the reverence that productivity has, communication has been voiced as an administrative value since the classical era of management. Chester Barnard considered communication the first function of the executive. [5] For Luther Gulick communication was a key process underlying POSDCORB, particularly the functions of directing and coordinating. [6] More contemporary scholars of management have also noted the importance of communication for policy formulation, decision making, implementation, administrative control, and other management processes. Simon, Smithburg, and Thompson; Downs; Kaufman and Couzens; Gortner, Mahler, and Nicholson; Hood; Rainey; and Garnett make such a contribution. [7] Practitioner and scholar John Gardner has noted its centrality by stressing that "communication is at the very heart of the leader–follower or leader–constituent relationship." [8]

The administrative ideal assumes a direct, supporting relationship between communication and productivity: better communication leads to increased productivity. Faulty communication leads to lowered productivity. Ammons describes how faulty information dissemination serves as a barrier to productivity. [9] Banks and Rossini examine research showing how poor communication between political officials and managers and productivity-oriented technocrats (a relationship they call the political–technical interface) hindered productivity efforts. [10]

Some, although hardly enough, empirical research has tested the relationship between productivity and communication, most of it in the private sector. [11] In public sector research, O'Reilly and Roberts found in a study of military personnel a significant relationship between communicating information and individual and unit performance. Employees rated high performers tended to communicate information more consistently and openly. Gatekeeping (filtering information) and information overload were associated with lower performance. [12] In another study, Roberts and O'Reilly found that personnel in military research and development organizations who actively participated in information networks typically had higher performance ratings than isolates. Roberts and O'Reilly were not using a strict input–output definition of productivity, but a more general measure of performance that is still consistent with the concept we are using here. [13] Research in hospitals found significant relationships between an employee's communication behavior and performance ratings. [14]

Not all research has shown a direct, positive relationship, however. Some research indicates the communication–productivity relationship may be nonlinear or has found some negative consequences of communication. [15] Hawkins, Penley, and Peterson found in a military organization that employees who viewed their superiors as receptive and responsive and who did not value upward communication tended to get higher performance ratings from supervisors. [16] Underscoring both the subjectivity of performance ratings and of reactive survey research, it is hardly surprising that superiors value subordinates who think highly of them and who are basically content with receiving downward communication. In a large-scale study of local government productivity in the United States, Ammons and Molta found an inverse relationship between perceived importance of community relations and mayoral-manager rankings on productivity improvement. [17]

Such research has tended to examine the statistical relationships between aspects of communication and productivity without emphasizing the potential conflicts between these two administrative values. Even instances where the relationship is weak or inverse tend to be explained as measurement problems or as possible anomalies rather than as fundamental conflict between these administrative values.

Administrative Reality: Clashes between Productivity and Communication

Potential conflict between productivity and other administrative values has been observed by other researchers. In two administrative classic studies, Blau and Lipsky note that attempts to promote productivity may conflict with service *quality*. [18] In his pioneering study of "street-level bureaucrats," Lipsky observed that efforts to hold frontline employees accountable through efficiency/productivity measures could force employees into emphasizing quantifiable productivity objectives at the expense of quality or effectiveness objectives. Other researchers such as Chitwood, Okun, Hatry, and Wilenski stress the potential and often actual incompatibility between productivity and *equity*. [19] In a more recent examination, Brudney and Morgan attempt to overcome some of the conflict between productivity and *equity* and quality by emphasizing performance measurement that captures multiple administrative values. [20]

In a discussion of ethics surrounding government communication, Garnett describes how similar value conflicts can occur between productivity and the administrative value of *communication* which involves openness, access to information, accuracy, and honesty. [21] Reality often conflicts with the administrative ideal that assumes productivity and communication are both desirable values and are mutually reinforcing.

This chapter goes on to identify types of potential value conflict between productivity and communication and in so doing discusses some of the leading legal, administrative, and political causes or conditions for this value conflict and offers a conceptual framework for public managers to help them understand such conflict.

Conflict between Core Administrative Values

That administrative values compete and can even conflict has been grounded in the study of management. Gulick recognized competition among values in ways to organize. [22] In contrasting Theory X and Y, McGregor emphasized conflicts in assumptions about how workers behave and are motivated. [23] Contrasts in values about leadership highlight Burns' and Kouzes and Posner's comparisons of transactional and transformational leadership. Recognition that administrative values can compete is hardly new, although these and comparable works used the competing values to underscore other concepts rather than as an emphasis in its own right. [24]

Two recent efforts at a more self-conscious and comprehensive exploration of competing administrative values have been undertaken by Quinn and Goodsell. [25,26] In his *Beyond Rational Management: Mastering the Paradoxes and Competing Demands of High Performance*, Quinn contends that understanding organizational contradictions is crucial to improving and maintaining organizational effectiveness. To that end, Quinn develops a multi-dimensional Competing Values Framework that reflects alternative management models: Human Relations Model, Open Systems Model, Internal Process Model, and Rational Goal Model. In his framework, Quinn views communication and productivity not as directly competing values, but as two values that both emphasize organizational control.

Goodsell articulated his *Five M* framework more to enlighten decisions over ethical dilemmas than to serve as an overall framework for achieving organizational effectiveness. Goodsell contends that five basic value orientations predominate in American public administration: means, morality, multitude, market, and mission values. The *means* orientation casts public administrators as the passive tools or means to serve higher authority. This orientation stresses the duty of public managers to implement policy made by the legislature, executive, or the courts. Taking this orientation, managers stress the values of productivity, efficiency, and effectiveness in faithfully carrying out their charge to serve the public through its democratically elected representatives.

Morality is another potential administrative value orientation discussed by Goodsell. In a morality orientation, administrators do not just serve their democratic masters but are also guided by moral values such as "equality, justice, honesty, fairness, and the protection of individual rights." [27] The morality orientation, rooted in higher moral law, represents the kinds of emphasis often reflected in government ethics codes.

The *multitude* orientation is grounded in the normative foundation of populist equality. Taking this orientation, managers respond "neither to elected officials nor to a higher morality, but to the citizens themselves, directly and immediately." [28] Consistent with this orientation are efforts by public administrators to promote citizen participation, support coproduction of services, serve as advocates for citizen rights and welfare, and communicate directly and regularly with citizens. Just as the multitude orientation is a product of radical and liberal groups in the 1960s, the *market* perspective stems from conservative groups in the 1970s. Administrators taking this value orientation are guided by market economic forces rather than higher authority, higher morality, or populism. The public choice school of political economy embodies the market orientation. Values stressed under this orientation include economic competition, deregulation, privatization, and fee for service. Economic efficiency provides the normative foundation for the market orientation.

Under the *mission* value orientation, administrators "obey their own emergent conceptions of the proper missions of their agencies." [29] These missions are articulated by legislation and by executive and court orders, and news media coverage. And over time, public managers develop their own sense of their agency's mission through experience, contact with other professional managers, and professional activities. Under this orientation

> administrative agencies are seen as legitimate actors in the governance process in their own right, along with elected officers and the courts. Hence, their institutional strength and health are inherently of value, as is satisfactory service to their clients and other publics. These agencies pursue the public interest, which in this context is defined as fulfilling the adapted mission in the long-term interests of all affected parties, proceeding on the basis of an agency's past experience, and judiciously weighing competing claims and arguments in policymaking and implementation. [30]

A sense of the "public interest" serves as the normative foundation for the mission orientation.

Goodsell contends that each of these orientations is justifiable and has legitimate underpinnings. Public administrators need to recognize that these competing value orientations are sometimes incompatible, forcing decisions about which values to emphasize.

Types of Value Conflict between Productivity and Communication

Building on the theme of value conflict among core administrative values, we have developed a typology of productivity-communication value conflict shown in Figure 22.1. In this first iteration, the typology is based on two dimensions: *communication role* and *communication flow*. *Communication role* involves roles as sender or receiver. *Communication flow* pertains to the direction of communication: internal sender to internal receiver (internal flow), internal sender to external receiver (outward flow), external sender to internal receiver (inward flow), or external sender to external receiver (external flow). In most cases two way communication exists making internal and external actors and both senders and receivers. For our purposes, however, attribution of sender and receiver is determined by two criteria — who primarily *initiates* a message and which role is of longest *duration*.

Type I: Internal Sender/Internal Receiver

Type I value conflict occurs when internal intra-agency communication among government managers and employees hinders rather than facilitates productivity efforts. Productivity advocates

	Receiver: Internal	Receiver: External
Sender: **Internal**	Type I Internal Agency Communication (Internal Flow) Agency employees and management sending to other employees and managers within the same agency e.g., internal reporting, memos, grapevine, intra-agency publications	Type II Public Information (Outward Flow) Official and unofficial communication to clients, media, constituents, co-producers, other agencies e.g., public information, trial balloons, leaks, official reports
Sender: **External**	Type III External Feedback (Inward Flow) External clients, constituents, others sending to internal agency management and employees e.g., requests, complaints, competing demands on agency	Type IV External Exchange (External Flow) Clients, media, constituents, other agencies, co-producers, and other external actors communicating with each other e.g., news reports, bargaining among other actors, coalition politics

Figure 22.1   Types of Value Conflict between Communication and Productivity

may articulate the needs or successes of their program, generating opposition and resistance from competing agency programs or projects. Communicating honest assessments of shortcomings and resource needs may prompt agency superiors to kill or reduce the productivity effort. Requests by agency superiors for frequent and perhaps detailed progress reports may detract from the actual attention to productivity.

A clear illustration of Type I conflict is provided by the construction of agency ethics codes. Many federal, state, and local government agencies have developed their own internal ethics codes for employees to follow. Such codes typically go beyond requirements of law, dealing with such issues as policies on accepting gifts, nepotism, outside employment, and employee relationships with agency clients. These codes are intended to guide employee conduct. Agency ethics codes can interfere with agency operating productivity. Much communication effort is necessary to have an effective ethics program rather than one which only pays perfunctory attention to the issue.

Communicating to its employees, to elected officials and to citizens that an agency takes ethics seriously usually involves the use of multiple media — briefings, regulations, statements, meetings, workshops, and behavior of top administrators — to convey that the agency does more than pay lip service to ethics. It also involves varying and repeating these messages as appropriate to the different audiences inside and outside the agency. The content of these messages evolves as the agency addresses such issues as why ethics affects the agency, individual employee, and public to be served; what the relevant ethics policies are; what behavior is acceptable and unacceptable and under what conditions; who is responsible for fielding questions about what is acceptable behavior; how employees should report violations; what the real consequences of ethics violations are; and the agency's belief that ethical dimensions extend beyond illegalities or improprieties and that willful failure to communicate needed information or otherwise giving less than a best effort in serving the public is unethical. [31]

Time and energy consumed in processing ethics complaints or investigations and in the considerable communicating task involved detract from time and energy devoted to service or product delivery. On the other hand, an agency that has no ethics code or program may be less distracted from productivity efforts, but be less ethically alert. These choices involve a conflict between Goodsell's orientations of *morality* and *means*.

Affirmative Action reviews are sometimes an example of Type I conflict. Such reviews by the Affirmative Action unit of another organizational unit's workforce composition often pit these two units against each other because of the different roles they perform. The more fully the operational unit reports its Affirmative Action status and the more communication with the Affirmative Action unit, the less time and attention the operating unit will be able to devote to operational productivity. Both Affirmative Action and productivity values are supposed to be pursued within our system, but conflict between them is possible.

Type II: Internal Sender/External Receiver

Type II conflicts involve primary internal senders whether official (e.g., news releases, agency reports) or unofficial (leaks, rumors) communicating to external receivers (clients, constituents, news media, or other government agencies).

Sometimes the value conflict occurs over communication between government agencies themselves. For example, Meltsner reports how the volume of reports, memos, meetings, briefings, and other communications provided by the United States General Services Administration to satisfy the demand for information by the Bureau of the Budget and other actors in the 1970s delayed proposals to replace government vehicles sooner in the government motor pool. [32] In this instance, the value of supplying increased information to a greater number of audiences was favored over attempting to push through swiftly reforms that promised to produce (and later delivered) increased productivity in terms of lower down time, lower repair cost, and a more useable vehicle fleet.

Some of these delays could certainly be attributed to "stalling tactics" by the Bureau of the Budget and others who opposed this change or wanted to be more certain of its results. Yet the General Services Administration chose as a tactical and value choice to promote communication instead of pushing for early closure on this issue. Keeping communication channels open and conscientiously supplying information even when so much study and analysis had already been provided ultimately proved successful in later adoption of revised standards for vehicle replacement.

In other situations, Type II conflict can occur when government agencies provide or choose not to provide information to external constituencies, clients, and news media.

In the early 1970s, Mayor John V. Lindsay's administration in New York City embarked on a program involving systematic analysis of municipal service need and delivery patterns and led to redistribution of many services on the basis of need. For example, extra trash pickups and extra police patrols were scheduled for East Harlem, the South Bronx, and other neighborhoods where litter and crime were worse than in most parts of the city. Such changes made more effective use of strapped city resources by redeploying them on the basis of greater need. These redistributive productivity efforts were publicized by the city as responsive government and were reported in detail by *The New York Times* and other news organs. When residents in more affluent areas of New York City, areas where residents were more likely to vote and pay higher taxes, discovered through the press that this redistribution was occurring, they opposed decreased services for their neighborhoods. The Lindsay administration responded to substantial voter and taxpayer pressure by retrenching its reform program and restoring some services to more affluent, more powerful neighborhoods.

This is an example where the rights of voting and taxpaying constituencies to be informed about productivity improvement efforts jeopardize attempts to improve service to indigents and other clients whose needs are greater, but who lack the political clout of those who fear their services or tax bills will suffer if service to others is improved.

Another case of Type II conflict comes from the realm of ethics enforcement. A few American states have legislated ethics codes for local governments, imposing additional administrative burdens upon these governments. In New Jersey, a 1991 Local Government Ethics Act requires most public officials to file financial disclosure forms. These officials must list the names and addresses of sources of income over $2,000; the sources of fees over $250 for speeches and writings; the sources of gifts, reimbursements, or prepaid expenses exceeding $400; the names of all businesses in which an interest is held; and the addresses of all real property held in the state. The purpose of this filing is to disclose potential conflicts of interest.

The state agency responsible for enforcing financial disclosure statements has only five employees assigned to handle the 35,000 to 50,000 statements received annually. It is doubtful that individual forms can be scrutinized carefully enough to identify conflict of interest, yet the major reporting of this information by local government officials detracts their attention from productivity issues. Other requirements of this Ethics Act mandating complaint procedures and hearing processes also make the process so burdensome to local governments that the Act not only detracts from credibility, but, ironically, likely hinders the effectiveness of ethics policy implementation itself.

Type III: External Sender/Internal Receiver

Type III conflict occurs when the primary sender is external and principal receiver internal. This can take different forms. Demands of elected officials for information about service delivery efforts can put productivity improvements at risk by raising expectations of performance or by calling into question managerial tactics or the effects on constituents. For example, Shumavon describes how city code requirements to communicate bid specifications in the Cincinnati, Ohio *City Bulletin* to prospective suppliers can add weeks to the purchasing process, particularly if errors are made or if minority businesses are involved requiring a special process to give them a better chance of competing. [33] These delays not only hamper the efficiency of the procurement system itself but also can reduce overall municipal productivity since city agencies experience delays in getting needed equipment and supplies. The purchasing department receives complaints about the cumbersome nature of the process. Department officials and employees believe that many of those in other agencies who complain, blame the department for being inefficient rather than understand and accept that other values — openness and equity — are being pursued, thus limiting pure productivity. But pressure from minority and political groups is also expressed to the city manager and purchasing department officials that supports the bidding process and the extra requirements that apply to minority businesses. Such communication stressing the values of openness and equity conflicts with the messages lower purchasing department employees receive about the need to make procedures more streamlined and economical. Officials and employees in the purchasing department felt this tension.

Another example of Type III value conflict stems from requirements for citizen participation. Aron chronicles how a provision in the 1970 Migrant Health Act requiring that "persons broadly representative of all elements of the population to be served [be] given an opportunity to participate in the implementation of such programs" led to delays and inefficiencies in establishing a health clinic for migrant farm workers in Bakersfield, California. [34] Invited participation by competing community groups and organizations emphasized communication (Goodsell's multitude orientation) but at the expense of service effectiveness and productivity. Aron reports that the results of much negotiating and attempts at implementation showed a small percentage of appropriations actually spent on clinic operations.

One official from the United States Department of Health and Welfare was quoted as saying: "I would say that we've been more interested in using the clinic as an instrument of long-range social change than in meeting the short-run health needs of the target community." [35] In this situation, communication values are placed above productivity values. Similar examples can be found from those environmental and consumer protection statutes which mandate citizen participation.

The Clean Air Act, for example, mandates a role for environmental groups in developing and implementing clean air policy. The Act fails to specify, however, which groups are to be represented and how strong a role they are to play in policy development and implementation. Active and open involvement between these groups and government agencies enhances the quantity of external communication agencies receive, but it can complicate the policy process since these groups may be vying for representation and influence in that process, overloading the agency with information and attempts to influence decisions. Skewed representation is also prevalent. Those organizations best funded and organized and best able to articulate their position typically gain representation and influence. Such skewed representation contradicts Goodsell's *multitude* orientation with its accent on true representativeness.

Type IV: External Sender/External Receiver

Type IV value conflict occurs when external actors communicate to other external actors. For example, agency clients may communicate their concerns over productivity improvement efforts to news media whose reporting may then be picked up and interpreted by legislators and other key constituents, making such productivity efforts vulnerable to agency changes or to budget cuts.

Type IV conflict also can occur when individual or organizational members of a coalition interact to work against productivity efforts. Efforts by Boston's Department of Health and Hospitals to deploy more productive measures such as increased emphasis on testing to combat the AIDS disease were opposed by certain members of a broad AIDS coalition who doubted the efficacy of testing the poorest or hardest to reach target populations such as intravenous drug users. [36]

Police-community relations sometimes degenerate into Type IV value conflicts involving community groups, legislative actors, news organizations, and others. The management of the Rodney King beating by several Los Angeles police officers in 1991 is a classic example of how allowing a Type IV conflict to get out of hand has disrupted the morale and productivity of that department for some time to come. News media organizations, external political actors, and even street gangs may be regarded as exogenous forces in this tragic episode. By refusing to discipline the offending officers via internal procedures, Police Commissioner Daryl Gates allowed the court, media, and other external actors to do most of the communicating and decision making among themselves. This loss of control over the situation allowed it to get out of hand. The resulting rifts damaged morale and productivity in more than the Los Angeles Police Department.

Productivity and Communication Clashes: Next Steps

In this chapter we have tried to take a new approach to the long-standing tensions between productivity, communication, and ethics. By looking at government issues with this trifocal conceptual lens, a more realistic insight is possible. Next steps after further refining the types of conflict are to conduct empirical research on situations involving one or more of the four types and exploring how public administrators attempt to resolve these types of value conflict between communication and productivity through *denial tactics* (denying that value conflict exists), *sublimation tactics* (sublimating one set of values to emphasize the other), *reconciliation tactics* (working to reconcile the differences between both sets of values), *redefinition tactics* (redefining the situation to produce a different value configuration), or through some other means. We think this research can make an important contribution to guiding public administrators in understanding conflicts among administrative values and in resolving such conflicts.

Acknowledgments

We wish to acknowledge the invaluable assistance of Alan Jarman in suggesting models for further consideration and John Hart for capable editorial and logistical support in preparing the transcript.

Note: *Originally published in Garnett, J.L. and Sigler, J.A., When productivity and communication clash: Ethical issues for government managers, International Journal of Public Administration, 19, 2235, 1996.*

Endnotes

1. Ammons, D.N. and Molts, D.J., Productivity emphasis in local government: An assessment of the impact of selected policy environment factors, in *Promoting Productivity in the Public Sector*, Kelly, R.M., Ed., St. Martin's Press, New York, 1988, chap. 3; Dalton, T.C. and Dalton, L.C., The Politics of Measuring Public Sector Performance, ibid, chap. 2.

2. Brudney, J.L. and Morgan, D.R., Local government productivity: Efficiency and equity, in *Promoting Productivity in the Public Sector*, Kelly, R.M., Ed., St. Martin's Press, New York, 1988, chap. 9.

3. Burkhead, J. and Hennigan, P., Productivity analysis: A search for definition and order, *Public Administration Review*, 38, 34, 1978; Dalton, T.C. and Dalton, L.C., op. cit.

4. Gulick, L.H., Interview with Garnett, J.L., November 30, 1976; Garnett, J.L., *Reorganizing State Government: The Executive Branch*, Westview, Boulder, CO, 1980.

5. Barnard, C.I., *The Functions of the Executive*, Harvard University Press, Cambridge, MA, 1938.

6. Gulick, L., Notes on the theory of organization, in *Papers on the Science of Administration*, Gulick, L. and Urwick, L., Eds., Institute of Public Administration, New York, 1937, chap. 1.

7. Simon, H.A., Smithburg, D.W., and Thompson, V.A., *Public Administration*, Knopf, New York, 1950; Downs, A., *Inside Bureaucracy*, Little Brown, Boston, 1967; Kaufman, H., *Administrative Feedback: Monitoring Subordinates' Behavior*, Brookings Institution, Washington, DC, 1973; Gortner, H.F., Mahler, J., and Nicholson, J.B., *Organization Theory: A Public Perspective*, Dorsey, Chicago, 1987; Hood, C.H., *The Tools of Government*, Chatham House, Chatham, NJ, 1983; Rainey, H.G., *Understanding and Managing Public Organizations*, Jossey-Bass, San Francisco, 1991; Garnett, J.L., *Communicating for Results in Government: A Strategic Approach for Public Managers*, Jossey-Bass, San Francisco, 1992.

8. Gardner, J., *On Leadership*, Free Press, New York, 1990, 5.

9. Ammons, D.N., Common barriers to productivity improvement in local government, *Public Productivity Review*, 9, 293, 1985.

10. Banks, J. and Rossini, F.A., Management science failures in the public sector, *Public Productivity Review* 10(4), 15, 1987.

11. Hellweg, S.A. and Phillips, S.L., Communication and productivity in organizations, *Public Productivity Review*, 6, 276, 1982.

12. O'Reilly, C.A. and Roberts, K.H., Communication and performance in organizations, paper presented at the Academy of Management Annual Meeting, Orlando, FL, 1977.

13. Roberts, K.H. and O'Reilly, C.A., Some correlates of communication roles in organizations, *Academy of Management Journal*, 22, 42, 1979.

14. Szilagyi, A.D. and Sims, H.P., A Causal Inference Analysis Between Organizational Climate Perceptions and Individual Performance over Three Different Time Lags, paper presented at the Academy of Management Annual Meeting, San Francisco, 1978.

15. Hazen, M.D. and Balthrop, V.W., A Causal Analysis of the Relationship Between Communication Satisfaction and Productivity, Role Discrepancy, Need Level, and Organizational Position, paper presented at the International Communication Association, Chicago, 1975.

16. Hawkins, B.L., Penley, L.E., and Peterson, T.O., Developing Behaviorally Oriented Communication Scales for the Study of the Communication-Performance Relationship, paper presented at the Academy of Management Annual Meeting, San Diego, CA, 1981.

17. Ammons, D.N. and Molta, D.J., op. cit.

18. Blau P., *Dynamics of Bureaucracy*, rev. ed., University of Chicago Press, Chicago, 1964; Lipsky, M., *Street-Level Bureaucracy*, Russell Sage, New York, 1980.

19. Chitwood, S.R., Social equity and social service productivity, *Public Administration Review*, 34, 5, 1974; Okun, A.M., *Equality and Efficiency: The Big Trade Off*, Brookings Institution, Washington, DC, 1975; Hatry, H.P., Performance measurement principles and techniques: An overview for government, *Public Productivity Review*, 4, 312, 1980; Wilenski, P., Efficiency or equity: Competing values in administrative reform, *Policy Studies Journal*, 9, 1239, 1980.

20. Brudney, J.L. and Morgan, D.R., op. cit.

21. Garnett, J.L., op. cit.

22. Gulick, L., Notes on the theory of organization, op. cit.

23. McGregor, D., *Human Side of Enterprise*, McGraw-Hill, New York, 1960.

24. Burns, J.M., *Leadership*, Harper & Row, New York, 1978; Kouzes, J.M. and Posner, B.Z., *The Leadership Challenge: How to Get Extraordinary Things Done in Organizations*, Jossey-Bass, San Francisco, 1987.

25. Quinn, R.E., *Beyond Rational Management: Mastering the Paradoxes and Competing Demands of High Performance*, Jossey-Bass, San Francisco, 1988.
26. Goodsell, C.T., Balancing competing values, in *Handbook of Public Administration*, Perry, J.L., Ed., Jossey-Bass, San Francisco, 1989, chap. 40.
27. Ibid., 577.
28. Ibid.
29. Ibid, 578.
30. Ibid.
31. Garnett, J.L., op. cit., 246.
32. Meltsner, A., *Policy Analysts in the Bureaucracy*, University of California Press, Berkeley, 1976, 246–250.
33. Shumavon, D.H., Productivity and social goals: A case study from Cincinnati, Ohio, in *Promoting Productivity in the Public Sector*, Kelly, R.M., Ed., St. Martin's Press, New York, 1988, chap. 10.
34. Aron, M., Dumping $2.6 million on Bakersfield (or how not to build a migratory farm workers' clinic), in *Public Administration: Cases and Concepts*, 5th ed., Stillman, R.J., II, Ed., Houghton-Mifflin, Boston, MA, 1991, 89.
35. Ibid.
36. Scott, E., Planning for early intervention in HIV infection: Judith Kurland and the Boston Department of Health and Hospitals, in *Public Administration: Cases and Concepts*, 5th ed., Stillman, R.J., II, Ed., Houghton-Mifflin, Boston, MA, 1991, 404.

APPENDIX VII

Questions for Review and Discussion

1. Describe the environment in which government public relations is practiced.
2. What are some of the factors that contribute to government public relations being vulnerable to outside forces?
3. As a public administrator, what steps can you take so that your agency has a robust and effective public relations program without triggering criticism from the outside?

Additional Reading

Dimock, M.E., Selling public enterprise to the public, *National Municipal Review*, 23, 660, 1934. [Path-breaking essay arguing that it is legitimate for public agencies to sell to the citizenry the need and justification for government programs.]

Lee, M., President Nixon sees a 'cover up': Public relations in federal agencies, *Public Relations Review*, 23, 301, 1997.

Lee, M., When Congress tried to cut Pentagon public relations: A lesson from history, *Public Relations Review*, 26, 131, 2000.

Lee, M., The image of the government flack: Movie depictions of public relations in public administration, *Public Relations Review*, 27, 297, 2001.

Lee, M., The first federal public information service, 1920–1933: At the U.S. Bureau of Efficiency!, *Public Relations Review*, 29, 415, 2003.

Lee, M., When government used publicity against itself: Toledo's Commission of Publicity and Efficiency, 1916–1975, *Public Relations Review*, 31, 55, 2005.

Stoke, H.W., Executive leadership and the growth of propaganda, *American Political Science Review*, 35, 490, 1941. [In the run-up to World War II, this political scientist was concerned about the danger to democracy of combining the powers of a strong chief executive and public communications techniques. Based on modern-day government, were the author's concerns indeed valid or not?]

Yarwood, D.L. and Enis, B.M., Problems in regulating federal executive branch publicity and advertising programs, *American Review of Public Administration*, 18, 29, 1988.

THE EXTENDED PUBLIC SECTOR: PUBLIC RELATIONS BY NONPROFIT AGENCIES

Introduction to Section VIII

In the 21st century, Americans have become more aware of the existence of a third and separate sector in our political economy. While 20th-century rhetoric tended to differentiate solely between government and business, the increasing size and importance of the nonprofit sector now justifies considering it as a third sector, along with the public and private sectors. Reflecting this changing awareness, more and more institutions of higher education have begun offering professional training in nonprofit management (or nonprofit studies) independent of their pre-existing public administration and business administration programs.

Therefore, given its status as an independent sector, the practice of public relations in the nonprofit sector would be considered a different activity from its uses in business and in government. Certainly, the qualitative differences among the three sectors justify viewing public relations as inherently different in each sector. For example, many nonprofits engage in advocacy efforts, mostly focusing on trying to influence public policy. In these instances, the *target* of an advocacy project would likely be government. But, there is no converse phenomenon in government public relations. American political culture looks askance at government agencies engaging in high profile advocacy efforts to change public policy. That would quickly be denounced as propaganda. (See Chapter 19.) That means advocacy can be part of nonprofit public relations, but not government public relations. (It's also, of course, found in business administration, usually called lobbying or governmental affairs.)

Despite inherent differences in the practice of public relations between government and the nonprofit sector, there is one important reason to include in this volume a brief section about nonprofit public relations. Increasingly in the 21st century, nonprofit agencies have become the deliverers of government-financed goods and services. In a trend that began largely (but not exclusively) on the national level with the implementation of President Johnson's Great Society programs, government more and more is only the *financier* of public policy. Instead of having government employees provide, say, welfare services, these are increasingly delivered by nonprofit agencies under contracts with government. (Sometimes, of course, the contracting-out phenomenon includes private business.) Fewer and fewer health and social service programs are provided to the public directly by a civil servant. Instead, governments hire nonprofits — sometimes through competitive bidding, sometimes not — to provide those services. Clients and customers may never come in contact with a government agency or employee, but the goods and services they are receiving are paid for by the taxpayers.

There are advantages and disadvantages to this approach to service delivery. Given the purpose of this reader, there is no need to delve into the philosophical and practical arguments for and against third-party delivery of government-financed services. Rather, with this increasing role of nonprofit agencies in providing the citizenry with public services, it is quite relevant to note the practice of public relations in the nonprofit sector. When nonprofits front for government, they are part of a broadly defined public sector. However, given the factors that differentiate nonprofit management from public administration (such as ownership, accountability, and independence) it is useful to focus on nonprofit public relations as an activity that is slightly different from government public relations. While the source financing the service is the same, the context of the program deliverer is distinctly different.

Given these realities in the relationship between government and nonprofits, Chapter 23 provides a *tour d'horizon* of the practice of public relations in the nonprofit sector. It seeks to provide an overview of nonprofit public relations, especially focusing on activities that are ancillary to the core purpose of most nonprofits, namely, the provision of goods and services. In this context, public relations supports the mission of the agency by enhancing the organization's external communications activities. The key theme to focus on is how nonprofit and government public relations are similar and how they are different.

Chapter 23

Public Relations for Nonprofit Organizations

Mordecai Lee

Contents

Introduction

A focus on external relations in nonprofit organizations assists in understanding that an agency consists of more than the sum of its tangible components, such as employees, finances and real property. Similarly, the skill sets needed by a nonprofit executive extend beyond managing these 'in house' components, such as human resources, budgeting and asset management. An external relations perspective helps emphasize that the totality of a nonprofit agency includes people and entities that are outside its formal and legal boundaries and the duties of a nonprofit executive include leading 'beyond the wall,' such as through management of external relations.

Increasing Importance

Several recent trends have contributed to the increasing importance of external relations in non-profit organizations. First, the emergence of instant communications technologies permits and facilitates new forms of external communication that previously were cumbersome or expensive. For example, an Internet newsletter to contributors has many financial and temporal advantages over a hard-copy version that is mailed to a constantly changing mailing list.

Second, in an era of increasing privatization, subcontracting, third-party service delivery, alliances, public–private partnerships and social entrepreneurship, more and more of the totality of a nonprofit agency is outside its formal boundaries of, for example, activities in which its salaried employees engage.

Third, one manifestation of external relations, advocacy, is becoming an increasingly visible activity in the nonprofit sector. Nonprofit organizations with a primary mission of public advocacy are a fast-growing category within the nonprofit sector. Salamon estimated that the number of nonprofit advocacy organizations grew 68% between 1977 and 1992, increased their employment by 48% and through 1995 increased their revenue by 216%. [1] For other categories of nonprofit agencies, advocacy is an important secondary activity. For example, a 1996 conference on the contemporary role of foundations identified their increased "need for professional communication capabilities to educate their publics and influence policy debates." [2]

Fourth, the Guidelines for Graduate Professional Education in Nonprofit Organizations, Management and Leadership issued by the National Association of Schools of Public Affairs and Administration (NASPAA) include external relations as one of 14 subjects that should be included in a curriculum. [3] Similarly, Wish and Mirabella list public relations — within the larger rubric of 'fundraising, marketing and public relations' — as one of the seven major categories of a curricular model of nonprofit management education. [4] A survey of faculty, practitioners and students regarding the skills needed by nonprofit administrators listed public relations as one of eight 'most important' core subjects. [5]

Fifth, management theorists have increasingly emphasized the importance of external relations. It is both a specialized staff function within large organizations as well as an operating concept shared by the agency's management. The higher a manager moves up the hierarchy, the more she or he deals with external issues and constituencies. This necessitates a greater need for having and using public relations skills. In the private sector, corporate CEOs are now estimated to spend 25–75% of their time on external relations. [6–9]

Scope

There is a lack of uniformity of nomenclature for this subject matter. External relations, as an overarching moniker, is sometimes also called public affairs, public relations, external communication, community relations or governmental affairs. [10] The critical decision point is what external relations encompasses. A literal definition of external relations would encompass all interactions between the salaried employees of a nonprofit agency or its board members with any other individuals or organizations. This, however, would include activities that are the core mission of a nonprofit agency, such as the marketing and delivery of its services to clients or its relationships with donors and volunteers. It would also cover business activities such as purchasing and vendor relations. These latter activities are generally ministerial in nature from the perspective of external communications strategies. When external relations is defined to cover the totality of the agency's out-of-house contacts, it then loses any analytic or applied utility. Focusing on everything is tantamount to highlighting nothing.

Similarly, a broad approach to external relations, as defined by the NASPAA guidelines, would include all advocacy organizations. However, for these nonprofit agencies, external relations is their *raison d'être*. [8] The study of their external relations would be tantamount to a review of the entire agency's operations. In this situation, too, the prism of external relations adds little to the observer or practitioner.

A pragmatic approach to external relations focuses on those discrete activities that are important to the life of a nonprofit agency, but are ancillary to the agency's central mission and purpose as well as its ministerial external business relationships. External relations contributes to broad, amorphous goodwill towards the agency on behalf of the public-at-large and other more selected populations.

External relations is defined here as an agency's secondary out-of-house activities, whether planned or unplanned, that affect its standing with the public-at-large and with specific groups, exclusive of its ongoing external relationships with clients, volunteers and funders. Specifically, external relations includes media relations, lobbying/advocacy, citizen relations, community relations and crisis management. An effective external relations operation must be fully integrated into the primary mission of the agency, by working to further the agency's strategic plan, as well as its marketing, development, volunteer and employee training programs. For more information on conducting all aspects of external relations, see Endnotes [12,13].

Media Relations

The most common purpose of nonprofit external relations is to deal with reporters from the news media. This can be reactive and/or proactive. As a reactive activity, agency staff handle inquiries initiated by journalists covering a story that has some connection to the agency, such as its programs, financing, operating policies or expertise. When answering media inquiries, two approaches are possible for larger agencies with specialized media relations staff. Some agencies prefer to rely on their expert staff to deal directly with the media. This is a way to protect less expert employees of the agency from common mistakes when talking with a reporter. Using this approach, the spokesperson for the agency is the media relations professional. Other agencies use the media relations staff as facilitators. With this latter approach, staff focus on connecting the reporter to the optimal agency employee for that particular issue. In these situations, instead of having one person as the agency's permanent 'face' and 'voice,' the agency has multiple spokespersons.

With proactive media relations, a nonprofit agency initiates an interaction with the media, in an effort to persuade reporters or editors that a specific story idea is worth covering. In these cases, the reason for contacting the reporter is usually structured around an upcoming agency event, such as an unveiling of a new program, the announcement of a major contribution or the laying of a cornerstone of a new facility. These events are planned and intended to make the agency look good. Coverage is unpredictable and often dictated by the press or absence of other 'breaking news' in the same news cycle as the agency event.

The scope of an agency's media relations activities should not be limited to the traditional mass media of daily newspapers and the news departments of commercial television and radio stations. In addition, nontraditional mass media can be a further means for the agency to promote its message. The latter can include weekly newspapers, shoppers, public television and radio, student newspapers and radio stations, regional magazines, organizational newsletters and specialized publications intended for such groups as businesses, women, residents of a particular neighborhood or hobbyists.

Sometimes, a nonprofit agency needs to bypass the media so that the public-at-large or a specific audience hears the agency's message despite a lack of coverage by the traditional mass media. In that case, communication activities fall under the rubric of citizen relations, rather than media relations (see below). For more information on conducting media relations, see Endnotes [14–16].

Lobbying and Advocacy

This area consists of two separate but related activities. First, lobbying (sometimes called government relations) describes the direct efforts by a nonprofit agency to affect public sector decision making. This can occur at the local, state or federal level and can be targeted towards the legislative branch, the chief elected official of the executive branch (mayor, county executive, governor or president) or a government agency. This form of lobbying focuses on issues, not direct funding of the agency's programs. Hence, lobbying by the American Heart Association of Congress and the president for increased federal funding for heart research would be considered part of the agency's external relations activity. On the other hand, the association's communications with a specific federal agency about grants and contracts to fund the association's direct services would generally not be considered external relations.

The difference between the two examples is that the former reflects the disinterested views of the organization while the latter concerns its self-interest. This distinction is the effect of the definition of external relations used here, namely, that it is not about the core mission and in-house operations of an agency, such as its ongoing relationships with clients, volunteers and funders. This latter activity involved in government funding is sometimes called program funding, grantsmanship or contract management. In addition, as mentioned earlier, this overview of external relations is not applicable to nonprofit agencies whose main purpose is issue advocacy.

The second activity by a nonprofit agency under this rubric is usually called grass-roots advocacy. This is different from lobbying because its focus is on efforts by the organization to affect public sector decision making indirectly. A nonprofit agency sometimes tries to mobilize its existing networks of volunteers, donors and other supporters to express their opinions to a particular government official, agency or institution. Grass-roots advocacy activities can also be aimed at the public-at-large, trying to mobilize any citizen to voice the agency's views to a particular government agency or person.

Grass-roots advocacy is sometimes contrasted to 'astro-turf' advocacy. The latter describes efforts by for-profit businesses to mobilize public opinion through misleading appeals, front organizations that hide their true identity, efforts that are geographically pinpointed to influence the views of a small number of key elected officials and the use of advanced technology to forward the calls of individuals from the front-organization's 800 telephone number directly to, for instance, the Washington office of their representative in Congress. For more information on conducting lobbying and advocacy, see Endnotes [17–19].

Citizen Relations

A nonprofit organization interacts with many selected publics, often identified by their relationship with the agency itself, such as clients, volunteers, donors, government agencies and the media.

Sometimes it interacts with groups identified by socio-economic or ethnic status (such as low income or Hmong), by geography (residents of southern Smith County) or by affinity (animal lovers or HIV positive). Yet, a nonprofit agency also interacts with the broad and undifferentiated public-at-large. The phrase 'public relations,' in its literal meaning, conveys this activity. However, that specific phrase has evolved to represent a different and generally negative meaning. Nonetheless, in its original meaning, the phrase is helpful because it identifies a distinct population group with which a nonprofit agency interacts, namely the citizenry as a whole. To avoid misinterpretation, another title for this activity is 'citizen relations.'

Akin to government agencies and commercial products, a nonprofit agency has an image. This is a broadly held set of perceptions about the organization by public opinion as a whole, rather than by a small select group within the general population. For example, a nonprofit might be viewed as 'classy,' 'in trouble,' 'successful,' 'elitist,' 'caring,' etc. These images evolve slowly (and change slowly) based on the invisible civic network that aggregates individual opinions held by the public-at-large. Nonprofit agencies need to pay deliberate attention to the large and small details that contribute positively or negatively to its public image.

In that respect, citizen relations is brand management. An agency can design its casual interactions with the public-at-large along with its formal relations with its specialized publics (clients, volunteers, supporters) to create a consistent image. These can include such details as its name, logo, graphic look, signage, web page, public service announcements, media coverage, etc.

Citizen relations is not involved with the core mission of an agency, such as its customer services and fundraising. Rather, citizen relations is aimed at building goodwill towards the agency with the public-at-large. It enhances the image of the agency in civil society.

In public administration, citizen relations has a direct impact on the future of an agency. For example, the 'favorability' ratings of federal agencies can be measured. [20] A NASA astronaut, indoctrinated in the agency's sensitivity to public relations, stated bluntly that "public opinion helped determine funding." [21] An official of a state agency observed that "name recognition is important in gaining support from the state Legislature." [22] Elected officials want to be viewed as supporting popular agencies and criticizing those with low favorability ratings. This connection between image and funding, while more amorphous, also occurs in the nonprofit sector. Agencies that have favorable images with public opinion are more likely to be successful, whether in fundraising, expansion, new programming or political support. Through a well-planned and comprehensive approach to citizen relations, agencies can gradually improve their public standing and, therefore, enhance their success.

Community Relations

A separate external relations activity is community relations. It is regrettable that the word 'community' has become so overused in contemporary times that is has lost most of its previous substantive meaning. Nonetheless, as an organizing concept, it can be helpful in focusing attention on two distinct aspects of a nonprofit agency's external relations.

First, community relations refers to populations living in close physical proximity to any of the agency's facilities. By their very nature, the locations of a nonprofit agency's buildings can create problems and even opposition to their existence. That is why a nonprofit agency benefits by directing deliberate attention to the populations in the neighborhoods in which it is located. This might include ongoing neighborhood liaison, frequent contact, a hotline for reporting problems, open houses, advisory committees and regular newsletters. Given the predominance of the NIMBY syndrome ('not in my back yard') in contemporary times, agencies are well advised to deal pro-actively with potential neighborhood problems. For example, before any public announcement of its plans to establish a group home in a specific neighborhood, the agency should work intensively with the residents near the site to alleviate the automatic fears these proposals normally provoke.

Second, community relations refers to concentrated relationship-building with a particular and identifiable segment of the population that would have a discernable interest in something the agency is doing or planning to do. These are not publics with which an agency routinely interacts for client service, volunteer recruitment or donor development. Rather, there may be racial or eth-nic groups that have a discernable but indirect sensitivity to the agency's activities.

For example, a housing redevelopment agency might have selected a specific neighborhood for its efforts. Certainly, current residents of the neighborhood might have concerns about gentrifica-tion pushing up property values to the point that they could not afford to continue living there. That would require the first category of community relations activities. However, there may be other population groups that are not directly affected, but are traditionally concerned about such issues, such as the leadership of the city's African-American population or Hispanic population. In this example, effective community relations would call for initiating contacts with these demo-graphic groups although they are not affected, as a whole, by the project in question.

Crisis Management

All crises have external relations implications because that is when an agency gets the most atten-tion from the media, government and the public. Sometimes an emergency is isolated to the agency itself, such as a major physical disaster at one of its facilities from a fire or the release of an extremely negative government audit or newspaper exposé. At other times, the emergency is com-munity-wide and the agency is playing a major remediating role, such as in response to a public health epidemic, a major disaster such as a transportation-related accident, etc.

In all cases, the agency not only needs to respond substantively to the crisis, but also have a mech-anism to handle smoothly the sudden increased public attention. The guiding principle for these situ-ations is the advertising tag line that 'one never has a second chance to make a first impression.' This requires significant advance planning, both managerial and logistical, as well as a close integration of senior external relations staff with the agency's decision-making group. For more information on conducting the external relations aspects of crisis management, see Endnotes [23–25].

Note: *Originally published in Lee, M., Nonprofit organizations, external relations,* in Encyclopedia of Public Administration and Public Policy, *Marcel Dekker, New York, 2003, 835.*

Endnotes

1. Salamon, L., *America's Nonprofit Sector: A Primer*, 2nd ed., The Foundation Center, New York, 1999, 140–141.
2. Spann, J., *Foundations: Exploring Their Unique Roles and Impacts on Society*, Nonprofit Sector Research Fund, Aspen Institute, Washington, DC, 1998, 19.
3. National Association of Schools of Public Affairs and Administration (NASPAA), Commission on Peer Review and Accreditation, *Guidelines for Graduate Professional Education in Nonprofit Orga-nizations, Management, and Leadership*, 1998. http://www.naspaa.org/guidelines/guide_npft.htm#3 (accessed 2001)

4. Wish, N.B. and Mirabella, R.M., Curricular variations in nonprofit management graduate programs, *Nonprofit Management & Leadership*, 9, 99, 1998.
5. Tschirhart, M., Nonprofit management education: Recommendations drawn from three stakeholder groups, in *Nonprofit Management Education: U.S. and World Perspectives*, O'Neill, M. and Fletcher, K., Eds., Praeger, Westport, CT, 1998, chap. 6.
6. Ehling, W.P., White, J., and Grunig, J.E., Public relations and marketing practices, in *Excellence in Public Relations and Communication Management*, Grunig, J.E., Ed., Lawrence Erlbaum Associates, Hillsdale, NJ, 1992, chap. 13.
7. Simon, H.A., *Administrative Behavior: A Study in Decision-Making Processes in Administrative Organizations*, 4th ed., Free Press, New York, 1997, 294.
8. Herman, R.D. and Heimovics, D., Executive leadership, in *The Jossey-Bass Handbook of Nonprofit Leadership and Management*, Herman, R.D., Ed., Jossey-Bass, San Francisco, 1994, chap. 7.
9. Grunig, J.E., What is excellence in management?, in *Excellence in Public Relations and Communication Management*, Grunig, J.E., Ed., Lawrence Erlbaum Associates, Hillsdale, NJ, 1992, chap. 9.
10. Lee, M., Public information in government organizations: A review and curriculum outline of external relations in public administration, *Public Administration and Management: An Interactive Journal*, 5, 183, 2000. http://www.pamij.com/5_4/5_4_4_pubinfo.pdf (accessed 2007) (*Editor's Note:* See Chapter 1.)
11. Lee, M., A Jewish 'March of Dimes'? Organization theory and the future of Jewish community relations councils, *Jewish Political Studies Review*, 12, 3, 2000.
12. Booth, M., *Promoting Issues and Ideas: A Guide to Public Relations for Nonprofit Organizations*, 2nd ed., The Foundation Center, New York, 1995.
13. Levine, M., *Selling Goodness: The Guerilla P.R. Guide to Promoting Your Charity, Nonprofit Organization, or Fund-Raising Event*, Renaissance Books, Los Angeles, 1998.
14. Salzman, J., *Making the News: A Guide for Nonprofits and Activists*, Westview, Boulder, CO, 1998.
15. Martens, T., *Nonprofits and the Press: Newsmaking Strategies for California*, Nonprofit Sector Research Fund, Aspen Institute, Washington, DC, 1998. http://www.nonprofitresearch.org/newsletter1531/newsletter_show.htm?doc_id=16180 (accessed 2007)
16. Muehrcke, J., The 10 media trends that will drive your future and how to get ready now, *Nonprofit World*, 17(2), 36, 1999.
17. Pidgeon, W.P., *The Legislative Labyrinth: A Map for Nonprofits*, Jossey-Bass, San Francisco, 2001.
18. Smucker, B., *The Nonprofit Lobbying Guide*, 2nd ed., Independent Sector, Washington, DC, 1999.
19. Rees, S., *Effective Nonprofit Advocacy*, Nonprofit Sector Research Fund, Aspen Institute, Washington, DC, 1998. http://www.nonprofitresearch.org/newsletter1531/newsletter_show.htm?doc_id=16986 (accessed 2007)
20. Pew Research Center For The People & The Press, *Performance and Purpose: Constituents Rate Government Agencies*, 2000. http://people-press.org/reports/display.php3?ReportID=41 (accessed 2007)
21. Lovell, J. and Kluger, J., *Lost Moon: The Perilous Voyage of Apollo 13*, Houghton Mifflin, Boston, 1994, 155.
22. Associated Press, Historical society name change doesn't sit well with everybody, *Milwaukee [WI] Journal Sentinel*, June 5, 2001, 3B.
23. Thompson, R.L. Contingency and emergency public affairs, in *The Nonprofit Handbook: Management*, 3rd ed., Connors, T.D., Ed., Jossey-Bass, San Francisco, 2001, chap. 13.
24. Ogrizek, M. and Guillery, J.-M., *Communicating in Crisis: A Theoretical and Practical Guide to Crisis Management*, Aldine de Gruyter, Hawthorne, NY, 1999.
25. Berry, S., We have a problem…call the press!, *PM. Public Management*, 81(4), 4, 1999.

APPENDIX VIII

Questions for Review and Discussion

1. In what ways is public relations as practiced in the nonprofit sector and in the public sector (as outlined in Section I) similar?
2. Conversely, in what ways is public relations as practiced in the nonprofit sector and in the public sector different?
3. If you were given the choice of being appointed to run an agency's public relations office, would you prefer that the agency be nonprofit or governmental? Why?

Additional Reading

Feinglass, A., *The Public Relations Handbook for Nonprofits: A Comprehensive and Practical Guide,* Jossey-Bass, San Francisco, 2005.

Kenny, B.B. and Rasmussen, J.C., Best practices in communications: Ten tips for improving communications and setting the stage for your success, *Public Manager,* 34(1), 19, 2005.

McAdoo, S. and Pynes, J., Reinventing mental health service delivery: One nonprofit's experience, *Public Administration Quarterly,* 19, 367, 1995. [The experience of a community-based mental health nonprofit agency with a public relations campaign designed to increase awareness about its government-funded programs and services.]

Thrall, A.T., The myth of the outside strategy: Mass media news coverage of interest groups, *Political Communication,* 23, 407, 2006. [An important empirical study indicating that a nonprofit's size and budget have a substantial influence on the potential of garnering media coverage.]

FUTURE TRENDS IN GOVERNMENT PUBLIC RELATIONS

Introduction to Section IX

Having made it to the last section of the book, by now you have a pretty good idea of what government public relations is, what it does, and the multiplicity of ways that it can help a public sector agency accomplish its mission. Therefore, the volume appropriately concludes with an effort to look forward, to assess the current trends in government public relations and identify the likely developments that will be occurring in the foreseeable future.

Based on the rapid advances in digital, computer, and communications technologies, we are most certainly in the 'information age.' More and more of government's work, as well as its interactions with external stakeholders, is becoming computerized and virtual. In such a context, it seems fair to predict that government public relations — itself an information-based activity within public administration — will increase in importance and centrality throughout the 21st century.

As presented in Section VI, during times of crisis government public relations becomes nearly tantamount to public administration. As we progress through the century and benefit from additional advances in computer and communications technology, it's likely that more and more aspects of government management — not just in emergencies — will become public relations-based. That's because so many public sector functions will be reliant on external communications and public outreach. If this prediction is close to being on the mark, then the uses and benefits of government public relations will expand and become more central to the work of public sector bureaucracies. Agency leadership will become, increasingly, a daily practice of public relations. The top managers who are sure-footed about using the techniques of external communications will be the successful civil servants of the 21st century.

These trends are already becoming faintly apparent as we approach the second decade of the century. A quick review of the daily schedule of a U.S. federal Cabinet officer in Washington, D.C., demonstrates the importance of government public relations. What do they do all day? Increasingly, a majority of the time of a departmental secretary is spent testifying before Congress (and in a way that can be understood by reporters and C-SPAN viewers), holding press conferences, meeting with citizen advisory groups, traveling around the country to highlight departmental services, and participating in public service advertising campaigns that announce new programs and services. These Cabinet secretaries are engaging most of the time in external communications. They have to leave the internal management of the department to others. Public relations is their first and foremost consideration.

In this context, the two chapters in this final section focus especially on two of the key purposes of government public relations: media relations and public reporting. Chapter 24 reviews the impact of globalization on public administration, particularly the internationalization of media coverage of government. While most of the contemporary journalistic trends first started in the United States, a review of the literature demonstrates that such reportorial templates are becoming standard around the world, certainly in the developed and western nations. Civil servants everywhere need to be ready to deal with the negative media coverage of their work and to seek alternative methods of reporting to the citizenry.

The imperative of finding new ways to report directly to the public, as identified in Chapter 24, is a good segue to the last chapter in the book. Chapter 25 reviews the application of e-government and e-democracy technologies to the 20th century practice of direct public reporting. Government managers now have new ways to engage the citizenry and to perform their democratic duty of public reporting. Called e-reporting, this opens up new ways not only to reach the public-at-large but, also in turn to engage in two-way communication. E-reporting also facilitates improved responsiveness to the citizenry by creating new channels for public administrators to be able to listen to the public.

These early applications of e-reporting are likely to be only a foretaste of the ways that government public relations will further grow due to the communications and technological revolutions of our times. New methods and applications of public relations to public administration are likely to become apparent in the future. Such an enhanced role of government public relations will strengthen government management and the ability of public sector agencies to achieve their missions, which is precisely what the entire theme of this volume has been.

Chapter 24

Effects of Globalization on Media Coverage of Public Administration

Mordecai Lee

Contents

Abstract: One aspect of the globalization of public administration that has received only scant attention has been media coverage and media relations. Yet, the CNN-ization of media coverage has led to an American style of reporting about public administration globally: superficial, negative, scandal-oriented and episodic. Public administrators everywhere can adapt to this emerging global phenomenon by honing their media relations skills and by finding ways to bypass the media and communicate directly with the citizenry. In particular, the parallel global trend of e-government presents the possibility of updating the 20th-century practice of public reporting. Government-to-citizen (G2C) e-gov technology permits public managers to report directly, effectively, frequently and inexpensively to the citizenry, irrespective of media interest. This form of 21st-century public accountability is called e-reporting.

Introduction

Comparative and international administration has generally paid little attention to media issues. For example, administrative–media relations are not addressed in the overviews and handbooks edited by (in reverse chronological order) Heady, [1] Hyden, [2] Garcia-Zamor and Khator, [3] Baker, [4] Dwivedi and Henderson, [5] and Rowat. [6] While the first edition of Farazmand's handbook did not include any entries for media relations, the second edition had one. [7,8] That entry, by Kalanatari, focused on the role of the media in the United States, its impact on the political system and a short discussion of the implications of these trends for public administration. [9] While a helpful contribution, it did not address the broader scope of agency–media relations from international and comparative perspectives. A contributing factor to the minor attention paid to media relations is partly related to the limited ability to draw generalizations between the wide variety of the governmental and media systems of contemporary nation-states. [10,11]

An attempt to find such literature in other related fields provides equally meager results. In public administration writings, according to Martin, the study of agency relations with the press "is one of the more dramatic examples of a subject from which Public Administration has borrowed only a scattering of the available literature." [12] According to Garnett, all aspects of communication, whether internal or external, have "been underemphasized in public administration practice and scholarship relative to its importance to the enterprise of public administration." [13]

Similar results are found in political science. It has dedicated substantial attention to the reporter–politician relationship in democracies, both regarding coverage of candidates, campaigns and elections as well as coverage of elected officials once in office. [14–21] However, the field generally focuses less on the relationship between the administrative side of government and the news media. Nearly 40 years ago, Hiebert noted that there were very few studies of the public information function in the U.S. federal government or research that would be relevant to public information practitioners. [22] Since then, little has changed. McKerns noted that the focus of the government–media literature "has been largely myopic, i.e., the primary focus has been on the relationship at the federal level and between the president and the news media in particular." [23] Nimmo and Swanson summed up research in political communications by noting that "even more rare are analyses of bureaucratic communication." [24]

Finally, the literature of media studies regarding government generally focuses on elected officials, politics and public policy making. Little separate attention is paid to the non-elected side of government, the bureaucracy. For example, Asante's comprehensive review of the literature did not identify a subfield regarding media coverage of public administration in the section on the government–press connection. [25]

The following two sections provide a brief summary of the limited available knowledge about how the media covers public administration from a comparative and international perspective.

Media Coverage of Public Administration: First World Nations

An assessment of trends in media coverage of American public administration concluded that it has been diminishing quantitatively. Further, the reduced coverage has been assuming a greater negative tone; with reporters often framing their stories with archetypal story lines, such as 'wasteful bureaucrats,' 'citizen victimized by bureaucracy' and 'agency ignoring real needs.' [26] The overall impact is that "the bureaucracy and other institutions of government, with little influence and access to the media, get victimized and condemned without proper investigation" by reporters who are driven by a different agenda. [27]

These patterns are spreading to other countries. Negrine and Papathanassopoulos reported on the Americanization of political communications throughout the world: "Indeed, as television becomes the main source of information for most people, the fact that its own development has been greatly influenced by the U.S. experience increases the connections between practices in the United States and elsewhere." [28,29] Similarly, the growing importance of talk radio in the United States has spread to other countries as well, such as Hong Kong. [30]

Several reports by the Organisation for Economic Co-operation and Development (OECD) suggest that the trends regarding U.S. media coverage of public administration are also occurring in other First World countries. OECD consists of 30 of the most advanced nations economically, which have a free-market economic system and a democratic political system. At its "Ministerial Symposium on the Future of Public Service" representatives expressed concern about pressures from the media for rapid responses to problems. In particular, they felt that "the part played by the media, clearly vital to the functioning of democracy and oversight of administrative action, can be disruptive if decision makers are subjected to permanent inquisition." [31] As a result, a year later OECD issued a public management paper noting general trends in media coverage similar to ones occurring in the United States, including a basic 'spin' that is increasingly cynical, superficial and sensationalist. This negative trend was compounded in OECD nations by a media focus on scandal, real or fabricated crises and policy failure. Another trend in media coverage is a sense of urgency and expectation of immediate response that has the effect of skewing policy agendas and decision making. However, "what is urgent is not always what is most important." [32]

While Japan is similar to the United States as a democratic and economically advanced nation, media coverage of the bureaucracy has been significantly different. Notwithstanding its modern media institutions on par with the United States, Japan's media gives much greater coverage to the administrative state than U.S. media. According to Krauss, Japanese television has had an "exceptionally large percentage of stories related to the bureaucracy and its advisory councils in Japan (together occupying 36 percent in the Japanese sample versus only 2 percent for mentions of bureaucracy in the American sample)." [33] While U.S. media is executive-centered and input-oriented, Japanese media is bureaucracy-centered and output-oriented. Krauss concludes that "the portrayal of politics and government, particularly the administrative state, is one of the most important and seemingly distinctive aspects of the content of NHK television news compared to American network news." [34]

This significant difference can be partly attributed to general cultural factors, but Freeman attributes it largely to the prevalence of press clubs in Japan. [35] These press-based information cartels limit competition between reporters from different media outlets who are assigned to the same beat. Furthermore, most assignments are institution-based, normally corresponding to major administrative departments. Press clubs have the effect of giving bureaucrats the ability to assert control and define their own agendas.

One similarity between U.S. and Japanese media trends is that "saturation television news coverage in Japan of bizarre events easily rivals its American counterparts" that can have the effect of slowly crowding out the current extensive coverage of bureaucracy. [36] This, again, confirms the trend of the globalization of American-style media coverage of public administration.

Media Coverage of Public Administration: Eastern Europe

According to Édes, one of the ongoing problems for government information officers in the transitional countries of Eastern Europe is what he called "immature media." Somewhat comparable to some Western media trends, he noted that "some newspapers make little effort to report in a balanced, objective manner, and resort to sensationalism to attract readers." [37]

Earlier, O'Neill had noted the Americanization of television coverage of government news in Eastern Europe, describing it as aggressive, critical, reckless and sensational. [38] He concluded that "however much these trends may vary from country to country, they are traveling in the same general direction: toward various degrees of mediocrity, in which TV politics replaces old patterns of governance,… and instant public emotions override reflection and deliberation in the making of policy." [39]

A newspaper reporter from Germany who was assigned to cover southeastern Europe noted "because of a journalist's constraints always to cover 'headline-news,' important background stories on subjects like public administration reform never or seldom are written." [40] Kimble suggested that in the successor states to the Soviet Union, which had been dominated by the administrative apparatus, the emergence of market economies, personal freedoms and democracy meant "government is becoming irrelevant." [41] Diminished media coverage of the bureaucracy, she argued, reflected evolving citizen perceptions of which institutions are now important in their lives and those which no longer are.

What to Do? Practitioner Responses to the Globalization of Media Treatment of Public Administration

The preceding sections have demonstrated that academic research and reports from practitioners indicate early signs of the globalization of the trends regarding press coverage of public administration in the United States, including reduction in quantity and an increasingly negative tone in quality. These patterns are gradually manifesting themselves in other countries as well. This trend is currently most noticeable in First World nations, which are economically, socially and politically at levels comparable to the United States. However, as a broad generalization, the 21st-century era of globalization suggests that these trends will eventually encompass all nations, not just First World ones. If so, what is the modern-era public administrator to do?

Training

Public administration education has gradually reduced its focus on the importance of external communications, public relations and media skills. [42] However, with the emergence of the digital era as one of the most important factors driving globalization, training in the use of information outside the bureaucracy is as important as it is in-house. If 'knowledge is power,' then certainly in the information age effective government administrators need techniques for communicating with the public. In fact, information has become such an important commodity in the globalized world that some theorists are now suggesting that, in the next phase of the digital era, the citizenry will assert that it must be given formal legal and constitutional rights to information from government. [43] In this context, government managers-in-training need to have their curriculum include external relations and current practitioners would benefit by seeking continuing education and professional development in this area.

In a separate piece, this author has suggested a specific and detailed curriculum outline for public information, including the purposes, audiences and techniques that government managers can use to accomplish their responsibilities. [44] The key is to avoid the temptation of focusing on learning techniques in a sterile context. Rather, the appropriate techniques emerge from the purpose and audience in each specific circumstance. Therefore, selection of communication techniques should be the last step of the process for the practitioner, rather than the first. Certainly, media relations is a narrower subject within the larger rubric of external relations, but public administrators can use public information and external communications strategies very effectively for many other related and important missions, not just media relations. [45,46]

Given the global trend of the Americanization of media coverage of public administration, practitioners particularly need to hone their skills for dealing with an increasingly unfair, distracted, trivia-obsessed and crisis-driven press corps. Some specific recommendations include:

- Becoming a policy entrepreneur, especially focusing on the importance of the 'problem definition' stage of public issues and concerns.
- Learning to speak in short and pithy sound-bites, being able to express a position in 10 words or less.
- Making it as easy as possible for reporters to cover the agency.
- Communicating through multiple mass media, not just the 'traditional' ones.
- Seeking allies in the press corps, especially individual reporters who are concerned about a problem and would be willing to publicize it.
- Involving the agency's public affairs staff in decision making at the highest levels of the organization.
- Putting a human face on the issue in which the agency is involved by bringing forward a client or customer who would be likely to appear sympathetically to reporters and the audience. [47]

Some practical and useful handbooks on conducting media relations have been published for U.S. practitioners including (in reverse chronological order) Brown, [48] Cohen and Eimicke, [49] Krey, [50] Bjornlund, [51] and Wade. [52] Assuming that the globalization of media relations in public administration is indeed a gradual Americanization of it, then some elements of these training guides can be useful for international practitioners where similar trends are occurring.

E-Government and Direct Reporting to the Citizenry

The emerging global concept of e-government has the potential of revolutionizing many elements of public administration, governance and democracy. [53,54] In particular, direct government-to-citizen (G2C) e-gov and the emerging phenomenon of e-democracy offer the practitioner an efficient, inexpensive and mass reaching way to communicate *directly* with the citizenry. For the first time, by using e-gov technology, the public administrator can bypass the press corps and exchange information with the public-at-large. In this respect, e-gov provides an alternative to the traditional reliance of government on the mass media to provide information to the public. Up to now, public administrators could only communicate this information to the citizenry *indirectly* through the press. That, of course, has meant that reporters had the power to define the agenda and control what information would reach individudal members of the public. However, in traditional public administration theory, government managers were also assigned the normative obligation of *direct public reporting* to keep the citizenry informed of their activities and record. [55,56] One of the fullest flowerings of institutionalizing public reporting in the United States was the establishment by President Franklin D. Roosevelt of the Office of Government Reports within the Executive Office of the President. The mission of that agency, which existed from 1939 to 1942 and then from 1946 to 1948, was to keep the public informed of the programs and activities of the Executive Branch and to report back to the president on public opinion. [57]

When it is considered from the perspective of purpose, the obligation of the public administrator to engage in media relations is to account to the citizenry, albeit indirectly through the media. If, then, the rationale for media relations is to engage in public reporting, then the emergence of the digital era permits the practice of public reporting to continue, simply doing it in a slightly different way, directly to the citizenry rather than indirectly through media relations.

The technological capability provided by e-gov for government managers to be able to report directly to the citizens without being dependent on the media has been called *e-reporting*. Increasingly, public sector organizations are using the Internet to provide information to the citizenry. This helps contribute to the basic need for an informed public in those forms of governance that call for, whether directly or indirectly, the consent of the governed. Certainly, notwithstanding the many variations on democratic government, the sine quo non of popular sovereignty is an informed public. Regardless of the details, the expectation is that in a republic, public opinion is important.

Up to now, the role of the free press has been to serve as an instrument of democracy, by being the only channel that governments can use to inform the citizenry of their activities and then be held accountable by public opinion. Now, G2C e-gov technology permits public managers to engage in e-reporting by keeping the citizenry informed through the Internet, websites, email and other digital technology. [58] In a sense, the technology contributing to the globalization of public administration includes the expansion of the definition of traditional media relations to include direct e-reporting to the citizenry. Some best practices in e-reporting include:

- Report consistently, for example at least annually.
- Make it easy to find on a government's homepage.
- Make it easy for a lay citizen to read and understand.
- Include photographs, charts and other visual aids to communicate the record of the agency in non-verbal forms, as well.
- Keep it short because lay citizens are not interested in too much detail.
- Present performance management information.
- Use performance management results that closely correlate to the interests of the citizens, rather than those that would interest managers and policy decision makers.
- Create a feedback loop for citizens to give their opinions, ask questions and get involved.

More generally, OECD has strongly encouraged public managers to enhance their direct interactions with citizens as a way of promoting citizen engagement. Efforts such as providing information to the public, engaging in consultation with the citizenry and increasing public participation in policy-making contribute not only to better public administration, but also help balance out the traditional dependence of the government manager on press relations to reach the public. [59–61] In fact, improved standing with the public can strengthen the political standing of a government agency and help it withstand future pressures and unwanted interference.

In conclusion, the globalization of media relations in public administration presents both problems and responses to the government manager. The Americanization of press coverage of government is contributing to a style of coverage that is increasingly negative, episodic, scandal-driven and uninformative. However, to counterbalance that spreading phenomenon, the global trend towards e-government is providing the public administrator with new capabilities of communicating directly with the public. This has the potential of discounting the possible harmful effects of the international trends in media coverage. In this regard, the 20th-century focus on press relations in public administration is being superseded, thanks to technological advances, into a managerial activity that could be called public relations — in the best sense of that term. The key, as always, is for public administrators to be adaptable and fleet-footed in implementing their role of keeping the citizenry informed of their activities, stewardship and record.

Note: *Originally published in Lee, M., Globalization and media coverage of public administration, in* Handbook of Globalization, Governance, and Public Administration, *Farazmand, A. and Pinkowski, J., Eds., Taylor & Francis, Boca Raton, FL, 2007, chap. 8.*

Endnotes

1. Heady, F., *Public Administration: A Comparative Perspective*, 6th ed., Marcel Dekker, New York, 2001.
2. Hyden, G., Democratization and administration, in *Democracy's Victory and Crisis; Nobel Symposium No. 93*, Hadenius, A., Ed., Cambridge University Press Cambridge, UK, 1997, chap. 11.
3. Garcia-Zamor, J.-C. and Khator, R., Eds., *Public Administration in the Global Village*, Praeger, Westport, CT, 1994.
4. Baker, R., Ed., *Comparative Public Management: Putting U.S. Public Policy and Implementation in Context*, Praeger, Westport, CT, 1994.
5. Dwivedi, O.P. and Henderson, K.M., Eds., *Public Administration in World Perspective*, University of Iowa Press, Ames, 1990.
6. Rowat, D.C., Ed., *Public Administration in Developed Democracies: A Comparative Study*, Marcel Dekker, New York, 1988.
7. Farazmand, A., Ed., *Handbook of Comparative and Development Public Administration*, Marcel Dekker, New York, 1991.
8. Farazmand, A., Ed., *Handbook of Comparative and Development Public Administration*, 2nd ed., Marcel Dekker, New York, 2001.
9. Kalantari, B., Media and the bureaucracy in the United States, in *Handbook of Comparative and Development Public Administration*, 2nd ed., Farazmand, A., Ed., Marcel Dekker, New York, 2001, chap. 61. (*Editor's Note:* See Chapter 7.)
10. Grunig, J.E., Public relations management in government and business, in Garnett, J.L. and Kouzmin, A., Eds., *Handbook of Administrative Communication*, Marcel Dekker, New York, 1997, chap. 12, 270-71. (*Editor's Note:* See Chapter 2.)
11. Lenn, D.J., International public affairs: Managing within the global village, *Practical Public Affairs in an Era of Change: A Communications Guide for Business, Government and College*, in Dennis, L.B., Ed., Public Relations Society of American and University Press of America, Lanham, MD, chap. 30, 441.
12. Martin, D.W., *The Guide to the Foundations of Public Administration*, Marcel Dekker, New York, 1989, 148. (*Editor's Note:* See this book's Appendix.)
13. Garnett, J.L., Administrative communication: Domain, threats, and legitimacy, in *Handbook of Administrative Communication*, Garnett, J.L. and Kouzmin, A., Eds., Marcel Dekker, New York, 1997, chap. 1, 6.

14. Alger, D., Megamedia, the state of journalism, and democracy, *Harvard International Journal of Press/Politics*, 3, 126, 1998.

15. Gans, H.J., What can journalists actually do for American democracy?, *Harvard International Journal of Press/Politics*, 3, 6, 1998.

16. Nimmo, D. and Newsome, C., *Political Commentators in the United States in the 20th Century: A Bio-Critical Sourcebook*, Greenwood, Westport, CT, 1997.

17. Nye, J.S., Jr., The media and declining confidence in government, *Harvard International Journal of Press/Politics*, 2, 4, 1997.

18. Jacobs, L.R. and Shapiro, R.Y., Toward the integrated study of political communications, public opinion, and the policy-making process, *PS: Political Science and Politics*, 29, 10, 1996.

19. Lipset, S.M., *American Exceptionalism: A Double-Edged Sword*, W.W. Norton, New York, 1996, 285-87.

20. Patterson, T.E., Bad news, bad governance, *Annals of the American Academy of Political and Social Science*, 546, 97, 1996.

21. Patterson, T.E., Bad news, period, *PS: Political Science and Politics*, 29, 17, 1996.

22. Hiebert, R.E., Introduction, in *The Voice of Government*, Hiebert, R.E. and Spitzer, C.E., Eds., John Wiley, New York, 1968, 6.

23. McKerns, J.P., *News Media and Public Policy: An Annotated Bibliography*, Garland, New York, 1985, xx.

24. Nimmo, D. and Swanson, D.L., The field of political communication: Beyond the voter persuasion paradigm, in *New Directions in Political Communication: A Resource Book*, Swanson, D.L. and Nimmo, D., Eds., Sage, Newberry Park, CA, 1990, chap. 1, 28.

25. Asante, C.E., Ed., *Press Freedom and Development: A Research Guide and Selected Bibliography*, Greenwood, Westport, CT, 1997, 11–49.

26. Lee, M., Reporters and bureaucrats: Public relations counter-strategies by public administrators in an era of media disinterest in government, *Public Relations Review*, 25, 454–55, 1999.

27. Kalantari, op. cit., 881. (*Editor's Note:* See Chapter 7.)

28. Negrine, R. and Papathanassopoulos, S., The "Americanization" of political communication: A critique, *Harvard International Journal of Press/Politics*, 1, 53, 1996.

29. A similar point is made by Patterson, T.E., Time and news: The media's limitations as an instrument of democracy, *International Political Science Review*, 19, 55, 1998.

30. Lee, F.L.F., Radio phone-in talk shows as politically significant infotainment in Hong Kong, *Harvard International Journal of Press/Politics*, 7, 57, 2002.

31. Organisation for Economic Co-operation and Development, *Ministerial Symposium on the Future of Public Services*, Session Two, Organisation for Economic Co-operation and Development, Paris, 1996, 4.

32. Washington, S., *Consultation and Communications: Integrating Multiple Interests into Policy: Managing Media Relations (Public Management Occasional Papers No. 17)*, Organisation for Economic Co-operation and Development, Paris, 1997, 30.

33. Krauss, E.S., Portraying the state: NHK television news and politics, in *Media and Politics in Japan*, Pharr, S.J. and Krauss, E.S., Eds., University of Hawaii Press, Honolulu, chap. 3, 99.

34. Ibid, 102.

35. Freeman, L.A., *Closing the Shop: Information Cartels and Japan's Mass Media*, Princeton University Press, Princeton, NJ, 2000.

36. Pharr, S.J., Japanese videocracy, *Harvard International Journal of Press/Politics*, 2, 136, 1997.

37. Édes, B.W., The role of government information officers, *Journal of Government Information*, 23, 463, 2000.

38. O'Neill, M.J., *The Roar of the Crowd: How Television and People Power are Changing the World*, Random House, New York, 1993, 155.

39. Ibid, 156.

40. Rub, M., Press relations with governments in emerging democracies, in *Effective Communications between the Public Service and the Media, SIGMA Papers No. 9*, Organisation for Economic Co-operation and Development, Paris, 1996, chap. 5, 47. http://unpan1.un.org/intradoc/groups/public/documents/NISPAcee/UNPAN006712.pdf (accessed 2007)

41. Kimble, D., Postcards from the edge: Reflections on international and comparative administration at mid-life (panel session), 59th annual national meeting of the American Society for Public Administration, Seattle, May 9–13, 1998.

42. Lee, M., Public relations in public administration: A disappearing act in public administration education, *Public Relations Review*, 24, 509, 1998.

43. Bovens, M., Information rights: Citizenship in the information society, *Journal of Political Philosophy*, 10, 317, 2002.

44. Lee, M., Public information in government organizations: A review and curriculum outline of external relations in public administration, *Public Administration and Management: An Interactive Journal*, 5, 183, 2000. http://www.pamij.com/5_4/5_4_4_pubinfo.pdf (accessed 2007) (*Editor's Note:* See Chapter 1.)

45. Freeman, M., and Nelson, S., Communications in local government: A business planning model, *IQ Reports* (monograph series of the International City/County Management Association), 35(4), 2003.

46. Weiss, J.A., Public information, in *The Tools of Government: A Guide to the New Governance*, Salamon, L.M., Ed., Oxford University Press, New York, 2002, chap. 7.

47. Lee, M., Reporters and bureaucrats: Public relations counter-strategies by public administrators in an era of media disinterest in government, *Public Relations Review*, 25, 456–458, 1999.

48. Brown, L., *Your Public Best: The Complete Guide to Making Successful Public Appearances in the Meeting Room, on the Platform, and on TV*, 2nd ed., Newmarket Press, New York, 2002.

49. Cohen, S. and Eimicke, W., *The Effective Public Manager: Achieving Success in a Changing Government*, 3rd ed., Jossey-Bass, San Francisco, 2002, chap. 11.

50. Krey, D., Ed., *Delivering the Message: A Resource Guide for Public Information Officials*, 2nd ed., California Association of Public Information Officials, Sacramento, 2000.

51. Bjornlund, L., *Media Relations for Local Governments: Communicating for Results*, International City/County Management Association, Washington, DC, 1996.

52. Wade, J., *Dealing Effectively with the Media: What Local Government Officials Need to Know about Print, Radio and Television Interviews*, National League of Cities, Washington, DC, 1993.

53. Margetts, H., Electronic government: A revolution in public administration?, in *Handbook of Public Administration*, Peters, B.G. and Pierre, J., Eds., Sage, London, 2003, chap. 29.

54. Kakabadse, A., Kakabadse, N.K., and Kouzmin, A., Reinventing the democratic governance project through information technology? A growing agenda for debate, *Public Administration Review*, 63, 44, 2003.

55. Beyle, H.C., *Governmental Reporting in Chicago*, University of Chicago Press, Chicago, 1928.

56. Lee, M., Intersectoral differences in public affairs: The duty of public reporting in public administration, *Journal of Public Affairs*, 2(2), 33, 2002.

57. Lee, M., *The First Presidential Communications Agency: FDR's Office of Government Reports*, State University of New York Press, Albany, 2005.

58. Lee, M., E-Reporting: Using managing-for-results data to strengthen democratic accountability, in *Managing for Results 2005*, Kamensky, J.M. and Morales, A., Eds., Rowman & Littlefield, Lanham, MD, 2005, chap. 4. Also published as a monograph and available online: http://www.businessofgovernment.org/pdfs/Lee_Report.pdf (accessed 2007). (*Editor's Note:* See Chapter 25.)

59. Caddy, J. and Vergez, C., *Citizens as Partners: Information, Consultation and Public Participation in Policy-Making*, Organisation for Economic Co-operation and Development, Paris, 2001.

60. Caddy, J., and Vergez, C., Eds., *Promise and Problems of E-Democracy: Challenges of Online Citizen Engagement*, Organisation for Economic Co-operation and Development, Paris, 2003.

61. Gramberger, M.R., *Citizens as Partners: OECD Handbook on Information, Consultation and Public Participation in Policy-Making*, Organisation for Economic Co-operation and Development, Paris, 2001.

Chapter 25

E-Reporting: Using Performance Results to Strengthen Democratic Accountability

Mordecai Lee

Contents

Two key developments in contemporary public administration, performance information and electronic government, have converged to permit the transformation of traditional 20th-century public reporting (such as through printed annual reports) into 21st-century *e-reporting*. Generally, performance information was initially used as an internal management control tool as well as by oversight bodies, such as the legislative branch and other elected officials. However, more recently, performance information has also been used to strengthen and improve public reporting. By publicizing this information to the citizenry, agencies have a newer and concise format to use to report on their activities in ways that are meaningful and understandable to the lay public. Similarly, the emerging technology of electronic government had initially focused on transactional relationships between government and citizens, such as filing forms, submitting requests, and renewing licenses. Now, the evolution of electronic government towards e-democracy offers new opportunities for agencies to engage in e-reporting, by posting regular reports on their websites.

Based on the results of a review of federal, state and local websites, e-reporting is much more common on the federal level than in state and local government. This is partly due to the required reports that federal agencies must submit in compliance with the 1993 Government Performance and Results Act (GPRA). However, putting a several-hundred-page report with performance information on an agency website is not automatically good e-reporting. Exemplary e-reporting activities by federal agencies and in state and local government identified in the review are described as models for other agencies. Of all e-reports reviewed, only two agencies — both federal — earned the highest grade of A+. They were the National Science Foundation and the General Accounting Office. Both agencies had posted brief (under 50 pages), attractive and readable e-publications on their websites that provided lay-oriented *highlights* of performance information taken from, for example, more extensive GPRA-required reports.

Based on the results of the review, recommendations are made for public managers interested in fulfilling their responsibilities to democracy through e-reporting. These 'best practices' include general guidelines for e-reporting, as well as specific suggestions for using performance information and for utilizing the capabilities of electronic government.

What is E-Reporting?

In the 21st century, a meshing of performance measurement information as a management tool with the latest technologies of electronic government permits re-conceptualizing the 20th-century concept of public reporting into *e-reporting*. E-reporting is the administrative activity that uses electronic government technology for digital delivery of public reports that are largely based on performance measurement data. As a tool of e-democracy, it conveys systematically and regularly information about government operations that is valuable to the public-at-large, in order to promote an informed citizenry in a democracy and accountability to public opinion. E-reports are planned to be citizen-friendly by being understandable and meaningful to the lay public.

Linking Performance Information to Public Reporting

The development of the contemporary focus on performance measurement was partly driven by a need for more refined tools for internal management and for external oversight of government agencies by elected officials. Since then, the uses of performance information have gradually evolved to include external uses, such as by attentive external stakeholders such as clients and customers. Performance information can now also be used for systematic and credible public reporting.

Based on the study of 'citizen-driven performance measurement' at Rutgers University–Newark, public reporting is an important part of the performance measurement process. [1] Generally, it suggests "performance data should be presented in a way that is meaningful to citizens so they can understand what is happening in their neighborhood, as well as the community as a whole." [2]

One of the early and very successful approaches to performance measurement was the CompStat program in the New York City Police Department. CompStat became the nexus for monitoring the performance of each police district, holding district commanders accountable, identifying trends requiring attention and prompting a strategic approach to management. While originally developed to use performance data for *internal* accountability, CompStat's potential for *public* accountability rapidly became clear. Now, residents of New York can access current crime statistics for their neighborhood on the city's homepage. The New York City Police Department's CompStat concept has been expanded to include public reporting and accountability. [3]

In Baltimore, the use of performance data for accountability was extended beyond the Police Department and beyond internal management oversight. The Mayor's office utilized the performance measurement process to convene reviews every two weeks for all municipal departments. It helped accomplish accountability not only regarding performance on key policy mandates for each agency, but also for strict accountability for the management of the agency's human resources. For example, it helped monitor use of vacation time and sick leave by a department's employees, with the possibility of identifying trends and problems before they became too severe. In a refinement of New York's CompStat, one of the data streams for CitiStat came from service requests on Baltimore's new 311 One Call Center. That was a way to monitor the impact of performance on individual citizens. [4]

As shown by Baltimore's example of CitiStat, even though public reporting is a distinct activity, this does not mean the reports themselves have to be created from scratch. On the contrary. Much of the content used in public reports can originate from other reporting activities such as performance measurement systems. The information generated from those management reporting systems would simply need to be 'translated' so that performance data becomes understandable to the lay public. Public reporting does not need to be a major new burden to government agencies. There is no necessity to reinvent the wheel. Most information can be recycled from other uses.

Linking E-Government to Public Reporting

Along with performance information, one of the most important innovations in public management recently has been the trend to electronic government, called e-government. More and more governmental functions have been transferred to digital technologies and the Internet. This has increased the productivity of the public sector and improved government management. Some of these e-government innovations are largely unseen by individual citizens, in that they are based on computer systems that are used internally in government agencies. However, parallel to the expansion of performance measurement activities such as CompStat and CitiStat to civic communication purposes, e-government has also transformed the interaction between government and the individual citizen. Sometimes called 'government-to-citizen' (G2C) e-government, it focuses on using digital technology to permit a direct connection between government and individual citizens seeking to interact with a particular public agency. This helps differentiate this particular use of the Internet from other uses in the public sector, whether for internal or external purposes. For example, an internal use of digital technology in the public sector can focus on interactions between the agency and its staff, called government-to-employee (G2E). Other external uses include government-to-business (G2B) and government-to-government (G2G).

Much of the focus and emphasis of e-government up to now has tended largely to be on transactions and useable information. [5] In that respect, e-government has consisted of using an emerging technology so that pragmatic and tangible governmental missions could be accomplished faster, better, and cheaper. This has led, indeed, to a revolution in how government agencies did their jobs and delivered their goods and services. For example, citizens could find out when an agency would be open, whether a book they wanted was in the collection of the public library, what their neighbors' reassessed property values were, etc. Another aspect of e-gov has focused on *transactions*, such as renewing a driver's license, reserving a library book, and paying a fine. The recent innovation of extending geographical information systems (GIS) to public use on government websites is an indication of the potential of e-government to improve services to individual citizens. [6]

Now, e-democracy is engaging the attention of those at the cutting edge of the digital era. In these situations, agencies are stretching the potential of e-gov technology to provide information to the public that is both useful as well as accomplishing accountability to the citizenry.

Public reporting, too, can be greatly enhanced by e-government. Technology can be used to update the 20th-century view of public reporting. E-government permits "new forms of public accountability." [7] Instead of focusing solely on expensive hardcopy reports, as was done in the 20th century, public managers can use e-government to fulfill their obligation to democracy by delivering reports digitally. This facilitates access to information, direct reporting to the citizenry, and 24/7/365 use. It also provides the ability to revise and update reports without limitations.

Baltimore's CitiStat also showed how e-government can be used to strengthen public accountability through reporting. The municipality began using the CitiStat results as a "civic communication tool." [8] The data submissions for CitiStat were made available to the public on Baltimore's website. In that way, citizens could look over the same information that managers had:

> In keeping with the mayor's pledge to operate an open and transparent government, CitiStat has stimulated the accumulation of previously unavailable data regarding the operations of the municipal government. By making the agencies' data submissions available to the public via the city's website, citizens are able to access the same information that the administration uses to prioritize spending and gauge performance. [9]

The Benefits of E-Reporting

Public reporting continues to be a relevant and constructive way for government agencies to fulfill their obligation to democracy by making performance information available to the public-at-large. The rationale for such regular reporting and the principles of good reporting are little changed from the 20th, and even the 19th, century. As practiced then, governments viewed their annual reports as significant platforms to inform the citizenry of their stewardship of public funds, record of accomplishment, and future goals and challenges. Now, in the first decade of the 21st century, technology and management tools present an opportunity to perform this timeless attribute of democracy in new and more effective ways. The emergence of electronic government technologies provides cutting-edge, inexpensive, omnipresent, and efficient ways to convey modern-day reports to the citizens. Placing reports on agency websites has become relatively common in the United Kingdom. [10] Parallel to that new technology, performance measurement data can be used not only for internal organizational and control purposes, but also for democratic accountability. Performance information can succinctly present the results of an agency's activities over the previous year and in ways that can be easily understood by lay citizens.

Yet, effective and vigorous public reporting can also catalyze a more concrete benefit to a government agency. The motivation for public reporting can also be an agency's self-interest. As such, e-reporting can also be viewed as a pragmatic activity that helps accomplish more specific governmental goals. As part of an external relations and public communication program, e-reporting can contribute to the emergence of positive public opinion toward an agency. It is already recognized that having 'good press' and a positive public image can strengthen an agency vis-à-vis its overseers, even lead to expanded appropriations and new programs. [11] For example, astronaut Jim Lovell (of Apollo 13 fame) stated bluntly in his memoirs that "public opinion helped determine funding" for NASA. [12]

While politicians generally have a 'fingertip feel' for public opinion about government, the attitudes of the public toward government agencies is now quantified and tracked like other subjects. The American Customer Satisfaction Index, based at the University of Michigan Business School, measures the annual scores of the level of public satisfaction with individual federal agencies. [13] For example, in the report released in December 2006, it noted that "agencies like the Social Security Administration and the Veterans Health Administration continue to provide services that rate among the highest in government. The one decliner this year is the Medicare program, which falls 4% to 73, its lowest score since 1999, possibly impacted in part by the overhaul to its prescription drug benefit." [14] Similarly, the Pew Center has conducted polls of citizens rating government agencies and compared the results with other surveys. [15]

Elected officials want to be seen as supportive of government agencies that have high public support and be viewed as critical of agencies that are unpopular. Therefore, it is in the pragmatic best interest of a government agency to engage in activities that can have the indirect effect of contributing to public support. Effective reporting as described in this report can be a distinct and helpful component of such efforts. What was written half a century ago is still as valid today: "A well-conceived annual report, attractively presented, can serve a highly useful purpose in building understanding, good will, and public support." [16] E-reporting can indirectly contribute to the development of public support for the agency, which in turn is converted to concrete support from elected officials. Rourke summarized this dynamic succinctly:

> Basic to any agency's political standing in the American system of government is the support of public opinion. If it has that, an agency can ordinarily expect to be strong in the legislative and the executive branch as well. Because public opinion is ultimately the only legitimate sovereign in a democratic society, an agency that seeks first a high standing with the public can reasonably expect to have all other things added to it in the way of legislative and executive support. Power gives power, in administration as elsewhere, and once an agency has established a secure base with the public, it cannot easily be trifled with by political officials in either the legislative or the executive branch. [17]

Good efforts at democratic accountability lead to good things for government agencies. E-reporting that contains performance information can be part of that picture. It is good for democracy and in the best interests of the government agency, too.

The exponential growth of communications technology has revolutionized many aspects of society. The state of e-government now would have been viewed as political science fiction as recently as 15 years ago. The evolution of electronic government has reached a point that some theoreticians are now beginning to talk about information as a constitutional right. Some European governments are even moving in that direction. [18] It is unlikely, of course, that the United States Constitution will ever be amended to create a constitutional right to information. Yet, as a de facto practice, our form of government is most certainly moving in that direction. The availability, access, and use of information are gradually becoming baseline expectations by the citizens regarding all levels of government in the United States. One of the lessons learned from the corporate scandals in the first decade of the 21st century applies to the public sector as well, namely, the imperative to "overcommunicate, overexplain." [19] Government agencies should always err on the side of transparency and openness.

A planned and organized effort by governments to report performance information as part of their electronic government efforts would be a welcome, practical, and constructive step towards strengthening democracy in the information age.

A Snapshot of Current Practices

Instances of recent efforts at public reporting (though not in an overall annual report) have been by the U.S. Social Security Administration and U.S. Internal Revenue Service (IRS). For example, Social Security sends annual financial statements to all workers over 25 that summarize their estimated benefits upon retirement. The 2007 version included an introductory cover letter by the agency's Commissioner, reporting on the financial health and long-term prospects of the fund. His summary bluntly briefed the recipients that "unless action is taken soon to strengthen Social Security, in just 10 years we will begin paying more in benefits than we collect in taxes. Without changes, by 2040 the Social Security Trust Fund will be exhausted." [20] This is an example of reporting about policy issues facing government. It helps educate citizens about *future decision making* and invites them to become involved in this democratic process.

Another example, this one of post-hoc direct reporting, is by the IRS. In 2007, the booklet with instructions to citizens for filling out the 1040 income tax form for the 2006 tax year contained text and pie charts on "Major Categories of Federal Income and Outlays for Fiscal Year 2005." [21] This provided taxpayers with basic information about how the national government spends its tax revenues and the role of the income tax as part of the federal tax system. That information, strictly speaking, is beyond the ken of IRS's mission. Yet, the agency is connecting its narrow mission with the broader concept of citizenship by helping inform and educate the taxpayer about what happens to those tax payments.

During the first decade of the 21st century, an international organization of developed countries, the Organisation for Economic Co-operation and Development (OECD), released three reports urging increased efforts by governments to view citizens as partners. One of the major initiatives it recommended was providing citizens with more information about government activities and performance through regular reports. [22–25] That is beginning to happen. For example, a study of Australian governmental units confirmed that, indeed, a greater degree of direct reporting was occurring. [26]

To ascertain contemporary approaches to e-reporting and identify examples of 'best practices,' a review was conducted of highly rated and award-winning webpages of local, state, and the federal government. For the review instrument, the principles of good reporting from the 20th century were identified and refined for appropriateness to the 21st century. The goal was to establish basic and necessary elements of best practices in public reporting. Then, these principles were adapted into a questionnaire that covered effective e-reporting. The questionnaire paid special attention to two general topics of particular interest: the use of performance information and the degree of utilization of the capabilities of e-government technology.

Findings

Regarding performance information, the review showed that only about half the reports (28 of 54) had some performance measurement data. Of the reports that included performance information, the information was somewhat tailored to lay citizen readers. Statistics would be of interest to a lay citizen had a mean score of 3.5 (from a low of 1 to a high of 5) and the data were relatively easy to understand, with a mean score of 3.9 (from 'difficult to understand' as 2 and very easy to understand as 5). Similarly, about half the reports highlighted key results and were relatively easy to compare to previous years' data (mean of 3.1, from a low of 0 to a high of 5). It appeared that most of the data in the public reports came from the same management data system used for internal management control purposes.

Relating to the uses of e-government technology to accomplish public reporting, only about a third of the reports had hotlinks for additional information, most were well maintained and up-to-date, about two-thirds were searchable, and most included reports from previous years to permit comparison of current performance with earlier results. Similarly, most of the documents were shareable by one citizen with another. However, few permitted two-way communications, such as naming a contact person, having a feedback option, having a participation option or a sign up for future dissemination of like reports.

In general, the results indicate that regular reporting to the citizenry is not a common online activity by governments in the United States and that those entities engaging in reporting tend neither to focus on performance results in the reports nor to use the full technological and interactive capabilities of e-gov.

The outstanding websites that provided operational examples of best practices in e-reporting, especially combining the use of performance information with the capabilities of e-gov technologies are:

A+: U.S. Government Accountability Office
U.S. National Science Foundation

A: City of Portland (Oregon)
New York City
Oregon Department of Health and Human Services
U.S. Environmental Protection Agency
U.S. National Aeronautics and Space Administration
U.S. State Department

A–: U.S. Consumer Products Safety Commission

Regarding the practice of e-reporting by the federal government, in part due to the Government Performance and Results Act of 1993, federal agencies have better e-reporting than other levels of government. GPRA requires that all federal executive branch agencies (with some exceptions) submit annual reports that are based on the performance information. With almost all GPRA-required reports on agency websites, most federal agencies engage in a minimal and adequate degree of e-reporting. However, most GPRA reports fall under the jurisdiction of agency CFOs. This tends to mean that reports reflect the ethos of the profession of accounting, with its focus on comprehensive and detailed financial reporting. When reports are so long as to be intimidating to the average citizen, they lose their value from the perspective of e-reporting.

Two federal agencies are examples of e-reporting at its best. The General Accounting Office and the National Science Foundation both prepare a 'highlights' brochure as a separate publication from their GPRA reports. While containing key performance information, these lay-oriented brochures are citizen-friendly and are inviting to the less knowledgeable public.

Generally, state and local governments have also been affected by the trends of performance management and e-government. However, as would be expected in a decentralized system of government, there is a much greater variation in the e-reporting levels of state and local government compared to federal agencies. Lacking a uniform mandate comparable to GPRA, a much smaller proportion of state and local governments included performance information from their annual reports on their webpages. Certainly, many state and local government seek to implement a performance measurement orientation and seek to have accessible websites. However, only a small proportion of the sites reviewed engaged in any minimal form of e-reporting, consisting of performance-based reports on their homepages.

General Recommendations

Based on the results of the survey of contemporary e-reporting practices, some clear principles of best practice emerged:

1. When you do public reporting, do it electronically: Public managers have a general obligation to report on their agencies' record to the citizenry. Rather than doing this through old-fashioned 20th-century hard-copy annual reports, the emergence of e-government provides a technology that can greatly enhance and modernize reporting, called here e-reporting. Government executives are encouraged to post on their agency websites periodic reports to the citizenry that are presented in lay-oriented formats. In particular, a short and easy-to-understand 'highlights' brochure that is presented in a visually pleasing way constitutes exemplary e-reporting.

2. Use performance information in e-reports: Most agencies and governments already have performance information. E-reporting does not necessitate reinventing the wheel. Rather, existing data can be repackaged in ways that are relevant and understandable to the lay citizenry, with highlighting of key categories of performance results. To assure accountability, standardized performance categories need to be retained from year to year. Similarly, it should be possible for the reader to compare current performance results with that of previous years.

3. Create options to engage citizens in the use of performance information: E-government began with passively providing information on the Internet. Its second stage was facilitating two-way transactions. Now, agencies are able to advance to the next stage, e-democracy. E-reporting can engage citizens in government, particularly through the presentation of performance information. For example, some agencies are providing reports more frequently than once a year. Some are providing real-time reports with data that is useful

to the citizen. In particular, innovative efforts to distribute and disseminate e-reports are encouraged. It is not enough to simply post an annual e-report on the agency's homepage. Methods can include emails to previously created lists, speakers' bureaus, information kits for various age groups, interactive media, mailings to lists of opinion leaders and media events to get free coverage. Similarly, e-reporting can increase *interaction* with the public, including two-way communication features such as an opinion feedback option, the opportunity for citizens to volunteer to participate in agency public planning processes and a sign-up feature for receiving future reports automatically. When citizens experience a tangible benefit from accessing e-reporting information, it redounds to the credit of the agency through positive public opinion.

Specific Recommendations

What specifically would good public reporting consist of? Based on the results of this review of hundreds of governmental websites, exemplary e-reporting in the public sector would seek to include as many of the following features as possible:

Overall

1. Easy to find: It should be easy for a lay citizen, perhaps a first-time visitor to the agency's website, to find the e-report. On the opening page of the website, the existence and availability of the report should be highlighted. Then, the visitor should be able to click on the notice of the report and be hotlinked directly to it. The report should not be more than one click away from the opening page.
2. An integrated report: If this is the website of a general government (city, county, state), the report should provide an integrated, across-the-board and consolidated perspective. It should not be the electronic equivalent of separate agency reports merely 'stapled' together. Similarly, the e-report of a federal agency should be integrated, rather than a compilation of the reports of its separate component bureaus, services, or administrations. Citizens care about subjects, not organizational units.
3. Understandable: The front/cover page of the e-report should be formatted so that a lay reader can quickly grasp what this document is, what its purpose is, and what kind of information will be presented in it.
4. Navigable: The e-report should be easy for the reader to navigate. For example, if the reader is particularly interested in one topic, he or she should be able to click on the appropriate title in a table of contents and be hotlinked to that chapter. (This is one of the disadvantages of the current PDF technology, notwithstanding its many positive features.)
5. Contents: The report should be visually interesting, since not all people like to absorb information by reading. Also, a 'wall of words' can be repelling to the reader. Similarly, reports consisting only of words are harder to scan and 'leaf through' by a casual reader. Therefore, reports should include many photos, graphs, and tables. The technology of the Internet now also permits using multimedia inserts in e-reports, such as a short clip of a mayor speaking, an in-motion visualization of the work of the agency, etc. Finally, e-reports should be written in plain English and at a reading level that is appropriate for an average citizen.

6. Frequency: Annual e-reports are consistent with the traditional cycle of government operations. However, if possible, post e-reports with agency performance information more frequently than once a year, such as monthly or quarterly.
7. Current information: Minimize the time lag between the end of the period covered in the e-report and when it is posted on the website.
8. Who's on first? Designate an agency official to be in charge of the e-report and list his or her name and title in the website.

Performance Information

1. Relevance: Performance information presented in the e-report needs to be relevant to the casual and general interests of the layperson.
2. Statistics: Use statistics that are easy to understand, such as basic quantitative functions (percentages, proportions, fractions) rather than high-end methodologies that are hard for an average citizen to understand.
3. Box scores: Highlight key areas of performance activity with box scores, comparable to the presentation of sports news.
4. Permanent format: Stick to standardized categories of performance information that do not change from year to year.
5. Comparisons: Make it easy for the reader to compare this year's performance information with several previous years, not just last year.
6. Re-use existing data: Don't create unnecessary work for the agency. Maximize the use of performance information that is already being collected for other purposes, such as for internal management control, accountability reports to legislative bodies, etc.

Electronic Government: General

1. Length: Be sure to fit the length to the interest of the reader. Most citizens would only be interested in a short and concise report. Therefore, e-reports should not be encyclopedic nor be statistical compendiums. However, the technology of e-government permits creating hotlinks to in-depth information for readers particularly interested in more detail on a specific topic. Place throughout the e-report self-directed links to get more in-depth information, such as "If you are interested in more information about this topic, click here."
2. Up-to-date: The e-report site must be well maintained. In particular, the links from the front page of the website to the e-report need to kept up-to-date regarding content. Similarly, be sure that there is not a broken link due to changed URL addresses, etc.
3. Search function: Make the text of the e-report searchable, so that a reader can use the 'find' function to zero in on a very specific topic or term of interest. A limitation of some current PDF technology is the limited scope of the search function, such as only to the page being displayed on the screen.
4. Library: Archive e-reports from previous years and make them easy to reach so that a user can go back to earlier reports for comparison reasons.
5. A real person: List a contact person for the e-report with an email address, besides the usual Webmaster contact information.

6. FYI: Make it easy for users to share the e-report with someone else they think might be interested. For example, some newspaper websites have an 'email this page' function. Similarly, it is relatively easy to forward the URL of a PDF file.

Electronic Government: Interactivity

1. I was wondering: Create an informational and opinion feedback feature on the e-report. For example, at the end of the report, create the electronic equivalent of a 'tear-off coupon' to fill out and email back: "I read the report and here is my reaction" or "I read the report and would like more information on the following subject: _____."
2. How can I help? Create a participative feedback feature, permitting a reader to sign up to become involved in the agency's activities, such as advisory boards, citizen participation events, ambassador for the agency, be notified of future agency events, etc.
3. Keep me posted: Create a feature for a reader to be notified when the next e-report is posted and when other relevant reports are disseminated in the future.

An Idea for the Future: The Agency's Chief Democracy Officer

Most government agencies have CFOs and CIOs. For agencies seeking to reap the benefits of public support that is often a result of exemplary e-reporting, they similarly could have a Chief Democracy Officer (CDO). The CDO would work to modify already existing agency publications, performance data, its website and its public relations programs to assure that the agency would be making itself accountable to the public-at-large. With CDOs helping their agencies participate in the democratic process, they would be facilitating citizen understanding of agency programs and the benefits that emerge from an informed public opinion about the agency.

In terms of implementation, creating a CDO in an agency (or for a general level of government, such as at City Hall) does not necessarily mean creating a new position or hiring new staff. Rather, most agencies and governments have Offices of Public Affairs or somesuch (there tends to be wide variation in titles). The mission of these offices is closely related to promoting democracy. Therefore, perhaps with little need for significant reorganization, the Director of Public Affairs could be re-designated as the CDO. There might be a temptation to assign the responsibility for e-reporting to the CFO, since he or she probably handles performance information, or to the CIO, given the connection of e-reports to information processing and the agency's website. However, the central foci of these two officers could subtly pull them away from the public manager's obligation to the citizenry-at-large. Given the mission of Directors of Public Affairs, these professionals would already have an orientation that is largely in the direction of what would be expected of a CDO.

Acknowledgments

My deepest appreciation to the IBM Center for the Business of Government. The conditions attached to its grant — essentially, use the funding for whatever you think is right and then submit your report — are a researcher's dream. Mark Abramson, Executive Director of the Center, and John M. Kamensky and Jonathan D. Breul, both of IBM Business Consulting Services, provided very helpful guidance after reading the initial draft. They especially helped me relearn how to write in plain English, rather than 'academese.' To all three, my thanks.

Also, grateful acknowledgment to the Center for Urban Initiatives and Research at the University of Wisconsin-Milwaukee for conducting the review of local, state, and federal websites regarding current use of homepages for reporting. In particular, my thanks to Scott Sager, a researcher at the Center and Ph.D. candidate in Political Science, for his contributions to the review.

Note: *This is an abridged, adapted and revised version of Lee, M., E-reporting: Using managing-for-results data to strengthen democratic accountability, in* Managing for Results 2005, *Kamensky, J.M. and Morales, A., Eds., Rowman & Littlefield, Lanham, MD, 2005, chap. 4. Also published by the IBM Center for the Business of Government as a monograph and available online: http://www.businessofgovernment.org/pdfs/Lee_Report.pdf (accessed 2007).*

Endnotes

1. National Center for Public Productivity, Rutgers University–Newark, Citizen-Driven Government Performance: Case Studies and Curricular Resources. http://www.andromeda.rutgers.edu/~ncpp/cdgp/Booklet.pdf (accessed 2007).
2. Callahan, K., Performance measurement, citizen driven, in *Encyclopedia of Public Administration and Public Policy,* Marcel Dekker, New York, 2003, 915.
3. Henderson, L.J., The Baltimore CitiStat Program: Performance and Accountability, IBM Center for the Business of Government, Arlington, VA, 2003. http://www.businessofgovernment.org/pdfs/HendersonReport.pdf (accessed 2007).
4. Ibid.
5. Marchionini, G., Samet, H., and Brandt, L., Digital government, *Communications of the ACM,* 46(1), 26, 2003.
6. Perlman, E., Maps for the masses, *Governing,* 17(1), 26, 2003.
7. Margetts, H., Electronic government: A revolution in public administration?, in *Handbook of Public Administration,* Peters, B.G. and Pierre, J., Eds., Sage, Thousand Oaks, CA, 2003, chap. 29, 374.
8. Henderson, op. cit., 33.
9. Henderson, op. cit., 25.
10. Margetts, op. cit., 372.
11. Gormley, W.T., Jr. and Balla, S.J., *Bureaucracy and Democracy: Accountability and Performance,* CQ Press, Washington, DC, 2004, 19–21, 177–178.
12. Lovell, J. and Kluger, J., *Lost Moon: The Perilous Voyage of Apollo 13,* Houghton Mifflin, Boston, 1994, 155.
13. American Customer Satisfaction Index, Government satisfaction scores, 2006. http://www.theacsi.org/index.php?option=com_content&task=view&id=27&Itemid=62 (accessed 2007).
14. American Customer Satisfaction Index, Citizen satisfaction with federal agencies improves, 2006. http://www.theacsi.org/index.php?option=com_content&task=view&id=162&Itemid=62 (accessed 2007).
15. Pew Research Center For The People & The Press, Performance and Purpose: Constituents Rate Government Agencies, Washington, DC, April 12, 2000. http://people-press.org/reports/display.php3?PageID=225 (accessed 2007).
16. Richard, O., The public-relations value of the annual report, *Public Personnel Review,* 8, 150, 1947.
17. Rourke, F.E., *Bureaucracy, Politics, and Public Policy,* 3rd ed., Little Brown, Boston, 1984, 50.
18. Bovens, M., Information rights: Citizenship in the information society, *Journal of Political Philosophy,* 10, 317, 2002.

19. McGeehan, P., Quick: What's the boss making?, *New York Times,* September 21, 2003, sec. 3, 1.
20. U.S. Social Security Administration, Your Social Security statement: What Social Security means to you, 2007. http://www.ssa.gov/mystatement/currentstatement.pdf (accessed 2007).
21. U.S. Internal Revenue Service, 2006 1040 Instructions (Cat. No. 24811V), 83. http://www.irs.gov/pub/irs-pdf/i1040gi.pdf (accessed 2007).
22. Caddy, J. and Vergez, C., *Citizens as Partners: Information, Consultation and Public Participation in Policy-Making,* Organisation of Economic Co-operation and Development, Paris, 2001.
23. Gramberger, M.R., *Citizens as Partners: OECD Handbook on Information, Consultation and Public Participation in Policy-Making,* Organisation of Economic Co-operation and Development, Paris, 2001.
24. Macintosh, A., Using information and communication technologies to enhance citizen engagement in the policy process, in *Promise and Problems of E-Democracy: Challenges of Online Citizen Engagement,* Caddy, J., Ed., Organisation of Economic Co-operation and Development, Paris, 2003, part I, 43.
25. Forss, K., An evaluation framework for information, consultation and public participation, in *Evaluating Public Participation in Policy Making,* Caddy, J., Ed., Organisation of Economic Co-operation and Development, Paris, 2005, chap. 4, 51.
26. Mack, J. and Ryan, C., Is there an audience for public sector annual reports? Australian evidence, *International Journal of Public Service Management,* 20, 134, 2007.

APPENDIX IX

Questions for Review and Discussion

1. Based on the two chapters in this section, what are some trends that are affecting the practice of government public relations?
2. In what ways is government public relations changing as a result of those trends?
3. Can you identify any important trends in the practice of government public relations besides those mentioned in the two readings?

Additional Reading

Gramberger, M.R., Discussion of information dissemination, in *Citizens as Partners: OECD Handbook on Information, Consultation and Public Participation in Policy-Making,* Organisation for Economic Co-operation and Development, Paris, 2001, 18–20, 30–32, 38–39, 52–56, 71–75.

Seib, P., News and ethics in a real-time, online world, *Public Integrity,* 3, 313, 2001.

West, D.M., E-government and the transformation of service delivery and citizen attitudes, *Public Administration Review,* 64, 15, 2004.

Wise, K., Linking public relations processes and organizational effectiveness at a state health department, *Journal of Health and Human Services Administration,* 25, 497, 2002–2003.

APPENDIX

APPENDIX

Annotated Bibliography of Historical Sources: Agency Relations with the News Media

Daniel W. Martin

Editor's Note: The selections for the chapters in this book generally shied away from historical perspectives on government public relations. The focus was on more practical, contemporary, and useful readings. The only exceptions to the avoidance of historical chapters were Chapter 4 and Chapter 12. They provided specific examples of, respectively, what an all-out government PR campaign would look like and examples of a robust public reporting effort, the latter based on interesting experiments by municipalities during the first half of the 20th century.

However, given the central role of the media in 21st-century public affairs, it may be useful for readers interested in more historical context on that subject to have a starting point. This annotated bibliography, published as volume 37 in the Public Administration and Public Policy Series (the same series as this reader on government public relations), provides a helpful summary of the pre-1990s literature on the relationship of public administration and the news media.

Introduction

The media have become a political force of considerable weight and impact upon bureaucratic behavior. This is one of the more dramatic examples of a subject from which Public Administration has borrowed only a scattering of the available literature. The study of press relations in the governmental arena generates not only its own courses, but its own schools. A smaller selection of that literature has also been read and cited frequently by public administration audiences, and that literature is the subject here.

Notably, this review ignores all but a few studies on the press itself, as well as presidential–press relations, since both subjects have generated too much literature that is marginally relevant to public administration. It does, however, include the specialized issue of governmental secrecy, a topic that is an inherent part of government-press policies.

Finally, it should be noted that the overlap between this topic and public opinion is considerable. The press literature is often more focused on the mechanics of the media and the relations of reporters with the bureaucracy, rather than with the public. Both topics should be consulted, however, for a more representative sample of the literature.

In an interdependent world, relationships are not always what they seem. The literature of public administration generally argues that the bureaucracy has taken on roles that were reserved for other parts of our political machinery, but that have been more successfully fulfilled by the administrative function. Both the press and interest groups are making similar contributions from outside the governmental machinery.

By tradition and the Constitution, the press and government are rivals. By the heritage of the Progressive era, interest groups are similarly a rival force to be controlled. Yet, government has come to rely on both for its information about the electorate, and even about itself. The information function has not been "taken over" so much as it has been performed so well by these outside groups that government administration has not invested the resources to keep its own sources competitive.

Jefferson's adage about preferring a press with no government to a government with no press may never have been a serious proposal, but it was an imaginable scenario. Today, the possibility of eliminating either is too speculative to usefully imagine what might remain. The rivals are no longer prepared to operate without each other.

U.S. Supreme Court, *Totten v. United States*, 92 US 105 (1876)

Long before literature appeared on the role of the media in government, some rules of government's limited obligations were set. During the Civil War, Lincoln contracted with Totten to conduct espionage behind Confederate lines. When enforcement of the contract was later disputed, the Supreme Court held that the case could not be heard by the Court of Claims for fear that military secrets would be inevitably revealed.

Woodrow Wilson, *New Freedom: A Call for the Emancipation of the Generous Energies of a People* (New York: Doubleday Page, 1913)

Military questions notwithstanding, the general thrust of American literature since colonial days has been toward open governmental operations. The sentiment peaked during the Progressive era as the abuses of secret dealings between government and industrialists were fresh in everyone's memories. As Wilson noted in a 1912 campaign speech, "Publicity is one of the purifying elements of politics. The best thing that you can do with anything that is crooked is to lift it up where people can see that it is crooked, and then it will either straighten itself out or disappear" (pp. 115–116).

Leo C. Rosten, *The Washington Correspondents* (New York: Harcourt Brace, 1937)

In the 20th century, the press corps in Washington grew large enough that it became interesting as a subject for separate study, and Leo Rosten was one of the first to investigate their backgrounds. Using interviews, he found that Washington correspondents tended to be more educated and more heavily Democratic than the population. However, they were not well trained as journalists.

They also preferred concrete and personal stories to those about abstract concepts, reinforcing the "crisis" and disjointed nature of the news. They also frequently had difficulty with their editors over the content of their stories.

James L. McCamy, *Government Publicity: Its Practice in Federal Administration* **(Chicago: University of Chicago Press, 1939)**
and
J(ohn) A(lfred) R(alph) Pimlott, *Public Relations and American Democracy* **(Princeton, NJ: Princeton University Press, 1951)**
As the press grew, government also expanded its use of information policy. As early as 1913, Congress attempted to restrict the use of funds to publicize the achievements of those in the bureaucracy (38 Stat. 212). Such efforts continued, however, and these were some of the early attempts to describe them.

By 1937, when his information was gathered, McCamy found public relations offices to be common and highly placed in the bureaucracy. Nine agencies even had a network of regional publicity offices. Tactics varied from traditional press releases to large fairs to ten regular feature programs broadcast from government offices. The purpose was often public information rather than propaganda, and was not a threat to democracy so long as publicists remembered their duties as well as rights.

In 1951, Pimlott updated the description of expanded public relations, noting that everyone agreed that some public relations was necessary for government to work, but that the recent expansion in both "lobbying" efforts and publications unrelated to agency business had led to new controversy. He differentiated public relations from the more narrowly focused advertising, and from legislator-focused lobbying, and concluded that public relations reflected a professionalization of a function that had always been present, but that had grown more difficult. He also concluded that the media and public relations officers had become both partners and rivals in the information process.

Dwight D. Eisenhower, Executive Order 10501, "Safeguarding Official Information in the Interests of the Defense of the United States" (November 6, 1953)
In the 1950s, the issue of secrecy took on new urgency in American politics. In 1953, Eisenhower tried to arrest the growing tendency of government to classify documents having nothing to do with national security by replacing Truman's Executive Order 10290 of September 24, 1951. The new order redefined and tightened the categories and time frames of classification decisions, and eliminated the category of "restricted" material altogether.

Harold L. Cross, *The People's Right to Know: Legal Access to Public Records and Proceedings* **(New York: Columbia University Press, 1953)**
and
James R. Wiggins, *Freedom or Secrecy?* **(New York: Oxford University Press, 1956)**
and
Edward A. Shils, *The Torment of Secrecy: The Background and Consequences of American Security Policies* **(Glencoe, IL: Free Press, 1956)**
Academics soon joined the chorus of those who felt that government secrecy was endangering democratic accountability. Cross' book was particularly gloomy on executive department secrecy. "The entrance gates to records are shut and guarded except on those occasions when official grace is moved to set them ajar for light and air" (p. 183).

Both Cross and Wiggins recounted the revolution in access to information that accompanied the beginning of the republic, and the deterioration in that access that had become rampant in the 20th century with such new common-law concepts as the right to privacy, and especially with the delegation of more of government's authority to secretive executive agencies.

Shils argued that society should be pluralistic, which meant a balance of publicity, privacy, and secrecy. The problem of the 1930s to 1950s was that we had allowed publicity through our media to grow too large, resulting in a societal move toward greater secrecy. Secrecy, to Shils, was privacy made compulsory, or in other words, no privacy at all. We needed a coalition of the political spectrum to put our values back in order and restore a pluralistic society.

Douglass Cater, *The Fourth Branch of Government* (Boston: Houghton Mifflin, 1959)

Cater's book, which is by far the most frequently cited in the area of government-media relations (often incorrectly as the first), contained a general description of the business of Washington correspondents, which "has become specialized, compartmentalized, channelized, even routinized to a degree that would shock ... predecessor(s) of [a] few decades ago." He noted the tendency of correspondents to seek the sources of action: presidents rather than administrators, Congress rather than presidents. Once focused, however, he noted their tendency to routinize their sources of information.

Despite their regular patterns of behavior, Cater was impressed that Washington correspondents were more willing to dig for information when necessary than was the case in European nations, and that they played "an almost constitutional role" in the U.S. government.

Francis E. Rourke, *Secrecy and Publicity: Dilemmas of Democracy* (Baltimore: Johns Hopkins Press, 1961)

Rourke argued that secrecy and the government's need for publicity were parts of the same governmental weapon for increasing control over society. He documented the growth of government secrecy, noting that it had been encouraged by Congress, the president, and the courts. He also described the ways in which controlled publicity could coerce private actions that could never be forced by law, although he noted that the courts were becoming more concerned about the use of public "exposure" to control behavior. He concluded with no appropriate balance among secrecy, publicity, and democracy, arguing that society's best protection was to avoid apathy on the subject.

Daniel J. Boorstin, *The Image: A Guide to Pseudo-Events in America* (New York: Harper & Row, 1964)

Underlying much of the media literature is a concern with the disjointed and incomplete picture of public events that is presented to the public through the tactic of reporting only developing crises. Boorstin followed the pseudo-events that are created by the media's practice of compressing the world into incidents that are interesting and quickly reportable. He also described the ways in which government administrators and politicians have adjusted to the practice by creating packaged events for public consumption to generate favorable publicity.

Bernard C. Cohen, *The Press and Foreign Policy* (Princeton, NJ: Princeton University Press, 1963)

The second of the three almost universally cited works on government–press relations (after Cater's) is focused specifically on foreign affairs. Using the themes of the press as observer, as participant, and as catalyst, Cohen reinforced the image of reporters as both captives and occasional unwitting framers of foreign policy news. He saw the conflict between the needs for secrecy and publicity as essential, although he did suggest that the information function would be better served if the reporting was not geared toward mass audiences, who paid little attention anyway.

Dan Nimmo, *Newsgathering in Washington: A Study in Political Communication* (New York: Atherton, 1964)

The third book cited by virtually all later studies is this study of the relationship of news reporters and agency officials. Nimmo found that such relations fall into three major categories: cooperative, marked by continual, informal contacts between the two sides; compatible, marked by less frequent, more formalized contacts; and competitive, marked by very formalized contact with little real communication. Compatible relations are the norm, although the likelihood of each style depends on shared views of the roles and functions of each, mutual respect for each other's status in their professions, and the type of agency.

William L. Rivers, *The Opinion Makers* (Boston: Beacon, 1965); *The Adversaries: Politics and the Press* (Boston: Beacon, 1970); and *The Other Government: Power and the Washington Media* (New York: Universe Books, 1982)

In each of his works, Rivers combined anecdotal descriptions of the Washington press corps with analytical discussions of the appropriate role of the press in democracy. He acknowledged that the press and government need and help each other, and that "information policy has been at the very center of governing the United States from the beginning" (1965, p. 1).

The cooperation that goes with such arrangements, however, seemed increasingly dangerous to him as he moved into his 1970 sequel, and added the data of the Johnson and Nixon administrations. "The power of political journalism is dangerous, but it is also necessary . ... The only way for a reporter to look at an official is skeptically" (pp. 252–253). He was equally harsh on the press corps, repeating Lasswell's proposal that the press corps could be cleaned up through an industry-staffed Committee on Public Communication, which could rid the industry of those "whose distinguishing characteristic is their questionable choice of vocation" (1965, p. 200).

By 1982, some of those concerns seemed more distant. He spent more time on the internal workings of Washington media. He described the way in which press "wisdom" has often framed later presidential reputations. He noted, however, that the bureaucracy still receives almost no television coverage.

Ray Eldon Hiebert, Ed., *The Press in Washington: Sixteen Top Newsmen Tell How the News Is Collected, Written, and Communicated from the World's Most Important Capital* (New York: Dodd Mead, 1966)

This is a compilation of sixteen guest lectures from Hiebert's advanced journalism class at American University, including such diverse contributors as Art Buchwald and Clark Mollenhoff. Much of the content is personalized and conversational, with little analysis of how the press and Washington fit together. An exception is Mollenhoff, whose discussion of "Secrecy, Classified Information, and Executive Privilege" updated Cross' and Wiggins' earlier works on the subject.

James Reston, *The Artillery of the Press: Its Influence on American Foreign Policy* (New York: Harper & Row, 1967)

Reflecting the renewed skepticism of the Johnson era, Reston's "theme is that the rising power of the United States in world affairs, and particularly of the American President, requires, not a more compliant press, but a relentless barrage of facts and criticism, as noisy but also as accurate as artillery fire" (p. vii). His focus, in these lectures before the Council on Foreign Relations, was foreign affairs. As is common for inside accounts, Reston often seemed to be harsher on his industry than on politicians, and he used anecdotes freely as he described the role of the press in spreading information for the government, resulting in both manipulation by, and influence over, the government.

Ray Eldon Hiebert and Carlton E. Spitzer, Eds., *The Voice of Government* **(New York: John Wiley, 1968)**

Recruiting highly placed current and former officials as contributors, Hiebert and Spitzer compiled a set of readings on government's public information activities. The theme, similar to Lippmann's, is that the press alone is not sufficient to shape public opinion. Government needs public information officers to help describe its programs to the press, Congress, and affected interests. Unfortunately, two of the authors complained, such officers are often treated as stepchildren in their agencies, hindering their effectiveness.

Delmer D. Dunn, *Public Officials and the Press* **(Reading, MA: Addison-Wesley, 1969)**

As a political scientist, Dunn used 75 interviews among the press corps and officials of Wisconsin state government to analyze more systematically the role of the press in providing information for public policy makers. He noted that reporters often try to be objective, although the pressures of their jobs steer them towards disjointed, crisis coverage. As a corollary, political events receive more attention than administrative ones. Officials' views of the press depend on their recent success with it. In general, Dunn found that the press has its highest impact on government when policies are new, although it serves an important informational role at all times.

Dale Minor, *The Information War* **(New York: Hawthorn, 1970)**
and
William J. Small, *Political Power and the Press* **(New York: W.W. Norton, 1972)**
and
David Wise, *The Politics of Lying: Government Deception, Secrecy, and Power* **(New York: Vintage, 1973)**

These are three of the better-known examples from what Stephen Hess later called the "Outrage School" of journalism that flourished during the Johnson and Nixon administrations. To the extent that such a term is accurate, it may be more a reflection of the time than of these authors. Two of the books, Minor's and Wise's, used narrative descriptions of events of the era as data. Both also concluded with a point similar to Boorstin's, that what appears in the media is a set of events tailored more to the media than to reality.

Small's book is the most historically based and the most analytical. However, he also treated the press as the captive of politicians who make the news, whatever its value or honesty. Of the three books, Wise's is the most adamant in its solution. "Lying and secrecy have no place in a democracy." Minor concluded with a set of ethical dilemmas for the reporter, while Small pushed for greater research and diversity in reporting.

Leon V. Sigal, *Reporters and Officials: The Organization and Politics of Newsmaking* **(Lexington, MA: Lexington Press, 1973)**

Sigal studied the operation of the *Washington Post* and the *New York Times* to determine how national news is made. After reviewing the operations of reporters and officials, he concluded that news "could be seen as the product of the interaction of two bureaucracies — one composed of newsmen and the other of officials." Disagreeing with the mythology of individualized reporting, he saw information as coming mainly through "routine channels," and news decisions as being consensual. Furthermore, he felt that consensus is needed to adjust for the limited perspective of individual reporters, the need of government and the press to work together, and the disjointed nature of both sources and newsworthy events.

David Morgan, *The Capitol Press Corps: Newsmen and the Governing of New York State* (Westport, CT: Greenwood, 1978)
From the state level (New York), Morgan found that a triangle of distrust develops among the media, the agencies, and the legislature. Instead, all parties rely on individual relationships that develop over time. He argued that while governmental elites often ascribe great power for mischief to the press, the press actually has little power. Individual reporters can easily be cut off from sources. Also, the common complaint that the press lacks competence is probably justified. Finally, he marveled that none of the actors felt that the public demands more information than is being offered.

Stephen Hess, *The Washington Reporters: Newswork* (Washington, DC: Brookings Institution, 1981); and *The Government–Press Connection: Press Officers and Their Offices* (Washington, DC: Brookings Institution, 1984)
In these books, Hess described first the journalists and then the governmental-press officers who work in Washington. He found that reporters tend to come from elite backgrounds, are more liberal than the population, and prefer "exciting" beats to more developmental matters such as economics. They receive less resistance from editors than Rosten reported in the 1930s, but the headline writers tend to give their stories a presidential flavor even when Congressional sources have been used.

Press officers are "semibureaucrat/semireporter, in the bureaucracy but not truly of it, tainted by association with the press yet not of the press." They are generally more competent than their reputations indicate. However, they seldom manipulate the news because they are not skillful enough, they are given too little room to maneuver in the bureaucracy, and alternative sources of information are too easily available.

Lewis M. Helm, Ray Eldon Hiebert, Michael R. Naver, and Kenneth Rabin, Eds., *Informing the People: A Public Affairs Handbook* (New York: Longman, 1981)
This book of readings was an attempt to update and expand the topics in the then-dated *The Voice of Government* on government communications policies. The basic theme, summarized by Scott Cutlip, was that the press and government are adversaries, but each needs the other since neither can do its job alone. The book also described new publicity tactics and the new conflicts under the Freedom of Information and Privacy Acts.

Note

Originally published as Martin, D.W., Agency relations with the press, in *The Guide to the Foundations of Public Administration*, Marcel Dekker, New York, 1989, chap. 9, 148–155, 161.

Index

Q